D0046234

SEP   - 1997

SIMENON

SIMENON

a biography

PIERRE ASSOULINE

*translated from the French
by Jon Rothschild*

Alfred A. Knopf   New York   1997

92
S4894AS

TEMPE PUBLIC LIBRARY
TEMPE, AZ 85282

THIS IS A BORZOI BOOK
PUBLISHED BY ALFRED A. KNOPF, INC.

Copyright © 1997 by Alfred A. Knopf, Inc.

All rights reserved under International and Pan-American
Copyright Conventions. Published in the United States
by Alfred A. Knopf, Inc., New York, and simultaneously in
Canada by Random House of Canada Limited, Toronto.
Distributed by Random House, Inc., New York.

http://www.randomhouse.com/

Originally published in France as *Simenon: Biographie* by
Julliard, Paris, in 1992. Copyright © 1992 by Pierre Assouline.
Copyright © 1992 by Julliard, Paris.

ISBN: 0-679-40285-3
LC: 97-71924

Manufactured in the United States of America
First American Edition

TO MARCEL ASSOULINE, TO HIS RADIANT MEMORY

The most important date in a man's life is that of his father's death. . . . It is only when they no longer need him that sons realize that their father is their best friend.
—Georges Simenon, *Le Fils,* 1957

When you write a biography, either you tell the truth
or you do a bogus biography.
—Georges Simenon, 1982

CONTENTS

Contents

PREFACE

At the heart of Georges Simenon's life lies a paradox: here was a man famous mainly for his notoriety. His obituaries spoke of books sold, records set, and stunts performed, as though the writer had long been eclipsed by his image. "You feel like applauding him as you would the courage and daring of a juggler or an acrobat at the circus,"[1] his friend Federico Fellini once said, unaware that the intended compliment would not have pleased him. Yet Georges Simenon was the person most responsible for his own reputation.

Excess was his watchword. He thought of himself as the main character in the novel of his life, and his personality was so exceptional and his work so vast that to attempt his biography seems an almost demented undertaking. If ever a man lived a life too far out of the ordinary to be reduced to a listing of dates, names, and events, it was Simenon. And how can a body of work outstripped by its own legend be analyzed?

Simenon's biography cannot be a mere mosaic of his life and times. Any assessment of his world that sought to banish the element of mystery would be incomplete and therefore misguided. Where a novelist is concerned, reality must take a back seat to truth, as Simenonists—an engaging tribe that has yet to find its Lévi-Strauss—have long been convinced. This may explain why the field of "Simenon studies" has drawn so many bibliographers, critics, and essayists but so relatively few biographers, as though the latter were stymied by some occult force. And it must be said that the subject himself did what he could to ward them off.

The many interviews he willingly granted from the earliest days of his career to his retirement as a novelist, combined with his impressive output of autobiographical writings—from the multivolume *Dictées* (1975–1981) to the *Mémoires Intimes* (1981)—gave Georges Simenon almost complete control of the interpretation of his past. This was far more important to him than guiding the exegesis of his work. An insatiably curious man, he knew better than most that indiscretion is fatal to myth.

He always managed to remain the principal source of information about himself. During his decades of triumph he was taken at his word, and his words were a flood that nothing and no one seemed able to stem. Yet they were in part clever artifice, meant to conceal his secret garden.

A lot of it was lies, though not the crude and vulgar lies of "a man like any other." Had he really been as ordinary as he claimed, no one would have paid any attention to him. His were novelist's lies, told with all his considerable genius. They were felicitous, too: lies that told the truth, lies by omission, selective amnesia. The novelist's gift, after all, is to dwell in an oneiric universe in which reality and fiction are so intimately intertwined as to become one. In personal matters he did not so much invent or distort as build legends, sculpting his own myth. By middle age he was no longer able to tell truth from falsehood, real from imaginary.

As he grew older, his self-intoxication grew to the point where he sincerely believed everything he said and wrote about himself. He became the worst possible source of information about Georges Simenon, until finally author and readers alike were lost in a hybrid form of autobiographical fiction.

Inquiries in the field and a study of the successive versions of various stories cast doubt on what Simenon had to say about himself. He must be constantly challenged, especially when he is the sole source of his own ego-history. In many cases, his memory will be confirmed. In others, inaccuracies will be corrected. But sometimes he must be ruthlessly refuted, even if it means demystifying the legend.

"As I see it, everyone is free to write whatever they please about me, which many people have already done, in France and especially abroad, without any intervention from me," he wrote to me in 1983. Several years later, when he gave a biographer unrestricted access to his considerable personal archives for the first time, he informed me:

"Do what you want, but don't expect me to help. Nor will I ask to read your manuscript before publication. That way you'll be free and so will I."

The confidence thereby expressed just a few months before his death was also extended by his companion, Teresa Sburelin; by his faithful collaborator, Joyce Aitken; and by his three sons, Marc, John, and Pierre. Without it this project would have been doomed. But there was a commensurate risk: it meant I had to read everything and tell all, without reservation. Simenon stretched the traditional boundaries of self-restraint, secrecy, and modesty so far that the biographer has no choice but to follow suit. Such are the rules of the game, and the game is worth the candle, for the hidden face of this writer's life and work is far more fascinating than the official version. It restores his contradictions, making him more vulnerable, and more human.

To separate Georges the man from Simenon the writer would be as absurd as trying to divide form from content. It would be equally absurd not to view Simenon's writings as documents revealing his life on the pretext that his work, allegedly resistant to Time and History, is equally refractory to biography. Simenon's entire experience reappeared in his work, albeit transfigured and transposed. Without his uncanny gift for absorption, this alchemist would never have been able to turn the lead of life as he lived it into the gold of his literary fiction.

True, we must avoid the pitfall of viewing the work as the mere reflection of the life and the life as the matrix of the work. But anything goes when exploring the areas of shadow and exposing their deeply hidden mechanisms: analytical study of the texts, journalistic investigation, interviews with witnesses, psychiatric diagnosis, literary criticism, and the decoding of archives. Is it too ambitious an undertaking? Probably. But the attempt is possible only because of the incredible labors begun long ago by researchers of various persuasions, weekend and full-time Simenonists, a veritable intelligence service without whose efforts a book like this would be stillborn. One is always indebted to one's predecessors, but especially so when they are pioneers.

"When my plan is done, the play is done," said Racine. A biography, too, may be judged by its plan, the most delicate aspect of which is to discern the turning points that can disassemble and reorder the chronology of a life. The book is divided into four parts: Belgium, France, America, and Switzerland. The choice is not arbitrary, for these countries marked four well-defined epochs in Georges Simenon's journey on this earth, and they correspond to four women: his mother, Henriette; his first wife, Tigy; his second wife, Denyse; and his companion, Teresa.

Georges Simenon did not like introductions. In fact, he recommended that they be deleted immediately after being written, since their sole purpose was to get the author started by stoking the locomotive.[2] I have enough critical admiration for Simenon and his work to end this preface here. But not enough to delete it.

BELGIUM

1

ALTAR BOY

1903–1919

ive forty-five in the morning. The alarm clock rings as the first bells toll for six o'clock mass at the parish church. A light goes on in a window at 53 Rue de la Loi. Moments later a child slips out of the building and disappears into the moonless dark.

The town of Liège lies sleeping under a blanket of drizzly rain. The child, eight years old, walks quickly, fear gnawing at his belly—fear of being late to the chapel at Bavière Hospital, where he is to serve mass; fear of the unknown shapes that might spring out of the shadows of a doorway. He tries to lift his spirits by murmuring to himself. He clings to the sidewalk's edge, carefully choosing the path that offers the fewest surprises, midway between the double threat of the roadway and the building façades. It is a ritual he performs daily, with clockwork regularity.

The nuns consider him a good little boy, pious and sensitive to the warmth, mystery, and poetry of the dawn mass. His teachers, too, see him as a model child, a little boy who knows his place.[1]

It is nearly six o'clock, and he is running now, through the working-class neighborhood of Outremeuse. Though it is still too dark to see, he sniffs the reassuring smells: the scents of Hosey chocolate from the Rue Léopold and of schnapps from the door of the first open café; the aromas of the dairies and of the fish, flower, and vegetable stalls in the deserted markets. These little alleyways "bombard passersby with the stench of poverty, an odor not unpleasant when you have known it since childhood."[2]

He stops to catch his breath, turns to see that no ghosts are in pursuit, and then moves on: past the benches of the Place du Congrès, down the Rue de la

3

Province, with its lovely middle-class homes, then onto the Boulevard de la Constitution, the Rue des Bonnes-Villes, and finally to the hospital and the welcoming smile of Sister Mathilde, the sexton. At last he breathes easy. If only he had a bicycle, he would be free of this dread. He has dreamed of it often, praying for one during mass and planning to borrow money for it from his mother. But she refuses his requests, with a disconcerting obstinacy that will mark him forever.

Years later, Inspector Maigret will buy the much-desired bicycle for another altar boy as a reward for his honesty:[3] little Justin, the hero of the short story "Le Témoinage de l'enfant de choeur" (The Altar Boy's Testimony, 1947), is Georges Simenon himself, as he will one day admit.[4]

Nervous anxiety, simmering conflict with his mother, obsession with time and ritual, spiritual unease—the Simenon boy's character is already taking form.

In 1911, at the age of eight, he was a pupil at the Institut Saint-André des Frères, 48 Rue de la Loi, a Catholic school across the street from his house. So far, he had shown no sign of rebelling against the rigid education dispensed by the Christian Brothers. An industrious student, he seemed destined to become an upstanding bank employee. But he had already shown a flair for French composition, his best subject, and at the end of the school year he won a prize for excellence, scoring 293.5 points out of a possible 315. He had become a teacher's pet. In class, the Brothers assigned him the first desk, and he was in charge of refueling the stove. He also rang the bell to announce times of prayer and recreation. He held the key to the spigot in the cobbled sandstone courtyard. Whoever wanted a drink had to see him first.[5]

At home, religion was embodied by his mother, who saw only its more petty aspects but was nonetheless entirely devout. She would never have allowed her son to learn to read and write elsewhere than at the Sainte-Julienne school, run by the Sisters of Notre Dame on nearby Rue Jean-d'Outremeuse. The boy's educational itinerary was set with an iron hand: first the Sisters, then the Brothers, and finally the Jesuits of the Collège Saint-Louis on the Quai de Longdoz.

The child's early, rare instances of misbehavior elicited severe reprimands from the Brothers: "You're as bad as those little hoodlums in the state schools."[6] When he began to depart from the straight and narrow, his mother responded by adding yet another item to her list of no-no's, forbidding him to play with the pupils of the nearby nonreligious school: "Don't let me catch you hanging around with workers' sons!"[7] Workers who were often better off than the Simenons.

The memorialist would later be unstinting in his praise of what he learned from the Brothers, but he would also be quite open about his hatred of their social attitudes, especially their peculiar penchant for holding the state schools up as a bogeyman and for harping on class divisions. This may well have been the leavening of a powerful conviction that never left him: that humility is the greatest of all human values.

At the age of eleven, he no longer served the dawn mass but had not yet broken free of his teachers' grip. The day after the German mobilization, with the Old World poised to plunge into the bloodiest conflict of its history, the child wrote to his aunt, Sister Mary Madeleine of the Ursuline convent:

"We trust in God Who brought our fathers out of Egypt and Who will once again blind the eyes of His enemies with His power."[8]

But at the same time, he became a kind of gang leader to his classmates, winning their admiration with his fertile imagination, his astonishing facility in absorbing the world around him, and his skill at marbles. He was always the first to finish his homework, but he began to pay the price, making slipshod errors,[9] a foible that enhanced his charm in his friends' eyes while further alienating his teachers.

At home, his parents were slow to understand. The boy who had seemed a conformist well cast in the mold was fast becoming a dissident cheerfully flouting all norms. He would never work in a bank, nor would he be a priest or an army officer, though he had been told that either of these professions would leave him ample time to indulge his hobby: writing.

The city of Liège was the source of much of what would emerge from the Simenon word factory. This little patch of Belgium where his memories were forged would become his main character and the focus of his nostalgia. The Rue de la Loi was a wide, paved thoroughfare lined with squat buildings. It had no scent, but it did have a hue: the color of brick. The Simenons lived at number 53, the fourth house they had occupied since Georges's birth on February 13, 1903. They were a family of four: the father, Désiré; the mother, Henriette; the elder son, Georges; his brother, Christian, three years younger. "There was born to me a brother," he would later recall, savoring the elegant formulation.[10]

These four often paired off in twos. When Désiré said "your son" to his wife, he meant Christian. When Henriette said the same to her husband, she meant Georges.[11] They were like two different worlds coexisting under a single roof, at times clashing, at times supporting one other, and sometimes even sharing love, in their way.

Désiré Simenon was born in Liège in 1877. Exacting genealogical research[12] has traced his family tree back to 1662. Originally from the Liège district, the Simenons emigrated to Limburg in Flemish Belgium before resettling in Wallonia. Civil and parish registries tell us that family members exercised various trades: plowmen, day laborers, brewers, skilled workers, domestic servants, weavers, makers of straw hats.

Désiré's father, Chrétien Simenon, was a hatter with a shop on the Rue Puits-en-Sock in Liège. The family was well rooted in Outremeuse, and Désiré never dreamed of living anywhere but in this neighborhood. A good Walloon not at all enamored of the Flemish, he nevertheless considered Wallonian a low-class dialect and did not want it to rub off on his son Georges's French. Désiré was educated in religious schools and grew up in an atmosphere of such middle-class warmth and engaging geniality that family members were loath to part from one another.[13] He was eager to transmit this sense of well-being to his children.

He loved the theater, and had once worked as a prompter for a small amateur troupe, typically preferring this modest role to that of actor. He had a wide, domed forehead, a prematurely receding hairline, a lush handlebar mustache, a ready smile, and a firm handshake, but a withdrawn air. The essence of his personality found expression in his most salient social characteristic: his complete lack of ambition.

He was timid and discreet, modest, reserved, and undemonstrative. In fact, he was so uncommunicative that his underlying tenderness was difficult to perceive. Watching him sit quietly in his armchair night after night, reading his paper, you might call him happy. He seemed in perfect harmony with his fate, at peace with himself. He knew his limitations and claimed to like everything and everyone. He was the embodiment of humility and resignation, but without the flavor of melancholy and quiet sadness commonly associated with such traits. Désiré was a sensible man who had let life take its course with a serenity only cynics would call naïveté.

When he wrote the word *office,* he spelled it with a capital *O,* the way you might write "Church" to refer to the institution rather than the building. His was at 18 Rue Sohet. His employer, Jules Monoyer, was the regional agent for two insurance companies. Désiré chose to specialize in fire insurance at a time when life insurance was touted as the future of the industry. But fire insurance required less initiative. It was the field least likely to disturb his peaceful Liégeois existence, allowing him to live as an upright, average man who stood midway between rich and poor while feeling no scorn for either. His salary of 180 francs a month was stable for a very long time. Younger colleagues who ventured into life insurance were soon bringing in more.

Young Georges was a great admirer of his father, and as an adult he placed Désiré in the uppermost niche of his personal pantheon. *Je me souviens* (*I Remember,* 1945) and *Pédigree* (*Pedigree,* 1948) are in part monuments to his memory, and many of Georges's other books bear the father's shadow. They all strive to grasp the essence of the father-son relationship, viewed through the prism of difficulties of communication, "a kind of inability to express family feelings."[14]

"Good day, son."

"Good day, father."[15]

That was how they greeted each other in the Simenon household.

This attitude of distance and respect was disorienting to the adolescent, who never quite succeeded in interpreting Désiré's thoughts. They understood each other best during times of shared silence. They never talked of politics or religion—that was too personal.[16] But at dinner, when the mother grumbled, a wink from the father and a grin from the son sufficed to mark their secret complicity. "As though the child could already understand."[17]

And so he could. Years later the novelist would have one of his characters say that there were two kinds of people in the world, those who bowed their heads and those who did not.[18] It was a summary but lasting judgment, even if he would come to regret having formulated it so starkly.

Désiré's working life was timed to a nearly maniacal exactitude, and he had a horror of stopped clocks. The household clock that rocked Georges's cradle ruled the family's daily routine, and the rhythmic swing of its pendulum would never leave his ears. When Georges's grandfather divided up his worldly goods before his death, Désiré asked for just one thing: the clock. It seemed a small enough request, but he was given a coffee-grinder instead.[19]

Désiré was inconsolable, and so was Georges, as though denying the father the sole object of his desire had also deprived the son of a part of his memory. Both saw it as unjust, but they bore it with characteristic silence.

Georges's mother, Henriette, came from the Brüll family. Her Dutch and Prussian genealogy has been traced back eight generations. In 1691 her ancestors moved from the Dutch to the Belgian part of Limburg, and later to the provinces of Antwerp, Brabant, and Liège, before finally settling in the city of Liège itself. They were farmers, burgomasters, day laborers, bakers, stewards, wood merchants, and irrigation engineers.[20]

Henriette was born in the northern quarter of the city in 1880, the youngest of thirteen children. At twenty-two she married the twenty-five-year-old Désiré in the church of Saint-Denis. He was already working for an insurance company, and she was a sales clerk at L'Innovation, one of the town's department stores.

When Henriette was a child, her father's wood-shipping company went bankrupt. He sank into alcoholism, and when he died in 1885, the family was left poverty-stricken, a fate especially harsh for being unexpected. Henriette, the "little one," would long retain a painful memory of the shock.

The Brülls, like the Simenons, were Catholic, but Henriette was far more devout than Désiré, by temperament, conviction, and choice. She never missed mass and was considered a model parishioner. She had clear, bright eyes; a narrow face; and a dignified, severe demeanor. A tense and anxious woman, nervous and hypersensitive, she was humble, proud, and haunted by the specter of poverty. Though basically honest, she was ready to cut corners when she had to. Her own mother would hurriedly put empty saucepans on the stove when visitors dropped in, trying to suggest a lavish meal to come, when in fact the cupboard was bare but for bread. Poverty must always be hidden. The image stayed with young Georges and would reappear often in his books.[21]

Henriette was as high-strung as her husband was serene. The more evident his quietude became, the more she chided him for his lack of social and professional ambition. Their lifestyle, origins, and milieu were classically petit-bourgeois, but Désiré's relaxed attitude to life prevented them from acquiring the resources with which to climb the social ladder.

Henriette invariably saw the slightest proletarian agitation, from the most ordinary strike to genuine riots, as a threat to the still shaky status of the Simenons. She was obsessed by the prospect of workers streaming into the streets, an intrusive, repellent mass overturning everything in its path. She felt permanently menaced. Often defensive, she was convinced that lies and self-interest were the sole driving forces of human nature, though she had proof enough to the contrary in Désiré. The alert young Georges knew that his mother's family had been ravaged by reversals of fortune, alcoholism, and madness. His mother had nightmares in which a carriage came to take her away to an asylum, a fate that had actually befallen one of her sisters.

There seems little doubt that the source of Georges Simenon's instability and anxiety must be sought in his mother's side of the family. Professor Mathieu Rutten, who has done extensive genealogical research, is categorical: "Professionally, socially, and psychologically, the history of the Brülls is an uninterrupted sequence of difficulties: temporary residences, unstable trades, relative lack of success. In short, a perilous and even gloomy fate. . . . Unlike Désiré Simenon, Henriette Brüll bore the memory of a past laden with problems, anxiety, and tragedy."[22]

Would Georges have become Simenon without chronic and often painful conflict with his mother? In the absence of a definitive answer, we may at least assemble the pieces of the puzzle. She lied about the very first event in Georges's life: his birth. Henriette was too superstitious to admit that her son came into the world shortly after midnight on Friday the 13th. She therefore told the registry office that the birth occurred at 11:30 p.m. on February 12, 1903.

Three years later, when she gave birth to Christian, she made no secret of her preference for her younger son, and for the rest of her life she missed no opportunity to recall this predilection. She saw Christian as handsome and gifted, full of charm and talent, while Georges was ill-favored, ugly, and plodding. The younger son was obedient, the older was not.

Georges was a perennial problem to Henriette. She had no faith in him and was never satisfied with him. Suspicious of everything, she was particularly distrustful of Georges.[23] Her older son was a proud boy, a trait that often has its good side. But not as she saw it. "His was a very ill-placed pride."[24]

The boy developed a strong sense of guilt, closely linked to a low self-image. He felt his mother treated him like a stranger. He could not remember her ever taking him on her lap. She never kissed him, instead offering him a perfunctory cheek or forehead, a token of estrangement and indifference that affected him deeply enough to reappear in several of his novels.[25] In his terrible memoir *Lettre à ma mère* (*Letter to My Mother,* 1974), written three years after Henriette's death, the seventy-one-year-old Simenon made this wrenching confession:

"As you are well aware, we never loved each other while you lived. We both pretended . . . 'Why have you come, Georges?' A little phrase that perhaps explains your entire life. . . . There was something excessive in you that lay beyond your control, but you also had an extreme lucidity. . . . A single thread bound us together, and that thread was your fierce desire to be good—for others, but perhaps most of all for yourself. . . ."[26]

A father, a mother, a brother. The immediate family circle was broadened by the visits of aunts and cousins and by spats and reconciliations with many other relatives. Young Georges had a special fondness for Uncle Léopold, who was scorned by everyone else except Henriette. A virtual outcast, he was an anarchist by conviction and a drunk by temperament, a jack of all trades and a master of none, a flamboyant nonconformist who had actually attended a university but without getting a degree.

Vagabondage was Uncle Léopold's true vocation, and he had spirit enough to ignore what people might say. It is hard not to think of him when observing the familiar figure of the tramp throughout Simenon's work, the easygoing, likable, and basically happy fellow with whom the author long dreamed of identifying. Uncle Léopold's great strength was his indifference to the humiliation of his own failure.

The grandfather also held pride of place in young Georges's personal mythology. A self-proclaimed master of dikes in a world where water was all-important, he took regular dawn swims in the Meuse River with a group of friends. Most of them were former craftsmen turned merchants, but one was a police inspector in Saint-Hubert. As the gentlemen undressed in the cabin they shared, young Georges would listen, rapt and fascinated, to the policeman's descriptions of his caseload.[27]

There was also Aunt Maria Croissant, née Brüll, wife of a basketmaker. The child would never forget her grocery shop on the Coronmeuse dock, and the adult would put the memory to use in *Chez Krull* (*Chez Krull,* 1939). At the counter she served the bargemen schnapps whose aroma mingled with the scent of cane and spices.

Young Georges felt at home in Outremeuse, a sealed and well-protected island where the provincial middle class defended traditional values and held disturbing questions at bay. The blows striking the planet never seemed to penetrate this little world in which unbroken tradition preserved the communal character of daily life.

At an early age, the child perceived the gulf between his parents' mentalities and characters. He saw that they did not want the same things out of life, and he witnessed and remembered their disputes, even though he did not always understand them at the time.

When Henriette complained that her husband had turned down a better job in Brussels, Désiré replied that nothing could ever make him leave his neighborhood, where he knew everyone and everyone knew him. What more could a man want? When she complained that her husband had not provided for his family's future by taking out life insurance—an amazing dereliction for a man in the insurance business!—he fell silent, hanging his head as his wife raised her voice. That particular quarrel dragged on for years, and one day the adolescent learned the reason for his father's attitude: the doctors had rejected his insurance application because of his precarious health.[28]

A father as happy as a peasant tilling his soil, optimistic but dominated, ever ready with a smile of resignation; an unstable, discontented mother, plaintive and domineering, fearful of the future; an older son who leaned instinctively to his father's side; a younger son under his mother's wing. This was the Simenon family in the years before the First World War.

Then, one day, Désiré's life was turned upside down. When he came home from work at the usual time, he found no free hook on the hallway coat rack. Someone else was sitting in his wicker armchair. Someone else was reading his paper. Dinnertime had been changed, and the dishes were different too. His home was no longer his. Henriette had taken in boarders, thereby turning her husband into a boarder as well—the least important one in the house, for the customer is king, and Désiré was not a customer.

Georges would never forgive his mother for inflicting this unspeakable humiliation on his father in his own sacred nest. For the moment, however, nothing could be done. Henriette had stopped working when her first child was born, and this was her way of augmenting the family income. Liège was a university town, and renting out rooms to students was an obvious move.

Not all of Henriette's boarders were foreigners, but most were of central European origin, from Russia or Poland, Romania or Czechoslovakia. Some were

Jewish. And several made quite an impression on the adolescent Georges. The boarders spent most of their time not in their upstairs rooms but in the kitchen, the heart and soul of the household. They cooked their own meals, but that never stopped them from sampling Henriette's dishes as well. Georges spent many hours observing them, and he put what he learned to good use.

In *Le Locataire* (*The Lodger,* 1934) the main character, Elie Nagéar, goes into hiding after committing a murder. He finds refuge in a student rooming house in Charleroi run by one Mme. Baron, his mistress's mother. He spends most of his time in her kitchen, eyeing the reactions of the other tenants, who grow increasingly suspicious. The first part of *Crime impuni* (*The Fugitive,* 1954) takes place in Liège in the home of Mme. Lange, who rents out rooms to students from central Europe. The novel's main character is an ugly, impoverished Polish Jew by the name of Elie Waskow. When a new tenant, a well-to-do Romanian who offers him aid and friendship, seduces Mme. Lange's daughter, Waskow loses control and kills the Romanian.

Young Georges's only objection to the boarders was that their presence humiliated his father, calling attention to his inability to raise his family's standard of living. Désiré was no longer master in his own house, for his wife was at the boarders' beck and call. Georges was hurt not only for his much-loved father, but for himself as well. He was relegated to the background and given the smallest room in the house. He and Désiré had to wait until the boarders finished dinner before they could sit down to eat. Very often they had to make do with leftovers.[29]

But Georges never managed to detest these intruders. He was fascinated by their conversations, and they soon made friends with him, astonished and delighted that an adolescent would show such interest in discussions about literature and anatomy, politics and biology, or the likelihood of a revolution in Tsarist Russia. In his memoirs, Simenon paid tribute to them for having introduced him to their great authors, Chekhov and Dostoevsky, Pushkin and Gorky, and of course Gogol, creator of *Dead Souls,* the greatest writer of the nineteenth century in Simenon's eyes.

Even given his admitted precocity, however, it seems unlikely, as he later claimed, that he read these Russian authors when the boarders' influence on him was at its peak. They had all left by 1914, when Georges was only eleven. Surely he backdated their impact on his reading by several years. On the other hand, it is likely that their influence fueled his inner revolt, sharpening his determination to break free of his family and his desire to violate the social conventions he found increasingly stultifying. He grew ever less tolerant of a world that seemed riddled with cowardice and hypocrisy, and he was frustrated at his own inability to express his revolt against the authoritarianism, discipline, and dishonesty that governed social relations both at home and at school.

Neither his mother nor his father read any "literature" apart from newspaper serials, but at least his father did not mock his son's passion for reading. Georges loved the novels of Alexandre Dumas, and some ten years later used the pseudonym Aramis. He soon found himself unable to put down the works of Dickens, Balzac, Stendhal, Conrad, and Stevenson. His admiration for the latter two in particular would never wane. He discovered most of these writers in the stacks of the Liège public library, from which he borrowed books at a dizzying pace—three a day at one point—sometimes checking out up to a dozen volumes at a time on his parents' unused library cards.[30]

In 1915, Liège was occupied by the German army. The streets were like barracks, and air raids blackened the nights. But Georges, like his classmates, was less concerned with problems of supply and the vicissitudes of the front than with the girls at a nearby school.

The Jesuits had enrolled Georges as a "day pupil" paying a reduced rate, and he was distressed by the psychological consequences of this favor granted his mother by the superiors of the Collège Saint-Louis. It made him feel downgraded and singled out. Yet he was still a good pupil, earning particularly good marks in French, spelling, and grammar.[31] Despite his increasingly rebellious character, his family and his teachers had him earmarked for the priesthood. But that summer everything changed: he fell in love for the first time.

It happened while he was on vacation in Embourg, very near Liège. He was twelve years old, while Renée, at fifteen, was almost a grown-up. One day Georges tried to impress her by climbing to the topmost branches of a holly tree to pick red berries for her. When he came down, he was bleeding all over. Sixty years later he recounted the details of the incident:

" 'Lie down over there,' she said to me, and I lay down. She began to clean off my legs, and then to lick them. Afterward she did the same to my chest. She told me to turn over, and when I obeyed, she licked my back. Then she pulled down my shorts and I felt her climb on top of me. It hurt like mad, because the foreskin was not completely peeled back. That's how it happened. She practically circumcised me."[32]

It would be an understatement to say that Georges was never the same again. By the end of the month, when he went home to the Rue de la Loi, he was determined to see Renée as often as possible. Since she was enrolled at the Institut Sainte-Véronique on the opposite bank of the Meuse, he solemnly informed his teachers and parents that he had decided to renounce the priesthood in favor of—a military career. The Collège Saint-Servais, which boasted an excellent science department, just happened to be located on the Rue Saint-Gilles, on the left bank of the river, closer to Renée's school.

At the Collège Saint-Servais, Georges fell under the spell of a Mr. Renchon, a short young professor of literature with red hair and a pockmarked face who was himself preparing for the priesthood. "He is probably the man who had the greatest influence on me," Georges later affirmed,[33] without further explanation.

His teacher was so pleased with him that he let the boy choose his own subjects and raised no objection when he took the liberty of signing his homework "Georges Sim." But this indulgence fell far short of luring Georges into academic life, especially since at the slightest misstep the dean unfailingly reminded him of his special status: day pupil paying half-tuition. There could have been no better way of showing an adolescent from an ill-favored family that he was more tolerated than accepted, and Georges got the message loud and clear. It is no accident that in his novels school is often a metaphor not for the transmission of knowledge but for the relationship of subordination between masters and disciples.

Georges spent three academic years at this institution, but did not take the final exam that would have allowed him to enroll in the scientific high school. Instead, he dropped out in the summer of 1918, and no effort seems to have been made to change his mind. His withdrawal had nothing to do with Renée, whom he had forsaken on the first day of school, when he saw her leaving the grounds arm in arm with a man of about twenty who was waiting for her at the exit.

Why, then, did he quit? Simenon later offered a version of this event that became an invariant fixture of his autobiographical writings, an element of his mythology: One day he was summoned to the office of Dr. Léon Fischer, his father's physician. "I have bad news for you, Georges," the doctor told him. "You're going to have to quit school and go to work."

"But why?"

"I saw your father a few days ago, and in my view he has no more than two or three years to live."[34]

The doctor felt that Désiré would not recover from the chronic angina pectoris from which he suffered. Georges therefore had to sacrifice his own ambitions to prepare for assuming a higher responsibility: supporting the family, providing for his mother's needs, and seeing to the education of his younger brother, then twelve years old. This mission was so compelling that his own plans were instantly swept away.

Much later, however, several doctors to whom he recounted this painful incident expressed surprise that their colleague would confide such critical information to a fifteen-year-old instead of to his mother. Simenon's response was not entirely convincing: "My mother, you know, was a very nervous, excitable woman given to sudden fits of anger."[35]

Perhaps. But it is also possible that the frequent repetition of this story afforded the writer a convenient explanation for the sudden interruption of his studies. Not that he made it up out of whole cloth. But here, as elsewhere, the novelist seems to have prevailed over the man. The truth is that at the end of the 1918 school year, Georges was gripped by internal turmoil unrelated to his father's health. He was increasingly less interested in his schoolwork, which was reflected in his grades. And he was having trouble keeping his bent for insubordination in check, especially when he was made to feel inferior to richer but less brilliant pupils. But most of all, he had a crisis of faith that led to a violent rejection of his entire Catholic education. Sin had given him a taste for women, and the priests' insistence on treating sex as an absolute taboo dissolved his lingering doubts. In a later interview he described the sexual exigencies of the Catholic Church as "impractical, unreasonable, and absurd."

"I wanted to get laid," he explained, "and the Church told me I'd be damned for it. So I left. The other reasons came later, with their own reality. But I have to tell you the truth: at the origin, at the root, was a categorical rejection of the supposed sexual morality of Catholicism."[36]

Education and religion had been one and the same in his mind ever since he had learned to read and write, for they were dispensed by the same people. To reject the one was to jettison the other. He did not return to the Collège Saint-Servais in September 1918. Instead, he struck out on his own, at a time when Europe, bled white, was counting its dead and preparing to sign an armistice. He was fifteen and a half years old.

2

CUB REPORTER

1919–1922

What Georges wanted most was to get out of the house, to escape the oppressive silence of the no-man's-land between his father and mother. For a time he drifted, nurturing little hope and few illusions about his future. Sometimes discouragement overwhelmed him, but one thing he was sure of, and it served to steel his character: "From my earliest childhood I was convinced that I would never be given anything for nothing, that I could never count on the thing called luck. It was an idea I got used to."[1] Expect nothing from anyone. It was a rule he would never break.

All he really knew how to do was smoke his pipe, a habit he had acquired at a very young age. His writing was still just a hobby, perhaps a pleasure, but not yet a passion and certainly not a vocation. It wasn't something you could live on. For the moment all he wanted was a real job that would give him a monthly check, just like his father.

One foggy night, as he walked across the Pont des Arches with a few friends, he solemnly informed them that at forty he would be a minister of state or a member of the Academy.[2] An absurd dream for a youth on the fast track to nowhere. His parents gave him plenty of advice. Henriette, already worried about her son's old age at a time when he had no idea what to do the next morning, urged him to take any job that came with a pension. Maybe something in the railroads, for example. When she realized that a job like that would hardly accommodate the character of a boy with such a "thirst for life,"[3] she recommended occupations that would let her remain a constant presence in his life. Maybe he could open a shop. In her wilder dreams, she

15

may have pictured herself working the cash register while her sons stood behind the counter.

In the autumn of 1918, Georges signed on as apprentice to a pastry cook at a shop very near his home in Outremeuse. This experiment lasted no more than two weeks. A little later he found a position that might better suit his penchant for reading. George Renkin, owner of the George bookstore in downtown Liège, was looking for a salesclerk. Simenon was hired and set out every morning for the Rue de la Cathédrale. At first he found it embarrassing to serve his former classmates of the Collège Saint-Servais, but discomfort waned as necessity prevailed over self-esteem. The owner, however, had trouble getting along with his clerk, whose insolence seemed boundless. The boy actually had the temerity to correct his employer in the presence of a third party.

One day a customer asked for a copy of *Le Capitaine Pamphile*. Renkin, probably confusing the title with *Le Capitaine Fracasse*,[4] began looking under the letter *G,* as in Théophile Gautier. The clerk, who knew his classics, suggested that he might try under *D,* as in Dumas, Alexandre. The customer sided with the clerk. Georges tried to apologize, but he was paid off and found himself on the street. He had lasted a month.

He went back to pounding the pavement, but this time his wanderings paid off, and he wound up a journalist. However improbable it may sound, his version of this historic day deserves to be reported.

He comes upon the Rue de l'Official, site of the headquarters of the *Gazette de Liège,* one of the city's leading dailies. He happens to go inside. He has recently read *Le Mystère de la chambre jaune,* and his head is spinning with thoughts of Rouletabille, Gaston Leroux's reporter-hero. He has not yet acquired the hat and raincoat—that will come later—but he does have the stubby pipe, and he is wearing long pants for the first time. He asks to see the manager. When he is shown in, he says without further ado, "I want to be a reporter."

The manager asks to see his references, and the young man doesn't hesitate: the bishop of Liège is his cousin and namesake, and one of his uncles, a grocery wholesaler named Scroten, is on the board of directors of a bank. What a coincidence! The manager holds a seat on the same board. A few phone calls, and Georges is hired.[5]

That is his story. But is it history? There were no other witnesses, but a careful study of Simenon's multiple versions of this incident, recounted in many interviews, turns up a few false notes. Sometimes he claims to have been talking to the manager, sometimes the editor in chief. True, these two posts were held by one and the same person, but it is far from certain that he was in Liège at the time. In some versions, the applicant is asked to write an article on the spot, and passes the test so brilliantly that the boss is instantly won over, delighted to add such a promising recruit to his team. In others, he hesitates before making a decision.

The bit about the cousin-bishop-namesake is also worth a look. Here we have a prime example of how reality is reshaped when the novelist turns memorialist. The man's family name was indeed Simenon, but his first name was Willem (Guillaume), not Georges. Also, he was not a bishop but the vicar-general of the diocese of Liège. Finally, he was not exactly the young man's cousin, but the cousin of a cousin of a second cousin of Désiré's.[6]

It seems likely that Simenon's entry into the *Gazette de Liège* was less dramatic than he tells it, and it is unlikely that he ventured into this terra incognita without collecting some solid recommendations first. Immediately after the armistice there were plenty of job openings in the editorial department of the *Gazette de Liège*. The paper had refused to appear under German occupation and was now being relaunched. It was an opportunity the young Simenon would not let pass. However it happened, he joined the staff in January 1919, a month before his sixteenth birthday.

The *Gazette,* as it was commonly called, was one of the oldest Belgian periodicals. Firmly conservative and Catholic, it prided itself on covering the entire eastern portion of the country, influencing both rural and urban opinion. Simenon could well have looked elsewhere, for the daily press in Liège was quite varied. There was the liberal *La Meuse,* the progressive *L'Express,* the leftist *La Wallonie socialiste,* the Catholic *Le National liégeois,* and others linked to industrial and financial circles, like *Le Journal de Liège.* It is hard to believe that chance alone guided him to the city's most conformist and traditionalist newspaper, especially since the ethic and ideology it championed so closely matched the attitudes of his family.

The *Gazette* was the flagship of a Liège dynasty: the Demarteau family. Joseph Demarteau, third of the line and a lawyer by training, now headed the enterprise. Upstanding and inflexibly right-wing, he wore wire-rimmed glasses, a black frock coat, and an ever-lengthening pointed beard. Not surprisingly, severity was his most obvious trait. But Simenon was eternally grateful to have been a special beneficiary of what he considered Demarteau's greatest characteristic: indulgence. The novel *L'Âne rouge* (*The Nightclub,* 1933), for instance, is clearly a fictionalization of the author's early career. Its hero, Jean Cholet, a cub reporter barely sixteen years old, works for a Catholic newspaper, the *Gazette de Nantes,* run by the very understanding Mr. Dehourceau.

Simenon sincerely admired his new employer, whom he regarded as the father of his career. The image was not entirely innocent, since Georges felt that Demarteau had qualities similar to Désiré's: both had a broad spirit of tolerance that helped the young rebel curb his inclination to go to extremes.

The young man was soon burning candles at both ends—learning the ropes in the editorial offices of the *Gazette,* rushing from desk to desk, joking and arguing with the other staff members, telephoning each of the city's six police stations twice a day to find out what was new, hurrying to police headquarters at eleven o'clock every morning for the daily press conference, writing several articles a day, closing out the shift with a ritual stroll through the courthouse corridors, spending what time he could in nightclubs, and dropping in on prostitutes at any moment. It is hard to imagine him living any other way. At sixteen he was already a phenomenon.

His salary started at 45 francs a month, but rose steadily. Within a year he had passed the symbolic figure of 180, the amount his father earned with twenty years seniority.[7] The money allowed Georges to savor his first revenge on his childhood. One of the cub reporter's first purchases was the bicycle the altar boy never got. He had dreamed of pedaling through Liège, and now he rode each day not only to police headquarters and the newspaper but also to the conferences, banquets, and ceremonies that formed the regular beat of an apprentice assigned to what was commonly called the "dog run-over" department. The pejorative designation notwithstanding, the young man spent nearly three years absorbing the events and foibles, colors and odors, of all levels of society. The insights thus acquired would permeate his work.

Georges quickly learned to make himself indispensable to the pressroom during the nerve-racking hours when the paper was put to bed. Apparently able to write on anything and everything with disconcerting ease, he would sit in his office amid his smoldering pipes and churn out whatever copy was required. All you had to do was get him started and tell him when to stop, and he could spin gold from the most trivial event. Many of his articles were unsigned. Others were bylined with his initials or a pseudonym: usually Georges Sim, sometimes simply Sim. His colleagues in the editorial office began to call him "Young Sim."

His editor in chief was astute enough not to confine him to a single topic. He began by covering speeches: the attorney Collignon's address on alcohol and Father Humblet's on classicism; the Amitiés Françaises colloquium on French influence in the world and Father Henusse's lecture on the doctrine of Marshal Foch. But he also reported on conferences held at the University of Liège on modern, "scientific" methods of police investigation.

Then there were the crime stories and local events, ranging from the often arcane world of municipal government to accounts of bicycle races and the inevitable postwar memorials to the brave men who had fallen on the battlefields, to the undying gratitude of a thankful Belgium. He wrote a smattering of articles on political, social, and economic themes, and a very few theatrical, literary, and artistic reviews.[8] His fingers were in every possible pie.

The author's energy and enthusiasm are evident in his articles, but his writing was marked by a complete absence of discipline. His style still had a high school quality—not exactly surprising in a sixteen-year-old. Rigor was not his strong suit. He wrote as quickly as possible, using the vocabulary and turns of phrase of a Collège Saint-Servais sophomore.

> Immersed in the crowd, I attended a patriotic festival. Ringed by banners, the echoes of the brass band still floating in the air, an orator gave a speech. Cheers and frantic applause greeted his every phrase. Yet I remained absolutely calm, surprising myself by coolly analyzing every phrase and every pause, in which the same sonorous words were inevitably repeated. I strove to uncover the oratory procedures. The crowd listened religiously, awaiting the brilliant finale to let its enthusiasm explode.
>
> A thought occurred to me and tyrannically imposed its will on my thought. Is it really from these resonances and these fluttering banners that the people draw their patriotism? Or is this feverish atmosphere only an occasion for them to give their exuberance free rein? I know not. My reason nevertheless refuses to accept that such a phrase, such a gesture, such a parade, arouses love for the Fatherland. Are there not, indeed, other links, perhaps more subtle but certainly more profound, that bind us to our native land, causing us to love it despite everything, despite ourselves? Are speeches necessary for a child to love its mother? It is an old and even banal comparison, but it seems to me fair. Do not the passing years leave a little of ourselves in all that surrounds us? . . . I love my country for the hours of happiness I have enjoyed here, and for the memories it awakens in me daily.
>
> I love it with my feelings, and cannot understand how reasoning or words alone can exalt this love. But perhaps I am only a dreamer.[9]

Less than a year after joining the *Gazette*, Young Sim was assigned a regular column by Joseph Demarteau. This promotion gave Simenon the chance to loose his overflowing reservoir of words and impressions. Initially entitled "Outside the Henhouse" (and later "Let's Talk"), the column ran for 784 installments, slightly more than half of which were signed "Mr. Rooster," the rest "Georges Sim." His columns were generally well constructed. The content was often trivial or frivolous, but Mr. Rooster usually managed to be funny, in a style unusual for such a conformist paper.

Simenon's nearly three-year apprenticeship afforded him entry into the inner sanctums of worlds he found fascinating. Since the *Gazette* refused to assign him to opera or theater reviews, he turned instead to the circus. Liège had a large, permanent big top, and Simenon became such an ardent fan that he used the paper's loge seats two or three times a week whether the program changed or not. He was as curious about what went on behind the scenes as in the ring,[10] and he was particularly enthralled by the artists who worked without a net. Their attitude tallied perfectly with his own philosophy of life.

One summer's day in 1919, he was assigned to cover an apparently minor event: a drunken brawl in a hotel-café involving the owner's son and a demobilized soldier. It started with an exchange of insults but degenerated into a mob scene as supporters of the protagonists gathered in the Place de la République Française.[11]

In the course of the scuffle a man was chased onto the roof of the Hotel Schiller. He stumbled as he ran, and clung desperately to the cornice to keep from falling. The populace below turned into a howling lynch mob, as a vicious rumor swept through the crowd: "a traitor . . . a spy . . . a Judas!" They began to demand that the "Kraut" be handed over. As the rumor spread, seemingly upright passersby became aspiring assassins uninterested in the niceties of a trial. Police and firefighters were called out, and the hotel-café was ransacked.

Simenon was long haunted by the episode,[12] in which unfounded rumor triggered collective psychosis in a context that inflamed human cowardice. It gave him a phobia for mobs, traces of which appear in several of his novels. In *Les Fiançailles de M. Hire* (*Mr. Hire's Engagement*, 1933), the hunted hero tries vainly to escape over the roofs in similar circumstances. In *Chez Krull* (1939), the populace of a small village lays siege to a house to do away with the "Kraut" Hans Krull and the "sex deviant" Joseph Krull, each suspected, without any evidence, of the murder of Sidonie, a village child. And in *Il pleut, bergère* (*Black Rain*, 1941), the seven-year-old narrator tells of Gaston Rambures, his friend's father, an anarchist suspected of an attempted assassination, who fled across the roofs to escape a lynch mob gathered in the square below.

Simenon would rarely witness the morbid power of ordinary hatred as intensely as during this manhunt. Yet however trying the experience may have been, this kind of journalism satisfied his deepest aspirations, giving him the illusion that he had seen the underside of history.

He had that same feeling whether he was covering politics or the circus. Slipping unnoticed into the appeals court, listening in on the conclaves of the managers of the *Gazette,* joining meetings of the provincial council, he was convinced that he had penetrated "the secret of the gods."[13] Later he would say that he was well aware that it was just a game, but at the time he seemed intoxicated by his role as a prying young reporter.

He now felt at home with any kind of assignment, from covering speeches by famous writers to everyday crime reports. Apart from his Mr. Rooster columns, he wrote about gambling in Liège and about doctors' views of physical education. He covered the Liège-Bastogne-Liège bicycle race, following the contestants on a big Harley-Davidson, and he did a piece on smugglers in occupied Germany.

In March 1920, a little more than a year after being hired, Simenon brought in a major scoop—or at least that's how he remembers it. As he tells it, he was puttering around the office one Sunday morning when Joseph Demarteau sent for him:

"Get to Brussels however you can, but quick. Marshal Foch's special train is scheduled to pass through at 11:30. He's on his way to the Ruhr."

"Okay, but what do you want me to ask him?"

"Ask him if he's going to Warsaw."

"That's it?"

"That's it. It's very important."

Young Sim leaps on his motorcycle and heads for Brussels. At the station he threads his way through a crowd of onlookers, cops, and reporters; jumps onto the platform of the marshal's car; and presents his request to an aide-de-camp. The aide consults briefly with his chief and then escorts Simenon into the inviolable compartment just as the train pulls out of the station.

"You're nothing but a kid!" exclaims the renowned victor of the Marne.

"Well, I'm sixteen. Just getting started."

"And you're here to interview me?"

"There was just one thing I wanted to ask, and it's not that complicated: Are you going to Warsaw?"

"Of course. Within the next two months."

Georges Sim now has what he needs, and it is Ferdinand Foch's turn to ask a few questions about the reporter and his newspaper. When the train stops in Liège, the cub excuses himself and gets off. The next day the *Gazette* runs a huge front-page headline announcing an interview with the marshal.[14]

So goes the memorialist's account of the incident. But he told several variants of it. In one, the aide refuses to let him see the marshal. Sim therefore waits on the steps of the coach and then slips into the corridor, where Foch happens to notice him and takes pity on him.

"What are you doing here?"

"I was sent to interview you, Marshal, but they wouldn't let me see you. Your aide-de-camp told me to wait here."

"What do you want to know?"

"Well, just one thing: Are you going to Warsaw?"

"Yes, of course."

"That's all."[15]

But that was not all. If we check Simenon's report as published at the time,[16] we find a slightly different "live" version of the event. Here the stationmaster plays the role later assigned to Foch's aide, and the exchange between the venerable officer and the young journalist takes place not in the comfort of the coach but on the platform. Finally, Foch's reply to Simenon's one and only question is not nearly so laconic as "Yes" or "Of course":

"I have indeed decided to go to Warsaw. Is it not my duty to greet the Polish army, to which alone among our allies I have not yet paid personal homage? As for the date of my departure, it cannot yet be set. It is in any case certain that my first official journey will be on behalf of the Polish Republic, which, like Belgium and France, suffered martyrdom in the Great War."

This was a Sunday in Brussels. The Monday morning edition of the *Gazette de Liège* reported that Foch had passed through, but in a brief, unsigned article containing no exclusive information. Curiously, it was not until Tuesday that the paper published Young Sim's big scoop, though the technical facilities for doing so the day before were available. So what happened?

What is certain is that Marshal Foch, the former supreme commander of Allied troops, signatory of the armistice, and president of the war council, did pass through Brussels on that day. It is also certain that the Poles were seeking French support against the advancing Red Army and that all the chancelleries of Europe were wondering whether the marshal would go to Warsaw. For the rest, the author's successive versions bear a whiff of fabrication.

Which of the Simenons are we to believe? Perhaps the most reliable is the one called Mr. Rooster, who, shortly after the publication of this increasingly suspect "scoop," produced two withering columns deflating sensationalist reporters like . . . Georges Sim. In fact, it transpires, Marshal Foch was not surrounded by a crowd, no one was jostling to question him, and some reporters are only too eager to exaggerate an event's importance in order to supply their editor with a flashy headline.[17]

Marshal Foch was never interviewed by Georges Simenon. The reporter simply elicited a sibylline statement in far-from-heroic conditions. The scoop was not a scoop. What are we to make of these Mr. Rooster columns? Self-criticism? Self-derision? Either way, the important thing was that Sim had called attention to himself. People were talking about him, and that was all that mattered.

In October 1921, he struck again. Having noticed three large crates that had been lying in the corridors of City Hall for some time, he conducted a private inquiry. It turned out that they had been there for two years and were meant for the alderman, who was to transfer them to the Bibliothèque des Chiroux. But the alderman was in no hurry. The crates contained a complete collection of French periodicals—*La Revue des Deux Mondes, La Revue de Paris, L'Illustration, Le Miroir*—that constituted a precious source of material for researchers on the history of the war. It was a gift to the city from a private citizen.

The reporter decided to expose this flagrant instance of administrative negligence. He and a colleague got a wheelbarrow and carried off one of the 165-pound crates (demonstrating, in the process, that anyone could take anything out of City Hall). Simenon liked to do things with panache, so he personally delivered the crate to the librarian, who had given up hope of ever laying eyes on it.

The subsequent article, suitably caustic and ironic, caused an uproar. The alderman filed a police report but withdrew it the next day when the rest of the Liège press picked up the story. Sim won the polemic hands down: he was the talk of the town, readers were delighted, and his employer rewarded him with a box of cigars.[18]

Sim's investigations were not always so mordant, especially when the theme was politics. About six months after he joined the paper, as the campaign for the November legislative elections began, Jules de Géradon, a rich scion of one of the region's well-connected families and a director of the *Gazette,* announced plans to run for office on a platform of defense of the middle class. Demarteau asked Simenon to help Géradon get elected, and Georges began looking into the city's various associations, beginning with those with the largest membership.

Having ascertained that fishermen were the region's biggest single occupational group, he convinced Géradon to run as their champion. The tactic worked, and Géradon was elected on a platform in which the pollution of the Meuse River figured prominently.

"I waged a campaign on this issue, writing articles and speeches castigating the factory owners for killing off the fish. . . . This was the sole political exploit of my life.[19] . . . For several weeks I was secretary to a candidate for parliament, and my work consisted of writing newspaper articles for his electoral campaign," Simenon would later say.[20] In fact, there was only one well-crafted propaganda piece. It turned out to be enough.[21]

Later, in 1921, Simenon would dabble in real political journalism when he produced a trenchant polemic on the language question. A bill had been proposed calling for the use of both French and Flemish in the civil administration. In his report on a rally held at the Variétés, Simenon vehemently attacked Wallonian nationalists and liberals. He was on the front page of the *Gazette* for several days in succession, firing shot after shot in an ultimately victorious battle against three other newspapers hostile to his positions. The exercise took nerve, pugnacity, and wit. Simenon was honing his writing skills on the job, tempering them in the fires of controversy. Clearly, he was also enjoying himself.[22]

This precociously talented boy showed flair where it was least expected, a valuable trait that could sometimes be hard to live with. Though he seems to have had no sense of limits, even his most daring and explosive choices can usually be reconciled to some moral or professional logic. But one of his forays remains enigmatic, even in hindsight: a series of articles wholly atypical of him in length, tone, style, and content. In the middle of 1921, Young Sim launched a violent and apparently inexplicable crusade against the Jews.

Between June 19 and October 13, 1921, the *Gazette de Liège* published a series of seventeen long articles entitled "The Jewish Peril," a sweeping denunciation of the omnipresence of Jews in the upper echelons of everything from Bolshevism to international high finance. After disconnected references to the philosophy of Karl Marx, the economics of David Ricardo, and, most of all, the notorious *Protocols of the Elders of Zion,* the journalist listed the influential Jews in the entourage of the leaders of the Great Powers, claiming that Sassoon stood behind Lloyd George and Georges Mandel behind Clemenceau. He then moved on to a systematic pinpointing of the Jews in the League of Nations and in the governments of various European countries.

"In the light of this enumeration," he wrote, "which could be extended far longer, it may perhaps be understood that the role of the Jews in international affairs is not purely imaginary and that a Jewish peril really exists, against which national and especially Catholic forces must struggle."[23]

The author of the series made copious use of the *Protocols of the Elders of Zion* as source material, while admitting that there was no evidence of their authenticity. He claimed to cite them while reserving judgment and without denying their "possibly" apocryphal character, but with such meager criticism and such spirited approval that he effectively sanctioned them. His intent was clear: he called himself a "historian of the role of the Jews in modern society,"[24] and article after article authenticated the *Protocols.*

According to him, the Israelite ideal was nothing less than the establishment of a world super-government that would corrupt the nations with gold and demagogy. "The Catholics alone have preserved their independence and, together with clear-sighted patriots, remain the enemies of the Jewish ideal."[25] He assured his readers that the Jewish conspiracy was aimed at universal domination. "It may be said without exaggeration that the Jews were the real beneficiaries of the war, even if they were not its authors,"[26] he affirmed without the slightest supporting argumentation.

While scarcely a European country escaped his denunciation, Protestant England held pride of place in the dock. He contrived to demonstrate through historical acrobatics that the Anglo-Saxon, the Puritan, and the Jew had hatched a plot to lay the planet low. He then moved on to a detailed review of the ministries of Westminster and the British administration in India. He listed the Jewish Masonic lodges in the city of Leeds and took inventory of the Jewish nobility of the United Kingdom and of mixed marriages between aristocrats of French origin and rich Jewish heiresses. From this erudite "demonstration" he concluded:

"The Jewish octopus thus extends its tentacles into all classes of society and into all spheres, where its influence is soon felt. And so it will be until the world finally decides to react. Unless by then it is too late."[27]

The longer this stream of articles flowed on, the more peremptory its author became. In the last installments, seeking to prove collusion between Belgian Jews and Socialists, he claimed:

"Everything hangs together and is quite clear in this nefarious movement now threatening the Old World: through their rage for destruction and thirst for profit, the Jews have given birth to Bolshevism. They used Germany to weaken a troublesome enemy and to reduce him to helplessness. So glaring a truth cannot possibly be disputed."[28]

Before examining the origins and consequences of this episode in the life and work of Georges Simenon, it may be useful to point to some of its more bizarre elements, beginning with its style. None of these articles bears any trace of "Young Sim." Biting irony, recalcitrant insolence, sharp sense of observation, small literary touches—all are absent. For the first (and apparently the last) time, he assumed the trenchant, unyielding tone of the dogmatic propagandist.

The author of these lines portrays himself as a serious, well-informed publicist with intimate knowledge of the mechanisms of international politics. This expertise entitles him to juggle historical references with confidence and to manipulate his documentation with assurance. It is hard to believe that an eighteen-year-old high school dropout who had hardly ventured out of Liège could be such a man. At least not alone.

Curiously, the first seven articles of the series carried no byline. The rest all bore the signature of Georges Sim. Had the editor in chief insisted that he take responsibility for his work? Or was the journalist himself deliberately laying claim to what was initially supposed to represent editorial opinion? One way or the other, Simenon now referred to himself as the author of the entire series. The tenth article made abundant use of the first person singular: "I do not think . . . I would like to point out . . . I hope that . . . As I have said . . ."[29] And the very first paragraph of the fifteenth installment employed a formulation that attributed paternity to all the earlier pieces: "I would now like to return to an assertion made in one of the first chapters of this study. I wrote then . . ."[30]

This was not a fit of bad temper but a press campaign in the most traditional sense. Though its appearance under young Simenon's byline is surprising, it was common fare for the *Gazette de Liège,* a conservative paper peddling traditional Christian anti-Judaism. Garden-variety anti-Semitism was widespread in Catholic circles in Liège, and French-speaking Belgians generally held pro-Maurras and anti-Dreyfus views during the "affair" that tore France apart. Two years before the series on the supposed "Jewish peril," readers of the *Gazette* were informed that "what the Jews in the modern world embody most of all is materialism, the abject tyranny of gold."[31] Several months before Simenon's outburst, the editors published a letter from an "independent Belgian" complaining of the favors the authorities had granted the Jewish "sect." Another article denounced collusion between Belgian Jews, Zionism, and Bolshevism. A year later there was even a brief anonymous article calling for "the physical elimination of this evil race."[32]

It is therefore hardly surprising that after this campaign the *Gazette* renewed its denunciation of Jews as "the worst evil enemies of Christ,"[33] or that in 1923, unlike several of its competitors in Liège, it saw fit not to devote a single line to the death of Abraham Bloch, the grand rabbi of Belgium.[34]

Simenon's articles on the Jews were part and parcel of two traditions: the deeply rooted anti-Judaism of conservative Catholic circles, and the anticapitalism expounded by certain socialist theorists. The author forged his own synthesis of these traditions, citing as sources a pamphlet by Georges Batault on Judaism, clippings from the international press, and, most essentially, the inevitable *Protocols of the Elders of Zion*.

This forgery was concocted in Paris in 1897, at the height of the Dreyfus affair, by agents of the Okhrana, the czarist secret police, in an effort to justify pogroms. It outlines a supposed secret plan for world domination and ruin drawn up by a group of Jewish conspirators. The *Protocols* were initially circulated among diplomatic circles in mimeographed form and then quickly popularized throughout Europe. The first printed version appeared in Germany in 1919. An English edition was published in early 1920 and received a favorable mention in the *Times* of London some months later. Several right-wing French newspapers published accounts of the English translation. By the mid-1920s the *Protocols of the Elders of Zion* was Europe's best-selling book after the Bible.[35]

Simenon produced his seventeen articles by shamelessly cribbing from this text. But that was by no means a record. At around the same time, the *Dearborn Independent*, a weekly owned by the overtly anti-Semitic industrialist Henry Ford, managed to squeeze no less than ninety-one articles out of the same source. These were published between May 1920 and January 1922 under the general title "The International Jew: A Major World Problem."[36]

The articles of "Young Sim" were therefore part of an international propaganda campaign generated by one and the same source. When the French edition of the *Protocols* (published by Roger Lambelin in 1921) arrived in the offices of the *Gazette,* Joseph Demarteau decided to give it the greatest possible play. Since Demarteau considered Freemasons the reincarnation of the devil and socialists the Antichrist, it is not hard to imagine what he must have thought of the Jews. He therefore had no hesitation in publicizing a document that was already highly suspect. The rest of the Belgian press, regional and national, also received copies of the *Protocols,* but most papers were more circumspect than the *Gazette*.

Le Soir of Brussels expressed initial reservations about the text's authenticity and ultimately denounced the deceit, refusing to lend the *Protocols* the slightest credibility, even while sharing the *Gazette*'s views on collusion between Jews and Bolsheviks. The *National Liégeois* was also suspicious and finally decided that the *Protocols* were a hoax. *L'Express,* a liberal newspaper in Liège, loudly denounced the "fraud" very early on, going to the mat with the *Gazette* on the issue.[37]

In the late summer of 1921, as Simenon was hard at work on his denunciation of the "Jewish peril," three successive issues of the *Times* of London carried the results of an investigation by Philip Graves, its correspondent in Constantinople. Tracing the origins of the fake, Graves produced compelling evidence of forgery. The *Protocols,* it turned out, were not merely the fabrication some had suspected, but also a gross plagiarism of a pamphlet that had nothing to do with Jews at all. The original, written by Maurice Joly, was published in Brussels in 1864 under the title *Dialogue aux Enfers entre Machiavel et Montesquieu* (A Dialogue in Hell Between Machiavelli and Montesquieu). The great British daily concluded that there could no longer be any doubt about the hoax, a judgment whose impact was enhanced by the fact that the *Times* had itself been responsible for catapulting the *Protocols* to public attention a year and a half earlier, lending them credence in an editorial entitled none other than: "The Jewish Peril."[38]

But even this was not enough to shake the convictions of the *Gazette,* which continued its campaign unabated, using the same arguments from the same sources. Simenon was completely engrossed in the effort, evincing breathtaking determination and vigor.

What did he know of the Jews before the "revelation" of the *Protocols of the Elders of Zion*? "Young Sim" came from a petit-bourgeois neighborhood suspended between the worlds of rich and poor, a place where people were almost casually anti-Semitic by habit and tradition. There were very few Jews in Liège. Before the 1914 war, they worked mostly in the food trade and in the butcher shops that had attracted Jewish immigrants from Alsace. In the popular mind they were associated with shortages, rationing, and the profiteering such conditions often engender.

Anti-Semitism in Liège was a widespread phenomenon transmitted by one strain of Christian tradition and fostered by the contagion of Parisian publications, like the daily *La Croix* and the books and articles of Charles Maurras and Edouard Drumont. Simenon had heard scant mention of Jews in his adolescence: names like Bernheim, the assistant director of Innovation, the department store where Henriette Simenon had worked, or Roskam, director of a large clothing store.

"But I never heard it said that they were aliens," he later recalled. "Nevertheless, there was a family in the neighborhood of whom it was said, without reprobation I might add: the Jews. This had to do with the fact that the man, the woman, and the children had retained the characteristics of the Israelites as depicted in ancient paintings and in contemporary caricatures."[39]

When he was a schoolboy with the Christian Brothers, Simenon had one Jewish classmate by the name of Schoof, the son of a salt fish merchant on the Rue Puits-en-Sock. If Schoof was not well liked by his schoolmates, it was because of his odor rather than his origins: he reeked of pickled herring, dried cod, and carob.

"This odor was not typical," Simenon commented in 1981. "I have known many Jews in my life, and I never noticed that they had any particular smell."

The artlessness of the statement is intriguing, especially since several lines later he adds:

"In Russia, Poland, and Hungary, a Jew is generally recognized at first sight. In America they have changed so much in two or three generations that they are no longer distinguishable from Americans."[40]

The fact is that most of the racial and ethnic clichés about Jews and central Europeans in Simenon's work come from his observation of his mother's boarders before 1914. *Pedigree* (1948) is revealing in this regard. It was by listening to these boarders that he learned to distinguish "real Poles" from Polish Jews, Safts from Feinsteins.[41]

Was the author of the *Gazette*'s "Jewish Peril" series a convinced anti-Semite or simply an opportunist pursuing his career? Office rumor had it that Young Sim was ever ready for any ingratiating mercenary task. His propaganda piece for Jules de Géradon was a kind of odd job. His denunciation of the Jewish threat was of quite a different dimension.

Prolix though he was, Georges Simenon never felt the need to clarify the ambiguity of this episode until 1985, when he responded to the publication of a book by the young Liège journalist Jean-Christophe Camus by sending him a brief letter correcting several trivial errors. Then he added:

"I would like to mention just one point that may be of some importance. It concerns the two or three articles I wrote about the Elders of Zion. These articles, in fact, in no way reflected my thought, then or now. I was ordered to write them and was obliged to do so. During the same period, more than half my mother's Polish and Russian boarders were Jews with whom I got along perfectly. I have had Jewish friends all my life, including the closest of all, Pierre Lazareff. I am therefore in no way anti-Semist [*sic*], as these assigned articles might suggest."[42]

What are we to make of the ravages of memory here? Simenon scales down his participation ("two or three articles" instead of seventeen particularly long ones) and confuses the source (*The Protocols of the Elders of Zion*) with the target of the denunciation (the Jews).

It is quite probable that the series was ordered by Joseph Demarteau. But the least one can say is that the young reporter did himself no violence in accepting the assignment. He and his editor seem to have been well in tune on the issue. The force of conviction resounds in every article. It is also difficult to credit his claim that he had no choice but to carry out the assignment, especially when we recall his rebellious personality and strength of character. In fact, he himself acknowledged that he had considerable freedom of action in his columns:

". . . My positions were not always in harmony with those of the newspaper. But the director, Demarteau, Thank God, was broad-minded and indulgent with his impatient chick, who sometimes showed a bent for rebellion."[43]

The origins of the anti-Semitism manifested in the "Jewish Peril" series are worth examining at some length, because although these articles are atypical of Young Sim's output, his subsequent work is riddled with stereotypical Jewish characters. The Jew-according-to-Simenon was born in his adolescence and youth and owed little to his adult experience. It is as though the characterization was frozen in time.

In a 1923 magazine profile of the writer Henri Duvernois, Simenon emphasized his subject's physical features, beginning with his "bourbonesque nose. Bourbonesque in the manner of the noses of Fischer, Bernstein, Tristan Bernard, and the rest of the tribe. . . . All the Bourbons . . . of Israel."[44] The characters physically typed as Jews in several of his pulp novels of the late twenties are not very pleasant.

In *Un monsieur libidineux* (A Libidinous Gentleman, 1927), there is a psychiatrist—or *aliéniste*, the term still in use at the time—called Professor Goldenstein, "a short, pudgy gentleman with a nasal appendage as modest as possible for a child of Israel. A lighthearted mien. Large, protruding eyes."[45]

In *La Jeune Fille aux perles* (Young Girl With Pearls, 1932), the banker Isaac Reiswick is a cynical, fat little old man, spineless and calculating, fish-eyed, with flaccid cheeks, huffing and puffing like a walrus.[46]

In *Lili-Sourire* (Lili-Smile, 1930), a romance novel in which a female employee loves her employer so dearly that she will do anything to save her company from bankruptcy, the role of the "bad guys" naturally devolves to the Brothers Lévy, Parisian bankers who specialize in debt collection and repurchase. It is because of them that the hero is threatened with prison: "What swine these Lévy and Lévy are! Have they no heart? . . . When your name is Lévy you have it in for no one. But you have it in for everyone's wallet."[47]

In *Deuxième Bureau* (Deuxième Bureau, 1933), a spy novel, a chapter title introduces a character who becomes ubiquitous: "The Polish Jew," an international vagabond with a disquieting glance, a thoughtless man devoid of feeling, with readily recognizable physical features:

"There exist some suits of clothing that emit the unmistakable odor of international trains, proclaiming that the man inside them has just crossed Europe from end to end. This man was blond, with frizzy hair, a long nose that revealed his race, lips with a bitter curl." When he greets someone, he shakes both hands at once, which is surely a "ritual." He inspires "nervous repugnance," and his name is Shalom, "Hebrew translation of Simon[?]," but the author prefers to call him simply "the Jew."[48]

In *Pietr-le-Letton* (*The Case of Peter the Lett,* 1931), Inspector Maigret deals with Jews in his very first official investigation, primarily in their Paris ghetto between the Rue du Roi-de-Sicile and the Rue des Rosiers, "half a Jewish quarter, half a Polish colony." Roaming the teeming courtyards and rancid elevator cages, Maigret finally catches up to Anna Gorskine, the Lett's mistress. The encounter affords the author yet another opportunity to deduce a character's Jewish origin from her physical features:

"She looked older than the twenty-five years listed in the records. Probably that had to do with her race. Like many Jewish women of her age, she had thickened, though without losing a certain beauty."[49]

Simenon would repeat this theme in other novels, sometimes with a bit more tact. Jews are often associated with financial manipulation, like Jacob, the blackmailer in *Monsieur Gallet, décédé* (*The Death of Monsieur Gallet,* 1931), or Bleustein, the Brussels money changer in *L'Aîné des Ferchaux* (*The First-Born,* 1945), to cite just two examples. In *Le Fou de Bergerac* (*The Madman of Bergerac,* 1932), Inspector Maigret has considerable trouble exposing the true identity of Samuel Meyer, a Polish Jew who, operating under the cover of the stamp trade, is an underworld forger to whom borders mean nothing. It also transpires that he is a pimp, shipping Jewish women off to South America:

"There were hundreds of people like Samuel available for study in Paris and elsewhere, and he had always observed them with a curiosity tinged with embarrassment, if not quite repulsion, as though they were a different species from the ordinary human kind. . . . Samuel was a Jew. The Jews generally have their feet on the ground. They venerate the family: knitted socks. They venerate saving money, too: three-year-old suits, of hard-wearing cloth."[50]

As we see, there is no shortage of clichés in these portrayals. In the short story "Les 3 Rembrandt" (The Three Rembrandts), the main character is Wahl, who wants to sell one of the master's paintings to raise a dowry for his daughter: "He is Jewish, which means very patient . . ." But sometimes the cliché is less insipid, as in *Pietr-le-Letton* (1931): ". . . a whole interbreeding of garlic-eating Jews who kill beasts differently than others . . . scattered everywhere, they nonetheless form a people apart."[51]

Did the novelist's perception of Jews ever change? Two of his most powerful books, written more than twenty years apart, afford us an answer: *Les Fiançailles de M. Hire* (1933) and *Le Petit Homme d'Arkhangelsk* (*The Little Man from Archangel,* 1956).

Monsieur Hire is an ageless bachelor beset by nature itself. He is ugly, has no clear occupation, and is considered an undesirable tenant. He poses as a policeman and does not even have a first name. He is believed to engage in petty swindles on the fringes of legality. He was born Hirovitch on the Rue des Francs-Bourgeois, close by the Place des Vosges. His father, a tailor from Vilnius who spoke only Yiddish, was a religious man and a part-time usurer.

Monsieur Hire is inevitably suspected when a sadistic murder is committed. But he accidentally discovers the real guilty party while peeping through the window of his neighbor Alice, with whom he is secretly in love. When he proposes to Alice that they flee together, she sets him up. The police now have their man. Jeered by a mob, Monsieur Hire escapes over the roofs. Caught in extremis by the firefighters, he collapses in their arms, dead of fright.

We would like to sympathize with the poor man, but it isn't easy, for the author never invites us to do so, as is powerfully pointed out in one study devoted to this theme: "His tragic end arouses only reluctant pity, for Monsieur Hire's past is too deeply compromised."[52] Yet Monsieur Hire is a hunted man—as, in his way, is Jonas Milk, the "little man from Archangel."

Married to the unfaithful Gina, childless, about forty years old, Milk leads a simple and uneventful life as a stamp merchant in a small town in Berry. An agnostic of Jewish origin, he has converted to Catholicism in an ingratiating effort to avoid sullying the landscape. One day his wife disappears, along with some valuable stamps. She has probably run off to join her lover—or maybe not. Maybe the little man is himself responsible for her disappearance. The town suspects the worst. Milk, after all, is different from the rest: a Jew from Russia, a country of which he knows nothing, not even the language:

". . . because the Milks had reddish-blond hair, fair complexions, and blue eyes, the country people seemed to take no notice of their race. Everyone thought of them as Russians. And in a sense they were."[53]

Milk is finally able to prove his innocence, but declines to do so. In the deepest dark of loneliness, he kills himself instead—out of weakness, out of resignation. His body is found hanging from a branch of a tree in the courtyard of one of the houses in town. Milk's death is infinitely more tragic than Monsieur Hire's, for his suicide, as one study points out, represents "the Jew's becoming aware of the fatal nature of his destiny and his submission to this absolute." It is as though "the ancient curse that, according to the Church, condemns them to wander persecuted among the nations, serving as scapegoat, weighs upon Georges Simenon's ordinary Jews."[54]

Half-breed, man without a country, nomad, parasite. Whenever Simenon's main character is a Jew, we have a rootless personality who—wherever he may be, whatever his efforts, and however self-effacing—will always remain a displaced person in the image of the little tailor with the eternally apologetic expression:

" 'Excuse me,' he murmured. He was always excusing himself. The Kachoudas had always excused themselves. Transported like parcels from Armenia to Smyrna or to Syria, they had acquired this prudent habit centuries ago."[55]

Simenon perceived this kind of alienation so sharply that he was able to reconstruct its psychology masterfully, through small touches. *Le Petit Homme d'Arkhangelsk* was enthusiastically received by the Jewish press. One critic, while pointing out errors of detail in Simenon's portrayal of Milk's social milieu, acknowledged that the author had "succeeded in penetrating the deeper nature of the Jewish being."[56]

Another, equally eminent Jewish critic also praised *Le Petit Homme d'Arkhangelsk* and congratulated the author for having seen fit not to stir the pot of racism among the antagonists: "He no doubt regards anti-Semitism as a manifestation of bad taste."[57]

Yet even with the best will in the world, we cannot ignore the reportage of the mature Simenon. In his articles about his European tour of 1933, for example, he boasts of being able to discern ethnic mixtures with dispatch. When it comes to Jews, he is especially precise. Vilnius is "40 percent Jewish." As for Poland: "Ten percent of the total population is Jewish above all else!"

When a "fat Jew" in Cernowitz goes into business, it is "on credit, of course." When the reporter likens Poland to a house, he reserves the upper floors for the officer, the aristocrat, and the bureaucrat, and the ground floor "for a filthy Jew selling furs and sausage." When he strolls through a square and indiscreetly eavesdrops on a conversation through the half-open door of a phone booth, he hears "a Goldstein" discussing some suspicious deal. In Ankara, he stays at the Palace Hotel, where the porter is "a Jew, naturally." When he stops off in Piraeus on a Mediterranean cruise, he immediately surmises that the Jewish merchants he encounters are involved in fraudulent bankruptcies.[58]

Georges Simenon's attitude toward the Jews was long a taboo subject. Having examined the issue more closely, can we detect "a striking example of the populist anti-Semitism that so deeply permeates an entire fringe of French literature"?[59] As we have seen, when asked to explain himself, Simenon issued categorical denials—embarrassed, artless, awkward, and unconvincing. In a private letter he admits that when he created the "little man from Archangel" in particular and his Jewish characters in general, he invariably had his mother's boarders in mind, especially one of them, a Polish scholarship student who did not wear shoes and lived on an egg a day.[60] That confession might help to account for the novelist, but it cannot excuse or justify the journalist.

Liège, the editorial offices of the *Gazette*; a day like any other in 1921: "Young Sim" has been "mixing the plaster" for two years now. He will later say that it was here, as he breathed the mythic air of rolling presses, that he got his true education, ". . . amid the thick smell of melted lead and printer's ink."[61]

He is gaining self-assurance day by day, and it shows in the tone of his articles and in their subjects. It is hard to say whether his stunning progress is the product of genius, energy, and ambition or of rashness and arrogance. Both Georges Sim and Mr. Rooster are voicing an ever more nonconformist spirit that runs counter to the newspaper's line. His colleagues regard him with both jealousy and admiration. "He could turn an everyday crime story into a breathless intrigue," one of his competitors at the *Journal de Liège* admits.[62] In other words, he is, body and soul, a journalist.

But what does it mean to be a journalist? Here is his answer to that question in 1921:

"He is a man capable of leading a solitary life amid the crowd without succumbing to its lure; a man with the fortitude to attend dreary vaudeville shows and twenty-scene dramas; a man skilled in the science of finding relatively honest ways of praising rich poseurs in all the arts; a man who can stay awake at political meetings; a man who knows the language of poets and of hooligans, who can sit at a table adorned with flowers or at one with wobbly legs; most of all, a man who writes a column or two on a subject he knows absolutely nothing about."[63]

A man who writes. To the end of his life, this man would give an invariant answer to the ritual question, "Why do you write?"

"I write because ever since childhood I have felt the need to express myself and because I feel uneasy when I don't."[64]

He was eighteen years old and about to publish his first novel.

3

BUDDING WRITER

1921–1922

ew would have believed that this frenzied young man was already leading a double life. When Simenon joined his colleagues at the Café de la Bourse for the ritual early-evening beers, it was less to celebrate the end of the workday than to mark the debut of a night of promise.

Disappearing into the dark Liège streets in search of women, he would drop in at cabarets and generally wind up at a bordello. His heated pursuit of prostitutes was a habit he retained to an advanced age. In part it helped to satisfy the imperious demands of an exuberant sex drive, but he also craved the spectacle, the contact, and the atmosphere. Simenon would often say that he felt most at ease with hookers, whom he considered the most direct, most pleasant, and least hypocritical of all "females."

In 1920 and 1921 he often headed from the brothel to the offices of *Noss'Péron* or *Nanesse,* two local magazines whose verve, nonconformism, and willingness to do battle with the establishment placed them poles apart from the *Gazette de Liège*.

Noss'Péron, a rather humorless enterprise, was uncompromising in its devotion to its watchword, "Belgians first, Walloons forever," a slogan "Young Sim" would make his own in several charming chronicles, among them his "Letter to a Woman of the Petite-Bourgeoisie." But although he shared the magazine's outlook and tirelessly trumpeted both his Wallonian identity and his pride in his origins, his zeal was ultimately found deficient. When the other Simenon, the one with the day job at the prestigious *Gazette,* dared to criticize the speakers at a Wallonian rally, *Noss'Péron* broke relations with him, closing its columns to the young man and announcing the decision in an article that called him "an ill-intentioned little urchin who deserves a good spanking."[1]

The atmosphere at *Nanesse* was quite different. This rebellious, satirical weekly, while as demonstratively Wallonian as its name suggested—Nanesse and Tchantès (Agnès and François) being popular characters in a Liège puppet show—was also suspect in various respects. An anonymous article attributed to Simenon, for instance, ridiculed the powerful Jules de Géradon, the future deputy for whom Young Sim had written propaganda in the *Gazette*. The magazine had a pamphleteering spirit and a taste for hoaxes and pranks.

Simenon's mother was ashamed of her son's collaboration with a magazine she considered lewd and dangerous, a judgment that was not far wrong. The owner of *Nanesse*, Ferdinand Deblauwe, eventually abandoned journalism for pimpery, selling the magazine to the unsavory Hyacinthe Danse, a libidinous secondhand bookseller whose shop Simenon had been frequenting for several years. *Nanesse*'s new management took it further in its natural direction, basically turning it into a blackmail sheet.[2] Both Deblauwe and Danse were later convicted of murder.

Simenon spent little time at the *Nanesse* offices, but he never forgot the characters he met there. They come up briefly in his autobiographical *Les Trois Crimes de mes amis* (My Friends' Three Crimes, 1938) and are represented more diffusely in *Maigret chez le ministre* (*Maigret and the Minister*, 1955) and in *Les Quatre Jours du pauvre homme* (*Four Days in a Lifetime*, 1949), two novels dealing with blackmail.

Many years later, Simenon said that he came close to drifting into a life of crime in those days, not as a bourgeois slumming for a few hours a week, but as a confirmed outcast lured by the unknown and by the thrill of walking on the edge. But three guardians held him in check: his father, his boss, and Régine, the woman who would soon become his wife.

The circumstances of their first encounter were hardly propitious. They met through a semi-secret club to which Simenon was initiated by Henri Moers, his friend and colleague at *La Meuse*. "I'll say you're a poet," Moers suggested. The subterfuge was requisite, for it was not easy to gain admittance to this peculiar institution that began in the attic of a mansion on the Rue Louvrex and then moved first to a dead-end street near the Church of Saint-Pholien and finally to a garret on the Rue Basse-Sauvenière. It also had three names: Le Cénacle, l'Aspic, and finally La Caque. The club was not much more than a poorly furnished room lit by an oil lamp or a candle planted in a human skull. The atmosphere was thick with pungent smoke redolent of various alcohols.

The dozen or so members, mostly second-rate painters with a penchant for long hair, snappy fedoras, and black cravats, were an informal late-night coterie. Bottles of ether were passed around with the wine. Girls were shared as well. Sim fit right in, inhaling the alcohol fumes and the carnival illusion, getting high on empty speechifying and vacuous invective. At times he seems reminiscent of the hero of *L'Âne rouge* (1933), seeking to forget a father resigned to humiliation and a mother who plays the eternal victim.

Apart from painters (Morsa, Mambour, Kleine, Bury), the group included engravers (Lempereur, Bonvoisin), philosophers (Nuez), musicians (Betet), decorators (Caron, Veckmans), literary figures, poets, and bohemians. The guru was a pale young man with jet-black hair by the name of Luc Lafnet, a painter, engraver, and draftsman with an already substantial portfolio. Lafnet considered himself an expert on both the philosophy and the history of art. A magnetic personality, alternately anxious and enthusiastic, he savored the adulation of his little circle.[3]

Basking in his authority and prestige, the members of La Caque sat up until dawn remaking the world, much like the Compagnons de l'Apocalypse in *Le Pendu de Saint-Pholien* (*Maigret and the Hundred Gibbets,* 1931). They thought of themselves as libertarian aesthetes, decadent and romantic, and they played the part with ebullience, drinking, screwing, and reciting Villon. But most of all they talked and talked: Marx and Nietzsche, Moses and Christ, as well as more exotic varieties of mysticism. Consistency was not the prime concern. The Liège bourgeoisie could rest easy in their beds despite the din from this sordid alleyway into which no reasonable man would ever venture alone, for the only dramatic incident in which La Caque was ever involved concerned the club itself.

One morning the sexton of the Church of Saint-Pholien found the body of Joseph Kleine hanging from a clapper on the front door, his woolen scarf wrapped around his neck. Was it suicide or had the young cocaine-snorting painter been murdered in a drug deal gone wrong? Simenon held out for suicide. He was one of the last to have seen Kleine alive the night before, having helped to put him to bed. But if Kleine had been too drunk to walk, how had he found the strength to get up, go back to the club, and hang himself several hours later? If someone else killed him, was his death the result of some bizarre La Caque ritual? Was it murder made to look like suicide? The mystery was never solved, and the tragedy marked Simenon deeply. The incident recurs in *Le Pendu de Saint-Pholien* (1931) and *Les Trois Crimes de mes amis* (1938).

On New Year's Day 1921, the members of La Caque gathered in a more temperate venue, the home of a young architect from a middle-class family.[4] Simenon arrived half drunk. The young lady of the house, the host's sister, answered the door and helped him to a couch, where he promptly collapsed. Her name was Régine Renchon. Three years older than Simenon and a student at the Royal Academy of Fine Arts, she was regarded by her professors as unusually painstaking and hardworking. She was a virgin and not really pretty, but she did have a kind of charm, more intellectual than physical.[5] As

Simenon recovered, they began to talk—about art, philosophy, literature. It was not quite love at first sight, but several weeks later they were engaged.

Simenon was now sure that he wanted to be a writer, and his determination to achieve that goal would be the organizing principle of his life. He thought of himself not as a man of letters producing Literature, but as a humorist of the Mark Twain type.[6] Young Sim had already published about twenty short stories in the *Gazette de Liège,* but that was just practice, a raw and rather naïve sampler.[7] The much-heralded sequel would not be long in coming.

His first book was called *Au pont des Arches.* Signed Georges Sim and subtitled "A short humorous novel of Liégeois mores," it was published by Bénard, a printer, in early 1921. Bénard decided to take the risk of producing this work by a reporter not yet eighteen years of age only because the author agreed to guarantee sales of the three hundred copies required to cover the costs of a first printing of fifteen hundred.

The novel was ninety-five pages long, consisting of twelve chapters. It was illustrated by four of his painter friends, among them the famous Luc Lafnet. The story began this way:

"Joseph Planquet, owner of the Pont des Arches pharmacy, did not sleep late that Sunday. He was awakened at eight o'clock by his wife, who returned from mass with a wet, red nose and said, in a slightly hoarse voice, 'Hurry up! You know what task awaits us today . . .' "

It is not necessary to plow through the whole book to guess that the father shares certain character traits with Désiré (though physically he looks more like Joseph Demarteau) and that the mother has many of Henriette's flaws. The son is primarily concerned with providing for his mistress. An uncle, who lives with them, is driven by a single-minded aspiration: to develop a laxative for pigeons. In choosing a pharmacy, the novelist did not go far afield. There really was a Pharmacie Germain at 13 Rue Pied-du-Pont-des-Arches, and it specialized in medications for dogs, cats, and other animals.[8] And there was a clothing store in town called Au pont des Arches.[9]

Foretastes of the great novelist to come can be glimpsed here and there in this effort: his unerring sense of detail, his knack for chiaroscuro portraits, his idiosyncratic manner of capturing a city by re-creating its colors, scents, and sounds. Two well-intentioned critics mentioned the book's appearance, one in *Noss'Péron,* with which he had not yet parted ways, and the other in *Le Journal de Liège.* There have been less honorable debuts, especially at such a tender age, but many years later, Simenon stubbornly refused to authorize the reissue of his first novel, which he considered unpublishable.[10]

Georges Sim committed his second offense just a few months later, in April 1921. The novel *Jehan Pinaguet. Histoire d'un homme simple* was meant to be both picaresque and philosophical. It tells of the peregrinations of an ordinary man of Liège, recounting his successive occupations (carriage driver, café waiter, bookstore clerk), encounters, and experiences, particularly his rather offhand quest for wisdom. The author acknowledged the influence of Rabelais and Anatole France. Here is the opening:

"Jehan Pinaguet opened his eyes that morning with voluptuous sloth, Rabelaisian noises rattling from the long nose that jutted from his face like a fishing boat's sail. Contrary to his custom, however, Jehan did not feast his eyes on the wallpaper's symmetrical bouquets of pink flowers, nor did he pursue the phantoms of his dreams, still floating in a corner of his brain. Instead, he was absorbed in his contemplation of the window, or rather the skylight, which gleamed sparkling and warm in the brightness and warmth of a beautiful August sun."

Pinaguet is an engaging character not entirely unlike his creator. As he walks off into the sunset at the end of the tale, one is reminded of something the novelist would later say about himself: "The real Simenon is an eternal adolescent who wanders off into the sunset, hands in his pockets, breathing the air of the quays and the alleyways."[11]

Despite the interest expressed by a printer other than Bénard, this book went unpublished until 1991. Whether out of caution, sycophancy, or lack of self-assurance, "Young Sim" decided to submit the manuscript to the owner of the *Gazette*. Demarteau pored over the manuscript with special care, probably because he did not appreciate his employee's parallel collaboration with *Nanesse* and the resemblance some detected between himself and the pharmacist Joseph Planquet, the hero of Simenon's first novel. When he finished, he summoned Simenon to his office and read him the riot act for the first time. "My dear young Sim," he said. "You have a choice. Either publish your book and leave us, or abandon it and stay with us."[12]

Simenon chose the second option. What could have motivated such a stark ultimatum from a man whose indulgence Simenon had constantly hailed? The budding novelist was convinced that Demarteau was unhappy with the character of the Abbot Chaumont, who not only initiates Pinaguet into the world of knowledge and culture but also represents the very antithesis of a good priest, at least from the point of view upheld by the *Gazette*. He smacks of heresy and alcohol, and has a greater taste for pleasure than for asceticism.

This "negative" character was undoubtedly part of the reason for Demarteau's attitude. But there were probably other, more directly political motives as well. The entire sixth chapter and part of the seventh have a revolutionary tinge that a right-wing employer might well have considered subversive less than four years after the Russian revolution. Jehan Pinaguet plays a leading role in the formation of a union of hotel and restaurant workers; he frequents the "hotbed of socialism" known as the Maison du Peuple and consorts with aspiring trade unionists demanding wage increases and a shorter workweek.

"It is high time that we stand up and tell the bosses once and for all that there are limits to the exploitation of the people," writes Georges Sim. "He was filled with an immense pity for these people, whose poverty weighs increasingly heavily once they become aware of their own strength and of their right to happiness."[13]

It was more than enough to disturb a devoted businessman. The manuscript went into a drawer for decades, but the author did not abandon his pen. In November 1921 he drafted a pamphlet of about twenty pages meant to be printed in a very limited run as a Christmas present for his fiancée, with a few copies being given to his friends at La Caque. In fact, they were the prime audience. *Les Ridicules,* typeset on *Gazette* equipment, was a series of acid portraits of several of them.

No one was spared, not even the writer himself. The victims, who were also the sole readers, were not named, but no one had any difficulty identifying the characters in this gem deposited by Simenon in Régine's Christmas stocking. None of them appreciated it. *Les Ridicules* was trenchant rather than outright nasty, but one wonders why Sim felt the need to indulge in such unkind attacks, referring to his dear friends as "pedantic prigs," "naïve ephebes," "pitiful wild men," and "effete puppets." Contrary to what he seems to have expected, his portrayal of himself as a fool was not regarded as adequate atonement for his indelicacy.[14] The work's confidentiality was its sole redeeming feature.

If we bracket *Les Ridicules* as a mere curiosity, then Simenon's third book, *Le Bouton de col* (The Collar Stud), was a parody of a detective story. Written in 1921 or 1922 in collaboration with Henri Moers, it reads as though its authors had plenty of fun writing it but did not take it too seriously, much like a couple of high school students perpetrating a prank. They did not openly admit that they were parodying masters of the genre like Gaston Leroux or Maurice Leblanc, but that seems highly likely, for the *Gazette* was serializing the work of these authors at the time.[15]

The manuscript was partly handwritten, partly typed. The plot is virtually impossible to follow, the superabundance of characters does not facilitate comprehension, and the number of chapters (47) is disproportionate to the number of pages (144). But no matter. This homage to Sherlock Holmes was meant to be funny, and sometimes it was.[16] It, too, however, was never published, for Simenon considered it execrable, as he admitted in 1975:

"If anyone ever sent me a manuscript this bad, I would consider myself duty-bound to recommend that the author apply himself to any profession, be it garbage collection, other than literature, even comic literature."[17]

Fortunately for us, Simenon spared himself this sort of murderous reply, having sent *Le Bouton de col* to no one at all.

November 1921 found Simenon in Antwerp, with two days left before having to report for military service. The *Gazette* sent him to the land of Jordaens and Van Dyck on assignment, but he took the opportunity to arrange a tryst in a hotel that rented rooms by the hour. His stay in Flanders was pleasant enough, his return far less so. As the train pulled into the Liège station late in the afternoon, he saw Régine standing on the platform waiting for him, accompanied by her father. He realized immediately that if they had come to meet him in person, it was to transmit the kind of news better communicated by a glance than by words.

"Dear Georges, you must have courage . . ."[18]

Désiré was dead. It happened in his office, on the Rue Sohet. He was at his desk, eating lunch at the usual time, as he had done for years, when suddenly he collapsed. Dr. Fischer had been right after all: it was the chronic angina pectoris that killed him. Stunned, Simenon went straight to his parents' house—he was not yet ready to call it his mother's. Désiré was laid out on the bed, hands crossed over his chest, ringed by candles, frozen in a decorum sadder than death itself. Georges found the ritual repulsive, but a slew of staring and whispering women had gathered, and he felt he had to go in. He suppressed his lingering reluctance and leaned over to kiss his father.

The burial was ghastly. Simenon attended without speaking a word. His only gesture was to kick a spray of flowers into the grave. Then he walked away, more rebellious and outcast than ever, going home to do his crying alone.[19] He was Jean Cholet, the feverish, unbalanced hero of L'Âne rouge (1933) on the day of his father's funeral:

"All the right people were there, and they were all so serious, displaying overbearing kindness. As though death had purified everything! As though all the little bits of filth had been burned, their ashes scattered. No one even remembered them anymore. Jean followed the coffin through a dull green world traversed by trolleys that seemed to mute the clatter of their wheels. People on the sidewalks waved."[20]

Désiré died with 300 francs in his pocket, the sole liquid assets of a man who had been treasurer of the Association of Honest Poor, a neighborhood alliance of simple folk who could not make it to the end of the month without help but preferred to suffer their poverty in silence rather than ask for it.[21] The sum was insufficient to cover funeral expenses, and Simenon asked his more fortunate uncles to pitch in. They refused, and in the end the newspaper advanced him the money to give his father a decent burial.[22] He would never forget any of it. Years later he would stipulate in his will that his own children be informed of his death only after his cremation, in order to spare them "all that."

He had no one to talk to, no one to whom he could express ineffable emotions that went far beyond sorrow. Simenon had always esteemed his father above all others, but after that fateful November 28, he would idealize him in book after book. Le Fils (The Son, 1957) is among the many examples.

In this novel, written as a father's letter of confession to his son, the protagonist, forty-eight-year-old Alain Lefrançois, an employee in an insurance company, recounts his family's past, beginning with the death of the grandfather. But the memorial is primarily a pretext for unburdening himself of a guilty secret: a young girl pregnant with his child has died of complications after an abortion. The father sacrifices himself, going to prison to save his son's future:

"I believe, too, that I have understood why the death of the father is so very important: because all at once you change generations, becoming an elder in your turn."[23]

On the day of his father's death, Young Sim truly became an adult. Like his future hero, he realized that the most important date in a man's life is that of his father's death.

One shock follows another: first death, then the army. Draftee Georges Simenon, 18½ years old, was 5 feet 8 inches tall and weighed 154 pounds. Scheduled to be called up in 1923, he joined early in order to get it over with as soon as possible. His goal was to get out of Liège, and to do that he had to complete a formality he regarded more or less as forced labor. He was sent to the Rote Kaserne in Aix-la-Chapelle for basic training. Offered his choice of assignment, he opted for a motorcycle regiment, probably hoping that he would soon be riding Harleys just as he had when covering the Liège-Bastogne-Liège bicycle race.

A cruel delusion: a month later he found himself in the Mounted Service Corps, assigned to the Lancers barracks in Liège. As the sole support of his family, he was granted certain privileges. Not only was he stationed very near his mother's residence, he was also allowed to continue his collaboration with the *Gazette,* writing a daily chronicle that he sent to his editor by courier. All this helped to ease the bleakness of military life, but he did not escape it entirely. He learned to peel potatoes, to make a bed with squared corners, to hold his tongue when he felt like speaking, and to stay put when he felt like leaving. If it wasn't discipline, it was a pretty good imitation.[24]

He could truthfully say that he was in the cavalry, but the reality was less sexy than it sounded. He spent most of his time guarding stables, keeping watch over 160 horses along with three comrades, sleeping on straw amid the stench of manure. Actually, the memory became a pleasant one after he learned to ride. The worst of it was having to wake up in the middle of the night, hungry, in the freezing cold, to water and groom the horses.[25]

Fortunately, it did not last long. Gradually and unobtrusively, he managed to detach himself first from the daily routine, then from the barracks, and finally from the army itself. He was given permission to spend the day at the

Gazette, provided that he returned to the barracks to sleep. "If you need me, telephone the *Gazette* and I'll come immediately," he told the colonel, who, it transpired, was an old friend of Demarteau's.[26] There have been experiences of military life grimmer than Simenon's. His passed simply and without incident, which may explain why there is scarcely a trace of it in his work.

A year after being drafted he left not only the army but also his family, his city, and the world of his childhood. Joseph Demarteau was the first to hear about his new plan: Paris.

"Inspector Delvigne regarded his colleague [Maigret] with the involuntary deference reserved in the provinces, and especially in Belgium, for anything that comes from Paris," Simenon wrote in *La Danseuse du Gai-Moulin* (*At the Gai-Moulin,* 1931).[27] Brussels was a political and administrative capital for Liège, but Paris was its cultural reference point.[28]

Simenon now felt stultified in his hometown. His three-year stint of workaday journalism had given him insight into all social layers and afforded him an impressive stock of experience. "There comes a time when you face the necessity of determining your fate, of doing the deed that really counts and from which there is no turning back. It happened to me at twenty," the hero of *Le Fils* (1957) would say.[29] It happened to Simenon a few weeks short of his twentieth birthday.

The director of the *Gazette* tried to change Simenon's mind, even offering to rehire him immediately if things did not work out. But he had always appreciated Simenon's flair and ingenuity in attaining his goals, and he was well placed to realize just how determined the young man was.

"I would sooner starve to death than admit I was beaten by Paris,"[30] the reporter said. He was too ambitious to remain in Belgium when Paris was the place to be. But he would never forget or deny his city. On the contrary, he would carry it with him to all continents, resurrecting it in varying forms throughout his novels and short stories. An old Liégeois feels right at home in Simenon's fictional world.[31] Certain towns—some named, some not—are mere transpositions of Liège, with its alleyways and little shops, its church and its main square. The city that would be "his only true nostalgia and the main character of his work"[32] would crop up everywhere.

So natural was his habit of viewing the rest of the world through the prism of his childhood haunts that Liège would long remain his standard of measurement. He was imbued with its tastes and smells, its light and sound. These sensations, the raw material of his inspiration, reconnected Simenon with the child and adolescent he had been.[33] "All my novels are phantasms of my childhood," he later acknowledged.

Years later, the memorialist would cherish the illusion that he abandoned a pure and human world for a universe perverted by money. That feeling, however, was not contemporaneous with his decision. It was created later by nostalgia.

December 1922: As the train pulls out of the Liège station, the young man gazes out the window, dreaming of stronger brews. On the platform stands Régine, who has been urging him to take the plunge, though he needs no encouragement. Her father is at her side. The train's cars disappear one by one into a thick fog.

One thinks of Murnau's phrase: "Across the bridge, the ghosts came toward him . . ."

FRANCE

4

CROSSING THE LINE

1922–1924

I will always resent the Gare du Nord for the way it greeted me. . . ."[1] Though we do not know the exact date of Simenon's arrival in France, we do know that it was hardly triumphal. As dawn rose over the capital, he could not shake the somber images of his journey through the awakening working-class suburbs. In hindsight, Simenon had a tendency to paint the admittedly bleak atmosphere of his early days in Paris darker than it really was, emphasizing his great moral and material poverty. But things were not really all that grim. He had some pocket money and a letter of recommendation from Joseph Demarteau, and he was met at the station by a very dear friend.

The painter Luc Lafnet, guru of La Caque, had made the move from Liège to Paris several months before him. The very first question Simenon asked him was emblematic of his anxiety: "How are you getting by?" Lafnet's reply was to gesture theatrically at a fence and scaffolding, where several white-cloaked painters wielding large brushes were just finishing an enormous billboard for a well-known baby food.[2]

Before long Simenon was again immersed in the familiar atmosphere of his nights at La Caque. In Lafnet's studio on the Rue du Mont-Cenis in Montmartre, he met many expatriates like himself. Their host—the consummate bearded artist, earnest and tormented—served as a cheerleader of northern nostalgia. Some nights they scraped together enough money for wine and cold cuts.[3]

It was here that Simenon met the painter Jean Hélion, a compatriot whose moral rigor and lofty view of art precluded the slightest concession to fashion

47

or the marketplace. Architect's drawings were as low as he would stoop in his effort to raise himself, however sporadically, out of the poverty in which he somehow survived. Though they had little in common, the two men soon became friends. Simenon, who became a cynical bon vivant at the first drop of alcohol, boasted of his plans to write novels the way Henry Ford made cars: "I'll manufacture Fords for a while until enough money comes in. Then I'll make Rolls-Royces for pleasure."

The purist Hélion held that Beauty was the supreme value. To its dominion alone would he submit. "You'll starve to death," the reporter happily informed him. He was right about that.[4]

In the end, Simenon seems to have lost his fondness for this ambience for the same reasons that had impelled him to write the unflattering portraits of his La Caque friends in *Les Ridicules*. Echoes of this sentiment are found in *L'Aîné des Ferchaux* (1945), which contains a detailed re-creation of Lafnet's studio. The young and ambitious Michel Maudet, a man in rapid pursuit of success, is not enamored of the people he meets there: "He scorned them. 'Failures, believe me!' "[5]

Simenon was in an even greater hurry. Unlike many provincial expatriates who spend a year or two living within walking distance of a station from which they can catch the train back to their "homeland," Simenon did not despair when he found "no vacancy" signs in all the hotels around the Gare du Nord. He had decided to spend no more than 50 francs a month on housing, and he found what he wanted in the Seventeenth Arrondissement, a district not wholly unlike Outremeuse: a city-bound village with its own shops and artisans, a place where everyone knew everyone else.

The proprietor of the Hotel de la Bertha on Rue Darcet near the Boulevard de Batignolles offered him a small room in the attic. A month later he moved on to the most bourgeois section of the arrondissement, near one of the wide boulevards emanating from the Arc de Triomphe in honor of the Empire's battles and the Republic's generals. Strolling down the interminable Rue du Faubourg Saint-Honoré, he came upon a middle-class building not far from the Boulevard Haussmann. An elderly Englishwoman agreed to rent him a room if he promised not to cook there. After careful consideration, he decided that making a Camembert sandwich did not qualify as "cooking." Just to be on the safe side, he hid the cheese in the chimney, where it generally lasted several days. Unfortunately, the landlady's suspicions were apparently aroused by the crumbs of Camembert she found scattered on the apron of the fireplace, and Simenon was evicted before the month was out.[6]

He soon found better accommodations on the Rue du Faubourg Saint-Honoré itself. Across the street from Pleyel hall, famous for its piano recitals, was the Villa Wagram-St Honoré, a cobblestoned dead end lined with artists' studios, its serenity protected by a lovely wrought-iron grille. This unusual setting struck him as "something special, an intimate little corner of bustling Paris."[7] He had two rooms, one of them tiny, and a little glass panel instead of a proper window. Not ideal, but it would do, especially since he soon found an office nearby.

Though Simenon had not left Belgium simply to become the Paris correspondent of *La Revue sincère* of Brussels, he was grateful that one of the directors of that literary monthly encouraged him to write short stories and profiles of writers for the review.[8] The protective shadow of his employer at the *Gazette de Liège* still hung over him as he settled down in Paris, and Demarteau gave him a boost in France just as he had three years earlier in Belgium. This time it was a letter of recommendation to Georges Plumier, a Liège businessman living in Paris.[9] Plumier knew someone who knew someone who . . . and so on. Georges was on his way.

Number 248 Avenue Beaucour, at the corner of the Rue du Faubourg Saint-Honoré, was an old building with peeling walls. It was here that Georges Simenon was interviewed for a position that sounded grand: secretary to a great writer. He would be Pierre Gaxotte to Charles Maurras, or Jean-Jacques Brousson to Anatole France. He could already picture himself writing his own equivalent to Brousson's *Anatole France en pantoufles.*

The writer in question was Jean Binet, better known as Binet-Valmer, a physician turned author born in Geneva in 1875 to a Protestant family originally from Touraine. Binet-Valmer was a Swiss who tirelessly trumpeted his French nationality. His first critical successes had appeared in two magazines, *Mercure de France* and *Revue de Paris*. His first novel, *Le sphinx de plâtre* (1900), was acclaimed by the critics, but it was with *Les métèques* (1906), a novel of manners, that he attracted wide attention. Binet-Valmer was a prolific author who wrote everything from love stories to monographs. Though determined to bequeath a great body of novels to posterity, he was equally devoted to cultivating his popularity, especially through *Le Journal*, which published his short stories regularly. He was a man of impressive savoir-faire, one of the publicists with clout in Paris. He had once been secretary to a well-known playwright, François de Curel.[10]

Hired on the spot thanks to his references, Simenon was shown to a small, shoddy-looking office. At first his only task was to address envelopes, stuff them with press releases or invitations, and stamp them. Later, he was dispatched to the post office to send parcels and registered letters and to pick up the mail from Binet-Valmer's mailbox. Then it was off to the Opera quarter to deliver urgent communiqués to the forty-five or so editors who shaped public opinion and the political personalities who supposedly represented it.

Binet-Valmer assigned Simenon all kinds of scut work. He taught him to forge his signature and asked him to represent him at weddings and funerals. The signature *Binet-Valmer* in the register of condolences for the great tragic actress Sarah Bernhardt is in Simenon's handwriting. Was this what it meant to be secretary to a great writer? He felt more like an errand boy.

The scales fell from his eyes when he realized that Binet-Valmer spent most of his time speaking at Action Française meetings. The texts his Belgian mail-boy delivered were mostly tracts extolling "manly friendships, solidarity, and Duty."[11] Binet-Valmer was in fact the leader of a shadowy political organization. By Simenon's own admission, it was "of the far right, of course, like the *Gazette de Liège* that I had lately left."[12]

Naturalized in August 1914, three times wounded and three times decorated during the First World War, a dragoon second class at the outbreak of the conflict and a tank commander four years later, Second Lieutenant Binet finished out the war as an attaché in the office of the minister of war. Immediately after the armistice he founded and became vice president of a "League of Section Commanders and Combat Veterans," one of a number of associations that aspired to form a "veterans' organization" to demand that the traditional political parties accord proper honor to those who had risked their lives for France. Binet's league, unlike some others, was overtly political. Its membership consisted of demobilized soldiers whose prestige was at its height and who were therefore in a position to make demands. It played an organizing role for the large national veterans' associations.[13]

Binet-Valmer, sometimes credited with having coined the French equivalent of the expression "wild blue yonder,"[14] was obsessed with several issues, among them having an unknown soldier buried under the Arc de Triomphe. He was the author of the inscription on the veterans' monument erected in the Glade of Rethondes in 1927: "Here, on 11 November 1918, succumbed the criminal pride of the German Empire, vanquished by the free peoples it sought to enslave." A formulation some considered marred by "jingoist grandiloquence."[15]

Such was the writer with whom Simenon now worked. In March 1923 he turned literary critic to help promote Binet-Valmer's latest novels, *Le Désir* and *Le Péché*. In an article it would be euphemistic to call accommodating, Georges Sim wrote:

"Intense drama unfolds in his works. Individuals are fully revealed, the darkest corners of their souls bared. . . . In form these works have a simplicity that might suggest facility: short chapters, few descriptions, the usual transitions lacking. Tightly packed scenes, almost always breathless. The essential scenes of the drama. In each of them the atmosphere is sketched as though in dry-point, with an exacting, almost cruel touch. . . . Two small novels: two bleeding wounds. Flesh torn by passion; turbulent souls in agony."[16]

Was that the extent of Simenon's contribution, or had he also become Binet-Valmer's ghostwriter? There is no decisive proof, but the memorialist implicitly raises the question when he admits having authored two novels for "a French writer" at exactly that date.[17]

Simenon believed that he had finally made the big time by being hired by a famous Paris writer. But that was an illusion. In fact, he had taken but one step forward, a feeling he expressed very clearly in *Le Passage de la ligne* (Crossing the Line, 1958), a novel in which the League is transposed to a stationery shop on the Rue de Richelieu. But it was elsewhere that he put his experience as Binet-Valmer's secretary to use: in *Les Noces de Poitiers* (*The Couple from Poitiers*, 1946), one of his most autobiographical novels.

Its hero, twenty-year-old Gérard Auvinet, is desperate to find work in order to help his family after his father's death. He becomes secretary to Jean Sabin, a great writer who is also president of the French Patriotic League. Auvinet's title and the importance of his mission soon go to his head. He is swept into the whirlwind of ministerial antechambers and the magical atmosphere of the city rooms of major newspapers. But one day, as he is carrying packages around Paris, Auvinet begins to wonder whether the writer really needs him:

"It would be unfair, odious, and horribly undeserved if, seething inside as he was, he were to remain Jean Sabin's fake secretary. . . . For he had finally understood. The great novelist was living off the League. All the rest was a joke. It was in the name of the few thousand imbeciles of the League that he shouted so loud that the telephone buzzed; it was in the name of the League that he worked his way into the offices of newspapers. . . ."[18]

There is a good reason why Gérard Auvinet's letters to his mother are moving in their authenticity.[19] Simenon had really sent such letters in his day.

They are written on Georges Sim letterheads and are undated, but cross-checking we know they were composed at the beginning of 1923. In them, the son apologizes to his mother for his angry outbursts, ascribing them to the suffering of a young man who believes that these are "the most terrible times" of his life. He says that he is working relentlessly, preparing a major article for *Le Journal* and a series for *Le Soir de Bruxelles*. Binet-Valmer, "who is ever more charming with me," has promised to sponsor not only his stories but also his picturesque news reports. He feels he is on the right track, on the brink of success. All he asks is time, convinced that by assuring his own happiness, he will also guarantee his family's. He sets himself a deadline of no more than two months, for he doubts he can tolerate his destitution and solitude much longer. He makes it a point of honor to repay the 750 francs he borrowed from her as soon as possible:

"The sacrifice I ask of you is strictly necessary to my own existence. . . . Think of my father and of what he would have done in your place." After all, he, too, had made sacrifices. He will support his mother because he believes it is his duty to do so. But she should make an effort, too, being patient with him and recognizing that her monthly payment might be late if he had other priorities.

His wardrobe, for instance, is in a wretched state, and he will have to re-plenish it if he wants to attend the right parties. He calculates a budget for Henriette and says that he will send 200 francs a month. This, combined with the 200 francs she was getting from her other son, Christian, should enable her to make ends meet. If not, she might think about going back to work, as she did before her marriage. He even offers to approach certain well-connected ac-quaintances of his in Liège to find her a position as a salesclerk. All this is dif-ficult, he admits, especially after the misfortune they had weathered together. But he believes in the future. Better days will come. In the meantime, he is working, writing articles and stories. He feels his father's shadow over him, so obsessed is he with being an example in his eyes.

On March 24, 1923, Georges Simenon, no longer Young Sim, married Régine Renchon, known as "Tigy," in the Sainte-Véronique church in Liège. Henri-ette had insisted on a religious ceremony. The new Mrs. Simenon, an intellec-tual raised in a family of atheists "who swear only by Zola,"[20] was therefore compelled to bow to the rites of baptism and communion, after an intensive three-week catechism course. Simenon's colleagues, who took up a collection for a heart of cut crystal, were more numerous at the civil ceremony than they were at the church. But the groom seemed in a hurry to get it over with—not only the formalities, but the party as well.

He seemed ill at ease, and not because of the tuxedo he had bought from Carlo Bronne, a Liégeois expatriate in Paris who would one day be a royal prosecutor and member of the Belgian Academy. Perhaps he was hurt by his mother's ill-concealed hostility to Régine's family, and to the bride herself, whom she considered ugly. But what bothered him most of all was having been compelled to journey back to his starting point, albeit momentarily. He was eager to be through with Liège once and for all, hoping to catch a train to Paris that very afternoon.[21]

He was only twenty years old and seemed unable to control his thirst for women. Why, then, was he so eager to get married? He offered a rather en-dearing explanation—"I had always dreamed of two shadows on a dimly lit shade, and I thought it would be nice to be with her of an evening, behind that shade, as one of the two shadows"[22]—but part of the reason was hardly romantic, as he confided in a letter to his mother.

". . . you can be sure that it was out of necessity. It was impossible for me to do otherwise without working myself to death." He then went on to ex-plain that he did not want to waste any more time preparing his own meals, and housekeepers in Paris were outrageously expensive: 2.50 francs an hour.[23] "I am not the type to live alone," he admitted.[24]

The truth is that Simenon felt uneasy as a bachelor. He was a troubled man who lived in constant fear of Sundays in the deserted capital, of other people, of being crushed by his responsibility as family head, of being misunderstood, of giving up when he was so near his goal, of yielding to his urge to steal, of remaining a minor employee all his life.

Not long after the marriage there was another change in Simenon's life. Binet-Valmer made him a new offer:

"Would you like to become the private secretary to one of our great friends who has just lost his father? A man who bears one of the very great names of France."[25]

So it was that Simenon, armed with Binet-Valmer's letter of recommendation, presented himself at 37 Rue La Boétie, the impressive mansion of an aristocrat about whom he knew nothing. The interview was brief, and he was hired immediately. Later he would say of his new employer: "He was my second father, one of the men I owe the most, along with Désiré and Demarteau. . . ."[26]

The château was in Paray-le-Frésil, in the Allier, just fifteen miles from Moulins. Its architecture was so heterogeneous that the structure, which dated from the reign of Louis XIII, had no particular style at all, a condition aggravated when the bulk of the main building was reconstructed after a fire during the Second Empire. The surrounding countryside failed to compensate for the chateau's lack of grace. No plain, mountain, or forest. "Nothing impressive, nothing pretty," Simenon wrote when he transposed the site into *Deuxième Bureau* (1933). He found the interior more attractive:

"It has a touch of the cloister and a touch of the guardroom of a medieval castle. Cold and severe, but with much nobility and even charm." But he went on to note the absence of comfort:

"Absolutely no general plan; wings added on, doors thrown in at random, stairways repeatedly redone, colossal proportions . . ."[27]

The courtyard was ringed by a broad corridor paved with polished blue stone. Heavy oak doors led into the building at various points. Ten rooms covered an area of five hundred square meters.

The grounds included nearly five thousand acres, half agricultural land, half woods. The land was worked by a small number of sharecroppers who lived in conditions of barely disguised feudal servitude. Crops were rotated to preserve the soil's fertility, wheat alternating with oats from year to year. It was a long way from the bustle of the Rue du Faubourg Saint-Honoré.[28]

Raymond d'Estutt de Tracy was known as the marquis de Tracy. His family, issued of a venerable line of Scottish origin, had settled in the Bourbonnais in 1420. The château's archives, of course, had been burned during the Revolution, but it is known that Tracys had lived in the region since the reign of Francis I. Raymond, the latest of the line, was a tall, broad-shouldered man with a drooping mustache and thinning hair. He had charm and was reasonably adept at seduction. Some considered his strong personality intrusive, and while he prided himself on his open-mindedness, he was highly authoritarian. In the past, he had lived the high life in Paris, organizing parties in the ballroom of his mansion on the Rue La Boétie, but now, at forty-five, he declared himself weary of the society whirl, bending to it only out of necessity. Devoted to the perpetuation of his name and title, he was imbued with a strong awareness of the duty of preserving his rank. Yet he also had a reputation as a nonconformist. When he resigned from the exclusive Jockey Club of Paris, for instance, he justified his decision in these terms: "They're just a bunch of assholes."

He was a night person, but not because he had insomnia. He simply lived on a different schedule, rising at eleven o'clock in the morning and breakfasting in his robe. He hated horses, having had quite enough of them in his youth, when his father had owned a racing stable. But he was fond of the hunt, and he accompanied his guests perched on a half-track inherited from Citroën's Croisière Jaune. The marquis de Tracy was a lover of fine cars and a chain-smoker of cigars. He hated being photographed, did not talk to his children, and enjoyed dining with his wife, even though he believed that a woman must never participate in her husband's life.

At a time when the low cost of food made the admittedly sumptuous life of aristocrats in the countryside less extravagant than it seemed, the Tracys employed a cook, a maître d'hôtel, three chambermaids, and two governesses for the children. Then there were the gardeners, two game wardens, and the fifteen servants supervised by the steward.

Politically, the marquis de Tracy was a man of the right—reactionary, conservative, or monarchist, depending on the mood of the moment. But although he had served as a lieutenant and was wounded in the war, he did not share the veteran mentality. An assiduous reader of *Le Figaro* and *Action Française,* he made no secret of his anti-Semitism. "I did something wrong today," he mused to no one in particular on his way home one day. "I bought a car from a Jew."

He had inherited a handsome fortune on the recent death of his father, but he was not the owner of the many châteaux in Italy and rice fields in exotic domains attributed to him by legend. He was quite happy with his estates in the Allier (Paray-le-Frésil) and Nièvre (Tracy), and his mansions in Paris and Nevers. Having now become a proprietor of land under cultivation, he was not so free to make long trips abroad and was therefore less inclined to accept mysterious "diplomatic" missions on behalf of the Quai d'Orsay like the ones he had made to Tsarist Russia, though no one knew how much these voyages owed to his own imagination.[29]

The marquis de Tracy was active in running his newspaper, *Paris-Centre,* and that was one of the reasons he hired "Young Sim," as he, too, called him. Simenon was initiated into his duties within days of his arrival in Paray-le-Frésil: filing papers, putting books away, answering the mail, lunching with Monsieur le Marquis, accompanying him to the headquarters of *Paris-Centre* in Nevers, drawing up plans indicating each guest's position during hunts, summoning the banker Saint-Phalle in the middle of the night for this or that urgent matter.

Simenon learned fast, though it took him some time to grasp his employer's attitude toward money. The boy from Outremeuse had always assumed that the point of making money was to spend it. At first he failed to notice Tracy's extravagance and even thought him stingy:

"He was so afraid of being cheated that he always took 20 percent off every bill. It was supposed to be an honor to work for him."[30]

As he went through a huge packet of mail on his very first day, Simenon came across a thick stack of second notices on unpaid bills, many of them from Cartier. When he expressed his astonishment, the marquis told him, "We don't keep current on bills. We pay when we feel like it."[31]

Indeed, the marquis was systematically in arrears to his suppliers, paying late as a matter of principle. He apparently considered the expression "cash on the barrelhead" as vulgar in its semantic content as in its form. Tracy saw his behavior as proper for a noble lord. It was this attitude that Simenon had in mind when he put these words into the mouth of Emile Vannier, the businessman in *Les Noces de Poitiers* (1946):

"The more debts a man has in Paris, the more highly regarded he is, and the more credit he gets. The one unforgivable sin, on the other hand, is poverty. Well, my good friend, and I mean no offense, what you are is worse than poor. . . . What really looks bad, the thing that'll hold you back for sure, is to skimp, to act like some honest little clerk."[32]

It was a lesson Simenon would remember. In the meantime, he worked relentlessly, absorbed in a world he discovered with mounting trepidation. And every night after dinner, he faced the dreaded specter of solitude. Tigy, though close by, was no longer at his side. Tracy never met her and of course would not hear of her presence in the château, women being inevitably burdensome. To see her Simenon resorted to deceit, renting her a room in the nearest village and slipping away unnoticed whenever he could, bicycling to join her for dinner at an inn. He would then spend the night with her and hurry back to the château before dawn.

It took a few weeks for the two men to get to know each other, but they soon achieved a certain rapport. Their rooms were joined by a hidden door. Each spent part of the day on his own side of the wall, and they would meet at lunch or late in the afternoon to go to the *Paris-Centre* offices together. Before long Tracy began dropping in on his secretary more and more often, just to chat.

At first, Simenon was so busy that he had little time to think, but once he established a routine, gloom, sadness, and discouragement began to haunt him anew. He came to find the château intolerably boring. Infuriated to find himself still at the table at four in the afternoon and nine at night, he found it harder and harder to endure the endless meals. He couldn't stand being separated from Tigy, sometimes becoming so bitter that he complained about his master in private letters, occasionally simply spewing venom to relieve his resentment: "Tracy doesn't even notice that his wife is not here. The assh . . . !"[33] In Simenon's eyes, the clearest evidence of his employer's lack of appetite for life was his attitude toward his beloved books, which he never read but only fondled.

He was glad when the marquis had to travel and asked his secretary to accompany him, either to a cure in Aix-les-Bains or to his various domains. But it was the trip to Nevers that excited Simenon most. The offices of *Paris-Centre* were at 3 Rue du Chemin-de-Fer. The paper was a six-page "regional daily" with genuine influence, having a circulation of more than sixty thousand in Allier, Nièvre, Saône-et-Loire, Cher, Loiret, Yonne, and Puy-de-Dôme. Alongside the inevitable hallmarks of the provincial press large and small—glowing reports of agricultural fairs and Légion d'honneur award ceremonies, market hours, and obituaries—it featured extensive local crime news, ever popular with its readers, as well as more political fare. The death of His Royal Highness the duke de Montpensier, brother of the pretender to the throne of France, was front-page news for several days. Communiqués issued by our old friend Binet-Valmer received pride of place, being regularly featured on the front page and sometimes reprinted inside for any readers who may have missed them. But the prime concern of the paper's owners in early 1923 was to defeat the communists, radicals, and socialists in the upcoming May legislative elections. "The fatherland above all parties!" That was their slogan.

It was a familiar tune, and as the date of the vote drew near, it was trumpeted in one editorial after another. "The role of the state is not to bargain but to govern."[34] Or, "The man in the street may well wonder whether the first big saving ought not to be the abolition of Parliament."[35] Other articles, with titles like "The Reign of the Half-breed,"[36] denounced foreigners who supposedly sullied France and condemned "Anglo-Jewish finance capital" for having "induced France to accept international schemes for the settlement of the German question."[37]

Simenon got into the act with a two-column front-page article datelined Brussels and headed "Fall of the Belgian Government." It reported the collapse of the Theunis cabinet in the face of attacks by an alliance of normally bitter enemies: Wallonian socialists and far-right Flemings:

"From *Paris-Centre*'s special correspondent in Belgium[?]. No one can be unaware of the importance of the fall of the Belgian government, at a time when the struggle of international forces (socialism, Jewish and Anglo-Saxon finance capital) against French and Belgian national forces has attained its sharpest pitch." The article was signed "Sim."[38]

The elections were held on May 11, and the alliance of left parties defeated the National Bloc, in seats if not in popular vote. A month later, Gaston Doumergue replaced Alexandre Millerand in the Elysée Palace. The Radical leader Edouard Herriot was asked to form a new government. *Paris-Centre*'s campaign continued unabated, but Simenon's mind was elsewhere. His body would soon follow.

How could he stay in Paray-le-Frésil when Paris was the place to be? The marquis de Tracy understood. Young Sim could not continue writing stories in the boondocks and trying to get them published in the capital. The young man had shared his plan with the marchioness—"Make as much money as possible writing easy books, and then settle down to write literature"[39]—and the marquis considered the project courageous. He was not unduly astonished when he received telegrams from his former secretary asking for loans, and he later said that he was "amused" to learn of the young man's success.[40]

Georges Simenon would never forget the marquis de Tracy, though the memorialist expressed his gratitude somewhat gingerly: "My marquis was likable enough, but he sometimes wore a Talleyrand grin, since in his eyes I would always remain the little boy from Outremeuse. That only intensified my rebellion."[41]

Simenon learned a lot during his two years with this extraordinary man, and his experience fueled his novelist's inspiration. He became well acquainted with Pierre Tardivon, steward of the château in Paray-le-Frésil and one of the estate's most influential members, for he acted as a screen between landlord and sharecroppers. The character reappears as Joseph Tardivon in *Les Larmes avant le bonheur* (Tears Before Happiness, 1924) and *L'Affaire Saint-Fiacre* (*The Saint-Fiacre Affair*, 1932), as well as *Les Mémoires de Maigret* (*Maigret's Memoirs*, 1951). The Moulins region is Inspector Maigret's native land, and his father was steward at the Château Saint-Fiacre.

The marquis de Tracy, whom Simenon in all seriousness once called a direct descendant of Descartes,[42] also had enough impact on the young man to reappear in many of his novels. In *La Fiancée aux mains de glace* (The Fiancée with Icy Hands, 1929) he is the marquis de Tercy. The character is even clearer in *Deuxième Bureau* (1933), especially in the hunting scenes. In this novel Jean Colin—married, twenty-three years old but with the air of a kid, "a small young man, pale and thin, too blond, with skin too fair"—is secretary to Henrico de Peralta, a South American marquis. Colin hands out targets to invited guests at the hunt, also determining their place in the pack. In this alien world he learns to distinguish fine weaponry from ordinary rifles and discovers the rituals of a milieu in which local squires who do not work for a living call government ministers by their first names. At one point the novelist even slips and has the marquis call Jean Colin "Georges."[43]

In *Monsieur Gallet, décédé* (1931), one of the first Maigret novels, Aurore Gallet is the daughter of a former secretary to the last prince of Bourbon, now director of the newspaper *Le Soleil*, "which nurtures the hopes of a handful of country squires that a Bourbon might regain the throne of France."[44] Her husband, Emile Gallet, turns this hope to his own advantage by extorting money from monarchist families.

Simenon retained an undying fascination with the aristocracy and with château life. Both are legion in his pulp novels. He ranked the nobility in his own mind, ascribing the highest positions to great hereditary lords and the lowest to impostors who attained their status through baser means—calculated marriages, money, and so on. Here is how he put it in *L'Heureuse Fin* (The Happy Ending, 1925):

"Down-on-their-luck local squires perpetuating medieval traditions in modest country manors; newly issued noblaillons [*sic*] acquiring land and châteaus and scurrying to rub elbows with the real nobility; rich and powerful industrialists well received everywhere since millions are now equivalent to the most sonorous titles—all that . . . displeased her. She detested stiff, proud counts or barons whose only concern in life was the renown of their names and titles and for whom the hunt was the last vestige of the past, a privilege of noble stock. She had no greater fondness for rich merchants affecting manners intended to bury the memory of the shops they had come from and who, having purchased some old country house, blushed at their origins and spoke with sovereign scorn of the 'common people' of whom their own fathers were issued."[45]

In Paray-le-Frésil, Simenon had the heady feeling of having leapt across an invisible boundary, as many of his future heroes would do in the most varied circumstances. The accumulated emotions of this period of his life are expressed most sharply in a novel entitled *Le Passage de la ligne* (1958). The narrator, Steve Adams, a Franco-Englishman in his fifties, organizes his introspective and retrospective reassessment of his life around the crossing of three lines of demarcation.

Alvin Haags, his first ferryman, is an international swindler who brings him into the world of palaces. Gabrielle D., a widowed businesswoman of about fifty, originally from Bordeaux, "initiates" him into another life: the world of international big business. These two key characters seem to share aspects of the marquis de Tracy's personality.

When Haags, a seasoned jewel thief, accepts young Steve Adams as his assistant, he also undertakes to alter his habits, clothing, and attitudes to make him more accomplished at fraud:

"It was a little like the transformation of a girl you pick up in the gutter and groom for high society. . . . So it was that, with him, I finally ceased to belong, however tenuously, to any particular milieu. I moved from one square to another, but it was like a game. I learned to be the man from nowhere and everywhere that I had vaguely dreamed of being."[46]

In bits and pieces, Haags tells young Steve Adams so much about his murky past that the young man feels he has been led to the heart of true power and secret influence, to the wings of the theater of life, the place where decisions are made. He believes he is standing in the shadow of the men who really pull the strings, who hold genuine power far more surely than the princes who govern us.

Gabrielle D. then hires Steve Adams as her secretary. Served by a numerous household staff, she owns châteaux, mansions, factories, and a newspaper. He deals with all sorts of problems for her, arranging meetings, making reservations, organizing her social life.

"I also had to follow her almost everywhere, though I often wondered why, since people rushed to serve her wherever she went. In the end I realized that she lived in such a state of tension that she could never relax, for fear that she would be unable to set the machine in motion again at the appropriate time. Actors face a similar dilemma. Her way of never weakening was to be sure always to have an audience, to be performing all the time. Well, I was her audience. She tested her moods on me, rehearsing with me, thinking aloud instead of to herself."[47]

The narrator ultimately achieves social and professional success by his own resources. That is his third and final passage, one he owes to himself alone. The story might have ended there, but for the chronic dissatisfaction of the hero, who, tormented by a strange malaise, decides to throw it all away. He feels as though he is playing a part not his own:

"When I sat behind the wheel of a big American car and drove down the Rue Saint-Antoine or any of the other streets I had known, it was as though I had been seeking a path and, having found it, discovered forgotten pleasures. Or as though, moving from square to square, drifting ever farther from basic needs, from hunger and thirst, from a world in which everyone is subject to immutable laws, I had unwittingly wandered into an abstract universe in which nothing existed but signs."[48]

Had Georges Simenon crossed the line at the Paray-le-Frésil château? In any event, it was when he left the marquis de Tracy's employ that he finally took the plunge. He was twenty-one and driven by an unshakable desire: to make his living with his pen.

5

INTO THE WHIRLWIND

1924–1927

aris, the Hotel Beauséjour on the Rue des Dames, in the Batignolles quarter: the Simenons are living in one room, forbidden by order of the landlord to cook. They circumvent the interdiction with a hot plate balanced on the windowsill, making sure the smells drift out into the street.[1] Some nights they splurge, eating out in restaurants patronized by carriage- and cabdrivers, cozy places where family members cook the food and wait the tables, where the menu is scrawled in chalk on a slate and the wine is unpretentious.

Tigy is as good as her word. "It turns out she's a splendid housekeeper and a first-class cook to boot," Simenon writes to his mother.[2] She not only takes charge of the material aspects of their married life but also works for him, reading over his copy as he writes, correcting mistakes, digging up information, taking his pieces to newspapers.[3]

On his table Simenon has placed a small black notebook, a kind of diary inaugurated on the thirtieth of April. In it are recorded his receipts, but not his expenses. There are two categories, "paid" and "pending." There follows a list of articles, names of publishers, and magazine titles: *Paris-Flirt, Frou-Frou,* and so on. Sometimes the information is more detailed: "Paid, 50 francs, *Paris-Centre,* article on fall of Belgian government" (May 8); "Paid, Tracy, 1,000 francs" (August 22); "Brought Duvernois *Marie Ledru*" (October 8).[4]

He had been writing throughout his stay with the marquis. Between April and July 1923, *La Revue sincère* of Brussels published a series entitled "My Files."

In these brief portraits, Georges Sim taunted major French authors and publicists in much the same way he had parodied his La Caque companions in *Les Ridicules*. It is difficult to say whether his freewheeling tone, trenchant style, and polemical verve reflected naïveté, lack of opportunism, or a complete absence of what Parisian literary strategists would call political savvy.

The novelist and dramaturge Henri Duvernois (pseudonym of Henri-Simon Schwabacher), whose Jewish origins Simenon was pleased to recall, is so relentlessly described as a mass of flesh that Sim "forgets" to mention his abilities as a storyteller.[5] Claude Farrère, the naval officer who won the 1905 Prix Goncourt for *Les Civilisés,* fares no better, being treated as an egotistical skirt-chaser and hashish-smoker in a portrait not at all false but one-sided to say the least.[6] Paul Fort, the "prince of poets" whom the former *Gazette de Liège* reporter had the privilege of meeting, is gently mocked for the musical quality of his rhymes: "Tra la la, tra la la."[7] Léon Daudet, *Action Française*'s chief pamphleteer, would have made "a fine tyrant in a light operetta." He was "a caricature of majesty" whose personality was the product of his physical misfortune: he was a large, fat, sweaty man.[8]

And what of Maurice Barrès, who died several months later, though not of the effects of Simenon's article? The nationalist poet and former deputy from Nancy was portrayed as a lost sheep, a bitter man born in the wrong era: "He missed the Inquisition by a few centuries, missed the venomous intrigues of the Medicis. He missed Ruy Blas and the heroic epoch of drama. Missed Romanticism, too. He wanders sadly in a vaudeville world."[9] Tristan Bernard, the last "file" to be tacked to the board, was a disenchanted author spewing scorn for everything, including himself.[10]

Here, as in his earlier profiles, Georges Sim omitted any assessment of the literary qualities of the authors he was supposed to be writing about. Employing a procedure fashionable in the far-right press between the wars, he dwelt instead on what they looked like, deducing the essence of their personalities from their appearance.

Simenon had written a few portraits during his years with Tracy and had managed to get some of them published in risqué magazines. It was a situation he put to use in *Pour le sauver* (To Save Him, 1925), in which the young poet Albert Dulin is secretary to the Academy member Maxime des Courtières:

". . . Twenty-four years old, he eked out a living from articles placed with great effort in a few newspapers, without so much as a thought for the morrow, convinced that his day would come and that he, too, would taste glory. . . ."[11]

Georges Ista, a popular Belgian novelist then living in Paris,[12] gave him introductions to various magazines and journals with titles like *Frou-Frou, Sans-Gêne, Paris-Flirt, Le Sourire, Paris-Plaisir, Ric et Rac, Le Petit Journal, Le Rire,* and *Gens qui rit.* By Simenon's own admission, these journals published "a literature more suggestive than flirtatious, in which much time was spent skirting the issue."[13] One of the first things he learned was how to convey that a man and woman made love without actually saying so. Later the author grew bolder, and his risqué stories began to feature voyeurism and exhibitionism. These spicy tales not only earned him quick money, they also formed the first stage of what he saw as his on-the-job training in the novelist's craft.

He described it as "mixing the plaster," an expression he was especially fond of since it recalled the artisan spirit so dear to him. His aim was to examine the construction of a story from the inside out, studying the ways it could be put together regardless of how hollow the plot might be. The psychological mechanisms were primitive, the tone one of pathos bordering on sentimentality. "Success hinges on how you do things," he told his friend Jean Hélion, reiterating his determination always to aim at the broadest possible audience.[14] He soon found his stride, churning out an average of several stories a day.

Simenon might well have marked time much longer had it not been for an encounter with Colette, who had married Henry de Jouvenel, editor in chief of *Le Matin,* and was now in charge of the paper's fiction desk, spending three hours a day at the office. In 1923, Simenon sent her some of his stories in the wild hope that she might let him get his feet wet in the prestigious "Thousand and One Mornings" section. His works were consistently rejected, and he would pick up the castoffs at the *Matin* offices while delivering new efforts. Then one day there was no rejection notice. Instead, he was summoned to the office.

The fiction department and the cash desk were on the same floor. A good sign. You could smell the ink from the stairway. The day's paper had been put to bed, and the presses were ready to roll. An impressive jumble of papers covered Colette's American-style desk, and she grumbled endlessly, "Writing is stupid enough, but tinkering with other people's stuff, really!"[15]

If Simenon was impressed by the invitation, he was stunned by Colette's response to his work:

"My dear little Sim, this is not what we want. Almost, but not quite. You're too literary. No literature! Get rid of all the literature, and you've got it."

He went home to ponder the surprising advice of the author of the *Claudine* novels. He tried to take it to heart. In vain.

"Still too literary. No literature!" Colette repeated.[16]

Finally he got it right. On September 27, 1923, *Le Matin* published "La Petite Idole," a story by Georges Sim. It was the beginning of a long and fruitful collaboration.

From the day he met Colette to the end of his career as a novelist, he seems to have written and edited with her voice in mind, mercilessly banishing adverbs from his prose. "I tried to be as simple as possible. That was the most useful advice I ever got, and I am eternally indebted to Colette for having given it to me," he said.[17]

Now that he was settled in Paris, Simenon was able to work the way he wanted. To start with, he needed more creature comforts. He did not care that his typewriter was rented. It was housing he was most concerned with, and he soon left the Rue des Dames for the Place des Vosges, in the Marais quarter.

One day he happened to come across a one-and-a-half-room apartment on the ground floor of number 21, in the former mansion of Marshal Richelieu. Not surprisingly, he thought of his glorious predecessor less as the victor of Fontenoy or the architect of Franco-Austrian rapprochement than as a great libertine:

"He was most famous not for his battles but for his sexual exploits. If I am not mistaken, he was the lover of Ninon de Lenclos, who was still making conquests at eighty," the memorialist recalled.[18]

It was a quiet neighborhood. In the morning he could hear the bubbling fountains in the square even though his window faced the inner courtyard. He pounded his typewriter relentlessly, stopping only to fortify himself with red wine or to watch passersby come and go. Apart from the Simenons and the elderly widow Dreyfus, the building had few residential tenants. Most of the apartments were occupied by companies or craftsmen.

The Simenons had no intention of spending their lives in this neighborhood. At the local bistro they were more likely to rub elbows with tailors or Jewish workers from central Europe than with artists or journalists. As night fell they left this grim arrondissement and crossed the Seine for the lights of Montparnasse. They soon became regulars at all the fashionable restaurants, bars, and nightclubs: La Rotonde and La Coupole, Le Dôme and the Jockey Club.[19]

In Montparnasse, Tigy was his guide. Despite the many tasks she had taken on since their move to Paris, she still found the time to paint and to exhibit her work on the sidewalks of Montmartre. Her husband encouraged her by framing her pictures, trying hard to get the corners square. But as Simenon's production increased, she abandoned her paints and brushes to spend all her time helping him.

As always, Simenon immediately spent whatever he earned and soon acquired the habit of spending what he had not yet earned. When a larger apartment became available on the third floor of his building, he signed a lease without giving up the ground-floor flat. He now had a spacious living room overlooking the Place des Vosges. Why not? If they were short of money, he would write more stories.

The new apartment was decorated under Tigy's watchful eye. Enamored of Art Deco, a style wholly at odds with the detested decor of his childhood homes, Simenon had the walls painted colors that seemed loud even in the dark. He had a stylish bar put in, and he enjoyed the subtle play of light on the polished glass of the countertop. Large velvet curtains, high leather stools, and the respectable number of whiskey bottles lining the wall testified to his desire to re-create the ambience of an American bar. But the atmosphere Simenon achieved was Montparnasse, not America.

He went to the movies on the Left Bank as well, preferring small neighborhood theaters to the less intimate houses of the Boulevard Poissonnière. According to his memoirs, the first movie he ever saw was *The Cabinet of Dr. Caligari*, Robert Wiene's 1919 film based on an idea by Fritz Lang. This picture, whose aesthetic values and stunning atmosphere marked the beginnings of German expressionism, opened new vistas for him: "The sets made no attempt to mimic reality, and I saw this as a genuine revolution in cinema."[20]

Other films that Simenon saw again and again with undiminished enthusiasm included *La Charrette fantôme* (1920), by the Swede Victor Sjöström, which used the then-revolutionary technique of superimposition; *Entr'acte* (1924), a short farce in which René Clair had performers known for their genius in other fields, like Man Ray, Marcel Duchamp, Marcel Achard, and Georges Auric, act out a fantastic story conceived by Francis Picabia and set to background music by Erik Satie; the early films of Jean Epstein; and soon, those of Jean Renoir (*La Petite Marchande d'allumettes*), Alberto Cavalcanti (*Le Train sans yeux*), Josef von Sternberg (*Chicago Nights*), and of course Fritz Lang's *Metropolis*. These and many others had a lasting impact on his imagination.[21] He would come home late from the movies, sleep for a few hours, and then sit down at his worktable, wine and typewriter at hand, to churn out stories that were anything but avant-garde.

Mixing the plaster, practicing his scales, learning his craft—that was his obsession, and he set to work with a keen sense of organization and an already seasoned knowledge of public taste. Between 1924 and 1931, he published about 190 pulp novels under at least seventeen pseudonyms, among them Christian Brulls (his brother's first name and his mother's maiden name), Jean du Perry (after the Rue du Perry in Liège), Georges Sim, Jacques Dersonne, Luc Dorsan, Georges-Martin Georges, Gom Gut, Gaston Vialis, and, less often, Germain d'Antibes, Bobette, J. K. Charles, Georges d'Isly, Kim, Plick et Plock, Poum et Zette, Jean Sandor, and G. Violis.

His plots are recognizable from book to book, for he often recycled situations, characters, and even entire stories. There are also recurrent psychological stereotypes: the heroine who sacrifices herself for love, the intrepid young man driven to despair, the aristocrat in his château, the merciless financier, the blackmailer motivated by cynicism or need.

Simenon divided his novels into various categories corresponding to the titles of collections issued by his publishers: Lively Novels, Little Lively Novels, Crime and Police Stories, Adventure Novels, Romance Novels, Great Adventures and Exotic Voyages, Love Stories, Short Funny Novels, Dramatic Tales, Short Lewd Novels, Great Love Stories, and even Dramatic Love Stories.

For the most part, however, the output was played in three major keys: light novels, romance novels, and adventures in France and overseas.[22] The author was able to shift from one to another in a single day with apparent ease, from *La Fiancée fugitive* (The Fugitive Fiancée, 1925) to *Le Cercle de la soif* (Circle of Thirst, 1927), from *Nox l'insaisissable* (The Elusive Nox, 1926) to *Celle qui revient* (She Who Returns, 1929), from *Chair de beauté* (Flesh of Beauty, 1928) to *La Lac d'angoisse* (Lake of Anguish, 1928), from *Captain S.O.S.* (1929) to *Cœur de poupée* (Doll's Heart, 1929).

He often wrote so hurriedly that his plots lacked coherence. Characters changed names and occupations in the course of a book, and the spellings of their names seemed largely a matter of chance from page to page. But none of that mattered. The structure, the overall scaffolding, was the important thing, even if the writing and the theme suffered. This is what he meant when he spoke of learning the trade, and he ignored the mockery with which beginners are commonly treated by critics.

One might well imagine that at ten or twenty thousand lines per novel he ran the risk of picking up bad habits and being contaminated by the defects of genre writing, which are in fact well represented in his books: facile clichés, platitudes, conventions, poverty of vocabulary. In his own defense he claimed that this was not contamination but "vaccination." It was the only way to learn what not to do.

He acquired technical skills like a craftsman's apprentice. But he dispensed with the traditional tour of France. Instead, he made copious use of the illustrated Larousse, especially in his adventure novels. Constant resort to the atlas was a necessity, since he had never traveled. How else could he have turned out such titles as *Un drame au pôle sud* (Tragedy at the South Pole, 1929), *Le Monstre blanc de la Terre de feu* (The White Monster of Tierra del Fuego, 1928), *Les Maudits du Pacifique* (The Damned of the Pacific, 1928), *Les Nains des cataractes* (The Dwarfs of the Cataracts, 1928), *La Panthère borgne* (The Panther Sulks), *Le Secret des lamas* (Secret of the Lamas), *Le Sous-Marin dans la forêt* (The Submarine in the Forest, 1928), *Le Pêcheur des bouées* (Marsh Fishermen, 1930), *Le Roi des glaces* (The Ice King, 1928).

"I have never known such a thrill of adventure as in writing them," he later said. "While others ran to catch the bus or metro, I sat at home and spun the globe."[23]

Daylight dawned over the city. Simenon sat at his table, inhaling the mingled odors of coffee and pipe tobacco. He flipped through the pages of the Larousse:

P as in pygmy, *H* as in hacienda, *M* as in monsoon. He was convinced that the poetry of this kind of story lies wholly in the words and not in the plot or the action. He believed he had penetrated the secret of the adventure novel the day he learned to write "mangrove" or "baobab" instead of "tree," and "tomahawk" instead of "hatchet."[24]

He rarely revealed his sources of inspiration, but there are a few exceptions: in *L'Ile des hommes roux* (Isle of the Redmen, 1929), one of the characters dreams of becoming an island king after reading Kipling's *The Man Who Would Be King.* He acknowledges in the novel itself that the idea for *Le Gorille roi* (The Gorilla King, 1929) came from a pamphlet about cannibals in central Africa by the Baron Aucapitaine, an attaché in the Arab Bureau in Blida.[25] But it will be many years before an erudite interviewer elicits his confession that the details about the Mormons recounted in *L'Œil de l'Utah* (The Eye of Utah, 1928) were lifted from Robert Louis Stevenson's *The Dynamiter* (1894).[26]

He also draws unalloyed pleasure from his "steamy" novels, which he later describes as "more juicy than spicy," as "hot" as the decade in which they were written.[27] They often have a comic, burlesque dimension that redeems a flimsiness unconcealed by the dropping of such heavy names as Dostoevsky or Freud and his beloved libido,[28] the latter in a work entitled *Un monsieur libidineux* (A Libidinous Gentleman, 1927). *Une petite dessalée* (A Girl Who Learned a Thing or Two, 1928) features a character by the name of Joseph Fistullin, technical adviser to a decency committee assigned by the League of Nations to draft a report on the state of vice in France.

These novels, often more pamphlet than book, were not much to look at, but at least they were "written," by which Simenon meant "constructed." He was quite happy with them, though he had no illusions about their literary worth. He called them "novels for secretaries"—the very first of them, in fact, was *Le Roman d'une dactylo* (A Secretary's Novel, 1924)—and their avowed aim was to move the steno pool to tears. They were deliberately commercial. The author felt he was supplying a product for which there was a market demand.

"I disown none of my writings, not even my popular novels,"[29] the memorialist later declared, although privately he acknowledged their "absolute banality" and at first refused to make a list of them: "It really isn't worth it."[30]

Yet it is in this dense but uneven mass of stories that we find the genesis of his future work. The great Simenon can be seen in embryo in the pulp novels of young Georges Sim. Michel Lemoine, one of the few researchers to have studied Simenon's early work, concludes: "A broader reading of these unpretentious fictions permits us to trace Simenon's arduous progress toward a kind of realism rooted in the small, telling detail and in the multisensory portraiture that generates what has been called the Simenon atmosphere."[31]

As the workday ended, Simenon would "go into a trance," drafting a more ambitious short story in which he strove to weave the three dimensions of past, present, and future into a single action. Then, unable to bear the tension of the effort, he would go to the bathroom to throw up.[32]

He was now averaging eighty pages a day,[33] an output that included both novels and magazine articles. He hired the first in a long line of secretaries, thereby increasing his rate of production by dictating his novels, atlas in hand, improvising from hastily jotted notes.[34] The "Simenon organization" was expanding, and a third woman now joined Tigy and the secretary. Her name was Henriette Liberge but Simenon called her Boule.

The Simenons met this country girl during a vacation on the Norman coast, where she was a maid for some friends of theirs. Originally from a family of fishermen in Bénouville, she was nearly twenty and had but one desire: to escape. Simenon hired her for a year, but she wound up spending a lifetime with the man she called "my pretty little gentleman," becoming a key presence in his life and the sole eyewitness to all its stages. He saw her as the very embodiment of loyalty.[35] She was exactly his type: "blonde, plump, and simple."[36] Theirs was a unique relationship that fell into none of the usual categories of extramarital affairs. Genuine mutual affection accompanied the voracious, frequent, but cautiously furtive sexual encounters that began with her arrival at the Place des Vosges and continued ever after.[37]

Boule took charge of the kitchen and the household tasks, Tigy helped her husband, the secretary typed, and Simenon wrote or dictated. The train was on its way. For the moment, the engineer was content to let his publisher act as stationmaster.

Simenon considered publishers "industrialists" to whom he had to deliver a "product" shaped to a particular market. He often described himself as a supplier filling orders for which he was paid by the line or the pound: "Like an artisan, I sometimes calculated my cost price in terms of an hourly return."[38]

The publishers of Paris, and later their colleagues throughout the world, would soon find out what it meant to deal with an author with such a keenly commercial view of his craft. Joseph Ferenczi was the first to have the experience, in the late summer of 1924. A Hungarian Jew who emigrated to Paris in 1879, Ferenczi began his career selling books out of an upside-down umbrella. Later, he and Henry de Jouvenel opened a bookstore in the Odéon quarter, before moving into book publishing at the end of the century.

In 1920 he began bringing out low-cost unabridged editions of previously unpublished novels by contemporary authors, in a collection entitled "Les Œuvres inédites." Two books were issued every month, at 95 centimes apiece.

This revolutionary venture proved highly successful, and three years later he launched another list of a different type, borrowing an idea of Arthème Fayard's. "Le Livre moderne illustré," illustrated reprints of proven best-sellers priced at 2.50 francs a copy, soon became a popular favorite.

The first titles were by house authors (Francis de Miomandre, Colette, and Francis Carco), but when Ferenczi decided to broaden the list, he began republishing Mauriac, Giraudoux, Morand, and others whose works also found their way into the review *Demain,* which he launched in the spring of 1924. Colette was the editor of one of Ferenczi's lists, but it was not under her auspices that Simenon broke into this firm. This time, far from considering him "too literary," she thought him not literary enough. Ferenczi wanted Simenon not for one of his prestige lists but for down-market "popular" titles for which his varied output under his many pseudonyms would be more suitable. Over the next seven years, Simenon supplied Ferenczi with dozens and dozens of manuscripts, from *Le Roman d'une dactylo* (1924) under the name Jean du Perry, to *Victime de son fils* (His Son's Victim, 1931), under the pseudonym Jacques Dersonne.

Simenon was loyal to Ferenczi's house, in his fashion, but no single publisher could have exhausted his enormous reserves of energy and imagination. He worked at such a frenzied pace that the three key events in a book's creation—signing of the contract, completion of the manuscript, and printing—were telescoped. If he was not always able to keep track of the flow, Tigy was on hand to help, recording everything in the precious black notebook purchased at the Papeterie de la Bourse on the Rue de Richelieu. Under the heading "Receipts" for the year 1925, at the top of the first page, she wrote the figure 42,671 francs, a huge sum for the time but the smallest to be registered by the "Simenon enterprise" through 1941, the last year listed in the notebook.[39]

Since Ferenczi's printing and distribution services had trouble keeping up with Simenon, the publisher could hardly object when the author began offering manuscripts to his competitors: mostly Fayard and Tallandier, but also Rouff and Prima's "Collection Gauloise."

Arthème Fayard, the son of a lawyer from the Auvergne, began his business in 1855 by publishing songs in pamphlet form. His namesake and successor expanded the house in many directions, from classical theater and historical works to a series of pulp novels launched after the buyout of the Dentu list (Paul Féval, Michel Zévaco, etc.) and a right-wing weekly called *Candide.* Fayard, a handsome, silver-haired man who struck Simenon as a typical Parisian of the era, published everything from Barrès to "The Chaste and the Fallen." There was plenty of room for Georges.

Their first contract seems to have been signed on November 19, 1925, for *Dolorosa,* a romance novel under the pseudonym Christian Brulls. But it appeared only two years later, first serialized in *Paris-Soir* and then released in book form in 1928. The contract for *Le Feu s'éteint* (The Fire Dies), signed on January 15, 1927, gave the author an advance of 2,000 francs.[40]

In the beginning, Simenon dealt not with Arthème Fayard but with his son-in-law and collaborator, Fernand Brouty, a notorious tightwad. Whenever he needed a title to fill a suddenly empty slot in a list, Brouty would buttonhole young Simenon in the company's offices on the Rue du Saint-Gothard, where he regularly came by to drop off his freshly typed pages. You could always count on Georges: "For when? Four days from now? Fine."[41] Brouty never asked much—only that his authors deliver their manuscripts on time and not press to be paid. Neither Brouty nor the inaccessible Arthème Fayard was responsible for discovering the unsuspected talents of the ubiquitous Georges Sim. That distinction goes to one Baron Dillon, a highly colorful personality.

Although he insisted that he had sold his title to bail himself out of financial embarrassment, Charles Dillon still called himself "the Baron." A handsome womanizer and former army buddy of the boss, he was Fayard's great master of popular literature. His young assistant, Max Favalleli, would open the packages, but it was the Baron who read the manuscripts. Since both were accustomed to eccentrics parading in and out of their office every day, Simenon's advent must not have surprised them. Yet Favalleli recalls that he stood out among his colleagues:

"Solid on his legs, a short clay pipe stuck in his mouth, roast beef–colored cheeks. He dressed in the Rouletabille style: checkered suit, flat cap, knickerbockers. His inexhaustible productivity was a godsend to Papa Dillon. Whether we needed a 15,000-line romance novel or a detective story, all we had to do was call on our boy. Next Monday? Good enough. And he would deliver right on time, with a nonchalance that stunned Charles Dillon."[42] Confident that his own seasoned instincts were sound, the Baron would soon help Sim become Simenon.

The third of the trio of publishers to whom Simenon sent his manuscripts was Tallandier. He and Fayard were the kingpins of the pulp novel, Ferenczi following close on their heels. It is no accident that the neighborhood around the Rue du Saint-Gothard features prominently in Simenon's novels, for the offices of Tallandier and Fayard were on the same street, barely three hundred yards apart. At Tallandier, as at Fayard, Simenon had no direct contact with the owner. Jules Tallandier, a rich businessman and president of the publishers' and booksellers' associations, was an intimidating figure. The firm had been founded by various republican leaders under the Second Empire. Tallandier joined the staff around 1883. By the end of the century he had become the sole owner.

When Simenon went to the Tallandier offices, he would pause in the courtyard for a look at the boss's car, a luxurious Donnet ZL polished to a brilliant gleam by a full-time chauffeur. It was an image he would never forget. The same might be said of Tallandier's estate in the fashionable Fontainebleau suburb of Samois, a small town on the Seine that Simenon would re-create in *La Femme rousse* (The Redhead, 1938).

At Tallandier, as at Fayard, Simenon's contact was the boss's son-in-law—here Rémy Dumoncel, editor of the popular lists. A rich man in his own right, Dumoncel was nevertheless more accessible than Tallandier. Fifteen years Simenon's senior, he quickly established a friendly intimacy with the younger man, often taking him to lunch at La Coupole or at his large apartment on the Rue d'Aumale in the Eleventh Arrondissement, and even inviting him to his Avon estate in Seine-et-Marne.

Dumoncel was the publisher who accepted *L'Homme à la cigarette* (The Cigarette Man, 1931), rejected by Fayard and Gallimard but later regarded as "one of Simenon's best pulp novels."[43] Shortly after meeting Simenon and reading several of his early books, he found that the young man had not eaten for twenty-four hours. In an arrangement that would last for years, he promptly offered him a stipend in exchange for two sixty-page novels a month. Simenon was deeply touched. After the war he signed a copy of *Le Haut Mal* (*The Woman of the Grey House*, 1933) for Dumoncel's widow with this warm inscription:

". . . in memory of a man whom I long regarded as a father and continue even now to cherish."[44] In a letter to Dumoncel's son Maurice, who also became a publisher, he saluted ". . . the memory of the man who probably had the greatest influence on my beginnings—and from whom, in any case, I enjoyed the greatest kindness."[45]

Paris, 1925: in the cafés near the Palais-Bourbon the talk is of Caillaux's financial projects, the constant cabinet reshuffles and changes of government, the escalation of the war in the Rif Mountains against Abd el-Krim, and Marshal Pétain's efforts to raise an army for the pacification of Morocco. But the habitués of the bars of Montparnasse are more concerned with André Breton's *Surrealist Manifesto,* the first Surrealist exhibition at the Galerie Pierre, Le Corbusier's new essay on architecture, and Chaplin's *Gold Rush.*

Simenon listened to it all but paid little attention. He spent his days chained to his typewriter, working at the usual breathtaking pace. Only Tigy and Boule knew what a bundle of nerves he really was. His contracts with various publishers were a constraint and a stimulus. He felt he had now attained his initial goal, and he decided to raise his sights, aiming at the foreign market. He was only twenty-two, but he had a fair number of published books under his belt, and his determination and self-assurance were unshakable. Two positive signs fueled his optimism.

The first came from Italy. Augusto Foa, a literary agent and director of the Agenzia Letteraria Internazionale, with headquarters in Turin and later in

Milan, proposed to publish several of his novels in Italy. Surprisingly, Simenon rejected the offer. He did not want a one-shot deal, nor even an agreement covering several books, no matter how profitable in the short term. Convinced that he would eventually break into the international market anyway, he held out for a long-term arrangement. He wanted to sell the rights to his entire output, establishing exclusive relations with one publisher in each country. His patience was soon rewarded with an approach from another intermediary, Curtis Brown, acting for the Italian publisher Mondadori. They would later form an alliance that lasted for decades.

The second encouraging sign came from Paris: an article in *Paris-Soir,* the first of its kind in the French press. Its author, who actually took the trouble to visit the Place des Vosges, was a big name: Paul Reboux, forty-eight, famous for his prewar pastiches, written in collaboration with Charles Muller and published under the general title *In the Style of . . . .* The piece in *Paris-Soir,* however, soberly entitled "Georges Sim," was more paean than parody.

> Nine in the morning. The typist is hard at work, and Georges Sim had been waiting for her. Before noon he is to dictate two humorous stories, one tragic story, and the outline of a popular novel. This afternoon he will deliver what he has composed this morning, and tonight he will write, write, and write some more, for he has promised to complete two 1,500-line novels by next week! After midnight, when he is all alone, he will finally permit himself the luxury of writing "for real," in other words, for pleasure—though one is tempted to call it redemption. These after-midnight writings, I hasten to add, are not the ones most sought after. Georges Sim is twenty-two years old. At sixteen he was already a journalist producing a daily column, news reports, chronicles, and interviews.
>
> Great newspapers and lesser sheets were soon accepting his writings. He is one of *Le Matin*'s most esteemed story writers. He also feeds on green, pink, and salmon paper: light short stories, amusing anecdotes, jokes, saucy tales free of improprieties. Life is Georges Sim's raw material, and life, in Paris more than in most places, whether we like it or not, has little of the convent about it, at least if we consider monastic rules from the standpoint of principle rather than reality. His monthly output? Sixty stories, from fifty to two hundred lines each, plus three novels of three thousand lines each. All published under a good dozen pseudonyms.
>
> Such is your fate, young man from the provinces, when you come to Paris to "do literature" and your pen is your only resource! You will work twice as hard as any industrialist, and with twice the determination. You will squeeze your head like a lemon to make ideas flow. A

pity, young man, but it's what you wanted. Don't say you didn't know what was in store for you, for such is the lovely craft you dreamed of, instead of taking over your dear father's business. . . .

If he met Georges Sim, the young man from the provinces would reply that the task can be endured with a smile. So it can. But let me add that Georges Sim is a quite exceptional man, as you will see if you read these fruits of his inexhaustible imagination. There is something in all of them, . . . for if he writes to live, he also lives to write. It is his passion, his ideal. If he ever gets the time to work in peace, he will do great things. Patience![46]

But Simenon's great virtue was discipline, not patience. He worked like a man possessed, but since he did everything to excess, he was quite capable of taking vacations that were as long as his dedication to writing was intense. After spending a summer in Etretat, the Simenons set out for Porquerolles, spending the 800 francs earned by the sale of one of Tigy's canvases. They spent several months in the "earthly paradise" of a 2,500-acre stretch of Mediterranean coastline on the Giens peninsula. Porquerolles became their secret garden. It was a long way from Paris.

For the moment, however, Simenon felt more at home in Montparnasse than anywhere else. At Le Dôme or La Coupole, most often accompanied by Tigy, he struck up friendships with older artists and writers who had recently achieved some notoriety beyond the narrow circle of connoisseurs to which they had been confined before the war. Though generally sensitive to the spirit of the times (marked by a return to order and a certain classicism), these seasoned rebels had plenty of fight left in them. They included painters (the *fauves* Vlaminck and Derain, who drew in their claws along with their colors; the cubist Picasso, temporarily rather subdued; as well as Pascine, Kipling, and Soutine), graphic artists (Paul Colin), illustrators (Marcel Vertès), and poets (Max Jacob).

Simenon needed good reasons to venture beyond the sacred precincts of Montparnasse. The famous "house" maintained by Madame Hélène at 26 Rue Brey in the Etoile quarter was one such attraction. Several times a week or several times a day, depending on his financial resources (the other kind was never lacking), Simenon would drop in on Madame Hélène to visit "the most charming women in Paris."[47]

Then there were the artistic events. The great mechanical-music concert at the Champs-Elysées Theater, for example, which concluded in the most unexpected manner. Among the audience in evening dress were Jean Cocteau and Georges Auric. The curtain rose, to nearly universal stupor. The orchestra's place in the pit had been taken by an elaborate apparatus that turned out to be the superstructure of a new and improved phonograph. Stravinsky strode onto the stage, raised his baton, and tapped the podium. An assistant put a record on. The audience was flabbergasted: the great composer meant to demonstrate the rising importance of music in daily life thanks to instruments of progress like the radio and the phonograph. The audience broke out in boos and catcalls. Simenon and his friends, utterly delighted, contested the majority opinion. Scuffles erupted, and the concert ended at the police station.[48]

And there were the nights of madness at the Bœuf sur le Toit (Ox on the Roof), a magical place well worth a journey out of Montparnasse, to the Rue Boissy-d'Anglais, near the Madeleine, as "Right Bank" a venue as anyone could imagine. Opened in early 1922 and boasting the neighborhood's smallest stage but greatest concentration of personalities per square meter, this nightclub soon became a mecca where artists and writers of avant-garde Paris gathered to spend their money and tie one on after the show at the Champs-Elysées Theater, now more music hall than center of dramatic art.

The Bœuf, as habitués called it, was the kind of place where people threw their arms around one another to say hello while glancing over each other's shoulders to see who else was there. The supercharged atmosphere moved Tristan Bernard to comment, "Now I see why the ox headed for the roof." Wit was as compulsory as champagne: "One cocktail, two Cocteaus." Everyone who was anyone was there: Raymond Radiguet and Paul Morand, Maurice Sachs and Serge de Diaghilev, André Gide and Maurice Chevalier, François Mauriac and the Princess Murat, Coco Chanel and Léon-Paul Fargue, and many others, not necessarily together or in that order.[49] One night Jean Wiener and Clément Doucet replaced the orchestra and treated the clientele to some American tunes. In the wee hours of the morning a curious Florent Fels leaned over to glance at their music and saw a Simenon novel propped on the stand. The anecdote seems far-fetched, but it deserves to be true.[50]

These were the days when Simenon happily added a dash of hashish to his pipe tobacco and drank more than he should have.[51] He had become so thoroughly Parisian, so intimate with all the right places, that when the French government asked Firmin Gémier to take the visiting Soviet minister Anatoly Lunacharsky on a tour of the City of Light, the director of the Odéon Theater entrusted the delicate mission to his friend Simenon, convinced that Georges was truly the man for the job.[52] He was right. Simenon escorted the eminent Marxist-Leninist to all the attractions of Paris, finishing at the home of the woman who, in Georges's eyes, *was* Paris: Josephine Baker.

Like everyone else in his world, Simenon discovered her one evening in October 1925 at the Champs-Elysées Theater, where a graphically daring poster by Paul Colin announced a show entitled *La Revue nègre*. The girl from St. Louis with the short, conked hair was completely unknown at the time, but she was about to conquer Paris in a single night.

The revue consisted of twenty-five young but seasoned artists, including musicians (among them the clarinetist and saxophonist Sidney Bechet and the pianist Claude Hopkins), dancers, showgirls, a blues and spirituals singer, and Josephine, whose act so thoroughly flouted all conventions that it was impossible to characterize her.

Within a single hour she ignited the enthusiasm of Parisian society and polemics from the right-thinking press. No one had ever seen anything like it: her grimaces and squinting, her allegedly obscene contortions, the pink flamingo feather clenched between her thighs (the legendary banana belt appeared a year later), her provocative animal sexuality, the stunning contour of her muscled, ebony posterior, and the grace of her breathtaking nudity.[53]

Like just about everyone else, Simenon was utterly smitten. But unlike most everyone else, he did not leave it at that. Instead, he made his way to her dressing room, introduced himself, and asked her out. It was love at first sight. For a year or more they had a passionate affair in a city just as supercharged as themselves. She was twenty, he was twenty-three.

Friends and associates of this new queen of the night could not understand what she was doing with a kid when the rich and famous were at her beck and call. That she didn't care what people said was itself a sign of the freedom of spirit that had charmed Simenon in the first place. She did what she wanted, on stage and off.

Simenon was rarely so in harmony with a woman as he was with Josephine. They had the same inexhaustible energy, the same bent for showmanship, the same irrepressible desire to taste life in all its forms, the same exuberance and joie de vivre, the same sexuality, transgressing all taboos. To call them lovers is an understatement. He was bewitched, and he made no effort to hide it from readers of the fan magazines:

> Hers is, without question, the world's most famous butt, and the most desired. A butt so famous and so desired that it might well be an object of adoration, enveloped in dense billows of incense burned by the lust of thousands. . . . It is a photogenic butt. The screen captures its firm, sweet contours, its lascivious quivers and wild convulsions. . . . We have seen it wreathed in bananas glinting warmly of gold. We have seen it studded with pink feathers of delicate hues, bringing out the bronze of the flesh. We have seen it nude. . . . But most of all we have seen it so taut, jutting so far out from the torso in a sweeping gesture of defiance that it becomes a being apart, with a life of its own, far from Baker's face and eyes, comically crossed in stupor. What a synthesis! A synthesis of animal delight, as young and alive as jazz, vibrating and laughing, raw and guileless, but most of all joyous, with a child's healthy, exuberant joy, greedy perhaps, but never licentious. Why does Baker's butt move continents? Why are masses of men so stirred, and woman's jealousy disarmed? Because, by Jove, it is a laughing butt!

And it's not just the butt. Josephine Baker is a burst of laughter, from her comically lacquered hair to her nervous legs, whose curves we cannot see because they are never still. She is a wild child hurtling through the world, carried from continent to continent, dropping into a solemn salon, being hoisted in an egg to the ceiling of a music hall. And we all rush to see her, eyes gleaming in the very same way. Palms sweaty with the same desire. A thousand pairs of opera glasses and naked eyes focus on her, and trembling fingers reach out to her. Baker could keep from laughing only if she took herself seriously, if she let it go to her head and played the femme fatale. But she is far too healthy for that. So she laughs. She shakes her breasts, not big, but pretty and sweetly shaped. She shows her teeth. She laughs most of all with her eyes, with those big, improbably white eyes whose corneas glitter as brightly as her lacquered hair, while the black coals of her pupils wander, now in concert, now aiming at different objects. Try it, Madame! Grimace, make a face, and stay desirable! Or rather, grimace and look even more desirable. It is all so intensely alive, and it is the life that we desire, that we want to grasp for an instant and absorb, the life of the butt and the eyes, the life of a young girl who has become a star and loves every minute of it! . . . Next year she will make a European tour. There will be talk of her butt in Berlin, Vienna, Moscow. The lust will grow. Three million, ten million, fifty . . . someday a billion! And this, I say again, because it is a laughing butt, a laughing being flaunting its joie de vivre. And a body as voluptuous as can be, whether decked in gold lamé, bananas, or pink feathers.[54]

Baker and Simenon were so closely linked that a rumor spread through the bars and nightclubs that he was her secretary. It wasn't true, but it was not entirely without foundation either. Georges did act as her courier for several months, helping to guide her through the administrative shoals of stardom, putting her accounts and papers in order, making sure her mother in the United States received a monthly money order of $200, "a transaction she found too complicated to handle herself."[55]

But there was more to their relationship than that. Simenon would generally finish out the night by taking Tigy, who suspected nothing,[56] to Chez Joséphine Baker, the nightclub Baker had opened on the Rue Fontaine. Afterward he would often take both of them to El Garrob for a nightcap. Over drinks they would spin wild plans. For some time now they had been excited about the idea of a magazine devoted entirely to Baker. Simenon's most daring plans often took flight before anyone had the time to poke holes in them, and so it was that *Le Joséphine Baker's Magazine* (nearly) saw the light of day in Paris in 1927. The cover of the first issue sported a giant *M* in the center: *M* as in monthly, *mondain* (fashionable), modern, and *mondial* (worldwide).

Josephine and Pepito Abatino, her new impresario, were the producers, so to speak, Georges Sim the editor in chief and sole journalist. Editorial offices were to be in Simenon's apartment at 21 Place des Vosges. But despite the co-operation of Paul Colin and the promise of literary contributions from various prestigious sources, the project never got off the ground.

Suddenly there was trouble between the principals. Their friends were surprised when Josephine hired his colleague Marcel Sauvage instead of Simenon to ghostwrite her memoirs. The passion was still there, but Simenon was having second thoughts: "I had become the friend of Josephine Baker, whom I would have married but for my refusal, unknown as I was, to become Mr. Baker."[57] Daunted by that prospect, Simenon decided to run off with Tigy to the island of Aix, between Ré and Oléron. Flight was the only way to break free of a woman with whom he was still madly in love. He exorcised his inner demons through his writing, and the woman with the irresistible butt may be seen in the characters of Nadia, the dancer in *Chair de beauté* (1928), and Dorothée in *Défense d'aimer* (Forbidden Love, 1927).[58] But it is in *Dolorosa* (1928) that the portrait is most undisguised:

"To be husband or lover to a famous woman and to be nothing oneself—is this not the worst torture for a man's pride? A selfish sentiment, but one deeply rooted and therefore noble. Does not man need to feel himself the stronger, to protect the woman he loves, to be her guide and support?"[59]

Ensconced on his island for the entire summer, Simenon also wanted to forget Paris for a while, the better to be forgotten, for his favorite city had just done him the first wrong of his career. Early that year, 1927, Simenon had been drawn into the scheme that made him a phenomenon forever after.

Mr. Eugène Merle, cunning, crafty, and energetic, considered himself the Napoleon of the Paris press. Though short of stature, he always managed to get noticed, if only for his extravagant suits and loud ties. His tables in the city's leading restaurants were open to one and all, for Merle was as generous as he was broke.

A smooth talker with a husky voice, utterly cynical and sparklingly brilliant, he liked to take money where he found it and put it where it ought to be. Forty-three years old, the son of an Italian immigrant named Merlo, he proudly called himself a libertarian and a blackmailer, adding that blackmail, like probity, was merely a question of publicity.

He was a fixture of Parisian life, comical and captivating, fond of speaking of himself in the third person: "as the illustrious Merle has pointed out —" In journalistic circles he had a reputation as a nonconformist ever eager to give beginners a chance, sniffing out the most promising talents among young reporters with an unerring instinct. It was said that he was equally at home with gangsters and cabinet members. It was also said that he cheerfully bounced checks to his most cherished creditors, that he had done time in prison, that he drew an informer's salary from a secret slush fund in the Ministry of the Interior, that he kept up-to-date lists of colleagues slated to receive "envelopes" from government ministers and big banks, that he owned a château in Avrainville where he lived in grand style while doing his own cooking for his honored guests. Rumor also had it that he had done his undergraduate work in a dive in the port of Marseille, that he had an innate sense of spectacle, that he could predict public tastes, and that he was outrageous, amoral, and perfectly respectable.[60]

Simenon was immediately charmed by Merle's boisterous personality and soon came genuinely to admire him, passionately listening to his stories of his youth as an anarchist militant, his activism in the pacifist movement, and his battles in the pressroom at *La Guerre sociale* and *Le Bonnet rouge,* of which he had been the general secretary. These memories would emerge from the author's unconscious many years later, in *Le Destin des Malou* (*The Fate of the Malous,* 1947) and several other novels involving attempted blackmail by the editor in chief of a newspaper.[61]

In 1919, Merle launched a weekly called *Le Merle blanc* (The White Blackbird), "the paper that blows the whistle and tells the tales." Virulently satirical and polemical, this antiparliamentary broadside (whose main whipping boy was Georges Mandel, Clemenceau's cabinet chief) was an incontestable success. In three years, circulation rose from 34,000 to 812,000.[62] Merle put his promotional genius to good use, bombarding the public with billboards and opinion-makers with personal letters boasting of *Le Merle blanc*'s "rebellious bias, unfair polemics, and resounding bad faith." The paper's offices were on the Boulevard Montmartre, above the Café de Madrid. A stairway led to *Le Merle blanc* on the left and to *Frou-Frou,* a racy magazine also controlled by Merle, on the right.

Simenon was "hired" to keep things moving, and he wasted no time. He showed up at the paper's "offices"—actually a single room—every Wednesday at eight in the morning and stayed until ten at night, taking a short break for lunch at the bistro downstairs. When he opened the door to go out, thick clouds of smoke billowed from the room. By ten, when the typewriter ceased to clatter, Simenon had written most of the paper, and his copy was ready for the printer.

Le Merle blanc, now imitated by *Le Merle rose* (The Pink Blackbird), another house product aimed more especially at lesbians, soon began to show signs of running out of steam. The owner, however, was not unduly concerned, for he already had something else in mind: a daily, no less. On October 3, 1923, the indomitable Eugène Merle launched *Paris-Soir,* a paper he would sell, seven years later, to the textile industrialist Jean Prouvost, already the owner of *Paris-Midi.* When the first issue rolled off the press, he joined several collaborators on the balcony of the paper's offices and waited to hear the hawkers shout the first, inevitably historic headline. He then turned to Henri Jeanson and said:

"Well, that's it. . . . It's a lot like making love, you know? . . . Doesn't last. . . . Cigarette? . . . It's expensive, a daily. I have to come up with a hundred thousand francs a day . . . like squeezing blood from a stone. . . . Fortunately the days are long!"[63]

Merle was a man of successive enthusiasms, and soon he fell out of love with *Paris-Soir*. Instead, he was excited about a new project: the creation of a mass-circulation left-leaning daily to be called *Paris-Matin*. He sought out Simenon, but not to talk about editorial policies:

"What we want you to do is write a novel in public. Suggest a dozen or so characters, of which the audience will pick three. Then suggest a dozen or so titles, of which they'll pick one. Then you write while they watch, for three days and three nights."[64]

Merle's goal was not so much to promote Georges Simenon, who needed no help on that score, as to publicize *Paris-Matin*. It would be a circus stunt, staged in a glass cage either at the Moulin-Rouge or in the newspaper's offices. Simenon's pages would be posted as they came out of the typewriter, before being sent to the *Paris-Matin* linotypists.

Simenon rose to the challenge without hesitation. An architect was asked to design the glass cage. The plans would then be sent to a glassworker on the Rue de Paradis. In the meantime, Merle and Simenon, the "director" and the "man of letters," the manager and his champion, duly drew up a contract embossed with the seal of the French Republic:

> It is stipulated and agreed as follows:
>
> Mr. Georges Sim agrees to draft, in full view of the public and under its control, a novel whose subject, title, and characters shall be determined through a prior open referendum and communicated to him by a bailiff at the time of his entry into the site assigned him, which site shall remain continuously accessible to the public and in which Mr. Sim will occupy a glass cage or box largely of glass to the immediate vicinity of which the public shall have the broadest access day and night. Mr. Sim agrees to execute his novel at the normal hourly rate of pay for a newspaper feuilleton, the totality of the novel to be a maximum of sixty feuilletons and to be completed within one week, without Mr. Sim's having any possibility of communicating with any third party outside conditions of control established by the newspaper. The said referendum shall enable the readers of *Paris-Matin* to choose, from among twelve new novel titles proposed by the newspaper, the one that shall serve as the author's theme, it being understood that each title shall correspond to a subject of a genre determined in advance and that the twelve titles shall include the most varied genres. The said referendum

shall also enable the readers to designate, among fifty types of characters described in advance, the eight principal protagonists of the novel, the author retaining the right to add episodical or secondary characters but pledging to reserve the most important roles for the personages designated by the public. It is understood that the publication of this novel and the publicity it may directly or indirectly occasion shall be reserved exclusively for the newspaper *Paris-Matin*. The whole of the above shall be stipulated in accordance with the following conditions:

Article One. Mr. Georges Sim will receive from Mr. Eugène Merle the sum of fifty thousand francs (50,000 francs) upon the signing of the present contract and an additional sum of fifty thousand francs (50,000 francs) upon the execution of the aforementioned commitments.

Article Two. Mr. Georges Sim will likewise receive remuneration of one franc twenty-five centimes (1.25 fr) per line of the novel published by *Paris-Matin*, it being understood that the length of the said novel shall be determined by the management of the newspaper, though it shall not be less than ten thousand lines.

Article Three. It is further agreed that Mr. Georges Sim will receive a share of fifty percent (50%) of all benefits of any kind that may result from the present agreements, whether translations, adaptations, reproductions, or arrangements of commercial publicity, direct or indirect.

The present contract shall remain in force for a period of six months from the date of its signature. The date of its execution shall be sometime after the first of March next at the earliest and shall be communicated to Mr. Georges Sim at least one month in advance. In the event that within the time period thus described Mr. Georges Sim shall not have been afforded the opportunity to execute the present contract, he shall retain the sum advanced to him by way of indemnification. Drafted in two copies and in good faith in Paris, the fourteenth of January one thousand nine hundred twenty-seven.[65]

The die was cast. *Le Merle rose* announced the show in a full-page ad printed in large type:

"A sensational exploit . . . by one of the best novelists of the young generation . . . a record novel: record speed, record endurance, and, dare we add, record talent! . . . a young author not yet 24 years of age who, under various pseudonyms, has already written no less than 1,000 short stories and 60 novels, will accomplish this prodigious feat at the improbable speed of at least one feuilleton an hour! . . . This unprecedented celerity will in no way inhibit the rare qualities of imagination, clarity, and style commanded by the hero of this inimitable performance, our colleague and friend Georges Sim, with whom Mr. Eugène Merle, director of *Paris-Matin*, intervening to interrupt negotiations under way with other newspapers, has unhesitatingly signed a contract a copy of which is reprinted opposite and whose value to the beneficiary will represent no less than 300,000 francs!"[66]

Journalists in the pressrooms and watering holes of Paris talked of nothing else, Merle's announcement temporarily eclipsing the Franco-British accord on war debts, the impending withdrawal of French troops from the Saar, and the initial hubbub over Abel Gance's *Napoléon*.

Many of Simenon's colleagues were at first entranced by the project, as they were by its protagonist's precocity and fecundity. And he, in turn, was clever enough to play the game. Indeed, how could he take offense at being treated like an assembly-line worker when he himself boasted of his ability to turn out three hundred typed lines in forty-five minutes? But once the initial surprise had passed, reservations were expressed. Was such extreme eccentricity really worthy of a journalist? Wasn't it humiliating to reduce a man of letters to the status of a circus performer? And what about Merle, whose credibility was less than universal? How could anyone be sure what the real advance was? Maybe it was more like half a million francs.[67]

In an effort to defuse the rising criticism, Simenon let copies of his contract circulate in city rooms. He then advanced various arguments in his own defense. After all, Molière wrote his *Bourgeois gentilhomme* on command in one month, the young Victor Hugo produced his first novel, *Bug-Jargal,* in two weeks, and Voltaire his *Candide* in a single night. Before anyone had time to check whether these claims were true, Simenon opened fire on the promotional aspect of the enterprise as well, recalling that Colette had endorsed a brand of perfume, that Maurice Barrès had hired men in sandwich boards to publicize his *Taches d'encre,* and that Maurice Rostand had recited his poems in a music hall. In a final attempt to win over diehard doubters, he evoked two illustrious predecessors, Balzac for his wit and Dumas for the quantity of his output.

But all for naught. The project soon became a target of derision. In *Paris-Midi,* Noël Sabord predicted a new era in literature: the end of ghostwriting thanks to the transparency of the cage. "We will come to see writers at work, shout themes at them, and applaud their prowess as we do performers at the circus, the stadium, or the bicycle races."[68] In *La Petite Gironde,* Jean-François Plantier predicted that this project "would stretch the ridiculous to new limits." He went on to demonstrate his expertise by describing Simenon as "a 24-year-old novelist, and a Belgian and an Israelite to boot!"[69]

Even *La Wallonie* was divided. An initial article mocked Simenon: people in Liège had hoped he had gone to Paris in search of less tawdry glory . . . he used to be a writer, but now he's an acrobat, albeit courageous and perhaps even commercially shrewd. "But let us take pity on him: Georges Sim has committed suicide."[70]

But it was *Le Canard enchaîné* that expressed the greatest hostility to Simenon's project, in its characteristic style, its biting, ironic, and polemical tone. Treating Simenon as though he were a mermaid on exhibit in a sideshow, the satirical weekly proposed a contest pitting its own standard-bearer against *Paris-Matin's*. *Le Canard's*, however, would be not a writer but a professional reader who had proved his mettle by devouring the most indigestible fare: Proust's four sentences in fifty pages, the complete works of Michel Zévaco, every word of Charles Maurras, Raymond Poincaré's memoirs, Claudel without a translator. *Le Canard* even suggested locking its reader in a cage and making him read his counterpart's copy as it came. The public could observe his reactions and place bets on how long he would last.[71]

Simenon was taking a lot of heat. Some saw the entire affair as the ultimate debasement of the writer, a process that began when bookstores had authors sign their works at the cash register. Professional feuilletonists were furious at the discredit one of their own was bringing upon their craft. Editorial offices bristled with all sorts of threats: some suggested giving the upstart a spanking at the conclusion of his performance, others swore they would sue him if he went through with it. One chronicler by the name of Georges Pioch proudly announced that he would gladly be the first to open fire on the glass cage.[72]

It was a feeding frenzy, and he hadn't even done anything yet. His friend Marcel Sauvage, Josephine Baker's ghostwriter, was kind enough to interview him for *L'Intransigeant*.

"When?"

"In a month."

"And you won't come out of the cage?"

"No, except for one hour every evening, under close guard. My cage will be six meters square. . . ."

"Do you also write literature?"

"Yes, for myself. I don't want to talk about that now. Later we'll see. . . ."[73]

Then suddenly, the project was canceled. The press speculated as to why: Merle and Simenon had backed down in the face of the general outcry; the novelist's financial demands had risen in proportion to the hype; the local police had threatened to ban an exhibition likely to disrupt public order; the glassworker had defaulted on his delivery date; *Paris-Matin* had gone bankrupt before the stunt could be staged.

This last explanation is probably the correct one, since Simenon pressed on even after the daily went under, asking Marcel Sauvage to suggest the idea to Elie-Joseph Bois, owner of the *Le Petit Parisien,* and to Léon Bailby of *L'Intransigeant*.[74] Fortunately, he found no takers, for as the editorialist from *La Wallonie* had correctly pointed out, it would have been suicide.

The most incredible thing about this whole story is that Georges Simenon would forever after be known as "the man who wrote a novel locked in a glass cage." Various memorialists helped to sustain the myth.

"People thronged to the site. The newspapers heaped anathema upon him.

They reviled his name. The performance took place . . . ," Youki Desnos recounts.[75] "Simenon had done the impossible, writing an entire novel in record time while locked in a glass cage in full view of the public," recalls André Warnod.[76] "Merle mined this lode as well: Georges Sim, who, locked in a glass cage under the eyes of a flabbergasted public, had to write a saga, rushed page by page to the linotypists of *Le Petit Journal* . . . ," says Florent Fels.[77] Louis Martin-Chauffier even traced the origin of Simenon's uncanny contact with the broad public to this adventure. As he tells it, a newspaper promoter set the cage up in the street: "Showered with requests, Sim labored indefatiguably, writing to order."[78] Others, swearing that they had seen him at work, offered gripping color commentary: he never raised his head . . . he wrote very fast . . . it happened in the offices of *Le Petit Journal,* no, at the Cadet intersection. And so on. Even as late as 1986, despite the repeated denials of the protagonist, the very scholarly *Histoire de l'Edition française* still reported: "Soon famous, he could be seen writing in a glass cage under the watchful eye of readers awaiting the next page. Once having made his fortune, Simenon abandoned these exhibitions."[79]

What did he finally get out of this episode? Twenty-five thousand francs (which he needed badly) and a legend he would have gladly done without. The birth of the "Simenon phenomenon" can be dated to 1927, the year of this famous nonevent.

6

WAITING FOR MAIGRET

1928–1931

t's only a drawing, but far more telling than many a commentary. A small boat is moored at a dock. Simenon, the very picture of happiness, his pipe in his mouth, is sitting on board, one hand on his typewriter keyboard. In the other he holds a freshly typed sheet, which he is handing to a sailor who passes it down a line of other sailors extending all the way to a printshop. The cartoon, signed Ralph Soupault and published in *Le Merle blanc,* bears the caption: "Georges Siménon [*sic*], Citroën of literature."[1] The legend was on the march.

In 1928 he decided to set sail, literally and figuratively. He held on to his apartment on the Place des Vosges but sold his famous American bar to the painter Foujita. Accompanied by Tigy, Boule, and Olaf (a mastiff puppy from Ulm), he set out on a voyage through the rivers and canals of France. "I have spent my life on the move, probably because of my lack of an anchorage, for I have no country," he would later write,[2] convinced that the best place to do creative work was one where he spent no more than two weeks.[3]

He bought a boat and passed the test for a motorboat license. *La Ginette,* was an open craft a little more than four yards long and five feet wide, with a capacity of about sixteen hundred pounds. It cost 5,800 francs, including a three-horsepower Johnson motor, a canvas tent, and a canoe for camping equipment, towed by a line attached to the stern of the boat.

He knew nothing about boating, but was determined to learn just as he learned to write novels: on the job. He would make each mistake only once, learning the vocabulary of sailors and lock-keepers, the sole lexicon able to capture the magic of the rivers and the spirit of the canals.

An itinerary was traced out: Paris, Epernay, Chaumont, Langres, Chalon-sur-Saône, Lyons, Marseille, Sète, Carcassonne, Toulouse, Bordeaux, Montluçon, Orléans, Montargis, and home again.[4] He planned for everything except the rise of the Seine and the perversity of the Rhône. Both forced him to make changes in course.

Using hotels was out of the question (except for brothels). Simenon and Tigy would feel dishonored to sleep anywhere but on board, while Boule and Olaf camped in the tent pitched on the bank. At dawn he sounded the horn for Boule to make breakfast and carry the tray to the boat, wading waist-deep into the water if necessary. Then he sat down at his typewriter, which rested on a folding table. Sometimes he set up shop on the dock, as in Lyons, where early-morning spectators stared transfixed as he worked on a novel.

Six months and a few dozen stories and novels later, neither his sloop nor France itself was big enough for him. By now he knew the canals well. In fact, his flair for exaggeration and gift of gab allowed him to pass as an expert, at least when talking to neophytes. Some years later, when the filmmaker Jean Vigo was preparing to shoot *L'Atalante,* he asked Eugène Merle to ask Simenon, a "man of experience," for information about the locks and sailing villages of the Ile-de-France.[5] The waterborne novelist cultivated the illusion so well that even the normally competent magazine *Sporting* expressed admiration for the maneuvering, repair, and caulking skills of his amateur team.[6]

After a brief stopover at the Place des Vosges, Simenon took a course in seamanship while Tigy signed on as an apprentice mechanic in a garage.[7] *La Ginette* was soon replaced by *L'Ostrogoth,* a seaworthy cutter (ten by four meters, twenty tons) built and fitted to order in Fécamp. Moored at Pont-Neuf, at the tip of the Vert-Galant, Simenon's new "home" was baptized by the abbot of Notre Dame. A cheerful band of revelers then partied until first light.

"Captain" Simenon and his crew spent 1929 and 1930 sailing the continent, from the Meuse to Finnish Lapland, with stops in Liège, Maastricht, Dutch and Belgian Limburg, Amsterdam, the Zuydersee, Stavoren, Delfzijl, Emden, and Wilhelmshaven. Later, they boarded a commercial ship and headed north, to Kirkenes, Norway. This was more than mere tourism. Simenon had developed an irresistible yen for life on the water, and he was interested in only one sort of boat: "The kind you can live on, a houseboat, a floating home, a boat that can be your nest, your intimate warm, dry refuge in bad weather, when storms break and the sea rises."[8]

During these long months Simenon seemed to immerse himself in geography the better to flee history. The circumstances were as romantic as could be, and outside events generally had little effect on him. But at rare moments they caught him unawares. In October 1929, for example, he found himself in Hindenburg's Germany, just before the start of the Allied withdrawal from the left bank of the Rhine.

The economic crisis had just broken out, and the country was governed by a coalition led by a Social Democratic chancellor. The leader of the National People's Party had recently formed an alliance with Adolf Hitler. Within a few months the fall of the Müller government would seal the fate of the parliamentary republic.

The *Ostrogoth* was moored in Wilhelmshaven, a port in Lower Saxony at the tip of the Bay of Jade on the North Sea, and Simenon was visited by a man who gave every sign of being a plainclothes policeman. The author was not unduly suspicious, since on his arrival the police helped him find supplies and even carried them to his boat like so many porters. But he soon realized that this time he was dealing with a counterespionage agent.

The man asked questions for two hours, searched the boat's stores, expressed surprise when he discovered a typewriter and an easel, tried to decipher one of Simenon's novels as though cracking a secret code. Finally he escorted the author to the Polizeipräsidium to continue their "discussion." A high official asked Simenon to account for his presence in German waters. The authorities were concerned about several telegrams addressed to him from *Détective,* the title of a magazine launched by Gaston Gallimard a year earlier.

"Are you a detective?"

"It's a weekly police magazine."

"You're a policeman then?"

"No, I write police stories."

"Why?"

"Because they're commissioned."

"In other words, you perform tasks commissioned of you?"

The "captain" grew increasingly ill at ease. Droplets of sweat broke out on his brow. He realized that the mail he had sent to Paris the evening before had been opened. He was asked to sign a deposition. He read it, hesitated.

"I know little German."

"Where did you learn it?"

"At school, in Liège. But I was never good at it."

"Is that because you don't like our language?"[9]

Simenon decided to sign the deposition and get it over with. His expulsion was now inevitable. The *Ostrogoth* was ordered to raise anchor at noon.

Did this episode teach him anything about Germany's impending political evolution? His memoirs suggest that it did. But the article recounting the incident at the time is more lighthearted than anxious. It concludes: "How could I be angry at a police department that had lugged my potatoes and cabbages aboard?"[10]

He wrote constantly during this voyage, recording impressions he would later put to use. With few exceptions, he wrote his novels the way you make waffles: with a mold. Yet he says that it was on this trip that he wrote the first Inspector Maigret story. Ever alert to the promotion of his own legend and anxious to authenticate the official version of the birth of the myth, the memorialist spares few details of the historic moment.

The scene ostensibly unfolds in September 1929 in Delfzijl, a Dutch port at the mouth of the Eems, in the Gulf of Dollart. The *Ostrogoth* is in dry dock for recaulking, and he cannot remain on board while the workers see to the stanching of the hull. He therefore has an old, flooded barge refloated and has two crates brought aboard, one to sit on, the other for his typewriter. Settled on the barge, he begins a new novel, *Pietr-le-Letton*.

The story features one Jules Maigret, inspector of the Paris Judiciary Police, who cracks a complicated case mainly through his patience and intuition, which allow him to blend into his surroundings while awaiting the right moment to pounce, that fleeting instant when the prey vacillates, when he reveals his vulnerability, weakens, and collapses.

Simenon claimed that Maigret emerged fully armed from the brain of his creator:

"I can see myself now, sitting in a café one sunny morning. . . . Have I had one, two, or even three small schnapps spiced with a few drops of bitter? One way or the other, an hour later, slightly sleepy, I began to picture the powerful, impassive bulk of a gentleman I thought would make a passable inspector. I added various accessories as the day wore on: a pipe, a bowler hat, a thick overcoat with a velvet collar. And since it was cold and damp on my abandoned barge, I put a cast-iron stove in his office."[11]

A good story, but not exactly accurate. Since we are dealing with one of the century's most popular fictional characters, it is worth trying to get the details right.

Flashback to the early summer of 1928. A dock on the Saône, in Lyons. Simenon, dressed in sailor's trousers and a thick faded sweater, sits at the keyboard, writing *L'Amant sans nom* (The Nameless Lover, 1929), a novel whose hero, Yves Jarry, is a kind of adventurer who has read enough Maurice Leblanc to think of himself as Arsène Lupin. Suddenly, through a heavy fog, Simenon "sees" the Maigret character take shape in his unconscious mind's eye.[12] He is Jarry's adversary, agent no. 49. The profile fits perfectly, down to the pipe clenched in his mouth.

"He was tall and vigorous, but his face did not resemble the usual image of the perfect detective. Nor that of any character in a police novel. It was round and slightly ruddy. A good country fellow's face. The eyes were guileless, their naïveté further accentuated by a pug nose. His head bobbed gently as he walked, as though he were constantly talking to himself. His swinging arms were enormous. . . . It would be hard to depict a more powerful picture of calm, cold patience, obstinacy, and composure than by painting a portrait of agent no. 49, who at ten o'clock climbed to his room with a heavy tread. . . . An enormous, weighty man. Thick, immobile features. An air of clumsy naïveté, and of stubborn, mulish obstinacy. . . . He filled a pipe with the care he brought to all things, lit it, and began to smoke as he surveyed the room."[13]

Thus was born Inspector Maigret, though under a borrowed identity. The first book in which his name appears, *Une Ombre dans la nuit* (A Shadow in the Night, 1929), is not a detective story but a romance novel published under the pseudonym Georges-Martin Georges. The character who bears it is not a Paris policeman but a Saint-Macaire doctor who has only a minor role in the plot. This is itself somewhat unsettling, since both Georges Simenon and Jules Maigret would later acknowledge, each in his own way, their frustrated desire to become a doctor. Several other pulp novels written in 1929—*L'Homme à la cigarette, Captain S.O.S., La Victime, La Femme en deuil* (The Woman in Mourning)—feature police inspectors who prefigure several of the future hero's character traits, particularly his reliance on instinct, his capacity for blending into the surrounding milieu, and his ability to put himself in others people's shoes.[14]

Inspector Maigret appears full-blown for the first time, though in a secondary role, in *Train de nuit* (Night Train, 1930). Here he already shows a flair for insight into the minds of hunted men. He becomes a little clearer in *La Figurante* (The Extra)—just as gruff but slightly warmer, his personality still rather subdued, asserting himself only in interrogations and already illustrating the quintessential Simenon watchword: to understand and not to judge.

Things become clearer with *La Femme rousse*. Here the author draws the character of the future inspector more sharply.[15] But *La Maison de l'inquiétude* (House of Anxiety), written in the winter of 1929, contains probably the most complete prefiguration of Maigret. Not only is the portrait of the inspector more vivid but the character is present at all stages of the story, leading the investigation from start to finish.[16]

Simenon was getting close now: this fourth prototype worked well. Having tested it on both himself and his readers, he finally had his hero. All that remained was to baptize him, but that would require a little trickery, for the birth had to occur under the most auspicious possible circumstances.

Why was Simenon so insistent that *Pietr-le-Letton* was the first Maigret, when it clearly wasn't? The explanation reveals how determined he was—even at this young age—to construct and protect his legend.

The volume of copy he was supplying might suggest that he had the freedom to do whatever he pleased. But his silent partners had few illusions about his capacities. Georges Kessel, who had been named editor of *Détective* by Gaston Gallimard, was openly critical of him. When Simenon handed in the manuscripts of *Les Treize Mystères* (1932) and later *Les Treize Énigmes* (1932), both of which were hits with the weekly's readers, Kessel was initially quite unhappy. He considered the enigmas too contrived and the plots too sloppy.[17] Simenon was forced to make changes, even though he hated reworking what had already been written.

Though he had no problems with Tallandier or Ferenczi, things were different with Gallimard. In December 1928, Simenon sent the manuscript of one of his popular novels, *Tonnerre de Brest* (Brest Thunder), to Georges Sadoul, a member of the Gallimard reading committee, suggesting that the book was tailor-made for "Adventure Novel Masterpieces," the collection Sadoul directed. Whether out of courtesy, timidity, or simple editorial caution, Sadoul reported that although he liked the novel, he had reservations about publishing it. He felt the author had revealed the plot too quickly, but said he would be delighted to meet with him and, who knows?, perhaps publish another of his books.[18]

The door of Gallimard's prestigious NRF (Nouvelle Revue Française) was now ajar, and Simenon needed no prodding. Two months later he sent the manuscript of *L'Homme à la cigarette* to Sadoul. The first reader's report was favorable, but Sadoul wanted to see other works by Simenon before making up his mind.[19] Simenon, not used to this kind of evasion, wanted to know where he stood with the publisher of Gide, Proust, and Valéry. Sadoul then explained that the NRF reading committee was "unanimous in finding *L'Homme à la cigarette* of great interest." The firm very much wanted to publish one of Simenon's books and had no doubt that he would someday be part of the NRF list. Unfortunately, however, *L'Homme à la cigarette* was not quite what was needed:

"We think it preferable that the first work of yours to be published under our imprint be a novel with every chance of success."[20]

Simenon did not know what to think, especially inasmuch as his correspondent concluded by assuring him that Gallimard hoped to read more of his work and to be his publisher someday. *L'Homme à la cigarette* was finally published two years later, by Tallandier. In the meantime, Simenon was also having problems at Fayard—not with Baron Dillon, who was as accommodating as ever and as sure of the promise of this young talent, but with Mr. Fayard himself.

In 1928, Simenon had to negotiate each contract separately. In April, he was given an advance of 1,800 francs for *La Maison sans soleil* (House Without Sun); in July, 5,000 francs for *L'Amant sans nom;* and in October, for *La Fiancée aux mains de glace,* an advance of 3,000 francs on signature of the contract plus 50 percent of subsidiary rights, not including press serialization, which the author retained in exchange for promising to wait two years before submitting the text to a newspaper.[21] In 1929 and 1930, things were simpler: *L'Inconnue* (The Woman Unknown), *La Maison de la haine* (House of Hate), *Train de nuit,* and several other titles were published under identical terms— an advance of 3,000 francs for each. But the publisher stipulated that he reserved the right to make cuts and revisions, and to alter titles.[22]

Despite these laborious compromises, Arthème Fayard saw fit to reject *La Maison de l'inquiétude,* the novel that launched the investigations of Inspector Maigret. It was therefore in the columns of a daily newspaper, *L'Œuvre,* that readers first discovered the new character, in March 1930, two years before its publication in book form by Tallandier. On the other hand, two months after rejecting what was actually the first Maigret novel, Fayard agreed to publish *Pietr-le-Letton,* initially as a serial in one of his newspapers, *Ric et Rac.* (He also suggested that the author's name be changed: "Why not Georges Simenon?")

In the course of that year Simenon offered Arthème Fayard several other manuscripts, some of the usual popular, sentimental sort, others of a new type, along the lines of *Pietr-le-Letton.* Among these were *Le Charretier de "La Providence"* (*The Crime at Lock 14,* 1931) and *Monsieur Gallet, décédé.* When he went to the office to discuss these last titles, Mr. Fayard's reaction seemed peculiar:

"So, my dear young Sim . . . Not bad, not bad . . ."

"Oh?"

"Well, actually, catastrophic! Unpublishable!"

"Oh?"

"No love story, no really good characters, no really bad ones, no leading man, no heroine. No likable characters, nothing ever works out, no one ever gets married. . . . We need happy endings, and most of your plots are sordid. . . . Besides which, they aren't detective stories, they aren't scientific. They aren't based on one particular problem, like a chess problem. The hero is a second-rate bureaucrat, not strong, not handsome, not exceptional. . . . No allure and no panache. You're not even giving the public the elements of a novel. . . . There are no riddles, and therefore no mystery story. . . . What do you expect us to do with this kind of stuff? Believe me, it won't sell. . . ."

"In other words," Simenon said, reaching out to pick up his manuscripts, "you don't want them?"

"I've talked to the bookstores, and they won't sell. It'd be a disaster. You won't sell a thousand copies, and we'll lose money." He paused. "All right, look: give me one a month and we'll see what we can do."

Fayard and Simenon agreed that the publisher would be given six novels in advance. The author, tormented by the challenge, promised to keep up the pace. It would have been easier had Fayard agreed to let him work on it full-time, but nothing doing. Naïvely, Simenon wondered aloud whether these great novels to come might not be applied to his account, now 30,000 francs in the red. "Impossible!" Arthème Fayard replied. "First deliver the 30,000 francs' worth of pulp novels you owe me!"[23]

Simenon had little choice. He was already writing twice as much as he should, and now he would have to turn out twice as much again. He would bring his first "period" to a close while simultaneously launching the next.

Despite his initial reluctance and even hostility, Arthème Fayard later boasted that he was the farsighted publisher who suggested to Simenon that he invent a "likable cop" very different from traditional reporters and gentlemen-burglars like Rouletabille or Arsène Lupin.[24]

Simenon, too, would rewrite this "historic" episode. Although *La Maison de l'inquiétude* was in fact the first Maigret investigation, he felt it suffered from a number of flaws: it was not a commercial success; it was signed Georges Sim (which he now considered a pseudonym of his apprentice years); it had been rejected by his main publisher (Fayard) and eventually published by a competitor (Tallandier). *Pietr-le-Letton,* on the other hand, had more obvious charms: the plot was better constructed and more typical of Simenon's new style; it was the first book to be signed Georges Simenon; it was the first Maigret investigation accepted by Fayard, who would also publish the successors, with uncontested success. *La Maison de l'inquiétude* therefore had to give way to *Pietr-le-Letton.*[25]

A lot of ground had been covered since Edgar Allan Poe published "The Murders in the Rue Morgue" in 1840. Ninety years later, a new French crime novel that took liberties with the American model came on the scene. "All authors of detective novels were doing the same thing, except Georges Simenon," Thomas Narcejac would later say.[26] "The form had been so narrowly defined as to stifle imagination."

Simenon now knew how to construct a plot, compose a coherent story, create characters with some depth, control his most intrusive clichés, and mix past, present, and future in a single action with a little more skill. All this was just enough to reach an audience of higher quality and to make more money. But his characteristic lucidity kept him from rushing ahead too fast. He felt that he did not yet command the resources to produce real literature.

He admitted as much to Arthème Fayard during their famous meeting in September 1930, when he sought to justify his move to a literary genre the publisher felt was inappropriate for the Georges Sim he knew.

"I've decided to step up a notch."

"Meaning what?"

"After all the pulp novels, I want to try a semi-literary novel."

"What do you mean by 'semi-literary'?" Fayard's tone was doubtful.

Simenon then proceeded to expound a "theory" typical of him.

"There are maybe ten or twenty literary genres, which are like the various sections of a department store in that they exist only by tacit agreement between seller and buyer. Each category has its own rules, which commercial honesty forbids us to violate. Standing above all this is the realm of the pure novel, the work of art, which defers to nothing but itself and eludes all the rules of publishing. I don't feel I'm mature enough to enter that category yet. You can't write a novel—by which I mean a real novel—before your forties, because it presupposes a maturity difficult to acquire at an earlier age. The novelist is God the Father, and I'm still very far from that."[27]

This speech was not made to measure for his publisher. Soon afterward, when a favorable mention of him appeared in *L'Intransigeant,* Simenon got a call from Frédéric Lefèvre asking that he pay him a visit in his office at *Les Nouvelles littéraires.* Flattered, hoping that the journalist wanted to devote one of his famous "An Hour With . . ." interviews to him, Simenon took him up on the offer. Jacques-Emile Blanche, the art critic, painter, and novelist, sat in a corner of Lefèvre's office listening to their conversation with half an ear. Lefèvre found Simenon a "likable and original" young man, and Georges proceeded to "sell himself," something he was already quite adept at doing:

"Up to now I've been called Sim, Georges Sim, but I've had enough of that. From now on I'm going back to my real name, and I'll sign my books Georges Simenon. . . . I haven't written that much. I'm already 29 and I've only published 277 books. . . . It's not my profession. By profession I'm a traveler, or an explorer, if you will. I come in from the Baltic, and a month later I'm off again, maybe for Oceania." "Up to now I've been doing bread-and-butter literature that I'd rather not talk about. But now I want to change my style. Hence the name change."

"You'd like to do pure literature?" Lefèvre ventured.

"Not yet. You have to go by degrees. First I want to do semi-bread-and-butter literature, because I want to buy a bigger boat."

Jacques-Emile Blanche walked over to them, in undisguised stupefaction.

"Semi-bread-and-butter?" he asked. "What in the world is that?"

"Semi-bread-and-butter novels are the ones you read over once before sending them to the printshop. Call it semi-literature, if you prefer. Novels where I try to create real characters but still use conventional procedures and frameworks. As soon as I can dispense with the handrail, I'll try to write novels *tout court.*"

"*Tout court,* eh? From semi-literature to novels *tout court.*" Blanche guffawed. "It's a new one on me. And I thought it was going to be a wasted day."

The two men were obviously laughing at him. An unruffled Simenon put two volumes on Frédéric Lefèvre's desk: copies of *Le Pendu de Saint-Pholien* and *Monsieur Gallet, décédé.*

"Which one should I read first?" the literary journalist asked with ironic false deference.

"Le Pendu de Saint-Pholien," Simenon replied. "It's the latest, and therefore the closest to my developing aesthetic."[28]

No less. Yet it was this self-assurance that took Simenon where he wanted to go. Several months after this first contact, which a more testy person might have found humiliating, he was visited at his apartment by Georges Charensol, a *Nouvelles littéraires* journalist who was to interview him for a series of portraits of "unknown celebrities"—celebrities for the general public, unknown in that they were scorned by critics and intellectuals.

Simenon struck Charensol as a pleasant, picturesque character, an author who did not take himself too seriously. A novelist capable of writing anything at all for money[29] but not quite capable of saying anything, for there was far too much determination in his glance and precision in his choice of words when he turned suddenly solemn and announced:

"My ambition is to produce semi-literary novels as a step toward rising to the class of a Jack London, or, who knows?, maybe one day a Conrad."[30]

In the meantime, he still needed a ringmaster, someone who could discipline characters that might otherwise wander off, eluding the author if he let them go. Inspector Maigret would play this role, and would have to continue to do so until the novelist was capable of developing more than one character at a time.[31] He now began to fill in Maigret's physical and biographical features.

Jules Maigret is born in literature at the age of forty-five, almost exactly the age at which Simenon's father died. He is married and childless, as was Simenon at the time. He is neither Georges nor Désiré, but has flaws and virtues borrowed from both. He is plebeian, stable, intuitive, apolitical, suspicious, chaste, neuter, reassuring. He likes to eat, drink, and smoke his pipe. He is gruff, discreet, sedentary, and not very sociable.

He was born in Saint-Fiacre par Matignon, about fifteen miles from Moulins (the Allier). In other words, in Paray-le-Frésil. His father, Evariste, was steward at the château Saint-Fiacre for three decades. He had Jules at the age of twenty-four and died of pleurisy at forty-four; Désiré Simenon had Georges at twenty-five and died of angina pectoris at forty-four. The future inspector, orphaned from his father at nineteen as the future novelist was at eighteen, studied medicine before changing his mind. Other than that, he is a man like any other, not so much described as suggested by his habits and tics:

"Rubs his hand over his head against the grain; doesn't dance or play bridge, doesn't know how to drive, doesn't like sweets. In the early days stirred the embers of his office stove before relighting it, one hand behind his back. Can manage a few words of German, understands English and Breton. Favorite expressions: 'I don't believe anything' and 'Not at all.' Splatters himself when he washes; hates writing on a marble desk; tiny handwriting that looks like a row of blotches. Doesn't like to stay in Paris without his wife. Wounded three times in his career. Sometimes considered whimsical by his colleagues because of his method of work."[32]

Maigret is no intellectual: he is not wont to ponder. Intuitive and instinctive, he is intelligent but not cunning. He soaks up atmosphere like a sponge, penetrating a milieu so as to grasp its rules. It is his sense of smell more than his reflective ability that leads to his most daring deductions.

He is a beer-drinker—mainly because Simenon's exceptional olfactory memory had registered the smell of beer as the characteristic aroma of the Belgium of his youth, a country of cafés and bars. He is a ritualistic man. Goes to the movies once a week. When he comes home from work, he stops midway between the third and fourth floors to unbutton his coat and take his keys out of his pocket, even though he knows that his wife, Louise, will open the door for him before he puts the key in the lock. Though fond of drinking, he never gets drunk, however much time he spends in bistros during his investigations. A country boy still close to the earth, he has a kind of sluggishness he makes no attempt to conceal.

Forever attached to the social layer from which he had come, Jules Maigret would always be more touched by the distress of the humble than by that of the rich. He was a man of the French heartland, a world of peasants and nobles disturbed and even frightened by progress and modernism. The author admitted that he had borrowed some of Maigret's features from several of the police officers he had known: Inspectors Massu, Guillaume, Xavier, and Guichard.[33] But he always had trouble recognizing the unconscious connections between himself and his hero:

"I do not identify with Maigret. It never occurred to me that I resembled him," he would often repeat, in unyielding denial.[34]

Yet even if we admit that some of the intriguing similarities between the two are incidental details, Maigret and Simenon did have a parallel understanding of their principal activities. They saw police work and writing as uncomplicated crafts. Both had an aptitude for living the lives of others and for immersing themselves in a milieu. The policeman felt uncomfortable when he was between cases, the novelist when he was between books.

The inspector himself constantly identifies with others. It is by climbing into his suspect's skin that he tracks him down. Maigret reasons as Simenon writes. Both tend to have more sympathy for the perpetrator than for the victim. The investigator often says that he knows the murderer only by getting to know the victim well, and the novelist builds his tale in exactly the same way. In the investigation itself, as in the writing that engenders it, atmosphere, milieu, and characters are more important than plot, clue, and suspense.

Simenon read a lot of Conan Doyle in his youth, and he claimed that Maigret and Sherlock Holmes were complete opposites, that his hero had no need of a sidekick ("It is I who serve as Dr. Watson"),[35] and that "Sherlock Holmes is theoretical, whereas Maigret lives, exists."[36]

A peremptory and debatable judgment, but it does contain an insight that helps to illuminate what sets the Maigret books off from other detective novels of the 1930s, still generally characterized by a whodunit plot and by the unerring logical and observational skills of the hero. Two Simenon experts, Boileau and Narcejac, analyzed the point more sharply than most others.

Pierre Boileau, who was twenty-five when the first Maigret novels came out, remarked that until the advent of the inspector, "no one ever reread a detective story unless they had forgotten the ending." Simenon twisted the traditional rules of the genre so thoroughly that readers did not expect clear and simple answers to the standard triad of questions (who? how? why?). "The important thing," Boileau wrote, "was not identifying the murderer but understanding him, decoding his own enigma instead of the puzzle posed by his actions, no matter how mysterious they seemed."[37]

His colleague Thomas Narcejac argued in a famous essay that since Simenon's starting point is never the plot but always the characters, his "Maigrets" are not detective stories but classical novels. The fact that the author ascribed the inspector's genius to intuition rather than logic took him even farther from the genre. In any event, Jules Maigret was hardly a credible investigator, at least in the early titles: he makes too many technical mistakes to be convincing to professionals. This may be seen as additional evidence that only novelistic truth was of real import to his creator.

In the absence of realism, Maigret never strays far from verisimilitude. The less professional he is, the more he is like us. The policeman, like the novelist, is less interested in the criminal than in the man. So great is their empathy, Narcejac says, that they often view the perpetrator as not being responsible for his actions, leading us to dismiss the fatal crime as excusable: "Instead of following a phantom assassin for 250 pages, he gradually unmasks the criminal, quietly leading us to acknowledge the psychological necessity of his act."[38]

It is late 1930. Inspector Maigret is about to be officially baptized, as is the writer Georges Simenon. He has just finished several other Maigret investigations besides *Pietr-le-Letton: Monsieur Gallet, décédé, Le Pendu de Saint-Pholien, Le Charretier de "La Providence,"* and *La Tête d'un homme* (*A Battle of Nerves*, 1931). All save the last are datelined Morsang-sur-Seine, "aboard the *Ostrogoth*." The exception was written in the Aiglon Hotel on the Boulevard Raspail in Paris.

Contrary to his wish, however, Simenon has not been able to devote all his

time to this series in which he has given the best of himself. Timidly, he raises
the issue again, but Arthème Fayard is as unyielding as ever. Simenon's reasoning makes eminent sense: since he is paid more for a chapter of Maigret
than for a pulp novel of twenty thousand lines, why not pay off what he owes
in Maigrets? He could wipe out the debt in two weeks. But the publisher will
not mix his accounts. Ever cautious and sensible, he is determined to cover his
arrears—just in case the novelist's "new style" fails to score the expected success among the broad public he has targeted. Simenon will never forgive him
for this.[39]

He decides to rent himself a "pad" near Concarneau (Finistère), lock himself
up for three months, sleep less, drink more than usual. There he churns out
pulp novels at the rate of eighty pages a day, writing in eleven-hour clips.
Within a few weeks he has lost some weight but gained 30,000 francs. Literally obsessed by the task, he is determined to finish come what may, but the
inspector's shadow hangs over him during these days and nights devoted to
liquidating the past of one Georges Sim:

"Maigret lived inside me. I saw him as a flesh-and-blood character, I knew
his voice, the smell of his worn sweater, down to the tips of his shoes. He was
right there smoking his pipe, waiting, as I slaved away. We had faith in each
other."[40]

The author and his work were ready. All that remained was to launch them.
For Georges Simenon, the time had come to reveal a new facet of his genius.
The stakes were high. No one would let him off the hook if Maigret was a fail-
ure—not publishers, critics, journalists, or readers.

After the fiasco of the "glass cage," Simenon had no choice but to reach for
success under his own name. It was the start of his flight forward, and there
would be no respite until the publication of his *Mémoires Intimes,* almost exactly half a century later.

7

SIMENON MAKES HIS MOVIE

1931–1932

eorges Simenon did not have to be from Hollywood to agree with Samuel Goldwyn that the best way to launch a "product," whether a film or a book, was to get press coverage not in review sections but in the general news pages. The novelist's savoir faire now took a back seat to the Parisian's savvy.

He was determined to make sure that his books were seen as news events, and he would not be satisfied until people were talking about them without necessarily having taken the trouble to read them. In 1930 this was still a revolutionary approach in the republic of letters.

The trail had been blazed by the publisher Bernard Grasset, who organized a major advertising campaign in 1923 to promote *Le Diable au corps,* by the young and unknown Raymond Radiguet. Eight years later, most of Grasset's colleagues and a good number of critics still held their noses at the stir, despite the admitted qualities of the "product" sold by this technique.

Simenon, who had no patience with such prissiness, wanted to promote Maigret with a grand soiree—something exceptional, even historic. What he had in mind was a special kind of society "ball." If it worked, it would be the talk of the town.

"I am chided for my taste for publicity," Simenon confided to his friend Carlo Rim,[1] "as though God Himself had no need of his church bells! It's not enough to have talent. You also have to make it known."

Friday, February 20, 1931: Simenon's "Anthropometric Ball" is to be held at La Boule Blanche, a West Indian nightclub at 33 Rue Vavin, near the Luxembourg Gardens in Montparnasse, a neighborhood bursting with pride at having finally supplanted Saint-Germain and Montmartre in the hearts of artists and writers. The event is advertised as the greatest "prison gathering" ever held in Paris. The invitations look like summonses and "anthropometric" sheets: in other words, police booking cards. The novelist has also sent out thousands of postcards bearing breathless extracts from some of his Maigrets.

Ten p.m.—two hours to showtime: the decorations have been left in the expert hands of three of Simenon's artist friends—Marcel Vertès, Don, and Paul Colin, designer of the poster for the Revue Nègre, who will later claim that this event was his idea.[2] They have opted for a "Quai des Orfèvres" motif. The walls are covered with pictures of handcuffs, bloody hands, and headless corpses. Large question marks add a literary touch. Technicians from Fox Movietone, a company Simenon has contracted for the occasion, install tripods and cameras at the entrance to film people as they arrive. Throngs are already gathered outside, stamping their feet. It is impossible to contain them until the scheduled hour.

Three extras are posted at the entrance: a prostitute, a pimp, and a butcher in a bloodstained apron. A black man of impressive stature stands near them, looking on. Contrary to the claim of the cynical Henri Jeanson, the guests have not been selected for their criminal records. At least not all of them.

Midnight: The crowd is so thick that the doors of La Boule Blanche are forced open. The West Indian band swings into action. Within moments this nightspot, where perhaps three hundred people would normally be packed into its one hundred square meters, is invaded by a good thousand revelers who will not go home before dawn.

The guest list is a who's who of Paris. The Clermont-Tonnerres, Philippe de Rothschild and Misia Sert, and the writers Paul Vialar, Francis Carco, Armand Salacrou, and T'Sterstevens mingle with true aristocrats of the night like Tonton of Montmartre and Kiki of Montparnasse; the art critic Florent Fels and the actor Marcel Dalio rub elbows with the painters Derain and Kisling and with the architect Mallet-Stevens, under the ironic gaze of Pierre Lazareff. The reporter from *Paris-Soir*, who relishes hearing proper people talk dirty, busily takes notes: "Who knows how many tuxedo-clad pimps and plainclothes policemen were among the horde of guests?"[3]

Since evening dress is not required and its absence strongly recommended, many get into the spirit, slumming "at Simenon's" as they would at some dubious dive. Formal men slip off their jackets, well-formed women their dresses, one chronicler jokes. A masquerade contest is held upstairs in the packed mezzanine. Kisling, dressed as a Vice Squad informer, wins first prize (a chronometer). Celebrities sport disreputable sideburns while high-society ladies dress down as feminist militants.

The Anthropometric Ball is a kind of throwback to the Apache tradition, the snobbish fad of often questionable taste that had swept the salons of Paris before 1914, when the underworld was all the rage. The Black Misery Ball, advertised with great fanfare at the Champs-Elysées Theater in the 1920s, nearly finished off the trend, the organizers being forced to close up shop when massive numbers of real tramps and beggars representing the poorest the City of Light had to offer threatened to crash the ball. These undesirables, whom high society was only too happy to mimic with utter cynicism, apparently intended to infect the prestigious theater with the real-life cachet of the Court of Miracles.

The party is in full swing. Fake policemen in uniform posted at the entrance demand that guests have their fingerprints taken before being admitted.

"Your prints, sir?"

"No, thanks. Bad memories, you know."[4]

Damia, who will shortly break out in song while perched on a painter's shoulders, offers the red outline of her painted lips along with her prints. Eugène Merle, of the "glass cage," declines the invitation: "They're already on file."[5]

Inside there is no room to move. It is a miracle that no one is crushed or asphyxiated. The artists, invited to "sign" the wall, clear a path through the crowd as best they can, knocking over Derain, who is busy painting a portrait on the bathing suit of a female guest as a senator hollers, "Take him downtown!"[6]

Four in the morning. Waiters from Le Dôme have been steadily resupplying the buffet. The place is still packed with hookers and members of parliament, actors and writers, journalists and lawyers. The music is deafening. The most indefatigable party-goers strip off their clothes and take champagne showers. Meanwhile, Simenon, pipe stuck in his mouth, is signing copies of his new novels. He has spent most of the night on the mezzanine, scarcely looking up from the table, so imperturbable that some are inclined to wonder whether he is finishing his latest novel as the party peters out.

Seven in the morning: time for supper at La Coupole. Anyone who is anybody agrees that it's been a long time since so much fun was had in the capital.[7]

The Anthropometric Ball, partly financed by Simenon's advances, cost less than a classical publicity campaign. Maigret was on his way, and so was Simenon. The party was reported as a news event, not a literary function. In principle, all these people had gathered to attend the launching of two detective novels, "but the crowd was so thick that no one could have launched anything at all, not even a witticism," noted *Le Figaro*'s special envoy.[8] The critic André Thérive called it "the Misdemeanor Ball."[9]

Literary circles, however, reacted as negatively as Simenon could have feared. They treated him with such condescension that he might as well have perpetrated the glass-cage stunt. Some considered the party especially unseemly in a climate of economic depression. *Le Canard Enchaîné* weighed in with its customary wit, portraying Simenon as an insatiable publicity hound and speculating that if the Anthropometric Ball had failed, he might have tried to write a novel while walking on his hands around the lake in the Tuileries—which may have been a way of suggesting that he wrote with his feet.[10]

In the meantime, Simenon pressed on. Between March and December of 1931, he followed up the first Maigrets with eight others—*Le Chien jaune* (*A Face for a Clue*), *La Nuit du carrefour* (*The Crossroad Murders*), *Un Crime en Hollande* (*A Crime in Holland*), *Au Rendez-vous des Terres-Neuvas* (*The Sailors' Rendez-vous*), *La Danseuse du Gai-Moulin*, *La Guinguette à deux sous* (*The Guinguette by the Seine*), *Le Port des brumes* (*Death of a Harbour Master*), and *L'Ombre chinoise* (*The Shadow in the Courtyard*)—plus one novel, *Le Relais d'Alsace* (*The Man from Everywhere*), in which the inspector does not appear. And he continued his frenetic lifestyle, dividing his time between the *Ostrogoth* and the Château de la Michaudière in Guigneville-sur-Essonne. It was his usual pace.

Once the initial surprise generated by the Anthropometric Ball had passed, he had to deal with reactions to his "new style." At police headquarters on the Quai des Orfèvres, there were ironic suggestions that Inspector Maigret lacked authenticity: he went on stakeouts and tailed suspects as though he were a beat cop; his investigations took him to the provinces (Fécamp, Sancerre, Reims) and abroad (Bremen, Liège), although he was assigned neither to the Sûreté Nationale nor to the Flying Squad.

The novelist, of course, could claim that he had taken such liberties deliberately, the machinery of the police bureaucracy being too complex to render accurately anyway. But the police decided to help him get it right. Xavier Guichard, director of the Judiciary Police, invited the novelist to visit headquarters.

"Your books are fine," Guichard told him. "Very amusing. Your Maigret is just like our inspectors. But there are too many administrative errors. You ought to do a tour of duty with one of the inspectors." Simenon was more than willing. After the tour, he dropped in on the boss in his office.

"What I'd really like to do is sit in on some interrogations, feel the vibrations . . ."

"As long as you can promise me I won't read about it in the papers."

Simenon spent a day with Inspector Guillaume, commander of the Criminal

Brigade. He attended the morning roll call, the meeting of brigade commanders in Guichard's office, and even psychiatric examinations at a prison infirmary.[11]

In the end, he had a lot less trouble with the police than with the press. Some of his colleagues didn't like him, and they did not hesitate to let him know it. *D'Artagnan, Le Canard Enchaîné, Le Coup de Patte,* and *L'Œil de Paris* were particularly hostile. *L'Œil de Paris* was so determined to discredit him that it even claimed that "Simenon" was just another pseudonym and that his real name was Simminger.[12]

With the publication of *Le Charretier de "La Providence"* (1931), his third novel in three months, the word *record* became increasingly linked to his name. But few of his contemporaries had any notion of the labor and creative energy that went into his easily denigrated novels. At the time, little was known of his writing ritual, his idiosyncratic manner of immersing himself in a story of which he claimed utter ignorance at its start. He was a tightrope walker, his only net the manila envelope on which he scrawled a few notes as a kind of outline. The envelope for *Le Pendu de Saint-Pholien* (1931) is typical for its chaos:

"Neuchanz . . . bistro . . . Herstal revolver . . . 30,000 francs . . . Mr. Louis Jeunet, 18 Rue de la Roquette, Paris. Born in Aubervilliers . . . Shop on the Rue Neuve . . ." And the one for *Le Chien jaune* (1931): "Hotel de l'Amiral/Quai de l'Aiguillon . . . Mr. Gloguen wine merchant . . . Dr. Ernest Michoux . . . Mr. Le Pommeret, Danish vice-consul . . . Jean Servières, the Brest Lighthouse . . . Emma Grémillon . . . Friday November 7 . . ."[13]

He willingly granted interviews in his effort to defend himself, but they often had effects opposite to his hopes. One polemicist punctured this "instant novelist's" consuming ambition and parvenu boasting. Another portrayed him as a grotesque megalomaniacal clown. Simenon's complete lack of modesty grated.[14]

It must be said that he made no effort to cultivate the critics. He cared little that nitpickers complained about his alleged confusion of genres, his illegitimate mixture of the detective story, the adventure novel, and the roman feuilleton.[15] In fact, he boasted that since the publication of *Le Relais d'Alsace* (1931), the first of his nonpolice novels to be published under his own name, he had decided not to read contemporary authors so as not to subject himself to their influence. He announced his preference for Rabelais, Goethe, and Gorky, adding that these were "real writers" whose power lay in their ability to move readers through clarity of expression, unlike the petty despots of French literature, with their affected turns of phrase.[16] This was not the way to make friends in Paris.

Simenon even managed to arouse the ire of devotees of popular radio serials. When a Paris station broadcast a live sketch taken from *Le Pendu de Saint-Pholien* (starring, among others, the author himself and his friend Luc Lafnet), to a background of gunshots, screams, and footfalls, a professional newspaper scolded him for exploiting radio for personal promotion and for showing contempt for public taste: "He was primarily concerned to sow panic and fright among the peaceful race of wireless listeners," the commentator wrote. "This was Grand Guignol of the airwaves."[17]

But enmity was not his sole daily bread. He also had ardent supporters, some of them unlikely. Maurice Leblanc was one. When a critic suggested that the creator of Arsène Lupin could learn a few tricks by having a look at Simenon's work, Leblanc took the advice and wrote an "Open Letter" praising his young colleague.[18]

But even interviews with those of his peers who wished him well sometimes came off badly. The journalist Odette Pannetier of *Candide* tried to discuss Simenon's work with him but could not get beyond his strutting and boasting:

"It's absolutely unheard of, my dear, and I just can't take it anymore. . . . So next week I'm leaving, fleeing. Off on a tour of Africa, a land I instinctively detest, though I've never been there, and I want to see if I'm right. . . . I wish I could be anonymous again, walk around unrecognized. It's terrible, you know, not to be able to go into a bar or a restaurant without people elbowing each other and whispering, 'Look, it's Georges Simenon!' They read my books all over the world, you know. . . . In New York they say I'm the world's best detective novelist. . . . They're copying me everywhere now, so I want to make some changes in the genre. I was the first to do it, and now I'll have to create a new one, that's all there is to it. . . . I know that the style of my Maigret series is already pretty good, but I want to do even better. They say the novel is dead in France, you know. Well, I want to show all these literary lights that novels can still be written, that a genre in its death throes can be re-created. . . ."[19]

Simenon somehow managed to give his detractors ammunition every time he opened his mouth. He seemed to feel a need to justify his lifestyle even when it had not been questioned. Unfortunately, he sounded insincere:

"Believe me, I have no taste for the life I lead. If I spend half a million francs a year, it's only because I have to see the world. I have to know how it feels to lose a fortune in Monte Carlo, or to own a yacht and have a chauffeur. But as soon as I've amassed the material I need, it'll be over with, and I'll go back to a quiet, peaceful life."[20]

In an interview with J. K. Raymond-Millet for *Le Courrier cinématographique,* Simenon truly outdid himself. The conversation took place at an outdoor café, as Simenon's chauffeur dozed behind the wheel. The novelist talked expansively about his favorite subjects—himself and his work. The word *I* occurs thirty-four times in the text of the interview. The journalist was impressed by Simenon's self-assurance, his rate of production (a book a month at that time, soon to be one every two weeks, he promised), his readiness to take risks, his insolent good health, his florid complexion, and his flamboyant good humor: "Everything's fine. Life is beautiful. My books are selling well. I expect to die old. I'm happy."[21]

Simenon's interlocutor, dazzled by this fascinating self-assurance, yearned to uncover the secret of his subject's productivity. The author obliged by explaining how he spent his time.

> My existence is divided into periods of fifteen days. In each period I compose one novel. On the first day I wander alone, at random. I might run, sit for a while, or walk. I watch the people passing by. I make appointments with my characters, introduce them to one another. I watch. Later, when I go home, I have the "starting point" of my story, the "site" where the action takes place, and the "atmosphere." That's all I need. I don't think about it anymore. I go to bed. I sleep. And dream. My characters grow inside me, without my help. Soon they no longer belong to me: they have lives of their own. The next day and in the days that follow all I have to do is act as their historian. Did I mention that I type my books myself, directly, without writing them out by hand first? No touchups or modifications. My books are done in one take.
>
> I never write with an outline. I let my people act and the story evolve according to the logic of things. My books generally have twelve chapters. I compose one chapter each morning, no more. This takes only about an hour and a half, but then I'm "empty" for the rest of the day. Okay, twelve chapters, twelve days, plus the preparation day, for a total of thirteen. On the fourteenth day I reread the manuscript, correcting typographical errors, punctuation, maybe a dozen or so words in the whole book. Then I take the text to my publisher. On the fifteenth day I have friends over, answer letters I've received during the past two weeks, and grant interviews. Then it all begins again, exactly the same way, for the next fifteen days.[22]

Simenon's discourse on method was delivered with such self-satisfaction and insistent will to be believed that his interviewers found it embarrassing. He knew this, but didn't care. His prime concern was to get people talking about him and to live in harmony with his own inner nature, however unpleasant some found it.

Since Fayard could not decently publish more than one novel a month by a single author, Simenon accepted a proposal from Jacques Haumont, a young publisher just breaking into the trade. Haumont was promoting a new, illustrated series of detective stories called "Photo-Text." The authors would be paid a flat fee of 2,500 francs for every 25,000 copies printed. Four Simenon manuscripts were commissioned and a new character was introduced: G.7, one of the few police inspectors to own a private car. Titles were even determined: *G.7, Deux Cadavres, La Marie Gallante*,[23] and finally *La Folle d'Itteville* (The Madwoman of Itteville), illustrated by photographs by Germaine Krull.

On the night of August 4, Simenon threw a party aboard the *Ostrogoth*, which was moored at Anjou pier, near the Pont-Marie, to celebrate the launch of the new list. Champagne flowed from 9:00 P.M. to midnight, to the strains of banjos and accordions played by musicians from a local band hired for the occasion. Simenon and Krull signed copies of the first title. Tramps mingled with the dancers as amused passersby leaned over the railing of the bridge to watch. The art critic Florent Fels poured drinks for proud veterans of the Anthropometric Ball, who boasted of their attendance at that memorable gathering. The novelist Pierre Véry was there, and the Academician Marcel Prévost, along with the publisher Simon Kra. When Kra went into the cabin to get his signed copy, Simenon reminded him that when Kessel's *Le Coup de grâce* came out, "your colleague at Editions de France announced: 'the first Kessel in three years!' " Kra was perplexed, until he looked at what Simenon had written as his dedication: "For Simon Kra, the first Simenon in eight days."[24]

The party was a success, but *La Folle d'Itteville* was not. Simenon took it badly, and his relations with Jacques Haumont soon soured. Simenon wanted to be the sole author of the new series, but titles had already been commissioned from Germaine Beaumont and Pierre MacOrlan. They parted ways, and the new series was aborted.[25]

Eleven days later, on August 15, Arthème Fayard arranged for Simenon to sign copies of his works at the Hachette bookstore near the docks in Deauville. The novelist sailed down the Seine at the helm of the *Ostrogoth*, while his chauffeur followed along the riverbank in the Chrysler. Another "record": the first author not to take a car or a train to Normandy for a book signing.

"That morning the world was my oyster," he would later recall. The signing was notable for the presence of a dignified old gentleman who presented Simenon with copies of the first novels to appear under his own name, rebound and stamped with the family coat of arms.[26]

People who had been in regular contact with Simenon during his nearly ten years in Paris noticed a change in his behavior. The man of letters was now a businessman, too, formidable manager of his own affairs and uncompromising defender of his rights, attending to the smallest details personally. It was only the beginning.

He conducted the negotiations with photographers assigned to illustrate the covers of his titles: André Kertesz, Block, Martin-Vigneau, and others. When Man Ray complained that he was getting only 500 francs per cover, it was Simenon who arranged for his fee to be doubled.[27]

Fayard was learning to treat Simenon in accordance with his enhanced social status. Several contracts signed in 1931 stipulate advances of 6,000 francs against royalties of 10 percent, an improvement over the earlier terms.[28] But he was not satisfied. He complained that he was not getting enough publicity,[29] and he came up with a few unusual promotional ideas. At one point he proposed a deluxe reprint of one of his novels, with a pair of handcuffs to be given away with each copy. He was respectfully informed that the idea would never work, since gift books were aimed mainly at children. But he dug in his heels and insisted that three thousand pairs of handcuffs be ordered, promising to buy back any unsold stock, which he would resell to the manufacturer, who would make a film out of the event.[30] It became increasingly difficult to say no to such an enterprising author, especially since the public was now on his side. Simenon was popular. The Maigret books were selling well. And not only in France.

In 1931, translation rights to his new books were sold in the United States, Britain, Spain, Italy, Norway, and Portugal. Pirated editions soon came out in Japan.[31] The New York literary agent Curtis Brown, bidding to become Simenon's American representative, put him in touch with Covici, Friede, Inc., which issued *La Nuit du carrefour* under the title *The Crossroad Murder—Inspector Maigret Investigates*.[32]

This publisher planned to "adapt" Simenon to American tastes, but for the moment he was published as is, with a boost from Janet Flanner, writing under the name Genêt in *The New Yorker*. In the autumn of 1931 she helped launch Maigret on the Atlantic's western shores, devoting her "Paris Letter" to his creator.[33]

Georges Simenon was already a very busy man, but he was about to add a new string to his bow: films. At first he saw them as a quick and easy way to augment his income. He was not yet aware of the role they would play in popularizing and perpetuating his work.

His interest in the so-called seventh art antedated his discovery of the early German expressionists in the avant-garde cinemas of the Left Bank. Back in Liège he had moonlighted as a correspondent for *La Cinématographie française*, official review of the French film industry. Some of his "Outside the Henhouse" columns also dealt with the issue. In those days Young Sim considered movies an American Trojan horse sent to conquer the Old World, and he roundly condemned "Chaplin mania," Tom Mix, Douglas Fairbanks, and all the other actors who fired the public's passion.[34] But Simenon's relations with the film industry were to change completely with the publication of the

Maigret books and the mounting enthusiasm of directors and producers for the character.

In December 1931, the Simenons sold the *Ostrogoth* and rented Les Roches Grises, a villa on the Boulevard James Wyllie in Antibes owned by the writer Henri Duvernois. Although winter on the Côte d'Azur appeared very chic, the author spent most of his time at work, writing three Maigrets—*L'Ombre chinoise* (1932), *L'Affaire Saint-Fiacre* (1932), and *Chez les Flamands* (*The Flemish Shop*, 1932)—in two months. Around New Year's he also found time to don his businessman's hat and hold meetings with an American agent, a French publisher who happened to be in town, an Italian translator, and, most important, various movie people.[35]

Le Chien jaune (1931) was filmed barely a year after it appeared in print. This Maigret investigation, which takes place over four days in November, is laden with mystery and suspense—attempted murder, a strange disappearance, a poisoning. The three victims have one thing in common: they play cards together at the Hotel de l'Amiral in Concarneau. Maigret saves the fourth player, Dr. Michoux, by taking him into protective custody. The prime suspect seems to be a vagrant, but Maigret learns his real identity and provokes a confrontation that shakes the truth out of him: the murders were a vendetta, a settling of scores among former partners in a drug deal.

The producer of *Le Chien jaune* was Pierre Calmann-Lévy, son of the publisher. He paid 25,000 francs for the film rights. His contract, however, was not with Simenon but with Arthème Fayard. It stipulated that the author would receive the same sum for collaborating on the screenplay, the editing, and the dialogue.[36] The two parties quickly agreed on a director: twenty-eight-year-old Jean Tarride, who had made two earlier films, *L'Homme qui assassina* and *Prisonnier de mon cœur*. Tarride picked his father, the actor Abel Tarride, to play Inspector Maigret. Dr. Michoux was played by Robert Le Vigan.

Simenon insisted on being closely involved in the production and on being credited as coadapter. His concern was not purely financial. He felt that the film should reflect the spirit of the book it was based upon. He would not let them tinker with his hero, and he continued to propose script changes well into the shooting:

"P. 9: in a city where there are five or six pharmacists, no one would say 'the town pharmacist.' . . . P. 29: it is not in character for Maigret to say that the service is better at the hotel. He wouldn't give a damn. . . . P. 53: there is no reason for the mayor to call Maigret 'My dear sir.' . . ."[37]

Simenon also had another film project in the works: *La Nuit du carrefour*, written in April 1931, published soon afterward, and in production before the year was out. The financial terms were the same: 25,000 francs for the film rights and another 25,000 for the author's participation. This time he sold the rights not to the production company, Europa Films, but to Jean Renoir personally. He also added a paragraph to the contract, stipulating that the director and the author would have "the right to choose the actors, by common consent."[38] You could never be too careful. Simenon was already suspicious of the film industry, in whose ethics he had no faith.

Jean Renoir, whom he first met in 1923, now became one of his closest friends. The painter's son, as he was still called in those days, drove all the way to Ouistreham (Calvados), where Simenon was finishing out the summer, to discuss the film. Simenon would never forget how Renoir looked as he climbed out of his luxurious Bugatti, a broad smile on his lips and a copy of *La Nuit du carrefour* in his hand.

Simenon already respected this great creator, and he would now come to love him. He considered Renoir guileless, childlike, and unaffected—in the best sense of all three terms. Spontaneous and ingenuous, he was a nineteenth-century personality, too much the "gentleman" for the movie business. He had several literary adaptations under his belt (Zola's *Nana*, Feydeau's *On purge bébé*, and Georges de La Fouchardière's *La Chienne*).[39] But there was something else about Renoir that Simenon especially appreciated: he was fiercely determined to keep his distance from the industry and tried to maintain his independence by acting as his own producer. He therefore sought to finance this new project from private sources.

The two men closeted themselves in the Antibes villa for several days, working relentlessly to visualize this story of a murder committed at the Trois-Veuves crossroad near Arpajon. The body of an Antwerp diamond merchant by the name of Goldberg is found in the trunk of a car, in a garage. The inspector spends four days questioning the inhabitants of the three houses situated at the fatal intersection. The novel had a powerful unity of place and time, and Renoir was convinced that the film was implicit in the book itself:

"My ambition was to render in images the mystery of this intensely mysterious story. I wanted to subordinate the plot to the atmosphere. Simenon's book marvelously evoked the bleakness of this crossroads some thirty miles from Paris. I don't think there's a more depressing spot on earth. These few houses, lost in an ocean of fog, rain, and mud, are superbly described in the novel. They might have been painted by Vlaminck. My enthusiasm for the atmosphere Simenon had created led me, once again, to violate my strictures on the danger of turning a literary work into a film."[40]

They felt that once they had a clear vision of the characters, starting with Maigret himself, the script would come. They went through about a hundred possible actors and finally settled on Pierre Renoir, the director's brother,[41] a twenty-year veteran whose career had begun with Abel Gance's first film, *La Digue*. He would be the inspector.

La Nuit du carrefour was very much a "family affair." Apart from his brother, Jean Renoir also hired his nephew Claude as assistant cameraman,

Marguerite Houllé-Renoir as editor, and other friends in various positions: Jacques Becker was the production manager, Mimi Champagne the script girl. In filling out the cast, he could not resist bringing in his own people, even if it meant using amateurs in supporting roles. Among those putting in appearances were the painter Dignimont, the playwright Michel Duran, and the film critic Jean Mitry.

The interiors were shot in a studio in Billancourt, outside Paris, the exteriors at the intersection of Routes 1 and 309, in La Croix-Verte. Simenon was careful to show personal interest in the proceedings, visiting the set many times between January and March 1932.[42] Marcel Lucien, the director of photography, submerged the images in a thick fog. The atmosphere was truly sinister, and the overall effect had a rare poetry.

A month before the commercial release, Simenon was invited to a small private screening. When the lights came on, he could not contain his emotion. Eyes wet, he put his arms around Pierre Renoir, not sure whether he was embracing the actor or the inspector.[43] The producers, however, seemed unmoved by the work's poetic qualities and its atmosphere. In fact, they were downright upset, for they found the film incomprehensible. Pierre Braunberger, a colleague of Renoir's who had been invited to the screening to give an expert opinion, expressed stupefaction. He had read and liked the screenplay, but the film seemed incoherent.

"Maybe there was a reel missing," he said to Renoir.

"There was nothing missing, Pierre. That's my film!"

"I don't understand, Jean. Why did you make all those cuts?"

"I swear I made no cuts. The entire script was shot and mounted."

Renoir took out a copy of the screenplay and began to go through it with Braunberger. He was stunned to find that page 73 was followed by page 90. Sixteen pages were missing, and no one had noticed during the shooting. The financial backers took it as confirmation of what they had suspected all along: for Renoir and Simenon, plot was secondary to setting and atmosphere.[44]

The director later advanced a different explanation for the perplexity that inevitably assailed viewers:

"As far as mystery goes, the results exceeded our expectations, especially since the two lost reels made the film more or less incomprehensible even to its author."[45]

Two lost reels? Much later the critic Jean Mitry, who had a supporting role in the film, claimed that he had misplaced them on his way to the lab.[46]

Simenon's version, however, differs from both Renoir's and Mitry's. According to him, the director was in the process of breaking up with his wife, Catherine Hessing. He was depressed during the shooting and drank more than he should have. One day, dead drunk, he forgot to shoot some of the scenes.[47] But this may not be accurate either, since Simenon also said that they had been unable to shoot these scenes because they ran out of money.[48]

The producer was nonetheless determined to salvage the film. He made a proposal to the novelist:

"Look, why don't you introduce the film—for a fee of 50,000 old francs. We'll shoot you close-up, and you say something like, here is the story you are about to see."

"And then what?"

"Then you explain what happens in the missing parts."

"What kind of an asshole do you think I am?"[49]

Despite the hefty fee, Simenon categorically refused. But the episode fueled his resentment of producers, whom he considered ignorant, arrogant fools.

When the film opened on April 21, 1932, at the Pigalle Theater, its poetic dimension eluded the audience. Critics were not pleased either. The future film historian Maurice Bardèche, for instance, wrote that Renoir had "completely failed" to surmount the difficulties associated with the adaptation of such an "atmospheric" novel.[50] But Simenon always believed that Pierre Renoir was the best Maigret ever filmed. As for Jean Renoir, forty years later he admitted:

"*La Nuit du carrefour* remains a completely insane experience that I cannot recall without nostalgia. Nowadays, with everything so well organized, no one could ever work like that."[51]

Le Chien jaune and *La Nuit du carrefour* were commercial failures. For that Simenon blamed the producers, but he was also unhappy with the entire profession, including adapters, screenwriters, and directors (except his friends, of course). He was especially irate about the critics' claim to define the canons of the detective film. He had written his Maigrets by violating imperatives of exactly this kind, and he now railed against the conventions:

"There are rules, it seems, rules of the genre, which some seek to transgress and others obstinately defend. . . . To begin with, there is no such thing as a detective novel, nor a detective film. And there is no rule of the genre, and no formula either. . . . There are good and bad films. . . . The audience . . . doesn't give a f— about rules. And they're right! All the audience wants is a film that holds their interest all the way through, and they don't care how their interest is held. . . . If *Le Chien jaune* and *La Nuit du carrefour* are failures, the fault lies not with the people who made them but with the people who paid for them. Or rather, it lies with the rules and with the idiots who issued them."[52]

But the conflict between Simenon and the film industry went deeper. Individualistic novelist and solitary creator that he was, he was uncomfortable with the collective efforts and industrial procedures inevitably entailed in filmmaking. The ponderous chain of production annoyed him. Too many people had something to say about how the film came out. He was horrified by the sums of money and numbers of people involved and disoriented by a human and economic organization whose functioning eluded him.

When he wrote a book, he was the sole master. When a film was made of one of his books, his role shrank steadily as the date of shooting approached, until finally he was the fifth wheel on the cart, a condition that inevitably seemed aberrant to a man who was used to being the center of his own universe and the heart of his own production system. It was especially unpleasant for him to confront it for the first time just when his recent but promising success had fanned his most sensitive traits: vanity, egocentrism, and boastfulness.

Simenon was a stubborn man resistant to allowing his own personality to be dissolved in a project based on a gathering of talents of diverse origins. It was his book, his story, his script—and therefore his film. Even after collaborating on two screenplays, he did not understand that the director had to present in images what the writer tends merely to suggest in words. To depict without demonstrating, to suggest without describing, to be faithful to the spirit but not the letter—all this seemed inconceivable to him. He refused to admit that adapters might have to take liberties with the novels on which their films were based.

He therefore decided to make his own movies. He believed that if he had learned to write by doing it, there was no reason he could not learn filmmaking the same way. He would flout norms, schools, and rules, trust his own intuition, genius, and whims. Most of all he would get rid of all those irksome intruders who constantly urged him to modify, correct, add, or delete on the basis of criteria he did not share.[53] Some warned him of the difficulty of the enterprise and of the technical expertise required by this craft of which he knew nothing. He refused to listen. He made the proud announcement of his plans in an interview with *Paris-Midi.*

"Only the author can judge how his novel must be reincarnated," he declared,[54] adding that while he would merely oversee the production of *Le Charretier de "La Providence"* (1931), he would be completely in charge of *La Tête d'un homme* (1931).

In April, after writing *Le Fou de Bergerac* (*The Madman of Bergerac,* 1932) at the Hotel de France in La Rochelle, he moved to the nearby La Richardière, a sixteenth-century manor house between Nieul and Marsilly. He fell so in love with the place that he tried to buy it immediately, but the owner rejected his offer, and he had to be content with renting.

It was in these surroundings that "his" film was to be born. *La Tête d'un homme* was atypical in that it pitted Maigret against another major character, the murderer himself, who competes with the inspector in unraveling the threads of the investigation, thereby hoping to demonstrate his Machiavellian intelligence, unfairly overlooked by society.

The murderer in question is a twenty-five-year-old former medical student of Czech origin. The character was inspired by Simenon's friend Ilya Ehrenbourg, a Jew from Kiev who, like the author, was a regular at La Coupole.

Though he fled the Soviet regime, he had earlier participated in the 1905 revolution, and the police therefore considered him a Bolshevik propagandist. Once in Paris, he became a poet, writer, and journalist—the prototype of the exiled foreign intellectual. Simenon's murderer had many points in common with Ehrenbourg,[55] and to top it off he gave him the name Jean Radek. This was a clever touch: Karl Radek was a member of the Central Committee of the Soviet Communist Party and the presidium of the Comintern. Several years later he would be expelled on charges of Trotskyism.

Simenon wanted Pierre Renoir to play Maigret again. He was the right man for the role, and his mere presence in the film would suggest to audiences that the movies, like the books, were part of a series. Radek would be played by Valéry Inkijinoff, a Russian actor with Asiatic features who had recently been featured in *Le Capitaine jaune*.[56]

Simenon thought of everything, including the promotion of the film, which for the moment existed only on paper. When he invited Inkijinoff to his house in Charentes to work on the script, he made sure to alert a photographer from the movie magazine *Pour vous*. The subsequent article struck just the right tone: two pipe smokers walking dogs in the countryside, chopping and sawing wood, and most of all brainstorming—conceiving, writing, and dictating to a secretary what would surely be the film of the year.

In the end, alas, the film industry prevailed over Simenon's desire to go it alone. As he tells it, crooked producers paid him with rubber checks, thus forcing him to abandon the project.[57] Perhaps the results of his cogitations in Charentes struck them as too amateurish and therefore too risky. One way or another, a furious and disgusted Simenon was forced to pull out.

Marcel Vandal and Charles Delac, producers at the Films d'Art company, then assigned the picture to Julien Duvivier, a seasoned director with some thirty films to his credit, including several literary adaptations. With Duvivier there would be no unpleasant surprises. He kept Valéry Inkijinoff on in the role of Radek, but dropped Pierre Renoir in favor of Harry Baur, who would make a sober, taciturn, and physically powerful Maigret. He abandoned the existing script and asked Louis Delaprée and Pierre Caldmann to write another.

Simenon wanted nothing more to do with this picture or with films in general. Two commercial failures and his own aborted project convinced him that he would be boycotted by the industry, a prospect that did not concern him unduly. He expected his work to endure, and he was sure the movie companies would someday rediscover him, if only out of simple common sense: ". . . the cinema, abandoning its routines and repudiating its laws and prophets, will feel the need to assimilate the aesthetics of the novel, to delve into psychology, to come closer to man while stepping back from intrigue and from the theatrical clichés that have already half-mummified it."[58] When that day came, filmmakers who had learned to live with freedom would work unfettered. They would make movies the way he wrote. Until then he would renounce films. If he could not make "his" great picture, he would refuse to allow anyone else to make it in his place. Film rights to his books were no longer for sale, a boycott that would last for seven years.

But the false start had not been a total loss. He had made a fair amount of money, a hint of what he could get from the cinema if ever he decided to bow to its laws. "From the first Maigrets, the movies were a good fairy to me," the memorialist would later acknowledge.[59]

The frivolous image can easily be translated into more mundane terms. The little black notebook[60] in which Tigy recorded the Simenon company's annual "receipts" listed the following totals:

> 1925:   42,671 FRANCS
> 1926:   61,273 FRANCS
> 1927:   111,225 FRANCS
> 1928:   108,964 FRANCS
> 1929:   135,460 FRANCS
> 1930:   103,380 FRANCS
> 1931:   310,561 FRANCS

In 1931, movies were his second biggest source of income (75,000 francs), after the Maigret novels published by Fayard. If we take into account the financial resources the Simenons needed for their extravagant lifestyle, we get an idea of the strength of principle required to keep his inspector off the screen, albeit temporarily.

Shortly before his withdrawal from the cinema, Simenon sent this brief autobiographical notice to a reporter working on an article about him:

> I am twenty-eight years old. Until last year I pursued a funny kind of occupation, turning out novels at an average rate of one every three days. These, of course, were pulp novels: love stories, adventures, tales and short stories of all sorts, published under some fifteen different pseudonyms.
>
> I did not do this entirely by choice, nor entirely out of necessity. I wanted to make enough money to live in comfort before setting out to write somewhat more seriously. I traveled aboard my yacht for three years, and when I returned, I more or less perfected the formula of the police novels that have been issued since then.
>
> As you see, this is not wholly fascinating. I write no more than a novel a month or so. I continue to move around, for I have a horror of cities and am incapable of writing a single line in one. Since I have no imagination at all, I am obliged, moreover, to live for long periods in the surroundings and with the characters of my novels. All these are

real; my fictions are always based on real stories. While the Inspector Maigret novels will continue at the same pace, the same stories will now be appearing on the screen, since I have just sold the film rights to all my work.

Future plans? To continue the effort I have begun, which is someday to write a novel capable of capturing the interest of all audiences. This is not as easy as it sounds: not to repulse the learned while remaining comprehensible to simple folk. The Maigret series is a phase. I find it encouraging that I receive as many letters from workers as from students, snobs, and people of the world.[61]

That is how Georges Simenon saw himself, his life, and his work at the age of twenty-eight.

8

GREAT REPORTER, FAILED DETECTIVE

1932–1935

f you only knew how the provinces cleanse the heart and mind! To turn your back on the snake pit of the capital and put miles between you is the surest way of reexamining your values and regaining your balance."[1]

Simenon unrecognizable. The sailor turned gentleman farmer. It was as though he had been so badly burned by his misadventure in films that he now sought to heal himself by planting both feet firmly in the earth. Country life, close contact with nature and its people, would help him to gather his wits.

He seemed truly in his element at La Richardière. He had his own office and studio, Tigy was with him, and Boule saw to the housekeeping. Animals were everywhere. He claimed to be raising both crops and livestock. But when all was said and done, he was still more gentleman than farmer. Jacqueline, a local peasant whom he hired on his arrival in the region, commented:

"I showed him what to do, but he handled a pen a lot better than a cow's udder . . . and when we needed five kilos of fertilizer, he came back with fifty."[2]

The locals considered him a city slicker, but also an easygoing, regular guy who didn't care much about money. At first he seemed harmless, but there was some unease when he imported two magnificent young wolves from Turkey, procured by the captain of his boat. He had a cage built for them and was careful to sound a loud horn whenever he took them for a walk, prudently using a chain instead of a leash. But these precautions failed to placate his neighbors, especially when Biloko the cat ventured between the bars and was killed and eaten by Ghazi. In the end he had little choice but to consign his wolves to a zoo.

Simenon rode on horseback to the market in La Rochelle, which now became and long remained his favorite town. He found its layout pleasing; he loved its arcades and its port, its light and its people. Soon he was a local celebrity. A "premiere" of *La Tête d'un homme* was held at the Olympia, and he joined the local flying club. He bought an Arabian white stallion named Polo, and a fine mare for visiting friends to ride. The painful memories of his army apprenticeship were now forgotten, and he rode long distances every day. Nothing like it for clearing the head before pounding out *L'Ecluse no. 1* (*The Lock at Charenton*, 1933), *Le Haut Mal* (1933), or *L'Homme de Londres* (*Newhaven-Dieppe*, 1934) on his trusty Remington.

Carlo Rim, his most frequent visitor in the early thirties, often accompanied him on his rides. When the sky was gray, the wind icy, and the marsh deserted, Simenon seemed so proud a horseman that he looked like a figure in a Vlaminck landscape.[3] Except for one slight but significant detail: this character was anything but sinister or pessimistic.

"I observe my companion, erect in his saddle, pink as a baby, tender and serene, happy to be alive and happier still to show his happiness. Georges Simenon has just turned thirty, and already he can look back and measure the road he has traveled, be moved by his past, count his stages, assess his fellow men, forget the humiliations, and enjoy with childish pride but without resentment the small tastes of revenge that life has not been slow to afford him."[4]

When a newspaper asked him to list some of his "likes and dislikes" for a popular column, he ranked his preferences this way: his wife, Dumas père, Inspector Guichard, his farmyard, the Jesuit who had taught him Humanities, flat landscapes, and his new farmhand, who reported: "Sir, a gentleman phoned. He did not leave his name, but I didn't give him mine either." He concluded by announcing that he made more than a million francs a year (a gross exaggeration) and that his most intense memory remained "the time when I was hungry, very hungry."[5]

Rue Saint-Ferréol, Marseille; mid-summer, 1932: trying on a pith helmet in a hatter's shop, Simenon twists and turns in front of the mirror. He thinks it looks grotesque, but just then the shopkeeper says, "A perfect fit! And just what you need for the heart of Africa."

It was only an ordinary hat, but for Simenon it crackled with symbols. To put it on was to shed the illusions of his youth. Having re-created a mysterious and fanciful Africa in his pulp novels, he was now ready to cross the

Désiré and Henriette Simenon . . .

. . . with their sons, Christian (left) and Georges, in Liège, ca. 1908.
(Fonds Simenon)

Georges (right) and his little brother, Christian. (Fonds Simenon)

Portrait of the father in his element.
(Fonds Simenon)

Portrait of the mother in mourning.
(Fonds Simenon)

Joseph Demarteau, director
of the *Gazette de Liège*. (Fonds
Simenon)

As a reporter for the *Gazette de Liège* in the early 1920s, "Young Sim" covered everything from demonstrations by war veterans (at far right in photo to left) to bicycle races like the Tour de Belgique (below, left center, with pipe in mouth). In the picture at right, he is barely eighteen. (Fonds Simenon and Marc Simenon collection)

Behind the American-style bar
in his apartment on the Place
des Vosges. (Fonds Simenon)

Just a few years separate the man who wrote pulp fiction under seventeen pseudonyms (top left) from the well-established writer (bottom right). In the meantime, he wrote screenplays (left, with the actor Inkijinoff), hosted the Anthropometric Ball (above, left), and had an affair with Josephine Baker (above, right). The middle photograph shows Simenon with Josephine on his left and Tigy, his wife, on his right. (Fonds Simenon)

Rivers, streams, the sea: During the 1930s Simenon spent whatever time he could on or near water, whether at Porquerolles (above) or on canals, aboard the *Ostrogoth* (left above and at right). At left, in mate's costume, is Boule. (Fonds Simenon)

Simenou et [?]
moi à
bord d'un
paquebot en
méditéranée
1932

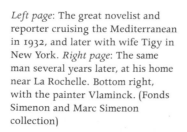

Left page: The great novelist and reporter cruising the Mediterranean in 1932, and later with wife Tigy in New York. *Right page*: The same man several years later, at his home near La Rochelle. Bottom right, with the painter Vlaminck. (Fonds Simenon and Marc Simenon collection)

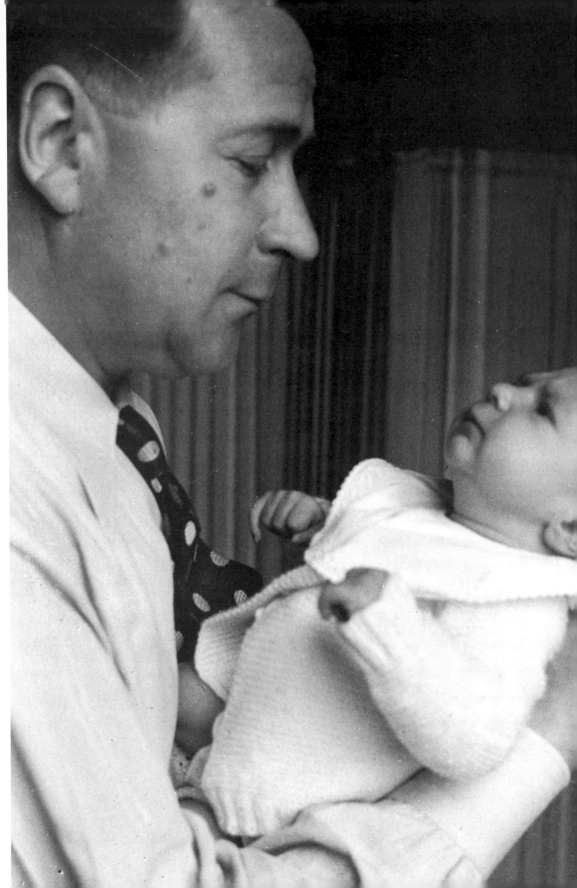

Simenon and his first child, Marc, 1939–1942. (Fonds Simenon and Marc Simenon collection)

At the Terre-Neuve château, at Fontenay-le-Comte in the Vendée, during the first two years of the Occupation. *Bottom left*: Simenon with the actor Jean Tissier. *Bottom right*: The family in town. (Fonds Simenon and Marc Simenon collection)

Christian Simenon, the brother, an absence and a taboo. "What a pity, Georges, it was Christian who died," said their mother. (Marc Simenon collection)

boundary between dream and reality. "That first helmet was my passport, my visa, to real life."[6]

Or so he thought. In fact, the world of adventure lay not ahead of him but behind him, in the atlas and the pink pages of the dictionary. He wanted to see the world, but the price seemed high: "timetables, tariffs, customs regulations, passports, bribes."[7] The magic of adventure was gone out of travel, as he found out when he wasted two days shuttling back and forth between the offices of Air France and the French Line. The world of travel turned out to be one of idlers who read escapist novels even on cruises, of letters of credit exchanged for empty promises in banana republics, of corrupt officials who had nothing but contempt for indigenous peoples, of unforeseen circumstances that ruined all preparations.

But he felt he had to get away no matter what. Boule stayed home to take care of La Richardière, while Simenon, accompanied by Tigy, meant to journey as deep as possible into the Dark Continent. Not as a tourist but as a journalist. Reportage was the best way to finance his curiosity.

As he set out for Africa, Simenon thought of himself as one of a long line of chroniclers like Londres and Helsey, Béraud and Kessel. His mission, like theirs, was to "recount living history."[8] He was a self-appointed member of the "club," the unofficial roster of leading lights of the Paris press.

He approached Africa not by the western maritime route (Antwerp to Matadi), but by the less frequented eastern gateway. His plan was to start in Egypt and go as far as the equator. For the moment, all he knew of Africa was what he had invented in his many pseudonymous novels, which teemed with the racist stereotypes that were part and parcel of the genre in the 1920s. Orientals were treacherous and deceitful, Arabs undistinguished for their cleanliness. Blacks were most often lazy and stupid. More generally, "the superiority of the white race is clearly affirmed, as is the superiority of the French over other whites."[9]

The first leg of Simenon's journey took him from Cairo to the Cataract Hotel in Aswan, on the upper Nile. He trooped through Egypt in summer, as he had through Lapland in winter: "If you want to see a country's real face, you have to visit it in all its intensity," he liked to say.[10]

After Aswan he went on to Khartoum, where he discovered the delights of the shorts, epauletted shirts, and kneesocks worn by members of His Majesty's colonial army. He fell in love with the fashion, ordering similar items from the last London suppliers of the British Empire.[11]

After Khartoum came Juba, the Belgian Congo, and the thousand-mile journey downriver to Kinshasa, then called Léopoldville. He stopped over in the port of Matadi near the mouth of the Congo River, where he spent five days with his brother. Christian Simenon was a representative of the port authorities, overseeing the secretariat of the commerce department and managing cargo-handling.[12] Four years earlier he had married Blanche Binet, and their baby boy was called Georget. Christian mistakenly believed that the honor would please his famous brother, none of whose children was ever called Georges.

The journalist made his African trip at breakneck speed. After stopovers in Port-Gentil, Libreville, and Conakry, he returned by way of Bordeaux. He brought back an object that would grace his office forever after. "Tiki," a totem bought in a village in equatorial Africa, was a statue made for tourists. It had no commercial value. A block of dark ebony weighing about ninety pounds and apparently carved with flint, it depicted the god of elephants (a local divinity half-man, half-ape) feeding the fruit of a breadfruit tree to a baby elephant.[13]

Apart from this formidable fetish, he also returned with impressions, anecdotes, and a series of articles entitled "L'heure du nègre," published in six issues of the illustrated weekly *Voilà* in autumn 1932. Also some 750 photographs, a good number of them depicting prepubescent girls and women wearing little or no clothing.

His trip taught him that the colonial enterprise was an absurdity meriting condemnation, that cannibalism still existed, that champagne was the only local diversion in Matadi, that the whites lived in constant fear, that the general atmosphere warped the moral and material values of the Europeans, and that the blacks were children in the process of growing up.[14] In *Je me souviens* (1945), Simenon offhandedly alludes to "those other children, the Negroes of equatorial Africa." Much later, however, he would recall his trip mainly as the symbol of a colonial epoch he "abhorred."[15]

It is true that one paragraph of his African articles triggered an uproar that Simenon later used to cast himself as a pioneer of anticolonialism, a claim that seems somewhat less justified when examined close up. In the wrap-up of his first article, he says:

"An old colonial official whom I told of my intention to write long reports on black Africa met my enthusiasm with skepticism: 'You think "Africa is speaking to you," that you hear its call, that Negroes and Negresses hold out their hands to you and that nature offers you her fruits? Africa? Believe me, what it says to you is sh..t!' "

He returned to the point in the very last lines of the series:

"My interlocutor, who never could stomach the fact that anemic young men from the prep schools arrive with their books and diplomas to administer this land, would have done better to say: Yes, Africa says sh..t to us, and quite rightly."[16]

It was daring for its time, and the formulation was especially evocative since the walls of Paris happened to be plastered with posters promoting a film of "La croisière noire" (The Black Cruise), an automobile race sponsored by Citroën. The poster proclaimed in gigantic letters: "Africa is speaking to you."

Simenon's crack was therefore emphatic and effective. But did it mean that he was a convinced anticolonialist?

It is true that he had no hesitation in deriding the colonial administration in virtually burlesque terms. He had seen the routinist sloth of petty potentates in remote villages who were incapable of responding to the expectations of the indigenous inhabitants. He knew that colonialism was tottering and that the religion of empire would soon be but a myth. Having searched far and wide for man in his naked state, he had finally found him in the land of nakedness. Yet it seems doubtful that his quest for paradise lost, for a land of innocence and purity (one of the keys to his work), found any fresh perspectives in Africa. The "noble savage," naked though he was, was nonetheless covered with tattoos.

Moreover, some of his criticism had already been made before him. In *Voyage au Congo* (1927) and *Le Retour du Tchad* (1928), André Gide, writing in quite a different tone and spirit, scathingly indicted the methods of exploitation and subjugation of both governments and private enterprise, attacking not the system itself but its perverse effects and abuses, for which he felt guilty.

Simenon went scarcely any further. His denunciation of the Congo-to-the-Atlantic railroad, which "on the average kills one Negro per sleeping car and one white per kilometer,"[17] was also nothing new. Albert Londres had already recounted the whole story in *Terre d'ébène* (1929), a far more powerful series of articles later issued as a book. Neither Londres nor Gide had any intention of undermining the foundations of French society or of challenging the legitimacy of empire. Simenon may have had the intention, but not the means.

His critique, however hasty and superficial, did strike a nerve, for there was still a broad consensus in favor of colonialism at the time. But his return from Africa caused less uproar than Gide's or Londres's. Granted, he lacked their credibility. It was not so easy for the man of the "glass cage" and the Anthropometric Ball to denounce abuses, injustice, and the treatment of blacks.

Simenon seemed truly convincing only when he took up what would now be his standard refrain: that dignity, the only truly universal value, was a necessity for all men, whatever the color of their skin. Anyone whose moral compass had that true north would inevitably see colonized peoples as humiliated. On that ground alone they had to be defended against a system that sought to crush them through scorn or indifference.

Three of Simenon's novels were inspired by his African tour: *Le Coup de lune* (*Tropic Moon*, 1933), *45° à l'ombre* (*Aboard the Aquitaine*, 1936), and *Le Blanc à lunettes* (*Talatala*, 1937). One of these threatened to do him real harm. For the first time in his career, he faced a revolt by one of his characters.

Le Coup de lune takes place in contemporary Libreville. It features a sensual and enterprising hotelkeeper by the name of Adèle Renaud who seduces a younger man, a bachelor drawn to Africa by the colonial mirage. After

Adèle's houseboy is murdered and her husband dies, the Machiavellian widow hatches a plan to escape with her lover. Unfortunately for her, she has reckoned without the famous *coup de lune,* a fit of hallucinatory madness known to local legend.

Simenon often claimed to be devoid of imagination, and sometimes it is a mistake not to take him at his word. During his time in Gabon he had stayed at the Central Hotel, the sole European establishment in Libreville, run by the widow Mercier. The hotel in his book is called the Central, and the local colons are portrayed in an odious light. They had no trouble recognizing themselves, starting with the hotelkeeper herself, whose character, it must be said, was especially well crafted: she is immoral and unscrupulous, shrinking from no crime whatever. When the novel was serialized in *Candide,* the widow Mercier sued for slander, demanding 200,000 francs in compensatory and punitive damages, plus the seizure of the manuscript. The colonial press picked up the story, and polemical communiqués were soon flying back and forth. Various celebrities wrote to Fayard to express support for the persecuted author: "Stand firm! Truth is on your side!"

The newspaper *Les Annales coloniales* fumed with indignation on the day the trial opened in the twelfth chamber of the correctional court of Paris: "He might have at least reserved his calumnies for his own colony."[18] This paper was not alone in noting that since the writer was Belgian, he would have done better to vent his spleen in the Congo. The plaintiff's attorney accused him of having extorted confidential information from his client and of having used it to damage her, under a transparent fictional mask. The lawyer spent considerable time on the atrocious picture of life in Libreville painted in *Le Coup de lune.* In an effort to disarm his adversary's probable resort to character witnesses, he brandished a petition signed by five hundred angry white citizens of Libreville pillorying "this forger's novel."[19]

Maurice Garçon, the talented attorney Simenon hired for his defense, argued that a novelist had every right to draw material from reality. In the end, the plaintiff was nonsuited: since her name had not appeared in the book, she had not been defamed.

Simenon was victorious, and the widow Mercier was ordered to pay costs. But he learned his lesson. He would be more careful next time. Two years later, a dumbfounded Simenon was to witness the same phenomenon in reverse: the owner of the hotel in Concarneau that had served as his model in *Le Chien jaune* (1931) renamed his establishment the "Hotel de l'Amiral," the better to capitalize on the tie-in with the novel and the film it had inspired.[20]

So much for Africa. Europe was next. The year: 1933.

Voilà, the "weekly newsmagazine" launched two years earlier by Gaston

Gallimard, was about to get a new editor in chief, Georges Kessel being succeeded by Florent Fels, one of Simenon's close friends. This journal, printed in gravure and tinted in sepia, had broadened its coverage from crime news to the national and international scene, though its photographs remained its greatest selling point, along with memoirs of femmes fatales ghostwritten by authors whose real identities were closely guarded secrets.

Voilà had financed Simenon's curiosity for Africa, and it now agreed to do the same for Europe. He roamed everywhere, from Belgium to Poland, Romania to Czechoslovakia and Hungary.

Germany was a particularly choice morsel. Simenon arrived in the midst of the collapse of the mark, and he visited Düsseldorf, Cologne, Frankfurt, and Berlin, where in January and February he witnessed the burial of the Weimar Republic. The National Socialist Party, big winner in the elections of July 1932, was the country's most powerful political organization.

Adolf Hitler, whom Reichspresident Hindenburg had not wanted in the post a short time before, was sworn in as chancellor on January 30, 1933. Three weeks later, the Reichstag fire set by Van der Lubbe enabled Germany's new master to decree a state of emergency and order thousands of arrests. World public opinion wondered about the nature of the terrorist: Was he a zealot, a mental case, a communist, an outcast manipulated by the Nazis, or all of the above?

Simenon claimed to have heard the answer from the best possible source: Hitler himself. The two men had indeed "met"—or at least their paths had crossed, which enabled Simenon to assert disingenuously, "I met Hitler ten times in the Kaiserhof."[21] In fact, he had had the good sense to check into the Berlin hotel where Hitler and his general staff had their apartments, so it would have been hard to miss the man Simenon derisively referred to as "the Messiah." Four days before the Reichstag fire, Simenon reported, he learned from an unnamed "very reliable friend" that Hitler and Göring had planned the whole thing in order to give themselves an official excuse to launch the repression against the communists. He immediately cabled the news to *Paris-Soir,* which according to Simenon preferred not to print it.[22]

More interesting is the tone of his reports on the new Germany, for it reveals his state of mind at the time. On the whole, Simenon sought to play down the horror of the situation, sometimes through irony. The more alarmist the news published by the Paris press became about the violence across the Rhine, the more Simenon wrote about Germans bored with bloody exactions and lethal clashes between rival extremists. Was he aware of the looming danger so clearly inscribed in the past, the program, and the speeches of the new Führer? Since people far more "political" than he failed to see it at the time, it would be unseemly to rebuke him for missing it. But the wrap-up of the sixth of his "Europe '33" articles is nonetheless edifying:

And there you are. A few dozen million Germans now feel that it's all over, that they have recovered their equilibrium and have finally been given a goal in life. The man who has done it? Hitler! The people were swarming in disorder, seeking amusement where they could, without conviction, each pursuing his own idea, which wound up creating general grief. Now Hitler has called them to order. He will polish them, straighten them out, make them over from top to bottom, just as I saw them parading through the streets in 1914, sure of themselves, confident in their destiny and in their corporals.

No further need of individual unease, of books of theosophy, esotericism, or eroticism. To feel the great shiver, to rediscover the pride and joy of being born a citizen of Great Germany, all you have to do is march to the music and holler "Hoch! Hoch! Hoch!"

Now, if you speak to me of Jews, communists, outrages, atrocities, and all the rest, I will remind you of what I talked about at the beginning: the gunshots on the tramways, the butchery of little boys, the mom with the chocolate bar, the suitcases full of millions of marks and the bare cupboards, Schopenhauer, Wagner, and the vampire of Düsseldorf.[23]

The formulation is so ambiguous that it is difficult to discern its intent. As usual, the memorialist would later cast himself in the best possible light, calling Germany a country "in which I no longer agreed to be published after the advent of Hitler."[24] A claim, however, that does not withstand scrutiny. As we shall see.

After Hitler, Trotsky—but this time it was more than an exchange of glances in a hotel elevator. *Paris-Soir,* no longer the property of Eugène Merle but the mass-circulation daily of Jean Prouvost, asked Simenon to try to interview the former organizer of the Red Army.

Legions of reporters pursued Trotsky, but few managed to make contact. Expelled from the Soviet Union in 1928, he was now in Prinkipo, the Princes' Isle, in the Sea of Marmara in Turkey, where he wrote, worked, and received literary and political personalities.[25]

After repeated approaches to Trotsky's Dutch secretary, Simenon was finally granted an appointment with the revolutionary leader, a favor and privilege for which he sought no explanation. But Trotsky insisted that he would supply written answers to written questions. Take it or leave it. The journalist decided to take it. He then received a letter from the secretariat: "In order to have the time to draft his answers and have them translated, Mr. Trotsky requests that you come to see him only the day after tomorrow, Tuesday, at around four-thirty." Simenon arrived, on time and impatient. A quick inspection of Trotsky's library showed that he had just read, among other things, Céline's *Journey to the End of the Night:* "He found it deeply disturbing," his secretary explained. "As far as literature is concerned, by the way, it is French that he knows best." At last Trotsky appeared, typed pages in hand. Simenon flipped through them: ". . . I am far from believing that race will be a decisive factor in the evolution of the coming epoch . . . democracy may be defined as a system of switches and insulation designed to control the powerful currents of national and social struggle . . . I consider an explosion of war from fascist Germany absolutely inevitable . . ." Simenon had his scoop. But Trotsky suddenly took back his text and appended a handwritten postscript: his answers had to be published "word for word and *in extenso*" or not at all.[26]

The journalist promised, and he kept his word. In his article introducing the interview, he reported one harmless human detail: the exile's passion for fishing, a ritual to which he devoted himself daily, preferably at dawn.[27] When alluding to the encounter long afterward, however, the memorialist claimed that Trotsky had taken him fishing, even adding that a bodyguard went to sea with them.[28] What can you do?

A few months passed, and one morning Simenon received an overseas call in Paris. Trotsky. He had an important declaration to make, and he asked Simenon to join him forthwith. Simenon refused, with genuine regret.[29] Not even a promise of exclusivity could lure him. He could not leave France, for he was completely caught up in something new: the Stavisky scandal and its sequels. Nothing else mattered, for this time his reputation as a journalist, novelist, and public figure was truly at stake. He had committed a sin of pride, confusing himself with his own creation, Inspector Maigret.

The "Stavisky affair" erupted on December 29, 1933, with the exposure of a swindle that ruined many small investors: Crédit Municipal of Bayonne had issued 200 million francs' worth of counterfeit cash vouchers. The instigator and major beneficiary of the scam was not at all unknown to the police, but because of his intimate connections with political, financial, and business leaders, he had been able to exchange the notorious vouchers for fake or stolen jewelry.

Alexandre Stavisky, known as Monsieur Serge, was a Jew of Russian origin, born in Kiev in 1886. His father moved the family to Paris when Alexandre was twelve, and father and son became French citizens two years later, in 1900. The young man had a knack for all sorts of operations—diversion of funds, con games, rubber checks—and this particular hustle was in full swing when the scandal broke. Stavisky was confident he had everything under control, but he overestimated the power of his connections and failed to foresee the consequences of an audit by the Ministry of Finance.

On January 3, 1934, the press unleashed a broadside against this upscale crook, who managed to elude the police and make good his escape. Public opinion demanded that the guilty parties be named, along with all their accomplices, for there was little doubt that Stavisky would never have been able to operate on such a grand scale without powerful allies. Several days later, the police picked up his trail in Chamonix. They surrounded his villa, but when they went inside, they found him dying. Stavisky had committed suicide. Or so the official story went.

Few believed it, for it seemed far too convenient to the Palais-Bourbon and the highest levels of government. The opposition parties, left and right alike, were convinced that Stavisky had been murdered to shut him up.

One minister resigned, and soon the entire Camille Chautemps government quit. The far-right press began a campaign of rare violence, employing its usual tactics. Peddling a mixture of half-truths and outright lies, unsubstantiated rumors and proven facts, it denounced the usual enemies: the Jews, the wogs, rich financiers, Freemasons, and corrupt parliamentary deputies. But the right-wing press was not alone in reviling the regime. Just about everyone joined in, for such was the mood of that eloquent yet unidentifiable beast known as "public opinion."

On February 6 there was a riot at the Place de la Concorde. The Republic tottered. The veterans' leagues clashed with mobile guards protecting the Palais-Bourbon. Damage reports next morning listed some fifteen dead and more than two thousand injured. The new Daladier cabinet was forced to resign. "It was the first time in the history of the Third Republic that a government was driven from office by rioting in the streets," one historian wrote.[30]

On February 12 the country was paralyzed by a general strike, but popular agitation subsided rapidly when Gaston Doumergue, the new president of the council, was granted the right to rule by decree. Pacification, however, proved temporary. On February 20 the mangled body of Albert Prince was discovered on the railroad tracks in La Combe-aux-Fées, near Dijon. Prince, a court of appeals magistrate and chief of the financial division of the Seine prosecutor's office, had recently been assigned to draft a report on a man whose activities he had been following for several years: Alexandre Stavisky. Another alleged suicide, another scandal. A confidential police report gives a sense of the atmosphere: "One cannot help noting that some degree of excitability is now sweeping through normally peaceful circles who do not ordinarily react to political events."[31]

At this point Jean Prouvost, owner of *Paris-Soir*, decided the time was ripe for something flashy: he summoned Inspector Maigret to entrust him with the investigation of his career.

Georges Simenon was in Porquerolles when he got word to return to Paris as soon as possible. He found Prouvost waiting for him in the *Paris-Soir* office, along with Pierre Lazareff, his chief collaborator on the editorial board.

The Paris press was convinced that public opinion was as excited about the Stavisky-Prince affair as it had been by the cases of Landru and Violette No-zières. *Paris-Soir* was not about to let such an opportunity slip by. Prouvost had bought the paper from Eugène Merle four years earlier for three or four million francs, and daily circulation had since risen from about sixty thousand to nearly a million. The expansion had been built on sensationalism: garish layout, blaring headlines, a magazine style, ample use of photographs, frequent resort to prestigious bylines, and a policy of supplements, scoops, and contests.[32] Hallmarks of Prouvost and Lazareff.

Simenon made no secret of his admiration for the former, whose success, power, and personality impressed him. His relations with Lazareff were quite different. Already colleagues, drinking buddies, and nightclub companions, they were soon to become close friends. They were of the same generation and shared similar temperaments. Both were self-educated and equally adept at getting things done.

Prouvost and Lazareff generally saw eye to eye, but when they did not, the journalist had to defer to the industrialist. That had been the case since the February 6 riots. "If we want to keep its trust, we have to go with the crowd," Prouvost said. Follow, don't lead. Lazareff was disappointed, but did as he was told.[33] "A suicide will cost me two hundred thousand readers; what I need is a murder," Prouvost is reported to have said at the height of the Stavisky affair.[34]

At the time, even newspapers with the greatest reputation for honesty were reluctant not to fall into line behind the predominant hypothesis: murder rather than suicide. The crowds in the street not only brought down the government but also inspired the management of the mass-circulation dailies, determining their headlines.

Prouvost wanted Maigret, and he offered Simenon alluring terms: complete control of the investigation, all the necessary resources, and freedom to say whatever he wanted.[35] The mission was to investigate the death of Albert Prince, in direct competition with the French police. It was hardly necessary for Mr. Prouvost to add that he would be disappointed should his esteemed inspector conclude that Prince had killed himself, or should he fail to uncover the obvious political connections between the deaths of Stavisky and Prince.

Simenon accepted the challenge—for the glory, the publicity, and the money. It was right up his alley. After all, he was the man who had said in his youth that a journalist was first of all a man who writes a column or two on a subject about which he knows nothing.[36]

Which was exactly the case here. There was, on the other hand, a famous precedent: the murder of Mary Cecilia Rogers near New York around 1840. Two years after the killing, Edgar Allan Poe studied the press coverage of the event and resolved the enigma "by the force of logic and reasoning alone," without even visiting the scene of the crime. The result was "The Mystery of

Mary Rogers," and Poe's hypothetical solution was confirmed when the guilty party confessed.[37] Could intuition be as effective as deduction? Simenon was determined to prove that it was.

The editorial offices of *Paris-Soir* were turned into a crisis-management center. A special desk was set up for the case. Two agents of the Sûreté, rather less inconspicuous than they believed, staked out the door in shifts. About fifteen reporters were assigned to the task full time, and a few heavyweights of the editorial staff were called upon to pitch in. Readers were also invited to help out, and thousands of letters poured in, offering testimony, hypotheses, clues. But even that was not enough. Jean Prouvost was worried about competition, and he decided that "Georges Maigret" could use some help.

"Inasmuch as the French police have gotten nowhere and your collaborators seem to be no more clever, we shall call upon the world's most renowned police to aid us in our inquiries," he told Pierre Lazareff.[38]

The Quai des Orfèvres was not amused, but Prouvost didn't care. On behalf of *Paris-Soir* he summoned three retired "aces" of Scotland Yard: Sir Basil Thomson, one of the directors of the intelligence service during the war; former Inspector Collins, and former Superintendent Wensley. The British press now had a local angle, and they began calling Simenon "the French Conan Doyle," a title that did no harm at all to his image.[39]

Armed with his pipe, fedora, and notebook, Simenon set to work. His first stop was Chez Fernand, on the Rue Bergère, where he shared his initial idea with colleagues gathered on the imitation leather benches: he would look for men likely to have bumped off an officer of the court in return for a hefty payment from the mafia.[40]

Next he made the rounds of the capital's worst dives. "You see," he told his friend Carlo Rim, "this is just like a novel, so it makes sense to ask a character from a novel to run the investigation. It's only natural. Thirty years ago they would have called in Sherlock Holmes. Today it's Maigret."[41] Rim understood perfectly. But when he wondered aloud whether Prince might not have killed himself after all, Simenon merely shrugged.

The two men wound up at Chez Nine on the Rue Victor Massé, a fashionable Montmartre watering hole where the underworld could meet the elite, where high-priced lawyers and their clients, politicians and bordello owners, enjoyed the southern cuisine of Nine, the owner, a colorful woman on first-name terms with everyone and anyone. She had just ejected the retired Scotland Yard sleuths, and when Simenon went to say hello to her in the kitchen, he got an earful:

"Son of a bitch, Sim, what are you doing mixed up in this mess? Don't dirty your spats with this crap! Believe me, you're in way over your head. You're a writer, a poet, not a damn cop! Leave your Maigret to his murderers, head-breakers, and whores! A fish out of water croaks, you know what I mean?"[42]

The warning was clear, but Simenon was undeterred. He continued his inquiry by patrolling the Bermuda Triangle of the Paris underworld, eventually winding up at Cotti's, a favorite restaurant of gangsters and celebrities owned by Mssrs. Cotti and Borelli. Tirelessly haunting such places, in the heady illusion that he was "behind the scenes with mobsters, secret policemen, senators, and compromised ministers,"[43] he finally found the man he was looking for, someone who really knew what had happened and was ready to unburden himself to the famous Georges Simenon.

Maigret's creator was a good deal more credulous than his hero. He listened carefully to his informant, who told him that the Prince case was "an organized hit." The man gave only his street name: the Baron. He wouldn't say too much, lest he compromise the influential personalities with whom he often dealt, though it wasn't clear exactly what he did. When pressed, he claimed he made his living as a freelance publicity agent, but he had various sidelines as well, such as buying and selling shares. He could be reached at the Hotel Carlton, and he urged the investigator to rent a room in that same establishment, since the mafia held meetings on the floor below. Names? Okay, but it would cost. No problem. *Paris-Soir* would pay.

Simenon swallowed the story whole. The Baron in question was in fact one Gaetan L'Herbon de Lussats, a bachelor born in Monaco in 1888. He had no office, no employees, no bank account. And for good reason. Gaetan was a familiar fixture in dives and racetracks, a bookmaker and part-time snitch who had done time more than once.[44]

Georges Maigret made little effort to assess the reliability of his source, especially since the Baron's "revelations" supported his initial assumption: that Stavisky was not simply a crook but a gangster. The trail therefore led to organized crime. His informer dropped various names but kept coming back to one in particular as the "brains" behind the Prince killing. He neglected to mention that he had an old score to settle with this man, but Simenon was delighted to have a real suspect at last.

Georges Hainnaux, a thirty-nine-year-old ex-boxer from Boulogne known as White-Haired Joe, lived in room 53 in the Hotel Chartres, a small building at the corner of a little alleyway and Avenue Victor-Hugo. After trying unsuccessfully to get in touch with him, Simenon asked a colleague with underworld connections to help. While the colleague conducted an "interview" on his behalf, Simenon paced up and down the avenue with a conspiratorial air. A deal was made: Jean Prouvost would supply 800,000 francs in small bills plus a quick plane out of Paris in exchange for a confession, check stubs from Stavisky, the address where the jewels were hidden, and the names of the killers.[45]

During the first two weeks of March 1934 the daily *Excelsior* published three articles on the case by Simenon. On March 20, *Paris-Soir* began an eleven-part series announced with great fanfare several days before. The articles were a hodgepodge of innuendo and hasty conclusions unredeemed by any sign of talent. There is no trace of the novelist in them.

But worse was yet to come. In an effort to give his inquiry more substance, Simenon published dozens of names normally mentioned only in whispers in the back rooms of "mafia" restaurants. What had been mere rumor now took definite shape under Simenon's pen. People were publicly identified as involved in the murder of Prince. Apart from Georges Hainnaux (renamed Joe Terror for the occasion), there was also mention of Paul Bonaventure Carbone, "a sports promoter in Marseille," and a man called Spirito, another habitué of circles less than literary.

Maigret's "intuition" soon bore fruit. Summonses were issued. People were searched, taken downtown, booked, locked up. The Baron, who was among those brought in, told the examining magistrate, "I don't know any Georges Simenon. I never talked to him. He never came to see me."[46]

In the meantime, Chief Inspector Bonny, "the number one police officer in France," was assigned to draft a report on the case. The minister of justice wanted arrests, even if he had to release the suspects later. Simenon's "mafia" theory was tailor-made for this charade, aimed exclusively at public opinion.

The inspector's report was submitted on March 27, the day the seventh of the novelist's articles appeared. The report concluded that the killing was not an ordinary murder, but a political assassination. According to Bonny, the Baron was the real instigator. He referred to Joe Terror as "one of my informants." The police would have solved the case earlier were it not for "the meddling of *Paris-Soir*," whose "tendentious campaign" was certainly "suspicious." The inspector was convinced that the Baron had tricked Maigret "for the sole purpose of obfuscating his own role and guilt in the assassination." He described Simenon as "one of those journalists who engage in these kinds of maneuvers for the sole purpose of thwarting the course of justice and preventing the police from concluding their investigations." He demanded that the novelist be brought in to make him reveal his sources.[47]

Simenon was now way out on a limb. He decided to meet with a lawyer, Philippe Lamour. After reviewing the entire case, examining all the hypotheses one by one, the attorney looked Simenon in the eye and asked: "Suppose there was no murder?" A surprised Simenon took his pipe out of his mouth and shook his head. "For the moment, that's not what the public expects," he said.[48] He refused to entertain a possibility that now looked increasingly likely: they had found nothing because there was nothing to find.

He was now becoming a target of ridicule. When Carbone and Spirito were released for lack of evidence, he acquired a new nickname: Sime-non-lieu. In the bistros of the Rue du Louvre, people were calling Jean Prouvost "the editor of Simenon's famous detective novel *Paris-Soir*."[49] In the publishing industry there was speculation that the entire Prince investigation was nothing but a publicity stunt to promote Simenon's next book. Cartoonists had a field day. Even the Union of Wine Merchants and Restaurateurs of Paris chimed in, complaining that Simenon had depicted bistro owners as "individuals of dubious morals."[50]

Meanwhile, Georges Hainnaux, who thanks to Maigret was now known as Joe Terror, apparently decided to live up to his new name. From his cell in the Santé prison, where he was serving a one-month term for his trouble, he let it be known that upon his release he would consider it his duty to knock out a few of Simenon's teeth. Gossip columnists warned the novelist to be careful, reminding him that suicide was all the rage these days. Hainnaux seemed really annoyed. Granted, this was not exactly his first brush with the law, but this time he hadn't done the crime. On the other hand, his newfound notoriety was not a total loss. His *Memoirs of Georges Hainnaux, a.k.a. Joe Terror* would appear before the year was out.

"Police novels are one thing," Joe commented in his book, "but journalism is another."[51] Even Hainnaux saw fit to lecture Simenon.

His position became all the more precarious when the Scotland Yard detectives concluded that Prince had killed himself after all. In fact, they found the suicide so obvious that they were almost embarrassed to be associated with the case. When Pierre Lazareff informed Prouvost, the boss flew off the handle:

"It is absolutely out of the question to publish their report! We cannot run counter to the view of the people, who believe a crime has been committed, who want there to be a crime. If we say it's suicide, it'll look as if we're taking sides politically, which would do terrible damage to our sales."

The owner of *Paris-Soir* undertook to convince "the English" that they had made a mistake. He asked them to start from scratch, offering them more money. The detectives bluntly refused. Prouvost then upped the ante, arguing that the political background of the Prince case made it far more sensitive than some Sherlock Holmes story. He brandished the specter of civil war.

Lazareff was called in to mediate, and a compromise was reached. The report of the Scotland Yard detectives was published, but the conclusions were edited out.[52] *Paris-Soir*'s competitors jeered. "What they really proved was Simenon's guilt," noted *Le Canard enchaîné.*[53] The satirical press was now writing more articles about the novelist-journalist than about Stavisky and Prince. *Paris-Soir* was losing heart, and readers began to abandon ship.

Finally Simenon backed off. The memorialist would later claim that he was informed by "well-placed sources" that since he was not a French citizen, he could be deported at any moment. The minister of the interior reportedly threatened to withdraw his residency permit, and Jean Prouvost strongly suggested that he take a world tour as soon as possible.[54]

Threats seem to have come in from unofficial quarters as well. One evening the Simenons went to Carlo Rim's for dinner. Pierre Lazareff was also there.

Rim's wife made every effort to make her guests feel at home, but there was tension in the air. Suddenly the telephone rang. It was Paul Bonaventure Carbone, who had just been released.

"I know Simenon is a friend of yours," he told Rim, "and I'm a friend of yours, too. So when you see him, tell your friend Simenon that he has nothing to fear from your friend Venture. Friendship is sacred to Corsicans. But from now on let him stick to writing novels, which he's very good at. His latest was excellent. Please give him my congratulations. I just read it in the Santé [prison], where it helped pass the time."[55]

"That was Venture," Rim said when he went back to the table, hoping to lighten the atmosphere. "He says hello."

"I'm glad to hear that," Simenon replied, looking relieved. Everyone laughed, but the laughter was hollow.

In April, Simenon retreated to Porquerolles to write a new novel, but late that month he was interrupted by a disturbing long-distance phone call from Paris. One of the editors of *Paris-Soir* wanted him to write a few more articles on the Prince case. He felt it was out of the question to deal with this issue again. There was money to be made—45,000 francs was on offer—but the losses in image and prestige would be enormous. He no longer wanted to be distracted by the bait of improbable glory, and he was completely absorbed in working on his next book. But he decided to take the opportunity to clear up any misunderstandings with the great daily. He therefore wrote to Jean Prouvost.[56]

He began with a list of complaints: the first *Paris-Soir* headlines featured only the English from Scotland Yard; he had been given office space but no staff; the reporters later assigned to help him acted as freelancers; there had been no coordination of the work team; he had been forced to endure the unpleasant impression of never being supported as he would have wished; his articles had been implicitly censored whenever he tried to challenge the Sûreté in general or Inspector Bonny in particular; he had been obliged to tiptoe as though he were a politician.

"I am convinced that I got as close to the truth as possible, and that no trails other than the ones I reported will ever lead to anything," Simenon wrote, apparently still convinced that the official investigation would eventually confirm his theory that Stavisky and Prince were murdered.

But the scandal itself was now fading. The news would soon be dominated by the "night of the long knives" in Germany and the assassination of Chancellor Dollfuss in Austria. Simenon rented the *Araldo,* a two-masted schooner with a crew of six, and set off on a six-month Mediterranean cruise, writing a series of nine articles dedicated to the glory of Mare Nostrum. In August, Inspector Guillaume, assigned by the government to conduct an investigation of the investigation, submitted his report. For Simenon it was a heavy blow, particularly since Guillaume was one of the "top cops" after whom Maigret was patterned. The report stated that Inspector Bonny ultimately decided that the original "mafia" suspects were not the perpetrators of the alleged crimes. The case within the case, created by Maigret in *Paris-Soir* and caught on the fly by Bonny, was a waste of the investigators' time. It muddied the trails, and "weighed negatively on the progress of the investigation." Indeed, that may have been the aim of some of the protagonists.[57]

Inspector Guillaume came to the same conclusions as his ex-colleagues from Scotland Yard: Albert Prince, driven to depression by the scandal, probably killed himself. *Paris-Soir* procured a copy of Guillaume's report and published it in its entirety, the most honorable way of finally burying an increasingly dishonorable story. Philippe Lamour, a well-known attorney and an advocate of the suicide hypothesis, presented his case in a two-page spread in *L'Œuvre*. Simenon wrote Lamour a letter stating that he now agreed completely with him, but refrained from admitting it publicly.[58] The "truth" about the death of Alexandre Stavisky and Albert Prince would never be known.

The case had an epilogue. A meeting of the Union of Journalists held on the morning of November 17, 1934, placed an explosive item on the agenda: an examination of charges that officials of the Judiciary Police and the Sûreté had personally participated in the *Paris-Soir* investigation. The management of the newspaper strenuously denied the allegation, while admitting that its daily headlines on the case were communicated in advance to Mr. Mondanel, director of the Sûreté's research center, and to his deputy, Commissioner Yves Le Gall.[59]

News of the polemic reached Simenon, now temporarily living in the Château de la Cour-Dieu, near Ingrammes in the Orleans forest, the lease on La Richardière having expired. Appalled, he broke off the chapter he was writing and sent a telegram to Jean Prouvost:

"Am stunned and outraged to learn from press in course of trip that you had me work unwittingly in Prince investigation with Sûreté Générale inspector to whom I was never introduced and whose name and face I do not even know."[60]

Some years later, Pierre Lazareff devoted an entire chapter of his midlife memoirs[61] to the Prince affair as seen from the *Paris-Soir* city room. All the protagonists are in it: journalists and gangsters, policemen and politicians. The only missing character is Georges Simenon. His name is not even mentioned.

Nineteen thirty-four was not a good year for Simenon the journalist. As it drew to a close, his one and only wish was to get away and to forget. A five-month world cruise would be just the thing. His itinerary was typical for great travelers of the pretourist age: from The Hague to New York by steamer, then Panama, Colombia, Ecuador, Galápagos, Venezuela, Costa Rica, Peru, Tahiti,

New Zealand, Australia, India, the Red Sea. Departure on December 12, estimated arrival back in Marseille on May 15.

Jean Prouvost encouraged him. *Paris-Soir* would publish his articles, as would *Marianne* and *Le Jour*.[62] The voyage would also inspire several short stories and six novels: *Ceux de la soif* (They of Thirst, 1938), written in Tahiti; *Quartier nègre* (Negro Quarter, 1935); *Long Cours* (*The Long Exile*, 1936); *Touriste de bananes* (*Banana Tourist*, 1938); *L'Aîné des Ferchaux* (1945); and *Le Passager clandestin* (*The Stowaway*, 1947).

Each stopover left its mark on Simenon, but two were of special importance. Ever since leaving France, Simenon had been planning to look into a "case" that had made news back in Europe: the adventures of the baroness of Wagner and her companions, a handful of Europeans who renounced civilization for the Galápagos Islands, an archipelago some six hundred miles off the coast of Ecuador. Two of the group died under mysterious circumstances, while their ringleader disappeared. Simenon reveled in the thought of telling *Paris-Soir* readers of this tale that "neither Conrad nor Stevenson" would have dared imagine. In some respects the story was a throwback to the late Georges Sim's tropical adventures, but with two big differences: the turn of phrase was vastly improved, and the author was dealing with a subject he knew something about. Unlike Sim, Simenon was careful to avoid the excesses of exoticism. In setting *Touriste de bananes* (1938) in the backwaters of Papeete, he took his readers behind the scenes, revealing the island's less paradisiacal aspects.[63]

His long stay in Tahiti was as important as the stopover in the Galápagos. It was first of all the occasion of a moving pilgrimage retracing the path of a writer he admired as few others: Robert Louis Stevenson, who had lived in Tahiti. The author of *Treasure Island* died in 1894 in his beloved Samoan Islands, where he had spent the last years of his life. He was buried by natives at the peak of a mountain overlooking the Pacific. Simenon extolled Stevenson for having managed to combine the best of Poe and Verne and paid frequent homage to "his manner of writing for a very broad public without making concessions."[64]

Simenon returned from his grand tour a new man. He had matured. He seemed seasoned, wiser, at peace. For some eighteen months his literary output reflected this evolution, and at around the same time he left Fayard, as though the man had to change his livery when his books changed their covers. As always, the break was not a whim but a carefully premeditated move. First he drew up his accounts.

In 1932, Arthème Fayard had paid him advances ranging from 6,000 to 10,000 francs on graduated royalty rates of 10 percent up to 10,000 copies, 12 percent on all copies from 10,000 to 25,000, and 15 percent on all copies beyond that.[65] His royalty statement from Fayard for that year showed a total income of 237,821 francs, while his moviemaking brought in 79,000 francs, his essays 4,200, and his articles 51,900.[66] But it wasn't just a question of money.

An article by Daniel Rops entitled "The Detective Novels of Georges Simenon" began with what sounded like an apology: "I fear that my readers may not take me very seriously when they see the subject announced in today's heading."[67] Small points like this were not a matter of indifference to an author as attached to his press notices as Simenon was.

At the beginning of the summer of 1933, in Porquerolles, he had finished his nineteenth Maigret novel, entitled simply *Maigret* (*Maigret Returns*, 1934). A young police officer working on a murder case asks for help from his uncle, former inspector Maigret, now in retirement in his country house on the banks of the Loire. The circumstances were quite deliberate. Simenon wanted to go beyond his hero, free himself from his soothing notoriety, carve himself a new niche in the hierarchy of literary recognition, and strike out once and for all in search of something new.

The meeting with Arthème Fayard was stormy. Having proudly informed everyone that he had launched Maigret like a brand of soap, the publisher was astonished to find him slipping through his fingers. But Simenon seemed determined:

"It's over, I'm quitting."

"You're insane! You'll never make it trying to write anything else but detective novels!"

"Let's put Maigret on the shelf. I don't need handrails anymore. I think I can write a real novel now."

"Just like Conan Doyle. He always wanted to kill off Holmes and write a real novel. You'll regret it for the rest of your life. No author of detective novels has ever succeeded in other domains. Believe me, it's an illusion. You'll be back."

But Simenon wasn't listening. His mind was already elsewhere—in his next book, with his next publisher.

9

A NOVELIST AMONG
THE LITERATI

1935-1939

eaving Fayard for Gallimard was part of Simenon's plan and involved no change in his style. Indeed, no publisher, however influential, could have had any serious effect on the creative process of an author with Simenon's strength of character. Contrary to the claims of certain critics who evince a very French penchant for classification, there are no grounds for dividing Simenon's career into "Fayard" and "Gallimard" periods somehow akin to Picasso's blue or red periods. Granted, his work has its fissures, but it cannot be defined by the financial or administrative terms of his contracts. Simenon crossed the threshold of Gaston Gallimard's illustrious house as his own man, and he had no intention of trimming himself to anyone else's measure.

On the other hand, his move did coincide with a new stage of his literary maturity. It was not simply the author who had evolved but the man as well. He was becoming bourgeois, in every sense: plump cheeks, early signs of stoutness, hints of a double chin; Savile Row suits, custom-made silk shirts, designer ties and fedoras; a large green Delage sports car; a fat line of credit from the Banque Worms on Boulevard Haussmann; fine wines ordered directly from the great châteaux of Médoc; gourmet meals at the best restaurants in town; a regular afternoon table at Fouquet's café; personalized invitations to dress rehearsals and premieres of shows; supper at Maxim's; a bottle reserved in his name at Chez Florence.

If Simenon had ever been a sailor or a gentleman farmer, it must have been in another life. Far from making any attempt to disguise his thirst for luxury and creature comforts, he now cultivated it ostentatiously, as though it were incontrovertible proof of his success. When his friend Vlaminck visited him at one of the châteaux he had rented, the painter was struck by the contrast between his host's obvious pride in his recent fortune and his claim to be close to the salt of the earth: "He has a marked taste for the social distinctions of the rich."[1]

These were the days of the Popular Front. The fight for collective bargaining, paid vacations, and the forty-hour week was at its height, but Simenon played the great bourgeois as never before. He had two official domiciles for tax purposes, in Neuilly and Porquerolles.[2]

The first was his primary residence: 7 Boulevard Richard Wallace, on the edge of the Bois de Boulogne, a high-toned address with a phone number to match: Maillot 28-25. Parisian society measured prestige by the quality of one's letterhead, and Simenon was quite alert to such considerations, protestations to the contrary notwithstanding. He would later claim that he had chosen Neuilly only to make Tigy happy, decorating the handsome apartment as a gift for her: "Just to have a bit of peace. The life I led there was as far as could be from what I wanted. I felt like a hair in the soup and dreamed only of escape."[3] The truth is that he was leading exactly the kind of life he wanted. His choice of apartment, far from an isolated act, was perfectly tuned to the image he was cultivating, albeit temporarily. His wife may have appreciated this lifestyle, but she was certainly not responsible for it.

When not in Neuilly, he spent most of his time in Porquerolles, the only place where he could truly relax. The island had not yet become a fashionable resort, and there were no casinos or tennis courts. But it would not remain unspoiled for long. Louis Renault's yacht was already moored in the port.

After trying several houses, the Simenons finally settled on Les Tamaris, a little walled villa named for the tamarisk shrubs that grew in the garden. Nestled in the port, it had a view of the sea and of the Maures mountains on the mainland. The ground floor had half a dozen rooms, but it was the ochre and white square tower that made the house special. A sort of minaret with one room downstairs and one upstairs, it had a railed terrace on top, accessible by a steep staircase. It was here that Simenon wrote *Le Blanc à lunettes* (1937), *Le Testament Donadieu* (*The Shadow Falls*, 1937), *Touriste de bananes* (1938), and *Monsieur la Souris* (*Monsieur La Souris*, 1938). A reporter who visited him in Porquerolles described his home as "part fishing port, part casbah, part exotic garden, part Uncle Tom's cabin, and part Algerian villa."[4]

Simenon soon began making improvements, renovating the house and adding a fifty-foot dock and a cabin for Boule and Madame Miche, a secretary from Avignon whose father was a chef at the Grand Hotel of Porquerolles. "Everyone on the island realized that the new residents of Les Tamaris had a lot of what it takes to get along," commented Angelo, their gardener.[5]

Indeed, Simenon bought himself a shiny new roadster, a set of fishing gear, including nets and casting equipment, and a canoe for Tigy. He also hired a professional deep-sea fisherman named Tado. Visiting journalists were treated to his seasoned-sailor, weathered-captain image: cap, thick blue sweater, pipe clamped between his teeth. He talked about the sea as though born to the bounding main, tirelessly answering questions about his passion for fishing and expounding on the art of preparing a proper bouillabaisse with an aplomb and a wealth of detail that dazzled those who were more used to seeing him in Neuilly, walking his great Dane through the pathways of the Bois de Boulogne.

His daily routine was adapted to the climate and to local activities. Rising before dawn, he would settle into his tower at six in the morning. The room was packed with files and manuscripts, Polynesian mats and hats, shell necklaces and antique maritime instruments. But it was devoid of books. A huge map of the Mediterranean hung on the wall over his worktable. He would fill six pipes, line them up, and begin to write. Three hours later he would come out, beaded with sweat, a chapter completed.

Later he would either meet the boat bringing mail and supplies from the mainland or take a three-mile stroll to the tip of the Langoustier, dressed in his Indian army shorts and wearing a Panama he had brought back from Tahiti. After the ritual afternoon nap, he would sit in the shade of a fig tree facing the Tour Fondue and chat with Raoul Noilletas or Victor Petit. Then he would organize a round of volleyball in his yard or join in the traditional game of *petanque* on the town square, followed by a pastis at the bar of the Hotel L'Arche de Noé with his friend Maurice Bourgues.

When the bells of the local church tolled evening angelus, Simenon and Tigy would go home for dinner, then drop in "at Maurice's" to play *belote* with Chapeau, the mailman, and Mozenti, the carpenter, while Bertrand, the poacher, leaned against the bar and offered acerbic comments as this or that card was played.[6]

It was a miniature Tahiti, except that Simenon, who had had a dose of real life on that mythic isle, knew that in the long run this kind of existence was a trap. Paradise on earth had deleterious side effects: sloth, numbness, erosion of will. In six months or so he was ready to head back to Paris or Charentes. But before long, pursued by the demon of instability, he would long to return to the island again. It was as if two different people waged a constant war inside him: "a man of the North keen on order and discipline, and a man of the South lying in his hammock under a fig tree as the Mediterranean licked the shores at his feet. I'll never know which of them won."[7]

For a French writer there was no more prestigious site in all of Paris than 5 Rue Sébastien-Bottin, in the Seventh Arrondissement. Many would have gladly given body parts to be able to instruct their readers to write to them here, in care of the magazine *La Nouvelle Revue française,* the NRF publishing house, or Gallimard. To be published between the stark, white typographical covers of the company that issued Proust, Valéry, Gide, and so many others was often an end in itself.

Gallimard and Simenon met for the first time in the publisher's office in 1933. They had been put in touch by a mutual friend, Florent Fels, editor in chief of *Voilà,* one of the house weeklies. Now free of any contractual obligation to Fayard, the novelist was master of his own output. It has been said that a contract negotiation is always a test of strength. If so, Gaston would soon realize that this author would be no joy to deal with. It is unlikely that he would ever say of Simenon, as he did of Marcel Aymé: "He's my favorite writer, never gives me any shit."

Gaston began with flattery ("André Gide is a great admirer of your work, you know"), proclaiming his happiness that Simenon's name would finally appear in the Gallimard catalog. He then proposed that they adjourn for lunch in a fine restaurant, figuring that contract discussions might profitably be sandwiched between the fruit and the cheese. Gallimard had Simenon pegged as a man of determination, and the author's response to his invitation gave him no reason to revise that assessment:

"To begin with, we will never share a meal. I detest business lunches where everything is discussed except business, followed by an appointment for another business lunch. This contract will be discussed in your office, in the presence of a secretary, with the door closed and the phone off the hook. We can settle everything in half an hour. Moreover, I will never call you Gaston, as everyone around here seems to do, nor will I ever say 'my good friend' to you, since I also detest that kind of talk. Whenever you want to see me, let me know the day and time, and I'll come to your office. Then we'll discuss everything. But after that you'll have to call me. If you want to renew the contract, you'll have to come and see me."[8]

Georges Simenon was definitely not Marcel Aymé. The author and publisher signed their first contract eight days later, on October 18, 1933. Its annual extension and revision gave Gaston Gallimard the opportunity to make a few extra trips to the countryside.

From the outset Gallimard considered Simenon's contract terms draconian. They called for six books a year at royalty rates of 10 percent up to the first ten thousand copies sold and 12 percent thereafter, with a nonrefundable advance equivalent to the royalties owing for sales of fifty thousand copies. But Simenon's demands for subsidiary rights were even worse. Income from translation and movie rights was to be split fifty-fifty, except if the author himself conducted the negotiations with the eventual buyers, in which case he would get 75 percent of the take.[9]

An author as greedy as a publisher—unheard of. But the flabbergasted Gaston signed, even though it would mean publishing Simenon at a loss initially. Contractual secrecy was rarely so well guarded, for Gallimard feared reactions from some of his other authors who were dissatisfied with their terms.

The first problem caused by Simenon's plunge into the tranquil waters of the NRF was purely technical. He was the company's most prolific author, and Louis-Daniel Hirsch, Gallimard's marketing director, was soon tearing his hair out trying to keep up. He and his colleagues in the production department found themselves hopelessly entangled in the intersecting manuscripts, galley proofs, page proofs, and corrected proofs of the six novels that were in the pipeline at any given time.

Simenon was the only one who could keep it all straight, and he was never around. Instead, he was in constant motion, on his way to Neuilly, Porquerolles, Nieul, or one of many hotels throughout France to which he would sometimes disappear without prior warning. When they finally managed to track him down, he would balk at having to interrupt the novel he was working on to deal with another at least several months old.

Promotional campaigns were especially problematic in such conditions, and Louis-Daniel Hirsch had to adapt to attitudes more common for newspapers than for books: "I think we have to make sure that both the bookstores and their customers know that they can count on a new Simenon arriving, for example, on the fifteenth of every month."[10] A clever suggestion, since the novelist would soon be turning out a book a month, the rate he felt his public expected.[11]

The bottleneck was never completely cleared, but Gaston preferred to leave the day-to-day worries to his staff. He had another sort of obstacle to deal with: the house itself rejected Simenon. The denizens of the Rue Sébastien-Bottin considered his image contemptible: he was a profuse purveyor of pulp crime novels, a Philistine, at best a phenomenon, at worst a boor. He was identified with his promotional outrages: the glass cage, the Anthropometric Ball, his errant life on the canals, his boastful interviews, his reputation as a tabloid journalist. He was too easy to read and sold too well. His writing was too transparent to be honest, his shameless self-promotion revealed a manifest lack of tact. He actually claimed to write by the sweat of his brow, as if artistic creation were some kind of labor. That alone was proof of his complete lack of genius, if not of talent. Simenon simply did not fit the discretion, elegance, and classicism of the NRF style.

The whispering campaign was started by Jean Paulhan, grand old man of the reading committee and director of *La Nouvelle Revue française*. He did not like Simenon and never would, tolerating him only because of Gaston's misguided indulgence. He would let him into the NRF catalog purely as a means of refilling the company's coffers when they had been depleted by the feeble sales of an Henri Michaux or a Max Jacob.

When Paulhan had to write something about Simenon or his books in the review, he did so with an utter lack of grace, employing his peerless ability to complicate the simplest questions. He took a malign pleasure in deflating this new contributor. Once, for example, he praised *La Rose de Java,* noting that its author, Joseph Kessel, "never shows greater finesse, force, and talent than when resorting to memory rather than invention." Several lines later, on the same page, he taunted Simenon for "stating publicly that he lacks imagination but has an excellent memory."[12]

Paulhan and Simenon could not have been more dissimilar. The former was among the most influential of Parisian literati, exercising a fascination over young writers but quite capable of demolishing them with withering comments on their first manuscript. Simenon, on the other hand, had a horror of the exercise of power, hated judging others, and was suspicious of intellectuals. When he strode down the corridors of the NRF, promised land of whisperers, he sang—not hummed, but sang.[13] Secretaries clung to the walls in stunned terror of such insolence.

Later in Simenon's career, Paulhan would claim that the novelist had no sense of tragedy, an especially troubling charge, since if there is an Ariadne's thread that runs through many of his books, it is precisely the tragic dimension of daily life. The author's response was emblematic of the gulf dividing him from the critic: ". . . walled up in his office as he is, I don't think he's ever had the slightest contact with life. How vulgar I must have seemed to him!"[14]

No doubt. In 1937, the year Gallimard published *Faubourg (Home Town),* *L'Assassin (The Murderer), Le Blanc à lunettes,* and *Le Testament Donadieu* (the latter widely promoted as Simenon's great novel), the author was snookered by his past. In that same year Ferenczi released *L'Ile empoisonnée* (The Poisoned Isle) and *Seul parmi les gorilles* (Alone Among the Apes), two exotic adventure novels written ten years earlier under the pseudonym Christian Brulls.

However bourgeois Simenon became, he remained socially anomalous. This was the last battlement of his resistance: he refused to become a man of letters, with all the compromises and concessions it would have entailed. Admitted to the Société des Gens de Lettres, he soon walked out, describing the organization as unprofessional. When he was slapped with a 500-franc fine for failing to fill out some documents despite several reminders, he charged the official assigned to oversee his rights with intolerable incompetence and resigned in his own inimitable way: asking for the address of a literary prison, explaining that he preferred to serve time rather than send them the money for the fine.[15]

His attitude sometimes made him aggressive with his peers. He boasted that he did not read their works, saying that he would always prefer Pliny the Elder and the Guillaume Budé collection to any of his contemporaries.[16] But he did ask Gallimard to send him a copy of Faulkner's *Sanctuary,* which he was apparently anxious to read.[17]

His articles and interviews in the early thirties bear scarcely a single favorable mention of any writer from his own or the previous century. Curiously, it was in discussing de Maupassant with an Armenian colleague from New York that he revealed one of the keys to his literary identity.

> I am as remote as can be from anything to do with criticism and more generally with the realm of ideas. My opinion therefore has little value. But for my part, I have always maintained that de Maupassant was the victim of an injustice in France, where he has never been accorded the status he deserves, which foreigners, especially in central and eastern Europe, do not deny him.
>
> At a time when literature was almost always encumbered by ideology (Victor Hugo, Zola, and so on, anticlericalism, comtisme, scientism, etc.) and when quarrels between contending schools seemed uppermost (the artist style of the Goncourts, naturalism, etc.), de Maupassant seems to me the most sincere and direct of French writers, the most inspired, if I may use the term, for he was the least affected by fashionable trends and attitudes. I also think that at a time when the man of letters was only a man of letters, he was one of the few to live real life and to draw his inspiration from it. (Was it not around the same time that Zola, before writing a chapter of realism, would spend several hours in a foundry or a cabinetmaker's shop, carefully noting the name of each tool?)
>
> As I see it, de Maupassant is as close as can be to a pure artist—somewhat like Van Gogh, with whom I see some affinities. But this is just the opinion of a man who forbids himself to have any ideas.[18]

Could an author shun the literary establishment while simultaneously seeking its support for literary prizes? Simenon was never short on contradiction. Prizes were on his mind even before he signed with Gallimard, and his choice of publisher may not have been entirely unrelated to this concern. Gaston Gallimard was the kingmaker in year-end awards, New Year's gifts to writers of all calibers. Only Grasset and Denoël occasionally threatened to breach his monopoly.

In 1932, Simenon nearly won a prize for *Le Passager du "Polarlys"* (*The Mystery of the "Polarlys"*), his only non-police novel to be published in a year that saw six Maigrets. According to Lucien Descaves, one of the ten members of the "Academy" established by the Goncourt brothers, the Prix Goncourt was to have gone to Céline for his *Journey to the End of the Night* (Denoël), the Prix Renaudot to Simenon. But after some last-minute maneuvers, the

Goncourt went to Guy Mazeline for *Les Loups,* published by—Gallimard. Walking out in a huff without even staying for the luncheon, Descaves broke the tradition of secrecy and divulged the "intrigues" that led to Céline's being given the Renaudot by way of consolation, while Simenon got nothing at all.[19]

Goncourt Academy records demonstrate that not a single one of Georges Simenon's novels was ever considered for a prize.[20]

Nevertheless, signs seemed favorable in 1937, a year when Gallimard published four of his novels, among them *Le Testament Donadieu.* Rumors swelled as September drew near, those in the know swearing that Simenon was finally a Goncourt prospect. In fact, the rumors did not exactly specify Simenon, but "a French-language novelist," later said to be Belgian, and later still Liégeois. Simenon's supporters rejoiced, especially when it was learned through an indiscretion that Lucien Descaves, the committee's enfant terrible, had taken steps to ensure that lack of French citizenship would not be an obstacle to a potential Belgian laureate.

On the eve of the awarding of the prize, Descaves visited the elder Rosny, president of the Goncourt Academy. In the course of the conversation he reminded Rosny that he, too, was of Belgian origin, having been born Boex, in Brussels, and that he had acquired French nationality at the beginning of his career, when he moved to Paris.[21]

The point was taken, and the next day the Prix Goncourt was awarded to Charles Plisnier, a novelist from Liège now living in Paris. The Ten had taken the unusual step of giving the prize to a collection of short stories, *Faux-Passeports,* for its moving portrayal of "certain problems of international communism."[22]

Simenon was deeply disappointed. Several years later, when his mother wondered why he had never been given this most prestigious of prizes, he wrote to her:

"For the love of God, don't talk to me about the Goncourt! It's just a little thing, and I'll never win it now, for the simple reason that I am to be the one awarding it."[23]

To his new secretary he commented: "Believe me, Carel, I'll be in the French Academy, no doubt about it, even if I am Belgian."[24]

Both claims were less pretentious than they sound. In 1936 he won several votes from the Goncourt Academy as a nominee to fill the seat vacated by a deceased juror, Léon Hennique. Ultimately, Léo Larguier was selected, but the mere fact that Simenon had been considered shows that his links to the literary establishment were not quite as tenuous as he claimed.[25] And soon afterward one newspaper did mention his possible election to the French Academy.[26]

It never happened, but the important thing was that there was public speculation about it. At thirty-three this man with a mania for planning could boast that his career was running ahead of schedule. He was determined to reduce unforeseen eventualities to a minimum, but there was one factor that entirely escaped his control: criticism.

Contrary to common belief, André Thérive was not the first literary critic to praise him. True, in the May 9, 1935, issue of the austere and respected *Les Temps* (daily newspaper of the Third Republic), Thérive hailed Simenon's emergence as a writer, discussing three of his new Gallimard novels. But by that time Simenon had been signing his books with his own name for four years, and there had been no dearth of press notices, sometimes mere passing mentions, sometimes genuine reviews. They were generally quite favorable, though reservations that would be expressed regularly in the future crop up here and there: monotony, platitudes, lack of pacing, improbable coincidences. But his virtues were said to far outweigh his defects, and some compared him to Conan Doyle and Edgar Wallace, Gaston Leroux and Maurice Leblanc, and even to Bergson and Tristan Bernard.

But while Thérive's article did not mark Simenon's "discovery," it did herald his arrival. The reviewer noted that the author had earlier committed the strategic error of appearing as a wholesale supplier to the literary industry, aiming exclusively at the general public's fondness for detective fiction and lacking the Parisian good taste and intelligence to submit only his most accomplished writings to criticism. But he had enough talent to overcome that handicap. It was now time to abandon the snobbery of literati who pretended to be slumming when they admitted that Inspector Maigret might have a thing or two going for him:

> I am firmly convinced that what I have just read is a masterpiece, raw and unrefined. . . . Mr. Simenon's *Le Locataire* [1934] could be the transition between his former style and the one he now evinces. . . . *Les Suicidés* [*One Way Out,* 1934] is already clearly superior, while exhibiting the same gifts. . . . They offer a dose of a Russian novel, lacking only the sprawl and tortuousness. . . . In all seriousness, fatality is the main character of *Les Suicidés,* and its filigreed image lends genuine grandeur to this slender story. . . . But *Les Pitard* [*A Wife at Sea,* 1935] is a fully realized work. . . . *Les Pitard* can be read as a crime story or as a novel with true depth. In either case, and I say this openly, it attains sublime pathos. No romanticism, no didacticism, just unprecedented force in making us feel truth. The "rendition," as they say in painting, is truly extraordinary. I shall always protest when Mr. Simenon is accused of writing badly: he writes very well, which is to say, just as is required. (I found just one tiny Belgicism.) Read this astonishing book, so dense yet so simple, and tell me that the word perfection is not made for it.

Thérive remained an ardent Simenon supporter despite a few reservations, as did René Lalou of *Vendredi* and Ramón Fernandez of *Marianne*.

In the years just prior to the Second World War, critics in Paris, the provinces, and Belgium were generally favorable to him. Some rebuked him, often justifiably, for this or that flaw, but Edmond Jaloux summed up his colleagues' overall attitude when he wrote in *Excelsior* that "Simenon remains exceptional even in his less polished works."[27]

More important than the favorable reception, however, was the mere fact that critics took notice of him. Most writers dread a reaction worse than scorn or hatred: indifference. The risk is real, especially since many critics are also novelists and therefore rivals for the same literary recognition, if not the same audience.

Simenon was already well known. What he needed now was recognition and consecration, and this, as usual, was a step-by-step process. First the critics brought Simenon out of the "entertainment" section. In 1938, a record year during which he published thirteen books (better than one a month), 366 articles were devoted to him (better than one a day). But even in 1936, when he published "only" three novels—*L'Evadé* (*The Disintegration of J.P.G.*), *Long Cours*, and *Les Demoiselles de Concarneau* (*The Breton Sisters*)—there were 185 articles, a staggering figure.[28]

Simenon preferred his notices to be unequivocal, for good or ill. Mixed reviews left him distraught, disturbed, and anxious, feelings he could ill afford when he was in the middle of writing. He admitted that he was disconcerted by critics who reproached him for awkwardness and imprecision while hailing his novelistic genius in the same breath. André Thérive, for instance, waxed rapturous about his technique but seemed to have no notion of his efforts to make his characters' words "sound" right. Keeping dialogue simple was far more complicated than it appeared, and it annoyed him that even those who praised him failed to notice the care he had taken:

"Damn! I've been killing myself for years trying to make what a farmer or a fisherman says come out right. It would have been easy to put words in the mouths of people like myself. Complex characters are easy to create, since the writer, by definition complicated, senses and understands them better than any others. But to write novels about people who live without thought—without what we call thinking!"[29]

This complaint was particularly aimed at critics who appreciated his Maigrets, like Robert Brasillach, another ardent admirer. In an article entitled "For and Against the Police Novel," Brasillach compared Simenon to Malherbe, raved about the power with which he describes a canal in *Le Charretier de "La Providence"* (1931), hailed the portrait of decay and degradation in *L'Affair Saint-Fiacre* (1932), and called Maigret the Monsieur Bergson of the police novel. But in the end he criticized Simenon for neglecting the action.

"The police novel can be the springboard for a renaissance of the novel in general, provided that it maintains an equal distance from pure mechanics and excessive analysis," Brasillach argued.[30] But the author remembered mainly the reproach.

Striving to justify himself in a letter to the critic René Lalou, he could not resist this confession, which many a "theoretician" of literature would do well to ponder:

"For my part, I write for a living, and I can assure you that deadlines may well account for a certain degree of negligence."[31]

Deadlines. It is true that they often dictated his conduct. Writers are usually loath to discuss such material issues, which, however, weigh as heavily on their work as the influence of any great master. But deadlines were not the sole reason for Simenon's errors of detail. He detested rereading his own work, and it was not easy to get him to make changes. The idea that emotion could be corrected by rules was alien to him. That which instinct produced had to stand with its own strengths and defects. Revision had to be minimal, and so it was. The truth is that Simenon liked writing less than having written.

By the middle of the 1930s he felt satisfied with his progress. But he would soon feel the need for an outside opinion from a more disinterested source than a publisher. He knew that he had mastered narrative technique. He was now able merely to suggest where he had earlier expounded. But that did not ease the anxiety that oppressed him whenever he emerged from an intensive period of writing: the fear of losing his psychic balance, of wandering into a terra incognita from which it would be impossible to escape without suffering irreparable damage.

Convinced that there were certain walls that could not be scaled without sacrificing one's mental health, he suffered the torment faced by other creators who had gone before him: Van Gogh, Lautréamont, Nietzsche. On finishing *Le Bourgmestre de Furnes* (*The Burgomaster of Furnes*, 1939), he told his publisher of his irresistible desire to get away for a while: "By the end I was working in a genuine hallucinatory state."[32]

So long as Simenon remained Simenon, critics of the mid-thirties were generally kind to him. But when he raised his sights and claimed finally to be writing the "great novel" that had been demanded of him, his supporters were less willing to stick with him, as though they were embarrassed by his efforts to break into the literary major leagues.

He had a bitter experience with this in 1937, when Gallimard published *Le Testament Donadieu*. Unusually long for a Simenon novel (318 pages of small type), the book chronicles a family's drift from unity to fragmentation. The collapse is triggered by the mysterious death of the patriarch, the shipowner Oscar Donadieu. The terms of his will throw the family into complete confusion. His widow, known as "the queen mother," believes herself particularly wronged. Alliances are formed among various members of the clan, and the ambition and jealousy, hatred and narrowness, previously suppressed by Oscar Donadieu's unchallengeable authority, rise to the surface.

Reviews were mixed.[33] Some critics considered the novel's structure, style, and language slipshod, unbalanced, and dense. The usual chorus of syco-phants was ever ready to laud this "masterpiece" by "one of our greatest writ-ers." René Lalou was one of the few reviewers lucid enough to raise the right question:

"It remains to be seen whether he will succeed in freeing himself from the lien of violent death that has so far weighed upon all his writings, or whether he needs this initial boost to deploy his visionary power."[34]

The author himself admitted that *Le Testament Donadieu* was his "first novel"—his first truly literary work, even though it begins with an enigmatic death. It is hard not to recall the epigraph André Gide appended to *The Coun-terfeiters* (1925), for identical reasons: "To Roger Martin du Gard I dedicate my first novel, in token of profound friendship."

Not long before, Simenon had been saying that he would write his "first novel" at forty, and that it would be a *Master and Servant,* or at the very least *The Idiot.*[35] Once again he was ahead of schedule.

The critics had begun likening him to other writers even before *Le Testament Donadieu,* and the process continued afterward, as if facile comparisons re-lieved them of the trouble of analyzing the originality of his fictional world. There are some real gems in this menu: "a false Mauriac," "a false Julien Green." The names of Gorky and Dostoevsky, Pierre Benoit and Charles Dick-ens, Zola and MacOrlan, Gide and de Maupassant, Dumas and Poe, Francis Carco and Pierre Loti also came up. Even Shakespeare and Virginia Woolf. All of which tells us less about Simenon's qualities than about the addled state of criticism. But most of all he was compared to Joseph Conrad and Balzac, the former because of the exoticism of his settings and the shadiness of his char-acters, the latter because of *Le Testament Donadieu*'s length, the complexity of its composition, and the psychological motivations of its heroes.[36]

Was Simenon the Balzac of the twentieth century? In the provocative days of his early triumphs, he might have replied that Balzac was the Simenon of the nineteenth. In any event, the parallel soon became a critical cliché, and it must be said that Gallimard encouraged it, putting it to use in a promotional campaign some years later, when an advertising pamphlet described *Le Tes-tament Donadieu* as "the most Balzacian" of Simenon's novels.[37]

Later still, when Simenon was asked about the Balzacian atmosphere of the Donadieu family, he simply shrugged, explaining that all he had done was to depict a milieu well known to him, that of the shipowners of La Rochelle. Admitting that the novel's length was more typical of Balzac than of Simenon, he claimed that the story was originally ordered as a long serial by *Le Petit Parisien*.[38]

Simenon was only too happy to bask in the rather hasty amalgam of himself and Balzac, one based on superficial resemblances: overproduction, relations with publishers and with women, discipline, and so on. At bottom, however, the comparison does not withstand scrutiny. Simenon's characters are rarely motivated by ambition, money, or power. One searches his main characters in vain for a Baron Nucingen, and still less a Rastignac. Marcel Aymé once called Simenon "a Balzac without longueurs." If he had to be compared to a glorious ancestor, Alexandre Dumas would probably be a more astute choice. But it is a pointless debate. Ordinary readers needed no help from professional critics and other official exegetes to realize that this author's work was quite unique.

Simenon was rarely as concerned with the reactions of his peers as he was in the case of *Le Testament Donadieu*. He sent out many review copies and soon began receiving letters of thanks. The cabinet minister Anatole de Monzie expressed great admiration for his art, which he had already noted in reading *L'Assassin* (1937). He blamed the mass-circulation press for "nearly causing us to misjudge you out of prejudice."[39]

The powerful literary critic Emile Henriot likewise hailed *Le Testament Donadieu* as "nothing less than a masterpiece," saying that he had been unable to put the novel down, so charmed was he by its hero, about whom, however, there was nothing charming at all.[40] François Mauriac, who saw great talent in it and assured Simenon that he was familiar with all his work, discussed technique with his colleague, but not without offering a few left-handed compliments:

"I never much appreciated your police novels, but in many of them I liked the gift so magnificently displayed in *Le Testament Donadieu*. The entire first part strikes me as admirable. You need to do a lot of work not on your style in the deeper sense (you have 'style'), but in the sense of 'corrections,' even if only to discourage nitpickers."[41]

French writers were sharply divided in their views of an author so difficult to classify. On the one hand there was Céline, who praised *Les Pitard* (1935). Simenon was grateful, though the admiration was not mutual. He would later say that he was so put off by Céline's "antistyle" that he had trouble reading him.[42]

On the other hand there was Paul Nizan, who had this to say in a review published in the communist daily *L'Humanité*:

"Back when he wrote stories in which the ignoble, sentimental Inspector Maigret unraveled his cases by tact and intuition, one was tempted to say that Mr. Simenon had the gifts of atmosphere that herald a genuine novelist. But since Mr. André Thérive hailed him as a great writer, Mr. Simenon has begun writing novels without police. We now realize that he was a good enough writer of detective novels, but only a mediocre writer of novels *tout court*."[43]

Meanwhile, despite Jean Paulhan's unyielding hostility, Simenon's novels found more and more supporters at *La Nouvelle Revue française*. Writers of all kinds read and liked him. Prejudices and preconceptions were the sole obstacles he had to overcome. Those who were not repulsed by the author's reputation unhesitatingly devoured his work. The case of Jacques Copeau is symptomatic.

The soul of the Vieux-Colombier Theatre, administrator of the Comédie-Française, and founder of the NRF decided to give Simenon a try. After several fruitless attempts, he picked up a copy of *Le Bourgmestre de Furnes* (1939) at a train station. This time he was hooked: "Austere technique, vigorous language, coiled force, poetic power," he wrote, identifying with the character of Joris Terlinck, owner of a cigar factory and local burgomaster, a man of intransigent moral stature.[44]

Emmanuel Berl was another story. He was the director of *Marianne*, a weekly launched by Gaston as a cultural organ for the left intelligentsia, a kind of counterpart to *Candide* and *Gringoire*, both decidedly right-wing. Berl, who had no taste for the exercise of power, accepted the editorial assignment as a favor to Gaston and for the privilege of attracting writers to the new journal. Simenon was one of them, and Berl compared him to Alexandre Dumas in all respects but one: "Simenon manages to make you forget your toothache for a while, but he does not make you happy like *The Three Musketeers*."[45]

Other eminent members of the NRF milieu soon came to share Gaston Gallimard's infatuation with this new member of the house. Jean Schlumberger and Roger Martin du Gard were among them. Their enthusiasm was important in itself, but it also encouraged others. Indeed, it appears that one or both of them were responsible for the discovery of Simenon's work by a writer who would henceforth play a significant role in his evolution: André Gide.[46]

One day in 1935, Gaston Gallimard summoned Simenon and informed him that André Gide wanted to meet him. "I'm giving a cocktail party. Please be sure to be there."[47] Simenon duly attended the ritual June soiree at the Gallimard offices, an event that would have provided an ethnologist with a broad sampling of the denizens of the literary tribe that dwelled along the banks of the Seine: great writers and their girlfriends, wordsmiths and bores, lurking gossip columnists and roaming sophisticates, literary jurors under the influence and the inevitable critics.

A man unknown to him approached and struck up a conversation: Gide.

"You're Simenon?"

"Yes."

"So, you exist in flesh and blood."

"So it would seem."

Gide led him into Gaston's office and closed the door. Knowing Gide's pro-clivities, Simenon got nervous—wrongly.

"Please sit down. I have a few questions."

There followed an hour-long interrogation. Many of Gide's queries were exactly the kind Simenon hated: Where do you get your ideas from? How do you write? How do you classify yourself? How this and how that?

Simenon cut him off. "Look, I don't know anything about all this. If I start analyzing myself, I won't be able to write anymore."

"But when did you create your character?"

"You mean Maigret?"

"No, yourself!"

"What character? I just am."

"I mean the character you've created for yourself out of your own idea of what you are."[48]

Simenon did not understand. Later he would, when he learned that Gide re-copied his own letters for posterity and he edited his private journal as though it were a public work. Himself an expert in self-promotion, Simenon was hardly wet behind the ears. But he was stunned by this degree of calculated affectation.

The future Nobel laureate in literature, then sixty-six years old, had al-ready completed the vast bulk of his work, save his monument, the *Journal*. He had begun reading Simenon only recently, starting with *Le Haut Mal* (1933), which he greatly admired.[49] The favorable first impression was soon confirmed by *Les Suicidés* (1934), the second Gallimard novel after *Le Locataire* (1934). This time Gide shared his enthusiasm with his entourage, telling them that this author, "after an abundant, indifferent, and quite unknown out-put, has begun to produce books of incredible psychological quality and value."[50]

Gide continued to read, enjoy, and comment on Simenon from then on, and Simenon increasingly solicited the master's advice, as their copious corre-spondence attests. But as excessive as Gide's praise sometimes seems, the crit-icism he expressed in his private reader's reports to Gaston Gallimard was equally intense. Not that he was two-faced. He seems to have wanted to cor-rect the younger author's defects without discouraging him.

He was charmed by the strength, energy, and vitality of Simenon's person-ality, and fascinated by the genius with which he produced what Gide him-self never managed to achieve: a great novelistic œuvre—not a few more or less successful books, but a veritable monument in paper, as coherent and massive as *La Comédie humaine* or *A la recherche du temps perdu*. Gide also seems to have taken some pleasure, not completely devoid of provocation, in defending an author who was often regarded with condescension because of his utterly plebeian literary origins.[51]

Gide, of course, was infatuated with many other writers as well. But Simenon was one of the few he promoted outright, as though determined that those around him share his discovery. One day his young secretary, Lucien Combelle, was chided for having read only Maigrets. Gide sat him down and read passages from *Les Trois Crimes de mes amis* (1938) and *Le Locataire* (1934) aloud. He then urged Combelle to have a look at the library in the foyer, where an entire shelf was devoted to Simenon. All his Gallimard novels were there, soon joined by some of the Fayard detective stories.[52]

Later, posing for a photograph alongside that same bookshelf, Gide proudly held a Simenon novel aloft and later sent the author the picture, with this dedication: "For my Georges Simenon, his old friend reading (rereading) *Monsieur la Souris* [1938]."

In private, Gide became increasingly enthusiastic as more Simenon novels appeared, though he admitted that the output was inevitably uneven. He was astounded by the artistry of composition, the economy of expression, the discipline with which all superfluous elements were excised, and the unrivaled authenticity of the dialogue. All of which, he told Simenon, should eventually clarify a mistaken interpretation from which his work still suffered:

"You are considered a popular author, but you do not address the broad public. The subjects of your books and the subtle psychological problems they raise are suited to the refined."[53]

What did Simenon think of Gide? This was, after all, the man who, during the Tunisian stopover on his Mediterranean cruise, ridiculed Hammamet as "the mecca of pederasty."[54] It is not at all certain that he actually read Gide's major works, except for the first volume of the *Journal,* which he claims to have "devoured" upon its appearance.[55]

Although we do not know Simenon's literary assessment of Gide, we do know what he wanted from him: advice and leadership. Just before the war, Simenon seemed burdened by creative solitude for the first time. He sought the professional opinion of his prestigious colleague, acknowledging the latter's expertise by sending him a copy of what he modestly called "my abortive little Donadieu effort."[56] Simenon and Gide were rarely in the same city at the same time, and their relations now took an epistolary turn, which may have made Simenon feel more free to express himself.

A few weeks before his thirty-sixth birthday, in reply to two letters from Gide, Simenon sent the man he now addressed as "My dear Master and great friend" a confession thirteen typed pages long. He would rarely say as much about his writing as he did in this letter.

> . . . And now I owe it to you to explain myself, which is far more difficult than explaining a character. Almost impossible, for one's own self is the sole terrain forbidden to knowledge, is it not? That, in any case, is often how I feel about it, and that is why I often cheat with myself. I

pretend not to know, so as not to defy fate. . . . Spoken aloud it would be false. Given a partner, I would automatically play a role, I would become a character in a novel, I would see my partner that way, too, and would lie quite sincerely. It is easier to be cold and stark in writing. And I owe you that, for I realize what you have done and can find no words to express my gratitude. . . .

The police formula allowed me to reach a broad public and to make money—and also to study my craft in the most comfortable conditions, with a ringmaster, so to speak. . . . After eighteen police novels I am tired of it—I feel stronger and I eliminate the ringmaster, namely Maigret. These are the days of *Le Coup de lune* [1933], *L'Âne rouge* [1933], *Les Gens d'en face* [*The Window Over the Way*, 1933], *Le Haut Mal* [1933], etc. But I'm still in a narrow framework. I need support, some big action. The only way I can hold attention is with a dramatic story. And above all, I can handle only one character at a time!

I think this is the key to all my effort, and perhaps to preferences that may seem strange. I want to be in full possession of my craft before writing the great novels I plan to write, and it's hard to imagine Sebastian Bach having to grapple with technical problems, which (in the sense I mean) are as complicated in a novel as in music or painting. In painting they say a hand doesn't live. In literature there are so many hands, and heads too, that do not live.

Now, one thing that is possible in painting, namely a living model, is not possible in a novel, at least as Zola conceived it. Excuse me, my dear Master and Friend. I'm getting carried away, speaking ex cathedra, but it's my whole life that's at stake, because if I'm wrong, then it's lost. Or in any event, the ten years I spent writing pulp novels are lost, under the illusion that I was learning my craft, mixing the plaster—and the roughly ten more I spent trying to live all possible lives whatever the cost. So as never to have to look for material. Never to have to study a character I needed. So that when the time came, ten characters would be right there in my office when I needed them. And most of all so as not to have observed them; I have a horror of observation. You have to try. Feel. You have to have fought, lied—I was about to say stolen. You have to have done it all, not in depth, but enough to understand. Which turns out to mean that I am second-rate in everything, from gardening to horseback-riding, and less than second-rate in Latin. Constant fear, not so much of what I think as of what man feels. And of what he says, of his slightest deeds. Not to be able to look at a field without figuring its yield and without knowing how the farmer eats, how he makes love with his wife. . . .

I wish I could know all crafts, all lives. . . . Now, after unburdening myself so much, it is difficult to speak of my novels. My method? It hasn't changed. First of all to have the people within you (the ideal would be to be able to say all people), to have lived all their lives. Even in miniature, to have suffered all their sufferings. I am far from that! With time I will come closer to that ideal.

But how can I sincerely describe the gestation of a novel? It's nothing but trickery with myself . . . to put myself in a trance . . . to neutralize myself . . . lie in the bath . . . in a state of grace . . . discipline, mania. . . . You see that there are no phenomena, or perhaps just a simple phenomenon of will, which is hardly extraordinary. Provided, of course, that I have not made a basic mistake about the goal! . . . This is the first time I've ever tried to explain myself. May it at least not cost me your friendship and encouragement! . . . There is a time for everything. Your extended hand, my dear Master, comes to me at the exact moment when, having labored so long alone, I might have fallen prey to lassitude. Thank you, with all my heart, from the bottom of my heart. Simenon.[57]

Gide's sustained attention, encouragement, and technical aid gave Simenon something no one else could have provided: self-confidence. Only a writer with such an aura of majesty in French letters could have given him a sense of his own importance at a time when doubt assailed him.

Soon afterward, in 1939, an entire double issue of *Cahiers du Nord,* a quarterly published in Charleroi, was devoted to Simenon, an impressive tribute to an author not yet forty years old. There were glowing contributions from Jean Cassou, René Lalou, Max Jacob, André Thérive, Vlaminck, G. W. Stonier, and others. Gide also answered the call, offering a judgment that would go down in literary history:

"I consider Simenon a great novelist, perhaps the greatest and most authentic novelist we have in French literature today."[58]

His encounter with Gide was an important stage in Simenon's life. But unlike the others, he had not planned it, and it impelled him to self-examination earlier than he had expected. The late thirties became a time of reassessment for him.

He now had one burning desire: to be a novelist and nothing but a novelist. He would do whatever he had to do to achieve complete independence. That meant financing his increasingly lavish lifestyle while making the fewest possible demands on his time, making more and more money without doing anything to damage his image. He was not yet the free man he wanted to be. Money and deadlines still cast their shadows over his work and various side issues complicated his schedule. These included the press, lawsuits, foreign rights, the theater, films, and relations with his publisher.

In 1937, Simenon began trying to extricate himself from entanglements with the press. In the mid-thirties he had been one of the most frequently serialized authors, his novels and short stories appearing in *La Revue de France, Radio-Magazine, Les Annales, Marianne, Le Journal, Aujourd'hui, Candide, Paris-Soir, Le Figaro, Le Jour, Gringoire, La Revue de Paris, Police-Magazine, Confessions, Votre Bonheur,* and *Le Petit Parisien.* Now, however, he felt that prepublication of his novels as newspaper serials would be prejudicial to his literary reputation as a Gallimard author. But at the same time, he wanted to maintain journalistic links with the papers that had financed his travels.

He had a number of projects in mind, including trips to Rhodesia, Transvaal, and Kenya, which would also supply material for a novel about diamond prospectors.[59] In August he reached an accord with *Paris-Soir* for a series of twelve articles on Africa under the general title "There are no more colonies, only lands of settlement." With Jean Prouvost's agreement, he hoped to induce the French to renounce "adventure" in favor of "dominion."[60] A contract was signed on September 10 stipulating a payment of 100,000 francs a year, a rather substantial sum considering that Simenon's royalties from Gallimard in 1936 totaled 156,000 francs, while his gross income for the year was 512,166 francs.

The contract, however, called for short stories and novels as well as reportage. Prouvost read fine print as carefully as he did articles, and before long he was on the phone to Simenon, furious:

"You've been my best collaborator, but your byline will never again appear in *Paris-Soir* or in any other paper of mine. You think you can cuckold me and get away with it?!"[61] The "boss" then ran down the list of his papers, from *L'Intransigeant* to *Marie-Claire, Match,* and others.

Simenon had committed the faux pas of serializing one of his novels in *Votre Bonheur,* a newly founded rival of the Prouvost group. This was unpardonable. But the novelist did not beg for forgiveness, since he had more than a few complaints against Prouvost.

He had laid out considerable sums for the African series and had sweated blood for two weeks collecting the necessary visas and authorizations. At the last minute Prouvost canceled the project, without reimbursing Simenon. Soon afterward, Simenon's novel *Touriste de bananes* (1938) was serialized under the title *Tamatéa de Tahiti,* which he considered low-class. Finally, when Simenon delivered *Cour d'assises* (*Justice,* 1941), a novel commissioned by Prouvost, the press and wool magnate rejected it on the grounds of "the total immorality" of the characters.[62] He objected in particular to the trio of heroes: Little Louis, a contemptible, small-time hoodlum posing as an underworld big shot; Constance Ropiquet, an heiress who passes herself off as the countess of Orval; and Lulu, a prostitute trying to get free of her pimp.

The breach between the two men was not definitive, for each was astute enough to keep future options open. In fact, the author admitted in private: "I gave him the book without giving any thought to the moral angle, and I confess that I often get carried away by my subject and lose sight of this aspect. From now on I will not publish anything in the newspapers." And in case the point wasn't clear, he added: "I am no longer collaborating with newspapers. I have withdrawn to my lair. And I am working for posterity!!!"[63]

For a time, Simenon and Prouvost communicated only through lawyers. The author-businessman was no mean hairsplitter when he had to be. Whenever he felt he had been done an injury, he called in the good Maurice Garçon, Esq. In his defense, it should be recalled that he had been burned by threats of legal action before.

The *Coup de lune* affair had left a bad taste in his mouth, and it was only the first in a sequence of lawsuits. In March 1935, when he was passing through Papeete, Simenon was introduced to François Hervé, administrator of the Tuamotu archipelago. Hervé, an amateur writer who prided himself on his expertise in literature, had written several texts inspired by Pacific mores and folklore. He and Simenon signed a "contract": If Hervé's writings were not accepted by a publisher, Simenon would rewrite them or use them as material for his own work. In either case, the products would be cosigned and the rights would be shared equally.

A year later several stories and tales inspired by his trip were published in *Marianne* under Simenon's own name. Among them was "L'Oranger des îles Marquises." Hervé asked his lawyer in France to file suit. Simenon replied that he had simply borrowed a theme from Hervé for two articles in a series of thirteen to be published by *Paris-Soir* under the title "Les ratés de l'aventure." As it happened, "L'Oranger des îles Marquises" was the only story rejected by *Paris-Soir*. *Marianne* picked it up and printed it before he had the time to review the galleys.

When the plaintiff was not convinced, Simenon brought out the heavy artillery, threatening a whopping exposé of the insatiable greed of the colonial administration. That seems to have done the trick. Hervé's lawyers decided that a lackluster settlement was preferable to a trial, and in January 1937 the case was shelved.[64]

But the respite was brief. A few months later the characters of *Quartier nègre* rebeled just as their counterparts of *Coup de lune* had done. The action of this novel, published in 1935, takes place in three cities along the Panama Canal: Cristobal, Panama, and Colón. As before, the complaint came from a French hotel-keeper, Pascal Canavaggio, who remembered Georges Simenon's three-week stay in his establishment very well. A reading of the novel convinced him that the author had taken a tad too much inspiration from what he had seen and heard there.

This time Simenon took the bit in his teeth. He admitted that he had had conversations with the hotelkeeper's son, but insisted that these were not the source of the plot, spirit, or atmosphere of his story, which deals with the decline of a young Frenchman and his wife, forgotten and penniless in this remote corner of the world. All his information about the French settlement came from a government official in Panama City, who told him in private that its population consisted mainly of traders of Syrian origin, procurers, and escaped convicts. In a deliberate effort to avoid any potential problems, the author had incorporated his impressions of Ecuador and Colombia, as well as of Tahiti and Nouméa. Both the hotel and the characters were composites.

Furthermore, Simenon explained to his lawyer, the plaintiff would have a hard time proving that he had been defamed by the novel, since everyone on the island was involved in smuggling. Not to mention the fact that the offended party evaluated his honor at the royal sum of 500,000 francs.

"These guys can always claim that novelists have used them as characters, especially if they think they can be well paid for it," he complained.[65]

The case dragged on for two years until the two sides finally reached a compromise. One morning in March 1939 readers of *Paris-Soir* were treated to a full-page article entitled, "Panama, Last World Crossroads," signed Georges Simenon and accompanied by an incongruous sidebar singing the praises of one Pascal Canavaggio. ". . . Fifteen or twenty men can be enough to reshape a country. A single man like Canavaggio is worth an institution. It was his efforts and his money that founded a popular library."[66]

These various legal experiences had taught Simenon one lesson: don't trust anyone. It was an attitude that sometimes entangled him in contradictions. In 1938, when *Les Trois Crimes de mes amis* (which he would later call "an autobiographical novel as true as *Pedigree*")[67] was published, he asked Gallimard to subtitle it "A True Story." When the publisher made him see reason, he grudgingly agreed to substitute "A Novel." But he was not convinced: ". . . since it is obvious that it is not a novel and that readers will realize it."

He preferred that there be no subtitle at all, but Gallimard pointed out the problem. The book features three people the author knew as a young reporter in Liège: Hyacinthe Danse, Ferdinand Deblauwe, and Le Fakir. The first two were publishers of scandal sheets, the third a magician. All three committed murders, and any one of them might well have filed suit for slander. Describing the book as fiction would help avert that possibility.[68] Gallimard carried the day, and *Les Trois Crimes de mes amis* was published as a novel.

In 1939, lawyers and magistrates who were among Simenon's readers were probably amused to find the following disclaimer on the copyright page of *Le Bourgmestre de Furnes:* "I have never been to Furnes and know neither its burgomaster nor its inhabitants. For me Furnes is no more than a kind of musical motif. I therefore hope that no one will claim to recognize himself in any of the characters of my story." No one was fooled, but Simenon's peace of mind now required such deception.

On the translation front, Simenon had covered a lot of ground since *The Case of Peter the Lett* was published in London in 1933. Six years later he was the most widely translated contemporary French-language writer in the world. With eighteen translations, he ranked with Sinclair Lewis, Jack London, and Maxim Gorky. Alexandre Dumas, with twenty-two, held the record for non-contemporary French authors, while the leader in all categories was still Edgar Wallace, with eighty-two.

Simenon was personally responsible for his own international fame, for his novels, especially the Maigrets, were full of ordinary characters with whom Finns could identify as easily as Japanese.

One writer in particular, a German named Hermann von Keyserling, understood this very early on, and the fact that he was a foreigner may well have helped the rapid international diffusion of Simenon's work. Famous for his *Travel Diary of a Philosopher* (1925), Keyserling was the founder of the "School of Wisdom." His subsequent essays (*Creative Understanding, America Set Free,* and others) enhanced his prestige. In 1936 he wrote to Simenon to express his admiration, thus beginning a correspondence that continued for three years. The many questions this philosopher asked the novelist showed that he considered him a kind of "phenomenon" to be studied more than merely read. He asked Simenon to send him all his books, and he repeatedly invited him to come to Germany for a visit.

"I hope you're not a teetotaler," he wrote. "Since I spend most of my time in silent, ascetic solitude, I require an atmosphere of excess for release."[69]

A good sign. But Simenon was reluctant to accept the invitation. He was put off by his correspondent's intellectual aura, though he should have been reassured by what von Keyserling had written about him in the French press, claiming, for example, that he was Balzac's superior in the art of describing events, in evocative power, in the ingeniousness of his plots, and in the scope of his talent. Confessing that he had long read detective stories as a soporific, von Keyserling reported that he now devoured Simenon to stay awake.[70]

Simenon was so flattered that in 1937 the two men finally met, at von Keyserling's home in Darmstadt, where the novelist was subjected to a three-day interrogation. From the moment they shook hands, von Keyserling struck him as a colossal figure, astonishingly perceptive and boundlessly curious. Simenon tried to answer all of his host's questions with unaffected simplicity, sincerely trivializing his "genius," his ability to copy real life, his habit of writing under deadlines, and his satisfaction with first drafts. When the three days were up, von Keyserling was as fascinated as ever. But he was more enamored of the Maigrets than of the other novels. He saw Simenon as confirmation of his theory that any human activity could be perfected by practice.

"I know of no more clearly gifted novelist in all of French literature," he later wrote in his memoirs.[71]

For his part, Simenon retained an astonished admiration for this great thinker. "Keyserling considers me an imbecile of genius," he said shortly after their meeting. "Which happens to be exactly my own opinion. I am absolutely unintelligent. I have no critical spirit and no imagination."[72]

Two years after this encounter, Simenon felt strong enough to impose his own conditions on the increasing numbers of foreign publishers bidding for his Maigrets. He wrote to Fayard to explain:

"The time has come to stop signing one-off translation contracts. From now on I will release foreign rights to just one leading house per country, provided that house agrees to publish a significant portion of my work, for example the entire Maigret collection."[73]

In the United States at least ten of his books had been published since 1933. Two firms competed for American rights. Little, Brown, while generally enthusiastic, cited two major obstacles to producing all the Maigrets: their length (Americans would never pay two dollars for such short books) and Simenon's highly psychological approach. The New York publisher Harcourt, Brace did not share these fears, and its willingness to sign a contract for the entire series carried the day.

Britain, however, was the main springboard for the international spread of Simenon's work. In an article published in *The New Statesman,* the critic G. W. Stonier compared *Le Locataire* (1934) to Cecil Scott Forester's *Payment Deferred* (1926) and assessed Simenon even more positively than the future creator of Horatio Hornblower. "Most of all he is wonderfully readable," Stonier wrote.[74]

Another Englishman who played a pivotal role in the propaganda process was not a critic but a translator, Geoffrey Sainsbury, who introduced Simenon's work to the London publisher Routledge. The firm was so impressed by Sainsbury's plea that they agreed to publish detective fiction for the first time.

Once the initial moment of enthusiasm had passed, however, T. Murray Ragg, Routledge's managing editor, hesitated at taking the risk of signing a contract for twenty-six novels all at once. He felt that the four Maigrets already published by his colleagues at Hurst and Blackett were not a sufficient test. He therefore had Sainsbury translate *La Tête d'un homme* (1931), just to see. Experience had taught him that many French books lost their flavor in other languages.[75]

The results of the experiment must have been felicitous, for Routledge soon took the necessary measures to become Simenon's exclusive publisher in Britain, intending to turn him into "an institution in the English language."

Like Gallimard in 1933, Routledge had to go through a point-by-point negotiation, especially on the question of the division of film rights. This author
definitely had no need of an agent.[76] Within a year, Routledge was satisfied
that they had done the right thing: sales rose steadily, and the novelist regularly sent review copies of his books to British and American critics.[77]

Simenon was no ingrate, and he soon offered his translator informal status
as minister plenipotentiary: "What I'd like for you to be, so to speak,
Simenon in England," he told him after dinner one night. Sainsbury felt
compelled to decline the offer, partly out of lack of availability, but also out
of pride. He considered himself an author in his own right, addressing his letters to Simenon "Dear Colleague." Had Simenon been swifter to recognize the
nature of this misunderstanding, he might have saved himself much disappointment ten years later. In the meantime, however, he had full confidence
in this man who carried the delicate notion of "translator–traitor" to fresh
heights.

From the very beginning Sainsbury freely altered names, psychological
profiles, details, and even plot elements when he considered them inappropriate, implausible, or contradictory. The results of his "re-creation" were
duly submitted for the author's approval, which was always forthcoming.
And for good reason: Simenon did not understand a word of English.[78]

For a time, admittedly brief, Simenon had the idea that the theater might supply fresh contributions to his prestige and his income. His first play—*Quartier
nègre,* in three acts—was performed by Jean-Pierre Aumont and fifteen black
actors at the Théâtre Royal des Galeries Saint-Hubert in Brussels in November
1936. Simenon's concept of the theater was as simple as could be: dip into real
life and put it on the stage.

"Who cares about a thousand combinations of ménage à trois?" he asked
one critic. "A raw theater for a raw epoch. Our young people have to look life
in the face at twenty, and life is far more dramatic than any sophisticated
drama."[79]

Specialists smiled at his pretentious innocence, but he didn't care. Increasingly excited, he followed rehearsals closely. So many reporters showed up
that they began to look more like press conferences.

"The time has come to reform the theater," he declared with authority. "We
are lost in banalities, the characters are no longer of interest."[80]

A few weeks after his triumphant "premiere," he took to the boards again
with *A bord du "Tonnerre de Dieu"* (Aboard "God's Thunder"), an adaptation
of *Les Pitard* (1935) broadcast by Le Poste Parisien radio station. It is not clear
exactly when he realized that he had little to gain, figuratively or literally,
from the world of the stage, foreign to him as it was. In any event, he gave it

up temporarily in 1938, though not for lack of proposals. Gaston Baty, director of the Théâtre Montparnasse, hectored him for months in an effort to overcome what he diagnosed as a bad case of "stage fright," bombarding him with
witty letters aimed at squeezing an adaptation of one of his novels out of him.
"I extend my hands to you," he wrote. "Give me your own, followed by a
manuscript." In the end, Simenon tried to get rid of him by sending him an
adaptation written by his friend Vlaminck. A disappointed Baty returned it
with this comment: "So great a painter need not be a good playwright as
well."[81]

Several years had passed since Simenon's first experiments with films. Despite
his declarations of principle, he had often been approached by producers. A
few synopses had been written, but the quantity of time wasted and ink ex-
pended confirmed his gloomy view of the industry. Toward the end of 1934,
he mandated Robert Aron to negotiate in his name. In the event, "negotiate"
meant turn down offers, a task Gallimard's subsidiary rights officer handled
easily enough.

Simenon's opinion of movie people was as low as ever. In the autumn of
1934, several months after the Stavisky affair, he authored a survey for *Le
Jour,* Léon Bailby's daily, entitled "Inventory of France: When the Depression
Ends." The thirteenth of this series of twenty articles was devoted to the
French film industry. In it Simenon denounced the industry's efforts to
squeeze money out of the government in the name of the fight against unemployment and derided producers as an unscrupulous crew—"most often
Moldavian, Illyrian, or Andorran, if not Hungarian or Transylvanian"—who
never had any money but somehow managed to find some to acquire the film
rights to a book.[82]

This article fit right into the atmosphere created by *France-la-Doulce,* Paul
Morand's anti-Semitic satire of French cinema, published that spring. Morand
had worked the miracle of not using the word *Jew* even once, but the Germans
made no mistake when they quickly released a translation.

On the other hand, it must be said that while Morand and Simenon exag-
gerated, there was a kernel of truth in what they said. The French film industry had attracted a significant number of opportunists, careerists, and
unscrupulous characters more concerned with lucre than with the quality of
their films. And since the industry was a magnet for producers fleeing Nazi
Germany or central Europe, a good number of whom happened to be of Jewish origin, the amalgam seemed irresistible.

In those days anyone at all could set up a production company for a particular film, use a known actor's name to get in to see financial backers, pay the
technicians with rubber checks, and make off with the bank account before

the film was shot. Something was truly rotten in the state of filmdom, and denunciation of the system, however cruel and caricatural, was often well received, not much thought being given to its racist political content.

Simenon's mistrust of "film entrepreneurs" was not quite as extreme as that of Henri Jeanson, who once sent in the even-numbered pages of a commissioned script, promising that the odd ones would follow when he had been paid in full.[83] But his *Mémoires intimes* (*Intimate Memoirs*, 1981) say that the few bounced checks he received always came from producers.[84] In *Le Testament Donadieu* (1937) all film producers go bankrupt sooner or later,[85] and producers are stereotyped in several other novels and short stories: Jean Bronsky in *Maigret et son mort* (*Maigret's Special Murder*, 1948); Art Levinson, the American agent for a film star in *Maigret voyage* (*Maigret and the Millionaires*, 1958); Weill in *Les Volets verts* (*The Heart of a Man*, 1950); and the crooked Elie Wermster, head of the Paris office of World Films in "Emile à Bruxelles" (Emile in Brussels), one of the short stories in *Dossiers de l'agence O.* (Files of the O. Agency, 1943). But despite his resentment, Simenon gradually retreated from his decision not to allow the people of this industry to "tinker" with his work. He seems to be backpedaling as early as 1936:

"I'm not saying I will never sell one of my novels to the movies again, but if I ever do, you can say to yourself, 'Simenon must have really needed the money.' "[86]

Soon afterward he announced his plans to produce adaptations of *Les Pitard* (1935) and *Quartier nègre* (1935), both to be shot on location, the former in Rome, Hamburg, Reykjavik, and Fécamp, the latter in Panama. He hoped that these films would star Jean Gabin, who, in 1937, at age thirty-three, had appeared in some twenty films and was about to score his greatest triumph in *Grand Illusion*.

In September 1937, Simenon finally did go back into films. His return to the screen, however, did not necessarily mean selling film rights to one of his novels. Instead, he wrote *La Marie du port* (*Chit of a Girl*, 1938) especially for the movies. In private he gave this explanation for his decision:

"There are two reasons. First, the producers finally accepted the principle of original scripts, for which I had always argued. Second, I want to make fewer and fewer concessions in my literary production, escaping the constraints of the mass-circulation dailies as far as possible. In other words, I want the cinema to give me the financial equivalent of what I got from the serialization of my novels. . . . As you see, the situation is clear. This is not a case of an author randomly selling the film rights of successful novels and viewing screen adaptations as extensions of his books. Once again, I have had that experience and consider the formula disastrous both for the cinema and for the writer's standing."[87]

Simenon hired Synops, the agency founded by Denise Batcheff-Tual, to represent him in his dealings with the film industry. The 10 percent commission was a small price to pay for peace of mind. A one-year contract was signed as a test,[88] and the agreement soon bore fruit: Synops brought in 85,000 francs in 1938 alone, for the scripts of *La Maison des sept jeunes filles* (The House of Seven Girls, 1941) and *La Marie du port,* neither of which would be made for several years. In the meantime, Simenon himself got 50,000 francs for the French film rights to *Les Caves du Majestic* (*Maigret and the Hotel Majestic,* 1942) which went to Imperial Films, headed by Joseph Lucachevitch, a German Jew who had fled Nazism.

Proposals poured in as word of Simenon's "return to the screen" got around. Raimu and Louis Jouvet wanted roles in *Quartier nègre* (1935). The enterprising Lucachevitch offered 50,000 francs for the rights to *L'Evadé* (1936). His colleague Gregor Rabinovitch, whom Simenon referred to in his letters as a "French" producer, with ironic quotation marks, was negotiating for the rights to *La Maison des sept jeunes filles,* hoping to cast Danielle Darrieux in the lead role. Simenon had a special fondness for this rather silly book, which he declined to have published in the same collection as his other novels. In private he admitted that he had written it "for budgetary reasons alone," and he was only too happy to have the film industry pick it up.[89] But he did not simply wait passively for proposals. He sent samples of his work to such people as the director Robert Florey, "the" Frenchman of Hollywood.[90]

As his movie work gathered momentum, Simenon declined to renew his contract with Synops, in part because he discovered that his publisher had been involved in setting up the agency. He learned from an advertisement that Synops was the exclusive agent for the NRF, and he suspected that Gaston Gallimard, despite his denials, was a silent partner. He now decided that film negotiations should be conducted directly by his lawyer, Maurice Garçon. "It's easier for you to be tough than for me," he told him.[91]

Despite the suspension of his boycott of the film industry, Simenon remained suspicious. He said he wanted the movie people to look upon his work as a "stock of ideas,"[92] but he was also afraid they would take him literally. When he sold the film rights to *Le Passager du "Polarlys"* (1932) to Nicolas Vondas, he warned the producer: "I've already been burned in the movie business, and I intend to insist implacably on the execution of our contract."

The warning, however, did not deter Vondas from sending Simenon a 25,000-franc rubber check, from hiring a third-rate director after "promising" to get Julien Duvivier or Pierre Chenal, or from altering the script without informing the author. When Simenon sued, Vondas complained that resorting to the courts was "inelegant."[93] Simenon definitely paid his dues. But in the end he became the contemporary French-language writer whose works were most often adapted for the screen, both big and small.

In 1935, less than two years after their first contract was signed, relations between Simenon and Gallimard took a turn for the worse. Simenon's on-the-scene investigation of the adventures of the baroness of Wagner on the Galápagos Islands produced not merely a series of articles for *Paris-Soir* but also a novel. Of course, he changed the names, locales, and various details, moving the action to an island called Floreana and calling his heroine the Countess von Kleber. He then sent the manuscript off to his publisher from Tahiti, explaining that this was "a slightly fictionalized account of the adventure of the baroness of Wagner and Dr. Ritter." He also suggested a title (*Galápagos*) and an introductory note designed to ward off any possible lawsuits. But it was something worse than a lawsuit that worried Gallimard when he read the manuscript. Experience had taught him that an author who tries to capture the public's curiosity by picking up a news item is courting failure.[94] The novel was eventually published under the title *Ceux de la soif* (1938). But Gallimard sat on it for three years before releasing it.

A year later, Jean Zay, the minister of national education, introduced a bill limiting the terms of contracts between authors and publishers to ten years. The bill was amended several times and finally buried by the Chamber of Deputies, which had more pressing concerns, but Gallimard took advantage of the legislature's brief debate to review his agreements with Simenon, suggesting that future accords be based on "commercial" rather than "sentimental" considerations. The records show that Simenon was paid advances of 43,500 francs per title for his first six Gallimard novels, while actual sales earned an average of about 15,000 francs each. In 1935 the annual contract was revised downward. For the six titles of that year he was paid advances of 28,800 francs each, but sales earned only 21,600 francs per book.

Gallimard found out from a printer that the standard Fayard print run for a Simenon novel had been 25,000, while sales of the Gallimard novels were running at an average of about 15,000 each. He therefore proposed to lower the guaranteed per-title payment to 21,600 francs, which seemed a more reasonable reflection of the commercial reality.

"It seems clear," he wrote to Simenon, "that your abandonment of the detective novel has resulted in a predictable decline in sales. All I ask is that you realize that it is only natural that now that you have made the turn to literature, your books will take on the sales rhythm typical of literary works, which means that their sales will be slower, but you will also find that they will become more regular and continuous, such that someday you will reap greater advantages."[95]

The publisher showed his author the figures. Times were hard, he said. The NRF's overheads were rising, printing costs were up, and fresh taxes had been levied on the company. The author balked. He wanted his royalty rate to stay at 12 percent of the retail price for each copy sold, while the publisher insisted on 10 percent. It was a stalemate, until Gallimard played his trump card, threatening to increase the price of the books. Simenon backed down.[96] It was a bigger defeat for the author as businessman than he realized. He could boast of fabulous print runs, but his publisher knew the truth. In late 1937, Gaston Gallimard informed his brother Raymond, the commercial "brains" of the house, that sales of the average Simenon novel stood at eight thousand copies.[97] Gallimard now realized that Simenon's illusions were rooted in the pace of his production. Sales of each title taken separately were mediocre, while the cumulative total was impressive. But as Simenon pointed out, all this was relative:

"How many authors do you have whose books sell eight thousand copies each twelve times a year without any promotion?"[98]

That was the real sore point. Simenon constantly complained that the NRF did not do enough publicity for his books, as if this debatable deficiency accounted for the low sales. When *Faubourg* was issued (in 1937), he suggested that Gallimard spring for thirty radio ads and even supplied the copy:

"Have you read the latest Simenon?"

"No."

"Well, take a look at *Faubourg!*"

Gaston refused. He found the idea too feeble and the price (50,000 francs) too high.[99] Simenon raised the issue anew for *L'Assassin,* released at around the same time. Disappointed again, he complained that Louis-Daniel Hirsch, the marketing director, had approved only a few leaflets.

"It is obvious that if the series continues to appear in these conditions, it will very much resemble a liquidation," he warned.[100] Tension mounted until finally, in November 1938, Gallimard lost his temper. The issue was the film contracts Simenon was negotiating without even bothering to have them countersigned by the NRF.

Gaston decided to speak his mind, politely but firmly:

> . . . It is now necessary for us to take stock of our affairs. I write to you in all candor. It seems to me crude and a bit unfair for the NRF to act as your banker, without ever having a chance to recover its advances. You know with what friendship I regard not only your work but your success in general. Nevertheless, if I draw up a Simenon balance-sheet for the NRF, I note that to date I have paid you 500,000 francs more in rights than I have collected in sales, and that the uncovered costs of production are in excess of 400,000 francs, making the total deficit nearly a million. . . .
>
> To continue in this way would inevitably discredit you. The reality is that you are asking too much of publishing, which is a modest industry, and it is not fair for it to assure the basis of your livelihood while, for example, the film industry, with its enormous resources, declines to make the efforts on your behalf to which you are entitled—the

film industry, or the press. . . . It is unhealthy for you to consider publishing as a means of supplying you, in difficult times, with the tens of thousands of francs you require, while offering works whose market value is not really what you expect and for you to rely on the publisher's desire to have all your work appear under one imprint, as is true for any publisher, the NRF or anyone else. . . .I ask you to think seriously about all this. There is no doubt that it will be difficult for the NRF to continue in this way, and I believe that it is dangerous for you to try to press matters so far.

Gallimard insisted that the situation had to be regularized as soon as possible, claiming that the large sums paid to Simenon were effectively "a line of credit extended to you by the NRF as a banker would." Finally, he argued that new contract conditions would spare Simenon having to rush through his manuscripts, scrape the bottom of the barrel for material, sell the same copy twice, and flood the market.[101]

Simenon was at his house in Charentes, absorbed in the writing of *Le Bourgmestre de Furnes,* when he received this shocking letter. He was so surprised by the onslaught that he broke one of his rules, suspending work on a novel in progress in order to reply. He adopted the cool and sarcastic tone of a man more hurt than annoyed. Responding point by point, he rebutted the most insulting allegations, rehearsed the history from his point of view, pointed to Gallimard's conflicts of interest as a shareholder in Gallimard, *Marianne,* and Synops, insisted that it was to the publisher's advantage to hold exclusive rights to an author's output, and complained of the derisory promotional budget allocated to his works. He then concluded:

> I am a novelist. I will remain a novelist. I abandoned reportage and press serialization of my works because complete independence is the most important thing to me. I will not chase after these gentlemen of the cinema, wasting most of my time and ruining my work in order to hand more than half my rights income over to an agency, to my publisher, and to the Société des Gens de Lettres. I will sell my books when necessary, when I feel like it, at a price that seems equitable to me, because I alone am responsible for my reputation. . . . I do not have time to concern myself with that [film rights], because I am in the middle of a novel that is far more important, not financially but morally. When I have finished it, we can talk, but I can tell you right now that I will never agree to the notion that a publisher acts as a banker. Each of us takes a risk. Let us take it faithfully. . . .[102]

To Gaston Gallimard, this letter sounded like a "machine gun," and he thought it quite unfair. There was certainly some bad faith on both sides, as well as pride and self-esteem. But the essential thing was that author and publisher had finally lanced the abscess. Gallimard, in his turn, contested Simenon's assertions one by one, while blunting the edge of his initial charges.

For instance, he denied that he meant to say that Simenon was selling him works scraped from the bottom of the barrel: "I only wanted to draw your attention to the difficulty of selling a large number of works by the same author within a given time period. I have observed that the booksellers pay less attention to each title."

As for the real reason for Simenon's print runs, it had nothing to do with promotion, whatever the author may have thought:

> The abundance of your production does not allow each title sufficient time to acquire the resonance it deserves. Publicity is highly ineffective. Books cannot be sold like soap. Word of mouth is the only publicity that counts. I believe the booksellers. I believe travelers. I believe specialized journals. Why don't you realize that this is in my interest even more than yours, because I have to make good on the biggest discovery of the NRF, selling as many of your books as possible. You are right to say that you are a novelist. You could even say that you are most probably the sole true novelist writing today. Really, I fail to understand your mood. Of course you alone are responsible for your own reputation. But is the friendship of your publisher really an obstacle? For me, an author like you can only be a friend, as are all those who helped to establish the NRF. . . .[103]

The emotion of rediscovered friendship gradually gained sway over aggressive commercial considerations. In February 1939 the two men spent several days together at Simenon's house in Nieul-sur-mer. Things went well. Gaston was delighted to sample Boule's cooking. Simenon was pleasantly surprised at the new project his publisher proposed as they strolled through the Charentes countryside: two complete editions of his work, one octavo for libraries and one mass market.[104]

Everything seemed to have worked out for the best. In August, Gaston appended a handwritten postscript to a business letter to Simenon:

"I've just read *Le Bourgmestre de Furnes*. An absolutely remarkable book. One of your best novels. I tell you this with enthusiasm, not only out of friendship, but also as a disinterested reader."[105]

Yet their newfound harmony was fragile, for the merest detail aroused Simenon's suspicion. Once again he became convinced that he was being denied the promotion accorded other authors, such that the books he considered his best—*Chez Krull* (1939), *Le Coup de vague* (The Breaking Wave, 1939), *Le*

Bourgmestre de Furnes (1939), *Malempin* (*The Family Lie,* 1940)—passed "unnoticed."

He complained to Gallimard of an exchange he had had with the owner of a bookstore in the Montparnasse train station in August:

"Do you have the latest Simenon?"

"Simenon? It's been a long time since he published anything."[106]

10

A TIME OF COMMITMENT?

1939–1940

n the spring of 1939, Simenon and Tigy withdrew to a château in Alsace to await an "event"—not the war, or the release of a new book or a film, but the birth of their first child. When Tigy was in her ninth month, however, they suddenly had to leave. A friend of the prefect told Simenon of an impending general mobilization: the evacuation of this sensitive region was days away, perhaps less. So it was that Marc Simenon was born, on April 19, in Uccles, a suburb of Brussels, sixteen years after his parents' marriage.

It had been Tigy's decision to wait. "When all is said and done, she may have done me a great favor," Simenon later admitted, grateful for the complete freedom he had enjoyed during the twenties and thirties.[1] According to Marc, Tigy resolved to have a child only when she decided that her husband was finally mature enough.[2]

The birth turned their lives upside down. Simenon insisted that the baby be baptized—just in case he wanted to marry a Catholic someday. The intensive catechism Tigy had undergone before their marriage was an unpleasant memory. The ceremony was held in the house in Nieul, of which Simenon had recently become the happy owner, having had enough of the artifice of life in Neuilly.

Godparents had to be designated, and though Simenon had earlier promised Raimu, he now picked two of his most prestigious friends: the painter Vlaminck and Professor Lucien Pautrier of Strasbourg, who had spent several summers with the Simenons in Porquerolles and to whom *Le Testament Donadieu* (1937) was dedicated. Vlaminck, however, was Protestant, and his daughter therefore stood in for him at the baptismal font in the small church in Nieul, as music by Bach was played in the background.

Family photographs taken at the time show an emotional father embarrassed and fascinated by "all the innocence and hope a baby represents," as he would write in *Le Fils* (1957).[3] One of his former secretaries, who paid a visit around this time, was struck not only by Simenon's elation but also by the care the parents took to meet any desire that might be expressed by the new baby, who was adulated more than adored.[4] What did fatherhood mean to a man like Simenon? The narrator of *Je me souviens* (1945) calls it a way of assuring affection in one's old age. Many years later, after his death, his three sons would remember him as an extraordinary father.[5]

He was resolutely nonconformist and hostile to petit-bourgeois standards and social conventions, refusing to subject his children to the oppression of authority.

Simenon finally felt in his element in Nieul. He liked the house and the village, and La Rochelle was less than six miles away. That old Huguenot town, until the seventeenth century one of the country's greatest Atlantic ports, was Simenon's favorite French city. He liked everything about it: its colors and odors, its Vermeer-style light, its long arcades, which enabled pedestrians to walk across the city in the rain without getting wet. Omnipresent in *Le Testament Donadieu* (1937), *Le Voyageur de la Toussaint* (*Strange Inheritance*, 1941), and *Les Fantômes du chapelier* (*The Hatter's Ghosts*, 1949), La Rochelle appears in some eighteen of Simenon's novels and short stories.[6]

He also had a favorite spot in this favorite city: the Café de la Paix on the main square. For years this magical site was a kind of refuge for him. He loved its mirrored decor, its marble, its pilasters, its paintings, and its large, round, lights.[7] Pierre Caspescha, the owner of the café and of the adjoining Olympia cinema, became a close friend, embedding an iron ring in the cobblestones for the exclusive use of Simenon's horse. For the novelist, there could have been no more touching testimony to friendship. When he gave Caspescha a copy of *La Tête d'un homme* (1931), he wrote on the flyleaf that he considered him "the most precious of La Rochelle's citizens." Much later, in 1966, he called his years in La Rochelle and its environs "the happiest period of my life." He often told the Caspeschas that he had two homelands: Belgium, because he was born there, and La Rochelle, because he had chosen it.

He finally had the sense that he had attained an inner harmony. He had a wife apparently fulfilled by maternity and a child who was a source of unsuspected happiness. He felt that his writing was coming closer to perfection with each novel. Gide was symbolically at his side, sending him warm encouragement from wherever he happened to be, whether the Rue Vaneau in

Paris or the Temple of Luxor in Egypt. He hailed the austere inevitability of the structure of *Long Cours* (1936) and likened *Le Cheval-Blanc* (*The White Horse Inn,* 1938) to a musical theme. And he repeated how mysterious he still found Simenon: "I really do not understand *how* you conceive, compose, and write your books."[8] Encouraged by Gide's unflagging enthusiasm, Simenon was as happy as could be. The same could not be said of Europe.

Nine in the morning, September 1, 1939. Hitler's troops cross the Polish border. Simenon hears the news an hour later in the Café de la Paix, where he is having a drink with his young secretary, Annette de Bretagne. The customers are stunned.

Two days later, France follows Britain in declaring war on Germany. Simenon is dumbfounded. Back home in Nieul, surrounded by Tigy and Marc, Boule and Annette, he reacts instinctively, in his own way. Bringing champagne up from the cellar, he proposes a toast: not to hail the onset of the war or Belgium's momentary neutrality, but "to give ourselves the courage to look the future in the face."[9]

It might be supposed that from this point on Simenon, like the rest of his generation, would live not at his own rhythm but to the pace of the events shaking Europe.[10] But that would be true only in part, for even in these exceptional conditions, Simenon was still Simenon, a novelist absorbed in his own work.

"I am ashamed to admit that I am more anxious about your opinion than about the war communiqués," he wrote to Gide.[11]

To ease his nervousness and fill the time, he wrote two novels he was not sure he would be able to publish: *Il pleut, bergère* (*Black Rain,* 1941) and *Oncle Charles s'est enfermé* (Uncle Charles Has Locked Himself Away, 1942).[12] Gaston Gallimard, with what remained of the NRF general staff, had withdrawn to Mirande, in the English Channel, taking the files and accounts with him. There he continued to work. Upon receiving the manuscript of *Bergelon* (*The Country Doctor,* 1941), another of Simenon's novels written in 1939, he managed to send him 5,000 francs by telegraph. Preparation for the gloomy days to come. But Simenon was worried for his family.[13]

Since he lived near the naval front, he was not permitted to telephone other *départements.* All calls had to go through a control commission, and he knew he would be cut off the moment he broached any subject other than "business" narrowly defined. Moreover, as a foreigner he was not allowed to leave Charente-Maritime and the Vendée. At his urgent request, Gallimard appealed to the journalist Marius Larique, director of the weekly *Détective,* asking that he intercede with higher authorities to get permission for "this important house author" to travel to Paris. In vain.[14]

Simenon was stuck. He expected to be drafted at any moment, but he had no intention of volunteering: "So long as the threat to our homes is not clearer and sharper, I feel no obligation to rush headlong toward heroism," he confided to Gide.[15]

Despite his belated "anarchist" professions of faith,[16] Simenon was and would always remain a man of the right. The milieu in which he grew up, his education, his formative years, his intellectual awakening at the *Gazette de Liège* under the tutelage of Joseph Demarteau and later under the influence of Binet-Valmer and the marquis de Tracy all linked him to a current of thought whose reflexes he unconsciously preserved even when he did not deliberately adopt its attitudes. His political sentiments (feelings more than ideas) were remarkably consistent—from his journalism of the twenties to his novels to the memoirs he wrote or dictated in the autumn of his life.

Populist and conservative rather than reactionary, he was not free of contradiction. Though he abhorred rituals and conventions, he was a devotee of order. He detested change and ceaselessly praised immobility. The more he traveled and moved from house to house, the more he drifted into a nostalgia for roots, land, and family, tokens of stability for a man ever haunted by a vagabond's vertigo.

The myth of the "noble provinces," a pendant to that of the "noble savage," is recurrent in his work. This fundamentally unstable man, who never managed to find his place in society despite efforts sometimes tinged with pathos, nevertheless cherished the illusion of an Old Europe of indestructible, immanent values. This imaginary region, buried deep in his memory and peopled with craftsmen, peasants, and nobles, was a world resolutely hostile to progress and the machine age, to industrial society and technology.

This was the only universe in which he felt safe. His famous quest for man unclothed, which he liked to call the alpha and omega of his work, was part and parcel of this outlook. His nostalgia for a golden age took the form of an inchoate yearning for the rediscovery of a vanished world that in his mind embodied the innocence of childhood. Social discipline horrified him, but his own life was discipline itself. He claimed to be a citizen of the world, but he was constantly assailed by fits of nationalism, which reminded him that he was Belgian above all else. His values were so rigid that what millions of "ordinary people" like his characters saw as progress (paid vacations, for instance, granted by the Popular Front government in 1936), he saw as a threat.

Politicians aroused his ire. The time he had spent with them in the corridors of power during his days as a reporter left indelible images in his memory. One in particular often came to mind: the Café de Paris, across from the Opéra. Baron Edmond, patriarch of the Rothschilds, would mount his private stairway to the mezzanine, where he would receive visitors as though he owned the place, while "the king"—Georges Mandel, minister of the interior, a post that put him in charge of "the garbage can of the republic"—held court on the floor below, wielding the occult power of his portfolio to subjugate the citizenry.[17]

What Simenon "hated" was not so much politics as political action. He would never see a polling booth except on television. As far as he was concerned, the people who exercised the arrogant profession of politician were swindlers and liars naturally inclined to despise others. In his system of moral values, where human dignity held pride of place, there was no place for such people, who were no more than mediocrities bloated with ambition.[18]

He "hated"—and the word is no exaggeration, he used it often in radio interviews—all great international associations, whether communist, capitalist, or cosmopolitan. He was a convinced advocate of the myth of "the two hundred families who control France." He believed that great international companies, breeding ground of stateless capitalism and anonymous vagabond fortunes, had supplanted governments in their will for world domination.[19]

Much of his work bears witness to this antiparliamentary, anticapitalist, and antiliberal attitude. It can be seen clearly in his articles, especially those on his cinematic misadventures, where speculators of foreign origin come in for special denunciation.

But examples can also be taken from his novels. "There are crooks in politics, and the worst they risk is to be named ministers," Georges Sim wrote in *Les Cœurs perdus* (Lost Hearts, 1928).[20] "Then you were a banker," Inspector Maigret says to one Atoum, a rug merchant of indeterminate nationality, in *Les Caves du Majestic* (1942), "because in France, too, a clean police record is not required of those who handle the citizens' money."[21] And in *Le Président* (*The Premier,* 1958), the narrator observes that no one could remain in the corridors of power as long as Augustin, a former head of government, "without witnessing countless acts of cowardice and countless villainies."[22]

Simenon's individualism was rooted in a fear of having to grapple with immediate history, which aroused anguish in a man who never managed to find his place in a world in constant motion. He feared being unable to grasp its essence in the heat of events:

"History is an everyday thing, and the importance of events becomes clear only after the fact," the memorialist later wrote. "One cannot live with History, or rather, one cannot live History. One lives one's own little life, the life of a group, of an instant of humanity, an instant in the life of the world."[23]

Yet there were times when he feared that his endeavors were pretentious, vain, and ill-timed:

"The globe is giving birth to History. And you, blind insect, sublime cretin, you invite people to read your little stories of other people, everyday and everytime people, people who come and go with their second-rate feelings and petty hopes, as though they were not participants, whether they like it or not, in the most prodigious of adventures. . . . I raised my spirits by persuading myself that people do not live History with a capital *H*, but their own histories."[24]

Later, possibly out of embarrassment at his passivity during the war, he often claimed that he had refused to allow his novels to be translated and published in Germany after Hitler's advent to power.[25] The truth is that in 1938 and 1939, Simenon was quite willing to sell rights to his books and articles to newspapers and publishers beyond the Rhine. If no contracts were signed, it was not for moral or political reasons. He explained to his translator, Franz Winckler,[26] that in Germany, as elsewhere, he wanted to sell rights to the entirety of his work instead of dealing book by book. He was even clearer with Robert Aron, who was in charge of subsidiary rights at Gallimard:

"I believe that at this time I have no interest in allowing German translations to appear, and that we must wait until the situation changes to authorize a serious complete edition, as I have just now obtained in England."[27]

Nowhere in his correspondence with German interlocutors, whether agents, translators, or publishers, does he allude to the political situation. What mattered to him most was that "the entirety of my work" be published and that he be able to collect the consequent royalties.

Simenon's frenzied individualism, however, did not make him wholly immune to history's grip. On two occasions prior to 1940 he emerged from his ivory tower to confront the upheavals of the epoch—in his way.

The newspapers with which he collaborated between the wars were politically diverse. He was quite capable of signing contracts with leftist (*Marianne, Le Populaire*) and rightist (*Candide, Paris-Soir*) papers at the same time. But he leaned more often right than left, and sometimes far to the right, as in his series "Peuples misérables," published by the *Revue de l'Ordre corporatif,* a reactionary journal of some intellectual quality. What was important to him at the time was to be published, noticed, and paid. But in 1935, after municipal elections that brought a leftist victory, he went a bit further.

Six months earlier, the very reverend monsignor the count of Paris had launched *Courrier royal,* first as a monthly, then a weekly. Above the masthead was a slogan coined by the count's father, the duke of Guise: "The monarchy is not a party." The legatee of the House of France and pretender to the throne intended to play a role in the country's future and was preparing to assume his rightful place. But to rally the faithful and improve his image he first had to wrest the monarchist cause from the grip of a particular organization, Action Française, and a particular man, Charles Maurras.

The tone of his journal would therefore be as moderate and tolerant as the militants of Action Française were aggressive and polemical. In the face of the mounting peril, the count of Paris felt that it was urgent to lead the partisans of royal restoration out of the ideological ghetto in which they had confined themselves. He wanted to warn against the perverse fascination with European dictatorships to which the French adepts of fundamentalist nationalism were prone. He knew that his approach would eventually trigger a crisis leading to fratricidal struggle, but that was the only way to curb Maurras's intellectual hegemony over the monarchist ideal.[28]

Its disagreements with Action Française, however, did not make *Courrier royal* any less corporatist, antiliberal, anticapitalist, and antidemocratic. It simply lacked its rival's doctrinal rigor and political intransigence. It preferred to unite rather than divide, but its essential content was as counterrevolutionary as Maurras's *Enquête sur la monarchie*. The main difference was in the tone.[29] *Courrier royal* did not hurl insults.

Henri VI, count of Paris, twenty-seven years old, lived on his estate in Anjou, near Brussels, exiled by the June 1886 law that denied access to the territory of the French Republic to all heads of families who had formerly reigned in France and to their direct descendants, in order of primogeniture. In the Belgian capital he had an office on the Avenue Eugène-Demolder, which he shared with Pierre de La Rocque, one of his closest collaborators. Meanwhile, Edouard de La Rocque held the fort in Paris. These two defectors from Action Française were brothers of Colonel François de La Rocque, president of the powerful organization of holders of the Croix-de-Feu.

In August 1935, as they were getting ready to turn *Courrier royal* into a weekly, the brothers de La Rocque began looking for a prestigious collaborator outside their own circles. At the count's suggestion, they approached Simenon and explained their project:

"It [the journal] intends to be the publication that will express both princely thought in the realm of politics and the reality of a toiling, artistic, and intelligent people whose efforts are now penalized in the absence of a regime rewarding all its qualities," they wrote.[30]

Three months later the editor in chief of *Courrier royal* visited Simenon to discuss his collaboration. He was offered the lower-right quarter of the front page for a column to be entitled "Histoires de partout et d'ailleurs." Enthusiastic at the prospect of a new regular outlet, the novelist agreed to write about what he saw, heard, and experienced in the course of his great travels.

He declined to produce anything overtly political. Most often his column was a series of brief notes, stories that, in the view of their author himself, "probably prove nothing."[31] His role was simply to amuse the reader, and his articles were for the most part harmless. But sometimes they complemented the less harmless viewpoint of the magazine's editors. For instance, citing an American's offhand remark about the imminent demise of Latin civilization, he commented: "I observed him carefully, for he had a funny accent. He may have lived in a building in New York, but something about him seemed familiar. I soon discovered what it was: he had been born in Vilnius. He was a Polish Jew."[32]

Simenon was well aware of *Courrier royal*'s content. He not only approved of its political orientation but actively supported it, even making financial sacrifices, which was hardly his habit. The editor in chief was quite delighted: "I told Mr. de La Rocque that you were pleased to collaborate with *Courrier royal,* under conditions that reflect true dedication to the royal cause. He will inform Monsignor the count of Paris. We are most grateful to you. . . . P.S.: I told Mr. de La Rocque that you would be happy to be received by Monsignor the count of Paris."[33]

Simenon agreed to discounted reimbursement for his articles and sent contributions to the "royal" social service agency for disadvantaged inhabitants of the suburbs. These did not go unnoticed: "your generosity far surpasses the average, not only in the elegance of the gesture but also in the amount of the donation."[34] The prince asked his editor in chief to convey to the novelist how touched he was by "the exceptionally generous terms" of his precious collaboration: "It is in large part thanks to you that subscriptions and sales of the paper are developing as they are."[35]

Everything seemed to be going well, but three months later, Simenon asked to withdraw from the project. The count of Paris, troubled, took the opportunity to thank the novelist for his dedication to their cause.[36] Simenon replied by suggesting that his columns might be too "soft" to respond to the increasingly tense political situation. The count hastened to reassure him, granting him an audience in Brussels.[37]

The meeting was postponed several times, but the play adapted from *Quartier nègre* finally provided an opportunity, Monsignor the count of Paris honoring the "dress rehearsal" with his presence. After the promised audience, they met for lunch at the Plaza to get better acquainted. The count retained a clear recollection of their conversation.

"It was my idea to give him that column," he explained. "I was looking for a talented columnist to increase sales of the paper, I had read and appreciated several of his novels, and in his statements I had detected sympathy for the monarchist and royalist cause. I had guessed his convictions from his writings and his reputation in Brussels, and I was not mistaken. We began by discussing the deterioration of the situation in France, talking politics before getting down to the essential matter. Very much attached to our cause, he made a point of his disapproval of the line upheld by Action Française. He wanted to help me. His Belgian temperament made him loyal to Albert I, the *roi-chevalier,* and to Léopold III, who had just succeeded him, and he transferred to me the sentiments he held for him. In any event, by the end of our conversation I was in no doubt whatever about his desire to aid in a monarchist restoration."[38]

A year after this meeting, the duke of Guise published a "Manifesto to the

French" condemning Action Française. *Courrier royal*'s readership quickly plummeted, and Simenon's collaboration grew increasingly sporadic.

The episode had no official sequel. Many years later, asked his opinion of democracy, he replied, "Christian democracy has all the defects of both religion and false democracy."[39] The filter of memory had done its work, softening his prewar political sensibility. In 1938 he had given this reply to a journalist who pressed him to explain his endorsement of the monarchist movement: "I love ordinary people, real ones, and I am therefore horrified by democracy."[40]

Simenon became politically active again after the publication of *Le Testament Donadieu,* but in an even more surprising fashion. During a stroll in Beauce in late 1937, he and his friend Lucien Descaves (of *Le Journal* and the Goncourt Academy) talked about the political situation. Simenon's feelings seemed very different from those he had expressed in *Courrier royal* less than two years earlier. He was now disgusted by the rise of violence in the streets, the general spread of intolerance, and the militancy of the far right. He feared that politics would eventually corrupt ethics, and he wanted to do something about it. But what? His idea was simple: oppose hatred.

"It seems to me there ought to be a way of raising a mute but steadfast resistance to hate, a kind of permanent dam to hold back the flow of pus," he told Descaves.[41]

He recalled having seen people in Switzerland wearing badges that said, "Don't talk about the depression," and he wondered whether a similar campaign might be launched in France under the slogan "SH" (*Sans Haine,* Without Hatred).

An insignia was designed—the two letters against the background of a sun and a dove—even before a patron was found to finance the project, and the badges went on sale at the headquarters of *Le Journal* and at kiosks owned by the Hachette distribution service. They cost one franc each. The promotional posters bore the message: "I have my ideas and you have yours; let us express them without hatred." A long article by Lucien Descaves in *Le Journal* announced the campaign to the public in early 1938. The regional press picked up the theme under the watchword "Pillory Hatred," and statements of support began pouring in from celebrities. For good reason: Who could possibly object?

But some skeptics did express reservations. The two vertical bars of the *H* embedded in the *S* were uncomfortably reminiscent of a dollar sign. Others doubted that an insignia arousing irony would have much effect in countering the terror inspired by two other common alphabetic symbols, SA and SS. The journalist Georges Blond suggested that in private Simenon wore a badge reading "SB," for *Sans Blague* (No Kidding).[42] There was considerable suspicion about his motives. More indulgent observers ascribed his campaign to naïveté, while the more cynical considered him the point man for the Simenon Party.

But the message did get out, and profits from the sale of badges went to the Red Cross. At a time when France was torn by extremism ("whoever is not with us is against us" was a common attitude), public-spiritedness took the form of "SH" buttons, tietacks, brooches, or pendants, in plastic, embossed leather, or even gold or diamonds.

In February an SH insignia was presented to Albert Lebrun, the president of the Republic and a member of the committee of sponsors, along with Marshal Pétain, Cardinal Verdier, Pastor Boegner, Rabbi Levi, the president of the Société des Gens de Lettres, the secretary of the French Academy, the commander of the Boy Scouts of France, and so on.

But some of the press was less than respectful: "One sees certain Gentlemen strolling down the boulevards of Paris wearing SH insignia. They seem not to think they look ridiculous." That was good old Jean Paulhan, writing under a pseudonym in Gallimard's review.[43]

More than a decade later, in *Les Mémoires de Maigret* (1951), Simenon observed that although the inspector had no wish to excuse criminals, he did try to observe them with insight. And: "Without hatred, of course."[44] That may well be all he retained of this stillborn experience.

Events moved rapidly after the Wehrmacht's invasion of Holland, Belgium, and Luxembourg in May 1940.

In Nieul, Simenon waited to be drafted. Belgium had ordered a general mobilization, and he managed to find his old military records, but not his uniform. No matter. He put on his horseback-riding costume (riding pants, thick sweater, jacket). With a bit of imagination, it had a military air. Then he headed for Paris.

A loudspeaker at the train station urged Belgians to report to their embassy in the Madeleine quarter. Simenon did so, but the atmosphere was too highly charged, and he was unable to get any clear information. He then went to the Quai d'Orsay, not the Ministry of Foreign Affairs but the home of Charley Delmas, a friend from La Rochelle. He sank into an armchair in her apartment, his head in his hands.

"War is no fun," he said, "but I'll wage it with everyone else. The worst thing is leaving my wife and son."[45]

He went back to the Rue de Surène, where the embassy was surrounded by crowds of Belgian citizens as disoriented as their diplomats. Elbowing his way inside, he found chaos, rumors, and denials of rumors. He finally managed to get in to see Carton de Wiart, who asked about his relations with various officials and notables in La Rochelle and its environs. Exceptional circumstances called for instinctive decisions, and de Wiart informed Simenon of his intention to phone the minister of the interior:

"I'm sure he will agree to appoint you high commissioner for Belgian refugees. You seem to be well acquainted with the region all the way to Bordeaux. Thousands of Belgians are already en route, and they will be channeled to La Rochelle. It will be your task to greet them. You have carte blanche, including the authority to resettle them in the region and the right of requisition. Leave tonight and get in touch with the prefect and the mayor tomorrow. I'll notify them. That's an order, Private Simenon."[46]

The question of commitment was thereby taken out of his hands. The military situation was hopeless: Belgium had already been invaded. But the diplomat had made him an offer he could not refuse. At the age of thirty-seven, for the first time in his adult life, the fanatical individualist would serve others.

On May 14 the Wehrmacht penetrated the French front, opening a breach between Sedan and Namur. It was the turning point in the blitzkrieg. German armored divisions rolled toward the Paris basin. On that day, as the flow of Belgian refugees into the La Rochelle station grew steadily larger, Pierre-Alype, the prefect of Charente-Inférieure, agreed to set up a reception center. The Quai d'Orsay approved. For the moment, the ministry had two priorities: to make the best possible use of the refugees and to prevent certain of them from doing any harm. In other words, to greet them was to control them. But it was essential not to make them feel "penned in" like suspects. They must not develop an interned mentality. Homesickness, discontent, and lassitude could be exploited by enemy propaganda.[47]

Between May 14 and May 28 the prime concern of the refugees was to get settled in and to get news of home. The center Simenon set up in La Rochelle began working immediately. It was supported by various personalities who agreed to serve on an honorary committee: apart from the prefect, there was the mayor, Léonce Vieljeux; the bishop of the diocese, Monsignor Liagre; General Eon; the Belgian consul, Brumaud des Houlières; and the military quartermaster, Auricostte.

The novelist quickly became a high commissioner, in fact if not in name, revealing an unexpected flair for organization and aptitude for command. A team of four women aided him in countless daily tasks: Madame Blanche, a nurse; Yolande de Meyenbourg, a guide; Madame Beckers; and Lina, the seventeen-year-old daughter of his friend Pierre Caspescha, owner of the Café de la Paix.

They, he said, were "the real soul of the center from start to finish," although others soon pitched in, notably four Belgian scouts from one of the arriving trains and Simenon's brother-in-law, Yvan Renchon, who came from Brussels with his family.[48]

Some Belgians went by car directly to Royan, a tourist town on the Atlantic coast, and Simenon set up another reception committee there to make sure they were not cut off from their compatriots in La Rochelle.

When the makeshift barracks repainted in Belgian colors opposite La Rochelle train station was packed to bursting, Simenon began lodging new arrivals in schools, in surrounding villages, and in Fétilly. Thanks to support from the local population and the energy of Madame Bigois and the Abbot Crampette, some three hundred refugees were given food and shelter.

It need hardly be added that Simenon was unable to write during these exhilarating, exhausting weeks. He would go home to Nieul to get some sleep when he could, returning at dawn behind the wheel of his lemon-yellow Citroën. But he spent many nights on a bench at the center, often being awakened by the emergency telephone line that had been installed.

To the eighteen thousand or so haggard and disoriented Belgians who eventually gathered in Charente-Inférieure, Simenon was no longer a famous novelist but the man they turned to for help with the thousand and one problems that inevitably arise in an improvised transit camp: the distribution of newspapers, gasoline coupons, and baby bottles; the care of the sick; the establishment of an exchange office; the replenishment of supplies; liaison with the camp police; the organization of a moral assistance service; the registration of every arriving refugee (in triplicate); the quest for information about missing persons; the explanation of contradictory reports; the settlement of the travelers who poured off trains; the establishment of a sanitation service under the direction of Belgian doctors; the temporary placement of Belgian workers in the arms factories of La Pallice and Aytre and of farmers, lumberjacks, bakers, and dockers who could not be left idle. Four days after it opened, the center had a budget of 90,000 francs, donated by the Red Cross and several private benefactors.[49]

And all this despite the fact that Charente-Inférieure had not been officially designated one of the *départements* slated to receive Belgian refugees, who were supposed to have gone to Saône-et-Loire, the Allier, Ardèche, Haute-Garonne, and the Côte d'Or.

On May 28 the refugees were rocked by news even more damaging to their morale than an explosion. King Léopold III, commander in chief of the Belgian armed forces, had surrendered unconditionally. Although the government declared his decision "devoid of legal standing," there was general consternation. The king's defection plunged the exiled population into depression and aroused the indignation of refugees in uniform. Officers complained openly of dishonor. Their tone was increasingly Francophilic. They referred to the "ex-king" and his "felony." Their opinions were discreetly tracked at the Hotel Thermal in Vichy, where officials of the postal service opened and analyzed the letters of Belgian refugees.[50]

Léopold's capitulation changed nothing for Simenon. His concern was primarily humanitarian, and like a lawyer or a physician, he saw neither good nor bad clients, but simply refugees in need. Well, almost. For while he made it a point of honor to receive everyone regardless of nationality, be they Belgian, Italian, or even French, he had a problem with a group of Jews. Since he did not consider them Belgian, he refused to treat them as refugees until ordered to do so by higher authority.

The refugees in question were Jewish diamond merchants from Antwerp, a redundant formulation to judge by the characters in several of his novels: Ephraïm Goldsmit, Isaac Goldberg, Michel Goldfinger, Victor Krulak.[51] In fact, in 1939 about a third of Antwerp's six thousand diamond merchants were Jews. They planned to evacuate to Cognac in the event of a German invasion, but in the confusion of the exodus they wound up in Royan.[52]

Simenon felt it necessary to refer to this episode twice in his *Mémoires intimes* (1981). "An order from the Ministry of the Interior informed me that Royan was reserved for the diamond merchants of Antwerp, who would administer themselves," he writes. And more than four hundred pages later: ". . . I received from Minister Mandel an order to reserve the city exclusively for Belgian refugee diamond merchants."[53] But his report of the mission written for the prefect at the end of the summer of 1940 gives a very different account of the incident:

"Finally, on the order of Mr. Mandel, then minister of the interior, Royan was compelled to accept about 1,200 diamond merchants from Antwerp. I observed—and reported to you at the appropriate time—that less than a quarter of them were Belgians. They were almost exclusively stateless Israelites."[54]

That was probably true. But why did it matter to a man who claimed to be willing and able to accept all refugees without distinction?

June 17, three days after the German entry into Paris, the Paul Reynaud government resigned, and the new president of the council, Marshal Pétain, formed a cabinet and withdrew to Bordeaux. His first act was to seek armistice terms from the Germans and Italians. He then took to the airwaves to explain himself.

The Belgian refugees in La Rochelle and its environs were jubilant. They believed that demobilization and a return to their homes were at hand. Belgians and French drew closer in misfortune and defeat.[55] Many factories closed, and the exiles began going home, on foot, by car, by train. Convoys were improvised. By mid-July you could make a reservation on the Paris-to-Brussels train and pay for it just like before.

The last of the Belgian refugees in La Rochelle left the city on August 6. Three days later, Simenon closed the reception center and returned the key to the prefecture. His mission was over. The citizen could now return to his writing.

People who spent these three exceptional months alongside him testify to the qualities he displayed. Powerful friendships were born in those tragic times, in "distressing and sometimes magnificent circumstances," as he acknowledged in a dedication.[56]

It is not clear whether the Belgian embassy ever officially appointed him high commissioner for refugees. His name does not appear on the list of high commissioners drawn up by the Quai d'Orsay. But as the Belgian consul pointed out, in practice Simenon was the "mainspring" of the enterprise.[57] Lina Caspescha in particular testifies to his complete selflessness in this endeavor.[58] Pierre Bonardi, a journalist who observed him in the heat of action, mentions "superhuman devotion."[59] Mr. Wansele, who led a fishing fleet from Ostende to La Pallice in the last days of May 1940, would never forget Simenon's efforts:

"Working day and night, always on the go, in his convertible, accompanied by the lady nurse, he tried to house the refugees with the inhabitants of the region and even farther away, in the farms, because the bombing was getting worse and worse. Everyone wondered about Simenon: When did he eat? When did he sleep? He was satisfied only when he saw packed buses driving off into the neighboring countryside. You can't imagine the ingenuity it took, or all the different things you had to do at times like that, to get hold of the necessary vehicles, gas, and food."[60]

Simenon would never forget, either. Circumstances had enabled him to outdo himself, to exhibit a civic and community spirit previously unknown to him. Human brotherhood in action—it was a revelation.[61] How was his work marked by the experience?

Although *Le Fils* (1957) is set in La Rochelle in 1940—"a date that seems to cut history in two"[62]—and *La Patience de Maigret* (*The Patience of Maigret*, 1965) depicts the bombing of Douai, the events of these three months are reflected primarily in two other novels: *Le Clan des Ostendais* (*The Ostenders*, 1947) and *Le Train* (*The Train*, 1961).

The characters of *Le Clan des Ostendais* were directly inspired by the events of 1940. As Simenon admitted in private,[63] this novel was based on his encounter with Wansele, the captain of the fishing fleet (four boats with 150 people, including crew and families) that left Ostende on May 16 for Fleetwood in the north of England but arrived twelve days later at the port of La Pallice.

The main character in the novel, Omer Petermans, a taciturn Fleming of about fifty, is the captain of a fishing trawler, very much the master of his feelings, and head of his clan. He continues to fish from La Rochelle, where he and his family live through the exodus and the beginning of the Occupation. As the spokesman for his group, he is also a link between French and Germans. Stoic and withdrawn, he endures the misfortunes of tragic times—boats sunk by mines, sailors lost in shipwrecks, ambiguous relations with the invaders— until finally he decides to lead his family secretly to England. Despite everything, he manages to save his clan, or what's left of it.

Everything Simenon saw and experienced during these three months appears in the novel: the reception center; the difficulty of communicating when your only language is Flemish; the unpleasant sensation of being considered "beasts in a zoological garden"; the spirit of the French, who always considered themselves more clever than everyone else; the separatist mentality of the Flemings, who wanted to continue to live free of rules set by others; the mayor of the city, himself a shipowner; the way news spread among the exiles; King Léopold III's "betrayal"; the desire for autonomy manifested by the women; the crates of fish generously donated to the reception center; the feverish, frightened entreaties and lamentations of the Antwerp diamond merchants ready to pay cash for a boat with which to escape to England.[64]

What he did not put into *Le Clan des Ostendais* later went into *Le Train*. But while the two novels were equally successful, the second caused him far more pain.

The life of its hero, Marcel Féron, a timid, nondescript merchant from the Ardennes, about thirty years old, would be turned upside down by the exceptional conditions of the exodus. He would act and react as never before, not out of a spirit of sacrifice or spontaneous idealism, but to be a better man in the eyes of his children.

On May 10, as he is about to embark on a train packed with civilians in the chaos of the evacuation, he is separated from his wife, seven months pregnant, and his young daughter. They wind up in a first-class compartment, while he is far behind in a cattle car. En route the train is uncoupled, and they are separated more definitively. During this journey into the unknown, Féron meets Anna Kupfer, a Czech Jew of about twenty who has just been released from prison. They go through tense moments of bombing together, and though they know little of each other's lives, they are finally joined in both mind and body. When he gets to the station in La Rochelle, Féron manages to track down his family. He leaves Anna and resumes his former life. Later, during the Occupation, she suddenly reappears, upsetting his snug existence. She is on the run from the German police, and she needs help. Will he sacrifice his family's security for her? Anna realizes his dilemma and disappears. Some weeks later, he learns that she has been shot.

Apart from the gripping factual details, *Le Train* is remarkable primarily for what it reveals of how Simenon viewed the events of the summer of 1940: war as a personal encounter between man and his destiny; the cowardly relief manifested at the announcement of the armistice; the way life changes in a city in turmoil; the satisfaction of finding food and the anger of going hungry; and finally, the abolition of time, collapse of social conventions, and eclipsing of egotism in circumstances in which nothing occurs on a merely individual scale.

Simenon usually let a memory ripen for several years before resuscitating it in his writing, but in this case he felt an obsessive desire to produce this novel as early as July 1940. It was initially entitled *La Gare* (The Station), since his intention was to recount the war as seen from a station platform. Images writhed before his eyes, but when he sat down at his typewriter, he found himself unable to achieve a "state of grace." He would have preferred to take some distance from the events, but could not resist the compulsion to write this tragic story while the memory was still fresh. He was haunted by the theme: "a terrible yet magnificent subject that scares me a little."[65] He made a second attempt to write *La Gare* in September 1940, as this intense interlude in his life drew to a definitive close. Once again he could not manage it. "It's too soon. Maybe in a few months."[66]

The day would come when he would be able to write this novel that he was carrying within himself. Twenty-one years later.

In the meantime, he passed the hours visiting the region's bookstores. He had a feeling that reading would be a great escape from the war, and he wrote to Gallimard to suggest a new promotional poster:

HAVE YOU READ
ALL
THE SIMENONS?
(followed by a list of the NRF titles)
YOU WILL THIS WINTER![67]

Once again he had guessed right. The hour of commitment had passed. Simenon was his sensible self again.

11

OCCUPATION

1940–1944

s Europe went to war, Simenon's sole concern was to find personal peace. He would spend four years fleeing the Occupation by burrowing deeper into the French countryside, more determined than ever to escape the anguish, division, and conflict of History in the mad hope that he could seal himself off in a universe of stability, harmony, and unity. There he would pursue the goal he had failed to reach with *Le Testament Donadieu:* produce his great novel.

It has been said that the Occupation was one of those exceptional times that bring the qualities and defects of those who live it into the sharpest possible relief. Georges Simenon was no exception to that rule.

In the late summer of 1940 the Simenon family left La Rochelle for a farm in the Vouvant forest in the Vendée. His mission with the refugees now over, he returned to work, writing *La Vérité sur Bébé Donge (The Trial of Bébé Donge,* 1942). But it was not so easy to become a novelist again. He was so worried about his financial problems that his day-to-day activities were paralyzed. Foreign publishers could no longer make royalty payments, and the French publishing and film industries had not yet adapted to the new situation. His lifestyle being what it was, Simenon looked forward to the end of the year with undisguised dread. He had been harried by the threat of want ever since leaving Liège seventeen years earlier. Now that threat was all the more intolerable, for he had a family to support.

He had some reason for panic, since his liquid resources were few and there was nothing in the pipeline. He would have made a total of 232,500 francs in

1940, less than in 1939, which was already a bad year in which he had to dip into his savings to make ends meet. That was no longer possible. The "receipts" scrupulously recorded in Tigy's black notebook show that Simenon's income was more or less at its 1930 or 1931 level, before Maigret and the movies, far below the "vintage" year of 1934, for which a grand total of 717,216 francs was listed.

Publishing was still his major source of revenue, the press and films filling in the rest. Since payments from America and Britain were now cut off, he turned to Gallimard. In early September, while Gaston was still away, he wrote to Brice Parain, the company's general secretary for current accounts. Pride and self-esteem were thrown to the winds. Not long ago he was still playing hard to get with the NRF, but now he was a man at bay. "I am just about at the end of my tether," he admitted.[1]

Unfortunately, Gallimard, like most other publishers, took a wait-and-see attitude. Temporarily shut down by the Occupation, the firm would reopen in late November, by which time management of *La Nouvelle Revue française* would have been entrusted to the fascist writer Pierre Drieu La Rochelle, in conformity with the wishes of the Propaganda Abteilung. Authors would then be able to collect royalties again.

But Simenon could not afford to wait. The sums he got from Gallimard or *Gringoire* would not be enough to satisfy his creditors and assure his family a decent end to the year. With a heavy heart, he therefore decided to take a big step backward, offering his services to third-class magazines. The illustrious Simenon, determined to devote himself exclusively to his great novel, was instead reduced to accepting—even to seeking—bread-and-butter assignments in the hope that three months of this diet would take him through to better days.

He would never forget this humiliation, for which he held Gaston Gallimard largely responsible. Despite the mitigating circumstances, Simenon would not forgive him for being out of reach for several weeks, for sending him a mere 5,000 francs to tide him over, and for not taking the necessary steps to reopen the house sooner. Gallimard, however, was used to unjust complaints from his authors.

At the end of the year Gaston invited Simenon to his home on the Rue Saint-Lazare (the NRF offices being too insecure). There they had a long chat. Simenon was still annoyed, but he reassured his publisher: yes, he had visited *Notre Cœur* and several other similar magazines just to make the point, but he had not sold any rights to his work.[2]

His "mercenary task" consisted mainly in writing "Annette et la dame blonde," an inane, insipid story published by *Pour Elle,* a women's weekly on the Rue Pierre-Charron.[3] He did not want Gallimard to release a book version of this piece of fluff.[4] Gaston promised to send Simenon 25,000 francs at the new year—for starters. That was enough to tide him over. He would now be able to return to the only thing that mattered to him: his work.[5]

Fontenay-Le-Comte, in the Vendée, never recovered from the Empire's humiliating transfer of the prefecture to La Roche-sur-Yon. In the sixteenth century it had been an intellectual center. In the twentieth it subsisted on the memory of the few Fontenaisians who had achieved national glory, like the mathematician François Viètre and the magistrate Nicolas Rapin, better known as a poet and coauthor of *La Satire Ménippée* (1594).

It was to this city that Simenon moved in the autumn of 1940. After a brief stay in comfortable quarters rented from the lawyer Jacques Chaumel at 12 Quai Victor-Hugo, he was delighted to discover the jewel in the local crown: the Château Terre-Neuve. Its owner was Count Alain du Fontenioux, local landlord and president of the chamber of agriculture. Simenon went to see him.

"They tell me the Germans now occupying part of your residence are about to leave for Russia."

"Yes."

"I would like to take their place."

"By all means. I prefer you to whoever will surely come after them."

"I can assure you that if I'm living at your place, they won't come back."[6]

Simenon, Tigy, Marc, and Boule, along with a maid and a nanny, would spend the next two years in the privileged surroundings of this château—for the modest sum of about 500 francs a month.

Located on the outskirts of the city, Terre-Neuve had been built in the late sixteenth century for Nicolas Rapin, who received some of the great intellectual figures of the Renaissance there. Later, the estate was bought by Lazarist missionaries, who, in the nineteenth century, ceded it to the count of Vassé, the deputy mayor. It was his grandson Octave de Rochebrune, a sculptor and etcher who died in 1900, who restored the edifice to glory, adding architectural structures, art objects, and furnishings donated by or purchased or recovered from other decaying châteaux. The porch and the ceiling of individually carved stone coffers came from the Château Coulonges-les-Royaux, the monumental fireplace with the mantel carved with alchemical symbols from the Château Coulonges-sur-l'Autize, the Louis XIV paneling and the door of the dining hall from the workshop of Francis I in Chambord.

The façade of Terre-Neuve was adorned with terra-cotta statues of the nine muses of the Italian Renaissance. Above the door the poet had had verses inscribed that accurately captured the spirit of the site:

Winds of all seasons,
Smile upon this house,

That never fever nor pestilence,
Nor evils born of excess,
Nor envy, quarrel, and trial
Shall beset those who dwell here.

The seventeenth- and eighteenth-century furnishings were as lavish as the exterior: a Louis XVI bed and inlaid Dutch writing desk, a clock given as a gift from the king, a branched torchère and a Persian carpet, Chinese crockery from the East India Company, a credenza with allegorical motifs and ancestor portraits, collections of weaponry and of bronze mortars for spices and medicines. In wartime, of course, the château looked less like a museum than this inventory might suggest. Some of the furniture and art objects had been put in storage, but the atmosphere of architectural richness was intact.

While continuing to live on the upper floors and in the left wing with his family, Alain du Fontenioux rented the Simenons a large part of the ground floor of the right wing, including the large salon, the dining hall and kitchen, and four upstairs bedrooms. Relations between the two men were cordial, and they talked often. Simenon let his host know whom he was dealing with at their very first meeting: "Great minds say that there are two great writers in this country, Gide and me."

Mr. du Fontenioux got along well with his tenant, whom he considered vain and self-seeking, chatty and boastful. He was especially amused by the embarrassed, complicitous smile he saw on Simenon's face whenever he happened to run into him on the stairway to the upper floor, on his way in or out of Boule's bedroom.[7]

Here, as everywhere else, he was ever in motion, displaying a stupefying vitality. It was a vast château, and the count was convinced that his guest had a gift for ubiquity, for he seemed to encounter him everywhere. Shortly after his arrival, Simenon had Lina Caspescha send some stakes and a volleyball net from La Rochelle. When he was not dining with his landlord, he organized grand luncheons to honor visiting friends, including Vlaminck; the writer Claude Farrère; the actor Jean Tissier, who played golf with little Marc; and the entertainer Spinelly.

Dressed in his riding clothes or in shorts and no shirt, depending on the weather, he seemed at ease, though never quite at home. And for good reason: nothing here was his. "It was like borrowing shoes from a stranger," he noted in *Je me souviens* (1945). He is reminiscent of Alain Lefrançois, the hero of *Le Fils* (1957), saddened that his two-year-old son was growing up in a place foreign to him, fearful of bumping into antique furniture or knocking down portraits of a family not his own.

Simenon soon became a local celebrity. He knew everyone, and everyone knew him. What he saw and heard was put to use in *Le Voyageur de la Toussaint* (1941), *Maigret a peur* (*Maigret Afraid,* 1953), and to some extent in *Une confidence de Maigret* (*Maigret Has Doubts*, 1959). In *Le Fils Cardinaud* (*Young Cardinaud*, 1942), eight-month-old Denise's parents call her "Bébé rose," which was the count and countess du Fontenioux's nickname for their son Henri.

Michel Ragon, a local adolescent from a working-class family who later became a popular author, vividly remembered the count's wartime visitor, though he did not even know he was a writer.

> Mr. Georges was the squire of Fontenay. . . . From his terrace in front of the château, Mr. Georges could survey all of Fontenay, as though he were its lord. Every day at around six o'clock he would arrive at a gallop in his single-seat buggy drawn by a small, pretty horse. He would ride up the Rue de la République as far as the station, just for pleasure and to show off, then turn around and, still at a gallop, ride back down to the saddlery, where he would pull up. He liked to chat with Cousin Suzanne. . . . Not that Mr. Georges was handsome. Stocky and of average height, he wore tortoiseshell glasses like a lawyer and combed his hair straight back in fashionable style. Yet the dashing material of his suits, his extravagant shirts, and his colorful ties made him look good. I must say that his elegant carriage and lively pony, which looked like a circus horse, did not go unnoticed. The truth is, I envied him. He seemed to me the very prototype of distinction, nonchalance, wealth, and happiness. Only in the movies would you see people like him.
>
> After his daily visit to the saddlery, he would tie his horse to an iron ring on the Place des Marronniers and walk through the covered passageway leading to the Rue de la République. In this passageway, flanked by two palm trees in green-painted pots, was the entrance to the Hotel de France. Mr. Georges would go inside and say hello to the two ladies who kept the hotel.
>
> These two ladies, though of a certain age, were rather pretty. They always dressed flirtatiously, and I couldn't understand why they were called "the two spinsters," with a touch of mockery. They say Mr. Georges was courting them, and indeed he did strut like a peacock in the lobby of the Hotel de France, bowing and scraping, making extravagant declarations. I followed him and spied on him, not trying to catch him out, but with slightly idiotic wonderment. The two ladies cooed like doves when Mr. Georges came in. . . . Every Saturday there was a big outdoor market from the Place Vrètre to the Rue des Orfèvres. I liked to walk around there whenever I was in Fontenay-le-Comte. So did Mr. Georges, and I would take the opportunity to observe him whenever I happened to run into him. He spent a lot of time looking at all kinds of harnesses: for the big horses the peasants rode in on, for donkeys with long red hair. Sometimes he would stand motionless for a long time, a

finger at his lips, with an inquisitive air. He was thinking, but about what? . . . What was such a rich, elegant gentleman doing in that plebeian crowd?[8]

Contrary to appearances, Simenon was not thinking, or even watching. Here, as elsewhere, he was soaking up atmosphere, most especially in places where the worshipful adolescent could not have followed: the bistros.

He dropped in regularly at eleven in the morning and six in the evening. Sometimes at the Café du Commerce to have a drink, buy some tobacco, or play a game of *belote*. More often for his bridge game at the Café du Pont-Neuf, a more fashionable venue, with faded beveled mirrors, marble tables with cast-iron legs, imitation leather benches, and painted murals. The ritual card game, a leitmotif in *Les Fantômes du chapelier* (1949) and many other novels, was not merely a favorite pastime, it was also his way of sounding out the locals.

The Café du Pont-Neuf, owned by Mr. Thaboré, was the seat of an informal bridge club several of whose members became his friends: André Guiller, a young bicycle manufacturer; Grimaud, a hauler; Trojet, principal at the high school; Soulard, a baker; Martin, a retired municipal employee; Chaumel, a lawyer; and finally Drs. Urbain-Monnier and Sauvaget, the subprefect and the former commander of the local gendarmerie, who were occasionally joined by visiting young people.[9] There was also the mayor, Roger Guillemet, and the accommodating police commissioner Mamert, who excused Simenon from having to report daily to police headquarters, as foreigners were supposed to do.

Laughing and talking, smoking constantly, downing one glass of red wine after another, Simenon hardly seemed like a man who believed he was living on borrowed time. But according to his *Mémoires intimes* (1981), that was exactly the situation: a doctor had condemned him to an early death. The reality was quite different—and far more Simenonian.

First, his version of this crucial episode:

The Vouvant forest, late summer of 1940: Simenon is carving a stick for Marc. He slips and accidentally jabs himself in the chest with the piece of wood. He flinches but shakes it off. The next day he is awakened by pain and goes to a radiologist in Fontenay-le-Comte, convinced that he has cracked a rib. The six-mile walk into town takes two hours.

The doctor takes a radioscopy, draws some mysterious markings on the image of his heart, makes solemn inquiries into family medical history, and informs Simenon that he is strictly forbidden to smoke, drink alcohol, write books, or make love. Rest and slow walks are the only permissible activities.

"What exactly is wrong with me?"

"You have an old man's heart."

"Is it very dangerous?"

"You have two years to live—if you follow my instructions."[10]

Stunned by the tragic news, by a diagnosis that seems to amount to a death sentence, Simenon walks home in despair. He is in the same situation as his father, except that Désiré suffered constant pain from the angina pectoris that eventually killed him. No matter. The whole way home, Simenon cannot stop thinking about his father. He is convinced that the same fate now awaits him.[11]

Simenon believes the end is near. "I was a man who had done everything," he will recall, "and now they were asking me to do nothing."[12]

When he gets back to the house, he seems in shock. "I'm done for, Carel," he says soon afterward to Viviane, one of his former secretaries who has come to visit.[13]

"My little gentleman is very sick," Boule informs Odette, his current secretary. "He can't see anyone and won't write any more novels, so you might as well go home."[14]

"I was ordered to avoid all exertion," he writes, "and I obeyed. I did not protest. . . . How can you disobey fate?"

His life now changes completely, his work taking a new and unfamiliar turn. It is only two years later, when he consults "the best radiologist in Paris," that he learns the truth: his heart is perfectly normal, the Fontenay doctor was a quack.[15]

So goes his version. Can we pinpoint where autobiographical reconstruction leaves off and fiction begins? In fact, Simenon did live like a man on borrowed time. Except that the doubt and anguish lasted not for two years, as he claims, but for two weeks. Tigy is our witness. She questioned Dr. René Brémier (the only radiologist in the city), who immediately reassured her: "It isn't that serious. Nothing to be alarmed about."[16] Boule attests to this as well: "Two weeks later it was all over and he went back to his normal life."[17]

The condemned man apparently shared his anxiety with his landlord as well. "I went to the doctor," he told the count, "and he scared the hell out of me. You wouldn't happen to know a cardiologist in Nantes, would you?"

Soon afterward, Dr. Veran, to whom the count had referred Simenon, phoned the count with the verdict: "If this examination is accurate, your guy is already dead."[18]

The doctor reassured Simenon, suggesting that he simply cut down on tobacco and alcohol. The diagnostic error was probably caused by poor positioning of the heart or misplacement of the apparatus. But that was not enough for Simenon. Not satisfied with a second opinion, he wanted a third, and a fourth. He had always enjoyed the company of doctors, and he now made the rounds of Fontenay-le-Comte. They all reassured him: he was just over-worked, he was not going to die. Dr. Georges Artarit, a general practitioner with some competence in cardiology, advised him to ease up a bit.[19] Dr. René Laforge, with whom he smoked his pipe, drank Saint-Émilion, and played cards, also examined him and tried to ease his mind.

"I saw him regularly for two years and never knew him to be ill," he re-called.[20]

It was a false alarm, as the prescriptions given to him in 1941 demonstrate. They amount to a standard attempt to ease tension and stomach pains and to ward off early signs of hypertension. At the Pont-Neuf des Lusson-Sourisseau pharmacy, where his prescriptions were filled, and at the analytical laboratory of Jean Pichot, where his cholesterol and urine samples were analyzed, specialists finally soothed his legitimate uneasiness: there was nothing wrong with him.[21]

Simenon was no hypochondriac. He did not manifest the typical aggressive, taciturn, or irritable behavior, nor did he harass his doctors with complaints. The only factor that could have predisposed him to this degree of concern was his fear of heredity.

He had been carefully examined by two doctors in 1937. He asked the first to check for an ulcer. After a radioscopy of the stomach and duodenum, Dr. Brunet reassured him: no parietal lesion.[22] The second went further, since he had to write a complete report for the Nationale insurance company. His con-clusions were unequivocal:

"Respiratory system: normal. Circulatory system: normal. Is there any dif-ficulty that would suggest fear of heart or circulatory disease? None."[23]

Several months later, Dr. Michelot, of Hyères, recommended that Simenon avoid noise, fatigue, and exposure to the sun. Dr. Trocmé, a cardiologist in La Rochelle, examined him twice in 1940, finding no abnormalities.[24]

Neither in his conversations with his bridge partners nor in his particularly rich correspondence with André Gide and Gaston Gallimard did he ever al-lude to a medical "death sentence." But he would resuscitate this tragic episode, in whole or in part, not only in his autobiographical writings, but also in *L'Homme au petit chien* (*The Man with the Little Dog,* 1964) and espe-cially *Les Volets verts* (1950), which, he privately admitted, had little fictional about it.[25]

It was therefore neither by conviction nor out of hypochondria that Simenon felt the need to believe that he had been sentenced to death at the end of 1940. Why did he turn two weeks of worry into two years of anguish?

Probably out of self-justification. This was a man constantly haunted by a sense of guilt, and he never took any important step without some excuse. The ephemeral death-sentence-cum-novelistic-tragedy not only enabled him to explain his withdrawal from history during dark years, but also—and more importantly—served as motivation for his literary metamorphosis.

Between 1940 and 1945, Simenon wrote *Je me souviens* (1945) and *Pedigree* (1948), the former a kind of rough draft of the latter. He would one day come to consider them the "matrix of my work."[26] Conceived in midlife, they shed light on his earlier writings and on those to come. *Pedigree,* which many would call his masterpiece, was written in a special context, as a deliberate effort to produce something completely different from all that had gone before: a portrait of his family, childhood, and adolescence drawn in an unprecedented form.

According to *Mémoires intimes* (1981), it was the Fontenay radiologist's "death sentence" that impelled him to begin this great work. On his way home from the doctor he decided that he owed it to Marc, fated to be orphaned within two years:

"And you, son, would know nothing of your father's youth, nor of your grandparents, nor of Liège, of your aunts and uncles and cousins. A new project, still vague, germinated as I walked. Dogs, horses, and bulls have their pedigrees, while you would know yours only on your mother's side. But nothing of the Simenons, and of your father only hazy images, yellowing photographs, and novels you might read but in which you would find nothing of me."[27]

A kind of swan song. Mired in melancholy, he grasped at the fragile thread of his ancestors. He believed that everyone comes from a childhood as from a country, and more than ever he yearned for an unspoiled innocence that seemed all the more alluring amid the convulsions of a world at war. Or so he explained the genesis of *Pedigree* much later.

In fact, its origin was far less romantic and tragic. Contrary to his later suggestion, this book was not a testament. As early as the beginning of 1939 he had told Gide of his desire to leave Paris so as to concentrate on producing his great book. Two years later, without reference to any heart condition, he commented: "I'm watching my son grow up. That may have been what inspired *Pedigree.*"[28]

All evidence suggests that ever since *Le Testament Donadieu* (1937), Simenon had been dreaming of producing something exceptional: "I have been thinking about a great work for a long time. Great in length, in any case."[29] Indeed, what he had in mind would run between fifteen and twenty volumes.

The circumstances of the Occupation were ideal for someone who wanted to withdraw from the outside world, and his "death sentence" was a perfect excuse. Gide's unwavering support also encouraged him to take the plunge.

In early autumn 1940, emboldened by these three factors, he bought several notebooks bound in marbled cardboard and began to fill them with a tale like nothing he had ever dared to write before.

"In Fontenay I have begun a great novel that will keep me here for some time," he said in a letter.[30]

Though the project was as yet unformed, he was determined that this return to his childhood would be true, if not necessarily accurate. Poetic truth would prevail over factual reality.

A few months later, in early 1941, he finished his last "bread-and-butter" commitments and settled down to his grand project. He had already filled about a hundred pages of his notebooks. The great work was beginning to take shape. In a letter to his publisher he explained that it would be the epic of what he called "the human herd, . . . the *chanson de geste* of ordinary people, those who do what they're told without knowing where they're going and who try nevertheless to go somewhere, the people who never quit, who stick it out through all the ups and downs, hoping, despairing, and hoping anew. From 1903 to—I still don't know. The personal aspect doesn't really matter. Everything is tragically true, including the names. I'm not sure yet whether I'll change them. For the moment, I am not concerned with publication. Except that I may need a whip crack, or a hammer blow, from a Gide to press on."[31]

At Gallimard they got the message. Gaston did what he could to free Simenon of material concerns, while his son Claude, who had been working with his father for several years, went to Fontenay-le-Comte and returned with a typed copy of the manuscript in progress.

Simenon now needed Gide more than ever. He had almost finished a first draft (which he refused to reread), and suddenly he was racked by doubt. His own enthusiasm seemed suspect to him. He had cut himself off from others so completely that he sometimes wondered whether he was losing his grip on reality, and he felt that Gide alone would be able to tell him whether he was on the right track. Renewing their epistolary contact after an interruption of several months, he told Gide of his paralyzing uncertainty:

"What concerns me is that in writing this way, for my own pleasure, for the joy of freeing myself of all rules, and even of any thought of immediate publication, I may wind up writing things that have flavor and value only to myself. . . . You may have to bring me back to reality. . . . I know that you'll be frank. I ask that of you. Beg you even. I have no right—because I am a writer by trade—to spend years on vain adventure."[32]

In March, Gallimard traveled to the unoccupied zone, delivering the first part of the manuscript to Gide, who was living temporarily in Cabris, on the Côte d'Azur. Simenon anxiously awaited an opinion that he said he would take as a "verdict."[33] The publisher, realizing how damaging impatience could be to the morale of an author in this position, quickly shared his own impressions with Simenon:

"I liked the tone. The characters hold up very well. The desire to know more about them and to follow them grows from page to page. I await the rest with impatience."[34]

That was reassuring but not sufficient. Contrary to his custom, Simenon had given the manuscript to various other people to read. But it was Gide's opinion that mattered most of all. At the end of May he finished reading the manuscript. At the beginning of June he reread it, making corrections and taking notes. He reported his initial impression to Gaston Gallimard. It was, in a word, "regrettable."

He expressed his disappointment bluntly: "It is touching, but somewhat doddering. More than ever, good intentions make bad literature." Although the story picked up in the last few pages, it was carried solely by its author's name and not by its own internal force. Gide considered it "lacking in art and tone, without texture, flaccid and strained." It had to be tightened or it would be a disaster. But most of all he chided the author for having fallen victim to his emotions, for having faith only in his memory. His characters were shadows and not flesh-and-blood beings. Obsessed by memory, he had not re-created them as a writer should. One searched in vain for the atmosphere so typical of a Simenon novel. Finally, the worst possible charge: the text was boring. "What one expects from Simenon," he wrote, "is to learn how he became what he is; but perhaps he is incapable of it."[35]

Gide wanted to inform Simenon of his disappointment, but was not sure how to do it. In the end, Gaston Gallimard, who praised Gide's report for its lucidity, decided to send a copy to Simenon, who was complaining that he was working in the dark. He himself had said that he would appreciate a frank opinion. Well, he would get one.

It was a shock, but Simenon took it well, even accepting the "schoolmaster" tone of some of Gide's more punctilious corrections.[36] In his own defense he reminded Gallimard that this was just a first draft, raw material made up of bits and pieces that had to be rewritten and reorganized. Definitive judgment would have to await the final draft, and in the summer of 1941 he was still far from that.

"As I move ahead, I came closer to the form and will increasingly build a world around Désiré and Henriette. That is my idea at this point. Tell Gide," he wrote to their common publisher.

After mentioning several alternative plans among which he had not yet chosen, he concluded: "For myself, I firmly believe that after the aristocratic period, which was followed by the bourgeois period, we will see not the workers' period suggested by 1936, but the era of ordinary people, which is very different. Somewhat in the Dutch or Scandinavian manner. In fact, all the great American successes of which you once spoke to me are books about ordinary people, are they not? Of whom I am one, and of whom I would like to write the epic. We shall see where it leads."[37]

Simenon worked step by step, unhurried. His refusal to write at his usual speed, his desire to organize parts and chapters before actually writing them, his recognition of the need to submit work in progress to the criticism of one of his most prestigious peers, and his attempt to involve his publisher in the genesis of the novel all indicated, if any proof were needed, that *Pedigree* would be a unique work.

Gide continued to read as Simenon pressed on. He saw indubitable progress once Simenon's mother came on the scene, and he encouraged him to continue in the spirit of this particularly successful portrait, convinced that he was now on the right track.[38]

By November 1941, Simenon had been working on the book for a year. Thanks to Gide, he believed he had found the right formula: abandon the notebooks and the pen, go back to his typewriter, drop the inopportune use of the first person and write like a novelist, in the third person. A month later the new draft of the first part was ready, and Simenon took two months off to unwind. He was physically exhausted and decided to recover his strength by walking, sleeping, resting, and reading the books that Gallimard sent him at his request: the *Diary* of Samuel Pepys and Margaret Mitchell's *Gone With the Wind*.[39]

Gide continued to edit Simenon during the summer of 1942, from the villa in Sidi Bou Saïd, Tunisia, where he had taken refuge. The typescript of *Pedigree* never left his desktop. Notes piled up as he reread it. He offered detailed advice: be careful not to make too much of the portrait of Elise; avoid conceits like ending incomplete sentences with three dots; be suspicious of your limits; not every hero is a failure; stop taking abulics as major characters; you're doing the right thing now; keep at it; don't quit.

"You owe us marvels," Gide wrote. "I feel them coming; I await them."[40]

As always when he sensed that he was evolving, Simenon felt compelled to announce it, even at the risk of having his own writings belie his claims. In a long newspaper interview he explained that he had turned over a new leaf:

"I felt that I learned my trade by writing popular books. I have therefore renounced all the subjects I've dealt with up to now. Complete renovation. The rest of my unpublished work is under lock and key. I will not publish anything before the end of the war." *Pedigree*, he said, was his fortieth birthday present to himself. It had no murders and little action, but he spoke of it as a roman-fleuve, its chapters less sequences in a narrative than autonomous stories.

The final volume was already clearly in view: "it will deal with the revolution I expect to occur someday, in which people will emerge from slavery."

No less. In the meantime, he could not judge the results, but one thing was certain—he had given the best of himself:

"In *Pedigree* I wanted to drain out all the pus. I went to the very end. I could press no further into the dark. And it gave me a feeling I had never had. I was delivered from anguish," he told his admiring interlocutor.

This book was clearly a catharsis releasing its author from his chronic pessimism. It brought him close to his ideal: the Mediterranean serenity of a Mérimée writing *Carmen*. Fortunately, however, *Pedigree* was ultimately not enough to free him of the demons that tormented him. Had it really been a successful exorcism, one wonders whether he would have survived it as a novelist.

After the war, Gide argued that Simenon was an author superior to his own reputation.[41] *Pedigree,* which finally appeared in 1948, would enhance that reputation considerably.

On January 30, 1942, a very Parisian event took place in the heart of the Vendée: a gala soiree in the Fontenay-le-Comte subprefecture. The Ciné-Palace on the Rue de la République was decorated for the occasion. There were green plants and a red carpet in the entrance way. Some seven hundred people filled the hall. The normal 11:30 p.m. curfew was lifted. There was no shortage of uniformed Wehrmacht officers in attendance, but this was not one of the three nights a week reserved for them. The film was not in German. Everybody who was anybody in Fontenay turned out.

Simenon was a regular here, but that night he had a special reason not to miss the show, for he was the guest of honor. Thanks to his connections, he had managed to get hold of an advance print of Albert Valentin's film adapted from his novel *La Maison des sept jeunes filles*. Premiering in Fontenay-le-Comte before Paris! Local celebrities were invited, along with the stars of the film—Jean Tissier, Gaby Andreu, and Primerose Perret.

Everyone was seated when the novelist made his entrance. On his arm was not his wife but his friend and special guest Titine, a picturesque, buxom, truculent fishmonger from Les Sables who called her customers by their first names while overseeing the division of the catch, just like the character in *Le Fils Cardinaud* (1942).

The film was greeted by wild applause. After the screening, Simenon presided over a charity ball to benefit prisoners of war. An auction was held, with various prizes, from a bottle of Pernaud to a pack of Craven A cigarettes, from a live pig to a portrait of Marshal Pétain. Then, after cocktails in the lobby of the Ciné-Palace and coffee at the Café du Commerce with the general of the Kommandantur and a number of his collaborators, Simenon gave a dinner at the Château Terre-Neuve for his Parisian friends.[42]

Anyone in Fontenay who may have doubted the credentials of their illustrious guest was now disabused of his doubts. The man really did have connections not typical of your average novelist. A few months later he brought to Fontenay a print of *Les Inconnus dans la maison* (*The Stranger in the House*, 1940) for his own personal use, before any Paris cinema screened the film.[43] He was about to set yet another record, as the writer most often brought to the screen under the Occupation. Nine of his books were turned into films during this period, as against seven of Balzac's and four of Pierre Véry's.[44]

> 1942: *Annette et la dame blonde, La Maison des sept jeunes filles,*
> *Monsieur la Souris, Les Inconnus dans la maison.*
> 1943: *Picpus, Le Voyageur de la Toussaint, L'Homme de Londres.*
> 1944: *Cécile est morte.*
> 1945: *Les Caves du Majestic.*

Granted, not all were of equal value, and some merited the oblivion into which they fell at war's end. But Simenon's preeminent position was clear enough. From the onset of the Occupation, films were a "divine surprise" for him. His income for 1941 (as listed in the little black notebook) was 867,800 francs, half of which came from the sale of film rights. It is an enormous sum, especially when we recall that up to then his best year had been 1934, with 717,216 francs, and that 1940 had brought in a grand total of 232,500, forcing his inglorious return to bread-and-butter literature.

Simenon knew where his interests lay, but he had not made his peace with the film industry. In an article hailing Raimu, he defended his friend's reputation in a tone that was typical for 1942:

"Did anyone ever calculate how many francs or dollars are racked up by a single phone call from a Rothschild or any other stock-market shark speculating against the franc? No! But an actor! A star! . . . Watch out! Raimu is greedy! Raimu makes too much per film! Raimu has no character, which simply means that he doesn't blindly sign contracts drawn up by an Ixovitch or a Zetovief. Indeed, has the press ever said anything about the profits made by these gentlemen?"[45]

Simenon was rarely vulgar in his private correspondence, but he fumed against "those movie sons of bitches."[46] Yet he had more friends in the film industry than among the literati, especially after the Vichy government's establishment of the Committee of Organization of the Film Industry (COIC). Marcel Pagnol and Marcel Achard were both members of the consultative commission—the former as a producer, the latter as an author. Achard even became codirector of the COIC on May 25, 1942.[47]

Simenon, however, had no need of personal intercession. Filmmakers came to him. In late 1940 a Mr. Keller, lawyer and counselor for a production company called Continental, came to see him in Fontenay-le-Comte. He wanted the rights to *Les Inconnus dans la maison* (1940), which were available. The parties negotiated for several weeks, for the author wanted a say in the project's artistic development. Georges Lacombe and Marcel Carné were mentioned as possible directors, but Henri Decoin was selected. Corinne Luchaire and Michèle Morgan were considered as actresses, but the lead role went to Juliette Faber. Henri-Georges Clouzot would write the screenplay, instead of Charles Spaak, Simenon's usual adapter. The rights went for 150,000 francs, a princely sum.

"I felt it was not possible to refuse," Simenon explained after the Liberation.[48]

Indeed. Before the war he willingly signed contracts with Jewish producers. Now he did so with their German colleagues. No big deal. Even if they had settled in France in the wake of their army of occupation.

The contract for *Les Inconnus dans la maison* was signed on February 28, 1941,[49] and Continental became Simenon's passport to the movies. Created in Paris in October 1940 with capital diverted from the Occupation budget and contributions from two large Berlin firms (Tobis and UFA, an arm of the Ministry of Propaganda), Continental was the brainchild and instrument of its founder and director, Alfred Greven.

A tall, elegant German of about forty, the energetic but standoffish Greven was considered an enigmatic loner. He was a seasoned professional, having worked in the German film industry for about twenty years. The former head of production at UFA and Universum Films and managing director of Terra Filmkunst, a firm whose credits included a feature-length movie about Sherlock Holmes and a notorious propaganda film called *The Jew Süss*, he was the man of the hour in 1940, when the Reich needed someone to run the French film industry.

Greven (like Göring) had been a flier in World War I, and he was adept at calling upon behind-the-scenes support from Berlin, though no one was ever sure exactly how high that support went. He seems to have prevailed in various conflicts with top bureaucrats in the Propaganda Abteilung. In any event, his credits were proof of his maneuvering ability: *Le Corbeau, La Symphonie fantastique, L'assassin habite au 21, La Main du diable, Premier Rendez-vous, L'Assassinat du père Noël,* and so on.

Few filmgoers had any idea what was meant by the "C," as in "Continental," that rolled by on the credits. Within the industry, however, everyone was au courant, including Simenon.[50] Any doubts he might have had could have been dispelled by his friend Henri-Georges Clouzot, head of the script department at Continental. Contracts and letters were quite open about the company's origin. When he went to its Paris headquarters, Simenon saw that the secretaries spoke both German and French and that Herr Greven had a sufficient sense of humor to hang his hat and coat on the bust of Hitler that stood in his office.

Simone Signoret would later comment, "If there was a division among actors, it could only have been between those who agreed to work for the Germans at Continental and those who refused."[51]

Simenon was one of those who agreed—again and again. It seems to have caused him no pangs of conscience, especially since Alfred Greven, though a staunch Nazi, was clever enough not to mix propaganda with the seventh art.

Since Vichy was concerned only with control of newsreel footage, the National Revolution was virtually absent from works of fiction. Paradoxically, the Occupation became the golden age of French cinema. There were objective reasons for this: an energetically reorganized profession, the elimination of foreign competition, and a public eager for distraction. But if Alfred Greven regularly opposed Joseph Goebbels in the interests of fostering "French quality," it was out of taste as much as calculation. In fact, "the Occupation authorities wanted French films to help in the preservation of civil peace, but they also wanted Germany to become the exponent of a great European cinema capable of replacing now-banned Anglo-Saxon films."[52]

From the signature of his first contract, Continental regarded Simenon as one of its stars. In May 1941, when Greven organized a dinner at Le Doyen to honor the great German film star Zarah Leander (the unforgettable queen of Scotland in Carl Froelich's *Mary Stuart*), Simenon was granted pride of place, along with Arletty and Harry Baur, Danielle Darrieux and Henri Decoin.[53]

He was particularly delighted to have been invited to this party since it gave him a chance to spend a few days in Paris. An official invitation to the capital was a windfall for a foreigner who had tried everything to obtain a travel pass. At the dinner he got better acquainted with the general staff of Continental, including Greven; his deputy, Baummeister, and Pierre Léaud. The company was particularly interested in an adaptation of *La Maison du juge* (*Maigret in Exile*, 1942), about which great things had been heard. They must have been well informed indeed, since this Maigret investigation, to be published by Gallimard, had not even been released yet.[54] The producers were eager to look at anything Simenon wrote. Rights to some of his novels were bitterly contested by other firms, but Alfred Greven was always given priority, partly because of his dominant position, partly because Simenon now had "amicably devoted feelings" for him.[55]

It took two years of close and fruitful collaboration for the Simenon-Continental tandem to reach its zenith. But their relations were as discreet as possible. The agreement between them remained secret, and the relative "brevity" of the Occupation prevented it from coming to complete fruition.

In a contract dated March 19, 1942, and valid for three years, Simenon ceded exclusive rights to the Maigret character to the German company. For the sum of 500,000 francs Alfred Greven was granted an option on three books: *Cécile est morte* (*Maigret and the Spinster*, 1942), *Maigret* (1934), and *La*

Maison du juge (1942). As was the common practice under the Occupation, Article 9 of the contract stipulated:

"I declare and certify that I am French and of Aryan origin and I pledge to supply you with evidence of this upon your mere request."

After signing the contract, Simenon was apparently gripped by remorse. He took back the text and crossed out "French."[56]

The film industry was not alone in pursuing him. Fayard tried to win him back by signing a particularly attractive contract for the republication of twelve of his novels—including *L'Affaire Saint-Fiacre* (1932), *Le Coup de lune* (1938), and *L'Homme de Londres* (1933)—in a new collection entitled "The Simenon Library." Sales of five thousand copies per title guaranteed.[57] Another house also tried to entice him: Calmann-Lévy, recently "Aryanized," to use the era's least felicitous neologism.[58]

But Simenon remained loyal to Gallimard. For the moment, Gide and *Pedigree* made that a necessity. On the other hand, he continued to complain about the marketing of his works: bookstores in the Vendée did not stock his novels, there was not enough publicity, the NRF review consistently denigrated him.[59] But the truth is that the entire house now supported him, as did the entire Gallimard family: Gaston, of course, but also his son, Claude, and his nephews Michel and Robert. In less than six months eighteen thousand volumes of his works were sold.[60]

What was he complaining about? The whole country and all its products, including books, were racked by supply problems; the NRF review was difficult to control, and Gaston still did not believe in promotion. The success of the French translation of *Gone With the Wind* (a Gallimard product that sold 160,000 copies with no publicity campaign) convinced him that he was right. He tried to mollify his author: "I would like to get better sales from *Cour d'assises* [1941] and *Les Inconnus dans la maison* [1940], admirable masterpieces to which I am deeply committed, than from this book which I have not even read. . . . I know that you are a great writer, a writer of substance and future."[61]

So be it. For the moment Simenon was happy, especially since the times were so good to him. If it wasn't the movies or publishing, it was the press. He was deluged by so many orders that he could not find the time to fill them.

"I can't take it anymore," he said, harassed but content, to Continental's lawyer.[62]

At the same time he confided to his mother:

"I am almost ashamed to show such satisfaction when I can sense so much misery down below."[63]

He had planned to devote himself entirely to literature, but he was working as hard as ever in all domains. The censorship jointly instituted by the French publishers' association and the Propaganda Abteilung was of little concern to him, for he was prudent enough not to publish anything that clashed with the dominant sensibility. The large German publisher Rowolt proposed to translate his works,[64] and the literary department of the Propaganda Abteilung in Paris issued no attacks or bans on him. It had been many years since Simenon's pulp novels painted Germans in negative terms, as enemies of the French Empire. His reportage had rarely been flattering either. In his series on the crisis in France in 1934, for example, he affirmed that the Hitlerite movement was attractive for Germans because it was composed of millions of failures and second-raters who, in midlife, finally noticed the futility of their efforts.[65]

Despite this, Georges Simenon's name did not figure on the "Liste Otto," the catalog of works banned by the Occupation authorities. (Paradoxically, Georges Sim was not so fortunate. Two of his books were placed on the index in September 1940 and remained there for the duration of the war: *La Femme 47* and *Deuxième Bureau*).

Like everyone else who wanted to write in the authorized newspapers, Simenon had to fill out a form for the "Corporative Association of the General Periodical Press." His answers to the questions are revealing of his state of mind. This was not a man of commitment, but an opportunist:

> . . . Father: Catholic, Belgian, Aryan
> Mother: Aryan (German by birth)
> Maternal grandmother: Dutch, German by marriage
> Newspapers: *Le Journal, Le Matin,* etc.
> Publishers: Fayard, Gallimard
> Translated in: Germany (Schlesische Verlag), England, etc. . . .[66]

Simenon submitted articles to many Paris newspapers and magazines, as if trying to make up for the period of abstinence during which he had concentrated exclusively on writing novels. Citing *Paris-Soir, Le Petit Parisien, La Gerbe,* and other Vichy organs to which he contributed novels for serialization, he acknowledged: "My collaboration with them is significant, since my novels are used for major publicity campaigns."[67]

Did he ever wonder about his responsibility as a writer? Did he have any pangs of conscience about the conditions and environment in which these texts were published? We don't know, since he never discussed the issue.

When *Gringoire* published his new short story "L'Épingle en fer à cheval," it was advertised on the front page. In the same issue, Colette and Roland Dorgelès rubbed elbows with such contributors as the polemicist Henri Béraud, who excoriated the British, Philippe Henriot of Radio Vichy, who hailed the New Europe, and anonymous gossip columnists who denounced Freemasons, Jews, and Communists.[68] Did Simenon pay any attention? We don't know.

When *L'Appel,* Pierre Costantini's fascist weekly, asked to serialize Simenon's *Les Gens d'en face,* an anticommunist novel first published in 1933, he agreed on condition that the reprint royalties be paid to a charity.[69] But we don't know whether the charity in question was an association to aid prisoners of war or the LVF (Legion of French Volunteers Against Bolshevism), of which Costantini was a founder.

When *Le Suspect* (*The Green Thermos,* 1938) and *Le Cheval-Blanc* (1938) were serialized in two Belgian collaborationist newspapers, *Le Nouveau Journal* and *La Legia,* did Simenon even bother to read them?[70] No one knows.

On the other hand, we do know that he was as concerned as ever about how his works were received in the press. He awaited reviews eagerly and was rarely disappointed, receiving favorable notices from Lucien Combelle in *La Nouvelle Revue française,* Ramon Fernandez in *Lectures 40,* Robert Desnos in *Aujourd'hui,* Roger Charmoy in *Révolution Nationale,* Robert Brasillach and Georges Blond in *Je suis partout,* and André Billy in *Le Figaro.* André Thérive weighed in with this encomium: "I would like to be alive fifty years from now, so I could defend a thesis on Simenon's work at the Sorbonne."[71]

Praise was virtually unanimous in a twenty-page pamphlet issued by Gallimard. "Simenon: His Beginnings, His Plans, His Work" has been attributed to Raymond Queneau, recently named editor at Gallimard and a passionate Simenon reader. The pamphlet contained biographical data, summaries of his books, a list of his works, and an anthology of comments by critics and writers. The aim seems to have been to prepare the ground for the impending publication of *Pedigree.*[72]

Simenon must have been delighted. The Occupation had brought a revival of his fame among his peers and the public alike. It also filled his coffers, allowing him to devote himself to his grand project. What more could he want? Only a travel pass, which now became an obsession despite the fact that he was making more trips to Paris than he cared to admit. He nonetheless felt trapped in the Vendée, and he grew increasingly impatient:

"There are days when I get furious, spinning my wheels in Fontenay while any Gaullist can circulate freely," he told the managers of Continental, requesting that they intercede on his behalf with their compatriots.[73]

One of his close friends of the prewar period was particularly well placed to help him in his quest for a permanent travel pass. Jean Luchaire was one of the "new gentlemen" whose influence was now at its peak, and his reach was long indeed. His daily, *Les Nouveaux Temps,* was secretly funded by Pierre Laval in Vichy and by the German embassy in Paris. Jean Luchaire was not content merely to intercede with the Propaganda Staffel on Simenon's behalf.[74] He also supplied pretexts for official trips to Paris, naming him, for instance, a charter member of the jury for the Nouvelle France literary prize, launched by his newspaper "to maintain a climate favorable to French belles-lettres."[75]

Simenon, who was already a member of the jury for the Prix Mérimée, a short-story prize established by the review *Tout et Tout,* thus found himself in interesting company, including such eminent colleagues as Sacha Guitry and Pierre MacOrlan and no less eminent collaborationist personalities than Abel Bonnard, Abel Hermant, and Alphonse de Chateaubriant.[76] One colleague of similar political views commented that the quality of the jury made this prize "a dangerous rival to the Goncourt."[77]

The awarding of the Nouvelle France prize in mid-summer was one of the social events of 1942. Photographers and society columnists gathered at the Tour d'Argent amid d'Aubusson tapestries and Louis XIV furniture to observe the arriving celebrities. "Mr. Simenon, the first juror, came straight from his Vendée château, carrying just one small valise containing a pair of pajamas and a ream of paper. He was immediately surrounded," noted one reporter.[78]

The event naturally made the front page of *Les Nouveaux Temps,* whose account made the jury's deliberations sound like the battle in *Hernani.* Simenon was reportedly "fiery."[79] After bitter debate, Robert Collard, author of "L'Aventure commencera ce soir," carried the day against his equally undistinguished rivals.

Many jurors voted by mail. Abel Bonnard remained in Vichy, Maurice Donnay in Mantes, Pierre Benoit in Toulouse, Léon-Paul Fargue in bed, Alphonse de Chateaubriant out of town. Each of them sent his excuses, generally mentioning difficulties in crossing the border—the real border, the line of demarcation between the unoccupied and the occupied zones.

Most of the French population considered this "the" problem of the hour, along with supplies and the fate of the prisoners of war. Simenon, however, was not directly concerned with any of these issues. He had no prisoners in the family and no worries about supplies. Everything was at hand in Fontenay. And thanks to his Paris connections, he got enough travel passes to arouse the suspicions of the local Resistance.

The Occupation was mercilessly revealing, for Simenon as for everyone else. Events crystallized the hazy ambiguity of his politics. Neither an outright collaborator nor a member of the Resistance, he flirted successively with both tendencies in the course of the Occupation. Like most of the occupied populace, he took a wait-and-see attitude. Simenon remained Simenon: an opportunist above all else.

The political ties of the friend to whom he owed his *Ausweis* mattered little. For him the important thing was to be able to get to Paris as often as possible, for business reasons and to make the rounds of the most luxurious brothels: the One-Two-Two, the Sphinx, and most of all l'Etoile de Kléber, which opened in the summer of 1941 in a mansion on the Rue Paul-Valéry, very near another mansion on the Rue Lauriston, where they drank champagne on the upper floors and tortured prisoners in the basement.

In the eyes of the local population of Fontenay, he was one of the people who did not visibly suffer from the Occupation. In fact, success impelled this old nouveau riche to fresh ostentation. In 1941 he bought Tigy a mink coat. At the same time he donated many books to charity sales, sent dozens of copies of *Le Testament Donadieu* to prisoners of war, and contributed to Secours National, an organization that aided disadvantaged families. But he also wrote to his mother in March 1941:

"For my part, I have confidence in the offensive, and I hope that the English will not hold out much longer."[80]

He always knew where his interest lay. If unexpected opportunities were associated with tragic times, so be it. He preferred to devote himself to the readers and moviegoers who appreciated him rather than seek to alter the course of history.

What of the Resistance? "It did not exist in the Vendée. I tried to make inquiries, but without success."[81] The implication being that if it had existed, then maybe . . . It is true that Resistance in Fontenay-le-Comte was organized only in late 1942, under the leadership of a telegraph employee by the name of René Serceau (known as Captain Jeannot) and the Gerbaud family of the Hotel du Chêne-Vert, from which the group got its name. What did they think of Simenon?

"We heard he entertained German officers at the Château Terre-Neuve. For us he was neither an evil collaborator nor an informer. And certainly not a potential Resister. More like a party-goer interested only in having fun."[82]

Advocates of collaboration, whether disciples of Pétain or outright advocates of German Europe, were active in Fontenay much earlier. They were recruited mostly from the middle classes, small shopkeepers forming the bulk of the battalion, along with craftsmen and white-collar workers. But card-carrying militants were a tiny minority. According to a report of the general intelligence service, of the 400,000 inhabitants of the occupied Vendée, 200 were members of Marcel Déat's RNP (National People's Union), 200 of the LVF (Legion of French Volunteers Against Bolshevism), 60 of Jacques Doriot's PPF (French People's Party), and 5 of Marcel Bucard's Francoist Party.[83]

There were no more than a hundred or so ardent collaborators in Fontenay itself. The group called, simply, Collaboration (whose views were expressed by the newspaper *La Gerbe* in Paris) had the largest local membership: sixty.[84]

The two best-known collaborationist personalities were Edmond Butraud, local leader of the LVF, and Dr. René Brémier, who headed the branches of both the PPF and Collaboration. Brémier was none other than the notorious radiologist who had given Simenon two years to live. Rumored to be an intelligence agent for the Germans, he left town with them in 1944 and was never seen again. Butraud was the only inhabitant of Fontenay to be executed after Liberation.

As for the occupiers themselves, their presence was weightier than Simenon cared to admit.

"You would barely see two or three Germans in uniform standing in front of a house like any other, which the occupiers had made their Kommandantur," he wrote in *Mémoires intimes* (1981).[85] The only Germans he mentions in *Je me souviens* (1945) are soldiers on leave walking in the grounds of the château or taking snapshots of the façade like tourists.

In fact, between June 22, 1940 (the date of their arrival in La Roche-sur-Yon), and September 17, 1944 (official date of the *département*'s liberation), some fifty thousand German troops were stationed in the region. This strong military presence was a response to fear of an Allied landing on the sand beaches of the Atlantic shoreline. Fontenay was a convenient town, because it had a prison.[86] The Kommandantur was more active than Simenon claimed, as he well knew, since now and then he invited some of its officers to the château. Not by choice or conviction, but out of necessity. Once again his obsession with the *Ausweis*.

In the autumn of 1942 he was determined to find a way to move to the unoccupied zone, Porquerolles if possible. But an unforeseen event suddenly sharpened his desire to leave, for whatever destination. His haste was now commensurate with his fear. Simenon was caught in an imbroglio that nearly destroyed him, like Mr. Klein in the Joseph Losey film. He was suspected of being a Jew. Quite a shock for the author of "The Jewish Peril." How could suspicion have fallen on such a man?

In early 1942 the Sûreté Nationale, using reports from intelligence services and the prefecture of the Vendée, listed sixty-six Jews living in the *département,* forty-three of them French, twenty-three foreigners. In Fontenay itself there were only two, both French: Madame R., naturalized at the beginning of the century, and her daughter. The latter's married name was one of the most famous and respected in all of France.[87]

In April, Theo Dannecker, chief of the Gestapo's Jewish Affairs service, asked Captain Sézille, director of the Institute for the Study of Jewish Questions, to draw up a list of Jewish writers living in France, including foreigners. The survey was to be as complete as possible, omitting no pseudonyms. The intent was to "blacklist" these undesirables. One month later, the list was ready. It contained two Simons, but no Simenon. The French officer, a rabid anti-Semite, promised his German superior to continue the search for authors about whom "there is no precise information but who are questionable since they can be considered Jewish by dint of their writings."[88]

At the beginning of September the general commissioner for Jewish ques-

tions sent the director of its investigation and surveillance section in the occupied zone a confidential note about Simenon, asking him to press ahead
with his research:

"Simon, known as Georges Simenon, author of crime novels, Jew, of Belgian nationality, has been living for eighteen months, along with his wife, also
Belgian, and their child, with the Count and Countess Alain du Fontenioux at
Château Terre-Neuve in Fontenay-le-Comte (the Vendée). He does not wear
the insignia [the yellow star]. A good speaker of German, he has managed to
establish links with the officers of the Kommandantur, from whom he obtains
what he wishes, notably permits to travel into the forbidden zone. He left his
villa in Nieul-sur-mer (Charf. Inf.) 'for fear of bombing,' he says, but there is
no reason why the region in which he now resides should not be as exposed
as any other site on the Atlantic coast. He also engages in black-market practices on a grand scale. It does not seem that he fought in the war."[89]

Simon—one of the few pseudonyms the author of pulp novels under seventeen different pen names had never thought of.

A few days later an inspector of the Sûreté from La Roche-sur-Yon showed
up at the château to question Simenon.

"You are a Jew, are you not?"

"We are Christians from father to son, and for several generations the word
Christian has been among our first names."

"Simenon comes from Simon."

"Ah."

"And Simon is a Jewish name."

"I assure you . . ."

"I have no need of your assurances. What I need is proof."

"I can show you that I am uncircumcised."

"Some nonpracticing Jews aren't either. . . . You trade on the black
market?"

"I have never sold anything but literary rights."

"Ham, butter."

"I bought some for our own consumption and never sold any."

"You are a Jew! . . . I never make a mistake. I can smell a Jew at ten paces.
. . . I'll give you a month to supply me with your parents', your grandpar-
ents', and your great-grandparents' birth certificates. . . . I repeat, one month.
And don't try to run. We're watching you."[90]

The policeman left Simenon in a cold sweat of anguish. He wondered what
they really had against him. Granted, as a non-German foreigner living in
France, he was automatically suspect. But what was this Simon business all
about? Who had a motive for denouncing him?

An etymological dictionary of family names would have informed him that
the biblical name Simon and the given names and surnames derived from it
were indeed forms of the Hebrew *Shim'on*. And while there were no grounds

for concluding that Simenon was a distorted form of Simon, anything was possible. After all, his friend Harry Baur, who had been such a great Maigret in *La Tête d'un homme,* had had similar problems because he'd played Jews in various movies. And Charles Trenet had to go all the way to the Propaganda Staffel to deny the wicked rumor that his name was an anagram of Netter.[91]

Simenon remembered that a hostile journalist had once written that he was "not only Belgian, but an Israelite to boot" and even that his real name was none other than Simminger.[92] But that seemed too slender a basis for an investigation.

Perhaps he should look for a motive more in tune with the times. Something like rancor, jealousy, or revenge. After all, it was curious that this problem had arisen just as he was preparing to rescind his contract with Hérault Films for film rights to *La Marie du port.* Since Robert Aisner, the head of Hérault, was Jewish, he could neither fulfill his contractual obligations nor accept the 75,000 francs that Simenon wanted to return to him. By law the money had to be deposited in escrow.[93] At the same time, he was also preparing to sign an important contract ceding exclusive rights to all Maigret films to Continental, a company owned by Germans. He could not understand what the problem was.

While awaiting clarification, he had to initiate complicated genealogical research in Belgium, Holland, and Germany to establish his Christian ancestry. But he had no way to get there. He could think of only one solution: call Rémy Dumoncel, his former editor at Tallandier. He had heard that Dumoncel, who happened to be acting mayor of Avon, regularly supplied false papers to Jews being tracked by the Gestapo. Perhaps Dumoncel could help him get to Belgium illegally.[94] But Simenon had no way of getting as far as Avon.

He decided to ask his mother and brother to comb the parish registries in Limburg. Baptismal records of the Simenons and Brülls had been preserved seven generations back. All they had to do was find them. Religious records then had to be authenticated by the local bishopric, and translations accompanied by the originals.[95]

The Sûreté inspector eventually drafted a fairly favorable report. He mentioned that Simenon held a permanent travel pass for the free zone, recently issued (on September 10) by the German embassy in Paris and duly countersigned by the French authorities. That was itself a vote of confidence. He concluded:

"The Simenon-Brüll couple lives in opulence, the husband's profession as a man of letters generating a high income. They would not resort to the black market, and the information collected about him is good from every point of view. Mr. Simenon, who says that he has relations with members of the Vichy government, has expressed his intention to repair to the South of France."[96]

This report, however, did not do the trick. Several days later, having decided that "the question of Simenon's race has not been clarified," the Jewish Affairs police requested a supplementary inquiry.[97] Letters indicate that there had been no change of heart in this division: the subject was referred to as "Georges Simon, alias Simenon." The chief of the Jewish affairs police considered the original inquiry inadequate. It covered everything except the subject's real origins:

"The fact that the Simenon-Brüll couple were Catholics and that they state that they are not Jews is insignificant in my eyes. Simon, alias Simenon, must supply proof of his nonmembership in the Jewish race as required by article I of the law of June 2, namely the baptismal certificates of three of his grandparents. In the event that Simon, alias Simenon, is able to supply baptismal certificates of only two of his grandparents, he will have to supply his own baptismal certificate dated prior to June 25, 1940, and in the event that he is married, proof that his wife is not Jewish. . . . The situation of fortune and the literary [illegible] of Simon, alias Simenon, shall in no case relieve him of the obligation of submitting to the prevailing law."[98]

The Sûreté inspector duly arrived at the château for a final interview with Simenon. According to Mémoires intimes (1981), the novelist supplied him with baptismal certificates and announced his intention to move farther into the Vendée countryside. The policeman left, and the case was closed.[99]

So goes Simenon's version. But the policeman's report to his superiors casts a somewhat different light on the episode. Here Simenon not only claimed that his namesake, the vicar-general of the diocese of Liège, was his cousin, but also verbally supplied a genealogy of the Brülls and the Simenons. This was all worthless. Having been unable to get the required documents, he submitted two others instead, less religious and more political: a specially drafted letter (dated October 16) from his friend the collaborationist journalist Jean Luchaire, director of Les Nouveaux Temps, president of the National Press Corporation, and intimate of Ambassador Otto Abetz; and a letter written by Simenon to the chief of the Jewish Affairs police in Paris. We do not know the tenor of that letter. Perhaps that is for the best.

He also insisted on his intention to leave Fontenay. Not to live in the countryside, but to spend two weeks in Porquerolles before going on to Italy, where several of his films were to be shot. Finally, he announced that he would be making regular trips to Paris and that he could be reached at the Hotel Bristol, Rue du Faubourg Saint-Honoré.[100]

His new arguments (especially the letters) seem to have done the trick, for by mid-November everything had been settled. While still requesting that he produce as soon as possible "official evidence of your nonmembership in the Jewish race" (in other words, baptismal certificates), the general commissioner for Jewish affairs agreed that despite this grave deficiency, "there is every presumption that your Aryan character is evident."[101] The case was shelved. But it had been a bad scare.

November 1942: Simenon was now determined to leave Fontenay. The whole nasty business had made him anxious. His beloved son, Marc, was having trouble with the climate and needed a change of air, while he himself needed a change, period. Two years in one place was a long time for such an unstable man.[102] He would retain pleasant memories of these streets, these people, and this château, in which he had made many a business deal but written few books, mainly *Le Voyageur de la Toussaint* (1941), *Signé Picpus* (*To Any Lengths*, 1944), *Le Rapport du gendarme* (*The Gendarme's Report*, 1944), *Le Fils Cardinaud* (1942), *La Fenêtre des Rouet* (*Across the Street*, 1945), and of course the first part of *Pedigree*. But it was time to move on.

Unfortunately, the very day he decided to set out for Porquerolles, all necessary authorizations finally in hand, history suddenly derailed his plan. At seven o'clock in the morning on November 11, 1942, after the Anglo-American landing in North Africa, the Wehrmacht crossed the demarcation line, invading the unoccupied zone. The Germans were now everywhere in France. "There was no longer any point in leaving, since it was the Occupation I was fleeing, and now I would find it wherever I went," he explained.[103]

Instead, Simenon decided to burrow in a little deeper. His efforts to avoid the inexorable march of events now focused on a town much smaller than Fontenay, still in the Vendée but closer to the border of another *département*, Deux-Sèvres. André Guiller, one of his bridge partners at the Café du Pont-Neuf, gave him some bicycles in exchange for signed copies of his books and contacted Julien Tocquerau, who agreed to rent Simenon a villa on the outskirts of Saint-Mesmin, on the route to Pouzauges. He arrived in this town of sixteen hundred inhabitants feeling even more shut in than he had in Fontenay, despairing of gaining the personal freedom he dreamed of. But eventually he got used to local customs and the slower pace, more rural than provincial.

Simenon's life in Saint-Mesmin between 1942 and 1944 soon settled into a pattern: long walks with Dr. Eriau; glasses of brandy with Henri Guitton at Pierre Pacheteau's Café-Hôtel on the town square; sampling Bordeaux during excursions in the gas-belching truck of Rémy Liboureau, the wine bottler; card games with Paul Proust, president of the agricultural cooperative of the Vendée farmland; offering books to the local child-care center and having them returned by the prickly priest; getting a new tire for his bicycle in exchange for a copy of *Les Fiançailles de M. Hire* (1933); receiving visits from such illustrious Parisian friends as Fernandel and Harry Baur; generously donating 5,000 francs a month to the son of a prisoner of war.

The local people most imbued with Catholic and royalist traditions did not understand him. They considered his behavior, ideas, and even the way he dressed on hot days unhealthy and amoral. Rumor had it that women walked

around naked at his home. Some claimed that he corrupted certain village notables, perverting them by luring them into his own sexual frenzy, sowing
disruption in the land and upsetting the moral order. Others thought him an
enjoyable braggart who paraded around his garden half-naked and prided
himself on his knowledge of livestock and agriculture despite his lily-white
hands. Still others were suspicious of him as a Parisian who watched them
constantly as though preparing to steal something from them to use in a novel.
They noticed that he asked people the most personal questions. In the bistro
or the bakery he would listen to sordid stories, rumors, and scandals. He was
nosy and indiscreet. He didn't take notes, but he might as well have. He was
clearly up to no good.[104]

It is true that he was as eager as ever to absorb all he could of his surroundings. But there was not much to do in Saint-Mesmin, and he spent more
time than usual reading, dipping into the classics again: Goethe and Molière,
Flaubert and Saint-Simon, Proust and Gide.[105] He also continued to work
along three tracks: books, the press, and the movies.

He wrote five novels in Saint-Mesmin: *Le Bilan Malétras* (*The Reckoning*,
1948), *L'Aîné des Ferchaux* (1945), *Les Noces de Poitiers* (1946), *La Fuite de
Monsieur Monde* (*Monsieur Monde Vanishes*, 1945), and *Le Cercle de Mahé* (*The
Mahé Circle*, 1964, whose hero, Dr. François Mahé, owed much to Simenon's
friend Dr. Eriau), as well as one Maigret, *L'Inspecteur cadavre* (*Maigret's Rival*,
1944) and the second and third parts of *Pedigree*.

The shortage of paper was a serious curb on print runs, and Gallimard, like
other publishers, had to do battle with those who controlled paper consign-
ments. Eight Simenon manuscripts were in the pipeline, awaiting better days.
In the meantime, he tried to arrange deals with visiting Belgians, mostly busi-
nessmen dabbling in publishing in an effort to take advantage of the situation
in their country, where paper was available on the semi-official black market
and industrialists could work around the regulations more easily.[106]

These plans came to nothing, but Simenon never liked to say no. When a
Frenchman whose book had just won a regional prize got in touch with him
and proposed to write an essay on his work, Simenon encouraged the young
man. The author, a journalist from Lyons, had been dazzled by one of
Simenon's prewar lectures. They had exchanged a few words and he became
a devoted reader. Disregarding the advice of his seniors in the Paris press, who
urged him not to waste his time and talent on subliterature, the man threw
himself into the project, after first requesting the subject's authorization.
Simenon was cooperative, even offering to read the manuscript to point out
any possible errors of detail. The young man's name was Frédéric Dard.
He was twenty-two years old and had not yet created his own inspector, San
Antonio.[107]

On the movie front, Simenon maintained friendly relations with Continental at a time when underground Resistance leaflets denounced Alfred Greven's stranglehold on French films and raised the slogan "Abandon Continental!"[108]

Simenon didn't listen. Instead, he sold the firm the rights to *La Vérité sur Bébé Donge* (1942) and *Maigret* (1934), on which it held an option.[109] He was so committed to Continental that he was even forced to retract certain decisions to mollify Greven. When it was reported in the press that Continental was planning a production of *Les Caves du Majestic* (1942), Simenon panicked, for he had already sold the rights to an American firm.[110] He immediately informed Greven of this in a letter in which his disarray is evident, for he calls him Arthur instead of Alfred. Greven replied that he was aware of the obstacle but didn't care. He wanted the novel and he would get it. It was a Maigret investigation, wasn't it? And he had an exclusive option on the character.

He assigned *Les Caves du Majestic* to Richard Pottier, who had directed *Picpus,* and signed Albert Préjean for his third portrayal of the inspector (after *Picpus* and *Cécile est morte,* directed by Maurice Tourneur). The film would also star Gabriello and Suzy Prim.

The adaptation was done in circumstances not even Simenon could have imagined. In 1943, as he was working on the script, the indispensable Charles Spaak was arrested and imprisoned in Fresnes on charges of Resistance activities—not his own but his brother's. In the latter's absence, the Gestapo decided to pick up the former. The film was blocked. Until one day a man was shown into Spaak's cell.

"Continental sent me," he explained. "They would like to go ahead and make this picture, but it has come to their attention that you have made so many changes in the novel that no other writer could finish the script. It is obvious that the murderer is no longer the same person as in the novel, but it is equally obvious that you are the only one who knows who it is. So, Mr. Spaak, would you be so kind as to give us the key to this enigma and tell us who the murderer is?"[111]

So it was that the famous screenwriter finished his script in prison, laying down strict conditions in advance: he was to be given tobacco, food, paper, pencils, and so on. Every other day a representative of the production company dropped by his cell to pick up his completed pages.

Simenon himself had an equally curious experience around the same time. At the request of the state radio station in Vichy, he had written a radio play entitled *L'Invraisemblable M. Prou* (The Improbable Mr. Prou, also known as *Le soi-disant M. Prou*). After acceptance and payment, the text was sent on to Raimu, who was to play the lead. The producer, Arys Nissotti of the Regina company, immediately decided that the play would make an excellent film. He assumed there would be no problem with the censor, since Vichy radio had been cleared to broadcast the play. Moreover, Simenon informed him that none of the twelve adaptations of his work filmed over the past three years had encountered any problems on that front. Nissotti therefore bought the rights, and the film went into production. Shooting was to start in August 1943.

Then suddenly the Ministry of Information refused to approve the project. The subject was considered "immoral" and the picture was too reminiscent of earlier films. The producers were stunned. How could it have been moral on the radio but immoral on the screen? The script was given to Charles Spaak, who was asked to soften the story's tragic aspects. A new draft was submitted. This time it was rejected by the "quality control" commission, whose most prominent members were Paul Morand and Marcel Achard. After an informal inquiry of his own, the producer wrote to Simenon, isolated in the depths of the Vendée:

"According to information we have been able to obtain (as you know, everything will out in the end), it seems clear that you have been personally targeted. This is essentially an attempt to prevent a new script based on your work from being brought to the screen. The honorable authors are offended by your popularity, and since they are now both judge and jury, they are taking the opportunity to break the long string of your successes."[112]

Jealousy? That was hard to believe. One of the three censors, Marcel Achard, was a friend and the author of the screenplay based on Simenon's *Monsieur La Souris* (1938), which was shot in 1942, with Raimu in the title role. It would be outrageous for Achard to censor both of them barely a year later.

Simenon was as disappointed as Spaak was furious. When he learned that the screenwriter had dashed off a stinging letter to the censors, he followed suit, though in more measured tones. Addressing Paul Morand as "Mon cher maître," Simenon requested his honest opinion of the literary quality of his text and asked that Morand not place him in such a delicate position vis-à-vis the producers with whom he had a contract.[113] His plea to Louis-Emile Galey, director general of the cinema in Paris, was more explicit. After citing the international success of his novels and the French triumph of the films made from them since the beginning of the war, he dealt with the two criticisms no one had officially expressed, defending the work's morality and originality:

"The ruling passion of the main character, Mr. Prou, is, of course, hatred. I do not depict this as in any way triumphant or admirable, but as bitter and wrenching. It is defeated by simple, humble, patient honesty, in accordance with the most classical rules of moral tales. . . . The essential elements of the story were taken from a criminal case that took place last year in Fontenay-le-Comte, a case I followed personally and from which I even borrowed part of the text of the anonymous letters now filed in the clerk's office. I would be curious to know whether there is a single novel, play, or film with a plot based on a case, unique in judicial annals, in which a man seeks vengeance by sending anonymous letters denouncing himself."[114]

Louis-Emile Galey took a month to reply. Long enough for consultations and—who knows?—perhaps for some pressure to be brought to bear. In any event, in the end he reassured Simenon, stating that the literary value of his work was beyond doubt and expressing concern only about the producers' solvency. He concluded by reporting that the commission had reconsidered its position. The censorship certificate was issued.[115] *L'Invraisemblable M. Prou* was never brought to the screen. But the radio play, broadcast in twelve episodes, was a hit.

A writer equally in favor in Paris and Vichy was inevitably suspect in the eyes of the citizens of the Vendée among whom he lived. They knew or guessed that, while not a "collabo," he was not suffering unduly from the war either. As the Occupation moved into its worst days, his byline appeared in such well-connected newspapers as *Je suis partout,* but these were serializations of his novels and not polemical articles or political editorials.

The talk in the bistros was of an opportunist well satisfied with the situation. Open the newspapers and magazines of Paris and you would see his name: articles by or about him. In May 1944 the *Chronique de Paris* announced the creation of a Grand Prix Balzac. Simenon was named to the jury, along with such noted writers as Drieu La Rochelle and Jean de La Varende.[116] And strange visitors dropped in at his villa, like the journalist Théo Claskin, special envoy of *La Legia,* a collaborationist Wallonian newspaper.

Simenon didn't care about the rumors. He meant to get along with everyone. When he sent out autographed review copies of his novels, he divided critics into three categories: "literary" (Marcel Arland of *Comœdia,* Maurice Noël of *Le Figaro*), "collabos" (Georges Blond of *Je suis partout,* Robert J. Courtine of *Die Pariser Zeitung*), and "Resisters" (Jean-Paul Sartre of *Les Cahiers du Sud,* René Tavernier of *Confluences*). But they all got copies, without discrimination.[117]

The Resistance became seriously active in the border region between the Vendée and Deux-Sèvres as of the spring of 1943, when a local branch of the Civil and Military Organization (OCM) was formed parallel to the networks of France Combattante. Intelligence-gathering operations for the coming D-Day landing were the first activities. After that there were raids, sabotage of the railroads, and ambushes of the militia.

It was not difficult for a citizen of Saint-Mesmin to make contact with the Resistance. Those who wanted to do so found ways. But you had to want to. Simenon never dreamed of it. He thought of himself as standing not above the fray but alongside it, apparently impervious to the tremors shaking the Old World. His abundant correspondence with Gaston Gallimard is devoid of any mention of political events. Anyone reading it without noticing the dates would have no idea of the state the country was in. But in February 1944 he made one fleeting reference to the postwar period to come. It was time to start thinking about that.

Some inhabitants of Saint-Mesmin say they heard his name mentioned on several occasions by the BBC, and the announcer did not sound like a literary critic: "We have the file on you, Georges Simenon. . . ."[118] The claim seems credible, since at the same time *Bir-Hakeim*, an underground Gaullist monthly, promised that he would be arrested, tried, and punished immediately after Liberation. "Georges Simenon, writer," was listed in the same category as Pierre Drieu La Rochelle and Lucien Rebatet, colleagues far more gravely compromised with the occupier. The threat was worth taking seriously, for the newspaper was well informed, regularly publishing the identities and addresses of militiamen, *département* by *département*. Its blacklist of writers was also broadcast by Honneur et Patrie, the clandestine Resistance radio station.[119]

Simenon could see which way the wind was blowing. He therefore reacted—in his way. Realizing that the books he had donated to prisoners of war would not be enough, one morning in the spring of 1944 he asked his friend Rémy Liboureau: "What would the Resistance be interested in?" That very night he had a young man take them a pig and a cask of wine.[120]

In July 1944, a month after the Allied landing on the Normandy coast, a company of British SAS commandos parachuted into the border region of Deux-Sèvres, the Vendée, and Maine-et-Loire. A Frenchman, Captain Fournier, was in command. At the same time, a Franco-British team commanded by Major Withy was blindly dropped into the Absie region. Officers and noncoms of the First RCP of Free France soon settled into the same region, particularly in Pouzauges, not far from Saint-Mesmin. Their mission was to sabotage enemy supply lines so as to prevent German units that were still operational from moving back toward Normandy.[121]

Captain Fournier's men were close by, in La Crépelle, their regional action center. On August 9, after a signal broadcast by the BBC ("The frog dives"), ten tons of arms and sabotage matériel were parachuted in. Operating instructions were in English. A few days later, there were three explosions on the Cerizay-Pouzauges rail line.

The occupier responded by ordering the municipal authorities to organize permanent surveillance of the rail line by the populace. One local inhabitant who spent a night on guard duty with Simenon retained a bucolic memory of the experience, his partner having had the foresight to bring a few bottles along to make the job more bearable.[122]

In his *Mémoires intimes* (1981), Simenon gave a full account of the visit of the British paratroopers, who, he says, virtually invaded the town, turning it into a center of operations. In hindsight, he retrospectively identified with them (as did many others, collectively known as the Resistance Fighters of August 32), calling them "our Maquisards" and "my paratroopers." He says that in the heat of the battle he loaned them his Citroën, which became a virtually mythological object in his version of events, a veritable engine of death and terror packed with arms and explosives.[123] Some years later, pressed to justify his conduct, he would even say:

"I went to offer them my car and place myself at their disposal. It was with my automobile, and often on my instructions, that a good number of raids were carried out, discussed at my place at night."[124]

The reality is less heroic, as Constant Vaillant, instructor of the local Resistance group, confirms: "We took his car without asking his permission. We simply requisitioned Simenon's, like the others; as for the paratroops, I'd like to know what they could possibly have been doing at his place."[125]

The Germans were intent on decapitating the Resistance, whose center of action was now in Cerizay, close by Saint-Mesmin. At three o'clock in the afternoon of August 23, one of their convoys sped along the road between Bressuire and Pouzauges firing into all the houses lining the route. Two days later, in the small town of Montravers, they pulled into the main square at dawn and fired into a crowd before executing some hostages. At two o'clock that afternoon their artillery pounded Cerizay, setting 172 houses on fire and killing five people.[126]

In nearby Saint-Mesmin a thick column of smoke could be seen rising over the town. This time Simenon was really frightened. But it is not clear which he feared more, the blind terror of the routed Wehrmacht or the accounting of his wartime behavior that would soon be demanded by the Resistance.

"Having been reported to the Germans, I had to hide in the countryside with my family for nearly two weeks," he later explained, adding, with typical novelistic flair, that "a blond lady accompanied by a German officer" had come to question him. He was saved by the quick wit and presence of mind of Boule, who answered the door.[127] Part of that is true. Except that the visitors in question were not Germans but members of the Resistance.

"Two young people, one of whom was a grain merchant in Saint-Mesmin, came to the house to arrest him in the name of the Resistance. I told them he had left town, and they went away," Boule recalls.[128] What happened later confirms her version.

Simenon had already fled from a city (Fontenay-le-Comte) to a small town (Saint-Mesmin). Now he moved on to a hamlet, La Roche-Gautreau, about four miles away, taking Tigy, Marc, and Boule to the farm of Eugène Devaud. Accompanied by his friend Dr. Eriau and a few others, he spent several nights in the fields. Days later, when the danger had passed, most of his companions went home. But not Simenon. He stayed another ten days or so, from August 25 into early September.

"He liked it there," Devaud's son recalls. "He and his friends drank all the time. Every morning we would find the empty bottles. We knew he was extravagant, but he was no tightwad. We were generously compensated."[129]

La Roche-Gautreau was the smallest, quietest, most isolated spot in the region at the time. Later Simenon would say: "The France I knew was the France of 1922 to 1939."[130]

One wonders in what imaginary country he spent the four years of war.

12

THE FLIGHT OF MR. GEORGES

1944–1945

aris was liberated, but France was not. Though the war raged on, Simenon might have been expected to turn up in the capital at any moment in the autumn of 1944, so loudly had he cursed the fetters on free circulation during the past four years. But no. Instead, he remained in the town of Sables d'Olonne, on the Atlantic coast.

He says he was bedridden with a nasty case of pleurisy, a disease that had to be taken seriously. But why didn't he move to Porquerolles? He had been trying to get to the island for months, supposedly because of the climate. But the truth is that he had been denied permission to leave town, a measure used against people about whom more information was being sought—in other words, people who were not considered above reproach. It was not the doctors but the local authorities who kept him in this seaside resort.

Simenon sat and moped in Les Roches Noires, a three-story pension-hotel facing the Atlantic on the Promenade Georges-Clemenceau. When not resting in bed, he had all the time in the world to stroll up and down the embankment, a mile-long oceanfront boulevard, contemplating the sea he now yearned to cross. It would be too much to say that his conscience was not clear, but he was certainly no longer at ease with the times.

That autumn's tone was set by the festival of Liberation, held one Sunday in the Château d'Olonne amid a plethora of national flags and Resistance armbands. There had been four years of simmering hatred, accumulated rancor, and painful privation. The prisoners of war had not yet come home, and no one knew if the deportees ever would. It was hard not to demand that accounts be settled.

Simenon knew something about unchained purges and vigilante justice, having had a taste of both at the age of sixteen, when he witnessed tragic, unforgettable scenes that he had recently relived, re-creating them in the final pages of *Pedigree*.

It was a delicatessen whose owner had worked with the Germans. Some men surged into the shop and started hurling hams and sausages around. Then furniture. Dressers, beds, a night table, a piano were thrown out second- and third-story windows. The police didn't know what to do, and the looters ran along the street with their booty.

"Destroy what you want, but don't take anything!" an officer tried to call out.

Ten, twenty, fifty delicatessens suffered the same fate, and the crowd was increasingly varied. Gangs of people from poor neighborhoods ran riot on the Rue de la Cathédrale. Some cafés began serving free drinks, and others were forced to follow suit when the crowd demanded it. Roger looked on uncomprehending as a human form struggled in a dark corner with half a dozen relentless men. They were stripping a woman, tearing all her clothes off. She was naked, on her knees on the sticky sidewalk. One of the attackers was cutting off her hair to the scalp with crude snips of a scissors.

"She can go now. We're going to do the same thing to all of them who slept with Germans. This way their husbands will know what they're dealing with when they get back from the front."

She fled through a chorus of boos, pale and shivering in the draft of the street. Kids pursued her as similar scenes unfolded everywhere, and you would give a sudden start as you saw a pallid, naked body in the dark, hugging the façades of the houses.[1]

That was Belgium in 1919. It may as well have been France in 1944. For Simenon the nightmare had only just begun. It would be a long time before his memory could separate the country from the date.

Jean Huguet, a nineteen-year-old from Sables-d'Olonne, was what you might call a romantic of the Resistance. Faced with a choice between forced labor in Germany or joining the underground controlled by the communists of the National Front, he did not hesitate. After Liberation, the military justice department of the FFI (French Forces of the Interior) assigned him and several others, mostly young police officers, to "investigate" cases of suspected collaboration. In effect, this was a political police, but there seems to have been no particular thirst for reprisals. Of the three hundred or so cases dealt with, only five death sentences were issued, and none was carried out.

One morning Huguet was approached on the embankment by a Mr. Bertrand, owner of Les Roches Noires.

"You know what? I have a distinguished guest. You'll never guess who, but he's a great writer, and since you're so interested in literature . . ."

The hotelkeeper then showed Huguet the Belgian passport and ration card of one Simenon, Georges, man of letters, born in Liège. Huguet went back to the military justice headquarters and announced to no one in particular: "Maigret is in town!"

His superior, Inspector Aumont, called him into his office and closed the door.

"What did you mean by that?"

"Well, Simenon."

The policeman then told Huguet that a warrant for the novelist's arrest had been received by telegraph.

"We have to go and arrest him, but we'll do it alone, discreetly, without any fanfare," the officer decided.

At six in the evening the two men, accompanied by a superintendent, walked over to the hotel. Mr. Bertrand, frightened by the repercussions of his loose talk, tried to dissuade them from going upstairs:

"I assure you, he's very sick. There's a doctor at his bedside."

Bertrand was telling the truth. Their quarry had a high fever. He was burning up. The doctor took the inspector aside:

"He'll give us all pleurisy."

The three men withdrew, but the policeman told the hotelkeeper:

"Don't be surprised if someone drops by morning and night to see how Mr. Simenon is doing."[2]

Simenon knew that they were not inquiring about his health. As a foreigner, he was concerned that everything be in order, and on his own initiative he had his identity card sent to the police. A few hours later, a gendarme arrived to escort him to headquarters, where he spent two frustrating hours overhearing bits and pieces of telephone conversations with members of the purge committee of the Vendée. Then they sent him back to his hotel, without a word of explanation.

Early the next morning, still in bed, he heard whispers in the hallway. The police were back.

". . . It's Paris that wants him . . . because of a novel that appeared in *Paris-Soir* in 1940."[3]

Tigy, who wanted to have him taken to the capital by ambulance, approached the authorities in La Roche-sur-Yon. She was not easily discouraged, but could find nothing but rumors. The case file was missing, and gossip thrived in its absence. Local people confidently asserted that, in 1940, Simenon greeted the Germans in Nieul with open arms, proclaiming: "I'm the burgomaster now!" A furious Tigy demanded evidence but received only shrugs. Apparently mere presumption of guilt was enough. If only they would question him, Simenon would have some idea of what he was accused of. But instead he was left hanging, and before long doubt became anguish. Naïvely, he signed up for a six-month subscription to *L'Humanité,* the communist paper, and read it ostentatiously.

Inspector Aumont and Jean Huguet, accompanied by their superintendent, were soon back in the picture. But this time it was Simenon who summoned them:

"So, gentlemen, where do we stand? Tell me what you have against me."

"We don't know," the inspector replied. "They haven't sent me the file. All they do is curse on the phone. Simenon is a piece of shit, his name comes up in all the *collabo* organizations, legion of this, legion of that."

"Look," Simenon replied, "this war was a pain in my ass. Every time anyone asked me for money, I gave just to have a little peace and quiet. That's why my name comes up on those lists, and that's the only reason."[4]

As he well knew, that was not the only reason, but he felt he could not answer such vague charges. Bedridden by a relapse, he panicked one morning when two FFI members came to arrest him. This time the doctor's certificate was of some use: he could not travel. When he learned that the arrest order had come from Paris and not from local purge officials, he immediately got in touch with Mr. Garçon, his lawyer in the capital, who in turn located a well-placed representative in the region: François Ropert, counselor in La Roche-sur-Yon and member of the Liberation Committee of the Vendée. Meanwhile, Simenon prepared his defense for his lawyers.

"Throughout the war," he said, "I never wrote a single newspaper or magazine article and never spoke in public." While admitting that he visited the Kommandantur for the sole purpose of obtaining a travel pass, he enumerated the charges that might be leveled against him, in effect compiling his own case file: yes, he sold one novel to *Paris-Soir* and another to *Le Petit Parisien,* but that was "before Montoire"; yes, he sold film rights to Continental as well, but "I had no choice." It all seemed harmless and inconsequential. He could not imagine what other charges there might be against him.[5]

As he listened to the rumors, he became increasingly certain that this "nasty attack" came from Fontenay-le-Comte and not Saint-Mesmin. His analysis was that those now trying to tar him with the infamous "collabo" label were probably the same people who had denounced him as a Jew and a black-marketeer two years earlier.[6]

His biggest handicap remained his inability to flush his detractors out of the shadows. His health was precarious. Confined to his bed by pneumonia, he panicked again when he received a letter from a phthisiologist who seemed certain that he was suffering from tuberculosis. It was now imperative to get to Paris for more thorough examinations.[7]

The subtle Mr. Garçon, a persuasive man of many wiles, set to work in high places, in concert with Gaston Gallimard and the Gaullist Félix Garas, director of the publishing house La Jeune Parque. Through his connections, Garçon obtained a copy of Simenon's "police file," a running inventory of accumulated charges: constant collaboration with large Parisian newspapers, the films for Continental, a permanent travel pass for the free zone, political articles in *L'Atlantique,* a collaborationist weekly directed by his friend Pierre Bonardi in La Rochelle, the vengeful comments of Radio London, his alleged pro-German boasting in Nieul in 1940.

It sounded impressive, but some of these claims would not hold up. Granted, he wrote for those Paris newspapers, but his contributions were exclusively literary and never political. He never wrote a word in support of the Germans. A careful search of the entire collection of *L'Atlantique* would reveal that nothing of Simenon's was ever published. The magazine did write about him on occasion, which may have given rise to some confusion. The Nieul episode? That rested entirely on the testimony of a "snitch," one Robert M., who changed his story when questioned anew. And neither the mayor nor the municipal secretary, both present when the Germans entered their offices, had any recollection of this alleged remark.

Simenon began to believe that his case was on the road to resolution, but his optimism hung by a thread. During his daily walk along the embankment he was intercepted by an agent of the Sûreté Nationale. After an identity check at police headquarters and an interminable phone call "to Paris," the agent finally asked:

"Do you know who's making these charges against you?"

"No, but I certainly would like to!"

"Here's what it says in your file: notorious propagandist, dangerous to state security, . . ."

Simenon tried not to laugh. A funny kind of propagandist who never produced so much as a single political article during the entire war. But there was good news, too: the Belgian embassy had taken up his case. With any luck at all, the internment measure against him should soon be lifted.[8]

He breathed easier and even began to read and write again. Twice a day, around noon and in the late afternoon, he took walks along the embankment, chatting with his new bridge partners, the architect Maurice Durand and the judge Raymond Riquet, an erudite, honest, and influential man whom Simenon held in so much esteem that he made him a present of the typescript of *Chez Krull.* (This original document, with handwritten annotations by the author, had not in fact been donated to a charity sale to benefit prisoners of war. Nor had several other manuscripts, contrary to a well-established legend invented by the author himself.) Anyone watching him as he stood in the Atlantic wind would have taken him for a pensioner. With good reason: history had forced him into a kind of temporary retirement, at the age of forty-one.

He rarely devoured books as greedily as he now did in Sables-d'Olonne.

Gallimard, his main supplier, sent him the volumes of the Pléiade collection that he asked for, and others as well. In the small apartment he rented near the hotel to have a place to work in peace, he received occasional visits from young Huguet, who was more keen on literature than on political policing.

When he was not reading, he wrote a few short stories. But this time of forced residence provided little inspiration for him. The hotel would be re-created in *La Chambre bleu* (*The Blue Room,* 1964) and the city mainly in *Les Vacances de Maigret* (*A Summer Holiday,* 1948). Watching one of the customers in the hotel struggling to make her children obey would give him the idea for a short story, "Madame Quatre et ses enfants," which would eventually be translated into twenty-five languages and published in many school anthologies.[9]

Simenon's hope that Belgian intervention would resolve his problems was soon dashed. A government commissioner in Poitiers informed Mr. Vermeiren, the Belgian embassy's special envoy in the Vendée, that the case was now considered "serious." Simenon was to be interrogated, and possibly imprisoned. The longer the investigation went on, the more paranoid he became. In early February 1945 he feared the worst, but his local lawyer was doing all he could in behind-the-scenes negotiations with the departmental Resistance committee. On March 20 the prefect of the Vendée authorized the tax department, the postal system, and the banks to lift the freeze on the accounts of administrative detainees under house arrest. On April 18 the government commissioner in La Roche-sur-Yon, examining the grounds for charges that Simenon had contact with enemy intelligence, concluded as follows:

"1. Books and articles: Investigations have shown that these publications had no political tendency.

"2. Attitude toward the Germans in June 1940: No specific act of collaboration has been imputed to him."[10]

The next day the prefect lifted the decree confining Simenon to his residence in Sables-d'Olonne. He was free to go. There were no outstanding charges against him, at least not in the Vendée.

Simenon set out for Paris in April 1945. The atmosphere was turbulent, hardly a day going by without some major event: the death of President Roosevelt, the Russian offensive against Berlin, the conquest of Siegmaringen, Stuttgart, and Ulm by French troops. Believing he was now safe, he checked into the Claridge Hotel in the Champs-Elysées quarter. But when he turned on the radio, the nightmare began anew. A newscaster announced that he had been charged with passing information to the enemy. It was even reported that he had been arrested.

He was frantic. After consultation with his lawyers, he demanded a correction, a communiqué—something. *Ouest-France* agreed to run a sidebar headed "Non-lieu in the Simenon case" on the page reporting regional news from La Roche-sur-Yon.[11] It was a minor incident caused by a misunderstanding, but he considered it revealing of the atmosphere. Even if he had forgotten it, others were intent on recalling the origin of his recent good fortune.

Journalists and writers he had known well before and during the war were now hit by the purges. Georges Suarez and Paul Chack were sentenced to death and executed. Jean Luchaire suffered the same fate the following year. Stéphane Lauzanne was sentenced to twenty years, as was Henri Béraud, after being reprieved from a death sentence. Drieu La Rochelle was also executed.

Brasillach, for years Simenon's attentive reader, was executed on February 6. The journalist's enthusiasm for Maigret's creator was well known, but was the admiration mutual? Twenty years later, asked to join a collective statement of homage, Simenon recalled a man enamored of literature, saying not a word about the collaborationist excesses that cost him his life.

We do not know whether Simenon signed the petition to General de Gaulle appealing for commutation of Brasillach's death sentence. He may well not have been asked, for he was himself sufficiently "compromised" (to use the common expression of the time) that his signature would not have had the desired effect. This was the era of the committed intellectual, of which Sartre and Camus were the archetypes. In a world in which they were everything, Simenon was nothing. His status as a disengaged novelist had rarely been so uncomfortable to bear.

On May 30, twenty days after the deportees and prisoners of war began coming home, a decree dealing with the purge of literati was published in the *Journal officiel*. Article 3 was as clear as could be. It sounded as though it had been written deliberately to provoke insomnia in the Sixth Arrondissement:

"The committee . . . can order a ban on the publishing, printing, or performing of works that have been sanctioned; the temporary interdiction of publishing, printing, or performing new works; the temporary interdiction of collaborating with newspapers, reviews, or periodicals . . . the partial or total interdiction of collecting royalties or of drawing any profit whatever from literary activity."[12]

From his Scandinavian exile Louis-Ferdinand Céline wrote a memoir in which, in his own defense, he affirmed that he never sold a single line to a newspaper during the Occupation, unlike certain other writers "who ceaselessly furnished amusing or serious copy to collaborationist newspapers and even to Franco-German reviews. And they are not doing too badly today." He then went on to cite some of these colleagues, among them Simenon.[13]

Simenon was also drawn into the polemic over Continental. Immediately after the liberation of Paris, ad hoc purge committees drew up a list of eight suspended filmmakers. Seven of them were under contract to Alfred Greven's firm. In the film industry, as everywhere else, accounts were settled in an atmosphere of rumor and false information. Mere suspicion shrewdly passed along the grapevine often did the trick, for this was a milieu in which reputation meant more than judicial records. It was not a matter of punishing the guilty, since anyone who worked in films in Paris inevitably bowed to conditions set by the occupier. A few scapegoats would therefore suffice. The important thing was that they be well enough known for their banishment to have the proper symbolic value.

Simenon must have been anxious. His friend Clouzot (in charge of scripts at Continental) and his famous film *Le Corbeau* were to pay for the others. It mattered little that Louis Chavance's screenplay had been written three years before the war. The director was nevertheless slapped with "sanction 1": a lifetime ban on working in the industry.

But *Le Corbeau*, one of the most powerful works of this "golden age" of French cinema, was not the only film to be proscribed. Albert Valentin's *La Vie de plaisir* and *Les Inconnus de la maison* were also banned. Some Resistance papers considered the latter pernicious "because of its systematic attempt to besmirch and belittle France."[14]

In fact, there was plenty in this film to irritate censors, whether in 1942 or 1945. The moral order of both epochs was challenged by its denunciation of moral decay and of the meanness of the provincial bourgeoisie, of Moulins in this case. But the two complaints most often lodged against this picture were actually external to it. *Les Corrupteurs,* a short-subject screened as part of the program when the film opened on May 16, 1942, was a propaganda piece denouncing the nefarious influence of Jews in the French film industry. Some argued that the joint distribution was "surely no accident."[15]

The film's other handicap was more directly connected to Simenon. It concerned a gang member who commits a murder. In the film his name is Ephraïm Luska and he lookes like a "wog." The purge committee succeeded in banning the film mainly by insisting that Greven, Decoin, and Clouzot had distorted the novel by emphasizing the murderer's ethnic origins. Otherwise, they argued, why would the filmmakers have called him Ephraïm, when Simenon had named the character Justin? It sounds good, but it isn't true, as a quick check of the book shows:

"Luska père was born in Batoum, in the foothills of the Caucasus, where twenty-eight races swarm in a single town. Did his ancestors wear silk robes, fezes, turbans? Be that as it may, one day he left, as his father had no doubt left before him. When he was ten years old the family lived in Constantinople, and two years later on the Rue Saint-Paul in Paris. He was dark, greasy, and flaccid. The outcome of this entire fermentation, young Luska, who now stood in the dock, was a redhead, with a frizzy shock of hair in the shape of a halo."[16]

In Simenon's book the father was called Ephraïm Luska and the son Ephraïm Luska, aka Justin. But his original first name is recalled often. It was, moreover, a name he had already used to type Gorskine, the furrier in *Pietr-le-Letton* (1931).

The purge committees in the film industry were too concerned with the top figures of the profession to worry about Simenon, at least for the moment. But things were more delicate on the publishing front. Nearly all publishers were targeted, though some more than others and Bernard Grasset and Robert Denoël in particular. Gaston Gallimard displayed his usual cleverness. Since Drieu La Rochelle was no longer an ace in the hole, he pulled several others out of his sleeve: Paulhan, of course, as well as Camus, Sartre, Eluard, Malraux (now minister of information), and Aragon, who was head of the purge in the National Committee of Writers.

These eminent "Resistance" authors (a magic label at the time) would eventually write the articles and letters that would fully restore Gallimard's reputation. In the meantime, however, his name would not help Simenon polish his own somewhat tarnished image. How was it that he sold articles to *Je suis partout, La Gerbe, Gringoire,* and other pro-Occupation sheets with no apparent concern for the content of these magazines? How could he claim to be a disengaged novelist while granting literary endorsement to organs of political propaganda in a country occupied and controlled by an enemy army?

This hectoring question was regularly hurled at "compromised" writers. Curiously, however, Simenon seemed to slip through the cracks. Though Aragon was said to bear a special grudge against him, his name does not appear on the blacklists and is scarcely mentioned in most articles.

Simenon had been wanting to leave Gallimard for some time. The purge period, with all its difficulties and uncertainties, afforded him the pretext for doing so, as he would soon confide to his future publisher:

"You know that for at least two years I've been waiting for Gallimard to give me the opportunity to break with him. He has finally done so, though I confess I provoked it."[17]

Simenon's disaffection with Gallimard was motivated by several complaints, most of all, his resentment of Gallimard's resistance to promotion. The author blamed his publisher for his "mediocre" sales during the war, a period indisputably favorable to the reading of novels. When their contract came up for renewal, Gaston offered concessions on royalty rates and dangled the prospect of a complete collection of Simenon's works under the prestigious Pléiade imprint. Just what the author had always dreamed of.

If he resolved to leave Gallimard despite this offer, it was because he was now determined to oversee the distribution of his books personally. In fact, if he turned out one book every two months, he could be a publishing house unto himself.

The trouble was that he detested the worries and constraints of the publishing business. Instead of setting up his own house, he therefore decided to become a kind of copublisher. He was well enough known that any large Paris publisher would have been only too happy to add him to the house list, but he would now throw in his lot with a small, unknown upstart.

Sven Nielsen, two years Simenon's senior, was the son and grandson of Danish booksellers. When he first moved to Paris, he worked for a firm that exported French books to Scandinavia and Romania. Then, after a stint in the foreign-rights department at Hachette, he set up his own export company, Messageries du Livre. But he did not want to limit himself to distribution, and in 1944 he tried to found a general publishing house. Supplies of paper, however, were granted only to existing companies, so he bought a small house of Belgian origin, Editions Albert, instead of creating his own. He sensed that exports would be problematic because of high costs and that the postwar period would see an influx of English-language authors from across the Channel and the Atlantic.

Even before the end of the Occupation, he arranged rights purchases through Scandinavia, and by the time the Germans packed up, he was ready with translations of Peter Cheyney, Frank Slaughter, Irwin Shaw, and James Jones.[18] The most important thing was speed: that was how a new publisher could get off the ground.

One of Sven Nielsen's new authors was Arthur Omre, a Norwegian for whose novel *Traqué* Simenon had written a preface at Nielsen's request. Nielsen had no idea how much to offer the novelist for this piece, and when he left it up to the writer, Simenon refused any honorarium. Nielsen responded with a gesture Simenon would always remember, sending him a Ropp pipe and some Prince Albert tobacco, both rarities in those years.

When he arrived in Paris in the spring of 1945, Simenon went to Nielsen's new offices on the Rue de Seine to get better acquainted with a man he soon decided was "a timid soul with a will of iron." As he listened to Nielsen's ideas about book-selling, he realized that this was the ideal man to publish his books under his own control. To believe, as some have claimed, that someone as shrewd as Simenon signed up with a minor publisher simply out of "generosity," "panache," or "sympathy" is to exhibit true naïveté.

The first contract signed by the two men, who would later become real friends, dates from July 14, 1945. Most publishers would have considered the terms draconian: a 300,000-franc advance on royalty rates of 15 percent up to 20,000 copies sold and 20 percent on all copies sold beyond that, the arrangement to remain in force for a term of ten years. The copyright, foreign rights, and film rights were retained by the author.[19] Neither Bernard Grasset nor Gaston Gallimard would have put his name to such a contract.

For a time Simenon tried to keep two irons in the fire, observing the letter of his agreement with Gallimard: his first manuscript for Nielsen—*Je me sou-*

viens, published in December 1945—was not a novel and therefore did not fall under the terms of the contract binding him to Gallimard until April 1946.

"Every family has a skeleton in its closet," was the epigraph Simenon chose for *Les Sœurs Lacroix* (*Poisoned Relations,* 1938). The skeleton in the Simenons' closet was Christian, Georges's brother, who had long been a taboo subject. Christian is a great looming absence in Georges's autobiographical works. We learn from fleeting references in *Les Trois Crimes de mes amis* (1938) and a few other writings that Christian adored Georges, that he had a loud voice and was easily excitable, and that he died a hero's death in a distant colonial war. But he remains an indistinct and enigmatic figure. He is cited by name in *Je me souviens* (1945) but becomes "my brother" in *Pedigree* (1948).

Simenon needed the mask of fiction to settle accounts with the other Simenon. It is hard not to think of Christian when Georges introduces a brother as a character in a novel, but three books are particularly revealing of emotional conflict.[20] In the first, *Pietr-le-Letton* (1931), Hans Johannson kills his twin, Pietr, and takes his place after having lived and suffered too long under his domination. A psychoanalyst's delight.

In *Malempin* (1940), Guillaume Malempin, the younger brother, practices a dubious profession, constantly takes money from his mother, drinks heavily, marries a woman rejected by his family. Edouard Malempin, the older brother, narrator, and positive hero, is a doctor, as Georges Simenon would have liked to have been had he not become a novelist. Their mother uses her influence to get Edouard to help his younger brother, even though she is convinced that "Guillaume is the great man of the family."[21]

But most of all, there is *Le Fond de la bouteille* (*The Bottom of the Bottle,* 1949). The hero, P. M. Ashbridge, a conscientious, hard-working lawyer and Arizona ranch-owner, is surprised by the sudden return of his younger brother, Donald, who has been away for several years. It turns out that he has escaped from a penitentiary, where he was serving a long sentence for shooting a policeman. He is now on the run. The police are hot on his trail, and border guards are trying to prevent him from leaving the country.

The older brother, who has always thought of Donald as a weak and irresponsible child, must violate his own ethical standards and transgress his basic values to save his blood brother. They arrange a clandestine encounter, and when their eyes meet, they look at each other "as only two brothers can, with a kind of hatred found only among people of the same family."[22] Despite their former differences, based on the deep and irreconcilable conflict of their temperaments and philosophies of life, the hero is ready to to anything to help save his brother's life. The certitudes of the older brother, who has always considered himself strong and virtuous, are shaken. Haunted by an old but vivid sense of guilt, he sacrifices his life to help his younger brother "cross the line" and escape to Mexico.

Simenon is careful to warn us in the traditional introductory formula that "the characters and events recounted in this work are purely imaginary and bear no relation to any persons living or dead."

The truth is that P. M. Ashbridge is Simenon, and his brother, Donald, is Christian. The confrontation that occurs in Arizona in the novel actually took place in Paris, on a bench at the Place des Vosges, in the late spring or early summer of 1945.

After his older brother left Liège to seek his fortune in Paris, Christian Simenon had spent most of his time working in the colonial administration in the Belgian Congo. In 1928 he married Blanche Binet, with whom he had a son four years later. Christian happened to find himself in Europe in July 1940. He was unable to return to his posting in the Congo, and therefore spent the war in Belgium. The brothers had never lost contact, writing to each other as regularly as possible. In June 1943, Christian spent about ten days with Georges in Saint-Mesmin, and Georges soon realized that something was wrong. Christian seemed weaker and more vulnerable, more touchy and impulsive, bewildered and immature. It was as if he had suffered some great sorrow he could deal with only through alcohol. Georges and Christian talked a lot, the former, as always, trying to bring the latter to reason without wounding his sensibilities.[23] When Christian turned up in Paris in 1945, Simenon realized that his brother had done the irreparable, becoming an active collaborator, probably as early as the end of 1941.

He was a member of Rex, the pro-Hitler organization led by Léon Degrelle, and had been a department head of the CNAA (National Corporation of Food and Agriculture), a post he owed to the general staff of the party, in which Christian Simenon was chief of Section II/Department III.[24]

Georges himself also had connections with the Belgian far right, particularly with Théo Claskin, special envoy of *La Legia,* a newspaper founded in Liège by Wallonian journalists inclined to "collaborate intensively with the Propaganda Abteilung." But we do not know for sure whether Georges Simenon actually shared Claskin's ideas.

Christian Simenon was a different story. He had been personally involved in one of the bloodiest episodes of the end of the Occupation: a punitive expedition to avenge the death of the Rexist burgomaster of Charleroi, Oswald Englebin, who, along with his wife and son, had been assassinated by the Resistance. The retaliation was organized by "Formation B," a kind of militia whose mission was to guard the residences of Rex leaders and which degenerated rapidly with its participation in reprisal raids. In February 1944 Formation B began assisting the Germans in the repression of communists, Resistance members, and Jews.

On August 17 and 18, 1944, Victor Matthys, interim leader of Rex, mobilized the leaders of his general staff to punish notable personalities in Charleroi and its environs. Several teams were formed, including top leaders of Rex and members of Formation B, the SS, and the Wallonian Guards. All were volunteers. Christian Simenon, wearing a black uniform with white facing, took command of one of these units. In all, twenty-seven civilians were arrested and executed on the spot, each with a bullet in the neck.[25]

Most of the members of the punitive expedition were executed or served long prison sentences.[26] Christian had been tried in absentia by the war council of Charleroi and sentenced to death. He had escaped, and was now on the run. He explained his situation to Georges, swearing that he had committed no act of treason. Basically, he had three choices: to flee to Spain or Portugal, whose regimes treated this category of refugee kindly; to surrender to the Belgian authorities; to enlist in the French Foreign Legion.

After careful reflection, Simenon advised him to opt for the third path. No threat of war was looming, and the Legion never pried into its recruits' pasts. It also seemed the most noble way of atoning for his error, and it was what their father would have recommended.

The two brothers embraced. Georges promised that someday, when all this blew over, he would do what he could to win Christian's rehabilitation, morally if not legally. In the meantime, he would use his connections to speed his acceptance by the Legion. Christian Simenon left. In June 1945 he ceased to exist, being replaced by Corporal Christian Renaud of the French Foreign Legion.[27]

Simenon saved his brother's life that day, though unlike the hero of *Le Fond de la bouteille,* he was not forced to sacrifice his own. In fact, one might well argue that he acted partly out of self-protection, for in urging his brother to enlist in the Legion, he may have had his own uncertain fate in mind. By dropping out of circulation for at least five years, Christian shed his surname, and Georges was only too happy not to have to deal with a "collabo" brother on top of all the rest. He now had to worry about his own salvation, and he decided that the best way out was to emigrate and settle in America.

Postwar France had disappointed him deeply. The country had become mean and spiteful, too envious and nasty for his taste. He would never forget the injustice of being placed under house arrest. Simenon had fared better in the war than in the Liberation, and he found the climate of denunciation of 1944 and 1945 "just too disgusting," as he explained to the publisher Maurice Dumoncel.[28] There is no indication that the denunciation that had ravaged this same country in the preceding years had ever disturbed him unduly.

At a time when French deportees, prisoners, and exiles were hurrying home, Simenon was doing all he could to get out of the country in which he had lived for the past twenty-three years. An attitude that was suspect, to say the least. In those days, people who left generally had some reason to feel guilty.

In an effort to disarm the inevitable criticism, he claimed on many occasions that he had planned to emigrate as early as 1938, but that the birth of his first child and the outbreak of the war had prevented him from doing so. To hear him tell it, he dreamed of giving little Marc a combined Old and New World upbringing. His brief glimpse of America had left him with the memory of "a paradise for youth."[29] Besides which, this continent-sized country seemed indispensable to his own experience as a man and as a novelist. He felt an irresistible need to replenish his stock of images and emotions.

While these motivations were real, they were certainly not decisive, as Tigy points out:

"I don't think the desire to bring Marc up in the United States, though sincere, is the absolute truth. We left for America for other reasons as well. I think Simenon was influenced by the possibility of a Communist takeover in France."[30]

It is true that the French Communist Party, bolstered by the prestige of its role in the Resistance, was the country's largest single political organization, with 380,000 members as of January 1945. Fear of the "Red Peril" was probably one of the factors that convinced Simenon to leave. But it does not explain why he chose America.

That choice was made by the writer more than the father or the citizen. Convinced that the Faulkners, Steinbecks, and Hemingways were "perhaps the most authentic novelists of the times,"[31] he wanted to confront them on their terrain, as though the time had come to seek adversaries his own size. He had the feeling that he had gained all the readers—and all the notoriety—he could in the Old World. As he saw it, in Europe a writer was only a writer; in the United States he was a star.[32]

He preferred to reach for internationalization and exile rather than settle for literary consecration in Paris. The risk, after all, was small. He was already more or less alienated from the French intellectual establishment. He had shown that he could stand apart from literary fashions, schools, and sects, and he felt he would have no difficulty enhancing this natural bent once he crossed the water.

To obtain a foreign visa it was absolutely necessary to prove that he had not collaborated with the Germans. The Belgian embassy in Paris, unstinting in its aid when he was being "held" in the Vendée, now helped him navigate these delicate waters. On March 25, 1945, the embassy procured for Simenon travel authorization no. 3382, countersigned by the Ministry of Foreign Affairs. The purpose of his trip was said to be "literary and cinematic business." Date of departure: "As soon as possible."[33]

When he found that visas for Canada were easier to get, Simenon, with the support of his embassy, managed to obtain an official assignment from the Ministry of Information of the provisional government of the French Republic. The document bears the number 5498 and is dated August 24, 1945. The purpose of his mission was to make "contacts with Québécois newspapers and publishers." Date of departure: "As soon as possible." Date of return: "When the mission is concluded."[34]

He seemed to be racing against time, as though he sensed an imminent turnabout in the situation. As it happened, the report of an investigation by Superintendent Jean Péchereau of the central headquarters of the 22nd Brigade of the Judiciary Police in Poitiers had just been delivered to an examining magistrate. This report, while confirming that no charges had been filed against Simenon, depicted him in an "extremely unfavorable" light.

His attitude, it said, had been "clearly contrary to French interests during the German occupation." The superintendent had scoured Charente and the Vendée, convinced that he would turn up something big. He found nothing in Nieul or La Rochelle, Fontenay or Saint-Mesmin, for the simple reason that there was nothing to find but the same old gossip. But he concluded that his subject was a "Germanophile opportunist" with a "detestable" reputation. There were "no overtly reprehensible acts." But: "From information gathered everywhere he went, it transpires that Simenon did not leave happy memories; considered a collaborator, he was held in suspicion and his words aroused distrust."

On August 30 the head of the Judiciary Police asked the director of aliens and passports to issue an expulsion order against Georges Simenon.[35] But it was too late. He had just left, expelled on his own initiative, duly issued visa in hand.

What do you call a man who suffered more from the Liberation than from the Occupation and who hastened to go abroad in 1945? Suspect, to use the title of one of his novels. Simenon would remain suspect in the eyes of those who were repelled by his wartime stance of opportunism, cowardice, and financial success. He had done good business with the occupiers and their French accomplices, but it is hard to say whether his collaboration was primarily economic, intellectual, or moral.

In *La Fuite de Monsieur Monde,* written in Saint-Mesmin at the very beginning of the spring of 1944, Simenon recounted the wanderings of a respectable man who had broken with his milieu: ". . . he was waiting for something to which he aspired and which had not yet come. . . . He was a man who had long borne his human condition unawares, as others unconsciously bear an illness. He had been a man among men, bustling about as they did, pushing through the crowd, now softly, now with determination, never knowing where he was going."[36]

As the summer of 1945 drew to a close, Simenon was in the same situation as Norbert Monde. Like his hero, he believed he had eluded the phantoms and shadows that haunted his conscience. He felt ready for a rebirth.

In writing this novel, he seems to have completed the process he had begun with *Pedigree:* ridding himself of the weight of his past. A few months earlier he had told Gide[37] that he had the feeling that one period of his life was ending, and a new one beginning. It was an emotion difficult to convey. Something like being able to write the words *The End* before turning the page.

AMERICA

13

A BIT OF HAPPINESS

1945–1950

Forty-two years old, 5 feet 8 inches tall, 165 pounds, and a name worth a fortune. At midlife he was determined to start over in a new world. He spoke only a few words of "steamship and hotel" English,[1] but that did not stop him from composing a hymn in that language to the blacks who built the Panama Canal. The song was recorded by the baritone Roland Hayes, and the author proudly added the record to his private library of his collected works.[2]

After a monthlong stopover in London, the Simenons made their way to Southampton, where they caught a Swedish freighter of the Cunard Line for the twelve-day crossing to New York. He had been to the city briefly in 1935 during his trip around the world, but this time he disembarked with a different ambition: to inaugurate a new career he hoped would be as successful as the one he had left behind in Europe.[3] As his resentment of France eased, he began to think about shuttling back and forth between the two continents. He even bought a house in Saint-Cloud in the Paris suburbs to reassure Tigy as to his future plans.[4] But from the moment of his arrival in the United States, he acted more like a resident than a traveler or a tourist.

One man who understood this immediately was Justin O'Brien, whom Simenon had met in Paris before the war. He found them a room at the Drake Hotel on Park Avenue and facilitated their first contacts in the United States. A native of Chicago three years Simenon's junior, O'Brien was a professor of French literature and a former leader of the French section of the OSS (forerunner of the CIA). He had recently been demobilized as a lieutenant-colonel and was now putting his talents to use in a different endeavor, literary history. A specialist on Gide, whose *Journal* he would translate and about whom he would write a subtle study,[5] O'Brien was to be a key figure in Simenon's conquest of American literary circles.

As far as relations with publishers were concerned, he would have to bite the bullet. Despite his aversion to intermediaries, he realized that literary agents were now indispensable to him. He therefore hired Maximilian Becker, known as Max, to look after the proper execution of his contracts. His short-term goal was to set up an organization that would free him of having to supervise the various translations of each of his novels, making sure that his books appeared regularly in several countries as soon as they were published in France.

Becker proved to be an astute adviser. Among other things he suggested that Simenon buy the French and German rights to *Ellery Queen's Magazine,* a leading American detective story review containing between six and ten stories per issue. Simenon felt the idea would work, provided the magazine was adapted to the European market. Since Manfred B. Lee and Frederic C. Dannay—two cousins from Brooklyn who signed their work with the name of their hero, Ellery Queen—were unknown to French readers, Simenon proposed a new title: "Maigret Magazine presents the best American short stories, selected by *Ellery Queen's Magazine."* He also planned to replace two of the American stories in the first issue with two previously unpublished Maigrets.

"It is of biblical simplicity," Simenon assured Becker, who took charge of getting the project off the ground.[6]

Simenon decided that Montreal was the best place to get better acquainted with the New World, and he soon set out for Quebec, a province whose motto was "Je me souviens." For a man who could express himself effortlessly only in French, this was the best way of easing the shock of plunging into a new continent.

The train trip to Montreal gave him only a superficial sense of this land of lakes and forests, so he rented a car and explored the Laurentides, a hilly, tourist-oriented region between Saguenay and Saint-Maurice. Rather than settling in the big city, he opted for Sainte-Marguerite-du-Lac-Masson, a village about thirty miles from Montreal, and more particularly the comfortable estate of Estérel, with its typical wooden houses, not far from a lake on which cars would drive with the first freeze in winter.

Once settled in, he began making regular trips to New York to put the finishing touches on his business arrangements. Some men might have used such trips as an opportunity for clandestine liaisons, but Simenon had abandoned such stratagems about two years earlier. When Tigy caught him in flagrante with Boule in Saint-Mesmin one afternoon, he rejected her demand that he choose between them. In the course of a long explanation, he confessed that he had been cheating on her daily for about twenty years with many different women. According to him, Tigy was stunned by the news, which may be a slightly inaccurate assessment of her naïveté.

"She strongly suspected it, and he knew that," says Boule.[7]

Deciding that a separation would be bad for their son, they agreed to stay together not as lovers (which they were only rarely by now) but as sincere friends, each maintaining sexual freedom.[8]

Simenon made full use of his during their long stopover in England and their stay in New York, as well as upon their arrival in Quebec, exploring the brothels of each region as conscientiously as though he had contracted to write a guide book.

Once back in Manhattan, he set out in search of a secretary. After interviewing several unsuitable candidates, he turned to Rudel Tessier, a collaborator of his Montreal publisher, who reported that he had come up with a jewel.

On November 6, 1945, election day, Simenon got a phone call at his hotel from the prospective secretary. They agreed to meet at the Brussels, a restaurant on 78th Street near Central Park. Outspoken and intelligent, Denyse Ouimet was not yet twenty-five years old. A scion of the Catholic bourgeoisie of Ottawa, she came from a family of lawyers, journalists, and government officials. Perfectly bilingual, she was working for the British Information Service in Philadelphia. She had never heard of Simenon and did not even know he was a writer.

"I've been waiting half an hour," she said as he walked into the Brussels. "I'm not used to that. If I had anything but a check in my purse, I would have been long gone. But I had two cocktails, and I didn't have the money to pay. . . . I'm not sure I want to be your secretary. I have an appointment at the Waldorf at three-thirty with the Canadian director of Air Liquide. He's looking for a secretary, too."[9]

A few hours later, she met Simenon for dinner, and before long she was not only his secretary but also his mistress, and later his wife. His encounter with a strong young woman seventeen years his junior turned Simenon's life upside down, as he would admit in *Mémoires intimes* (1981):

"For the first time I was to know the thing they call passion, a veritable fever that some psychologists and physicians consider a malady. . . . I who didn't believe in love at first sight."[10]

He drew a more complete portrait of Denyse Ouimet in other autobiographical works also published some thirty years later. From their very first meeting, he says, she seemed tormented by a guilt complex so powerful that she was haunted by suicide. Faced with such a vulnerable and disoriented personality, a strikingly thin and pallid woman whose eyes rolled upwards after making love, he soon began behaving like a Pygmalion.[11]

Her version of their first meeting goes like this:

"I was charmed the moment I heard his voice on the phone. I wanted to show him I was not some little Canadian girl chasing after Europeans. Half an hour later I was in love with him. Though very sensual, I was a latent androgyne, while he was a terrible misogynist. I met him at the Brussels at 1:45. I saw him again at the Drake at 4:45. At 7:00 we were making love. In me he had found someone who loved sex as much as he did. As far as that went, we had the same meeting of the minds as he did with Jospehine Baker. Since my first lover's name had been Georges, he asked me to call him Jo. That's how it started."[12]

Denyse moved to Sainte-Marguerite-du-Lac-Masson. Officially she was only his secretary, but no one was fooled for long. In *Mémoires intimes* (1981), Simenon speaks confidently of his son's tacit complicity—as though Marc guessed and approved of the nature of this household at the age of six.[13]

When his mother went to New York with a girlfriend from time to time, Marc was alone with his father. Earlier it had been just the two of them. The father would withdraw to the bungalow adjoining the house to work, and the child would wait, nose pressed against the window, eyes fixed on the door of the log cabin. He knew he was not allowed to disturb his father while he was writing. But now the waiting dragged on and on. His father was constantly locked up with his secretary, and not just to dictate letters.

"I was shaken," Marc recalled. "Things weren't the same anymore. I would still wait for him to finish his chapter, but he was spending more time out of the house, in the cabin with her. Suddenly I felt very alone."[14]

Two weeks after meeting Denyse, Simenon gave a lecture entitled "The Novelist" at the Institut Français in New York. But he was clumsy in theoretical matters, and he soon returned to the favored terrain of practice, writing his first novel on North American soil.

Trois Chambres à Manhattan (*Three Beds in Manhattan*, 1946) is a milestone in his work, for reasons more than chronological. By his own admission, it was the first time he dealt with the theme of passion.[15] It was also the first time he set his "action"—if such a word can be applied to the slow drift of lonely urban denizens—in the myth-laden megalopolis of New York. In fact, the city is the story's real protagonist.

Trois Chambres à Manhattan would later be read as a novelization of his affair with Denyse. It is true that there are certain correspondences, but it would be a mistake to consider this book a mere roman à clef. François Combe and Kay Miller meet in a bar. They consummate their liaison in an anonymous hotel room, then later in his room, and later still in hers. They talk, tell each other stories, make love. But they feel most at home on the streets, and as they wander through the city, along Fifth Avenue, in Greenwich Village, on Broadway, they confront their own disarray, solitude, and emotional misery.

François Combe, like Simenon, is a recent arrival in New York. Like his author, he is also more famous in his own country than in his new one. It is hard to say which of them is talking when we read, "I can go back there and take my place again any time I want."[16] Both meet a woman, Kay/Denyse, in a bar and are drawn into a spiral of wanderings, from Scotch to Scotch, listening to their own special song, secret cement of the new couple.

From the outset this novel seemed to him so unorthodox that he altered his work routine for it, drafting a sort of rough copy in pencil before retyping each chapter as he went along.[17] The effort was so trying that immediately afterward he wrote *Maigret à New York* (*Inspector Maigret in New York's Underworld,* 1947) to get back on track. Writing a new case was his way of relaxing after an ordeal. Someone else might have gone fishing.

Trois Chambres à Manhattan was his first great novel not published by the NRF. Gaston Gallimard had not protested when *Je me souviens* went to Presses de la Cité in 1945, since this was not a novel but a memoir. As a favor, he had allowed his author to give *La Fenêtre des Rouet* (1945) and *La Fuite de Monsieur Monde* (1945) to a small publisher, La Jeune Parque, whose director had helped Simenon escape the purges. But when *Trois Chambres à Manhattan* was issued by Presses de la Cité in 1946, Gaston had had enough, especially since the book was a great commercial success. But that was just what the wily Simenon had been hoping for.

From this point on he would be merciless with publishers. Determination, of course, was nothing new for him, but he now had the means to press it to unprecedented lengths. Whoever negotiated with Simenon had to deal not with a writer concerned with defending his interests but with a businessman who wrote novels. When a young colleague asked his advice, he was unhesitating in recommending pragmatism over the romantic view of the struggling writer:

"You did well to accept a contract that assures your material needs. I prefer that path (tougher and less glorious, but more virile) to that of small, private reviews and literary cafés. It is true that I have a tendency to grind my own ax."[18]

Gaston Gallimard could testify to that. In late 1945, Simenon launched an assault on Gallimard's company, which he would later describe as "a kind of citadel not always entirely accessible."[19] As usual, he and Gaston began by quarreling over a detail, in this case the publication by a Canadian house of French editions of Simenon's works in North America. Demonstrating a stunning mastery of questions of distribution, promotion, exchange controls, and the division of rights, the author sought to bury his publisher in an avalanche of figures. As the year drew to a close he announced that from now on Brentano would be his French publisher in New York and that he would have "another publisher" in France.[20]

Gallimard was flabbergasted. He believed he had a special relationship with this author that went beyond issues of interest and profit. He had acceded to Simenon's desires too often and rescued him from too many desperate situations to believe that a break was irrevocable. He held up the prospect of a "book-lover's edition" of Simenon's work similar to those produced for Proust, Gide, and Valéry, a project that would be more difficult to carry out if his work were scattered among various publishers.[21]

Simenon stuck to his guns. He was starting all over, and that meant wiping the slate clean. He informed Gallimard that he had signed a ten-year contract with another publisher, and he now revealed his name: Sven Nielsen. A "small" publisher, to be sure, nothing like the Lord of All Printed Words, but one who had published *Je me souviens* in hard cover, something Gallimard had never managed. Simenon listed his complaints with breathtaking self-assurance. But his bad faith was patent: he was seeking a pretext to dissolve his last contractual ties to Gallimard, and he would create one if he had to. He admitted as much to his new publisher:

"Despite the option they hold on *Pedigree,* I'm going to try to discourage Gallimard and give it to you. I don't know whether I'll succeed, but in any event I will do my best by making my terms as draconian as possible."[22]

Here Simenon was true to his word, proposing to Gallimard royalty rates of 15 percent and 18 percent, an advance (in Canadian dollars) equivalent to the payment due for twenty thousand copies, a deluxe edition of the work, and exclusive rights only in France and its colonies.

Gallimard resisted for a while, then yielded on all points save one: foreign rights. Here he was intractable, and so was the author, who refused even to discuss Belgian and American rights. With a heavy heart, the publisher gave up. He would not publish *Pedigree* under these conditions.[23]

The coup de grâce came in 1948, when that work was published by Presses de la Cité. But Simenon now wanted to make Gallimard drain the cup to the dregs, establishing precedents for the future, for he knew that the break between himself and Gaston would not be definitive, particularly since there were still some fifty-three Simenon titles on the NRF list. He therefore stirred up what he called "family quarrels," announcing that he considered it "immoral" to have to pay Gallimard 25 percent of the fee when a producer bought the film rights to one of Simenon's Gallimard novels.

"I must confess that in my heart of hearts I will never forgive your house. I feel this is a flagrant injustice. And the family quarrel will last as long as this irritant persists."

He suggested to the Gallimards that it was incumbent upon them to remove it. Gaston I, Emperor of the Book Trade, had met his match. Against all expectations, it was not another publisher, but an author.

Contrary to what some critics believe, the change in publisher brought no change to Simenon's style. He and Sven Nielsen respected each other, and over the years their friendship was indestructible. But Simenon had too much character and too strong a personality to allow anyone to judge his manuscripts before publication. The sole exception to that rule was André Gide.

A careful examination of Simenon's correspondence with Nielsen demonstrates this. Despite the added affection, it was on the whole quite similar to his correspondence with Gallimard, dealing primarily with technical, financial, and legal matters. When books are discussed, it is mainly to settle questions about the covers, titles, presentation, and typography. Allusions to content or style are rare, literary discussions exceptional.

In the Gallimard days Simenon's letters were sometimes highly complex. Arguments over the division of rights and attendant problems of subsidiary rights often made them a dozen pages long. Nielsen was friend and partner as much as publisher, and things went far more smoothly. He rarely resisted Simenon's demands, especially after May 1948, the date of their first collision.

Until then, apart from *Je me souviens* (1945) and *Trois Chambres à Manhattan* (1947), Presses de la Cité had published *Au bout du rouleau* (Running on Empty, 1947), *Lettre à mon juge* (*Act of Passion,* 1947), and *Le Destin des Malou* (1947), as well as several Maigrets: *Maigret se fâche* (*Maigret in Retirement,* 1947), *Maigret à New York* (1947), and the short stories collected under the title *Maigret et l'inspecteur malchanceux* (1947). Nielsen now felt more at ease with his star author, and he began to address him in a more familiar tone.

Basically, what he said was simple: give us a solid Maigret, which is what sells best; there's nothing like some good Simenonian atmosphere laid on with a trowel; this is not the time to publish *Pedigree;* the public won't go for it, times are hard, I'll let you know when things change.[24]

Simenon took it badly. He responded by objecting to the spirit of Nielsen's remarks: "It is the business letter of a hardware merchant to a supplier," he complained. He felt that this reflected a routinist, demagogic conception of publishing, one that boiled down to pandering to mass taste. Simenon was of course not unaware of the recession. But rather than viewing it as a constraint, he preferred to see it as a test. It was at such times that a publisher distinguished himself from a paper merchant, a true novelist from a supplier on demand:

"I will not write Maigrets to make quick money whatever the cost. In accordance with my inspiration, I will calmly continue the work I began twenty-five years ago, confident that temporary downturns will be compensated by upturns, for myself and my publisher alike. I do not expect to take off like a shot. I am not manufacturing soap or toothpaste."[25]

Nielsen got the message. *Pedigree* was published six months later.

American publishers were also discovering how intransigent Simenon could be. He considered them just as exploitative as the others. To paraphrase his colonial imagery, their business was to squeeze blood out of the natives, in this case the working writer. He boasted of being the first "American" author to retain the copyright to his own works. Most of his colleagues ceded it to the publisher, who also controlled film and television rights:

"This was not just a question of money. I didn't want the people who were merely printing and distributing my books to make a fortune at my expense. It was a matter of justice."[26]

This was language the owners of the publishing industry were not used to hearing. Here was an author quite prepared to say no to powerful figures used to getting their way. When one of the directors of the powerful Book-of-the-Month Club approached him with a proposal that he produce a "tailor-made" novel to be read, corrected, and possibly rewritten by in-house specialists, Simenon categorically refused.[27]

After six months in Quebec, Simenon got antsy again. So he moved his little world to a villa in Saint Andrew in the province of New Brunswick, where he wrote *Au bout du rouleau* (1947) and *Le Clan des Ostendais* (1947), the first of his two novels inspired by the war. In six months he was ready to move on again.

Pierre Lazareff, the director of *France-Soir,* had signed a three-year contract with Simenon giving his paper exclusive serialization rights to all Maigret stories. Apart from the novels, Simenon had also supplied Lazareff with "slice-of-life" reports from London, New York, and Canada. In September 1946 he embarked on a more ambitious project: a series of articles, written and dispatched daily, recounting a fifteen-hundred-mile journey down the east coast of the United States, from Maine to Florida, along Route 1.

Two vehicles were bought for the purpose. Tigy, accompanied by Marc's tutor, drove the Oldsmobile. Simenon, with his son and Denyse, took the Chevrolet. Only Boule was missing, kept temporarily in France by visa problems.

Boston, Cape Cod, New York, Philadelphia, Baltimore, Washington, Georgia, the Florida coast—Simenon was only passing through, but his was not a tourist's eye. His articles centered on the thousand and one details of everyday life: cafeterias and public toilets, hot dogs and bathrooms, chewing gum and rocking chairs, highways and buildings. He seemed not to have learned much about this country since 1929, when, in *Pietr-le-Letton,* he described America as "the land of standardization."[28] His reports were not short on platitudes and banalities.

"I would like to avoid the ridiculous posture of being the latest of many gentlemen to discover America," he wrote in one of the early articles. But that was exactly the trap he fell into. His series reads as though it were conceived only to pay for the gas. The canny Lazareff was not fooled. He published only eleven of the nineteen articles Simenon sent him, under a title that spoke volumes: "Mr. Everyman's USA."[29]

But the trip was not a total loss. Simenon decided to stay in Florida for a while, spending nearly a year in a house in Bradenton Beach, where he wrote "only" three novels: *Lettre à mon juge* (1947), *Le Destin des Malou* (1947), and *Le Passager clandestin* (1947). The first of these is remarkable enough to merit some attention.

The author himself sensed that this book was exceptional. In itself, of course, that was nothing new. His private correspondence suggests that he always sincerely believed that his next novel would be his best, bringing him to a new phase that stretched the limits of possibility. Only when working on a Maigret does he express routine rather than exaltation.

It was in early November 1946 that he got the idea for *Lettre à mon juge*. Between two quick trips to nearby Havana's world-famous bordellos, he was gripped by a raging desire to start writing. Half-naked on the beach he would write out three pages by hand on a pad of paper. Then, in the evening, he jotted down a few pages of notes on the chapters to come. This procedure was still exceptional, but he felt it would soon become the rule.[30]

One sign that this novel would be "different" was that he hesitated for six months before writing it. That augured well, since reluctance usually heralded what he called a "vintage Simenon."[31] It was not his first novel written in the first person, but that style of narration was still rare for him. *Lettre à mon juge* distills several major Simenonian themes (solitude, lack of communication). The opening lines: "Judge, it is my wish that one man might understand me, and I would like you to be that man."

The narrator, Dr. Charles Alavoine, convicted of the murder of his mistress, confesses in a long letter to the examining magistrate, Ernest Coméliau. He neither explains nor justifies himself, but instead recounts his life from his childhood in Bourgneuf-en-Vendée to the birth of his passion for Martine Englebert, a woman of Liège. Jealous of her past, he strangles her out of love, killing not the Martine he knew, but the other Martine, the one from "before," to save her. On the day the letter reaches the judge, the press reports that Dr. Alavoine has poisoned himself in the prison infirmary.

Summarized in this way, it sounds like an ordinary crime story. Even the moral is banal, reminiscent of Madame de Staël's famous comment, "To understand is to forgive." But Simenon's focus is not really the murderer, not even the way he will seek to excuse his deed. What interests him is the average man unable to control his own fate, ready to tumble over the edge once he reaches a threshold of psychological saturation. Alavoine is a casual criminal who might be a prototype of those who will appear in his later work.

An inner voice seems to have pushed Simenon west. He left Florida for Alabama, Mississippi, Louisiana, Texas, and New Mexico.[32] Eventually he found himself in Tucson, Arizona. Fascinated by the desert sunset, he decided to stay for a while.

A cynical critic might call this the beginning of his Coca-Cola period. Tucson was a charming caricature of most Europeans' image of the West: desert, pioneer spirit, nearby Mexican influence, the spirit of Spanish missions and Geronimo. Only a few years earlier gunfire could be heard in the street—though it came from the set of *Arizona,* a western starring William Holden and Jean Arthur.

Until 1950, Simenon had several addresses in this myth-soaked state, both in Tucson itself and in Tumacacori, some forty-five miles away.

He learned to love Arizona for its light, its climate, and mentality. City streets in the world of his novels were often wet, as in Liège. Here it rained only eleven days a year. The atmosphere at Christmas seemed unique. The frenzied week of the great rodeo reminded him of the carnival in Nice, except that the horses and cowboys needed no masks. He and Marc went more than once to watch the spectacle of the branding or castration of cattle.

In Florida he fished. In Arizona he rode horseback and played golf, took long walks or drives. The big small town of Tucson offered a peaceful yet energetic life. His neighborhood was ringed by trees and greenery, but the desert was barely two hundred yards away. Early to bed and early to rise. Only reading, music, or the movies (when Marc picked the film) could distract him from his craving to write.[33] And if that was not enough, it was only about sixty miles to the Mexican border and the famous bordellos of Nogales.

Sometimes he would dream of spending a few weeks in Europe, but he felt so good in America that the yearning quickly faded. When he thought about his fellow exiles in this land, he felt closer to Jean Renoir, who felt at home in America, than to the nostalgic Charles Boyer. Arizona's wildness had a salutary effect on his inner equilibrium.

"From here it seems improbable to me that literary cafés, newsrooms, and publishers' offices might exist," he wrote to Gide.[34]

Given his remarkable capacity for adapting to alien traditions and climates, it is not surprising that a man like Simenon should feel content in these conditions. But there was one big problem: he belonged to no social circle whatever.

Now capable of carrying on a conversation in English, he enjoyed using the expression "You have to belong"—a reference to all the elements of community, which he lacked. In his novels the verb appears more naturally in English, as in *Le Passage de la ligne* (Crossing the Line, 1958): "*To belong.* I tried. And sometimes had the illusion that I managed it."[35]

In official forms he filled in the blank "religion" with the word *none.* It might have been more accurate to write "Simenonian," though it would have been difficult for American society in the 1950s to accept a household in which three women lived under one roof: Tigy, his official wife and mistress of the house when he received guests; Denyse, his passionate mistress and indispensable secretary; and Boule, his cook, who had finally joined him. He admitted that the situation was "somewhat irregular."[36]

He suffered only moderately from this social rejection, but it did bother him. He expressed his disappointment in *La Boule noire* (The Black Ball, 1955), through the character of Walter J. Higgins, a supermarket manager in Connecticut who loses his grip when the aristocrats obstinately refuse to admit him to the country club.

In October 1947, he gave his first address in English, to a select group at the monthly luncheon of a leading club in Tucson. The event had no sequel, which was not without its effects on his relations with the writers of this country. We know he had a taste for Hemingway,[37] and his enthusiasm for Jack London was unabated.[38] When asked which authors he admired, he always mentioned Gide, but also Faulkner, Dos Passos, and Steinbeck.[39]

He also cited Erskine Caldwell as a great American novelist who knew something about real life. Curiously, the two never met, though they had many opportunities to do so, for the author of *God's Little Acre* (whose works were translated into French by Maurice-Edgar Coindreau and published by Gallimard) lived in Tucson at the same time as Simenon. We know Simenon knew this, since he referred to the coincidence in a letter.[40] He claimed to have run into Caldwell once at the barbershop. They might easily have met at the Old Pueblo Club, where descendants of the first families to have settled in the region welcomed new arrivals who qualified for membership in the local elite. The club had the best restaurant in the city and was famous for its library and reading room. But it was probably too posh and respectable for Simenon, a view Caldwell may have shared. After regularly attending the Old Pueblo for a time, he and a local correspondent of the *Arizona Daily Star* founded the Tucson Press Club, where they could play billiards and poker. But Simenon did not frequent that club either.[41] Clearly he was not trying to make friends. It was as though he felt he had to choose between a social life and his work.

Tucson, November 1947: Simenon had just finished the rewrite of *La Jument perdue* (The Lost Mare, 1948) and was relaxing by working on *Les Vacances de Maigret* (1948) and *Maigret et son mort* (1948).

The phone rang and Denyse answered. It was an American journalist.

"Is it true that your husband is dead?"

"Excuse me?"

"We heard he died with the Foreign Legion."

Denyse was flabbergasted. "Impossible. He's in the next room working on a novel."

Suddenly she remembered Christian, though Simenon had rarely even mentioned his brother to her. She put her ear to the door, on which a "Do not disturb" sign was hanging. She could hear the typewriter.

"Jo," she said, opening the door, "I have something to tell you, but it's going to hurt."

"Go ahead! Whatever it is."

"Christian is dead."

"Nothing about him would surprise me."

After a shower, a brief nap, and a few whiskeys, he recovered. "It's about the best that could be expected from Christian, you know," he told Denyse.

He began to talk about his brother. Denyse got her first glimpse of Simenon's vulnerability. When he called his mother in Liège to tell her the news, he crumbled under her accusations:

"It's your fault Christian's dead! Why did it have to be him instead of you? You killed him!"[42]

Several years later she would repeat that lament in Denyse's presence:

"What a pity it was Christian who died, Georges. He was so tender, so affectionate."[43]

When he hung up the phone, Simenon was devastated. "It's true I'm the one who sent him there,"[44] he said, nervously twisting his fingers. Christian had died in Tonkin.

It would be an understatement to say he felt guilty. His grief was deep and sincere, though short-lived. When he calmed down, he began to wonder about the exact circumstances of the tragedy. Maybe they had the wrong man. After all, he had received no official notification. The news had been confirmed by his nephew, Georget, but Georget had heard it from the family of another Legionnaire. Anything was possible: mistaken identity, some elaborate hoax by Christian to get himself off the hook in Belgium. A man who refuses to face a truth is capable of imagining anything.

On January 14, 1948, it became official. A telegram from Saigon signed by General Salan, commander of French troops in the Far East, wiped away his last illusions: "Regret to confirm decease of Christian Renaud. Stop. Detailed information to follow by letter. Stop. Accept sincere condolences."

Christian Simenon had been wounded on October 31, 1947, when his convoy was ambushed by "rebels" along colonial route 4, between Dong Kue and That Khe. Transferred to the infirmary of the Third Foreign Infantry Regiment, he died that night and was buried in the That Khe cemetery, Row A, Tomb 9.

Simenon made it a point of honor to take care of his nephew, then fifteen years old. That was a promise he had made to his brother. He had also sworn that if anything happened to Christian, he would make sure that when their mother died, Georget would inherit the house in Liège and all its contents.

In America, just after World War II.
New continent, new life, new wife,
Denyse. (Fonds Simenon)

In the streets of Liège, 1952. The triumphant
return of the prodigal son. (Daniel Filipacchi,
Paris-Match)

pour mon cher J. Simenon
son vieil ami

Simenon and friends. *Above*: With Jean Gabin.
Left page, left to right, top: With Michel Simon,
Federico Fellini, Jean Renoir; *middle*: Jean Cocteau,
Henry Miller; *bottom*: Maurice Garçon,
André Gide, Sven Nielsen. (Fonds Simenon)

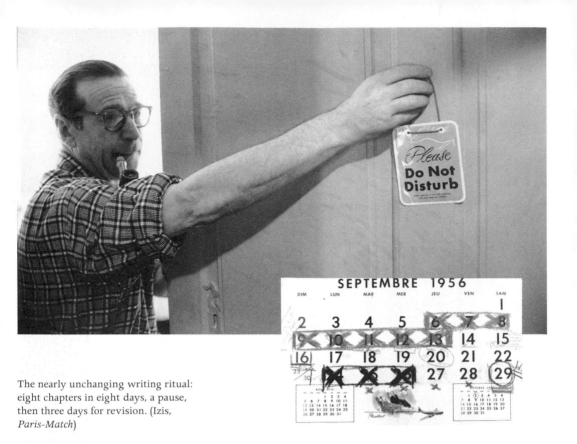

The nearly unchanging writing ritual: eight chapters in eight days, a pause, then three days for revision. (Izis, *Paris-Match*)

Simenon at Liège
with his mother, 1952.
(Daniel Filipacchi,
Paris-Match)

At home in Echandens: at left, with Marc and Marie-Jo (Quinn, *Paris-Match*); at right, Denyse Simenon. (Izis, *Paris-Match*) Below and on the following two pages, father and daughter. (Izis, *Paris-Match*)

Marie-Jo Simenon. (*Télé/7 jours*)

Epalinges, a
home made to
his measure.
(Fonds Simenon)

In his last,
and most
modest,
home. At
left, with his
son Johnny
(Jeannelle,
Paris-Match);
at right, with
his companion
Teresa.
(*Télé/7 jours*)

The movie Maigrets. *Left page, left to right, top*: Pierre Renoir, Harry Baur; *middle*: Albert Préjean, Michel Simon; *bottom*: Maurice Manson, Jean Gabin. *Right page, left to right, top*: the Japanese Kinya Aikawa, the Russian Boris Tenin; *middle*: the Italian Gino Cervi, the Englishman Charles Laughton; *bottom*: the stage actor Jean Morel, and the television actor Jean Richard, with Simenon. (AGIF DECAMPS, *Télé/7 jours*, Cinémathèque française, DR)

Simenon in 1967. (Letellier, *Paris-Match*)

It wasn't until Christian's death that Simenon realized how close he had been to his brother, despite everything. He now thought of Christian as a man with the courage to serve two years in the Legion without complaint. He had erred, but he had redeemed himself. It was in this spirit that Simenon wrote to his mother to confirm the news:

"Let no one today venture a criticism of him. He has paid. Not for his error, which, I am convinced, was venial if not nonexistent, but for the errors of a band of villains not even capable of facing their own responsibilities. . . . I know that I will not replace him for you. He did not have my awkwardness in tenderness; he knew, [illegible] the words of [illegible] to console you."[45]

Once the emotion passed, he returned to work. But his next novels were marked by his internal turmoil.

A few months later, in Tumacacori, Simenon wrote *Le Fond de la bouteille* (1949), an "American" novel of rare verisimilitude about two brothers opposite in everything but joined by adversity. It was preceded, of course, by the usual disclaimer.

In March, however, after the confirmation of Christian's death (in January) but before the novelization of his relation with his brother in *Le Fond de la bouteille* (August), Simenon wrote one of his harshest works, *La Neige était sale* (*The Stain on the Snow*, 1948). Once again he seems to have felt a need to go through stages, first exorcising his demon through an abject, cynical hero devoid of all moral center (Frank Friedmaier in *La Neige était sale*) before redeeming himself a few months later through a weaker, more vulnerable and excusable character (Donald in *Le Fond de la bouteille*).

Few of Simenon's books are as dark and sordid as *La Neige était sale*. Although "dirty" (*sale*) is a recurrent word in his work, it seems to explode in this title as if appearing for the first time. The story takes place during the Second World War in a city occupied by a foreign army. The country is unnamed, as are the nationality and profession of the hero, a bachelor under twenty years of age. It quickly becomes obvious that his cynicism and unsavory associations will lead him to complete abjection. He kills, first on a dare, then out of necessity. He steals. He sends a friend to rape his girlfriend.

As he worked on this story, Simenon altered his writing ritual again. Fifteen months earlier, with *Lettre à mon juge* (1947), he had begun roughing out the first few pages of each chapter in pencil. But now he composed entire chapters that way, making major modifications and sometimes even abandoning the draft entirely when he sat down at his typewriter the next morning. For the next several years he would divide his novels into two categories: the second, consisting largely of the Maigrets, were those written entirely at the typewriter.[46]

Published in 1948, the year it was written, *La Neige était sale* was a critical and commercial success. Curiously, although the author had tried to render the most universal themes, ideas, and values, not a few readers were intent on identifying the locales and characters. Since the German occupation was still very much in people's minds, many thought of the novel as taking place in northern or northeastern France. In the publicity campaign Sven Nielsen suggested that the action was set in Belgium.

Simenon was amused. He had deliberately left the location of his story undefined. Jean Renoir was one of the few to realize this immediately. He considered the theme so universal that when he decided to adapt the novel for the screen, he shifted the setting to America and even planned to shoot in Boston. As Simenon explained to a correspondent, his intent had been to show that a man could be drawn into this kind of downward spiral in any country occupied by any army:

"Germans are never mentioned in my book. Indeed, I wanted the occupier to be as neutral as possible, in order to lend the work more generality. The truth is that in my mind the action takes place in Central Europe, probably under Russian occupation. Both the interiors and the names are those of an Austrian or Czech city."[47]

At bottom the location mattered little. The book's violence was itself enough. Geoffrey Sainsbury, Simenon's official English translator, advised him not to offer the Anglo-Saxon public such a sordid story. The producer Stanley Kramer shared this view. Deciding that the novel's atmosphere was too bleak, he declined to pursue the film project with Renoir.[48]

Two years later, however, *La Neige était sale* was published in English, and its appearance earned the author one of the greatest compliments he could have hoped for. Dashiell Hammett, while offering a harsh and disenchanted view of the evolution of the *roman noir*, told the *Los Angeles Times* that Simenon was the best author of the genre: "In certain respects he reminds me of Edgar Allan Poe."[49]

A sign of the times: Simenon had become the most frequently stolen author in the municipal libraries of Paris.[50] There were days when he received more than a pound of copy from Argus de la Presse, his clipping service. Two more records for a man who was fond of keeping track of such things. And he was well on his way to a third: the French-language writer with the greatest number of film adaptations.

In America he was stimulated by a new factor: competition. Several writers of thrillers achieved fame and fortune between 1945 and 1947 thanks to the movies: James Cain (*Mildred Pierce* and *The Postman Always Rings Twice*), Raymond Chandler (*The Big Sleep, The Blue Dahlia,* and *The Lady of the Lake*), David Goodis (*Nightriders*), and of course Dashiell Hammett, who was several years their senior.

The industrialists of the movie business, as Simenon called them with a touch of scorn and defiance, no longer shunned him. It seems to have dawned on them that his work was an inexhaustible lode of story lines. But could the elusiveness of these stories be captured in pictures? It was a question that had already been widely debated.

"When you read him, you tend to say, 'What a great picture this would make!' But nine times out of ten, it turns out not to be so simple. . . . You think you have a density of action, but really it's all atmosphere, description, and painstaking character portraits," said Marcel Carné.[51]

In the spring of 1948, Simenon spent eight days in Hollywood. In less than a week he decided that the dream factory was "the most artificial city in the world, where people are valued only by the fees they command and are compelled, sometimes against their will, to lead lives commensurate with those fees."[52] Despite his considerable chameleon gifts, it was not a place he could adapt to. But he had received so many proposals that it seemed worthwhile to make the trip to talk directly with the leaders of the big studios.

The British film industry had opened the Simenon mine just after the war with Lance Confort's screen version of *L'Homme de Londres* (1934), released under the title *Temptation Harbour*. Now, some ten years after Julien Duvivier's version, Burgess Meredith and the producer Irving Allen were thinking about a remake of *La Tête d'un homme* (1931), casting the grumpy but powerful Charles Laughton in the role of Maigret and entitling the film *The Man on the Eiffel Tower*. They even planned to reconstruct 36 Quai des Orfèvres, the headquarters of the Judiciary Police, on a studio lot.

If Simenon hesitated to sell Allen the rights, it was for legal rather than artistic reasons. He had not yet settled all the outstanding questions of his position under the Occupation, and the character of Maigret was still owned by the state-appointed administrator of Continental's assets. The administrator in question, while delighted to act as coproducer, was not prepared to relinquish the rights, especially since several other projects were in the works.

Far from Paris as he was, Simenon was afraid of abusing the trust of his American partners. If one of them made a Maigret film and the French administrator sued to block its release, his reputation would be ruined and the market closed to him forever. In any event, for financial reasons he had already decided to sell as few rights as possible to the French film industry, reserving his most promising products for the Americans and the British.[53]

He stayed with Jean Renoir for most of his visit to Hollywood, and he brought his old friend a present: a copy of *La Fuite de Monsieur Monde* (1945). He was convinced that Renoir was the man to bring this novel to the screen, and he was willing to cede him the rights "without commercial considerations." A vague enough formula, especially as far as the money men were concerned, but one that could only encourage the project. Renoir read the book in one sitting. He was enthusiastic, and he had the means to act on his enthusiasm, for he had recently joined several associates in setting up his own production company, The Film Group.

During a dinner at Charles Boyer's home, the novelist himself suggested that the screenwriter Elliot Gibbons be asked to adapt Norbert Monde's story for American audiences. Renoir loved the idea:

"Transposing the story would let me shoot in real streets of real cities, giving it the 'documentary' flavor your books have, which the moviegoing public increasingly likes these days."[54]

The two men agreed to meet soon afterward in Arizona to discuss the project. But the film was never made. Confronted with the financial realities, Renoir abandoned hope of creating a truly independent production company. But he still wanted to make a Simenon movie. He was fascinated by *Trois Chambres à Manhattan* (1946), and had Leslie Caron in mind for the role of Kay. He gave the book to Charles Boyer to read, and Boyer loved it, but he had reservations about a film. He feared the wrath of the puritanical Hays office, the self-censorship committee of the American film industry.[55]

Boyer wanted cuts in the text. Renoir, unconvinced, consulted several friends conversant with such matters. Like many of his projects, this one would never be made. But Marcel Carné and Jean-Pierre Melville were soon in competition for the book. The former, better known and having a better reputation, had already filmed one Simenon novel, *La Marie du port* (1938). He therefore carried the day. His idea was to shoot the film on location, in an effort to shed his old image as a studio director. The picture was finally made years later, in 1965.

In early 1949, Simenon got a present from *Ellery Queen's Magazine:* the prize for the best detective short story of 1948. Despite Sven Nielsen's wry comment ("A Buick for a Frenchman"), he was less impressed with the $2,000 prize money than he was with the honor, which sincerely moved him. It was the first time a French-language author had won this award where Anglo-Saxons had been the unchallenged masters. Wilbur Daniel Steele came in second, Ben Hecht fifth.[56]

It showed every sign of being a vintage year. He had the sense that *Les Quatre Jours du pauvre homme* (1949), which had just been published, was his best novel yet:

"And besides that, it opens a new path I glimpsed long ago," he confided.[57]

In the meantime, he had recently been in one of his "trances," immersed in his next novel, *Un nouveau dans la ville* (A New Man in Town, 1950). The hero, Justin Ward, about forty years old, moves into a small town in the American North. He adapts, settles in, and tries to forget his past, while nevertheless rejecting any real communication with the natives, an attitude that only piques their curiosity. The more mysterious he is about his past, the more they seek to provoke a crisis that will force him to reveal the presumably sinister part of himself. They are ready to go as far as murder to restore the town's sense of peace and serenity.

In the midst of his work on this novel, having instructed his entourage not to interfere in his "state of grace," Simenon suddenly found himself in a situation not unlike his fictional character's. At forty-six, his past caught up with him.

The Occupation again. Apparently the institutions of justice of the Liberation had not spoken their last word on the matter. At four o'clock in the afternoon of July 16, the purge committee in charge of literary figures met in the Ministry of Arts and Letters on the Rue Saint-Dominique to discuss the disposition of its final case: Georges Simenon. The file had been passed back and forth from publishers to movie people, who had been unable to decide whether the subject of their investigation had been primarily a screenwriter or a novelist at the critical time. In the end, the prefect of the Seine declared that Simenon was above all a novelist.

At the close of this last session before the dissolution of their committee, the purge officials issued a sweeping condemnation of Simenon, who was declared "subject to the totality of the temporary interdictions of Article 3 of the decree of May 30, 1945, for a term of two years from the present date."[58]

This meant that for the coming twenty-four months he was denied the right to publish novels or articles, to give public speeches or radio broadcasts, to sell film rights to his books, or to draw any financial benefit from his literary activity. He was notified of the decision five years after the liberation of Paris.

Simenon was stunned when he read the letter from his lawyer announcing the news. Once he recovered from the shock, he was furious. He did not understand how they could condemn him without giving him the right to answer the charges against him, whatever they were. He forgot that he had received a summons in the middle of the summer, and had routinely forwarded it to his lawyer.

"I can go back and take my place there whenever I want," François Combe said in *Trois Chambres à Manhattan*. Combe's creator was not so fortunate.

Maurice Garçon wanted him to return to Paris. He felt the case was serious enough for his client to suspend his other activities. His strategy was simple: appear before the committee, offer an explanation, and have the decision rescinded. In the meantime, it had to be kept absolutely secret, even from Gaston Gallimard and Sven Nielsen, who would be very unhappy with a ban on selling their thousands of copies of books by Simenon.

Garçon felt the case could be won. He had seen the file, which basically consisted of a few letters between Simenon and the managers of Continental. Nothing really compromising, apart from a favorable allusion to the collaborationist Jean Luchaire, the expression of friendly feelings for Alfred Greven, and ill-contained impatience at being restricted to Fontenay-le-Comte "while any Gaullist can circulate freely."[59] A two-year ban for that seemed a bit much.

Simenon was eager to defend himself, but felt he needed a few weeks before leaving the United States. Apart from finishing *Un nouveau dans la ville* and the two Maigrets already in the pipeline—*Maigret et la vieille dame (Maigret and the Old Lady,* 1950) and *L'Amie de Madame Maigret (Madame Maigret's Own Case,* 1950)—it was absolutely necessary that he attend the opening of *The Man on the Eiffel Tower.* He was simply too busy to go all the way to Paris to seek forgiveness for a sin he had not committed. In his mind it was obvious that he had nothing to feel guilty about. While requesting that his attorney represent him before his self-proclaimed "judges," he drafted a five-page statement responding to the accusations point by point.

The portrait that emerges from this plea is of a hounded man prevented from reaching the unoccupied zone, a man in a panic because he had been denounced as a Jew. A man who spent four years waiting for an *Ausweis* that never came, who began working with Continental without realizing it was a German company and continued because he had no choice, "just as a merchant cannot refuse to sell his goods." A man who had to sell his rights at a loss, who hid Allied paratroopers in his house, who had to take refuge in the depths of the Vendée to escape the occupier. As for that offhand remark about Gaullists, he agreed that it was infelicitous but suggested a different interpretation: "Why go after altar boys when priests are left alone?"

If his colleagues on the committee did not agree, they might at least entertain the possibility of reducing the interdiction to a fine. Or of allowing the intervention of some influential personality with whom he had friendly relations, Louis Joxe, for example, the director of cultural affairs at the Quai d'Orsay. In any event, the proposed sanction seemed especially harsh. A two-year suspension would be harder to bear in 1949 than in 1945, since the public would assume that the delay had been caused by a long and difficult inquiry. The injustice would therefore be twofold.[60]

To be able to work more peacefully Simenon withdrew to Carmel-by-the-Sea, a small town on the California coast south of San Francisco, at the time a sort of Antibes for little old ladies. But he was unable to forget the case that now haunted him anew.

His lawyer's view was that the whole matter was more complicated than Simenon realized. There was some evidence that his file had been placed at the end of the queue by someone who had repeatedly postponed it in order not to damage the writer. As though time might bury it. Unfortunately, the writer Francis Ambrière, director of the Guides Bleu at Hachette and winner of the Prix Goncourt for 1940 (awarded in 1946), had ceded the chairmanship of the purge committee to an overenthusiastic magistrate intent on disposing of all outstanding cases and thereby bringing the final sequels of the Occupation to a close.

Simenon's exile counted against him. Garçon feared the worst: if some zealous commissioner shut down a play based on a Simenon novel, it would be a front-page scandal.[61] Simenon himself feared a more sweeping cataclysm: films banned, books confiscated, radio tapes placed under lock and key.

All the worrying turned out to be for nothing. Friendly pressure was brought to bear, and everything was settled quietly. Committee rules provided for no appeals, but rules could be adapted to circumstances. The Simenon case was closed, and with it the purge of French writers.

"Circumstances beyond my control"—that was the argument Simenon used in refusing to return to Paris to face the music. The "circumstances" in question were a baby, his second son, Jean, known as Johnny, to whom Denyse gave birth in Tucson, Arizona, in September 1949. Simenon seems to have been as moved by this birth as he was by his first son's. He was euphoric.

Barely a few days after completing *L'Amie de Madame Maigret* (1950), he threw himself into *Les Volets verts* (1950), while simultaneously considering Jean-Louis Barrault's informal proposal that he write the script for a police pantomime.[62] Brimming with projects, he was working as fast as he could and was more sure than ever that his next novel would be his best. He described *Les Volets verts* as "perhaps the book the critics have long been asking of me and which I have always hoped to write one day." Simenon considered this novel "a capital work" in his output. Even Gaston Gallimard admired it without reservation. Simenon was so exhilarated by the birth of his second son that he proposed to step up his rate of production, writing one or two literary volumes a year for his former publisher. Unfortunately, because of a downturn in the book trade, Gaston could guarantee Simenon no more than twenty thousand copies per title instead of the thirty thousand he demanded. Moreover, he took more than a month to inform him of the fact. Doubly offended, Simenon preferred to forget the whole deal. It would be a long time before these two men would work together again.[63] But no matter, three-month-old Johnny made the peccadilloes of business seem derisory.

"Even the sun has a different taste!" he confided to a female friend.[64]

Simenon was not the only one to be transformed by Johnny's arrival. Denyse would no longer accept the equivocal status of mistress-secretary midway between the official Mrs. Simenon and a cook utterly devoted to her master. She now wanted to be Mrs. Georges Simenon, in law as well as in fact.

For some time the novelist had made no attempt to conceal the situation. In many letters he describes Denyse as his companion, not merely a secretary but a collaborator of particular efficiency in that she was perfectly bilingual.

Denyse herself, responding to his important mail when he was in the middle of a novel, was less and less inclined to sign "Mlle Ouimet, Secretary." She gradually ceased referring to her "employer." They were now "Denyse" and "Simenon."

He had been thinking about divorce for several months, and if he had yet to take the step, it was not for moral reasons. Indeed, he had been one of the only people in the United States to send an affectionate message to Roberto Rossellini and Ingrid Bergman at the time of their "affair," when the American public refused to pardon one of its screen idols for having had an illegitimate child.[65]

He had but one aim: to keep his family around him. For that he was ready to negotiate, and lawyers soon became involved. Everything was put on the table: from the house in Nieul-sur-Mer to paintings by Tigy and by Georges's old friends in Montparnasse. Tigy was to be given a comfortable alimony payment, life insurance, and custody of their son. But she would have to commit herself to living within a radius of six miles of Simenon's residence, wherever it might be, so that he could see Marc every day.

On June 21, 1950, a divorce decree was issued in Reno, Nevada. The next day, in the same town, Simenon married Denyse Ouimet under terms of separation of property. In officially announcing his marriage to the press, Simenon introduced Denyse as his new wife, his secretary, and his manager. He said she would now be dealing with all his contracts.[66] Some days later, their bags were packed for Europe. It was a honeymoon, not a definitive return.

Having remarried, he also decided to change his residence. He was not sure where he would go, but improvisation had always served him well in choosing where to live. The priority was to find the best possible schools for Marc. During a stopover in New York, he talked to a Belgian diplomat who sang the praises of New England: Indian summer, concerts, lakes, forests, the gentle colors of the landscape, which also seemed to imbue human relations. He got himself a map and a DeSoto, and without really planning it found himself in Connecticut.

14

LAKESIDE

1950–1952

The enthusiasm of the first contact made him lyrical: "It looks like the Vosges or the Fontainebleau forest!"[1] He found his new home on July 4, Independence Day, and he was well pleased with everything about it—the region, the town, the house itself. For the first time in years Simenon sensed that he was settling down instead of merely dropping in.

Lakeville, founded in 1789 but built mostly in 1816 on the hillsides of Litchfield, near Lake Wononscopomuc, was a quiet place where little ever happened. In 1850 the population was 3,103; a hundred years later, it had increased by 29.[2] It was a town of permanence and tradition: one main street, a few shops, a post office, a Methodist church, the offices of the local newspaper, two well-regarded private schools (Hotchkiss and Indian Mountain), and Hugo the pharmacist. No industry, but there were trout-filled streams and snow three months of the year. No library or good restaurants, but you could find those in Salisbury, just a mile or so away. The houses were the opulent country homes of affluent New Yorkers. The city was only two and a half hours away by car or train.

Shadow Rock Farm, so named because it was nestled in the shadow of an enormous rock face, may not have been one of the town's most beautiful homes, but it was surely the best located and the most original. At the very end of Cleveland Street on the edge of town, it overlooked a lush valley unbroken by walls or fences. It was ringed by forest, had no immediate neighbor, and had a lawn bordered by tall trees. There was the pool on the terrace.

The jewel of the fifty-acre property was the house itself. Built around 1770, it had been turned into a foundry manufacturing rifles and cannon for General Washington's insurgents during the War of Independence. Successive owners added many wings. The overall effect was of a structure designed by a slightly inebriated architect: eighteen low-ceilinged rooms (eight of them bedrooms), six bathrooms, two soundproofed offices, several dens, garages, and a stable—all deployed in staggered rows. It was like a book whose chapters the author had forgotten to put in sequence.

The seller, who had made many of these modifications, was a flamboyant, controversial figure. The scion of an conservative New York family, author of two successful books on the war, an editor of such prestigious magazines as *Time, Fortune, The New Yorker,* and *Life,* Ralph Ingersoll was the talk of the town, both for his romantic liaisons and for his relations with communists. Since his new wife, recently divorced from a teacher at the Hotchkiss school, did not want to live in the same town as her ex-husband, Ingersoll decided to move to Pennsylvania, abandoning the house he had been steadily enlarging for twenty years.[3]

Simenon fell in love with it at first sight, buying it on the spot for a quite reasonable sum. We do not know the exact amount, but on his departure the real estate agent Cope Robinson set the selling price at $39,000. He bought most of the furniture he needed at very low prices at an auction, and he found a more modest residence in nearby Salmon Creek for Tigy, Marc, and Boule.

It was George Campbell Becket, known as Cam, who found this extravagant house for him. Becket, a lawyer who had fled New York for Lakeville, quickly became Simenon's legal adviser and his best friend in town, though it must be said that pickings were slim. The locals were perhaps more civilized than in Arizona, but hardly outgoing.

Soon after his arrival, an official visited from Washington and suggested that he become an American citizen:

"Here it's like a kind of club. They'll accept you as a guest for a while if you want to play golf or tennis, but eventually you have to join up and pay dues."

"But I pay taxes just like the Americans."

"Still, you ought to be naturalized."

Simenon refused.[4] But he was impressed by the government envoy's arguments, and when he was offered membership in the Royal Academy of Belgium, he wondered about the incongruity: Georges Simenon, American writer and Belgian Academician.

The idea apparently continued to percolate, for he wrote to his lawyer in Paris:

"I have been living in the United States for six years now, by choice, because I like the country and the kind of life I lead here. One of my sons is already American, the other more than half. I am somewhat in the situation of a guest at a club. I am still welcome, while free of all obligation, but it is obvious that the day will come when it will be more natural—and more elegant— to become a member."[5]

That was a decision he never made, though it is not completely clear what held him back. Perhaps he sensed that this country was not as morally irreproachable as it claimed.

During his automobile excursion down the Atlantic coast in 1946 he had been struck by the widespread quotidian anti-Semitism. Despite what he had written on the subject and what he would write yet again, he was shocked to see signs in Miami barring Jews from hotels and beaches. In New York he had a similar experience in a leading hotel where he had made reservations for a playwright friend who was both French and Jewish. He was stupefied when the director of the establishment discreetly informed him that the hotel did not accept such people as guests.[6]

His old friend Josephine Baker, who spent a few days in Lakeville during a tour of the region, told him that she had had terrible trouble being served in a well-known Manhattan restaurant, both the staff and the customers making it quite clear to her by look and gesture that a black woman's presence was inappropriate.[7]

In 1951, when Simenon was considering applying for citizenship, the U.S. Senate rejected a bill to set up a commission charged with preventing racial discrimination in hiring and firing. These were also the early days of the witch-hunt. Senator Joseph McCarthy had accused the State Department of harboring 205 communist infiltrators, and repression raged in artistic and intellectual circles. In June the convictions of eleven communist leaders on charges of sedition were upheld by the Supreme Court.

Simenon passionately followed the radio broadcasts of the hearings held by the senator-inquisitor's permanent subcommittee. The torrent of mud, hatred, and injustice dissipated his last illusions about a democracy he had tended to idealize:

"I was angry at McCarthy and his ilk for sullying 'my' America," he would later say.[8]

It was then that he definitively abandoned the notion of becoming an American. Though still convinced that America was a land of unbounded sexuality and record criminality, he now knew that its Puritan roots were nevertheless hardy.[9]

His schedule in Lakeville was virtually unvarying. He would awaken at six in the morning and lock himself into his soundproofed office for several hours. This part of the ritual was immutable in all latitudes: windows closed, curtains drawn, pipes filled and lined up on the desk, manila envelopes, white paper, directories, maps, dictionaries, coffee, and one new item—Coca-Cola. He would write a chapter and then walk into town, buy some newspapers at Hugo's, go to the supermarket, and to the post office. When he was not in the middle of a novel, he spent as much time as he could with Marc, picking him up at school, clumsily joining the other fathers in baseball games, taking the boy for walks in the woods to indulge his passion for zoology, particularly reptiles. That was about the extent of his social life, though he felt that the local bourgeoisie lacked the "haughty pride and petty ideas" of its Belgian and French counterparts.[10]

Once a month he and Denyse would break their isolation by checking into the Plaza Hotel in New York and spending several days sampling restaurants and nightclubs: the Latin Quarter and the Stork Club, the Copacabana and the Brussels, Sardi's and the Twenty-One Club. Here Simenon rubbed elbows with fashionable night owls as vain and superficial as those he had frequented in Paris in the mid-thirties (supposedly to make Tigy happy). Apart from his business associates (publishers, agents, lawyers, producers), his only friends in New York were Justin O'Brien and the composer Edgar Varèse, an American of French origin with whom he enjoyed exchanging ideas during walks in Greenwich Village.

Exactly a year after he moved in, the *Lakeville Journal* published an article about him, eloquently entitled, "Georges Simenon, A New American." His face in the accompanying photograph beams with happiness. The reporter took pains to point out how different this Parisian novelist was from the Left Bank cliché most Americans imagined when they pictured a French artist. With his charming accent and continental humor, he also failed to fit the stereotype of a creative genius in an ivory tower. His answers to the reporter's questions were downright disconcerting.

Writing was labor, inspiration, discipline. How long did he spend on each novel? Nine or ten days. Most important thing in the education of children? Personality development. Favorite music? Dixieland jazz. Favorite writer? Faulkner. The reporter from the *Lakeville Journal* had no doubt: this was a man ripe for naturalization.[11]

But Simenon would never be an American, though he would write twenty-six novels of various genres during his five years in Lakeville, from *Tante Jeanne* (*Aunt Jeanne,* 1951) to *Maigret et le corps sans tête* (*Maigret and the Headless Corpse,* 1955), from *Feux rouges* (*Red Lights,* 1953) to *L'Horloger d'Everton* (*The Watchmaker of Everton,*1954). But there would be no Lakeville style, just as there had been no Tucson, Saint-Mesmin, or Fontenay-le-Comte style.

His themes were always developed according to an invariant logic based on internal necessity. When America comes into his novels, it is usually in the landscape, settings, or social definition of his characters. Only exceptionally is there a more marked presence.

His linguistic evolution was more prominent. His daily use of what was now quite serviceable English is to some extent reflected in several of his post-Liberation novels. In *Trois Chambres à Manhattan* (1946) his characters take the "subway" instead of the "métro." They meet after "lunch" and get a "nickel" in change.[12] On the first page of the short story "Les Petits Cochons sans queue" (Little Tailless Pigs), written in Florida in 1946, Simenon describes a Paris bistro on the Boulevard de Clichy: "They had their own reserved table near the window. It was part of their home," the last word appearing in English, in roman type and without quotation marks.[13] On the other hand, italics and quotation marks abound in *Feux rouges* (1953), which is set on the coast of the United States: *log cabin, highway, jukebox,* and so on. In *La Mort de Belle* (*Belle,* 1952), Christine Ashby is one of the "trustees" of a school; people go to "parties" and take walks down "Main Street."

In *Le Fond de la bouteille* (1949), Simenon even uses a twisted Anglicism, describing Nora as "efficiente."[14] In *Maigret chez le ministre* (1954) there is a reference to *Le Globe,* a newspaper that "does not enjoy a large *circulation,*"[15] instead of *tirage.* Not only his fiction but also his correspondence was marked by his Anglophonic environment. He often reports that he and Denyse are "on the wagon" or "off the wagon,"[16] expressions few Europeans would have understood.

His newfound proficiency in English allowed him to begin an exercise he had long yearned to perform: checking some of the translations of his books. Where earlier he didn't care, he now began to quibble. He was no longer satisfied to entrust the task to Denyse. He insisted on reading proofs before publication. There were arguments about what Maigret should be called. Simenon wanted "inspector," his translator "superintendent." A suggestion aimed at satisfying both British and American readers was "detective."

He was irritated to find that translators had more trouble juggling past and present in the same sentence than he did. He noticed that they often altered his turn of phrase (for good reason), and he objected strenuously. If he, the author, had chosen to string words together in a certain order, it was deliberate. If the meaning wasn't clear, that was deliberate, too.

He knew, of course, that literal translations would be catastrophic. But he believed that his translators were taking too many liberties with the original. One of his major complaints was that he was often sent proofs when it was too late to make changes. He had a special horror of female translators: "They always put *dirty words* [sic] into my books," he complained, not without amusement. But things were far more serious when he found that additions or deletions had been made without his knowledge.

He was initially unaware that it was under the amicable pressure of T. S. Eliot that Herbert Read, his editor at Routledge in London, deleted a few *shits* from some of his Maigrets. Eliot and Read believed that British readers would be disagreeably surprised to encounter such vocabulary in high-class books.

When he found out, he did not insist. On the other hand, he was furious when he realized that Geoffrey Sainsbury, his first translator and one of his most lucid critics, had apparently arrogated a genuine right of review over his work. Since Sainsbury lived in Colchester, Essex, their duel was conducted through the post. The translator not only stuck to his guns but further angered the author by citing his "inalienable rights" to Simenon's novels in the English language, even declaring his willingness to slay a living character if the supposed tastes of "his" public seemed to require it. Simenon vigorously rejected Sainsbury's claim to authorship by proxy.

The inevitable ensued when Simenon discovered with stupefaction what had happened to *La Vérité sur Bébé Donge* (1942) in translation. In 1952 he broke relations with Sainsbury, guilty of having gone so far as to act on the advice the novelist had given him at the beginning of their collaboration in the thirties: "Be my ambassador in Great Britain"—a suggestion Sainsbury had translated a bit too literally for the author's taste.[17]

Simenon's feeling for French life, Parisian or provincial, was rarely stronger than in the forests of Connecticut. Distance in space and time was necessary to the strange alchemical process that he called the decantation of memory. The settings of the novels written during his first fifteen months in Lakeville were always French. But the atmosphere of America seemed to suit his morale. Denyse freed him of all administrative concerns, while Sven Nielsen saw to his finances in Paris. His readership was on the rise on both sides of the Atlantic. Reviews were generally favorable and, most important, regular. His New York publishers now planned to issue six of his novels a year. The success of *La Neige était sale* (1948) had something to do with that decision, as did Hollywood's enthusiasm.

"It does me good to have nothing to fear anymore," he confided to his publisher in a moment of abandon.[18]

But Simenon was not a man to rest on his laurels. He was too viscerally tormented to shed his chronic anxiety. His first months in Lakeville were so thoroughly harmonious that he displaced it to secondary matters.

For instance, when he sent the manuscript of *Les Volets verts* (1950) to his publisher, he was once again seized by his recurrent fear that it might be taken as a roman à clef. The initial reaction of his first reader proved this fear justified. Sven Nielsen recognized Raimu in the character of the hero, Emile Maugin, an actor of about sixty with a difficult personality, imperious with those around him, ostentatious in his crudity, too deeply anguished to be satisfied with his glory and too weak to stop drinking.

That was exactly what Simenon wanted to avoid, especially since Raimu, who died in 1946, had been one of his best friends. To prevent any possible misunderstanding, he and Nielsen agreed that the classic "Any resemblance . . ." disclaimer would be replaced by a foreword of about twenty lines categorically denying that his hero had been inspired by a famous actor:

"... Maugin is a portrait neither of Raimu, nor of Michel Simon, nor of W. C. Fields, nor of Charlie Chaplin, whom I consider the greatest actors of our epoch. However, exactly because of their stature, it is impossible to create a character of their import, in their profession, that does not borrow certain traits and certain foibles from one or another of them. All the rest is pure fiction. ..."

In private, while reaffirming that Emile Maugin was created out of whole cloth, he acknowledged having begun with an amalgam of Harry Baur, Michel Simon, Chaplin, and "above all" W. C. Fields.[19] The most perspicacious of his readers turned out to be not a critic but an ordinary fan in Medellín, Colombia, with whom he had a copious correspondence. Mauricio Restrepo had the temerity to wonder whether, on reflection, Maugin was not perhaps Simenon himself, since there were certain striking similarities. The author replied that with the exception of the very first pages, these were only disturbing coincidences. *Les Volets verts* (1950) opens with a medical visit similar in some respects to Simenon's fateful 1940 checkup in Fontenay-le-Comte, described thirty-one years later in *Mémoires intimes* (1981).[20]

In 1950, Presses de la Cité published a critical study that marked a significant stage in the consecration of his reputation. *Le Cas Simenon,* by Thomas Narcejac (alter ego of Pierre Boileau), remains a luminous and unparalleled analysis of his novels, despite the fact that there would be another twenty-two years of them after its publication. Narcejac's essay covered everything, though his periodization of Simenon's work was debatable or even erroneous: the Maigret epoch (Fayard), the epoch of characters victimized by fate (Gallimard), and what he called the era of will (Presses de la Cité), as though the characters of the later books somehow refused to submit to their destiny. That aside, rarely has a commentator so perceptively grasped the themes, mainsprings, and lines of force of such a complex and disconcerting novelistic universe.

Le Cas Simenon—a title whose emphasis on his "phenomenon" side irritated him—was also notable for the serene assurance with which the essayist disposed of the most hackneyed clichés: the author of detective stories, the man who writes too fast for his own good, who makes slapdash errors and has a penchant for seeming facile, the entertainer considered suspect by literary circles, the virtuoso whose art amounts to entertainment, the mere expert in technique. The book leaves the strong impression that Narcejac's primary aim was to rebut and combat an unfair reputation. Satisfied that he had attained that goal, he wrote:

"There is no need to belabor the point. Simenon's work can be apprehended at a glance. It has simplicity. Few truly essential characters. Several powerfully linked themes. Extremely varied settings, but grouped around

certain key images. The only problem to which Simenon has yet to find a solution: the problem of happiness, which is also that of duty."[21]

As welcome as Narcejac's effort was, Simenon eagerly awaited a study by a
far more prestigious author: Gide. Unfortunately, it would never be published, for Gide died in Paris on February 19, 1951. Four days later, Simenon
was already expressing concern about the fate of his library. He asked Sven
Nielsen to make the necessary inquiries in the event of a sale, and to be prepared to buy back copies of his own works annotated by Gide.[22] The mysterious study turned out to be not a manuscript but a brown folder soberly
labeled "Simenon" and referred to by its owner as "The G.S. file," the initials
standing not for "Georges Simenon," as might be imagined, but for "Gide
Simenon." Inside the folder were drafts of analyses of texts, press clippings by
the critics André Thérive and André Billy, dozens of notes scribbled on bits
of paper, critical reports probably written early on for Gaston Gallimard,
typed quotations taken from various works, a few letters from Gide to
Simenon, and many from Simenon to Gide.

In 1969 the file was given to Gaetan Picon, who was writing an article on
relations between Gide and Simenon for *Le Figaro littéraire*.[23] Later it was
pored over and partially reproduced by researchers.[24] But there were always
missing pieces: not only the majority of Gide's reading notes but also some of
Simenon's post-Liberation letters, which were never published, some because
they were considered too personal, others because Gide himself had marked
them "of no interest" or "of no importance." Yet these letters are among
Simenon's most revealing writings, retrospectively clarifying obscure areas of
both his private life and his creative genius as he saw it.

Gide may have been the only person to whom Simenon expressed his conception of love and the nature of his relations with women:

> . . . I remember that evening at the Claridge when you affectionately
> chided me for revealing nothing about my private life—by which I as-
> sumed you meant my love life or sex life. Today I'll do it, if you will,
> because these, too, are things of which I have never spoken to anyone.
> I think that recently they have had, and will continue to have, a great
> influence on my work. In the hundred or so novels I wrote up to 1946
> and which you have read, I believe I never spoke of love otherwise than
> as an accident, even a malady, I think almost a shameful malady, in any
> event something that could only belittle man by depriving him of his
> mastery of himself. And that was more or less the way I felt about it.
>
> Married at nineteen, I basically wanted a mate, almost a companion.
> And since I made a commitment, I made it a point of honor to respect it,
> almost scrupulously. Since, at the same time, I was devoured by curios-
> ity and had more than my share of appetites, I spent more than twenty

years settling for compromise. In other words, for twenty years I forced myself to avoid anything that could accidentally compromise the peace of my household—child, illness, scandal, etc. Perhaps this is what gave my work that [illegible] tone that is found everywhere in it, that note of cold, clear despair which I think I rendered in a particularly tangible form in *La Fuite de Monsieur Monde* [1945].

I, too, you see, am afraid of inflicting pain. And I was convinced that my wife would be devastated by any lapse in conduct. . . . A banal accident delivered me, and I now regret that it did not happen sooner. In 1944, shortly before Liberation, my wife surprised me [with] my maid. And I discovered that what I had assumed was love was in fact only pride, a need for possession, for domination . . . later I came to know love by chance, both love-passion, whose quasi-Greek beauty I discovered, and tenderness. Did I express it badly in *Trois Chambres à Manhattan* [1946]? I don't know. Did I fill it with too much of the romanticism I had so fiercely resisted until then? . . . It took me twelve months to write *Lettre à mon juge* [1947]. I don't know what it's worth either. I wrote it to rid myself of my phantoms and so as not to commit the act my hero did. Since then, for more than a year now, I have had the sense of leading a new life, one as full and as juicy as a fruit.[25]

Gide was one of the few people, if not the only person, to whom Simenon mentioned Christian, the skeleton in the closet:

"You're the only one to whom I have spoken of my brother. That's why it is to you alone that I have the sadness to announce that he has been killed in action on the Indochina front. He paid dearly, courageously, for a venial error, while those responsible escaped. I have long wondered whether I was wrong to send him there. Having thought about it, I don't think so."[26]

Gide was also one of the few people to whom he felt free to report what he thought of the critics: "I have been working hard. Next month I hope to begin a rather important novel. But I am stunned at the quality of the new crop of French critics. So much so that I have stopped reading them. Where do they get these people? They don't even have the elementary honesty to do a little research on material details, they mix up dates, titles, and soon authors. I far prefer American, and especially English, critics."[27]

Gide was one of the few people to whom he confessed the mainsprings and limits of his own writing mechanisms: "For relaxation I'm going to write a *Maigret*, since I'm not capable of writing two 'hard' novels one after the other. And also because I'm unhappy and grumpy when I go a long time without writing. A lot of people must be wondering why I go on with this police series. You can see that the explanation is quite simple."[28]

Gide was one of the few to whom he dared offer his view of his recent reading: "I suppose you've read Faulkner? To my mind, he has [illegible] life in the South (Georgia, Carolina, Virginia) better than anyone else. He is also, with Steinbeck, my favorite American writer. Much better than Hemingway, to my mind, who is very Europeanized. But as they say in Liège, 'what the hell business is it of mine?'"[29]

He expressed particular hostility to postwar French literature: "It's as though the French think all other epochs were dull and calm and that only today do people have a conscience. Well, what kind of era did Montaigne live in! It's too much, really. . . . I'm sure I sound incredibly pretentious, but while reading *Le Sursis* [Jean-Paul Sartre's *The Reprieve*] I thought of a mixture of Céline and Simenon concocted by a prep-school boy winking at other prep-school boys over coffee at the Café de Flore. My God, how detached from literature I feel, or how far literature is from me! Provided I'm right. It's a little scary to think about the thousands of pages I've blackened for nothing. . . . Don't tell anyone that I have the temerity to have literary opinions, so to speak. They'd only laugh at me."[30]

Strangely, Simenon is almost wholly absent from Gide's *Journal:* there is no mention of him in the first volume, completed in 1939, and only eight references in the second, which goes to 1949. Not much for a man Gide considered "perhaps the greatest and most genuine novelist we have in French literature today."

The truth is that Gide considered Simenon's work astonishing in its sweep but uneven in quality. He loved *La Neige était sale* (1948) but not *Pedigree* (1948), whose slow gestation he had closely followed but which he found boring, flawed, and all in all well short of the author's capacities. Nor did he appreciate *Trois Chambres à Manhattan* (1946) or *Lettre à mon juge* (1947), which he believed were too facile, contaminated by the author's newfound happiness.

At the age of eighty, he no longer considered his study of Simenon a priority, since its "subject" had not really fulfilled his promise. On reflection, neither the person nor the work had matched the high hopes the master had placed in them. Disappointed, he postponed the project so often as implicitly to abandon it.[31]

The bits and pieces of his projected essay are nonetheless instructive, for they afford us a hint of why Gide was so entranced by Simenon's talent. He was unequivocal in defending the author against his reputation:

> Simenon today is our greatest novelist, and tomorrow I will no longer be alone in saying so. Alone? Not quite, for even now he has many fervent admirers in Paris, the provinces, and abroad. I would not be at all surprised if he soon became fashionable in broader circles, even with some degree of snobbery mixed in, taste becoming fad. But in the meantime, Simenon is still being victimized by the public's mental laziness,

the tendency to adhere once and for all to first impressions. The success of some of his early books has earned Simenon a dangerous reputation as an author of crime novels, a suspect and discredited genre that confines him to the suburbs of literature. He has published ten, fifteen, twenty excellent books of quite a different nature one after the other, but nothing doing: once a detective, always a detective.

He was incisive in grasping the essence of the inhabitants of Simenon's novelistic universe:

> Much has been made of how ordinary Simenon's characters are. It is true that they are frightfully ordinary. But what strikes and touches me is their awful, harrowing awareness of this ordinariness of their lives, and the effort they sometimes make to escape it, an awkward and absurd effort that most often draws them into deeper grief. . . . The frightful mediocrity of their daily lives. The desperate, criminal effort to escape the boredom, the fatigue of the rat race. Then suddenly a random convulsive shift, brought on by some triviality, and all at once the automaton jumps the tracks. It is an inconsequential moment lasting but an instant, and he spends the rest of his life repenting. No, not religious repentance, but he no longer feels at home in the society of those around him, the same people as before. That path is barred to him. It is, then, the act of an abulic (which is what nearly all the characters are in Simenon's books, at least the main characters) who can escape this tedious circle only through crime. That is the subject of many of his books.

He kept copious notes on the individual titles of Simenon's work, rereading even those he felt were least successful and highlighting strengths and flaws. For instance: "I reread *Le Locataire* [1934] in Sidi Bou Saïd. There is no better portrait, no better dialogue; but the subject of the book remains (and had to remain) monotonous and develops, like Arab music, on one level alone. There is no double subject, as in those of Simenon's books that I like most; no secret subject. And yet the ever-growing interest that Mme Baron, the mother and landlady, has for her criminal tenant, the almost maternal and protective sentiment that develops in her, admirably observed and hinted at in delicate touches, lends the book a psychological value, a sort of depth and weight that joins it to the best of Simenon's narratives."

He read with an unyielding attention to detail, complaining, for example, that a single page of *Les Noces de Poitiers* [1946] contained "four paragraphs ending with points of suspension (the last three completely unjustified). Not counting four others in the body of the text."

He noted other stylistic quirks as well. Of *La Marie du port*, for instance, he wrote: "Excellent in all respects. Nothing lacking. One of the best. How is it that it was not more strongly noticed? . . . A few annoying manias. The most irritating is probably the abuse of the question mark. Simenon does not say: X wondered whether . . . , but: why, then, did X wonder whether . . . Or: Y then remembered . . . , but: why, at that moment, did Y remember that . . . The better the book, the more this bothers me."

But he also expressed admiration for Simenon's narrative innovations. He appreciated the attempt in *Malempin* (1940) to "bring the past back to life in and through the present. Here the memories of the past alternate with the notation of the present. The chapters of memory alternate with those of the present. Strictly speaking, there is no mixture. And yet the past casts light on the present, which would be incomprehensible without it. This establishes a remarkable parallelism between the relations of father and son, going from one to the other of two generations."[32]

This sampling of raw material gives us a better idea of what Gide's *Simenon* might have been like. And Simenon's Gide? During the master's lifetime the novelist ceaselessly expressed his recognition, but later the memorialist would take some distance, admitting that he was incapable of reading Gide's books through to the end, so put off was he by their "elegance of style," as always with the exception of the *Journal*.[33] "Tried to read Gide, whose friend I became," he wrote in his notebook. "Couldn't do it. Never told him."[34] Asked whether Gide had had any influence on his work, Simenon replied, "I don't think so."[35] He was too proud and solitary a creator to admit that the aid he had sought so avidly might have turned into influence.

Shortly before Gide's death, Simenon, too, found himself cast in the role of master to a young colleague. Frédéric Dard, like Gide (though for different reasons), had abandoned his essay on Simenon, who was nevertheless convinced of Dard's talent and wanted to aid and encourage him:

"I am following the stages of your career with amicable attention. I have never had the slightest doubt about you. . . . If I can put you in touch with anyone, let me know and I will do so with the greatest pleasure."[36] When Dard expressed a wish to work in films in order to make enough money to continue writing novels, Simenon offered to introduce him into this milieu that he knew so well, supplying him with letters of recommendation. This was unusual for him, but few young writers treated him as "master."[37]

It was inevitable that they would eventually work together. The opportunity arose when Dard suggested a theatrical adaptation of *La Neige était sale* (1948), which he found particularly fascinating since he had himself written a story based on a summary execution he had witnessed during the postwar purge. *La Crève* was published in Lyons in 1946 in a semiprivate edition (five hundred copies). Dard sent a copy to Simenon, who was enthusiastic:

"I read your very large little book with great passion. It contains four or five pages that I wish I had written, which does not mean that the rest is not first-class. I have had faith in you for a long time, but I did not expect you to rise so high so fast. Keep it at, my friend! . . . Be careful with the dialogue, which is still a bit too literary (if it wasn't, it would be frightening that you had written it at your age). Bravo, with all my heart."[38]

Soon afterward Simenon agreed to write a preface for Dard's next book, *Au massacre mondain,* an unusual step since he hated prefaces and introductions. The first dissension arose between them while they worked together on the stage adaptation of *La Neige était sale.* Misunderstanding was fostered by distance and the proliferation of intermediaries.

Simenon had sworn that he would never write another play. He did not like the world of the theater, which was too ingrown for his taste. Yet he agreed to the project after reading Dard's first draft, which he found generally satisfactory, though he continued to insist that the action be set in an imaginary country and not, as Dard wanted, under the German occupation. He suggested a number of changes:

"I have made the rape less prominent, or at least less spectacular, for otherwise I think the play would be banned, or in any case we would be accused of sensationalism. I have put more emphasis on Frank's personal tragedy. For Holst, we can talk about that later. As for Lotte, I assure you that she remains in the play exactly as I saw her in the novel. I confess that personally I don't like contrived 'changes of pace' in plays, comic eruptions in the middle of a drama."[39]

It was, after all, his book. As he often recalled, he was the author, Dard merely his "collaborator," though he insisted that the script be signed with both their names on a single line.

The play premiered on December 12, 1950, at the Théâtre de l'Œuvre, with Daniel Gélin and Lucienne Bogaert in the leading roles. It was a hit, and the reviews soon crossed the ocean to Connecticut. When Simenon read them, he was furious. He found that the director, Raymond Rouleau, had taken the liberty of adapting the adaptation, replacing the old gentleman of the novel with a narrator, a role he decided to play himself. Simenon was outraged by this "tinkering." It was not so much the changes that offended him as the issue of principle:

"No change should be made in my text without my consent," he wrote.[40]

This director had treated him like a wholesaler, thus putting him in a situation he abhorred: his signature sanctioned and assumed responsibility for a text to which he had not given his approval. Simenon assured Dard that he still considered him a friend. But nothing would ever be quite the same between them. One day, many years later, one of Simenon's sons heard him railing against some wretched books he had recently read, among them the adventures of one Inspector San Antonio.[41]

In March 1952, after several postponements, Simenon finally decided to act on a plan he had been nurturing for most of the nearly seven years he had been living in the United States: a great European tour. It would give him a chance to introduce his new wife to his old friends and to get reacquainted with his old haunts. In his *Mémoires intimes* (1981) he devoted fifteen pages to this trip. But the most precious document allowing us to follow the exhausting two-month marathon is his diary, which better captures the whirlwind nature of the tour.[42]

Accompanied by Denyse, a nanny, and Johnny (Marc staying behind in Lakeville so as not to miss school), Simenon leaves the Port of New York on *Le Liberté* on March 11. During the crossing the limelight is stolen by Dizzy Gillespie and several other musicians who happen to be aboard, but things change when they dock in Plymouth. The Paris newspapers have sent reporters to cover the story of the novelist's return to the Old World.

When the ship reaches Le Havre, there is a minor riot. Jostling for position to get the best shot, photographers call out his name as though they were old buddies who had just seen one another the night before. The first reporter to approach him is a Belgian, the special envoy of *La Meuse,* who asks him what he is most looking forward to. The hero's reply makes headlines:

"Eat fries with sauce in Liège and fried mussels on the Rue des Bouchers in Brussels!"[43]

Everyone competes for running interviews with the great writer. To his colleagues' great consternation, Paul Guth of *Le Figaro littéraire* manages to make the Havre-to-Paris trip with Simenon. Someone gets a great picture. It may have been on the dock at Le Havre[44] or on the platform of the Gare Saint-Lazare in Paris a few hours later,[45] but there is no doubt that the tableau itself is worth an Atlantic crossing: Gaston Gallimard, Sven Nielsen, and Jean Fayard standing side by side, each waiting for "his" Simenon.

He barely has time to say hello before reporters close in. He tosses off a remark that one of them records:

"Seven years go by pretty fast. I see they haven't forgotten me."[46]

The reference is clearly to his publishers.

March 18: Interviews all day.

March 19: Ditto, but the most trying and heralded event is scheduled for late in the day: a cocktail party hosted by Sven Nielsen at the Claridge, the hotel on the Champs-Elysées where the Simenons are staying. Everyone flocks to greet the man of the hour.

"It looked like the sacristy on the day of a society wedding or a theater on the evening of a triumphal premiere. Georges offered handshakes and smiles like a prelate," one guest comments.[47]

The crowd is packed with actors and screenwriters, directors and journalists, writers and editors, who all have one thing in common: Simenon. There is Michel Simon, who had given an unforgettable performance as Monsieur Hire in *Panique;* Carlo Rim, his old drinking buddy; Jean Fayard, Arthème's son; Victor Moremans, an old sidekick from the *Gazette de Liège;* Pierre Lazareff, his accomplice at *Paris-Soir,* now the brilliant editor of *France-Soir;* and also Fernandel and Marcel Pagnol, Danielle Darrieux and Henri Decoin, Gaston Gallimard and Francis Carco, Thomas Narcejac and Jean Gabin, and many others. Lost in the crowd is three-year-old Johnny, introducing himself as "little Maigret."

One radio reporter, struck by the new Mrs. Simenon's serenity in the midst of this chaos, holds out his microphone to the husband:

"Is she really always this calm and sweet?"

"She really is. Always. It's very soothing. And good for me, too, since I tend to be nervous. Otherwise it would be dynamite."

"Because you lead a pretty agitated existence . . ."

"She's never agitated. She always keeps her calm, and her smile."[48]

The writer Francis Carco takes Simenon by the arm and leads him over to Frédéric Dard, who hasn't dared make the first approach.

"Let me introduce our common adapter," says Carco.

"I have no adapter," Simenon curtly replies, turning around and wading back into the throng of admirers.[49]

Dard, who has so looked forward to this first meeting with his "master," spends the night in tears.

After the cocktail party, Simenon takes a walk with Denyse in Montmartre, revisiting the sites where he had helped Tigy sell her canvases thirty years earlier. Then, before turning in, he decides to say hello to his friend Jean Rigaud and to drop by his old apartment on the Place des Vosges. His first typewriter is still there, in the same place.

Back at the hotel the fearsome Doringe waits for him impatiently. Official copy editor of his manuscripts, this seventy-one-year-old Belgian has been an English teacher, a reporter (covering everything from the dog-run-over beat to film reviews), and a translator of American novels. She is a direct and unyielding woman who openly admits that she has been blessed with the temperament of a wirehaired terrier. Her letters to Simenon always begin, "Sim, dearheart . . ." He has told her so often that she knows his work as well as he does that she once decided, against his wishes, to write an essay about him, but the printer lost it during the chaotic collapse of Belgium. Like a jealous old mistress, she demands that the management of the Claridge assign her the room across the hall from the Simenon apartments. She leaves the door ajar day and night, the better to survey his words and deeds. Whatever "her" writer does, she is always on the scene.

"I hardly see him more than you do these days, Doringe," Denyse complains.

"Yes," Doringe replies. "But *you* sleep in his bed."[50]

It is a friendship Simenon considers somewhat intrusive. She is like a maniacal old maid: touchy, skittish, demanding—and indispensable.[51]

March 20: After lunch Simenon runs into Frédéric Dard in the corridor of the hotel. Dard asks for a moment of his time. Simenon agrees. The young writer enters the suite, where the Simenon factory is running full force, the secretary hammering away at her typewriter. He decides to take the plunge.

"You humiliated me last night."

Simenon throws his arms around Dard's neck and kisses him on the cheek, then begins changing his clothes as though he were alone in the room.

"Listen, my boy, it was just a passing mood. You know, you should have warned me that you were going to tinker with my play. But come on, we must see each other again!"[52]

More kisses on the cheek, loud backslapping. In the elevator Dard is bitter: humiliation in public, rehabilitation in private.

Simenon gives interviews all day. Then he climbs the stairs of the NRF offices on the Rue Sébastien-Bottin, where the Gallimards give a cocktail party in his honor, from six to eight that evening. Gaston, the patriarch, still considers him one of the house's most important authors. As late as 1967 he will refuse to allow *La Nouvelle Revue française* to publish a reputedly unfavorable note about him. Jean Paulhan, the author of the note, will quarrel with Gaston about it.[53]

At a quarter to ten Simenon and his wife are dropped off at the Rue de Rivoli for an intimate dinner with Marcel Pagnol, Jean Prouvost, and several others.

March 28: Lunch at Jean Fayard's. Meeting with Bernard Grasset at 2:30 and at 5:30 with the British director Carol Reed, still basking in the success of *The Third Man.* Eight o'clock, dinner with Paul Colin, designer of the publicity poster for Josephine Baker's "Bal Nègre," decorator of the Anthropometric Ball. Colin has done well. At the table are the Pagnols, the Achards, the Lazareffs, the Rims, the Guitrys, and of course the invaluable Maurice Garçon. The atmosphere is electric after a lively exchange between Denyse and the lawyer. Despite the host's attempts at levity, tension mounts inexorably. Simenon hastens to show solidarity with his wife, and the couple soon find themselves opposing the rest of the guests. The conversation turns sour when the subject of the United States comes up. Simenon loudly praises his adopted country, taking the opportunity to vent all the hatred of France he has built up since the war. The argument is still raging when the coffee comes.

"America is the land of liberty!" he proclaims.

"Except when it comes to Jews and blacks," Maurice Garçon suggests.

"France, America," Simenon mutters, sinking into an armchair. "I don't give a damn. I'm a citizen of the world."[54]

Denyse, in tears, takes refuge in the bedroom. Not a very auspicious first contact with the "gang" he has talked so much about.

March 29: Lunch with Guy Schoeller, from Hachette. Dinner at Lasserre with the movie producer Michel Simon and the culinary expert Robert J. Courtine, future author of *Cahier de recettes de Mme Maigret* (Mme Maigret's Cookbook).

March 30: The Simenons spend Sunday at the estate of the Nielsens, in Charmentray.

March 31: Reception at the Belgian embassy.

April 2 to 5: A stay with the Pagnols on the Côte d'Azur. Cocteau joins them for lunch. "It's curious that we three are the only ones who could get anything we wanted from America," Simenon comments. "I've thought it over, and I can't think of any others."[55] Dinner at Saint-Paul-de-Vence with Henri-Georges Clouzot, whom he has not seen since the Continental days. The director is working on a plan to bring *Les Volets verts* (1950) to the screen. Another dinner, this one at Monte-Carlo, with the producer Alexander Korda.

April 6 to 13: Milan and Rome. Couturiers for Denyse, paparazzi for Simenon. Interviews, cocktail parties, and contracts with the faithful Mondadori. Lunch and dinner with the Renoirs.

April 14: Return to Paris. Races at Longchamp. Dinner for two at the Claridge. "Alone at last!"

April 15: Dinner with Sven Nielsen.

April 16 and 17: Days off. Simenon goes off to find out whether the women of Paris can brook comparison to their Roman sisters he has just sampled.

April 18: Official reception at 36 Quai des Orfèvres, headquarters of the Judiciary Police, capped with a great luncheon. The writer is greeted like one of the family by the prefect and several inspectors and superintendents. The various men Maigret was modeled on have all retired, and the fireplace his hero liked to stir has been replaced by central heating. Before the novelist leaves, a silver badge, no. 0000, is issued in Maigret's name. Simenon will have it made into a key chain, and one day will use it to get the gendarmes off his back when he is stopped for speeding. He will also show it to the writer Jacques Laurent, who will be horrified that his illustrious colleague seems prouder of the badge than of any literary distinction.[56]

Eight o'clock: Radio interview with Paul Guth, then off to the Rue Vavin for a miniature replay of the Anthropometric Ball at the ex-Boule Blanche, appropriately renamed L'Anthropométrie. Forty well-behaved guests instead of the hundreds of unchained revelers who attended the historic soiree twenty-five years earlier. Paul Colin sent out the "summonses." But no one's heart is in it. You can't do the same thing twice without killing the spontaneity, spice of emotion. At dessert Simenon slips away and joins the Martiniquaise dancers in their dressing room:

"I make the most of it, not with all four, but with two of them, while the others watch, smiling with all their gleaming teeth. A crazy life. I am gripped by a sexual frenzy that D. [Denyse] finds greatly amusing."[57]

April 20 to 25: A mystery. In his diary we find the detailed program of a stay in London: lunches, dinners, interviews, cocktail parties with such eminent personalities of the literary world as Graham Greene, T. S. Eliot, Harold Nicolson, and Herbert Read, as well as the sculptor Henry Moore, the producer Alexander Korda, and the director Carol Reed, not to mention his publisher, Routledge. But the pages devoted to his European tour in *Mémoires intimes* (1981) bear no trace of any of it. And Denyse, who was never apart from him for more than half a day throughout these two months, is sure that they never went to London on this trip.[58] It seems likely that the London excursion was canceled because time was growing short.

April 29: After an interview with the journalist Michel Droit, lunch at Lapérouse with Desvaux of the Judiciary Police, Mr. Garçon, and the medical examiner Dr. Paul, on the occasion of the awarding of the Quai des Orfèvres prize. Then departure for Belgium. At last the true return to his roots.

His program was especially crowded. For several days the local press was full of talk of the much-heralded event. But Simenon was apprehensive. The attitude of the folks back home had bothered him ever since he abandoned Liège for the world beyond. In December 1934, when Carlo Rim told him that he was to give a lecture there and would take the opportunity to talk about him, Simenon's face suddenly darkened:

"I advise you to do nothing of the kind, unless you want trouble. They have bad memories of me back there, 'they' don't like me, I stuck it to them a bit too much when I was a reporter."

"Georges is hated in Liège," Tigy immediately added.[59]

Relations between Simenon and his home town took a turn for the worse after the publication of *Je me souviens* (1945) and especially *Pedigree* (1948). The jacket flap of the latter book explained: "In *Je me souviens* everything is true and everything is accurate. In *Pedigree* everything is true but nothing is accurate." Some of his characters, alas, took offense. They were now lurking in the shadows of courtrooms, on the lookout for the right moment to pounce.

This was not the first time, of course. After the publication of *Le Chien jaune* (1931), he expected problems with the inhabitants of Concarneau, where the mysterious deaths of the participants in a regular card game took place. The mayor, in fact, made no secret of his displeasure.[60] After *Un Crime en Hollande* (1931), he feared he would never be able to return to Delfzijl, having decided, on reflection, that the settings and characters of that novel were uncomfortably close to reality.[61] *Le Bourgmestre de Furnes* (1939) contained a disingenuous introductory note claiming that the author had never set foot in this corner of Flanders—an attempt to mollify the local authorities. And of course there had been the faintly ludicrous *Coup de lune* trial.

But things were more serious in Liège. As early as December 1948 several of the more illustrious inhabitants began to wonder whether the models ought not to profit from a novel as well as the author. Sven Nielsen was worried. Various Belgian sources suggested that *Pedigree* might be banned because of what some interpreted as its attacks on the local ruling class. Convinced that powerful figures would not subject themselves to such ridicule, the author was quick to reassure his publisher. But just to be on the safe side, he asked four people to read the manuscript before approving the proofs. Despite these precautions, however, one character did rebel, a commercial agent in Liège by the name of Albert M., a former classmate of Simenon's at the Institut Saint-André who figures in a passage in which the cook makes advances to a pupil after luring him to a cellar. Simenon had put this in the book because the episode on which it was based made quite an impression on him at the time. He told his lawyer that he did not recall the pupil concerned.

"I don't even remember the name. . . . Between you and me, I could not swear it was M. Once again, the name came to me while I was writing *Pedigree,* and I never realized that it was the real name of one of my classmates."[62]

Aware of his mistake, Simenon agreed to change the last name, less for the plaintiff's sake than to set his mother's mind at rest, for the Christian Brothers had summoned Henriette to denounce the novelist's conduct and to ask her to intercede. Albert M., who was present at this meeting with Henriette, reportedly told her:

"It would be a lot easier if your son were here. Then I would just punch him in the mouth."

The brothers are said to have added:

"We need money for our schools. Your son, a former pupil and a rich man, ought to help us."[63]

Albert M. charged that Simenon had portrayed him as a thief and a degenerate, inventing an incident out of whole cloth for the needs of the novel. It did not help matters any when the Belgian magazine *Face à main* selected precisely these controversial passages when publishing an extract from the novel. Albert M. demanded not only the deletion of all the offending lines but also a letter from the author acknowledging that he had used his name by mistake, plus 250,000 francs in compensatory damages.

Garçon sensed that if it came to trial, Simenon would lose,[64] for the "moral prejudice" was real, as was the relation of cause and effect between the author's error and the prejudice. He therefore suggested an out-of-court settlement.

Simenon tried to sort things out by writing a piece for the *Gazette de Liège* stating that *Pedigree* was not at all a roman à clef; that its characters, admittedly not entirely invented, were in fact composites of various real individuals; that it was not meant to be a gallery of portraits; and that although it was true that the action was set in Liège in the early years of the century, it was all simply reconstruction and recomposition.[65]

It had been a mistake to take this case lightly. He ought to have realized that Albert M. was quite unlike the plaintiff in the *Coup de lune* trial, and the people behind him were not a bunch of hicks from colonial Gabon but the Christian Brothers of the Catholic schools of Liège, powerful figures in their own backyard.[66] After several months of negotiations, he lost patience:

"I am beginning to get sick of people who think their honor can be redeemed with banknotes."[67]

The two parties finally reached agreement on February 7, 1950. The author agreed to delete the phrase "who lured his classmate M. into the cellar to engage in obscenities," as well as three other references to the same event. The name Albert M. would be stricken from the entire text. The offending volumes were to be withdrawn from the shops and replaced by a new, expurgated edition. Finally, Simenon would pay 70,000 Belgian francs in damages and court costs.

He was apparently satisfied with this arrangement, since he congratulated his lawyer for a "fine success."[68] He felt that the worst had been avoided. But that was an illusion. Garçon chided his client and friend—"You are wrong to depict real people too accurately in your books"[69]—and took pains to warn his colleagues during a trip to Liège. Eager to stanch the spring from which blackmailers commonly drank, he wanted to guard against future problems, since despite the agreement reached in the M. case, he knew he could no longer count on his client's willingness to negotiate.[70]

But none of this prevented Albert M.'s lawyer from taking the case of a lady who decided she had been libeled in *Je me souviens*—published five years earlier. Simenon was truly stunned by what he considered "contemptible blackmail" motivated by equal parts of bad faith and ill will.

"I have always heard that the spirit of the law stands above and beyond its letter," he complained.[71]

Apparently not, for in January 1952 he was ordered to pay the plaintiff 20,000 francs. But her demand that all copies of the book be confiscated was rejected, since the offending passages had been deleted.

The door was now open to all sorts of abuses. A certain C., unhappy that Simenon had written in *Pedigree* that Henriette used to lock him in his room to make him study, demanded 500,000 francs in damages. But the zenith of outrage came when the brothers of the Catholic schools themselves, led by Brother Félix, demanded 100,000 francs on the grounds that their congregation in general and the Institut Saint-André in particular had been libeled in *Pedigree*.

This time it was too much. Simenon categorically refused to negotiate with people who prattled on endlessly about honor while relentlessly trying to extort money from him.

"These people are crazy. . . . It's getting to be a joke."[72]

That was also the view of the local press. "Who's Next?" one paper asked, reporting the latest lawsuit. This book was beginning to look like a gold mine.

Simenon, however, was beyond laughing. He could not forget what the brothers had said to his mother, words she repeated in her letters like a leitmotif:

"Your son is so rich and we are so poor. He should remember his days in our school and send us a contribution. . . ."[73]

He was now ready to take them on. In May 1952 the time seemed ripe.

He arrived in Liège on May 4 and deposited his baggage at the Hotel de Suède. He wanted to take a walk with Sven Nielsen and Denyse in the streets of his old stomping grounds. Impossible. Daniel Filipacchi, a photographer from *Paris-Match*, had tracked him down, and Simenon agreed to let him come along. He would have no cause to regret that decision, for the reporter would take some of the most powerful pictures in the thirty or so years that Simenon had been posing for cameras.

His first visit, of course, was to his mother's. He went alone, since he wanted this rare moment to himself. It was a brief but intense stopover.

"For me there was something both mute and moving about it," he later wrote. "Had I stayed any longer, I might have cried."[74]

Yet in the seven years since he left Europe, he had never lost contact with Henriette, phoning her often and writing even more often, especially after the appearance of *Pedigree*. He was afraid she would be angry with him for the way he portrayed her through the character of Elise Mamelin, a picture too sweepingly severe to be wholly accurate, as he later admitted.[75] He repeatedly told her that this was a novel and not an autobiography, but as it turned out, he did not know her as well as he thought, for she was angered not so much by his filial ingratitude as by his allusions to family stories and his repeated attacks on the Christian Brothers.[76]

The next day, before assuming his expected role of prodigal son returning to his native land, he had to appear in court in Verviers to end these Liégeois quarrels once and for all.

The plaintiff was not the Institut Saint-André but the famous C., former boarder of Henriette's on the Rue de la Loi and one of *Pedigree*'s many characters. The lawyers dueled.

"My client does not claim to have written an autobiography. This is a novel in which everything is true but nothing is accurate."

"He wrote that Dr. C. was a short young man, thin and blond."

"Would you have preferred that he not say so?"

"And that he chased after the maid."

"But he never said he caught her, nor that he touched her! . . . Have you received letters from any of Dr. C.'s patients saying: we will no longer go to you because you put a skeleton in the maid's bed at the rooming house you stayed in when you were twenty?"

Mr. Garçon won the audience over by ridiculing his opponent's arguments, an effective tactic given the unusual number of reporters in attendance. The plaintiff's lawyer responded by reading extracts from the book aloud. The effect was striking.

". . . it seems clear that Simenon did not like his youth, he hates the students his mother had to take on as boarders . . . "

"But it isn't me who says that, but Roger," an outraged Simenon murmured from the defense table.[77]

He had rarely found himself so trapped on the borderline supposedly dividing real life from fiction, an invisible no-man's-land he had unwittingly crossed a hundred times and which the judge now sought to define objectively. Everything is true but nothing is accurate. You can almost see him smile. In the meantime, magistrates attending the trial asked the author to sign copies of the book for them.

Simenon was ordered to pay 100,000 francs in damages to C. and to delete his name and the contested passages from future editions of *Pedigree*. The damages were reduced to 6,000 francs on appeal. Manifesting his difficulty in defining the literary genre to which *Pedigree* belonged, the judge called it "a novelized biography." But critics were not reassured. When the book reached the best-seller lists in Britain, the *London New Daily* put it in the "fiction" category, while the *Birmingham Mail* called it "nonfiction."[78]

The Belgian courts, eager to resolve the issue, held that while the plaintiff did suffer damage to his reputation and violation of the integrity of his private life, the author had not intentionally libeled him.[79] But *Pedigree* nonetheless turned out to be good business indeed, and not only for booksellers.

Several controversial names and passages were deleted from the 1952 reprint. For the 1958 edition Simenon wrote a preface explaining how this unusual book came about and why he would not continue it as initially planned.

> . . . For the most part, the events are not invented. But above all, I have exercised the privilege of re-creating characters on the basis of composite materials, staying closer to poetic truth than to truth as such. This has been so badly misunderstood that, on the basis of a physical feature,

a tic, or a similarity of name or profession, many people have believed to recognize themselves, and some have sued me.

I am, alas, not alone in this, for many of my colleagues have had the same experience. It is now difficult to give a character in a novel a name, a profession, an address, or even a phone number without risking legal proceedings. The first edition of *Pedigree* concluded with the words: "End of the first volume." I still get letters asking me when the next volumes will appear.

I left Roger Mamelin at the age of sixteen. The second volume was to tell of his adolescence, the third of his beginnings in Paris and his apprenticeship in what I have elsewhere called the craft of manhood. But these books have not and will not be written, for I dare not guess how many of the hundreds of secondary characters I would have to depict would file lawsuits asking substantial damages.

For the 1952 reprint, which was reset, I cautiously and perhaps somewhat ironically left the offending passages blank, preserving only innocent punctuation marks. In a brief foreword, I ascribed responsibility for these lacunae to the courts.

In the present edition the blanks have been removed. Not without regret, I have abandoned even irony and pruned from my book anything that might appear suspect or offensive.

I nevertheless repeat, in the interests of accuracy rather than caution, that *Pedigree* is a novel, and thereby a work in which imagination and re-creation play the greatest part, which does not prevent me from admitting that Roger Mamelin bears a strong resemblance to the child I was.

There would be no sequel to *Pedigree*. Simenon was so badly burned by the experience that he later asked his publisher to postpone the expurgated reprint of *Je me souviens*. In this case he could not claim the book was a novel, and he feared a cascade of suits:

"They're lying in wait for me now."[80]

He was so concerned about this problem that he wrote a foreword to *Le Fils* (1957) explaining that since one of his characters was a prefect, he had no choice but to place him in charge of a prefecture; that since a prefecture was necessarily located in a large city, he had chosen La Rochelle; but that the man who had been prefect of La Rochelle in 1928 should not take it personally.

Once the legal problems were dealt with, however, Simenon was treated to a hero's welcome in his hometown, walking through the city streets with a throng of reporters and a crowd of onlookers so numerous that from a distance it might have been mistaken for a demonstration.

He went first to Outremeuse, where he gave a speech, shook hands with the merchants, walked around the docks, visited dives and puppet shows, prayed for the Simenon family at the Church of Saint-Pholien, made a nostalgic tour of the classrooms of the Institut Saint-André, and received the accolades of Brother Félix, despite the pending lawsuit.

The proceedings had been well orchestrated by his old friend Victor Moremans. Naturally, one of the stops was at the offices of the *Gazette de Liège,* where Joseph Demarteau, his beard a little whiter, was still on the job. Threading his way through the rows of linotypists and editors, he threw his arms around the city's enfant terrible:

"My dear Young Sim!"

"It was thanks to you that I turned out all right."

"I am proud to have been your employer. A post not many have held, if I am not mistaken."

"If only you knew how much I would have liked to remain your Young Sim, writing a little column!"[81]

Simenon was astounded to find familiar faces in the office. He signed books in the pressroom, while printshop workers gave him a present as a souvenir.

A reception was held in his honor by the municipal authorities. Another speech and more handshakes. Before sitting down to eat, he and several others witnessed a painful scene. Denyse switched the place cards, taking the seat reserved for Henriette at her son's right.

"It was one of the worst memories of my life," he would later write.[82]

Another incident, twenty-four hours later, also left a bitter taste, though it is so novelistic, so Simenonian, that its veracity may well be doubted. If it wasn't true, it should have been. It figures prominently in his moving *Lettre à ma mère* (1974):

> I found myself in a large, comfortable, even luxurious villa, where a lavish dinner had been prepared for me. In the afternoon the journalists of Liège had given me a pipe with a gold band, which I placed beside my plate. After dinner the lady of the house, still young, plump and rather pretty, came over to me, an excited expression on her face.
>
> "Did you know, Mr. Simenon, that relations between your family and mine go back quite a few years?"
>
> I did not know what to say. I had been dragged to so many dinners, luncheons, and receptions that I did not even know my hostess's name.
>
> "I am the daughter of Mr. X. He was a friend of your grandfather's."
>
> I stiffened and nearly left without a word. She was the daughter of the man who had caused your father's ruin. I stayed for a few more minutes, then left thinking of the little girl of five you had been. The next

day I noticed that the commemorative pipe my colleagues had given me was missing. I mentioned it to one of them, who immediately investigated. The pipe was found. My hostess's son had appropriated it, hiding it in his room. So as you see, we were robbed twice by the same family.[83]

Another episode of his trip to Liège may have left an even more indelible memory. It is not mentioned at all in his autobiographical writings, but he told his mother about it in a letter written shortly after his return to the United States. He had been deeply moved by his return to his roots, except for one thing: the visit to the Christian Brothers.

"It was the only moment of my trip at which I was compelled not to be sincere and to speak words I did not believe," he said.

He had not forgiven their position in the *Pedigree* case, and he considered their invitation nothing but a blackmailer's trap. One of the brothers, while shedding a tear during his welcoming speech, had slipped him a note whose content was "both sniveling and threatening." Money again. Simenon said he was disgusted that "the Catholic party" had nearly ruined his trip to his native land.

"I am a child of Liège and not of the Saint-Nicholas Church!" he protested.

He considered the clergy's attitude the sole cloud in an otherwise gleaming tableau, a sharp contrast with the warm, pure, and disinterested greeting he had received from his fellow citizens. He sensed that had he fallen into the brothers' "ambush," they would have taken it as an invitation to continue to ask for money after his visit. In this he was not far wrong, for just after he left Europe, Henriette was asked to intercede with her famous and very rich son.

"My response: nothing!" he told her flatly.[84]

After Liège, he went on to Brussels, checking into a hotel on the Place de Brouckère for three days that were as routine and boring as his stay in Liège had been spontaneous and moving. The purpose of the visit, it must be said, was as official as could be: Simenon was to be inducted into Belgium's Royal Academy of French Language and Literature.

"They forced my hand," he later said by way of justification, though no one had asked him for an explanation.[85]

Why didn't he refuse? Probably because the honor both flattered his pride and enabled him to send a personal message to the citizens of Liège, to Walloons, and to Belgians:

". . . I do not find this excessively amusing, but I take advantage of the opportunity to show my compatriots that I have remained one of them."[86]

Several French immortals were present as guests of their Belgian colleagues that day: Marcel Pagnol, Pierre Benoit, Monsignor Grente, Georges Duhamel, Jacques de Lacretelle, and Maurice Garçon, a man elegant enough never to mention his membership in the French Academy but clever enough never to let it be forgotten either. Some of the French participants had come to support their friend Simenon in this ordeal, and their presence was especially appreciated, for the National Assembly in Paris was in turmoil on that day, discussing candidates to fill the late Marshal Pétain's vacant seat.

The great hall of the Academy, in the former palace of the Prince of Orange, was packed with celebrities and journalists. Members of the Belgian and French Academies, in full uniform, sat in tight rows. Queen Elizabeth occupied her loge opposite that of Mesdames Simenon—Henriette and Denyse.

At three o'clock Academician Carlo Bronne, writer and magistrate, counselor at the court in which Simenon had recently been found guilty of libel, began his opening speech, an address riddled with clichés about the man and his work: Inspector Maigret, physician manqué, restorer of destinies, magic realism, human brotherhood, atmosphere, penetrating observation, influence of the great Russian novel.[87]

A safe speech from a man Simenon had known for nearly thirty years. Bronne sold him the tuxedo he got married in, and Georges Sim named the director of the Judiciary Police in *La Fiancée du diable* (The Devil's Fiancée, 1932) after him.

Perhaps realizing the inevitably soporific effects of the exercise, Bronne suddenly turned lighthearted and lyrical:

". . . you were sixteen, a rebel youth burning with desire to escape mediocrity, and from the Pont des Arches you cried loudly, within earshot of many others: 'At forty I will be a member of the Academy!' And so you are, sir, albeit slightly behind schedule, perhaps because your journey from Liège to Brussels took you first across the globe! . . . Yes, sir, you have earned the right to say: the craft of manhood is difficult."

Simenon then took the floor to reply. He wore a dark suit instead of a robe, dispensation he had insisted on for fear of looking ridiculous with a cocked hat and a sword. He seemed as tense as a schoolboy about to make a graduation speech.

". . . I stand before you like the little boy I used to be, and I cannot but feel the admiring respect due great personalities . . . "

He then launched into a paean to his predecessor in this chair, the regional writer Edmond Glesener, honest workman of the word and bard of his little corner of this earth. Whether out of emotion or lack of training, Simenon proved to be a wretched orator, often stumbling over his words. The content of his speech was disappointing, too. Something freer, more rebellious, less— well, academic—might have been expected of such a man. But his talk was conventional, sedative, boring.

And for good reason, for Simenon had deliberately written it that way. It was a speech of self-reflexive irony, meant to satirize his predecessor in particular and Academy members in general, its ferocity masked by its soothing tone. The truth is that he loathed literati like Edmond Glesener and detested the regional literature in which Glesener excelled. Simenon was so ashamed of the "eulogy" he had been forced to compose that he would not allow it to be published in France.

Shortly before leaving Lakeville for Europe, he had tested the understated irony of this speech by submitting it to the sagacious Doringe. After noting her reactions, he detailed his strategy and confided his true intentions:

". . . As for Bronne, who is a good boy, probably an intelligent man, I took him as the prototype of the Belgian academician, one of those people who have read everything and understood everything—lawyers, judges, novelists, critics who, from the roof of Sainte-Gudule . . . Well, you get the idea. It has to go unnoticed now, at least by the majority. But the day will inevitably come—fortunately too late for them—when everyone will surely get the point. I've followed the old tradition. It's not Simenon, you say? Of course not! They wouldn't even let me open my mouth! . . . I hope they all believe I'm coming to thank them humbly for the great honor—unworthy me—poor author of detective stories—and so on and so forth."[88]

Simenon was quite amused, but he was pretty much the only one to know it. The ceremonial ritual was such an ordeal that he hurried to get it over with. Afterward he was introduced to Queen Elizabeth, amid a flurry of hand-kissing. A journalist swore he edged his way close enough to overhear the exchange between Her Majesty and a blushing Simenon:

"I am delighted to meet you, sir. The entire country basks in your reflected glory."

"You are too kind, Madame."[89]

At five o'clock it was finally over. The new academician and his wife disappeared into a limousine that took them to more dinners, more medal ceremonies, more speeches, more photo opportunities and interviews.

He was exhausted. Never had he been forced to forgo his indispensable afternoon nap for so long. He returned to Paris just in time to spend a few happy moments with his dear friend Michel Simon. As they lunched together in a bistro in Les Halles, the actor reported his desire for a role in a screen version of *Le Cheval-Blanc* (1938). The author claimed to have forgotten what the book was about. Simon explained it to him, and the two men were soon showing off.

"I wrote that? Sounds fantastic. And?"

They began to parody the latest Simenon novel, speaking lines, parodying characters, ranting and raving, using condiments as props.[90] They then slipped out of the restaurant and jumped into a cab, heading for the Saint-Cloud laboratory to view the rushes of *Brelan d'as,* the film Henri Verneuil had just made of "Le Témoinage de l'enfant de chœur." Simenon was thrilled. Ever since Simon's performance as Monsieur Hire in *Panique* (1947), he had been convinced that he had finally found the actor capable of "being" his characters.[91]

The house lights came on, and the show was over. It was time to return to Connecticut. He was dying to get back to Marc, Shadow Rock Farm, and his typewriter.

The European interlude remained a good memory for him. He was not yet aware of its psychological consequences for his marriage.

15

THE COLOR OF BUSINESS

1952–1955

Simenon returned from Europe unchanged, but for his wife the trip marked a turning-point in an evolution that began with Johnny's birth and continued with the divorce from Tigy. Two months of being constantly hounded by reporters and of society functions in the glittering circles of the Old World had given Denyse her first real sense of her husband's enormous popularity. The whirlwind seems to have gone to her head, and their relationship would now change dramatically.

It might be expected that a novelist fascinated by all the various forms of what he called "crossing the line" would be especially sensitive to the moment at which Denyse's personality went through a sea change. But he wasn't, perhaps because he was too close. At most, he noted foreshadowings and symptoms.

In letters and interviews he had lavishly praised her efficiency in managing his administrative affairs, an especially complicated task since his geographical isolation forced him to maintain an increasingly bulky correspondence, both private and professional. Denyse did not have to try to make herself indispensable. It happened automatically, for Simenon considered it the height of discourtesy not to reply to a letter immediately. And since his writing compelled him to cut himself off from others for ten days or so several times a year, he also needed someone to protect him from the bustle of the outside world.

After their return from Europe, however, he noticed that his wife increasingly cast herself as his agent. And she seemed so swamped—locking herself up with her secretary for hours, having unreasonably long phone conversations with editors and producers in Europe and America, dictating endless letters—that he wondered whether she was not perhaps overdoing it, whether this flood of energy and activity was not superfluous. On reflection, he soon became convinced of it.

This curious febrility was an early sign of trouble, soon confirmed by others. He did not appreciate the rudeness with which she treated his secretary, Béatrix Czernin, known as Trixie or "the countess," because of her high-society European birth and her Austrian aristocratic ex-husband.

One day he noticed that Denyse had destroyed an object he prized as highly as a family photo album: an old black notebook in which he had recorded the names and addresses of friends, correspondents, and relatives (some of whom had died), since his arrival in Paris in 1922. On her own authority she had replaced it with a new one, innocent of this past in which she had played no role. He would never forgive this censorship of his memory.[1]

They had words, something that was happening more and more often, especially when the bottle was on the table. Simenon had started drinking at an early age. He liked his liquor, but he was no alcoholic. His "drunks" were memorable, for they made him even more intense, and the hangover might require two days in bed. But he was quite capable of going weeks without anything stronger than soda—simply out of a temporary indifference to drink.

His letters to his publisher suggest that it was in October 1948, in Tumacacori, Arizona, that he first stopped drinking. He had just finished writing *Le Fond de la bouteille* (1949), a novel set in America in which alcohol plays a big part, and was about to start *Les Fantômes du chapelier* (1949), a far more sober story set in La Rochelle. And all at once he stopped: no whiskey, wine, or beer. It was as if he suddenly decided that he had had enough to drink in the past thirty years. He stuck to Coca-Cola and ginger ale and seemed none the worse for wear. In fact, he felt rejuvenated, and his productivity did not suffer at all.[2]

Although this sobriety did not last, he never became a slave to alcohol. The same could not be said of Denyse, whose dependency he considered damaging to their relationship. As she settled ever more securely into what she now considered her rightful role, she increasingly tried to dominate this frenzied individualist whom no one had ever been able to control. Their relationship began to take a new tack: tests of strength, power struggles, outbursts of pride. Alcoholism didn't help, and traces of it would soon be seen in Simenon's novels: *Les Volets verts* (1950), *Antoine et Julie* (*The Magician*, 1953), *Feux Rouges* (1953), *La Boule noire* (1955).

Simenon believed Denyse capable of anything when she was drunk. He later said that she once threw herself down the stairs while she was pregnant, just to show him how far she could go when she wanted something. Hyperactivity and alcoholism were two symptoms of the change in Denyse. The third—no less serious in Simenon's view—was her maniacal preoccupation with cleanliness.

To some extent this was a concern he shared. In the early years of their life together he noticed that she carried cleaning products with her whenever they moved and that she thoroughly scoured the bedroom and bathroom before they settled into a new place. She did housework systematically.[3] But there came a time when he began to worry about this obsessional trait.

Denyse defended herself. She claimed that she had once found a used condom in the drawer of the night table in the Drake Hotel in New York on the day they checked in. She was so upset that she decided never to move in anywhere, no matter how briefly, without cleaning up first. At the time he considered this natural behavior for a well-born North American girl.[4]

But eight years into their relationship, Simenon no longer felt the same about this woman. They were in harmony only in matters of sex, and even that seems not to have been perfect. Despite their carnal accord, he continued to have extramarital encounters left and right, with a clear conscience and no remorse. Several years earlier, when his old friend Jean Renoir visited him in Arizona for the first time, he had taken his guest to a Nogales bordello on the night of his arrival. Denyse tried to explain his attitude:

"We made love three times a day every day, before breakfast, after an afternoon nap, and before going to sleep. We were insanely complementary. Sometimes I wondered whether he didn't think of me as a prostitute. Anyway, when he was drunk, he would deliberately treat me like a whore. He had contempt for women, but I'm the only one he respected while still showing that contempt. You want to know why he felt the need to cheat on me when he was getting what he needed at home? Definitely to reassure himself. He overdid everything: speaking, writing, publishing, and making love. This was a reflection of his temperament. But was the temperament commensurate with this prolixity?"[5]

Daily life resumed in Lakeville, almost as before. Writing, long walks, conversations. Simenon watched television more often than he had in Arizona. He understood it better and confessed a weakness for the comedian Sid Caesar. The routine was broken only by exceptional events, one of these being the birth in February 1953 of their second child, Marie-Georges, called Marie-Jo. A few months later he wrote *Feux rouges*, a novel whose hero is an alcoholic obsessed with "getting out of the rut." The book was dedicated to his daughter.

One special diversion was a visit from his mother. Dazzled by the lifestyle of her great-writer son, she was stunned when he took her to leading New

York restaurants where his arrival was publicly announced, to the theater to see Judy Garland, or to a nightclub to be introduced to his friend Josephine Baker.

He also enjoyed listening in on police broadcasts on his new short-wave radio, going to see the premiere of Jacques Tati's *Les Vacances de M. Hulot* at a charity function, and playing M. Hulot in his own small way, spending an idyllic month with his family in a small hotel on Martha's Vineyard, watching the passersby and the boats.[6]

Many friends and relatives came to visit. The Renoirs were of course among the first. Since they had "only" a continent to cross, they did so at the slightest pretext, such as the New York premiere of Jean's latest film, *The River,* which Simenon said he "adored."[7]

Also among his visitors was the publisher Maurice Dumoncel, son of the man who had given Georges Sim his chance at Tallandier so many years ago. After his stay in Lakeville, Dumoncel jotted down some impressions in his journal.

> Simenon is waiting at the Millerton station. Fur-lined jacket, pipe, and beret. Chrysler. We pick up one son at school, then drive over to Hotchkiss College, one of the most "chic" in the United States, where Marc Simenon is a pupil. On the way we pass Denyse's car.
>
> We are out of New York State and there is Lakeville. Houses large and small, whitened by the snow. They look very solid and bourgeois. A land of hills and valleys. We go up and down constantly. A turn, and then we stop. A long plank to walk over ice and snow. A long, low house that seems to turn in on and around itself. Former residence of Ralph Ingersoll. The "living room," with its great wooden table, old-fashioned fireplace. Shelves packed with books: the same collection of Alexandre Dumas as in Avon, the complete "Cabinet cosmopolite." Large, green leather armchairs. Another room also packed with books, a television, pipes, radios. The corner containing the works of the man of the house, all editions in all languages. The Simenonian Babel. A narrow ship's staircase takes us down to Denyse's office, and then Georges's.
>
> Metal furniture. Red leather. Large maps of the United States in her office, and files. All kinds of directories and phone books in his. A sofa along the bay windows that look out onto the gully and the pond. Table and typewriter. A radio like the kind they have in planes. It picks up Paris, Rome, or Moscow. Denyse's secretary: a countess, Czech or Viennese. Pool alongside the office. Rooms of the house at different levels. All very comfortable, simple, solid and secure.
>
> Talking about this and that over Pernod and Coca-Cola. Denyse joins us, interrupting the conversation by giving her husband long kisses on

the mouth. So it goes. From the general to the particular, the particular in this case being very moving: relations with my father, the birth of "Simenon," my mother's visit. His contracts, his income, Brouty, Canada, etc. Sensitive to the charm of this encounter in America, to the warmth of the house, to the romantic countryside around us, to the mutual emotion, as in New York last year. He says to me: "It's good you're here, after your mother. It would have meant so much to me if your father . . ." We both fall silent. [Arrested for his Resistance activities, Rémy Dumoncel was deported and died during the war.]

I tell him of my strong reaction to *Les Demoiselles de Concarneau* [1936], *La Veuve Couderc* [*Ticket of Leave*, 1942], *Le Testament Donadieu,* etc. He replies that most often he begins with a place, a city, a landscape, a momentary impression—for example, *Le Voyageur de la Toussaint* [1941]—without knowing where he's going. The novel is written in ten or twelve days, from 6:30 to 9:30 in the morning, typed directly, then he relaxes for the rest of the day. He doesn't read modern novels.

Visiting the house. Vast rooms, enormous (double) bed, bathrooms, kitchens, linen closets, etc. Intercoms in the children's rooms and a receiver alongside their bed, so they can hear what's going on. Guests sometimes sleep in Marc's room. Nanny, secretary, beautiful young colored maid, cook, cook's aide. A millionaire's lifestyle. Simenon is aware of it, pleasurably it seems to me, but he could no longer do without it. Simple and succulent lunch in an almost European dining room: from caviar to chocolate charlotte. The wine, a burgundy, is only for me and John Sargent [of Doubleday]. . . .

A moment in his wife's office, Simenon showing me their ultramodern filing system: photocopies of contracts, etc. He leaves us for an instant, goes to the "toilet" between the two offices, and, with the door open, continues the conversation while doing what he has to do. There are quite a few unusual things in this house. . . . Both accompany me to Millerton to get the train back. We arrive a few minutes before the train whistle. Simenon's last words: "I won't forget the *Figaro* article on your father: those twelve stations between Paris and Fontainebleau, and he could have got off anywhere. And now here's the little boy he told me about back in 1928." Like the other times in New York, he lets the silence grow, and once again, I am unable to reply.

On the train I read *Les Frères Rico* [*The Brothers Rico*, 1952], which he has just given me. It reads like a translation of an American novel: atmosphere, character, places, even plot. It could have been a Serie noire.

Eleven o'clock. Essex House. Tea, bath. I fall asleep thinking about the day, about G.S.'s ambiguous comments when one of the maids passed, about the atmosphere of "sexuality"—I can find no other word—in that house.[8]

Yet Shadow Rock Farm was also the headquarters of Simenon, Inc., a flourishing business concern: book contracts to sign, translations to check, proofs to read, letters to answer, contracts with television and movie producers, requests for speaking engagements and articles. According to the *Index Translationum,* as of 1951 he was the most frequently translated contemporary French writer in the world, with thirty-one translations, ahead of Gide (twenty-six) and Sartre (fifteen).

He checked everything himself, down to the smallest payment for reproduction rights from the regional daily *Ouest-Eclair.* Although he paid taxes only to the American Internal Revenue Service, he had long and exhausting disputes with the foreign exchange office.

"There are fat years and lean years," he once told a French publisher. "One must therefore take advantage of the former."

Fearful of devaluations and the whims of exchange rates, he asked his debtors to pay as they went. The last time he had to wait it cost him $70,000.[9]

Buried in mounting files, Simenon found the time to calculate that an average of more than one new book of his was published somewhere in the world every week: more than eighty that year.[10] His correspondence could fill several volumes.

"It's getting to be like a factory here," he complained.[11]

Immediately after a brief break between two novels, his life once again took on what he liked to call "the color of business."[12] His appointment book, sprinkled with titles of novels and numbers of chapters, also contains entries like this one for November 17, 1952: "11:00 A.M. to 9:00 P.M.: John Sargent (Doubleday). Discussions on basic contract. Nonstop!"

Much of his time was spent renegotiating publishing contracts. His ten-year agreement with Sven Nielsen and Presses de la Cité was due to expire in 1955, a deadline Gaston Gallimard had not forgotten. The NRF patriarch got in touch with Simenon immediately after his return from Europe.

This time he made few demands, not even exclusivity. Just a novel from time to time, under whatever terms Simenon wanted. But despite this show of goodwill, Simenon did not return to the fold. He didn't refuse either, but simply postponed the decision. At the moment he had no time for additional literary excursions, but in the future, who knows?[13] In an effort to encourage him, Gallimard launched a promotional campaign for *Le Bateau d'Emile* (Emile's Boat, 1954), a collection of short stories to which he still owned the rights. But Simenon was not taken in:

"If he's being so flexible and attentive, it's because he wants to lure me back. . . . In reality he's the most terrible of them all."[14]

Gaston Gallimard knew that Simenon was the kind of author who would not tolerate dealing with anyone in a publishing house other than the owner. His relations with his American publishers were similarly fraught, except that he seemed slightly more accommodating to them than to their overseas colleagues. He willingly submitted to Doubleday's demands that he cultivate critics in the corridors of New York conventions, show up at cocktail parties, and dine at the Brussels with his publisher's team.

Professional chores were more acceptable when imposed by Americans. Simenon was still convinced that American critics and the American reading public reacted better to his works than Europeans. Stunning productivity aroused admiration among a people who held work in high esteem, whereas in France it still provoked ridicule, being associated with "facileness."[15]

Though he claimed not to read contemporary novels, he did sometimes respond to his publishers' requests to look at books, manuscripts, and magazines. To read French authors, however, he needed some special inducement, as when Sven Nielsen asked for his opinion of "the book all Paris was talking about," *Bonjour tristesse,* the first novel by the nineteen-year-old Françoise Sagan. Influenced in advance by the negative opinion of his friend Jean Cocteau ("Rose water, albeit dirty rose water"), Simenon was even harsher after he read it: an insipid story; artificial characters; lack of freshness; contrived, feminine pornography; imitative of America. He could not understand why critics were so infatuated with the book and its author:

"It's like a Delly with sex scenes added. Very clever, to be sure, but the cleverness of pulp novels."[16]

He was far more enthusiastic about *Night of the Hunter,* by Davis Grubb (which Charles Laughton and James Agee soon adapted for the screen), Nicholas Blake's *A Tangled Web,* and especially *Le Juge et son bourreau,* by the thirty-four-year-old Swiss dramatist Friedrich Dürrenmatt. One man in particular played a special role in Simenon's conquest of the American reading public. Brendan Gill, a writer and journalist whom he met at a dinner at Cam Becket's home, was immediately charmed by Simenon, who seems to have been in especially good form that night, doing a marvelous imitation of Charlie Chaplin, cane and bowler hat in hand.

In January 1953, Gill wrote a fifteen-page profile of Simenon for *The New Yorker.* It was the first time since Janet Flanner's enormously enthusiastic piece in the same magazine twenty-two years earlier that Americans were exposed to so much information about Simenon's life and work. Gill spent five days in Lakeville, and Simenon was expansive, drawing a kind of midlife balance sheet. The mood was enhanced by the approach of his fiftieth birthday, a symbolic date he considered a turning point.

Simenon recounted the story of his life like a master filmmaker, with flashbacks, missing pieces, and jump cuts to pique the reader's curiosity. Gill's article covered everything: daily life in Lakeville; the looming shadow of the great Gide; Simenon's varied performances; the attitude of the critics; the genesis of *Pedigree;* his beginnings in Paris; Binet-Valmer and the marquis de

Tracy; his exotic novels; Colette's astute advice and the heroic epoch of the Place des Vosges; the birth of Maigret; the Anthropometric Ball; the war; the Fontenay-le-Comte radiologist's death sentence; his arrival in New York; his stay in Arizona and California; the status of the writer in society; his abandonment of alcohol in favor of Coca-Cola; the money he made and immediately spent; his writing ritual; his hellish pace.

Not a single superfluous word or unpolished formula, from the portraitist or his model. Simenon was careful to present himself as an idealist, to praise his wife's professional qualities, and to point out that if his novels were so full of fog and rain, it was simply because, according to meteorological statistics, it rained 185 days a year in Liège. He knew that the American public was fond of this kind of precision. He therefore made every effort, Hemingway-style, to enhance his legend as a record-holder, announcing that a Christmas story written in 1950 at the request of the *Illustrated London News* and bought by magazines and school anthologies in various countries and by Twentieth Century-Fox had brought in $30,000 for two days' work.[17]

Beyond the very New York literary consecration of its hero, this article is also notable for what it concealed, namely everything it was convenient to omit. The two men saw each other often after this first encounter, in both New York and Connecticut, where Gill had a summer home in Norfolk. Thirty-seven years later, as Gill was working on his memoirs, he learned of Simenon's death, and devoted an entire chapter to him. Its contrast with the *New Yorker* profile is edifying, even though it repeats large excerpts of the earlier piece.

In Gill's memoirs Simenon is a chronic hypochondriac, a "malade imaginaire" (in French in the text) obsessed by the prospect of death, his favorite topic of conversation. A man who often said that he regretted not having died at the age of forty-four, like his father. A novelist enamored of the role of great-writer-at-work, a comfortable pipe-smoker dressed in tweed, lucky in love, fulfilled by his family, satisfied with being finally recognized by the broader American public and never anxious about running out of inspiration. All in all, an excellent actor, though not everything in his ostentation was insincere. In Gill's portrait Denyse comes across as a well-behaved young wife gazing admiringly and submissively at her lord and master. Only Boule seemed truly natural, making no attempt to conceal the fact that she was more than merely a highly skilled cook.

When the *New Yorker* envoy visited Shadow Rock Farm, Simenon had just finished writing *Antoine et Julie* (1953), a novel whose hero, the magician Antoine Morin, is an alcoholic. He admitted that this book had been harder to write than most, since just before beginning it he had started drinking again, in order, he said, "to keep this poor guy company." He had had to call a doctor several times while writing the novel, for his blood pressure fell dangerously low. "One day I'll flicker out like a candle," he said, to the protests of his two women.

Simenon drew his visitor into his daily life. Though he did not write in his presence, he opened every other door. The only condition was that Gill not mention Tigy's proximity. In a tone of man-to-man confidence, he explained that Denyse would be more upset to find that he may have been having sexual relations with Tigy than with Boule.

"If one has a place in the country and if one has servants, what can one expect?" he asked, rhetorically. "One must take care of their needs."

The novelist and the journalist finished out the evening at a local inn, where Simenon recounted some of his countless conquests. Apart from several picturesque details (like the fact that Simenon claimed that in the thirties he had been "the private literary consultant to His Highness the Prince of Monaco, grandfather of Prince Rainier"), Brendan Gill's book also reported the novelist's version of the conditions of his second marriage:

He had to do something, "because Denyse had become pregnant. As Simenon had learned to his dismay, it was legally possible that as a resident alien he might be subject to deportation on the grounds of moral turpitude for practicing with Denyse what the immigration authorities called concubinage, to say nothing of violating the Mann Act by transporting her (and, for that matter, Boule as well) across state lines for carnal purposes. In recounting this period of his life to me, Simenon confessed to looking back on it as an intolerable mingling of tragedy and farce. He had always boasted quite openly of what he believed to be his exceptional sexual prowess, claiming to have made love to many thousands of women over his lifetime. Making love to two or three women concurrently was not an unprecedented feat for him; it was the confined circumstances in which the feat had to be performed that taxed his ingenuity. 'Imagine what it was like in that automobile!' he exclaimed. '*Quelle horreur!* I might have been driving a Frigidaire.' "[18]

Shortly afterward, *Life* magazine sent a five-person team to Shadow Rock Farm for a week. They produced a very nice photo spread more in the spirit of Gill's article than his book.

Simenon's links with American writers grew stronger as his rising popularity aroused their curiosity—sometimes for extraliterary reasons, such as the esteem in which he was held by the big Hollywood studios. Since 1945 he had become one of the most sought-after writers: three movies had been made—*The Man on the Eiffel Tower* (an adaptation of *La Tête d'un homme*), *Midnight Episode* (*Monsieur la Souris*), *The Man Who Watched Trains Go By* (*L'Homme qui regardait passer les trains*)—while rights had been sold for the novella *Sept Petites Croix dans un carnet* (Seven Little Crosses in a Notebook), *Le Fond de la bouteille,* and *Les Frères Rico,* the latter in an auction in which three producers participated. There were also plans for a film version of *Feux rouges* and for a remake of *Les Inconnus dans la maison,* twelve years after Henri Decoin's picture.

Apart from Dashiell Hammett, he met James Thurber through their barber, Robert Fiengo, Lakeville's best-informed citizen. Simenon considered Thurber a writer of the stature of Mark Twain and O. Henry. But though they had dinner together several times, they did not "talk shop," probably because of Simenon's lack of self-assurance.[19]

Despite *The New Yorker*'s promotion, he was still unsure of his stature in American eyes. In 1949 the Mystery Writers Association had given him the prize for the best short story of the year, for "Bénis soient les humbles" (Blessed Be the Humble), a variant of "Le Petit Tailleur et le chapelier" (The Little Tailor and the Hatter). A few months later he won the Edgar Allan Poe award, generally given to the best American detective story of the year, for *Sept Petites Croix dans un carnet.* Drawing up a list of the best writers of detective stories (a label he hated), a magazine published by Columbia University ranked him in tenth position, after Dorothy Sayers, Agatha Christie, Arthur Conan Doyle, Ngaio Marsh, Erle Stanley Gardner, Rex Stout, Ellery Queen, Margery Allingham, and Dashiell Hammett.[20]

Of these authors, Erle Stanley Gardner is the one to whom he is most naturally compared. They had in common their rapidity of execution, their rate of production, and the apparent facility with which they accomplished their task. It was no accident that Simenon's publisher decided to try something with him that had already been done with Gardner: the publication of one of his books under an assumed name. In 1954, Doubleday brought out *Tidal Wave* (a collection composed of *La Mort de Belle, Le Fond de la bouteille,* and *Les Frères Rico*), signed Georges Simenon, and *On Land and Sea,* a novel by one Victor Kosta. The copyright page of the latter revealed that it was in fact a translation of *Les Gens d'en face* (1933). But Simenon naturally disliked being compared on purely commercial grounds to authors he considered his literary inferiors.

There were only two well-known writers in the United States with whom he maintained ongoing relations. One was Thornton Wilder, whom he met in 1953. This writer and playwright, six years older than Simenon, had won several Pulitzer Prizes and was also a professor of literature and poetry. He was asked to introduce Simenon at a seminar on the novel held at Yale University, and they seem to have met again soon afterward, since Simenon's appointment book contains this entry for June 15, 1953: "Day with Thornton Wilder."

From his home in Hamden, Connecticut, Wilder wrote Simenon letters that often read like astute analyses of his novels. For his part, Simenon seemed incapable of talking about anything but himself and his work, though he did apologize for it. He told Wilder, for instance, how difficult it had been to write *Feux rouges* (1953). Frightened by the concentration it required, he gave up just as he was about to begin, writing another novel instead and coming back to *Feux rouges* six months later:

"In short, it was like living at highway speed for ten days without a break. At the end I was as exhausted as if I had driven for those ten days in the middle of Labor Day traffic."[21]

The other American writer with whom he corresponded even more regularly was the very antithesis of Thornton Wilder: Henry Miller.

Their exchange of letters seems to have begun in 1954, when Miller was sixty-three. Gallimard had just published *The Air-Conditioned Nightmare*. In the United States the ban on his work would be lifted only several years later, but French readers were already acquainted with *Tropic of Cancer, Tropic of Capricorn,* and *Black Spring*. From his years in Paris in the early thirties Miller had retained the habit of spending the morning writing letters as a way of jump-starting his brain before embarking on the day's literary creation. He saw it as exercise and as mental hygiene.[22]

The first time he wrote to Simenon it was to express his admiration for several of his novels, especially *Lettre à mon juge* (1947). Miller had long hesitated to read Simenon. In fact, he refused to believe that "such a popular and prolific writer could be so good." But on inspection he decided that he was even better than the public realized.[23]

"For us Americans who have just discovered you in translation it is like a new star rising on the horizon. You are absolutely unique among authors who have had great success among the public. . . . There is a 'tenderness' in you that I don't often find among French writers. Is it your Belgian side?"[24]

Too "broke" to travel even within the United States, Miller invited Simenon to spend a few days at his home in Big Sur, California, which he described as a sort of west coast Andorra. This might be the opportunity for a face-to-face exchange of views on sex, the only subject truly dear to both their hearts. In the meantime, Miller sent long letters singing the praises of the body of work he was steadily discovering.

"Like everyone else, the Simenon bug is gnawing at me.[25] . . . More and more I think you are the most popular author in the world today. A cruel honor!"[26]

No small compliment, but it was delivered quite spontaneously and without calculation. By common agreement their exchanges were more like impromptu chats than writers' letters for publication—not at all in the same spirit as Miller's correspondence with Lawrence Durrell. On the west coast Miller wrote by hand, while across the continent Simenon drummed on his typewriter. They often reminisced about the Paris they remembered, from Montparnasse to the Place Clichy. Bob, the bartender at La Coupole, was cast as the hero of their nightcrawler's mythology.

Now and then the subject of literature even came up, albeit not deliberately. For Miller it most often took the form of complaints about publishers, especially French firms that refused to admit that authors had to be paid the sums due them if they were to go on living:

"I am a book merchant because I cannot live on my royalties, which come in whimsically. Perhaps you know that Whitman sold *Leaves of Grass* door to door (what a commentary on America!). At the moment my agent in Paris (Dr. Hoffman) is fighting with Hachette for the several million francs they've owed me for years. It's a farce."[27]

One can well imagine how Simenon, the sharp businessman, must have smiled. He considered Miller a unique character, the quintessential nonconformist outcast, a poet to whom America owed a part of its moral revolution, a kind of secular saint.[28]

But did he read him? He says he did, after Miller sent him a selection of his works. He particularly admired *Plexus,* one of the volumes of the *Rosy Crucifixion* trilogy. But instead of discoursing on the qualities of Miller's work, he kept coming back to his own writings, remarking that in a sense, "*Pedigree* is my little *Plexus.*"[29]

Miller was clearly more generous. Not only was he sincerely interested in Simenon's novels (as was his great friend Anaïs Nin, who mentioned them often in her diaries), but he also shared his enthusiasm with his friends and correspondents. Informing Simenon that John Cowper Powys was one of his most eager readers, Miller urged him to read Powys's autobiography.[30]

Though he was probably unaware of the existence of the author of *A Glastonbury Romance,* Simenon nevertheless attached some importance to his opinion, for he was British, and nothing that came out of literary England left Simenon indifferent. But what would an author like John Cowper Powys have found so fascinating in novels like Simenon's? He explained it in letters to a friend in 1942 and 1943:

> My new favorite writer is Georges Simenon, a French novelist who adopts that admirable and rare form of narrative, the brief novel (each volume of the English edition contains two of them). The difference from my bête noire, the ordinary short story, is enormous and absolute. Henry James wrote brief novels of this size. Be that as it may, I find it an excellent form for fiction. Simenon's stories (I pray to heaven he is still alive and will continue writing now and forever!) have something of the look of crime novels (but this is only outward appearance, and these are not the best of them). I never thought I'd live to see the day that I'd be reading detective stories, but the detective element of Simenon's books is their weakest aspect, generally rather unconvincing. All the rest—atmosphere, composition, narration, and characters—is wonderful, at least for me. It's been years since I've come upon an author who has so pleased me, with so many books, all equally charming.

. . . Have you asked your friend whether he's read my favorite of all modern authors, English, American, or French: the great, the human, the wise, the noble, Balzacian, Dostoevskian, Dickensian, Rabelaisian, and Gorkian creator of the French Sherlock Holmes (but greatly superior to the original)? I am speaking of Simenon. The detective part of his novels is not really good—the crimes are the weakest and clumsiest aspect. But for atmosphere, character, intensity, humor, and above all for humanity and knowledge of the wretched, pathetic mass, adolescents in particular, he has no peer at all.[31]

Since this correspondence was published much later in London but never in Paris, Simenon was probably unaware of it. But it is likely that of all the compliments it contains, the acknowledgment of his superiority over Conan Doyle would have pleased him most, satisfying an old ambition and assuming special value since it was an Englishman who said it.

Simenon had never much liked Sherlock Holmes, considering his dear Watson a tad too elementary. "I am Maigret's Watson," he said in various interviews, in a tone of challenge. In the autumn of 1954 he had an opportunity to check on the state of his reputation on the scene, when his new British publisher invited him and Denyse to make a promotional tour of several major British cities.

For fifteen years his novels had been published in London by Routledge. Rather than deal with the firm's directors, like T. Murray Ragg, Simenon had chosen the eminent art critic Herbert Read as his special interlocutor and literary adviser. "An extraordinary guy," he called him.[32] In 1953, sensing that the novelist had some complaints about his British publisher, Read took the opportunity of a trip to the United States to drop in on the Simenons in Lakeville.

His fears turned out to be justified. Simenon was annoyed at Routledge for not being commercially aggressive enough. He wanted to flood the market with his books. "The more you publish, the more you sell," he confidently announced, "just as you have to add fuel to feed a fire." A dubious analogy that Read found cavalier to say the least.[33] Simenon also suggested that nothing had been the same since leadership of the firm had been delegated to "a lout," a manager by the name of C. A. Franklin.[34]

But all this may well have been mere pretext. As Gallimard could testify, Simenon was not above such tactics. The truth is that he no longer felt at ease with his British publisher. His only real complaint was that the firm had remained what it had always been, while the Simenon enterprise had steadily grown. They simply had not evolved in common. By 1954 he decided that Routledge was better placed to issue essays than novels.[35]

"I don't feel at home among these people, who are much too intellectual for me," he later explained.[36] His decision was irrevocable, and various British publishers began competing to take over from their unfortunate colleague. After examining the field, Simenon settled on three major candidates: Heinemann, Collins, and Hamish Hamilton.

Mr. Hamilton himself made a three-day trip to Lakeville to court his prospective author. He named some of the other writers on his list to show Simenon that he would be in worthy company if he signed on: Raymond Chandler, Stephen Spender, J. D. Salinger, John Dickson Carr, Nancy Mitford. Hamilton believed that he was better placed than anyone else to promote Simenon's work. After all, he had sold three times as many of Chandler's novels as were sold in the United States.[37] His enthusiasm seemed sincere. He said that he spoke of Simenon often with the fiction editor of the *Times Literary Supplement*, another ardent Simenon reader.

The director of Heinemann had already been to Lakeville the month before, and the head of Collins was due in the following month. But that trip was canceled, for Simenon decided on Hamish Hamilton even though his firm was the smallest of the candidates. There were three main reasons. Hamilton promised to take personal charge of Simenon's affairs; he seemed to know the books well enough to guarantee their success; and he was a perfect match to Simenon's idea of the English gentleman: Eton and Cambridge, club tie and umbrella, the best education if not the broadest knowledge, the very picture of courtesy.[38] The chemistry between the two men was good, and Simenon was ready to sign a contract as comprehensive as the one that bound him to Doubleday, his American publisher.

But if he wanted to go the distance, Hamish Hamilton was going to have to adapt to his new author's personality. He got a foretaste of what he could expect during their initial talks in Lakeville, when the subject of translators came up. Having already had several disagreeable experiences, Simenon was concerned that too many liberties were being taken. He therefore insisted that no changes whatever be made to his texts. Suggestions were one thing, but no corrections. In the meantime, he proposed that J. Seymour-Smith be named his official translator, the position once held by Geoffrey Sainsbury.

The publisher was nonplussed at the lavish sums this new author wanted laid out for his trip to Britain. He meant to stay at the Savoy, London's most fashionable (and expensive) hotel, and he specified a suite with a view of the Thames. Hamilton considered the plan ruinous, but in the end felt compelled to accept.

On October 29, 1954, after a six-day crossing aboard the *Ile de France*, Simenon went straight to Hamish Hamilton's offices for a reception in his honor. Then he was off to Liverpool, Manchester, Birmingham, Oxford, and Cambridge for book signings, press interviews, and meetings with professors of literature. Back in London on November 8, he attended parties and dinners at the Ritz and at his publisher's home, joined by such eminent writers, critics, producers, playwrights, and artists as John Hayward, Rose Macaulay,

Malcolm Muggeridge, Ian Fleming, the Baroness Budberg, Alexander Korda, Noel Coward, Peter Ustinov, Carol Reed, Raymond Mortimer, Harold Nicolson, and J. B. Priestley, not to mention reporters from the *Sunday Times, Evening Standard, Daily Mail,* and the *Observer.*

Hamish Hamilton did well, granting all Simenon's requests and letting him help draw up the guest list. He demurred only at inviting Herbert Read, Simenon's former editor at Routledge. Simenon even managed to connect with such personalities as Somerset Maugham and T. S. Eliot. He was interested in the former because of his medical training.[39] The latter, not wont to attend banquets, turned up nevertheless, driven by a combination of curiosity and a passion for detective novels. He later told Simenon of his fascination for *L'Horloger d'Everton* (1954), saying that he was especially impressed by the very personal way in which the author returned to one of his basic themes in order to treat it from different points of view through very different characters.[40]

The British may not have considered Simenon Conan Doyle's superior, but some definitely regarded them as equals. But as Julian Symons, an authority on detective fiction, remarked, although Simenon's most successful books were truly little works of art, they were nonetheless little:

"The books, hard novels and Maigret stories alike, can be more easily admired than loved. Their creator is in some ways the most extraordinary literary phenomenon of the century: but his talents have been those of a literary surgeon rather than a great creator."[41]

Simenon could not decently come so close to Paris without spending a couple of weeks there.

"The purpose of my trip?" he told a reporter. "Vacation."[42]

He and Denyse had a kind of belated honeymoon. This time he promised to do what he had been unable to do two years earlier: relax, rest, visit friends. But Simenon would have been untrue to himself had he not begun by making the social rounds: Marcel Pagnol at Fouquet's, Jean Renoir at the Joinville studios, and everyone else at La Coupole, the bistros, and the track. He was dying to attend the trial of Gaston Dominici, accused of the murder of the Drummonds, a family of English campers, but he resisted the temptation, fearing that he would wind up spending his whole stay in Paris in court.

On the other hand, he could not avoid a few professional engagements. One of these had an unexpectedly dramatic outcome. Like Paul Léautaud, François Mauriac, and several other writers, he agreed to read passages from one of his books into a microphone provided by Phillips in a studio set up in a former music hall on the Rue Pigalle. Simenon and the sound engineer took their places in a glass octagon, while twenty or so onlookers sat in chairs around them. The producer, Gilbert Sigaux, a seasoned professional with experience in radio, print journalism, and publishing, had chosen a passage on page 491. He handed Simenon the open book, with a note explaining that the reading would last for eight minutes and forty seconds.

Simenon was unaware of the content of the selected passage. When he began to read aloud, he found that it was the description of Désiré's death. Suddenly he choked up. Bursting into tears, he turned from the astonished spectators sitting outside the glass.

"I never reread the part about my father's death," he sobbed.

He then had a reaction that stunned the small audience. As if trying to conceal his sorrow and his shame at having lost control, he lay down on the floor so the others could not see him. Sigaux quickly evacuated the room.[43]

In 1955, Simenon was named a knight of the Légion d'honneur. The induction ceremony was held in February at the New York home of Count Jean de Lagarde, the French consul-general, in the presence of Belgian diplomats and his American publishers. It was followed by an evening at the Cotnaréanus, who gave a great banquet for him. The writer William Saroyan was there, along with the editor in chief of the *New York Times Book Review* and a Metropolitan Opera baritone who sang the *Marseillaise*. The hostess even cracked her last magnums of 1927 Bollinger for the occasion.[44]

Simenon must have been thrilled, especially since around the same time he was also named president of the Mystery Writers of America. But as soon as the party was over, he got gloomy again.

He had been irritable for several months, as if something were missing. He had finished *Les Témoins* (*The Witnesses*, 1955), his latest "hard novel," in September 1954. Since then he had done little more than keep his hand in with *Maigret et le corps sans tête* (1955). But the stint of unemployment was not the reason for his mood.

"Why is it that you stay in America?" Hamish Hamilton asked him during a visit to Lakeville.[45]

Simenon gave several reasons—the climate, the schools, the quality of life—but did not seem wholly convinced by his own answer. When he came home after taking his guest to the station, he watched television while Denyse filed some correspondence. Then he turned to her and asked:

"How would you feel about moving to France?"

She asked him why. He said he didn't know, but they talked about it all night, and by dawn they had made the decision. Simenon immediately wrote to Sven Nielsen to report the news, asking that it be kept secret, since he was afraid the Internal Revenue Service might demand a hefty sum as a guarantee against taxes owed. As he tried to analyze the reasons for his own wish to move on, he kept coming back to the simple fact that he was homesick. Not surprising, after ten years of exile. Once he got used to the idea of leaving Connecticut for the Côte d'Azur, he was euphoric:

"I feel like a fish in water!"[46]

He had been living at Shadow Rock Farm for five years, a record for a chronic wanderer who until then had never stayed in the same place for more than three years. He had been tempted to leave quite a few times, especially in 1947 and 1948, when a terrible devaluation of the French franc made him fear that he would have to reduce his annual budget (and therefore his status) by $50,000.[47]

What was it, then, that kept him in America so long? Very simply, America itself, a country with greater respect for the individual than any other. As he saw it, a democracy could be judged by its judicial system and by its capacity to allow him to assert his rights.[48]

It was a point he would come back to years later, after the assassination of John Kennedy. The journalist Christian Millau, who covered Jack Ruby's trial for the weekly *Le Nouveau Candide,* had the idea of turning the case file over to Inspector Maigret's creator. As far as the investigation itself was concerned, Millau's interviews elicited nothing more than banalities, speculation of the sort with which Simenon had filled the columns of *Paris-Soir* during the Stavisky affair. But when he moved to the more general terrain, he uncovered revealing elements of Simenon's attachment to this country. Simenon praised the American justice system as superior to the French.

"If I were guilty," he said, "I'd rather be tried in America. If I were innocent, I'd rather be tried in England. In France the laws change too often."

Skeptical about the "conspiracy theory," he affirmed his absolute confidence in the FBI, lauding its independence and incorruptibility. It is hardly surprising that this interview was the subject of a very favorable internal report by the American embassy in Paris. Nearly thirty years later, it turned up in the FBI's "Simenon File."[49]

Before leaving Lakeville, Simenon characterized his years in America as "the most important stage of my life."[50] They brought no change in his style, but replenished his stock of colors and odors, characters and landscapes, and enabled him to stretch his imagination in unexpected ways.

He had not really conquered America in the way he had hoped. He was better known now, but his sales never matched his ambitions. Some said that this was because he was too European. Others noted that his novels were translated by Britons and suggested that they be retranslated and adapted to the American language and mentality.[51]

His disappointment on this score may well have had something to do with his decision to return to Europe. But there was a narrower and more adventitious factor as well. Simenon was viewed with rising displeasure by the local populace in Lakeville. The arrangement whereby his ex-wife was compelled to live so close to him and his new wife (in far less comfortable material conditions) was viewed as cruel and unusual. There were rumors about his misogyny, his perversity, his escapades. One of the most tenacious had it that he had given his son a session with a New York prostitute as a birthday gift, after first sampling her himself.

He had been quickly accepted during his first few months in town. The inhabitants were pleased that this stranger was not just passing through, that he wanted not a second home but a place where he could put down roots. But they were disappointed when he refused to participate in the life of their community. This attitude would have been acceptable had he simply isolated himself in an ivory tower. But he didn't. Vicki Silvert, an editor of the *Lakeville Journal* who followed every little event in this small town, noted this evolution:

"He observed people like butterflies, as if he were an entomologist. He seemed more and more like a kind of voyeur at Hugo's and the inn, the two places he went every day. This was especially resented since he refused to get involved in the town. By spying on people as he did, he took something of their personality without giving anything in return. You sensed that he would leave when there was nothing more to take."[52]

He incorporated many details of these years into his novel *La Main (The Man on the Bench in the Barn)*, published in 1968. Lakeville became Brentwood; Shadow Rock Farm, Yellow Rock Farm. The nearby town of Canaan was respelled Chanaan, the Hotchkiss School became the Adams School, and the *Lakeville Journal* reappeared as *The Citizen*. Sutton Place, the New York address of his heroes, Ray and Mona, was the street where his publisher, John Sargent of Doubleday, lived.

La Main came out thirteen years after he left America. *La Mort de Belle* (1952), however, was written while he was still living in Lakeville. Its action clearly takes place there, and both the topography and several of the characters are identifiable. The story begins with the discovery of the body of eighteen-year-old Belle Sherman in the home of the Ashbys, a childless couple with whom she had been living for a month. On the night of the murder Spencer Ashby, a history teacher, was working at home, while his wife was out playing bridge at a friend's. Suspicion naturally falls on the husband. There is an investigation, interrogation, rumors. Little by little he is ostracized, though there is no proof of his guilt. An *M,* for "murderer," is painted on the front of his house. Then one night, finally cleared of all suspicion, he meets a woman by chance and takes her to bed. When he turns out to be impotent, he loses his head and strangles her, thereby committing the act the community had already attributed to him.

The novel was published by Doubleday in early 1954 under the title *Belle*. The *Lakeville Journal* gave it a rather wry review: ". . . it takes place in a town so similar to Lakeville that the post office and Hugo's store are recognizable. . . . But how many Americans will see themselves in these scenes?"[53]

The locals in Lakeville were not happy, and some of them let him know it.[54] The incident caused no more than a fleeting unease, but it deepened the gap between himself and his adopted town.

"I am periodically gripped by a need for change, even while remaining attached as by an umbilical cord to the places where I have been happy," he once wrote.[55] In that spirit, he claimed to have maintained ownership of Shadow Rock Farm, like the house in Nieul, "because we were happy there, we and the children, and later, perhaps . . ."[56] In reality, on August 20, 1955, the Salisbury real estate agent Cope Robinson put "the house of the famous detective story writer Georges Simenon" up for sale, along with its furniture, including the Chippendale chairs, the Renaissance buffet, the desks, the dictaphone, the Baccarat glass service, the gardening tools, and even the children's toys.

IV

SWITZERLAND

16

TO LIVE AND WRITE
IN NOLAND

1955–1963

hen he disembarked in France in the early spring of 1955, Simenon had no intention of becoming a Parisian again. Instead, he passed through the capital at the wheel of a Dodge, heading for Cannes, where he dropped off his wife, children, cook, and baggage at the Miramar Hotel. But that was only a stopover. He soon moved into the villa of his dreams, La Gâtounière in Mougins. Tigy and Marc checked into a hotel in town.

Four months later, after writing *La Boule noire* (1955) and *Maigret tend un piège* (*Maigret Sets a Trap,* 1955), he was ready to move on again. It was the usual pattern: initial euphoria followed by a period of drifting sometimes bordering on a mute anguish.

His plans were hazy. The main thing was to leave. Uncertainty about the future was still the best daily stimulus. He spent the next two seasons traveling around the country in a spirit of nostalgic pilgrimage, as though he had decided to introduce his family to some of his most personal memories: La Rochelle, Nieul-sur-Mer, Sables-d'Orlonne, Porquerolles.

Back in Mougins, he stayed long enough to write *Les Complices* (*The Accomplices,* 1956) and to find a new house. "Golden Gate," on Queen Elizabeth Avenue, was a far more spacious villa than La Gâtounière, and it was better situated, on Cannes's high ground. The fact that this city is the setting of eight of his novels might suggest that he was particularly attached to it. But he wasn't. Simenon would never put down roots in a place this corrupt, stamping ground for the shallow crowd among which he had already lived in Neuilly and elsewhere.

For him, Cannes was no more than a place of rest and recreation, despite the quality of its top-flight strippers and prostitutes. While there he wrote two "fun books"—*Un échec de Maigret* (*Maigret's Failure,* 1956) and *Maigret s'amuse* (*Maigret's Little Joke,* 1957)—and five "hard novels," several of which were among his most powerful: *En cas de malheur* (*In Case of Emergency,* 1956), *Le Petit Homme d'Arkhangelsk* (1956), *Le Fils* (1957), *Le Nègre* (*The Negro,* 1957), and *Strip-Tease* (*Striptease,* 1958).

This last was written at the behest of the director Henri-Georges Clouzot, who was eager to work with him again. But Simenon was still reluctant to do a screenplay, especially since he was deluged with other proposals—from the press and publishers, of course, and as always from the movies, but also from the theater. *La Chambre,* a choreography by Roland Petit based on a Simenon theme and *"Liberty Bar"* (*Liberty Bar,* 1932), performed at the Théâtre Charles in Rochefort, had given more than one playwright ideas. The director of a London theater even suggested a musical comedy based on Maigret.

But Simenon had more pressing concerns. He had to settle down somewhere, even if he sensed that it would be for only a few years. In the late spring of 1957, after combing a section of the canton of Vaud in Switzerland at the wheel of his new car, a Mercedes 300 S convertible, he fell in love with the Château d'Echandens, less than fifteen miles from Lausanne. The château was not for sale, but he was so enthusiastic that he agreed to sign a six-year renewable lease.

Why Switzerland? The saying has it that if it's a nice place to live, it's just as nice a place to die. Dying was not on Simenon's immediate agenda, but the choice of Echandens was not unrelated to his yearning for calm and serenity, withdrawal and discretion.

For him, Switzerland was the epitome of order and neutrality, two of his own character traits. Apart from the renown of its schools, he also felt that it excelled in the quality of human relations, a feature he deduced from its reputation for clock-making. He refused to believe that punctuality and organization were not the cardinal virtues of this people, and he thought of Switzerland as Europe's most unvarying country, the ideal spot for an ardent individualist who had always sought to flee History.

Jean Renoir was not surprised to hear of his choice:

"A few years from now we can expect the Simenon family to pull up stakes for the Cameroons or Patagonia," he wrote to his friend.[1]

A good guess, except that neither of those places would offer Switzerland's notorious fiscal advantages. Though he claimed otherwise, Simenon was especially sensitive to that argument. Eventually he would be subject to taxes on wealth and income, but for the first five years of his residence he enjoyed a privileged tax status by following the wily advice of a Lausanne fiduciary firm: he claimed not to be engaged in any profitable activity. So it was that throughout his stay in the château, from 1957 to 1963, he datelined his typescripts not "Echandens," but "Noland." This was not homage to Larry and Lil Noland, the main characters of *Le Fond de la bouteille* (1949), but rather his way of indicating that the twenty-five novels he wrote there were actually produced in a Swiss canton that cannot be found on any map: in no land.

Soon after settling in, his life took on the color of business again. The Simenon enterprise had become a genuine multinational. Only a fifth of his turnover now came from France.[2] The sales figures publicly reported by publishers are generally inflated, but those recorded in authors' royalty statements are reliable. A list, issued on December 31, 1962,[3] confirms that his French sales were not sufficient to sustain his increasingly lavish lifestyle. The figures range from a high of 92,000 (for *Maigret à New York*) to a low of 10,000 (*Une vie comme neuve* [*A New Lease on Life,* 1951]). On average, the print runs of the Maigrets were two to three times greater than those of the "hard novels," generally well under 30,000. The most prestigious of both were doing better than they had at Gallimard, but this was a different era. From the bookseller's point of view, the "Simenon phenomenon" had not changed: the basis of his success was the huge number of titles, not the number of copies sold per title.

His correspondence, too, was as massive as ever, though with his return to Europe the distances were smaller and he could meet people face-to-face more easily. Anyone who may have believed that negotiating in person might ease his pugnacity was sadly mistaken, as he proved in 1956, with a "coup" he was more than a little proud of.

Fernand Brouty, Arthème Fayard's son-in-law and now the owner of the firm, was eager to reacquire the worldwide French-language rights of Simenon's entire production, with the sole exception of the early pseudonymous pulp novels (which Simenon himself considered too wretched to reissue). Brouty's idea was to bring them out three by three. Simenon was willing to sign a contract authorizing this rights transfer, but he wanted something in return. Fayard would have to give up all subsidiary rights to these novels: mass-market paperback rights, film rights, television rights. Aware that Brouty was stingier than he was shrewd, Simenon proposed to buy these rights back, and he took his interlocutor by surprise, unfurling a towel full of cash on the desk in his office and putting the entire amount of the transaction on the table, literally. The ploy worked. Brouty agreed to what Simenon would later call the best deal of his life. It is hard to dispute that assessment.[4]

Simenon's reputation as a businessman was beyond challenge, but those who knew him well were convinced that the lure of profit was not what made him tick. Financial success was more a means than an end: a way of reassuring himself that he had made good. It sometimes seems as though he drew his energy from an adolescent image of his father: the naive, honest employee slumped dead at his desk after twenty years of loyal service.

He never accepted the prevailing principles of authors' rights, objecting in particular to what he called the injustice of having to share subsidiary rights with the publisher: "I have always struggled for this and will continue to do so. My literary property is my asset and my son's patrimony. I consider myself the only one qualified to manage it."[5]

During his years in America he was outspoken in defending authors' prerogatives. He felt encouraged in his battle when Raymond Chandler denounced the Hollywood studios' contempt for the writers they exploited and expressed his mistrust of "professional" literary judges in a merciless formula that epitomized his attitude: "Never ask for advice. Never show or discuss work in progress. Never answer criticism."[6] One of Chandler's articles, published by *The Atlantic* in February 1952, was eloquently entitled "Ten Percent of Your Life." Simenon felt a deep solidarity with his colleague. They were equally determined, and equally isolated.

In 1956 he spoke out in France as sharply as Chandler had in America. The occasion was a proposed bill on literary ownership, on which the cultural weekly *Arts* asked for his opinion. To the extent that the bill strengthened the rights of authors, he supported it. But he considered it no more than a palliative. He criticized its inadequacies, complaining that the bill ignored the most basic element of the injustice suffered by writers, the question of inheritance. Why was there a double standard? A author's descendants could retain a monopoly on the copyright for only fifty years after the author's death, but no limits were imposed on the descendants of bankers, arms dealers, and other captains of industry.

"... The writer? Fifty years after his death (much sooner in most countries), he is annexed by the state. His grandchildren might be starving to death, but the poor man in his grave, and his works along with him, comes into the 'public domain.' In a sense, there is beauty in it, for it amounts to official recognition of the preeminence of spirit. The state needs his name and his work. But I would like to know how this seizure of a man's work can be reconciled with constitutions and with democracy. Hereditary rights should be canceled after fifty years for everyone or for no one. Is the writer so indispensable to the country, to what we call civilization, that he must be made a being apart?"

Simenon asked that the legislature at least consider some compensation, the waiving of inheritance taxes, for example. When he realized that he had forgotten to say anything about his beloved publishers, he added a postscript:

"... The publisher today is no longer a man who publishes books, but a man who buys rights. Thus it is that in the United States the author is commonly referred to as a 'property.' ... Let publishers remain publishers. Let them take their risks as such, without trying to 'create' or 'inspire' talents. Let them have the dignity not to become agents or rights merchants and to leave to those who have built a body of work the profit from whatever has nothing to do with publishing itself."[7] Only exceptionally did Simenon commit himself in public, but when he did, it was noticed.

Brussels, Holland, Venice, Florence, Cannes, London, Versailles, Milan—he made many brief trips in Europe during his years at the Château d'Echandens, which were marked not only by the writing of some of his most important novels—*Le Président* (1958), *Le Passage de la ligne* (1958), *Dimanche* (*Sunday*, 1959), *Betty* (*Betty*, 1961), *Le Train* (1961)—but also by personal events of another order. Three years after moving in, Simenon became both a grandfather and a father again (Pierre, his third child with Denyse, was born in 1959).

For some time he had been complaining of terrible headaches, insomnia, and paralysis in one arm. Unable to type, he began writing *Le Fils* (1957) by hand. His marital relations were increasingly tumultuous, often stormy and violent, partly because of alcohol. Dissatisfied and discouraged, he hesitated to work. By late 1959 and early 1960 he was exhibiting symptoms of depression.

Eight months passed between the writing of *Le Veuf* (*The Widower*, 1959) and *L'Ours en peluche* (*Teddy Bear*, 1960), his next "hard novel." Between the two he barely managed to turn out *Maigret aux assises* (*Maigret in Court*, 1960). The inspector, weary of devoting himself to other people's problems, was contemplating retirement.

It is difficult not to see this as a reflection of the author's own discouragement, and not to think of Simenon's disarray when we read of Dr. Jean Chabot, professor and gynecologist, hero of *L'Ours en peluche*. Depressed, flirting with the idea of suicide, sagging under the burden of his responsibilities, he is sick of playing his role in society. An affair with a young night nurse and its consequences impel him to an increasingly melancholy introspection that drives him to a kind of "suicide"—he murders a foreign doctor.

At the time he wrote this stifling story, Simenon was himself gripped by the temptation to tear off the mask and break free of his entire entourage: family, employees, associates. He felt more alone than ever, forced to admit that his second marriage was a failure. His only friend and interlocutor was his fictional double, a fifty-seven-year-old man haunted by the specter of solitude and chastity. All he has is the memory of what had been his life's greatest and most genuine passion, three children more important to him than anything else, and a wife sinking deeper into alcoholism and neurosis.

Before removing himself from society by committing an irreparable act, Dr. Chabot gives expression to the inner turmoil of the author himself, who was also haunted by pauperization and "real" suicide:

305

He had to make a decision, just like Emma, except that he was loath to go away before having understood. So many people came to ask him to do their thinking for them, and he had no one in the world of whom he could demand the same favor.

It wasn't true that he thought of himself as stronger than the others. If they thought so, it was because of his sense of a kind of dignity related not to his person but to his profession. No one had understood him. He had always been aware of his own weaknesses, which was exactly why he forced himself to try so hard.

Even the title of professor. He was not particularly enamored of teaching. Perhaps, in the end, it was a waste of time. He had needed it to reassure himself of his own worth, and it was for the same reason that he had later been so obstinate about making money. Because he didn't want to feel crushed by people like those he was leaving, who crushed him despite himself.

In whom could he confide such thoughts? Like his need always to have someone at his side. . . . In the end, the truth was that he had had enough; he wanted a catastrophe, just as some people hope for a war to put an end to their daily troubles. To get rid of all his worries all at once, all the burdens piled on his shoulders, all his shame and remorse. No longer to have to be the infallible teacher ready to save everyone else.

It wasn't true and he had no right to tell them so. It was too late. He had always been too late, which was why he had continued to play his role, kept on going, like a robot. . . . A mysterious smile came to his lips, for he suddenly thought of his father and was tempted to imitate him. All he had to do was raise his arm: a car would take him home; he would pick his spot, his corner, the armchair in the den, for example, where he sometimes took his nap, and claim it once and for all. He imagined the consternation, the goings and comings, the phone calls, the questions, the problems it would cause, the doctors, the psychiatrists who would be called to the rescue and who would try to understand. . . . No more! Enough! From now on he would live alone, for himself, in inner tranquillity."[8]

Simenon resolved his own crisis through writing, purging his death wish through his characters. But in the early spring of 1960, just after this incident of depression, he also began a project unprecedented for him: a kind of private journal.

Apart from his family, his publisher was the first person to be informed of the idea. Simenon told Nielsen that his novels had begun to seem burdensome to him. He felt a need to rest by working on something completely unlike anything he had ever attempted.

"In short, I would like to put into it everything that is not in my novels.

That would relieve me of the unpleasant sensation of not doing a damn thing for weeks," he said.[9]

More fetishistic than usual, he set out in search of special notebooks like those he had bought as a child. They had to be spiral-bound, the paper narrow-lined, the shape a little more oblong than school notebooks, and no more than half an inch thick, so his hand would not be in an uncomfortable position near the bottom of the page. Their covers had to be of brownish-gray cloth.

Since notebooks like this were not to be had anywhere in Lausanne, Simenon asked his publisher to buy a few dozen of them at the Bourse stationery store on the Rue de Richelieu in Paris. He did not tell him why he insisted on that particular store: it was where he had bought the little black notebook in which Tigy kept track of his earnings from 1925 to 1941.

When Sven Nielsen found that the notebooks his author wanted were unavailable, he had them manufactured to order. He wanted to be as accommodating as possible. After all, Simenon had not ruled out the possibility of publishing this putative journal someday.[10]

The notebooks themselves, which contain entries dated from June 25, 1960, to February 15, 1963, are preceded by an epigraph from the physiologist Claude Bernard: "All I did was what I could, no more than what I could." Simenon released them to the public only in 1970, under the title *Quand j'étais vieux* (*When I Was Old*). An unusually long delay for him. But he came to regret publishing this book. Though he never quite repudiated it, he described it as insincere. Denyse had been reading the manuscript in progress, and he said that he felt as though he were writing under surveillance, which impelled him to exaggerate the feelings he had for her.[11]

Curiously, between the conception and the initiation of this project (April and June 1960, respectively), a time when he might have been expected to withdraw even further from the outside world before plunging into this internal adventure, he did something highly unusual. He presided over the jury for the Thirteenth Cannes Film Festival.

Back in 1958 he had chaired the Brussels Film Festival. This time he found himself unable to turn down the proposal of his friend Maurice Bessy, a close collaborator of Robert Fabre-Lebret, master of ceremonies at Cannes. Simenon later claimed to have been "forced" to attend,[12] but the truth is he had always loved the atmosphere of Cannes in May. He had attended the film festival three times since his return to Europe. It was one of the rare events that allowed him to indulge his voyeuristic instincts and his penchant for behind-the-scenes ambiences. Now he was determined not to miss a single moment of the show—the real one, the one most others never saw.[13]

By 1960 about fifty movies based on his work had been made, and he liked to surprise interviewers by claiming to have seen no more than five or six of them, which was not true, as his private and professional letters attest. Most often he was satisfied with, if not enthusiastic about, the scripts. His contracts generally provided for a right of review in the choice of director. But he was always most appreciative of the actors, whom he considered best qualified to judge a novel's cinematic potential, since they were the ones who had to assume the personae of the characters.

In the five years since his return to Europe, six movies based on his work had been released in France: *Le Sang à la Tête,* based on *Le Fils Cardinaud,* directed by Gilles Grangier and adapted by Michel Audiard; *Maigret tend un piège* and *Le Passager clandestin,* directed by Ralph Habib; *En cas de malheur,* directed by Claude Autant-Lara and adapted by Aurenche and Bost; *Maigret et l'affaire Saint-Fiacre,* directed by Jean Delannoy and adapted by Michel Audiard; and *Le Baron de l'écluse,* based on the short story of the same name, by the same team (along with Maurice Druon), which was released less than a month before the Cannes Festival. Five of these six films had an additional common feature: Jean Gabin. Besides playing Maigret twice, he also portrayed François Cardinaud in his search for his wife, Gobillot, a defense attorney who falls in love with a young delinquent, and Dossin, known as the Baron, at the helm of a borrowed yacht.

Gabin was fast becoming the quintessential Simenonian actor, in both the number of roles and the breadth of his characterizations. But while he loved the author's characters, he was less enamored of his outlook, which he found bleak and despairing.[14] In the meantime, Simenon made no secret of his admiration for Gabin's genius:

"I can no longer think of Maigret except through Gabin and Delannoy," he said, commenting on *Maigret tend un piège.* "It's very annoying. I think they may ask for royalties on my next book."[15]

The quip was an accurate reflection of his state of mind: "morally" he had taken his distance from an industry that nevertheless continued to supply a good part of his income. Jean Renoir agreed with him that it was well nigh impossible to ensure that the products of his imagination would not be distorted by the movie people.[16] Maurice Aubergé once said that not a single scene in *La Vérité sur Bébé Donge,* the film he had written for Henri Decoin, was actually taken from the Simenon novel on which the film was based.[17]

But as much as he hated screenwriting, he could never resist an offer. "Script," it says in his appointment book for the dates February 10 to 15, 1956. A big Hollywood studio had convinced him to write a screenplay based on his novel *Feux rouges* (1953).

Back in the thirties Simenon had sworn that he would never again do any such thing, and he drove a hard bargain with the studio: no more than ten days' work in Cannes to complete the script; Burt Lancaster or James Stewart in the lead role; and so on and so forth. When his demands were met, he could not get out of it. The producers flew back to California with the script in their bags. But the picture was never made. The studio owners were disappointed in the leading female character's lack of "glamour."

In the meantime more proposals flowed in. Henri-Georges Clouzot flirted with but gave up on both *Strip-Tease* (1958), which he considered too daring for the censorship of the era, and *Le Coup de lune* (1933). There were others as well. Jean-Pierre Melville tackled *L'Aîné des Ferchaux* (1945), and Jean Renoir was eager to renew the collaboration that had begun thirty years earlier. When his agent asked him for a project for M-G-M, he suggested two: *Trois Chambres à Manhattan* (1946), which he wanted to make in black and white, on location and with many exteriors, Leslie Caron playing the role of Kay; and a new version of *La Nuit au carrefour* (1931), in English, with José Ferrer and Caron.[18] Neither of these films was made. Instead, Renoir shot *Un déjeuner sur l'herbe,* for which he hired Marc Simenon as an intern.

The Thirteenth Cannes Film Festival opened on May 4, 1960, with a brief address by André Malraux, then the French minister of cultural affairs. On opening night there was a gala out-of-competition showing of William Wyler's four-hour-long *Ben-Hur,* and for the next sixteen days hardly anyone spoke of anything but Charlton Heston, the twenty-minute chariot race, the naval battle, the thousands of extras, the staggering budget.

Simenon was well aware that "his" jury would be closely watched—not only by producers but also by the special envoy of the Ministry of Foreign Affairs, anxious that the distribution of prizes take proper account of the diplomatic sensibilities of this or that country. The "feature-length" committee had four French members (the actress Simone Renant, the director Marc Allégret, the composer-conductor Maurice Le Roux, the critic Louis Chauvet), one Italian (Diego Fabbri), one Japanese (Hidemi Ima), one Soviet (Kozintsev), one German (Max Lippmann), one American (Henry Miller), and one Argentine (Ulysses Petit de Murat).

Some of the films on offer were noteworthy for the reputation of their directors or the promise of sharp controversy: Carlos Saura's *Les Voyous,* Vincente Minnelli's *Bells Are Ringing,* François Reichenbach's *L'Amérique insolite,* Peter Brook's *Moderato Cantabile,* Jacques Becker's *The Hole,* Jules Dassin's *Never on Sunday,* Michelangelo Antonioni's *L'Avventura,* Federico Fellini's *La Dolce Vita,* Luís Buñuel's *The Young One,* Ingmar Bergman's *Virgin Spring.* It was rather a vintage year.

For two weeks the members of the jury barely saw one another except at screenings. When the deliberations began, the festival organizers wondered whether they had done well to chose Simenon. The problem was not that he seemed less interested in the films than in the young actresses in attendance, or that he spent so much of his time talking about his own life and his women, or that he shepherded Jean Gabin around as though he had just discovered him. The president of the jury, after all, is primarily a personality. But he seemed so inattentive, so unconcerned with his mission, that they wondered whether he would be able to organize a quality vote.

A subdued but memorable incident occurred when Simenon denied Robert Fabre-Lebret, general director of the festival, access to the jury sessions. His presence was traditional, but since it was not stipulated in the rules, the novelist refused to hear of it. After a brief skirmish, the "intruder" was finally admitted.[19]

Some of the jurors seemed to view their task with a nonchalance bordering on frivolity. The Soviet member even left the room to make a phone call, a strictly forbidden act. Henry Miller spent most of his time playing Ping-Pong or lunching with old friends from France like Georges Belmont.

He had agreed to serve on the jury only because it gave him a chance to go to Europe, to meet a correspondent whose work he had long admired, to see Buñuel again, whom he had briefly met in Paris in 1929, and most of all to get away from quarrels with his fourth wife. Served with divorce papers while in Cannes, Miller was torn between his wife, his mistress (a young waitress by the name of Caryl Hill), and Renate Gerhardt, the German translator of *Nexus* (thirty years his junior), whom he met for the first time at the festival.[20] His friend Simenon was clearly far more intrigued by these problems than by arguments among film lovers.

Michèle Manceaux, the reporter from *L'Express,* noted after the screening of *La Dolce Vita:*

"As of five in the morning, the deskman at the Carlton and I had heard but one really favorable view of this film. It seemed out of the question that *La Dolce Vita,* belatedly admitted to the competition, would win the Palme d'Or."[21]

Twenty-four hours before the announcement of the winner, however, at a time when twelve films were under discussion and the contest was reportedly too close to call, Jean de Baroncelli, the critic from *Le Monde,* predicted that Fellini would get the nod after all. *La Dolce Vita,* ill-regarded just two weeks earlier, was now seen as "surely the most important" of the pictures under consideration, "despite its flaws."[22] Barely a week earlier, Baroncelli himself had described the film as too slow, too long, too disordered, too repetitive.[23] The day before the vote, the jury had lunch with the major distributors. It would be an understatement to say that they were contemptuous of *La Dolce Vita.* "I wouldn't give $50,000 to distribute that film," one of them commented.[24]

That was all Simenon needed. But his decision to champion *La Dolce Vita* was not simply the product of his taste for contrariness, defiance, and provocation. He fully shared Fellini's indictment of a decadent society of purebred aristocrats, demented careerists, movie people not so much evil as grotesque, and reporters more interested in filth than in life. And so much the better if it seemed a little outrageous. The final session was stormy. The jurors split into two camps: Fellini's supporters, led by Simenon, and Antonioni's, led by Maurice Le Roux.

The results were finally announced by President Simenon in the festival's great hall. Melina Mercouri and Jeanne Moreau shared the prize for best performance by an actress in a leading role. Since the jury had decided not to honor the "brilliant works" by Bergman and Buñuel, a special award, considered in remarkably bad taste, was given to them. To the catcalls of the crowd, Antonioni was given a prize "for his remarkable contribution to the search for a new cinematic language," while a storm of laughter greeted the announcement of a similar consolation prize for Kon Ichikawa's *Kagi*. But it was when the Palme d'Or was unanimously awarded to *La Dolce Vita* that the audience really went wild with gibes and jeers.

Despite the powerful microphone, Simenon was drowned out by the commotion. But he was not impressed by boos or invective, for he had won. He had initially been one vote short, but Henry Miller happily supplied it. "Tell me who you want me to vote for," he said without further ado.[25] The gala soiree ended with champagne and sirtaki parties honoring the two winning actresses. Several ladies plunged fully clothed into the pool at the Martinez, while an actress rode a horse into the lobby of the Carlton.

Simenon returned to Echandens and swore that he would not allow himself to be disturbed again. The hoopla of Cannes were soon forgotten. As promised, Simenon sent signed copies of *Le Roman de l'homme* (*The Novel of a Man,* 1959) to all the members of "his" jury. Though he was regularly invited to the festival after that, he declined to attend. But the episode had two pleasant results: the birth of a close friendship with Federico Fellini and the confirmation of his ties to Henry Miller.

Miller and Simenon got together again a few months later, when "Uncle Miller," as Simenon's children called him, stopped at Echandens for a few days. As unstable and uncertain as ever, Miller was thinking about moving back to Europe, but he was not sure where. Simenon urged him to settle in the hinterland of Lake Geneva, promising to help find schools for Miller's children and even offering his services as a real estate agent. But Miller couldn't stand Switzerland, despite the spirit of tolerance with which Simenon somewhat too generously credited it. He preferred Perpignan or the Costa del Sol. He was looking for a furnished house big enough for three adults, three boys ranging in age from eleven to thirteen, and a girl of sixteen.[26]

Observing Simenon in his element, Miller made no secret of his admiration for both the writer and the paterfamilias. He envied Simenon's ability to an-swer his children's harassing questions, retaining his patience and good humor in all circumstances.[27]

After meals the two writers would withdraw to the master's office to chat about the marquis de Sade or Gilles de Rais, about the strange and delicious neologisms coined by Miller, and of course about their respective sexual prowess, the author of *Plexus* claiming to be endowed with "a six-inch bone in his cock," the creator of *Strip-Tease* boasting of the several thousand fe-males he had bedded.

Just what it was that captivated Simenon about Miller's work is not quite certain, for the compliments in his letters are vacuous. It might be thought that exchanges between writers would stimulate his critical spirit. But he always seems to have been more familiar with their biographies than with their work, as though the former fascinated him to the detriment of the latter.

At around the same time, he was delighted to be visited repeatedly by Roger Nimier, a thirty-seven-year-old writer sent by Gaston Gallimard to smooth things over with both Simenon and Céline (two indispensable "pains in the ass"). He was much amused by Nimier's conversation and by his epis-tolary eccentricities. In an official letter written on NRF stationery, for exam-ple, Nimier warned Simenon against F., a mutual acquaintance:

"I know this squalid fortune hunter will be visiting you soon. To my knowledge, he has recently offered his services to the Mauriac and Monther-lant families. Since Montherlant has no daughter, he proposed to marry his former manservant. A distressing spectacle."[28]

Simenon was delighted by such joyous insolence. He was intrigued by this new friend, who died in an automobile accident just a few months later. But had he ever bothered to read *Les Épées* or *Le Hussard bleu*?

Paul Morand, a neighbor in nearby Vevey, also wrote to him, but in a very different spirit:

"You were right when you told me how happy you were with *La Vieille* [*The Grandmother*, 1959] in your office this spring. You have never written anything like it before. Magnificent! If you're free tomorrow, I have a few friends (seven or eight) coming for tea. Put me at Mme Georges Simenon's feet. All the best."[29]

A search of Simenon's notes and voluminous correspondence turns up not the slightest hint of any analysis of a single one of Paul Morand's books. He barely mentions Morand not as an author but as the director of the NRF's Re-naissance de la Nouvelle collection in the thirties.

This inability to engage the work of others is striking in Simenon's *Portrait-souvenir de Balzac*, written and narrated for French television in 1960 at the request of Roger Stéphane and Roland Darbois. A factual, chronological account of Balzac the man, Simenon's script barely even mentions that he was a writer. Most of it deals with illnesses, glory, marriages, mistresses, and money, and hardly any of it fails to lead back to Simenon's own biography, as though Balzac were but another excuse to defend and justify himself.[30] He claims to have prepared this essay carefully, methodically gathering documentation and apparently forgetting only to (re)read *La Comédie humaine*. But perhaps that wasn't necessary, since he was interested solely in those aspects of Balzac's life that might reflect on his own image. Simenon's Balzac is the man who wrote *Le Père Goriot* in three days, collected advances not due him, put his name to contracts he could not fulfill, ruined his life in order to succeed in his work, published six to eight novels a year, and married in an effort to find his equilibrium.

In most cases Simenon seems to have liked writers for extraliterary reasons. This is particularly noticeable with authors who had first been physicians. He envied them this twofold viewpoint, which enabled them to discern human weakness rather than strength: Chekhov and Conan Doyle, of course, but most especially W. Somerset Maugham, who visited him in Echandens in 1960, six years after their first meeting in London.

The eighty-six-year-old Maugham, whose last book, *Points of View*, had been published two years before, now described himself as "an unemployed writer" too alienated from the world to write anything but the memoirs that would be published after his death. But the suspension of his writing did not prevent him from leaving his Moorish villa in Saint-Jean-Cap-Ferrat for grand tours of Asia or Europe. The two men had lunch together, and Simenon told Maugham of his early years in Paris, in particular his meeting with Colette at the offices of *Le Matin*. Maugham's impressions were incorporated into his autobiography in progress.

Soon afterward, Willie was gracious enough to send Simenon two typed pages recounting their conversation, inviting him to make changes if he felt he had been inaccurately quoted. Actually, it was less the Paris anecdote than one of Maugham's personal observations that threatened to annoy him:

"I know of no better way of passing the time on a Nice-to-Athens or Rangoon-to-Singapore flight than to read a Simenon novel."[31]

Simenon was very forgiving of a man whose education he so admired. He would even quote him in a speech in Montreux to a congress of the International Federation of Writer-Physicians, of which Maugham was the honorary president:

"My friend and master Somerset Maugham, himself a doctor, has written: 'I suppose that one could learn much about human nature in a lawyer's office; but here, on the whole, one is dealing with men in control of themselves. They may lie, just as they lie to the doctor, but they do so more deliberately, probably because lawyers do not have such a great need to know the truth, the interests with which they are concerned being most often purely material. The lawyer sees nature from a specialized point of view. But the doctor, especially in hospitals, sees nature in the raw.' "[32]

Simenon saw primarily the man in the writer, and at most the doctor in the man.

When Somerset Maugham came to lunch in Echandens, Simenon was in the middle of reading not *Of Human Bondage* but *The Antibiotic Saga,* by Henry Welch and Felix Marti-Ibañez, a book that had been sent to him from the United States by one of his correspondents. He had begun "devouring" several medical journals a week, "like novels." His Testut anatomy manuals occupied a place of honor in his library. Medicine, which he considered an art more than a science, was his pet hobby, and he constantly reminded interviewers that, had he not been a novelist, he would probably have become a doctor.

He was most of all fascinated by diagnosis. He was delighted when Professor Leriche told him that whenever he started a Simenon novel, he tried to diagnose each of the characters and then checked his results at the end of the book, adding that few novels lent themselves to such an exercise, since few characters other than Simenon's had a liver and lungs and muscles and nerves as well as intellectual and spiritual lives.

The self-described "hypochondriac" and "neurovegetative"[33] Simenon expressed admiration for great doctors more readily than for great writers. His praise of doctors rings truer, for he felt he had much to learn from them. This was especially the case with psychiatrists, with whom he felt a special bond. One of his great regrets was that he never visited Carl Gustav Jung in his famous Bollingen tower on Lake Zurich. Simenon said that he read Jung assiduously from 1937, and that he felt a solidarity with his view of life: "He valued instinct and the subconscious, especially the creative subconscious, above intelligence."[34] He had been planning to ask for a meeting ever since moving to Switzerland, but dared not disturb the psychiatrist at work on his intellectual autobiography. He may also have feared that a discussion of the collective unconscious would go quickly over his head. This was a field in which he preferred to advance with caution.

In 1961 a Swiss journalist tried to arrange a meeting between Jung and Simenon. Both seemed enthusiastic, but the plan was aborted by Jung's sudden death. His obituary reported that a nearly complete and annotated set of Simenon's works occupied a prominent place in his library.

The novelist's fascination with medicine of both mind and body was of long standing. In 1920, at the age of seventeen, he discovered the psychiatric theories of Cabanès while covering a lecture for his newspaper.[35] Psychiatry plays a prominent role in *Les Scrupules de Maigret* (*Maigret Has Scruples,* 1958), in which the inspector consults his old friend Dr. Pardon, a modest neighborhood practitioner who cautions him about the pitfalls of the field while simultaneously offering useful suggestions. Maigret thumbs through a treatise on psychiatry: neurosis, neurasthenia, paranoia, ego hypertrophy, persecution psychosis. The more he reads, the less clear his case seems:

". . . In each category he found symptoms that applied to each of his characters. . . . Pardon was right: if you research the anomalies of human behavior, classify and subdivide them, you wind up not knowing who is of sound mind and who is not. Was he? After what he had just read, he was not so sure."

Maigret eventually solves his case in the usual way, by instinct rather than reasoning,[36] but his initial toying with psychiatric technique is nevertheless symptomatic of Simenon's state of mind in late 1957. His taste for medicine was gradually evolving into a passion for psychiatry, a fascination that was not unrelated to his marital difficulties. His ongoing "clinical" observation of Denyse's personality generated fresh questions about what he hazily perceived as mental disturbances.

Two years later he wrote *L'Ours en peluche* (1960), whose hero is a depressive doctor. But it was in 1962, with *Les Anneaux de Bicêtre* (*The Bells of Bicêtre*), that his concern with "the condition of illness" reached its height.

This novel, which from the outset he considered one of his most important, was dedicated to "all those—professors, doctors, nurses—who, in hospitals and elsewhere, seek to understand and relieve that most disconcerting being: the sick man." Simenon also marked the book's exceptional character by writing a foreword for it.

Les Anneaux de Bicêtre is a third-person account of the world as seen by a man partially paralyzed by a stroke. Lucid in his hospital bed, the patient listens and understands while those around him believe him barely aware of his surroundings. As friends come to visit, his personal reminiscences contrast with his new situation. Gradually regaining minimal use of his limbs and his organic faculties, he reapprehends his human condition, becomes aware of the man he had wanted to be, and is ineluctably drawn into a reevaluation of his life. He realizes that he has put all his energy into social and professional ambitions, sometimes to the detriment of his human qualities and his relation with a woman who has taken refuge in alcohol.

Simenon wrote two versions of this book simultaneously, one by hand, the other at the typewriter. He said that he had done this only six or seven times before, *La Neige était sale* (1948) being the most notorious instance. In the evening he wrote by hand what he would type the next day. At first it was a matter of ten lines or so at a time, then twenty, and finally entire chapters. This was not so much a draft, since he did not refer to it when he sat down at the typewriter, but a way of ridding himself of inhibitions before immersing himself in a world more troubling than others he had created.

The moment he felt he was drifting into "literature," he abandoned his pencil for the typewriter. Rarely had he been so concerned about the neutrality of his writing, as though he had decided to lend this novel the tone of a medical report. He was so ruthless in deleting what he considered "the fat" that he wound up with a typescript of only about 350 pages, where he had expected 500.[37] In its published form the book was 314 pages, about a hundred more than such recently published "hard novels" as *Betty* (1961), *Le Train* (1961), or *La Porte* (*The Door,* 1962).

In his mind it was not so much the hero as the people around him who would serve as the mainspring of the narrative. His secondary characters were all Parisian personalities (a dramatist and a novelist, both members of the French Academy, a leading professor of pathology, an official at the Ministry of Justice). At first there were thirteen friends, but only ten of them "made it," and in what state? Were success and recognition worth so many sacrifices and compromises? The questions arose as they lunched together in a private room at the Grand Véfour, one of the best restaurants in Paris, on the first Tuesday of every month over a period of twenty years. It is during one of these ritual meals that René Maugras, fifty-five years old, manager of one of the capital's great newspapers, is found unconscious in the bathroom.

From that starting point, Simenon was not sure how to reconnect his main character with the heroes of his childhood. After considering the problem from various points of view, he decided on partial paralysis. But since he wanted to be thoroughly credible, he had to do some preparatory research.

This was not the first time he had done this, however loath he was to admit it publicly. But it is doubtful that he ever collected so much material before beginning a novel. It was almost enough to write a book within the book.

He made a quick trip to Paris, spending an hour and a half at Bicêtre gathering details: how they picked up the garbage at dawn, the sounds of the doctor's car and of the bells of the neighboring church, the number of private rooms, the view of a bedridden patient when his door is left ajar, the meal schedules of the nurses.[38]

For an aphasic patient unable to move, sounds become life's true indicators. Simenon's character therefore expends his first efforts trying to hear, and the sense of hearing is echoed in the book's title. In most languages it was called *The Bells of Bicêtre.* In French, however, "bells" (*cloches*) has an unfortunate double-meaning of "idiots" or "bums." He therefore settled on "Les anneaux" (or "rings") of Bicêtre, a reference to a childhood memory of the hero: when bells sounded, forming concentric rings in the air, he felt another sensation, another vibration.

But Simenon was not content with the results of his own personal inquiry. On September 10, 1962, he drafted a ten-point questionnaire for Dr. Roger J. L. Pluvinage, a Paris physician familiar with the capital's hospices. He also consulted two other doctors: his own general practitioner, Dr. Samuel

Cruchard of Lausanne, former chief of a clinic; and Dr. Daniel Lemoine, an expert in motor rehabilitation in the neurology service of the Bicêtre hospice.

At Simenon's request, the former supplied him with a medical report on one Mr. Y., fifty-four years old. On February 2, 1962, this man was dining, "in time-honored tradition," with a group of friends, one of whom was a professor of medicine. At about ten o'clock he left the table to use the bathroom. A quarter of an hour later, he was found on the floor, in convulsions, his mouth twisted, the right side of his body immobilized, in a virtually comatose state.

Dr. Cruchard also listed the symptoms exhibited by this patient on his admission to the clinic (labored breathing, diminution of muscular reflexes, slightly ruddy complexion, etc.), the tests that were done (arterial pressure, blood work, electroencephalogram), the initial treatment (anticoagulant, tranquilizers, physiotherapy), the various stages of his recovery (regression of aphasia, limited mobility with a walker), and so on.

Also at Simenon's request, Dr. Lemoine sent him a copy of his lecture on the psychology of hemiplegia. Finally, the novelist summoned one last expert to his imaginary witness stand: Raymond Oliver, who had been chef-restaurateur at the Grand Véfour since 1948. Oliver sent him the menus of the Club of Twelve and informed him that one of its members had died "in conditions more or less identical" to those surrounding his hero.[39]

In late October, immediately after finishing the novel, Simenon turned to its promotion. This, too, was exceptional. Usually he preferred to forget a book once it was written, abandoning it to its publisher, the critics, and the public.

Sven Nielsen realized that his author considered this book important when he agreed to certain sacrifices to ensure its success: signings, a dinner with celebrities at the Grand Véfour, participation in a television broadcast.[40]

Back in 1948, convinced that *Les Fantômes du chapelier* might get some press, Simenon had considered organizing a psychiatrists' debate to publicize the book.[41] This time he chose a less artificial method, sending free copies of the novel to about five hundred "big names" in medicine, the courts, and the press, not only in Paris and the provinces but in Belgium and Switzerland as well. He eagerly awaited the reaction of medical circles. In fact, it sometimes seems as though he had written the story for that audience alone.[42]

The launch was a success. At the bar of the Hotel George V, where he granted serial interviews, Simenon greeted journalists in terms that brought them straight into the atmosphere:

"I'm glad you're on time. I don't mind having my wallet or some other object of value stolen, but not my time. Objects can be replaced, but who knows how much time any of us has left?"[43]

The television broadcast went well, too. Invited to appear on *Lectures pour tous,* Simenon overshadowed the other guests—Jean Dutourd, Pierre Gaxotte, and Arthur Adamov.

Some critics expressed reservations, among them, of course, Jean Paulhan.

In a very NRF tone of haughty condescension he complained of the author's popularity, the awkwardness of his metaphors, the banality of his plot, his lack of tragic sensibility, and his style, which, while "more or less" correct, nevertheless misused adjectives and adverbs.[44]

In this case, however, the views of Gallimard's master reader were shared by few other critics. Pierre-Henri Simon in *Le Monde* hailed the "important and distinctive" qualities of this novel even while scolding some of his colleagues for what he considered excessive enthusiasm for the author's work. He even took the opportunity to issue a mea culpa for having devoted only ten or so superficial and pedestrian lines to Simenon in his "History of French Literature in the Twentieth Century." But instead of accounting for his error of perspective, he justified it by repeating the common warning that Simenon's work threatened to sink without a trace under the weight of its own mass.[45]

In *L'Express,* the ardent Simenonian Thomas Narcejac assured readers that this new novel was a masterpiece just as significant as *Pedigree.* In his view, if there was any such thing as the "nouveau roman," Simenon was its authentic practitioner.[46] Robert Kanters in *Le Figaro littéraire* was also starry-eyed. But François Mauriac, in his column "Bloc-notes," published in the same weekly, produced an especially remarkable article:

> Here Simenon achieves a truth upon which no novelist before him has ever cast such a harsh, almost insupportable light. . . . The mechanics of a patient's day in a large hospital become the vantage point from which the rest of the world seems to dissolve into the nothingness described by the preachers of my childhood, who never managed to persuade me. Simenon is a better preacher. The effects of the illness he describes prefigure the distance old age creates between ourselves and life. It melts into illness on one essential point: the proximity of death—which it is useless to try to avoid, to try not to talk about or think about. Its mere looming presence, the feeling that we are within its grasp, is sufficient for the world to become that nothingness which is the real subject of Simenon's latest.[47]

By the middle of the summer of 1963 the novel had been on the best-seller list in *L'Express* for four months, alongside works by Joseph Kessel, Romain Gary, Marcel Pagnol, and Hervé Bazin. On its account an opposition weekly was threatened with indictment for libeling the chief of state, when it reported that Simenon had planned to ask three psychiatrists to draw up a psychological profile of General de Gaulle on the basis of one of his television speeches. The purpose was said to be to compare their reports and draw some conclusions about disagreements among experts to be used in *Les Anneaux de Bicêtre.*[48]

Simenon cared little whether the genesis of his novel was revealed, so long as it was not read as a roman à clef. Unfortunately, that was just what happened. Several Paris journalists quickly realized that the hero, René Maugras, was based on one of their own: the legendary Pierre Lazareff, boss of *Paris-Soir*.

The author's denials counted for nothing. Everyone knew that he and Lazareff had been friends for thirty years, and there were simply too many co-incidences. The devotee of the detail that rings true had let slip a few that left little doubt as to the source of his inspiration. Like Maugras, Lazareff arrived at his office in a Bentley; he was famous for always being in a hurry, for working without a break, for inviting ministers, stars, and bankers to Sunday parties at his impressive country home; he had been seriously ill a year earlier, and the first symptoms appeared during a dinner at the Grand Véfour.

Perhaps Simenon's imagination really was as feeble as he claimed, but it did not take a genius to detect the familiar figures of Marcel Achard (a playwright and member of the French Academy) or the Viscountess Marie-Laure de Noailles, née Bischoffsheim, a patron of the arts and literature whose salon at the Place des Etats-Unis was one of the capital's most brilliant. The book featured a Countess Marie-Anne de Candines:

"She was an Israelite, distantly related to the Rothschilds. Her father was a banker . . . Marie-Anne was the doyen of those who lead a certain kind of life and exhibit certain tastes. The young and the not so young gathered around her in her mansion in Alma and her château in Candines: writers male and female, filmmakers, couturiers, pretty girls who were in the theater or wanted to be, a couple of painters, and an undetermined number of pederasts."[49]

Apparently all those lawsuits had not scared him off. Perhaps he was even looking for trouble. The parallel to reality was even more striking in the case of Professor Henri Mondor, the obvious model for the novel's Pierre Besson d'Argoulet, a great physician and man of letters "who, between reports to the Academy of Medicine, wrote three books on the private lives of Flaubert, Zola, and Maupassant."[50] Mondor had written biographies of Verlaine, Rimbaud, and Mallarmé.

Curiously, no one sought to identify the character of Lina, the depressive alcoholic wife. That was because the collapse of the Simenon marriage was not yet public knowledge.

"He's afraid of her. She's mad."

That was the merciless judgment of the prestigious American publisher Kurt Wolff, who had seen Denyse in action, patiently listening to her exposition of extravagant financial demands on her husband's behalf. He also noticed that she talked for hours without stopping to take a breath and turned minor issues of contention into major ones.[51]

Wolff had recently made the Simenons' acquaintance in Bürgenstock, a fashionable summer resort overlooking Lake Quatre-Cantons. He and his wife, Helen, had learned that the novelist's contract with Doubleday was about to expire. It was Simenon's practice never to cede rights for the duration of the copyright (as most authors did), but to limit contracts to terms of ten years. He was displeased with Doubleday's refusal to reprint his early titles, only five of which were available in bookstores. That was enough to make him sensitive to the siren call of Doubleday's competitors.

He was impressed by the brilliant past of Kurt Wolff, a quintessential "Mitteleuropean," publisher of Franz Kafka, Robert Musil, and Joseph Roth (among others) in Germany in the twenties.[52] He also appreciated the intellectual probity of this couple, who proposed to publish *Les Anneaux de Bicêtre* immediately, letting Maigret wait a few years.

There was good chemistry between Simenon and the Wolffs. He would never have the chance to get better acquainted with Kurt, who was killed in an automobile accident on his way to the Frankfurt Book Fair several months later. But he often called Helen "one of the women I admire most." He considered her "my best female friend."[53]

Simenon accepted the contract the Wolffs offered him in the name of Harcourt, Brace and World, the New York firm in which they were associate editors. But on one condition: he wanted to speak to the company president, William Jovanovich.

"I absolutely must talk to the top man before signing," he explained. "After all, he's the one who makes the decisions."

The next day his wish was granted and the contract signed. Denyse played no part in the process. She had made the mistake of asking for too much. Her husband took the Americans aside:

"The way I see it, you always have to ask for the maximum, but not for more than that."

Kurt Wolff, a very intuitive man, was distrustful of Denyse from the start. He felt that she was so ill at ease, so unsure of her role and function, that she felt compelled to harp on her status as her husband's agent.[54]

Relations between Georges and Denyse Simenon had worsened steadily since their move to Europe. There had been violent scenes even in Lakeville, often involving alcohol. When the memorialist later wrote that their fifteen-odd years together had been a time of "passionate love,"[55] he, unlike Marc, forgot to point out that there might have been something "unhealthy" about this passion, this tendency to tear each other to pieces.[56] Apart from the delusions of grandeur Denyse acquired during their European tour in 1952, several other factors were involved in the evolution of their relationship.

In America, Simenon had been doubly isolated: by geography and by his initial hesitant command of English. Denyse was therefore indispensable to him. That was no longer the case, especially inasmuch as she had hired an efficient, multilingual full-time secretary, Joyce Aitken. In America, Denyse had been entirely devoted to her husband, relieving him of all administrative chores and satisfying his sexual fantasies. In Switzerland she transferred her abnegation to her own person. She spent hours pondering certain passages of *Le Fils* (1957). One of the narrator's statements had been put into italics: "A woman must be only a reflection of her husband and must sacrifice her personality to his."[57]

Her health had deteriorated, and not only because of alcohol. "My memory has often failed me since my 1955 illness," she admitted in a business letter.[58] Her husband was less enigmatic about the nature of that "illness," a reference to the painful operation she had undergone in a Mougins clinic, "losing a child due to be born in October."[59] The trauma did nothing for Denyse's morale.

Once he began to doubt her psychological equilibrium, Simenon began to notice symptoms he considered revealing. During the Cannes festival he remarked that the atmosphere had sharpened her need "to make herself feel important by rubbing elbows with important people."[60] Soon afterward, during a brief stay in Paris, he noted that her obsession with cleanliness had worsened. When they checked into their suite at the Hotel George V, she replaced the paper linings of the drawers and closets, scoured the bathroom, disinfected the telephones, and ran a vacuum cleaner over the furniture.[61]

Simenon also took her household demands as a sign that she was not getting any better. In 1956 she had six servants, a figure that rose to eight in 1959, nine the following year, and eleven in 1962. He saw this as symptomatic of an imperious need: "To reassure herself by increasingly asserting her importance." Denyse defended herself, pleading her concern to protect her master's work. But the master was not asking for so much. He was convinced that she had a need to assert her authority, to manage, oversee, and organize—in a word, to dominate, perhaps someday taking over his pen. It was an attitude that had less to do with megalomania than with a desire to arrogate power and glory to herself.

He felt that her febrility was the result of this useless expenditure of energy, matched by an equally useless professional hyperactivity (business letters three times as long as necessary, interminable international phone calls, and so on).[62]

Had he had the heart to joke, Simenon might have said of Denyse what Désiré said of Aunt Félice, that she was *brindezingue,* a charming euphemism for "drunk" also suggesting that the person was "nuts."[63] At first he tried to protect her, to help her become the "winner" she aspired to be. Denyse had the character and intellectual wherewithal for it, for she had a sharp intelligence that enabled her to quickly detect any interlocutor's flaws. But he gave up when he realized that her ambition amounted to a neurosis. He felt she was unable to measure up to her own perfectionism. She was too weak to be the best.

Soon after novelizing their meeting in *Trois Chambres à Manhattan* (1946), Simenon felt the need to record his exceptional passion for Denyse in *Lettre à mon juge* (1947). Charles Alavoine is Simenon, and Martine Englebert is Denyse, at least when he falls in love with this young secretary whose past heralds her future lack of balance:

"In all her being, judge, in her staring eyes, her open mouth, her pinched nostrils, there was an unendurable anguish, and at the same time—try to understand me—a no less desperate will to escape it, to burst the bubble, to break through the ceiling, in a word, to find deliverance. This anguish rose to such a paroxysm that it frightened me as a doctor, and I was relieved when suddenly, after a final, nerve-shattering tension, she would fall back as though spent, discouraged, her heart beating so powerfully in her small breast that I had no need to touch it to count its palpitations. . . . The great problem, the capital problem, was to discover why we loved each other. This was a problem that long haunted us, for on its solution depended the degree of confidence we could have in our love."[64]

Inquiring into Martine's childhood, Charles discovers the traumas that made her what she is. He wants to take her in hand to purge her of her dark memories. To deliver her from what she was "before," he strangles her. After his confession, he kills himself. Simenon would go not to those lengths, but to others, less radical and tragic. And they would turn both their lives upside down.

In June 1962, a few months before Simenon began writing *Les Anneaux de Bicêtre,* Denyse underwent the first of a series of detoxifications in Les Rives de Prangins clinic in the canton of Vaud, about twenty miles from Lausanne. Nervous exhaustion and advanced alcohol poisoning were the reasons for her stay, but she was convinced that it was actually a plot hatched by her husband in concert with a psychiatrist whom she would later blame for all her troubles.[65]

A pediatrician by the name of Roger Walter had introduced Simenon to the psychiatrist, Dr. Charles Durand. Seven years Simenon's junior, Durand was of French origin and had been the clinic's medical director since 1946. He had done his psychiatric training in various hospitals in Paris and its environs (Villejuif, Val-de-Grace, Sainte-Anne, and others) and later served on the staff at . . . Bicêtre. He had participated in a number of medical conferences, delivering papers on anorexia, neurosis and religious life, and schizophrenia.

Simenon told Dr. Durand that he was convinced that Denyse's alcohol dependence was a symptom of a disturbed psyche, but confessed his inability to analyze it in any greater depth. Though he had the general idea that she was a psychopath, he called in several doctors to try to help her achieve a state more tolerable for both of them. Even in the event of remission, however, he knew he would probably have to turn the page.

"An alcoholic who stops drinking is done for, isn't he?" the narrator of *La Passager clandestin* (1947) asked himself.[66]

Simenon wrote "only" three novels in 1963: *La Chambre bleu* (1964), *L'Homme au petit chien* (1964), and *Maigret et le fantôme* (*Maigret and the Ghost,* 1964). It was not one of his better years, for he was preoccupied with the threat of the collapse of the family nucleus to which he was so attached.

French television had recently spent many days filming a program at Echandens. The journalist Roger Stéphane, for whom Simenon had written and narrated the profile of Balzac, had convinced him to grant a long interview.

It did not go well, though the result was a first-class document. Simenon seemed nervous, irritable, and impatient. He was obviously eager to get it over with. He sometimes spoke aggressively to his interlocutor, which was unusual for him. Fearing that he would be perceived as a "case" or a "phenomenon" and powerless to prevent misinterpretation and misunderstanding, he lost his temper with the journalist. He later explained his attitude this way:

"I must say, too, that I find intellectuals and pederasts exasperating. And intellectual pederasts, well . . ."[67]

The interview was equally unpleasant for Roger Stéphane, though his admiration for Simenon's work was undiminished:

> . . . With no intention of fakery, falsely affable and genuinely distant in talking to someone he considered a mere network employee, Georges Simenon exhibited his extraordinary aptitude for work and the mechanics of his production. He displayed his wealth—not like a nouveau riche but like an industrialist of literature. He produced, and he sold what he produced. He talked about contracts, translations, and print runs.
>
> There was a very numerous staff in his residence, secretaries and servants ruled with a firm hand by Mme Simenon, who called them by their last names. Simenon did not seem to see them as people. He said he had only two regrets: not being recognized as a peer by psychiatrists and criminologists, and not being recognized as a master by the Nobel academy.
>
> Of the framework in which we worked I would recall three things. Fear of the future was one. Simenon dreaded a world war or some other catastrophe; hence the enormous laundry and operating room at his home, driven by a generator ready to go at a moment's notice. The house was replete with microphones, supposedly installed so that Simenon would know if one of his children was calling or crying, but I

think he also used them to eavesdrop on what others besides his children might be saying about him. And finally, he detested wood, in which any number of undesirable beasts might find shelter. The furniture was of glass, leather, and metal.

A curious impression: I listened to Georges Simenon for hours but never really got to know him.[68]

In 1962, when he learned that Echandens was about to be turned into a suburb with the establishment of a marshaling yard and the construction of a highway in the vicinity, Simenon began to think about packing his bags again.[69] But the impending upheavals were only a pretext. The truth is that he wanted a change of scene. He was tired of living in someone else's home. Whether as owner or tenant, he had yet to find a house that really suited him.

This time he needed a lot of space, for there were many people to house—children, servants, secretaries, employees—and many cars to park. On a vast plot of land in Epalinges, overlooking Lausanne and Lake Léman, he would now construct his Xanadu according to plans he himself helped devise.

It was not the happiest of portents. Citizen Kane ended his days in terrifying solitude.

17

DELIVERANCE

hen the house is built, misfortune enters."

Simenon pondered this Chinese proverb endlessly while Epalinges was under construction. It was as though he felt disaster looming. To those dumbfounded by the immensity of the structure, he would plead his wife's delusions of grandeur and his need to make sure that everyone had enough space. He wanted to be able to write while Johnny played the drums and Marie-Jo threw a party. But Epalinges was an accurate reflection of its owner. It was a house built to his own excess, both in the number of rooms and in their dimensions.

It would be charitable to call the overall effect unprepossessing. Both the façade and the interior evinced an utter lack of sense of color, form, and volume. The vestibule was as big as a hangar, the walls were white, the carpeting red, the bathrooms black. There were American-style bay windows, tiles imported from Belgium, paintings by Lorjou and Buffet, Matisse and Vlaminck. Solidity of construction was of prime importance to this fanatic of order and organization. A house was made of walls, and walls were meant to protect and defend him. Epalinges was his mask and his mirror.

The terraced lawn had a view of Lake Léman, the French and Italian Alps, and even the Juras. In the foreground was a sloping path leading to a little church. From the grounds you could watch baptismal processions, marriages, and burials. He didn't mind that, since it humanized the somewhat lifeless postcard view of a landscape slightly too grandiose for his taste.

Despite the dollar sign embedded in the gate and the impressive collection of automobiles parked out front (Jaguar, Bentley, Facel-Vega, Chrysler, Mercedes), the first visitors had the curious sensation that they had stayed in a fortress repainted after a war or in a futurist clinic. This latter aspect helped enhance an already colorful legend. Simenon's medical and hygienic concerns were well known, and little urging was needed for some to imagine him as a kind of Dr. Jekyll.

He made no secret of the fact that he saw the construction of this house and his purchase of parcels of land around it as more than an expression of his penchant for isolation. He genuinely considered it a good investment, since he felt the house could easily be turned into a clinic.[1] Apart from the sound-proofed rooms and the intercom, there was the notorious "operating theater." Some journalists, writers, and ordinary visitors claimed that it was so well equipped that the Simenons could have undergone serious surgery in it. But after all, more than half a century later, there were still witnesses who swore they had seen him writing a novel in a glass cage.

In fact, this infirmary was no more than a reasonably sized room with a large pharmaceutical cabinet, a massage table, and an ultraviolet lamp used mainly by the younger children to touch up their tans.[2]

Curiously, the mythical operating room got much more press than the immense playroom in the basement. A veritable paradise for Johnny, Marie-Jo, Pierre, and their classmates, the playroom said far more about Simenon than the supposed O.R.

Simenon had two offices in Epalinges—one for writing, the other for receiving visitors. His novel-writing ritual had not changed: rise at six in the morning; coffee; work from 6:30 to 9:30; a walk from 10:00 to 12:30, followed by lunch and a one-hour nap. Then he would walk again and read the papers. As night fell it was the secretaries' task to draw the shades and light the lamps, an absolutely imperative task, for otherwise Simenon would sink into torpor and depression.[3] Then dinner, television, and to bed at ten. Everything was timed with military precision.

When she returned from her first detoxification, Denyse tried to accommodate herself to this house, which was not yet really hers, even though she had helped supervise the design. Convinced that she was not "ill" but simply exhausted by the move, she found that her husband had consulted a psychiatrist about her, a discovery she made by chance as she was going over the household bills.[4]

Simenon's attitude toward her had changed. When she was in the clinic, he phoned regularly and tried to ease her mind. But he did not want her back, as he admitted to visitors:

"It's incredible when you think about it. She had three secretaries, and it took her all night to do what I do in an hour with one secretary, now that she's not here. I send telegrams instead of five-page letters."[5]

He felt she was out of place in Epalinges, no longer the indispensable collaborator she had been in America nor the submissive wife he was used to.

Nor was she a mother in the sense one of Simenon's characters meant it: "One of those women who smells of pastry."[6]

It would not have been enough for Denyse to replace alcohol with pastry. The antagonism was more complex, intractable, and irreversible. Immersed in his readings in psychiatry, Simenon was now deeply convinced that his wife was mentally ill, though he had trouble sorting out all the various terms: delusions of grandeur, megalomania, schizophrenia, misguided suspicion, obsessional cleanliness. Despite his protestations to the contrary, his approach to mental illness was still that of a novelist, not a scientist. But he did not have to go on noting symptoms. The specialists he consulted confirmed that he was, alas, on the right track.

Denyse's magnetism now left him cold. Until 1964 he tried to support her and to protect her from herself. Then his priorities changed. He decided to protect not his wife but the mother of his children, and later his children from their mother.

An apparently trivial event was decisive in this shift. One evening she was tottering around, glass in hand, presiding over the household again, more authoritarian than ever. He mentioned that it was getting late and that the employees had the right to get some rest. When she ignored him, he raised the tone:

"They're tired. Let them go home."

"*They're* tired? What about me?!"

There was a scene—one too many. Simenon's mind was now made up. It was all over. For good.

Denyse was soon back in the bucolic surroundings of the Prangins clinic. In 1966 she lived permanently in the Sans-Souci villa, an annex in which veterans of the clinic were free to walk around. The Paris journalist Yves Salgues, a forty-year-old heroin addict who had taken advantage of his frequent clinic stays to devour many a Simenon novel, was also a tenant, a position he owed to his employer, Marcel Dassault, the aeronautics tycoon and editor in chief of the weekly *Jours de France*.[7] In his memoirs Salgues pays tribute to both Dassault and Denyse, incidentally offering a remarkable snapshot of life in Prangins:

"I would credit a single person with revealing the true essence of my Prangins summers: Denyse Georges Simenon. She was witness to my exuberance, my fleeting happiness, and my irresistible dramatics: drinking so as not to succumb to the lure of the drug, suffering so as not to drink, drinking again so as not to suffer, and finally suffering endlessly—abjectly—for having drunk to the point of cerebral trauma. . . . With the shattering lucidity of hindsight, I am now convinced that by failing to take advantage of the five chances at a cure offered me at Prangins, I committed five homicides against myself."[8]

According to Salgues, 1966 was a crucial year for Simenon, a time of attempted conciliation when Denyse still hoped to regain his confidence, support, and love. But in vain. His visits were intermittent. He had abandoned the project he claimed to have undertaken with their very first encounter, in terms reminiscent of Charles Alavoine's confession in *Lettre à mon juge* (1947). Yet these are the words of the memorialist, not the novelist:

". . . I wanted to cure her. To cure her of herself. To cure her of the need she had felt ever since her youth to be something she was not. To cure her of the need to shine, which had earned her the nickname 'La Diva' from her brothers. A need to shine which, as I watched, little by little turned into the need to dominate."[9]

Simenon decided he had suffered enough. Like an exhausted boxer, he told the psychiatrist that he was throwing in the towel. From the depths of his own darkness, Salgues glimpsed her heartache:

"Denyse helped me a lot, though she was herself a great neurotic. She talked to me, mostly about Simenon, because she knew of my literary passions and because she couldn't help talking about him. She said he was monstrous, that all he wanted was to subjugate her, that he had driven her mad, that he was perverse and sadomasochistic. 'He's the one who put me in the snake pit,' she used to say, an allusion to Anatole Litvak's film."[10]

The summer before, Simenon had taken the whole family on a Black Sea cruise in a last attempt to salvage what could be salvaged. It was a nightmare. One fight after another. Between two of her stints in Prangins, he sent Denyse and their daughter, Marie-Jo, to a chalet in Villars for a few weeks of vacation. That was even worse. The adolescent returned traumatized, her heart heavy with a secret she would reveal, tragically, only years later.

The doctors now took a radical view of the case. Dr. Durand spoke for them:

"We are all convinced that nothing more can be done for your wife."

"Meaning she's incurable?"

"We have told her that there is no further reason to continue to care for her here, on one strict condition: that she no longer live with you or her children, that she have the right to see them only briefly, from time to time, until they are adults."

"And she agreed?"

"Yes. As for you, you can take her back if you feel like committing suicide."

"Where will she go?"

"Wherever she wants, as long as it's away from Lausanne."[11]

Denyse left Epalinges for good. Soon afterward, Simenon exchanged several letters with Tigy. They saw each other again. After one of these encounters, he turned to their son, Marc, and burst into tears:

"I was such a coward! A coward not to have tried to see her before now, to let myself fall under Denyse's spell."[12]

The people around him now feared that he would sink into depression again. More than ever, he needed someone to lean on. Tigy had filled that role for some twenty years. Denyse had been too unbalanced to play the part. It would now be assumed by Teresa.

A Venetian twenty-three years younger than Simenon, she had entered his employ as a housekeeper in December 1961, recommended by the secretary of his Italian publisher and friend, Arnoldo Mondadori. Several years later, Simenon had two occasions to be grateful for her presence at painful moments.

The first time was in Crans-sur-Sierre, during a winter vacation between two crises. For an instant Simenon was seized by a suicidal urge:

"What nostalgia gripped me that evening? I thought about D. [Denyse] alone among strangers, in Prangins, about our tumultuous passion during those first months and my obstinate efforts for so many years to make us a real couple. I tried everything, suffered everything in vain. She was lost to me, and probably also to herself. That evening, seized by a sudden despair, I decided to end it all. We were walking along a sheer rock face. I stopped, hesitated, stammered something like 'I can't take it anymore.' It was not an empty threat. At the time I was determined to end it, but Teresa held me back with her fortunately sturdy arms. She made me promise to give up walking on that path and gently led me toward the brightly lit, teeming streets."[13]

The second time was in Epalinges. Simenon had a nasty fall in the bathroom. Denyse was at the clinic. Teresa alone heard his shouts and came to help. He would never forget that. After having known friendship with Tigy and passion with Denyse, he would now discover tenderness with Teresa.

Le Petit Saint (*The Little Saint*), written in October 1964 and published the following year, bears the trace of this resurrection. It was the first of the "novels of destiny" written in Switzerland to be datelined not "Noland" but "Epalinges." No more trickery.

The "little saint" is the narrator and hero, Louis Cuchas, an artist who grows up in the chaotic environs of the Rue Mouffetard in Paris. His classmates nickname him "saint" because of his wisdom, serenity, and profound tranquillity. He is fatherless, and his mother takes care of her six children alone. Initially a street peddler, Cuchas builds his life around the rhythm of Les Halles and his affairs with women. As he grows up, he breaks away from this milieu to devote himself to his passion for painting, becoming a renowned artist without ever renouncing what remained the salt of his emotions: his mother's personality, the colors and odors of his childhood neighborhood, and his idiosyncratic way of taking things as they come.

Written at the conclusion of a dramatic period in Simenon's life, *Le Petit Saint* was one of the books he cherished most. In moments of enthusiasm, he even called it his favorite.[14] He wrote it entirely by hand in nine days, literally obsessed by its theme. Forty-eight hours after finishing it, when the routine of daily life still seemed tinged with strangeness, he mentioned that this story had been more onerous to bear than *Les Anneaux de Bicêtre* (1963), even though its theme and characters were far more optimistic. He had begun it in 1958, but abandoned it.

"For more than ten years I've been wanting to write a novel of this kind, but I was never able to do it," he told his publisher.[15]

Unlike *Les Anneaux de Bicêtre,* this novel required no research. He nevertheless made a brief trip to Paris to pick up the scent of the neighborhood, wandering through the streets at nightfall, climbing stairways, walking through hallways outside attic rooms. He did not go so far as to stay there, however, preferring to check into the Hotel George V.

Simenon needed these snapshots to recover the neighborhood's atmosphere and its light, the dreamlike light that dazzled his hero. In private he acknowledged that his painter owed something to Chagall and to Zadkin, though more in spirit than in letter. He also had Lorjou in mind, and when the novel came out he bought two of his pictures. He even thought about asking Lorjou to do some drawings and paintings for a deluxe edition of the novel.

His character is above all a man in harmony with himself who strives constantly for greater inner serenity. As egotistical as any true creator must learn to be, he takes from everyone whatever might be useful to his art, and so much the worse if he never gives anything in return. "From the 'career' point of view, the model is more or less Chagall. But from the 'character' point of view, he borrows much from myself. When someone slaps him, he does not respond," Simenon claimed in private.[16]

The little saint of the Rue Mouffetard has much in common with the altar boy of Outremeuse. But Simenon considered his hero an archetype. His writing was slowly evolving toward increasingly neutral characters purged of manias or idiosyncrasies, as though the psychological ordeal he had just suffered made him more aware of how much pathos the human condition could entail.

The book was delivered to the shops wrapped in an enigmatic promotional band: "At last I have written it."

It was his first "novel of destiny" in a year, since *L'Homme au petit chien* (1964). In the meantime, he had produced only two Maigrets. But the publicity slogan was meant to refer to the new stage he felt he had entered: he had finally produced a profile of an optimistic hero at peace with himself. For once he had written in a different key, and his effort was a striking success, though it was not to be repeated. Never again would he create such a radiant personality.

Booksellers were content, for readers were enthusiastic. But Simenon was surprised at the relative indifference of the critics. He found it particularly disappointing, since he was so fond of the novel himself. Once again he took solace from British and American reviewers.

The reaction of Helen Wolff, his new American publisher, was everything he could have hoped for. In a private note to William Jovanovich, owner of the publishing house within which she issued books under her own imprint, she analyzed *Le Petit Saint* at length, describing it as a novel of exceptional quality, a turning point in the author's career.[17]

Thomas Narcejac, too, would later call this book "a rare masterpiece,"[18] and Pierre MacOrlan also expressed his admiration in a letter to Simenon. As if trying to console the author for the lukewarm reaction of critics in Paris, MacOrlan assured Simenon that the subtle poetry of *Le Petit Saint* had simply eluded the soulless academic commentators.[19] MacOrlan was especially impressed by the book's final lines, which were indeed highly Simenonian:

"Had he not taken something from all of them, from everyone? Had he not made use of their substance? He did not know, could not know. Otherwise he would have been incapable of going all the way to the end. He kept trundling along, a smile on his face.

" 'May I ask you, master, what image you have of yourself?'

"It did not require much thought. His face lit up for an instant as he said, joyful and modest:

" 'I am a little boy.' "

Daily life resumed in Epalinges. Less than eight months after finishing *Le Petit Saint,* Simenon started *Le Train de Venise* (*The Venice Train,* 1965), having filled out the brief interlude with *La Patience de Maigret* (1965). A good sign. The regularity of visitors was another.

"Uncle Miller," still in search of a solitary retreat, had recently put in an appearance. During his four-day stay they were joined by a most distinguished guest: Charlie Chaplin, who lived nearby in Ban manor, a thirty-seven-acre estate in Corsier-sur-Vevey. Over after-dinner coffee one evening the conversation turned to the subject of psychology. Chaplin had strong opinions on the matter.

"We're all of us psychos. But a few, like the three of us, are unbelievably lucky. When they feel a crisis coming on, they don't have to spend a lot of money on psychoanalysis. You two start writing, I make a film, and we're temporarily cured. And we get paid for it to boot."[20]

This theory made a strong impression on Simenon. That it was somewhat simplistic mattered little. To him, Chaplin was the embodiment of complete success, and that was more important than what he said. Simenon made no secret of his admiration for Chaplin's relationship with Oona O'Neill. "Teresa is for me what Oona is for Charlie," he told his youngest son. "Oona is one of the few women I would have wanted to marry if I had met her first."[21]

The Chaplins and their children came to visit Simenon in Epalinges several times. They were fond of his food and drink, and equally of his pool. Conversations between the two "masters" were generally quite relaxed. Chaplin's

French was not good enough for him to appreciate the copy of *Le Petit Saint* that Simenon had given him as a memento, along with an electric pencil sharpener.[22] Rather than get embroiled in serious discussions, they preferred to amuse themselves comparing fan letters, especially the ones from golddiggers. They even discovered that they had a correspondent in common: a penniless single mother in Italy with eight children, who had sent the two of them exactly the same letter, almost to the comma.[23]

Simenon's attitude to Chaplin is significant, for once again he was more impressed by the man's life than by his work, by his marriage than by his genius. In his autobiography, Chaplin mentions Simenon only fleetingly. He makes a point of quoting Simenon's explanation for his tiny handwriting: "It's easier on the wrist."[24]

He could not have said much more, since the work was published in 1964. It was a commercial success, but reviews were lukewarm: too much name-dropping, too much pride and self-satisfaction, too many mistakes. The reaction convinced Simenon to decline repeated requests to write his own memoirs, especially since he knew that a real writer had worked with Chaplin on his. Otherwise it would have been worse. When Maurice Bessy later sent him his book of photographs of Chaplin, Simenon replied: "It would give me the greatest pleasure to tell you the name of the English writer who helped Charles Chaplin draft his memoirs. Unfortunately, he's a friend, too, and I cannot betray him."[25]

In a letter written before the book's publication, however, he revealed in confidence the identity of the person who had urged Chaplin to undertake the project, helped him in his dealings with the publisher, introduced him to the staff at the Bodley Head, and reviewed the organization of the material.[26] The author in question was Graham Greene.

Was Greene really a friend of Simenon's? The word loses much of its force when we recall how generously he tended to use it, especially if the candidate was English. On the other hand, he did not systematically abuse it. For instance, when Lord Snowdon did a photo spread on the novelist, Simenon said merely that the most aristocratic of Her Majesty's photographers was "very likable." In private he admitted that he found him "tiresome" in every sense of the word. He had insisted on innumerable poses, taking one shot after another and finally settling on a typical unoriginal setting: sitting on a bench at the foot of the cedar in the garden.[27]

On another occasion, Simenon was visited in Echandens by Ian Fleming, who was playing golf in the area. The historic encounter between James Bond and Inspector Maigret was arranged by a British journalist. The two novelists talked shop, discoursing on the merits of copy editors, the virtues of the exclamation point, action at the expense of psychology, critics' and readers' lack of gratitude, the cadence and rhythm of the sentence, the role of autobiography in imagination, the search for names for characters, and their common fondness for Goethe and Rupert Davies.

"Is it your ambition to write a great novel?" Fleming asked.

"Not a great literary novel," Simenon replied. "Just a true novel."

"You don't want to write something like *War and Peace*?"

"Not at all. Do you?"

"Me? I don't even want to write a true novel. I don't think I'll write anything else once I finish with James Bond. I'm almost at the end of my tether."

Simenon managed to get through the entire exchange without offering any opinion of Fleming's work. Fleming was more forthcoming, saying that he had been an eager reader of Simenon's novels in the original French for more than twenty years.[28]

None of which prevented Simenon from confessing his aversion to the James Bond novels to a Belgian journalist two years later: "a fossilized, schematized, artificial genre."[29]

Simenon generally regarded press interviews as a chore to which he submitted grudgingly, like a merchant servicing a commodity after a sale. He said he was especially exasperated by the banality of the questions and the mediocrity of the journalists. But there were rare exceptions. He was delighted to be interviewed for Belgian television by Henri Guillemin, a historian of literature and professor at the University of Geneva. From the first handshake the chemistry was good between Simenon and this Catholic who could talk with equal enthusiasm about God, Lamartine, and Victor Hugo. It was to Guillemin that he first admitted that it was the Church's position on sexuality that alienated him from Catholicism in his adolescence.

But what Simenon did not tell Guillemin about his views on religion is even more interesting. He considered the Old Testament a fascinating saga ("perhaps one of the world's most beautiful novels"), but his admiration was attenuated by what he saw as its lack of humanity:

"You find a lot more about hatred and curses down to the seventh generation than about love and clemency," he told a Protestant magazine in Geneva. He found the New Testament more admirable, but regretted that Catholicism seemed most devoted to imperatives to which he felt Christ was least attached.

One of Simenon's most unusual interviews was given to the magazine *Médecine et hygiène* in 1968. Five doctors spent the day "grilling" the famous author for an article to mark the journal's twenty-fifth anniversary. Dr. Pierre Rentchnik, professor of internal medicine and editor in chief of *Médecine et hygiène,* was joined by four colleagues: the psychiatrist Charles Durand; the general practitioner Samuel Cruchaud; the psychiatrist Dr. Kaech, who was also president of the Swiss society of medical writers; and Dr. Burgermeister, staff member of the University of Geneva psychiatric clinic.

They broached a long list of Simenonian subjects: the state of grace preceding the act of creation; its trigger mechanism; his nostalgia for order; the specter of pauperization; the former altar boy's guilt complex; his need to be kept in line by a spouse; his treatment of writing as therapy; his idealization of his father; his many changes of address; the predominance of the unconscious in his novelistic technique; his horror of money made by speculation; his fear of knowing himself too well; the genesis of *Les Anneaux de Bicêtre;* his terror of slipping across the line into madness; and of course Freud, Jung, Maigret, alcohol, medication, humiliation.

Some of these themes tallied well with his current concerns, such as Article 64 of the Penal Code, which defined criminal responsibility. Simenon had consistently denounced the article, believing as he did that man is never sufficiently evolved to be responsible for his actions, which were generally determined by such factors as tribal memory, social problems, and so on.[30] Juries, he felt, would do well to transfer their power to psychiatrists, an idea he had recently expounded in *Maigret hésite* (*Maigret Hesitates,* 1968).

The interview was not without value, but the concluding remarks attributed to the five physicians demonstrate the limits of the exercise:

"It is thanks to you that we have understood what can go on in the mind of a criminal and have been able to demystify the criminal personality. The physician's relationship to the patient parallels Maigret's to the criminal better than any psychiatric treatise or experiment. It is for this reason that we can say that the character of the doctor in your work is Maigret."[31]

Two of the five visitors—Durand and Cruchaud—were bound by professional confidentiality, since they had treated members of the Simenon family. Rentchnik was more detached, and with hindsight he noted how difficult it had been to get Simenon to talk freely:

"We did not discuss sex, a delicate subject in a group of six. Simenon needed doctors for reassurance, and the presence of his two physicians had that effect. On the other hand, we also spoke off the record, and we observed him carefully. Comparing our impressions afterward, we were struck by several things: his primitive sexuality, his conception of love (two-minute coitus), the lack of intimacy, emotional attachment, and romanticism in his sexual relations, his obsession with incest, which he said was shared by Chaplin, his remarkable sense of smell, his fabrications (he claimed to play eighteen holes of golf every day). When we visited his office, we were particularly aghast at his mania for detail. All the files were meticulously arranged in a special order of his own devising. Every object had its place, in accordance with a precise ritual. I left convinced that he was an obsessive-compulsive."[32]

In April 1969, Simenon returned to Liège, where his mother was being cared for in a rest home run by Ursuline nuns. In December 1970 he was summoned again. This time it was the end. She was in no pain, and her death was as peaceful as possible.[33]

He spent a week at her bedside in the Bavière hospital, the institution in whose chapel he had served mass more than half a century earlier. As his ninety-year-old mother lay between life and death, Simenon stood between two books, one that he had already written—*Le Chat* (*The Cat,* 1967)—and one that took shape in his mind as he watched her die, *Lettre à ma mère* (1974). In each he attained the summits of his art.

There is no lack of material on relationships between mothers and sons in Simenon's work, even in his early pulp novels: "Those who can love their mother without reservation don't know how happy they are" (*La Femme 47*); "She detested wealth. Perhaps she detested her son because he had money" (*Le Bourgmestre de Furnes*).

He rarely refrained from mentioning the subject in interviews, as though it were a less intimate theme than politics or religion. He had no compunction about publicly repeating a private refrain: "Everyone admires me except you."[34]

He often said that he had always seen writing as a way of defying his mother, that he had organized his life in opposition to the education she had given him (while being well aware that he had inherited her fear of the future), that he had always been determined to prove to her that he could make money.

When they promenaded arm-in-arm in Liège in 1952, it was he who was proud of her and not vice versa. She showered him with recriminations, his divorce and lack of morals being minor peccadilloes compared to the fundamental reproach: his brother's death. She wished Georges had died instead of Christian; Georges wished Henriette had died instead of Désiré.

He could be harsh when he spoke of her, especially when he knew there was no risk that the paper reporting his words might fall into her hands. He told Brendan Gill of *The New Yorker,* for instance:

"She was a miser, a money-grubber. She could never understand my becoming a writer. Her grand hope for me was that I become a pastry chef. Oh, how she wanted to see me at an oven and herself behind the counter! Once I put her in a novel, *Pedigree.* I admit that the likeness I drew of her was not only harsh but unmistakable, and at first she was very much offended. Then people started coming from miles around to look her over, and she turned out to enjoy it. She'd take visitors through the house and show them the table at which I wrote my first novel. But it wasn't really the same table. That table she sold."[35]

Simenon could also be cruel when he spoke of his mother in fictional guise, as in *Le Chat*. This novel of a couple who live only to tear each other apart was based on his mother's remarriage after his father's death. The widow Marguerite Doise is Henriette Simenon; the widower Emile Bouin, a retired construction foreman, is Joseph André, the retired railroad worker whom Henriette married in 1929, after having cared for his dying wife. The marriage lasted twenty years, until André's death.

In the novel the protagonists communicate only through increasingly lapidary notes. Emile suspects Marguerite of having killed his cat, wounding him through the animal he cherished. He avenges himself by doing away with Marguerite's parrot. The relation between them then degenerates into a pure hatred that they are unable to elevate to an even more powerful sentiment: indifference.

Seven years after completing this novel, Simenon would write in his *Lettre à ma mère* (1974):

"You and André soon began to distrust each other. He accused you of hoping he would die, so you could collect his pension for yourself. God knows whether he also accused you of hastening his first wife's death. The boarders were gone. The two of you were alone in the house on the Rue de l'Enseignement, strangers, if not enemies. No one recorded the words you exchanged, but they must have been terrible, full of deep hatred, for one day you decided to stop talking to each other and to exchange scribbled notes when communication was necessary. When I say hatred I'm not exaggerating. True, I wasn't there. But what other explanation is there when a man and a woman living together in marriage prepare their meals separately, keep their own locked food cupboards, wait for the kitchen to be empty before sitting down to eat. You were both afraid of being poisoned. It became an obsession, perhaps a compulsive one."[36]

Simenon made no special changes in his schedule or routine while writing *Le Chat*, one of his most anxiety-ridden works. As usual, his calendar—an advertiser's giveaway brought back from the United States: "Fly the Finest, Fly TWA"—not only lists appointments but also indicates days spent writing and rewriting. The former are circled and then crossed out in blue pencil: September 29 to October 5, 1966. The latter are in red pencil: October 17 to 20. Before, during, and after he was visited by Arnoldo Mondadori, Sven Nielsen, a newspaper reporter, and a television crew. He also went to the dentist and decided on the dates of the children's vacations.

When he realized that writing the manuscript by hand was too "concrete" and therefore too "conscious," he switched over to the typewriter. More than ever he wanted to purge his story of any trace of "literature."

"With a pencil you feel too much like a writer. It elicits elegant turns of phrase, lovely images, and so on," he explained.[37]

Simenon wanted more than the mere elimination of technique, of what his friend Derain called a novel's scaffolding. He wanted this book to be utterly bare of ornamentation, revealing humanity in its nakedness. When the cruelty of certain passages was pointed out to him, he replied that reality could be even worse: his mother's second husband had slowly and methodically pulled out the feathers of the parrot her beloved son Christian had brought back from the Congo for her.[38]

On reflection, Simenon wondered whether he had not finally written a love story. Did he realize that it was the tale not of two pensioners, but of a child's love for a mother who never accepted him for what he was?

Simenon finished *Les Innocents* (*The Innocents*, 1972), his latest "hard novel," on October 11, 1971, and *Maigret et Monsieur Charles* (*Maigret and Monsieur Charles*, 1972) on February 11, 1972. The inspector had recently acquired a television set. The eight o'clock news ruined his dinner.

These were not among his best books, but no matter. He had gone through less fertile periods. Unlike many novelists who swear that creative energy wanes after a certain age, Simenon at sixty-nine had not yet written his final words.

Denyse, out of the picture but still in the wings, now harassed him only through lawyers. Teresa was his companion. Marc, thirty-three, was a film and television director. Johnny, twenty-three, was studying at a university in the United States. Marie-Jo, nineteen, was trying, without success, to find herself. Thirteen-year-old Pierre was in school.

At nine in the morning on September 18, 1972, he sat down to begin his first novel in seven months. It was provisionally entitled *Victor*, a name he had already used in about twenty novels. But here it seems to have been of little significance, for he later referred to the character as Oscar, and even as Hector.

Following the ritual established decades ago, he began by jotting down a few biographical and topographical details on the back of a manila envelope. Less an outline than a safety net.

VICTOR

Gabriel Cavelli, 1880–1853 [*sic*], born Marseille 1880—son of a police superintendent—Rue Saint-Ferréol—law school in Paris—intern with Mr. Demange, esq.—lives at first Bd. Saint-Michel—pleads Legrain case (acquittal), which makes him famous—moves 14 Bd. Montmartre

His wife Berthe Chandolin, 20, his secretary dead in childbirth in 1908

Raymond their son born 1908—civil law—timid-calm—in 1935, 27, marries Martine de Brass . . ., daughter of a university classmate.

Works for his father. The father 73—moves Rue de Ponthieu—killed in 1951, age 43. Martine 10, Venezuela

Léonard born in 1938. Rue du Bucy. Old apartment with glassed studio. La Paternelle insurance company, Rue Laffitte. In 1962 marries Maud Couffée, secretary at the office—1 son Victor

Victor 10, Léonard 34, Maud 36

Cook Léontine. She worked Rue de Ponthieu, pupil Léonard—65

Annette d. of ch. 18

Law School, Rue du Panthéon

Lycée Montaigne, Rue Auguste Comte

Police headquarters, Rue Bonaparte

Police Station Rue de l'Odéon[39]

We can guess that the story takes place in Paris and involves a family of lawyers. From the first, discarded, draft we learn that Martine Cavelli was sentenced to ten years in prison for the murder of her husband, that she was released after serving seven years and then disappeared in South America.

More than that we will never know, for Simenon had written his last novel. As usual, after this initial stage he took a rest to give his characters some breathing space. He waited, but the trigger never came. Instead, he put his pencil down and put away his typewriter.

Why? An enigma. Simenon claims it was Denyse's fault, for she had begun hectoring him again, this time through the intermediary of a banker:

"I had had enough fighting, and I remembered that she had once boasted that she would 'break my pen.' She succeeded, but I did not lose heart. . . . D. [Denyse] got what she had wanted for a long time. From now on it was she, Mme Georges Simenon, who would write, trying to crush me definitively. After all, hadn't her long-standing dream been to be the widow Mme Georges Simenon and to take her place in the glorious world of 'overpossessive widows'?"[40]

The explanation is incomplete and insufficient, as Simenon himself later admitted. His shoulders were no longer broad enough to bear the burden of an imaginary world. He no longer had the strength to be a slave to his characters, to put himself in their skin for eleven days at a time, to accompany them sometimes as far as suicide. He did not want to plagiarize from himself, committing the sin of pride of writers too old to rejuvenate themselves but who fail to quit in time. The first novel to appear under his own name had been a Maigret, and so was the last. The circle was closed.

Simenon had long postponed this most fatal of all moments. He knew that when he finally reached the heart of man, when he was on the point of grasping the mythical truth that was his Grail, the pain might be intolerable. It was no accident that he described this process with a dentist's metaphor:

"I want to touch the nerve. There is still a small layer to drill through."[41]

Some ten years earlier he confessed that he feared this decisive instant above all else:

". . . I would be so devastated if I ever discovered that I was incapable of writing. It would be a terrible shock, and I don't see how any doctor could take me through it. He would certainly have to find some other activity for me, some compensation, as they say. But it would be really serious, for I really need to write."[42]

Had this imperious need deserted him? Simenon did not want to know. He did not seek truly to understand. Did it occur to him that he had published his first novel shortly before his father's death and his last shortly after his mother's?

Three days later he put the house and grounds of Epalinges up for sale. In giving up writing novels, he also abandoned the site of his writing, the house he had built to live and die in.

Simenon and Teresa soon moved to an apartment on the ninth floor of a building on Avenue de Cour in Lausanne. At the beginning of February 1973 he summoned Henri-Charles Tauxe to request that the Lausanne daily *24 Heures* carry an announcement of his decision: "Why I will no longer write." Two days earlier he had sent his collaborator Joyce Aitken to the Belgian consulate to make a change in his passport. The line listing his occupation now read "no profession" instead of "novelist." He felt that at last he had become a man like any other. But he alone believed it.

18

STYLE IS RHYTHM

1972

André Gide died without ever figuring out how the Simenon factory worked, though it must be said that Simenon never gave him any help, lest he kill his secret by revealing it. "How, *sincerely,* can I describe a novel's gestation? It's a form of self-deception, nothing more," he said as early as 1939.[1] But it was a methodical self-deception, a technique polished by decades of practice.

Simenon described the creative procedure as a ritual: a walk, a trigger of inspiration, a state of grace, material preparation, manila envelope, search for names in the telephone directory, isolation, rising at six in the morning and writing from 6:30 to 8:30, more walking, lunch, a nap, television, children, walking again, reading newspapers but no books, early to bed. Eight or nine chapters in as many days.

But the process was rather more complex than that. It generally began with a kind of malaise, an irresistible sluggishness. He would feel uncomfortable, like a displaced person. He would become increasingly gloomy and nervous, somber and irritable. Daily life seemed ever less tolerable, and he would feel a need to flee, taking refuge in a world of his imagination.

He would take longer walks than usual, always alone. This was an early sign that withdrawal was imminent, but also a way of attaining what he called the "state of grace," a condition in which he felt a void within himself that would soon be filled by his characters. The walks would get longer as he sought to elicit "the trance" he needed in order to enter "novel mode."

At times like this his withdrawal from the outside world was complete. Denyse recalls seeing him come back from one of his walks in Lakeville. Pipe in his mouth, eyes vacant, head lowered, he seemed to be looking into himself. She watched for long moments in silence, then approached.

"Hello," she said.

"Good day, madame," he replied impassively, tipping his hat and continuing on his way.

He had not recognized his own wife.[2]

In the early stages of the "trance" he would sometimes pick up his mail at the post office, just to have a destination for his long walk. The excursion would then become a ritual, repeated at exactly the same time each day, by the same route, for as long as it took him to complete the novel. Next he would clean his office and dispose of all correspondence and obligations. Then call his doctor. At this point the most important thing was to avoid the unpredictable. Illness was a grain of sand that might jam the mechanism, interrupting the writing process and ruining the novel in progress. He had acquired this mania for preparation back in his days at the *Gazette de Liège,* when he covered the circus. He had been very impressed by the concentration and meticulousness shown by trapeze artists before they hurtled above the void.[3]

He next jotted down names, addresses, phone numbers, and various topographical and biographical details on a manila envelope. His normally excellent memory often failed him when it came to names for his characters, so he was careful to assign them in advance. Last names sometimes came out of his past. In *Les Pitard* (1935), for instance, the shipbuilder from Rouen was called Bernheim (who had been assistant director of the department store where his mother worked before he was born). The name Donadieu, which occurs in several novels apart from *Le Testament Donadieu* (1937), was probably an afterimage of the advertisements placed by "J. Donnadieu, bonded warehouse of wines and beers in Nevers," in *Paris-Centre,* the daily newspaper owned by the marquis de Tracy when Simenon worked for him in 1923.[4]

First names were used repeatedly. Albert occurs in about twenty novels, as a valet, the owner of a café, a mechanic, a young boy, an apprentice, a chauffeur, a hotel concierge, and so on. In *Pedigree* (1948) he is one of Simenon's childhood friends. There are four nuns called Adonie: in *Pedigree, Le Bourgmestre de Furnes* (1939), *La Vérité sur Bébé Donge* (1942), and the short story "Le Matin des trois absolutes" (The Morning of Three Absolutions, 1963). His Adèles were more diverse. Three of them were maids or servants (*La Veuve Couderc* [1942]; *Le Nègre* [1957]; *Les Autres* [*The Others,* 1962]), while four were prostitutes (*Les Suicidés* [1934]; *Cour d'assises* [1941]; "La Tête de Joseph" [Joseph's Head]; *Le Destin des Malou* [1947]). His Arsènes were usually chauffeurs or valets, his Emmas domestic servants. On the other hand, almost all his bartenders are named Bob (after the man who presided at La Coupole for so many years), with a Jules tossed in here and there.

Most of Simenon's names, however, were taken from the inexhaustible reservoir of the telephone directory. At first he used a phone book from the region in which the action was set, but fear of lawsuits later convinced him to pick the Boston or Chicago directory for a novel set in New York.[5] When that failed to deter the litigious, he abandoned the phone book for the dictionary.[6] It is this procedure that accounts for the frequency in his later novels of names derived from verbs and adjectives, nouns and occupations: Emile Boulet, Nicole Prieur, Antoine Mature, Hélène Lange, Antoinette Vague, Robert Bureau, Victor Lecoin, Théo Porchet, Odile Pointet.

Once the names were selected, he would creep little by little into the skin of his still embryonic characters.[7] Fixing certain elements in space and time seemed to soothe his anxiety about plunging into a story of which he still knew little at this point. Experience had taught him that it was always easier to cut than to add, and nothing annoyed him quite so much as having to interrupt the creative process to research a detail.

The next stage was the writing itself. He began by drawing the shades of his office windows. The weather outside must not interfere with the weather in the story. He then filled six or seven pipes, so he would not have to stop in the middle of writing. Finally he sharpened the five dozen pencils bristling in a small cylindrical container. His handwriting was tiny, and he wanted to be able to change pencils as soon as the points were dull, again without having to stop. Despite the pencil collection, however, he worked far more often on the typewriter than by hand.

No one ever saw Simenon writing. The "Do Not Disturb" sign he borrowed from a hotel and hung on his doorknob was not a gag but a genuine interdiction. In *Mémoires intimes* (1981) he mentions that the only person who ever saw him writing was his son Marc, as a child. Marc denies it.[8]

He insisted on wearing the same clothes throughout each novel. For a while it was a sport shirt with large plaid checks on a red background, which he bought in New York. Ever partial to imaginative record-keeping, he would weigh himself before and after every novel. He estimated that each one cost him an average of nearly a liter and a half of sweat.

He claims to have had stage fright before every book, or at least every "hard novel." He would vanquish that fear with tranquilizers, which he kept in his shirt pocket. Generally, one was enough. Toward the end of his life he made every effort to portray himself as a sober creator, a man content to make do with large quantities of hot tea, the only liquid capable of wetting a palate dried out by a pipe. "No one has ever seen a bottle of whiskey on my desk, nor alongside my typewriter," he said.[9]

No one, that is, except the hundreds of thousands of readers who still remembered a famous photograph from the thirties: the novelist in his bathrobe, pipe in his mouth, fingers on the keyboard, in the foreground a glass and a bottle of whose contents there is little doubt. Despite persistent denials, interviews and articles attest that for many years Simenon drank while he

wrote. His taste in wine evolved: white at the Place des Vosges, rosé in Porquerolles, red in the Vendée. But he also liked beer, whiskey, and champagne.
Carlo Rim, who visited La Richardière several times in 1933, recalled another
ritual: ". . . the bottle of cognac that Georges would throw up in the garden,
two fingers down his throat, after he finished a chapter."[10]

The final element of his ritual was the trigger. This could be a smell, a setting, a detail, a color, a light, a sweet or oppressive sensation, or some unde-
finable thing in the spirit of the times. The trigger was often a character, rarely
a story. In fact, according to Simenon, it was never a story. Whenever he was
asked to explain his method, he always condemned the principle that a novel
was first of all a story. His awkwardness in summarizing his plots is evident,
especially when he tried to describe a novel he was about to begin. "It's something on the theme of father and child," he said about *L'Horloger d'Everton*
(1954), "of two generations, one man just entering life and another leaving it.
It's not exactly that, but I don't see it clearly enough to talk about it yet."

In 1968 he mentioned his next novel to the five doctors who came to interview him. The protagonist, theme, and starting point were set: the ordeal of a
man trying to suppress his penchant for violence. He wanted to set the story
in France, but decided it had to take place in the United States. But the novel
in question, *La Main* (1968), could have been moved to France simply by
changing the names, for it started and ended with the character.

His difficulty in describing his plots was equally obvious when it came to
completed novels. *Les Inconnus dans la maison* (1940), "A book about paternity." *Malempin* (1940), "The story of a father and his son."[11] In 1937, Gallimard asked him to supply information for the blurb for *L'Assassin*. He found
it a most disagreeable task, somewhat like writing an anonymous letter.

"The action takes place in a small city in Holland wreathed in rain or snow
in which people have to wipe the mud off the windows to see one another. As
I recall, there is a young girl who plays piano. Then several other characters
who play billiards. As for the victims, of which there are two, they are of
little importance, since we hardly meet them." Hardly likely to hook potential readers.

The trigger could come from a piece of music. Simenon did not deny the influence of Bach's fugues in his efforts to achieve a similar effect by superim-
posing words. Music also played a part in *Le Cheval-Blanc* (1938), whose
musical origin was recognized by Gide's practiced ear. Simenon acknowledged that it was inspired by "old memories of my German lessons, with
Schubert melodies playing in the background."[12]

One day Simenon was walking in the streets of Vichy. What would Maigret
be doing if he were here? he asked himself. Suppose a woman of means was
murdered while the inspector happened to be in town taking the waters. The
result was *Maigret à Vichy* (*Maigret Takes the Waters*, 1968).

But such admissions were incidental to a novelist who held that "character" was the alpha and omega of his universe. For him, every novel was organized around the life of an individual grasped at a particular moment. The world around him should stick to that character "like wet clothing" to his skin.[13] Simenon was careful to avoid psychological descriptions. Instead, the protagonist expressed his inner state through his acts, attitudes, and reactions. This was one of the reasons why Simenon always preferred peasants and white-collar workers to intellectuals, who, he felt, were more inclined to discuss and analyze their dramas than to live them. Novels about such characters might gain in analytical capacity, but at the cost of losing emotional intensity. In the Maigrets, too, he was rarely interested in professional killers, preferring opportunistic assassins, ordinary people not at all expected to kill or to suffer the consequences. His characters acted by instinct, just as he did, and he liked to claim he could not control them once he had created them.

"Simenon's characters are cavemen with a few neuroses added," Félicien Marceau once commented.[14] A penetrating formula more pointed than it seems, but Simenon put it differently: "My character is the man in the street at the end of his tether."

If plot is secondary, the famous "Simenonian atmosphere" that was the critics' bread and butter for decades was in fact never more than a poetic climate. This does not mean that it can be reduced to ambience alone, for it is sometimes expressed with such force that it becomes a theme in itself.

Although he strenuously rejected the cliché, Simenon was himself primarily responsible for his reputation as a "novelist of atmosphere." The word *atmosphere* occurs eleven times in *Monsieur Gallé, décédé* (1931) and sixteen times in *Le Port des brumes* (1932), which is only 220 pages long. In many of his books climate and ambience combine with smells to constitute what surely must be called an atmosphere—one broadly determined by the sensory world of his childhood. Simenon's was a porous mind able to capture the substance of existence after separating it from its soil. The olfactory and tactile dimension of his novels is testimony to this. In his books even night has an odor. Volumes, masses, proportions are rendered with an architect's eye.

He himself characterized this aspect of his style as an attempt to borrow from another artistic domain: "What the critics call my 'atmosphere' is nothing but the Impressionism of painting adapted to literature. The epoque of the Impressionists was the scaffolding of my childhood, and I was always in museums and at exhibitions. I acquired a certain sensitivity to it. I was haunted by it."[15] He seems to have absorbed Impressionism as if by osmosis. You can see it in the way he renders the vibration of light. He depicts water (a permanent element in his imagination) and luminosity very much in the manner of certain Impressionist painters, offering small touches of color and playing on the reflections.

The next step in the creative process was to determine the nature of the event that would upset his character's destiny, be it tragic (an accident, the death of a friend or relative, a betrayal) or otherwise (a minor unforeseen event, a misunderstanding). The novel then unfolds upstream and downstream from this crisis. Next he would put himself in the shoes of his main character, to the exclusion of the others. This rarely damaged the narrative, since most of the time everything would be seen from his point of view. The important thing was to bring this about by merging what he called the three dimensions (past, present, future) into a single action.

The theme of the story will often be the exploration of an ordinary man driven to the limit by the force of circumstance. The character's grandeur lies in his refusal to draw back from that borderline. Always in motion, in flight, he goes beyond it, preferring to tempt fate rather than stifle his instincts. In many of the novels this main character is a "deviant,"[16] who breaks from his moorings and drifts into an unknown world. The archetypical Simenon hero is a middle-class individual who loses his connection to the social context that had afforded him an illusory stability. Were his characters marooned together on a desert island, it is not at all certain that they would form a society

His heroes flee when they are overwhelmed by an existential weariness bordering on melancholy in the psychiatric sense of the word. Nearly spent, it is with their final burst of energy that they manage to cross the line, leaping out of routine only to face the vertigo of their sudden discovery of the void. By casting himself off from his milieu, the deviant provokes it, confronts it, and suffers its vengeance upon his return. He no longer speaks the same language as those around him, and the barrier between them is reflected in their divergent assessments of his act.

His characters often find redemption through confession, which becomes a means of achieving reintegration into their milieu of origin and reconciliation with themselves. There is a chasm between the true loner and the Simenonian individualist—an unstable man consumed by a sharp sense of guilt and by his inability to communicate with others. *Le Chat* (1967) is among the perfect illustrations of the point. Emile Bouin considers himself a loner, but only with his wife's death does he realize that his existence is meaningless without the object of his hatred.

Simenon's characters are often second-rate people. But as Gide pointed out, we are touched by them exactly because of their acute awareness of their own pathetic mediocrity. They are rarely optimistic. Nor was their creator, who was so often chided for it that he felt the need to defend himself. "Up to now," he commented shortly after the war, "I have encountered many weak people, scoundrels, unfortunates, and failures, but have not yet had the pleasure of encountering any saints—nor have I yet been witness to a full and harmonious destiny."[17]

345

Le Petit Saint (1965) was the book that filled that gap. But it was the exception rather than the rule. Reading a Simenon novel is most often a stifling experience. His universe is tragic. A month after completing *La Porte* (1962), he privately admitted his inability to achieve any sort of happiness through his characters: "I promised myself an upbeat novel, or at least an optimistic one, but my characters would not allow it."[18]

It was easy, of course, to blame the characters, who could hardly contradict their creator. The truth is that Simenon was an unstable, anxious man uninterested in people who were in harmony with themselves and their society. Fascinated as he was by neurotics, he felt that anyone who had effortlessly achieved success was a happy imbecile. He loved his characters because, like him, they feared their own inadequacy. "For me," he wrote, "the failure is the man who nurtures great ambitions in one or another domain, strives to achieve them, sacrifices everything, and one day, years later, realizes that he has gotten nowhere."[19]

Roger Nimier was quite correct to note that Simenon treated his readers as characters.[20] By talking to ordinary people about people like themselves, exposing their anxieties and repressed contradictions, conferring universality upon what they thought was their own private shame, he relieved their sense of guilt. Readers immersed in his novels not only escape their solitude; they also learn to share what they hazily perceive as some personal abnormality, thereby easing its gravity.

He would merge so completely with his character, living his life and breathing his air, that he would unwittingly mimic his physical gestures, attitudes, and expressions. His wife and children could usually guess the personality of the hero and the tone of the novel in progress without asking. When he was writing *Le Président* (1958), for example, he held himself and grumbled like an old man.

He always claimed to use only firsthand material, often rejecting characters or situations suggested to him by others.[21] Yet apart from his frequent use of events in his own life, he was compelled to acknowledge some borrowings as well, sometimes publicly. *Maigret chez le coroner* (*Maigret and the Coroner*, 1949) was a virtually straightforward account of a trial he attended in an Arizona court. Other admissions were private. Readers who saw in *Le Bourgmestre de Furnes* (1939) the direct influence of Gide's *La Séquestrée de Poitiers* (1930), especially the account of the trial, made no mistake.[22]

Many of his secondary characters were based on real people. In *Le Testament Donadieu* (1937), for example, Weil, "who controls every single grain of wheat consumed in France," is none other than Louis Louis-Dreyfus, known as Double-Louis, a banker and shipbuilder specializing in the import and export of wheat.[23] The rather unflattering portrait of Karensky, an impresario of indeterminate nationality in *Le Voyageur de la Toussaint* (1941), is based essentially on Marcel Karsenty, organizer of theatrical tours and codirector of the Karsenty-Herbert shows.[24]

This little game of who's who was not restricted to supporting players. The phenomenon is most obvious in *Le Président* (1958). The former president of the council, of whom the author gives only a first name (Augustin), is none other than Georges Clemenceau, although some elements of his personality are also borrowed from Aristide Briand, eleven times president of the council under the Third Republic. Simenon seems to have wanted to pay homage to the memory of the "Tiger," one of the few French politicians he admired.[25]

Since the resemblance was so striking, he naturally tried to cover his tracks, for example giving his president a former mistress in the person of the Countess Marthe de Créveaux. This society hostess, who presides over a sparkling political, literary, and diplomatic salon in her mansion on the Rue de la Faisanderie, is determined to trim the president's sails by initiating him into a milieu alien to him.[26] Which was exactly the role played in real life by the Countess Hélène de Portes, except that her victim was not Clemenceau but another council president, Paul Reynaud.

Simenon was implausibly but consistently astonished when attentive readers noticed such resemblances. But his struggle against the inner demon that made him pattern his characters after people he had known sometimes drove him to paradox. In 1934, for example, after sending a copy of his latest novel to his mother, he asked her:

"Did you recognize the tenants in *Le Locataire*?"[27]

Five years later, he implored her to cease identifying with this or that female character whose age or description seemed to fit, and to stop trying to match this or that family member with his other characters.[28] It was difficult to have it both ways, and the tension mounted with the publication of *Pedigree* (1948), which he described as an autobiographical novel or novelized autobiography, depending on whom he was talking to.

Books such as *L'Âne rouge* (1933), *Les Trois Crimes de mes amis* (1938), *Je me souviens* (1945), *Pedigree* (1948), and *Les Mémoires de Maigret* (1951) were so personal that he could not deny their origin. But he obstinately rejected attempts to identify him with any of the heroes of the vast majority of his other works, in particular his famous inspector. Admissions to the contrary are rare and generally private. Several weeks after finishing *Le Train* (1961), for instance, he wrote to Sven Nielsen:

"I've been wanting to write this novel for a long time, but I had to find the right tone. Reconstructing the atmosphere required no sorcery or wizardry. The gentleman in the barracks in La Rochelle is me. I was also the one who sent the trains where I could, stopped them somewhere in the countryside, and so on. The real risk was to put too much of myself into it."[29]

His memory was his archive. But a man with such a mania for detail could not afford mistakes, no matter how trivial. He therefore made sure that he was well informed, and since he usually lived far from large cities, he would call on his copy editor, his publisher, his lawyer, his former secretaries, and others for any information he felt he might need. Even if he made only limited use of it, he did not want to have to interrupt the creative process once it was under way. This suggests that contrary to what he claimed, he sometimes had a fully developed conception of a novel's theme before actually beginning it.

Occasionally he made inquiries that were not put to immediate use in any particular novel. These demonstrate that he was capable of mulling over several stories at once, despite his claim that he always had to throw himself into the task the moment his intuition took hold. For instance, several weeks after finishing *L'Ours en peluche* (1960), in a state of great fatigue, he asked for information about the German invasions of Europe: the exact date in 1940 of their entry into Norway, Holland, Belgium, and various cities of France—Paris, Orleans, Nantes, La Roche-sur-Yon, and La Rochelle; the dates of their evacuation of the northern regions, especially the Ardennes; the date the authorities advised Parisians to evacuate the capital.[30] Nearly a year went by between his receipt of this information and the writing of *Le Train* (1961), the book for which it was clearly intended. In the meantime, Simenon wrote *Betty* (1961), a novel having nothing at all to do with the war.

There were also requests for information he knew he would make scant use of, but which was nevertheless required for reassurance. In 1935, before attacking *Long Cours* (1936), he compiled a large file on navigation and on meteorological fluctuations on either side of the equator. In 1966 he did similar research on secondary education and university studies for *Le Confessional* (*The Confessional,* 1966), and in 1970, before writing *La Disparition d'Odile* (*The Disappearance of Odile,* 1971), he asked about the postgraduate program in sociology at the University of Lausanne and about the admission procedure at the nursing school of the canton hospital.

Finally, there were details he wanted even before knowing whether they would be of any use in a story. Before writing *Le Petit Saint* (1965) he had a photograph taken of a peddler's medallion in Paris: "This visual contact might be very useful to me for my novel," he explained.[31]

There were times when the title of a novel served as the trigger for the creative process. A careful study of his titles[32] shows that they can be grouped into five categories: references to the hero (*Betty* [1961]), the plot (*Crime impuni* [1954]), the site of the action (*Trois Chambres à Manhattan* [1946]), the event that causes the crisis (*Le Déménagement* [*The Neighbors,* 1967]), or a deliberately enigmatic formula (*Le Coup de lune,* [1933]).

In the case of *La Boule noire* (1955), Simenon acknowledged that the title had given him the story.[33] A black ball was the mark by which the members of a club in a small town in Connecticut voted against the admission of a new member, and the hero's internal drama is organized around exactly that ostracism. The same was true of *L'Escalier de fer* (*The Iron Staircase,* 1953). It was the title that gave Simenon the idea for the story of Etienne Lomel, a traveling salesman devoured by suspicion of his wife. As in many Parisian shops, an iron staircase led from the stationery store she had inherited to her bedroom on the floor above.[34]

The title was often of supreme importance, determining not only how a novel was to be read but also how it was written and sometimes its spirit if not its plot. Yet it is striking how variable titles could be. In the days of his pseudonymous pulp novels Simenon would often make changes just before publication, depending on the people around him, his publisher, the public's expected reaction, or the dictates of his instinct. His willingness to alter them at the last minute stayed with him throughout his career: at least fifteen were changed before publication.[35]

The rejected title was usually discarded because it sounded bad, was difficult to pronounce, or was already taken. *Cour d'assises* (1941) was to be titled *Petit Louis,* but Gallimard pointed out that there was already a *Petit-Louis* in his catalog, by Eugène Dabit. *Long Cours* (1936) was initially entitled *Cargo,* until Simenon realized that Palucl Marmont had published his own *Cargo* eighteen months earlier.

Once a title of a collection of short stories was inadvertently changed without his knowledge, when a distracted linotypist read *Maigret et l'inspecteur malgracieux* (Maigret and the Ungainly Inspector, 1947) as *Maigret et l'inspecteur malchanceux* (Unlucky). The book went to print with the altered title, and a highly irritated Simenon insisted that the mistake be corrected for the reprint, to the great pleasure of lovers of defective first editions.[36]

Simenon prided himself on using words that ordinary readers could understand. The deeper his art became, the more he strove for simplicity and sobriety, in a kind of quest for purity. He claimed to be less sensitive to the music of words than to their weight.[37] When pressed to define his style, he often used the expression "substance-words." These were not simply the palpable, three-dimensional words that enabled him to "sculpt" his novels as from a block of wood, but above all those that had the same connotation everywhere, easily translatable into all languages.

Syntax was less important to him than the poetic rhythm of the sentence. He felt there was no point in resorting to a sophisticated turn of phrase or in searching for the right word if the majority of his readers would not understand.[38] He liked concrete words: "table" instead of "furniture," "rain" instead of "shower." He considered these the most effective way of reducing the distance between author and reader, an imperative for someone who wrote in order to be read, as he explained when *Le Petit Saint* (1965) came out:

At bottom I am not a writer. If I were, I would fashion phrases and might not have been able to render the life of this man who aspired to put colors on canvas, on paper, or wherever. At the beginning, when he first goes to the paint store, Louis does not know the difference between watercolor and gouache. What he wants is pure colors. I, too, try to create the simplest phrases with the simplest words. I write with substance-words, the word *wind,* the word *hot,* the word *cold.* Substance-words are the equivalent of pure colors. . . . The word *love* is one I use very seldom. It has so many meanings you never know which one to choose. I am seeking a simpler, more natural truth, a material, biological truth. Take the word *dung,* for example. Now there's a great substance-word. There is in the odor of dung all the fermentation of the animal substance that lies at the root of biology. Whoever sniffs dung with pleasure has no fear of death. . . . With a substance-word we have some biological and philosophical depth.[39]

Nevertheless, he did have his tics. In *Le Clan des Ostendais* (1947) the sea is often "wrinkled." It is not unusual for sounds to "die" in a character's mouth, especially in *Un crime en Hollande* (1931). He particularly savored the verb *embobeliner,* which means both to envelop and to circumvent.[40]

Sometimes he violated his principles by using uncommon words his readers would have been hard put to understand: *guimpe* (a kind of shirtfront worn with a low-cut dress), *merlin* (a club used to stun cattle), *charte-partie* (a document attesting to the existence of a rental contract), *sapide* (flavorful).[41] Sometimes the meaning not merely of words but of entire sentences is doubtful: "And he threw a new pellet of earth on the hempseed near his line, to which a chub immediately clung."[42]

Ever the craftsman, Simenon liked technical vocabulary, especially when it came to seafaring. So what if the meaning isn't clear; the poetry of the phrase is enough. But how is a reader who knows nothing of bridge supposed to make sense of a passage like this:

"Do you want to play the Culbertson system?"
"If you do."
. . . He lost a trick and wondered whether it might not be a good idea to lose the game.[43]

Of course, you miss nothing in *Le Passager clandestin* (1947) if you don't know that Ely Culbertson revolutionized the game by insisting that a system was indispensable in contract bridge. But still . . . One wonders whether Simenon did not take some pleasure in throwing his readers a curve from time to time. In *L'Ours en peluche* (1960), for instance, he surely does not expect to be un-

derstood by the man in the street when he mentions the pathology of hy-
dramnios, the condition of a primipara, a patient's egocipetal tendency, or
Cattell, Rorschach, and Mira tests.[44]

If his language was unpretentious, his staying-power was modest. He may
not have known where he was going when he began a novel, but he rarely
went more than 220 pages. That was his rhythm and his distance, and there
were those who complained about both. Before the war he had established the
length of the Maigrets as a principle:

"I believe that a good detective story should not be long, otherwise you fall
into the Wallace style, with an accumulation of episodes at the expense of the
human element and the ambience. In addition, since a crime story should be
read in one sitting, it should not take more than two or two and a half hours,
like the old Maigrets."[45]

Unlike many other novelists, he used few formulas, but these were recurrent. The character of Maigret was one, of course. Other favorite techniques
included retrospective narration, reconstruction of the past in stages, confession by the main character, epistolary narration, private diaries, splitting a
story into accounts by antagonistic narrators, interior monologues, and the
parallel development of two themes.

Leitmotif was another. He used this technique often, for it meshed well
with his concern for the rhythm of the phrase, the pacing of paragraphs, and
the cadence of chapters. By marking the narrative at regular intervals, he offered readers an interpretative key.

The leitmotif could be a theme related to light: a stained-glass lantern (*Oncle
Charles s'est enfermé* [1942]), the light of a shop (*Trois Chambres à Manhattan*
[1946]), the lighted clock of a city (*Le Chien jaune* [1931]), the lights of the Place
Vendôme in Paris (*Il y a encore des noisetiers* [There Are Still Some Hazel Trees,
1969]).[46]

It could be the mention of a key event. The moving, nostalgic confession of
a father to his son in *Le Fils* (1957) is scanned by repeated references to "a
tragic event in La Rochelle in 1928."

It could be an obsessional return to the novel's theme: the corruption of the
body, for example, in *La Mort de Belle* (1952): "What they call love is a need
to sully, nothing more. . . . It is as if that purged them of their sins and somehow cleansed them."[47] It could be an incantatory formula repeated like the refrain of a song. It could be the mention of a buried secret, one of Simenon's
favorites: a letter (*Le Veuf* [1959]), a strongbox (*La Mort d'Auguste* [*The Old
Man Dies,* 1966]), a golden section (*Les Sœurs Lacroix* [1938]), the key to a
chest (*Le Voyageur de la Toussaint* [1941]), the papers in a suitcase (*Le Destin
des Malou* [1947]).

And finally, it could be a short, simple phrase that somehow sums up a
character's entire psychology: "One day I'll show them . . ." (*Le Nègre* [1947]);

"It's a lot of sh—! It would have been out of character for him not to say it. And he had a disgusted look, mired in distaste for the world. It's a lot of sh—" (*Le Cheval-Blanc* [1938]); "I don't know" (*Le Petit Saint* [1965]).

The leitmotif is often printed in italics to make it more obvious. Simenon always made sure that all his typographical instructions were scrupulously respected. Though he hated reading proofs, professionalism and sense of duty held sway over pleasure, and he devoted no less than three days to the task, two hours per chapter. When it went well, he even seems to have taken some small joy in it.

He hated correcting novels. To read what had been written was to relive a story he hoped to have left behind. When forced to do it, he discovered the novel anew, an exercise that, given his extremist temperament, had one of two results: either he felt that it did not stand up at all, which depressed him, or he was convinced that it was his best work to date, which thrilled him.

His primary aim in rereading was to trim away fat, to strain his sentences through a sieve so as to achieve maximum density. Subject, verb, and complement, but never a supplement. His stylistic ideal was the reflection of one of his most cherished myths: purity.

He mercilessly called himself to order whenever he detected too serpentine a sentence. But to correct did not mean to polish or to improve. He feared endangering the entire edifice if he removed so much as a single stone: "It's a success or a failure," he wrote to Gide. "But one way or the other, it is what it is and there's nothing I can do about it."[48] To make any concessions here would have been to violate one of his prized principles: "In the domain of art, technical perfection entails aesthetic regression."[49] Simenon wrote like a swimmer trying to regain the shore: he had no time to worry about his stroke.[50]

He corrected as he wrote, with feverish urgency. "Full speed ahead, so as to stay with it and get the chore out of the way as fast as possible." That was how he put it.[51] The only task more thankless than revising a "hard novel" was revising a Maigret, as he told his publisher in 1962:

"Began this morning the revision of *La Colère de Maigret* [*Maigret Loses His Temper*, 1963]. Luck of the draw, as usual. Some revisions are a pleasure and go quickly and smoothly. Others take me four hours a chapter or more. I never know in advance, and every time I start I feel a little anxiety, because I detest spending hours and hours sitting on my poor little butt doing a peon's labor. Curiously, it is not always the Maigrets that give me the least trouble, perhaps because I don't write them out by hand first. And also because I always mess up the dates, times, and so on, which are important in a detective novel."[52]

An examination of his typescripts reveals his constancy: barely a few changes per page, generally the deletion of adverbs, qualifiers, redundancies. He never made changes in the story. Characters and dialogue had to remain as he had lived them. Sometimes he changed his mind about names or places. Gérin would become Morin, and the dance hall Au Petit Robinson disappeared (*Chez Krull* [1939]); Boulevard Richard-Lenoir became Boulevard Voltaire, and the Barbès-Rochechouart neighborhood ceded to La Chapelle (*Maigret se trompe* [*Maigret's Mistake*, 1953]).

He attached special importance to punctuation and was capable of outbursts of rage if anyone tinkered with his commas without permission. While he considered the semicolon an affectation, he held the comma indispensable to the rhythm of the phrase. Its position could even change the meaning. He cited the last line of *Les Anneaux de Bicêtre* as an example: "One day he would go to see his father in Fécamp, with Lina." Without the comma, he explained, they are going off to Fécamp naturally, and the story has a happy ending. With it, they are still going, but there is a problem, and the happy ending disappears.[53]

But the fact remains that his haste to get the chore of correction over with sometimes led him to ignore obvious errors.

The critics noticed. In 1935, while praising the virtues of *Le Locataire,* André Thérive wondered whether the author's self-assurance did not perhaps border on negligence. Indeed, he had noted various improbabilities he considered crippling in a detective novel, such as a character's paying for a room in Belgium with French money taken from the stolen wad.[54]

A misplaced pronoun on page 91 of *G. 7,* a collection of short stories published by Gallimard in 1938, has Simenon describing a cadaver as having been killed. In *L'Evadé* (1936) the hero is called Jean-Pierre at the beginning and Jean-Paul at the end. One NRF copy editor scratched his head at this phrase on page 203 of *Le Voyageur de la Toussaint* (1941): "His hands rested on his feet."[55]

Simenon was horrified by these kinds of mistakes, but his publisher assured him that they were inevitable. Sven Nielsen would never forget a priceless phrase that slipped into *Philippe le Bel,* by the duke de Lévis-Mirepoix: "The French army of 120,000 men, 6,000 of them horses . . ."

Once he got to know his star author, Nielsen rarely reported blunders to him. Simenon was the kind of writer who groused about corrections, even when they were requested amicably:

"My sequence of tenses is not always strictly grammatical, and I seldom use the imperfect subjunctive. My sentence construction is sometimes rather personal. We must not lose sight of the fact that it is the people who, little by little, create language, while writers consecrate it, sometimes innovating, allowing dictionaries to catch up long afterward."[56]

Doringe, his official copy editor, was the only person with whom he was willing to discuss his grammatical and syntactical choices. Though she loved "her" author madly, she never hesitated to tell him exactly what she thought, often with "sadistic delight"[57]—for example, noting sarcastically that by age fifty he should have been able to tell grave, acute, and circumflex accents apart.

Since Simenon would not allow anyone to tamper with his manuscripts, Doringe peppered the pages with "little impertinent notes" whenever she came upon a problem. He respected her judgment, but did not always accept her suggested changes. "She's angry at me because I still haven't learned which words take two *n*'s or two *r*'s, never suspecting that if I had, I would probably be a copy editor instead of obstinately writing all these novels. On average, I accept about one in ten of Doringe's corrections. Otherwise my style would be as flat as hers," he told his publisher.[58]

Simenon considered it his privilege as a creator to violate language and twist grammar when he thought it necessary. His use of capital letters was neither grammatical nor logical, but reflected his desire to lend more general significance to certain words, making them emblematic. He defended the lack of clarity of his use of relative pronouns: ". . . as for the cascade of *who*s referring to different people, it is a deliberate representation of my character's (sometimes confused) train of thought, and it is more or less as clear as in Bossuet or Saint-Simon," he told his copy editor.

After several stormy arguments with Doringe, he established a correction procedure that left no room at all for interpretation. In 1960, a few days before giving her the text of *L'Ours en peluche,* he wrote her a sharp letter designed to avert any possible misunderstanding. From now on he would send her a photocopy of the manuscript instead of the original.

"This way you can of course correct the typos, spelling mistakes, and double letters on the first reading, but without changing anything and especially without adding or deleting commas, since I am a maniac on this point, whatever the correct grammatical usage may be. As for the other corrections, continue to send me those bits of paper. But when you see the proofs, don't be surprised if I have not responded to all your observations. I want you to make them, but I don't always agree with them. Often you are correct in terms of grammar. In certain cases, like repetition of words or certain infelicitous juxtapositions of syllables, I don't care about grammar. In this André Gide fully shared my point of view. It matters little to me if purists bristle."[59]

Doringe, "that dear old child," annoyed him, but she was indispensable. One of the few people willing to contradict the master, she was competent as well. At the age of eighty-three she continued to work for him from her solitary retreat in Pérouges, a small medieval town in Ain. In July 1964, ravaged by generalized cancer, she had but one concern: to finish copyediting Simenon's latest manuscript. Bedridden, her strength waning, she summoned the parish priest—but not to hear her confession. Sitting at her bedside, Father Gonnet completed the copyediting of *Maigret se défend* (*Maigret on the Defensive,* 1964) in her place. Then Doringe could die at peace.

———————

Simenon had many clashes with his publishers over the covers of his novels. In 1950, after Presses de la Cité had published seventeen of his books, he began to feel some nostalgia for Gallimard's cream-colored typographical covers with the red borders. Sven Nielsen's artistic choices struck him as vulgar. He found it hard to imagine that booksellers might want to exhibit such titles in their windows. "I never accepted the view that bad taste was a necessary feature of so-called popular publications," he remarked.[60]

He was convinced that garish covers could be an obstacle to sales among middle-class readers and intellectuals, who, he felt, admitted that they liked his books "the way you might admit you like rotgut red wine."[61] He wanted his publisher to switch over to British-style jackets, which had class while managing to help boost sales. He did not want his covers to be too direct, far preferring the symbolism of the jackets of his British and American editions: a wall representing a city, Maigret depicted in silhouette, a hat, a pipe. "The more detailed the cover is," he argued, "the more the reader is thrown off the track or disaappointed. Readers have their own images of the characters in a novel."[62]

Two proposed covers made Simenon particularly unhappy. For *La Neige était sale* (1948) the illustrator saw fit to detail the action and characters, even at the risk of misleading the reader. But Simenon never said why the snow was stained, or with what. For *Les Quatre Jours du pauvre homme* (1949) the designer chose to situate the action between 1945 and 1947, though nothing in the novel suggested those dates. On the contrary, the author held that the plot could be imagined as occurring at any time between the two World Wars.[63]

The truth is that it was virtually impossible to "illustrate" a Simenon novel. The NRF's somber typographical covers of the thirties may have been the most appropriate solution.

One day a friend and admirer of Simenon's taking a stroll in a Swiss city was surprised to find that his Zurich publisher, Daniel Keel, had put details of Picasso drawings on the covers of his novels. He wrote to the author suggesting a different technique: close-up photographs of men's and women's faces, anonymous, unposed subjects selected at random in the train stations, streets, and bars of Europe. The proposal was never implemented, despite the expertise of the man who suggested it: Federico Fellini.[64]

One hundred ninety-two novels under his own name, about 190 under pseudonyms, hundreds of stories and articles, with 20 or so autobiographical volumes to come: that was the Simenon continent. Was there any unity to this bloc of work? Maurice Piron divided it into "novels of destiny" and "Maigret novels," the former more psychological even when they had murders, the latter mainly detective stories even if not wholly innocent of psychology. Jean Fabre suggested that the "hard novels," associated with such sentiments as anxiety, instability, and dissatisfaction, appeared under the unlucky star of Henriette, while the Maigrets, reflecting happiness, satisfaction, and integration, were born under the lucky star of Désiré.[65]

Other commentators such as Boileau-Narcejac play down the contrasts between the Maigrets and the "hard novels": "The 'Maigret' cycle forms part of Simenon's broader cycle of novels. There is no important difference between a novel like *Maigret et le voleur paresseux* [*Maigret and the Lazy Burglar*, 1961] and one like *Le Train* [1961]. The aging Maigret merges with the mature Simenon."[66]

The critic André Thérive, who coined the term *Simenonism*, maintained that there was indeed a common theme in all these writings: "Development of remorse in a dim conscience after a crime that was not quite a crime so much as a mistake."[67] In other words, guilt.

We all bear our own flaws within ourselves. Simenon's thousands of pages teach this lesson, and his sweeping international success demonstrates that it came through in dozens of languages. "Simenon apprehends people and life instinctively, which bonds all humanity together," notes Gilbert Sigaux, editor of the seventy-two-volume Complete Works published by Editions Rencontre of Lausanne.[68] In this he was indeed a citizen of the world, even while remaining stolidly Liégeois.

His style, universally comprehensible as it was, is based less on atmosphere than on movement, measure, and cadence. "Style," he said, "is rhythm, the rhythm of the character."[69]

And the rhythm of the character's creator as well. Each of his chapters is about twenty pages long. After that he would instinctively stop. In a sense, his novels were written in one sitting, and we feel the need to read them that way, too. Reader and author are always in synch. His legendary rapidity of execution, of course, gave rise to myths. One day Alfred Hitchcock is supposed to have telephoned the author at home.

"Hello, may I please speak to Mr. Simenon."

"One moment, please. . . . I'm sorry, he's just started a novel."

"That's all right, I'll wait."

As he got older, his writing became more condensed. If his novels shrank from eleven chapters to nine, and then from nine to seven, it was because the "state of grace" contracted from eleven days to ten, and then from ten to seven. But at sixty, as at thirty, he was telling the same story: of a man who, in the wake of some exceptional event, understands that his life is false. Giving free rein to his most deeply buried instincts, he seeks to liberate himself from a gnawing guilt complex and to reconquer his place in life. At last he attains serenity—accepted, recognized, and integrated.

"I understand certain perverts, considered mad, who, having once tasted some particular delight in given circumstances, spend the rest of their lives reconstructing those same circumstances," Simenon once told Gide, justifying his own writing ritual.[70] That was just what he had done, tilling the same soil for forty years. When he gave up writing, Georges Simenon resembled one of his characters at the end of his quest, accepted, recognized, integrated. But he had not attained serenity.

19

UNATTAINABLE SERENITY

1973–1989

At the age of sixty-nine, for the first time in nearly half a century, Georges Simenon could no longer hide in imaginary worlds. His abandonment of fiction had delivered him from his characters, but not from his ghosts.

Despite his worldwide success, he was bitter at never having been awarded the only literary prize of truly international scope: the Nobel. He had been mentioned as a possible laureate as early as 1937. The prize for 1936 had gone to the American Eugene O'Neill, and the word in the corridors of the Swedish Academy was that a French-language writer should be the next to be honored. The 1937 winner was Roger Martin du Gard, but since rumors of his candidacy had been reported in the press, Simenon could not resist making a prediction:

"I will publish my first true novel at forty, and at forty-five I will have the Nobel Prize. In ten years, you'll see. I say this because I'm convinced of it, and I'm not afraid of looking ridiculous. So far everything I've predicted has happened. I will get the Nobel Prize in 1947."[1]

He felt that Gaston Gallimard had sufficient clout to win him this ultimate consecration. Gallimard had accompanied Martin du Gard to Stockholm to receive his prize, and on his return he told Simenon: "They talked to me about you."[2]

The publisher suggested that he was working on a strategy to garner the prize for his "chick": "As the reprints come out, I'll design new covers similar to those of Gide, Valéry. If we want to think about the Nobel, we have to make the books look as different as possible from the Fayard series."[3]

Long after Simenon's 1947 deadline had passed, he explained: "It was almost a done deal. Then I announced in the press that if they gave it to me, I would decline it. I'm not a country-fair animal. I want no blue ribbons."[4]

There was a done deal, all right, but it was André Gide who won the 1947 prize. Simenon did not have to reject an honor that was never offered him.

Four years later a press campaign was launched in France and Belgium in which his name was among the favorites. The Swedish Academy was reported to have compiled an impressive exploratory file on his work, a file that grew fatter day by day, as letters of recommendation poured in from around the world, even from India and Japan.[5] His hopes rose again.

"I confess that I would be delighted to be a Nobel laureate. In fact, it is the sole distinction to which I have always attached some value," he admitted in private.[6]

He even suggested that Sven Nielsen approach the Belgian government to gather some official support.[7] Unfortunately for him, the Swedish Academy preferred to honor one of their own that year, Pär Lagerkvist. In 1957 hope was kindled anew. Observers predicted that the Americans, the French, and the Belgians would all be pleased if the prize went to Simenon. Some even suggested a watchword for him: "If I win the prize, Maigret will be chief inspector."

Maigret got no promotion, for the Nobel went to Albert Camus. According to Denyse, Simenon took it badly:

"Every year he would complain: 'I'll never get it, I'm just a little Belgian.' But when Camus got it, he started drinking, and he hit me: 'Can you believe that asshole got it and not me?!' He couldn't calm down. He really wanted that prize. Not for himself but for his work. But believe me," she added, rubbing her cheek, "Camus's Nobel is one I'll never forget."[8]

By the sixties, when the press began to mention his name again, he was tired of the nerve-racking rumor-mongering: "I would have been pleased to have been given the Nobel a few years ago. Now I'm not sure I would accept it."[9] Believing that his chances were now nil, he claimed that he was not a candidate and had never even dreamed of being one. Maurice Maeterlinck, he said, would remain the only Belgian ever to win the Nobel Prize in literature. That was in 1911.

The Brazilian novelist Jorge Amado, who made no secret of his admiration for Simenon, ascribed this injustice to his reputation as a popular writer of detective novels, an image that did not work to his advantage with the Swedish Academy.

Image was a problem with another prestigious institution as well: the French Academy. There had been talk of his candidacy in the thirties, and during his visit to Darmstadt he told Hermann von Keyserling of his ardent desire to be accepted in that illustrious company. He feared that his lack of style might be an obstacle, unaware that this had long ceased to be a criterion.[10] The question arose again in 1949, when Jean Tharaud told Sven Nielsen, "It's high time for Simenon to put his name forward for the French Academy."[11] Ten years later Daniel-Rops brought it up again: "When will we see Maigret under the Coupole?"[12] For some time François Mauriac had been urging the Academy to change its rules and reserve seats for two French-speaking foreigners: Georges Simenon and Julien Green. The latter was elected to the Academy in 1972.

"We spoke of Simenon often at the Academy," says Maurice Druon, permanent secretary of the Forty. "But apart from the problem of his nationality, he was considered by many an author of crime novels. Moreover, since he lacked any club spirit, he didn't seem to be a company man."[13]

If he had a *Rosebud* in the late years of his life, it should perhaps be sought between the hands of a clock. Maniacal awareness of time was one of his enduring obsessions and was directly related to his memory of his father. The first thing Désiré did when he got to work was wind the clock. Georges himself yearned to have a watch from a very young age, and he was thrilled when an aunt gave him 5 francs to buy one on the day of his first communion. But his mother refused to let him spend the money, insisting that he save it instead.[14]

Years later, knowing he had not long to live, Désiré gave Georges a beautiful pocket watch engraved with the coats of arms of all the provinces of Belgium. He had won it in a national shooting contest. "Young Sim," however, soon traded the watch for a night of love with a "splendid Negress" in a Liège bordello. He then filed a police report declaring it lost, and repeated the lie to his parents.[15]

His betrayal of his father aroused a feeling of guilt. Watches and clocks became a leitmotif in many of his novels, even the early pseudonymous ones, giving his father a clandestine yet permanent presence in his work.

In *Au pont des Arches* (1921), a character gives his gold watch in lieu of payment for a hotel room. In *Un monsieur libidineux* (1927), the main character offers his solid gold watch to a woman in a transparent black silk bathing suit when she tells him that his 300 francs are not enough. In *La Femme rousse* (1933), the hero falters when he finds his missing daughter. The only solid purchase in the unreal-seeming room is his watch lying on the night table. He associates its ticking with his daughter's pulse. In *L'Âne rouge* (1933), Jean Cholet, Simenon's double, spends a portion of his 300,000 francs on a gold chronometer he has always wanted. The discovery of this object forces him to reveal to his parents the tangled web of lies in which he is entrapped, and this leads to his confession. In *Les Pitard* (1935), the commandant's watch is a metaphor for life. It "palpitates" like a human heart. In *Le Cheval-Blanc* (1938), the theft of a gold wristwatch by a servant in an inn is the trigger that reveals the innkeeper's jealousy of her employee.

In *La Veuve Couderc* (1942), Jean steals a gold chronometer from his father in order to join a poker game. In *La Neige était sale* (1948), the general is an ardent collector of antique watches. Old Vilmos, a clockmaker proud of his precious collection, wants his country to declare war on Egypt when he hears that King Farouk owns the world's most beautiful collection of watches. In *Crime impuni* (1954), we learn on the very first page that Elie Waskow has sold the silver watch his father had solemnly given him on his departure from Vilnius. In *Le Petit Saint* (1965), Vladimir sleeps with a watch against his ear. He is enraged when Alice finds it and takes it away.

Any number of additional examples could be cited. Apart from the "tiki" he brought back from Africa, the only object Simenon unfailingly took with him everywhere was an eighteenth-century clock that had been the pride of Houdin, clockmaker to the king. It was beautiful, but it weighed 770 pounds. It had to be embedded in the wall, and specialists were needed to reassemble it.[16] His "little pink house" was full of clocks and watches: "They live with us. I wouldn't say they impose their rhythm on us, but little by little theirs seems to come into harmony with our own."[17] If watches were alive, then so was Désiré.

Simenon's obsession with time seems to have intensified with age. It was a trait that was especially striking to outsiders. Alphonse Boudard, who came to Epalinges to write a film with Marc, came away with a cruelly ironic roman à clef instead of a script. *Cinoche* (1974) is a fictionalized portrayal of Simenon as the painter Ralph Galano, a tense, surprising, inaccessible man:

> At table he eats rapidly and wordlessly. He detests both idle chatter and never-ending meals. The guests, half choking, match him bite for bite. Lunches and dinners are finished in fifteen minutes. . . . Schedules and systems are draconian, as though he were running a railroad. At six in the evening he sits down at the head of the table. At six-twenty he gets up. "Good night, children." He climbs the stairs to his lair, and if you see him again it is as a wandering phantom from time to time in the middle of the night. His entire life is timed to the point of madness. Fifteen servants cater to him, their eyes on the clock. Everything is white, clean, waxed, scrubbed as in a clinic. Not a speck of dust, not a butt in an ashtray. In the rooms and hallways are laundry chutes leading to an enormous washing machine that never stops. Ralph had a pathological horror of dirt and disorder. . . . At Ralph Galano's you felt as if you were living in a laboratory. You didn't dare touch anything, and you walked with caution and in silence.[18]

For his seventieth birthday Simenon gave himself a tape recorder. He would now turn his attention to his own inner self. Over the next six years, twenty-one volumes of *Dictées* (Dictations), tentatively entitled "My Tape Recorder and I,"[19] emerged from his machine. The first, *Un homme comme un autre* (A Man Like Any Other, 1975), was dictated from February to September 1973; the last, *Destinées* (Destinies), was completed in October 1979. Curiously, *Quand j'étais vieux* (1970), which was written rather than spoken, was added to the series, while *Lettre à ma mère* (1974), which was dictated rather than written, was not, as though the former was inferior enough to blend into the mass of *Dictées,* while the latter was too good to be buried in it.

This verbal diary served a number of purposes, prime among which was to respond to a compulsive need for self-expression. Yet it would be an insult to him to take these volumes too seriously. By whatever standard we judge it, the writing simply does not measure up.

Not all commentators would agree with that assessment. Maurice Piron, for example, argued that Simenon "subjects the world and himself to an interrogation which, though not immediately perceptible, has a total, unmasked sincerity, always humble, sometimes anguished, without posturing and without 'literature.' "[20] One of his biographers, Stanley Eskin, assures us that the *Dictées* are sometimes reminiscent of Montaigne's essays "in their skeptical tone and their outlook hostile to any anthropocentrism."[21] The filmmaker François Truffaut was so enthusiastic that he considered the *Dictées* the third component of Simenon's work, after the "hard novels" and the Maigrets, even suggesting an overall title that might better reflect their mood: Elastic Memories, or the Elastic Memory.[22] On the whole, however, critics seem to have greeted these books with some embarrassment, as though concerned not to hurt the great writer.

Simenon was more exigent of himself. While not disowning the work, he denigrated it in the very course of the crime, the text itself:

"I consider myself less and less a writer, barely a novelist, and I feel I am moving further and further from literature.[23] . . . These *dictées* demonstrate that I am rather talkative by nature. . . . All this is nothing but chatter, like the rest of my dictations. I am sometimes ashamed of them. I dictate, therefore I am.[24] . . . At bottom, I have nothing to say.[25] . . . I cannot keep quiet.[26] . . . My *dictées,* however, have nothing to do with literature.[27] . . . Since dictating has become a need, so to speak, I will dictate every morning whatever comes to mind, whatever pops into my head while I'm holding the microphone."[28]

Indeed, at the outset of the project he set himself a model of quality: Samuel Pepys.[29] The British memorialist, however, produced a *Journal* that was both testimony for history and a portrait of mores. His curiosity and sharp sense of satire impelled him to skewer both others and himself, whereas Simenon was interested only in himself and put none of his talent into his observations. The twenty-one volumes of *Dictées* are no more than a litany of rarely insightful self-justifications, solemnly enunciated platitudes, increasingly clumsy ramblings, and endlessly reiterated incidents.

He let himself be carried away by the mood of the moment. Even his much-vaunted simplicity seems affected. Using and misusing the new instrument he called "my toy,"[30] he was like an old actor refusing to get off stage after saying his good-byes to his audience.

The autobiographical flood lacks the subtlety of his fictional works. The memorialist lectures where the novelist suggests. In his moments of self-criticism, Simenon used a terrible metaphor, comparing a painter's original canvas (*Pedigree*) to his "fake copies" (the *Dictées*).[31] Losing himself in a great outpouring that heralded what would soon become open warfare, he recounted his quarrels with Denyse and the details of their impending divorce, in the apparent belief that his notoriety was sufficient excuse to wash his dirty laundry in bookshops rather than in private.[32]

For decades his great strength had been his awareness of his staying power: a "Simenonian" novel of about 220 pages, divided into eight or nine chapters. He was a man of a single literary genre: his own. Why, then, did he take the risk of the *Dictées*? To exorcise the demons that haunted him: failure, old age, death. And once again, to justify himself. To ease a guilt complex reawakened by his conjugal heartbreak. Perhaps he could already feel the vultures of biography circling overhead. If so, the *Dictées* may have been meant to shape his own statue with more loving care than others might bring to the task. During the same period he gave many interviews as well, but with time these began to show the same flaw as the *Dictées*. Everyone has a tendency to aggrandize and embellish memories, but the inclination was carried to excess by a memorialist who already had a natural penchant for exaggeration.

Lettre à ma mère (1974), however, was an exception in his output of the seventies, a last burst of genius from a retired master. Some readers and commentators, in particular the doctors who had the privilege of knowing him, consider this brief, dense text the key to his personality. It is a chronicle of failure of understanding between two beings who never managed to love each other because they never managed to talk to each other. It reveals the core of his suffering as a great writer recognized by everyone except his own mother.

"You know, it's funny," Henriette once said in front of her daughter-in-law. "It's Georges who got the glory but Christian had the talent."[33]

The dichotomy between his letters to his mother and the *Lettre à ma mère* is striking. Indeed, the correspondence between Henriette and her son from the twenties to the sixties shows no sign of dissension at all. Simenon's letters are warm, devoted, and affectionate, full of touching attention and filial piety. He urges her to hire a maid, to move to a bigger place, to spoil herself. But money could always detonate their latent conflict.

We learn from his letters that in the sixties he continued to send her checks regularly despite her objections.[34] His book reveals that one day, on a visit to Epalinges, Henriette handed him an envelope containing the total amount of money he had sent her over the years.[35] She refused to be in his debt.

Lettre à ma mère was dictated in a few days with rare intensity. In it Simenon keeps the mask in place even while revealing himself. He loved her all the more because of his resentment of her:

"As you are well aware, we never loved each other while you lived. Both of us pretended. . . . I wonder if you ever took me on your lap. In any case, I have no memory of it, so it must not have happened often. . . . I was a stranger to you. . . . There was something excessive in you beyond your control, but at the same time an extreme lucidity. . . . What bound the two of us was just one thread: your fierce desire to be good—for others, but perhaps most of all for yourself."[36]

Simenon fell ill immediately after dictating *Lettre à ma mère*. For two months he was mired in a state he tried to analyze shortly afterward, sitting down at the microphone that now served as his cane:

"Sick probably for having discovered that I was not the man I thought I was, sick also from knowing that my mother had been no more than a woman, a very humble woman whose life was unbalanced from the outset and who deserved my tenderness and pity more than a certain indifference or a certain rancor."[37]

A little more than two years after this ordeal, a package arrived that plunged him into a new abyss of guilt. A French neuropsychiatrist and ardent reader of his novels had composed the *Lettre à mon fils* that Henriette might have written had she been capable of it. Captivated and stunned by the manuscript, which he described as "shrieking with truth," Simenon was deeply moved.[38]

His reaction would not have astonished the psychiatrists who knew him. In the absence of her admiration, he had never been able to win his mother's tenderness, and though there was no trace of tenderness in his visits to bordellos, he would seek it endlessly in his encounters with women. His exuberant sexuality may well have been a "compensatory rite" for his frustration, which would explain both the haste and the brevity of these encounters: knowing in advance that they would inevitably be unsatisfying, he made sure they would not be lasting.

An entire doctoral dissertation could be written on the rich theme of Simenon, sex, and women. He was loquacious on the subject, explaining that he felt powerful sexual urges from late adolescence onward and proclaiming his need to make love three times a day every day. It would be plausible but erroneous to write off his claims as hollow boasts or to view his behavior as symptomatic of latent impotence, suppressed homosexuality, or a need for reassurance. Anyone who revisits the places he lived soon finds that his boasts were not hollow. A large number of women have vivid memories of Georges Simenon, his inclinations, and his efforts to satisfy them.

He believed that the only way to know a woman was to sleep with her. "I would even say that sex is the only possible form of communication with women," he confessed to the writer Emmanuel Berl.[39] The celerity of his multiple copulations suggests athletic performance more than love, and his enumeration of his conquests smacks of a search for relief more than pleasure. He was proud of his sexuality and liked to flaunt it, referring to "females" instead of "women," and proclaiming his frequent resort to prostitutes, whom he called "professionals."[40] Encounters with them corresponded more closely to his animal conception of amorous relationships.

His novels, of course, are far from free of his preoccupation with sex. The heroines of *La Main* (1968) are often referred to as "females." In *Le Chat* (1967), he repeats that "a real woman is a female." Much earlier, in *Le Destin des Malou* (1947), he wrote: "Her entire being was rounded. She was nothing but flesh and shapes. She was a female. . . . And she smelled like a female." In *La Chambre bleue* (1964), he explained what he meant by animal pleasure: total joy, "with no afterthought, not followed by disgust, embarrassment, or lassitude." This conception of carnal relations is hammered down by the lawyer Lucien Gobillot in *En cas de malheur* (1956):

"What drove me most of all was probably a hunger for pure sexuality—if I may use the term without appearing ridiculous—in other words, without any admixture of sentiment or passion. Let us leave sexuality in its raw, or cynical, state. . . . Human beings sometimes have a need to act like animals."[41]

He was often accused of misogyny, a charge he rejected strenuously. When it was pointed out to him that he had never been able (or perhaps never wanted) to create great female characters, he countered by citing *Tante Jeanne* (1951), *Le Temps d'Anaïs* (*The Girl in His Past,* 1951), *La Main* (1968), and *Betty* (1961). But these were, indeed, few in number.[42]

In June 1958 the women's magazine *Marie-France* challenged him on this issue in an interview. He replied by explaining that if women in his novels were often background figures lacking any independent existence, it was because life was like that. But he clearly felt that a woman should be only a partner satisfied with the role of companion. She had no right to be jealous, since physical fidelity was of no importance. At the same time, however, he admitted that he could never stand the thought of his wife dancing with another man, since dancing was a publicly formulated invitation to sensuality.

We lack the data to quantify Simenon's readership by such factors as age, social class, and so on, but it would not be surprising to find that women were a minority among them. They would have few occasions to identify with his characters, and he generally received negative notices from women's magazines. Despite his claims to the contrary, he was considered an arrant misogynist, and the *Dictées* only worsened that image.

Perhaps paradoxically, however, the person who was most consistently devoted to him throughout his life, the only one who knew him intimately from his beginnings in Paris to his move to Switzerland, was a woman. She was with him in Charentes, the Vendée, and America, not exactly a friend and not merely a mistress, yet both at once, and something indefinably more as well. She was the one who lived through it all, saw it all, heard it all, and probably understood it all.

That person was Boule. It would be a gross error to believe that their relationship was based merely on occasional sex. The truth is that she sacrificed her life to her "pretty little gentleman." Incompatibilities of character with Teresa eventually caused her to leave Epalinges to live with Marc's family near Paris and later in Porquerolles. But she regretted none of it:

"When I was young, I thought writers were people who strolled around in big parks wearing capes. Later I learned. Without Simenon I would have married some idiot like myself in Bénouville. I would have had a lot of children like everyone else. What for? We were alike, he and I: animals. We did what we wanted. We loved each other very much. . . . What's he like? He's himself, he's human. The thing that marked our relationship was humanity. That's enough, isn't it? He's a normal man, with the faults and qualities of a normal man."

Boule's favorite Simenon books were *La Porte* (1962) and "that frightening novel" *Les Volets verts* (1950). She wrote a one-page Christmas story about Simenon at the end of his life, called "Le Vieux Navire" (The Old Ship), and regretted being unable to turn it into a novel.

In 1945–1946, when Simenon settled in the United States and Boule was unable to get a visa to join him, he wrote seven or eight love letters to her. She keeps these precious missives, read and reread a thousand times, in a safe-deposit box in a bank in Hyères. Like Doringe, his faithful copy editor, she has asked that her letters from him be destroyed at her death, and they will be burned in accordance with her wish. Her secrets are hers and hers alone; she will carry them to her grave.[43]

Boule may well be right: his sexual freneticism was simply part and parcel of a life given to excess. He fornicated just as he wrote, published, and spoke. It would have been surprising had he engaged in any of these activities with sobriety.

In 1977, at the age of seventy-four, Simenon solidified his sexual reputation—for better or worse, mostly for worse. In January of that year the producers of Federico Fellini's *Casanova* held a private screening for Simenon. Dazzled by what he called a "masterpiece," he announced his readiness to help his friend with the promotion in any way he could. The suggestion was well received.

Fellini and Simenon had had few occasions to meet since the stormy conse-cration of *La Dolce Vita* at the Cannes festival seventeen years earlier, but they had written to each other often—long, warm, and solicitous letters from one artist to another. "You are probably the person with whom I feel the closest links in the domain of creation," Simenon wrote to Fellini. ". . . Both of us have remained, and I hope will always remain, overgrown children obeying internal and often irrepressible urges rather than rules that have no greater meaning for you than they do for me."[44]

Simenon's admiration for Fellini was heartily reciprocated. In fact, the di-rector told the novelist that he had been an inspiration to him on the eve of beginning the shooting of *Casanova*. Fellini had had a dream: a leafy clearing, a man with a false beard in a shining, dewy garden, children at his feet. "What is he doing?" Fellini asks in his sleep. "He's painting his new novel. Look! It's already more than half done. A very beautiful novel about Neptune." Fellini was suddenly awakened by the clacking of a typewriter. The apparition was Simenon: "Master of life and creativity, he is part of an oneiric mythology and works miracles like a magus." The director emerged rejuvenated. His film seemed less contemptible, and he set to work having drawn a lesson from the dream. If my friend Simenon is capable of painting his novels, he said to him-self, then I can make *Casanova* in English.[45]

Such was the context of their meeting in Simenon's home in January 1977, a promotional move organized by Gaumont, the production company. The following month, a photograph of the two men appeared on the cover of the magazine *L'Express,* with the headline: "Fellini interviewed by Simenon about his *Casanova*." The article inside was titled "Fellini-Simenon: Casanova, our brother" and subtitled "A grand dialogue on the mystery of artistic creation."

The discussion took place in the bedroom. As might have been expected, the questions were as eloquent as the answers. Toward the end a genuine con-versation developed:

"You know, Fellini," Simenon said, "I think I've been a better Casanova than you. A year or two ago I figured out that since the age of thirteen and a half I've had ten thousand women. It wasn't a vice. I have no sexual vices, just a need to communicate. And even the eight thousand prostitutes among these ten thousand were human beings, female human beings. I would have liked to have known all females. Unfortunately, because of my marriages I couldn't have real affairs. But the number of times I managed to make love on the run, so to speak, is improbable."[46]

Indeed, the record to which Simenon laid claim struck the magazine's edi-tors as so implausible that they did not feature it, ascribing it, quite correctly, to hyperbole. After all, in the same interview the retired writer called Fellini's film "the most beautiful fresco in the history of cinema, a veritable psycho-analysis of humanity," and insisted that he had read Casanova's *Memoirs* at the age of sixteen. He also admitted that he had lost any sense of time two years earlier.

He might well have added that he had also lost any sense of proportion. The figure of ten thousand works out to about one woman every two days from adolescence to retirement.[47] Two years later, in one of his *Dictées,* he made the more reasonable claim that he had known "a great number of women."[48]

"Ten thousand? That was a joke," commented Tigy.[49]

Too late. The novelist in the glass cage now became the man who made love to ten thousand women.

On-the-scene inquiries cannot determine the real figure with any accuracy, but during his interwar European tour Simenon proved that he could sniff out a bordello in Lapland when the temperature was forty below.

How many female first names could he recall? That might be a relevant test, deducting the eight thousand paid encounters. In any event, there was one he was not likely to forget, even if he insisted on using only her initial: "D."

Within a few years of meeting her, he was already calling Denyse "D." in his correspondence.[50] He now did so systematically, but for other reasons: the better to efface the unnamed person.

Since 1971 they had been embroiled in endless legal and emotional conflict, both of them acting through lawyers. At issue was a divorce, a prospect Simenon considered too costly even to consider.

Denyse accused him of depriving her of her children, belittling her contri-bution to his work, evicting her from their home, ridiculing her in front of the family, preventing her from recovering her jewels and furs, and paying her insufficient support. He accused her of persecuting him, seeking to destroy him by all possible means, unfairly claiming professional collaboration, ad-vancing inordinate financial demands, and engaging in what amounted to blackmail in an effort to get what she wanted.

The stakes were commensurate with the value of the Simenon enterprise: a divorce under Swiss law would cost him a fortune. If Denyse could establish that she had really been her husband's "agent" for twenty years, she would be entitled to 10 percent of his income since 1945. She had never been for-mally named to that post, but she argued that she had played the role de facto.[51] There are indeed letters from America in which he refers to her that way, unhesitatingly praising the quality and efficiency of her work, of which he spoke highly even in public, as the famous *New Yorker* profile-interview of 1953 attests. "My wife is worth two agents and six lawyers: she takes care of everything," he said then.

To this argument Simenon invariably replied that he had only been trying to boost her self-confidence. She had gone beyond her function as interpreter and usurped his entire correspondence. In this he had decided not to frustrate her, though he would have liked to.[52]

Denyse stood her ground, convinced that he now hated her as passionately as he had once loved her. She sent him two threatening letters in June and October 1971, demanding that they never see each other again. That was fine with him, but she also wanted the right to see her children whenever and wherever she chose, as well as a monthly payment of 48,000 Swiss francs. Otherwise she would release the two articles she had written in reply to his *Quand j'étais vieux* (1970) to a press agency.

The sticking point in the negotiations was always the amount of the support payment. Simenon argued that he had already paid enough, particularly for his wife's repeated stays in the luxurious clinic-hotel of Prangins. But he was well placed to realize that she had now marshaled her formidable intelligence in the service of her litigious temperament. Proceeding in stages, she next threatened to grant interviews and even to publish a book exposing the great man.

Simenon refused to budge. In 1974 he rejected all her financial demands, definitively and permanently.[53] Behind-the-scenes negotiations continued, but after three years of hand-to-hand struggle, he realized that she asked for more whenever he gave any ground. He therefore instructed his lawyers to break off all talks. As he saw it, Denyse now had one and only one goal: to become a widow.

Several years earlier, Simenon's first wife had been repeatedly approached by publishers eager to duplicate the success of Françoise Gilot's *Living with Picasso*. Tigy had responded with a dignified refusal: "I don't want to exploit that."[54]

But Denyse was not Tigy. Simenon knew that she was quite determined to exploit "that," and he asked his former secretary Annette de Bretagne to make inquiries in the publishing industry in an effort to find out how advanced the manuscript was. If possible, he wanted to obtain a set of proofs.

As it turned out, two teams of two ghostwriters each spent seven months with Denyse, tape-recording her account of her life with Simenon, for a book to be issued by Jean-Claude Simoën, a Paris publisher who had just opened a new firm that bore his name. "She was obsessed with the idea of proving that she could write better than Simenon," one of the four reported.[55]

The manuscript seems to have lost whatever force it had in the transition from tape to print. When it finally appeared in 1978, after passing through many hands, *Un Oiseau pour le chat* (A Bird for the Cat) was no more than a collection of embellished personal anecdotes. It was a media event notable mainly for the notoriety of its target and the whiff of scandal that preceded its publication. The book came complete with an advertising band reading, "The Marriage of Madame Maigret."

Inevitably, the press sought reactions from the subject, and Simenon stated his position once and for all: the author hated him, the book was a tissue of lies. The entire exercise was of psychiatric rather than critical interest.[56]

In the end it was not as bad as he had feared. He had sufficient nerve, character, and endurance to absorb the blows. The same could not be said of his daughter.

Marie-Jo was twenty-five. She was outraged and distressed at the public sullying of a man she venerated madly—and that is not a figure of speech. Two months after her mother's book was published, she killed herself. The book was not the cause of her suicide, but it was the detonator.

Simenon adored all his children, but cherished Marie-Jo especially. She was his only daughter, and the weakest and most vulnerable of the four.

"Because she was a woman?" he was asked.

"No. I always considered her my little girl."[57]

Three crucial events marked her passage through childhood and adolescence.

When she was very small, Simenon had a premonition that all was not well. He was deeply affected by an apparently trivial incident that occurred in Lakeville when she was not quite two years old.

One morning at around nine-thirty, after finishing a chapter, he got into his car to drive to the post office and pick up the mail. Before embarking on this ritual journey, he would normally pull over near the garden, where the nanny was walking Marie-Jo, pick her up by her arms, and kiss her. But that day two cars coming simultaneously from opposite directions forced him to accelerate, and he continued on his way. When he got home twenty minutes later, he found Denyse, Boule, and the nanny in tears. Marie-Jo had fainted after his departure. Her body was lax, her face blank, her torpor frightening. The doctor advised Simenon to hold his daughter in his arms and speak to her softly. Her eyelids fluttered, a smile appeared, and she said:

"Don't go 'way again, Dad."

Simenon wrote that this dramatic incident determined his future relations with his daughter.[58]

"It's true that she said, 'Mommy, he didn't kiss me!' But she never fainted. All she did was cry," claims Denyse.[59]

Given the dispute between Simenon and his wife and their shared responsibilities in their daughter's death, their testimony is equally credible and contestable. But there is additional evidence from Christian Guy, a French journalist who spent a few days in Lakeville around the same time, working on a piece for the magazine *Votre Enfant*.

His article, published in February 1955, indicates that the little girl felt an inordinate love for her father, that she sometimes had fevers for which pediatricians could not account, that she feared above all that her father would cease to love her, that she had tantrums when he shut himself up while writing a novel, and that she would stop crying only when he came out of his office.

Simenon was so impressed by the fainting incident, which occurred shortly before his British tour, probably in September 1954, that he recounted it to a journalist, adding that the shock was so intense that he himself fell ill that evening. But what could he do? He says he tried changing his work habits. In vain. It was impossible to write a line.[60]

From the beginning, then, Simenon was aware that his daughter had a "problem." He wondered about his share of responsibility. But since he was powerless to react other than with more affection and attention, it only enhanced an already potent feeling of guilt.

Some years later, in Lausanne, they were shopping in the city, and Marie-Jo, looking in the window of a jewelry shop, asked her father to buy her a ring. Not a gaudy one with a colored stone, but a simple band.

"A ring like yours," she explained.

Believing that an eight-year-old had no idea of the significance of a wedding ring, he bought her one made to her measure. She had it enlarged over the years, attaching greater importance to it than to any other object. Simenon began to understand the import of his gesture when, every time she took it off, she asked him to put it back on her finger.[61]

According to Denyse, he was unable to resist buying her this present that was not a present.

"Marie-Jo is the only woman in my life besides you."

"You're crazy. You're encouraging her."

"But I love my little girl."[62]

The third event that marked Marie-Jo's childhood occurred in 1964, when she was eleven. Denyse had just returned from a stay in the Prangins clinic, and in an effort to smooth things over, Simenon sent mother and daughter on a winter vacation to a rented chalet in Villars-sur-Ollon. Marie-Jo returned traumatized. Something had happened that she refused to talk about. She sulked, brooded, and kept her secret, which she was to reveal only many years later.

She sank into illness. She was ashamed of something but refused to say any more. The initial symptoms alarmed Simenon, because they recalled those Denyse had exhibited in America. After her return from Villars-sur-Ollon, the adolescent was increasingly obsessed by cleanliness. She felt stained. Everything seemed "dirty" to her; the word came up constantly. She washed her hands compulsively, twenty, thirty, fifty times a day. She demanded that the floor under her bed be vacuumed, that the sheets be changed in the middle of the night, that dishes and glasses be cleaned during meals. She felt constant anguish that she might never become a "clean" person again.

Simenon had dark forebodings. The child of Outremeuse had grown up with the anxious fear that a hackney might come to carry his mother off to the insane asylum as it had come for his aunt. The grown man in Epalinges began to wonder whether Marie-Jo might fall victim to the same pathology as Denyse.

Marie-Jo, who according to one of her brothers[63] read her father's novels "relentlessly," felt crushed by his literary genius, anxious that she would never be up to "his" level. She believed that he harbored high ambitions for her and feared she would be unable to satisfy them. She was at a loss how to make him happy, though he did not ask much from her. Sometimes at dinner she was so entranced listening to her father talk that she was unable to eat.

She was deeply convinced that her parents had not desired her birth and that her mother considered her a substitute for a stillborn baby. Of Georges Simenon's four children it was Marie-Jo who suffered most from the degradation of the family atmosphere, especially around the time they left Echandens for Epalinges.

Marc, born in 1939, was already an adult, married and himself a father. He was living his own life, and Denyse was not his mother. John, born in 1949, had great strength of character. He had built himself an internal fortress that enabled him to resist external storms. He was too solid and well armed to be shaken. Pierre, born in 1959, was too young to understand everything. He was sheltered by his own equilibrium, his closeness with his brothers, and his passion for his father.

Marie-Jo, born in 1953, was in the center of the storm from the outset. Apart from hereditary factors, her personality made her vulnerable to the latent tension often exacerbated by alcohol abuse on both sides and by violence, scenes, and insults. She was born and grew up in a world of paroxysm that sharpened her sense of insecurity and instability. She never knew whether her father or her mother was telling the truth, for there were so many different truths, so many crises. A buffer between her parents, she felt increasingly disoriented.

She began to exhibit symptoms of a profound neurosis diagnosed by psychiatrists as obsessive compulsion: feelings of distress, anxiety, depression, phobia about filth and contamination, but also rigidity, coldness, indecision, inability to manage her time, perfectionism. She fell into a vicious circle: clinics in Lausanne and Prangins, repeated flight, psychiatric hospitals in the Paris area, suicide attempts.

During one stay in the Clinique du Lac near Rueil-Malmaison, known for its nonmedicinal therapies, she had serious problems with anorexia nervosa. The moment she was alone, she sought to starve herself into exhaustion. She hid behind large dark glasses, affecting a contemptuous and megalomaniacal façade. Fascinated by death, she claimed not to fear it. She tried to delude herself that she was a compulsive liar, but could not find the strength to carry it off. After treating her for a serious depression, the doctors discovered what they believed was the motor force of her difficulties: depersonalization.

"My thoughts are not my own," she told them repeatedly.

Acting on the principle that a trauma could account for a neurosis but not for a psychosis, and seeking the origin of her anxiety that she was the replacement for a stillborn child, they dug deeper into the archaeology of her symptoms, uncovering upheavals dating back to her prenatal life, when her parents were already fighting.

Simenon visited once a month. Long enough to drop off a check. He was less and less able to see her in this state, though he knew he was not the first father, nor the first "writer of crushing genius," to face such a situation. He did much more than an Evelyn Waugh, a man of monstrous egotism who would not even visit the bedside of his gravely ill son, agreeing to do so only when death was imminent. But he did much less than a James Joyce, so completely devoted to his daughter Lucie that when she slid inexorably into madness, he corrected the proofs of *Finnegans Wake* at her bedside, his eyes filled with tears.

There is no doubt that Simenon loved his daughter. But he did not know how to love her. He encouraged her to leave Epalinges, for her relations with Teresa were not good: it was inevitable that she would be jealous of her father's companion. He bought her a two-room apartment in the Lido Galerie on the Champs-Elysées. He was pleased when she moved in with her older brother for a while, correctly convinced that she would find balance and comfort in the home of Marc and his wife, the actress Mylène Demongeot.

Though she had tried and abandoned nearly every art, from dance to painting, he encouraged her to believe in her vocation as an actress, paying for lessons at the famous Cours Simon and helping her get walk-on parts in films by such "Simenonian" directors as Pierre Granier-Deferre (*La Race des seigneurs*) and Bertrand Tavernier (*Que la fête commence*).

He was not happy with her friends. Rumors and indiscretions from Paris had it that Marie-Jo went out only with married men in their forties or fifties, men who reminded her of her father. Most of them worked in the film or publishing industries. Some of his *Dictées* bear traces of his reaction, particularly when he proclaims his hatred of fifty-year-olds who take but never give, abusing the vulnerability of young girls, playing on their weaknesses the better to flaunt them as trophies.[64]

Simenon was filled with hope when Roger Mirmont came into Marie-Jo's life. The couple spent several days in Epalinges, and the young man seemed to be of a generous temperament, ready to hold out a hand to a drowning woman. They had met in a café. He was twenty-seven, she twenty. Athletic, energetic, and well balanced, Mirmont, originally from Bordeaux, had moved to Paris to pursue his career as a theater and film actor.

Marie-Jo often talked about her father. She wanted to astonish him, living through him by proxy but never managing to like herself, with a complex about her body like a child who had never been looked at. She was very inhibited where her father was concerned, alternately giving an impression of absence or excess. Sometimes she took so many tranquilizers that she fell into a kind of vegetative state. Even when we went on a motorcycle vacation in Corsica, Nice, or Saint-Jean-de-Luz, her pleasure was never very deep. I was at a loss what to do to make her happy. I didn't know how to help her. She was a defenseless child. She wasn't given to happiness, but seemed to finally find it when Mylène was at the piano, Marc on the harmonica, and me on the guitar. That's what she wanted. It was like she was in search of a missed childhood and an autonomy she never managed to find. Marie-Jo was seeking the impossible star.[65]

The young man stabilized her for a time, but not for long. When they separated, she sought solace in the arms of a champion swimmer at the Deligny pool, which had the fortunate side effect of making her more athletic. But soon she fell back into a downward spiral.

To the very end she sent Simenon heartrending letters that left him speechless:

> I can no longer bear the thought of leaving to others the task of making me live, that responsibility for oneself that is the first any "grown-up," or anyone "in the process of growing up," has to have the dignity to assume on his own . . . and even if I really sink, it won't matter anymore, since it won't be in front of you, Dad. . . . I could lower my guard a little without having the feeling that I was losing my dignity in front of you. . . . Oh Dad, if only you could be here, near me, take me in your arms like when I was small and make me forget everything. Forget everything and start all over, as if cleansed by you of all this past in which I'm stuck and from which I can't pull myself. . . . It is too late. I've gone too far adrift, and I'm too old to curl up on your lap. . . . The most incredible thing would have been to have a Daddy, and then a Dad, to have loved "the man," from afar, like a lover, to have read nearly all "Simenon," with a lump in my throat, to have finally taken in the whole "human being," from the little boy to today, through the pages and through my own memories. . . . A "Gentleman," too, magnificent in his silk suit, who carries me in his arms, borne by the music. A tenderness I would never find again. . . . And yet, something happened, something between Mom and Dad, the Why of both their books. Unfortunately, these books are packed with the lies that form their truth and which bring me only discomfort, if not more panic. How,

why, did they separate that way? Why was I stuck between the two?
. . . "Save me Daddy"—I'm dying—I'm nothing more, I don't see my
place—I'm lost in the space, the silence of the death. Forget my tears
but please, believe in my smile, when I was your little girl, many years
ago. Be happy for me—Remember my Love, even if it was crazy. That's
for what I've lived, and for what I die now.[66]

There was no way out. He didn't quite give up, but he might as well have. Yet
Marie-Jo had finally unburdened herself of her secret, confiding it to her father not long before, telling him of her stay with her mother in Villars-sur-
Ollon and explaining why she had come home traumatized. Now it was their
secret. But it was too late. Too much damage had been done.

After much hesitation, the psychiatrists now spoke of a "borderline state."
How could he allow her to weather the ordeal while preventing her from
doing the irreparable? How to lower one's guard when one knows that deliberate death lies at the end of the tunnel? Simenon had been haunted by suicide from his youth, ever since the death of Kleine, one of the members of La
Caque. It had been a recurrent theme of his work since *Le Pendu de Saint-
Pholien* (1931).

In May 1978 his daughter was twenty-five, the age Denyse was when
Simenon met her in New York and she was, as he put it, "deliberately preparing her suicide."[67]

Marie-Jo was revolted by *Un Oiseau pour le chat*. She made notes in the mar-
gin and phoned her father to share her outraged reactions. The book plunged
her head back under water just when she was beginning to breathe again. It
is not hard to see why: it dragged the man of her life through the mud.

This attitude, attested to by everyone who knew the young woman well,
was denied by her mother:

"She liked my book very much. Marie-Jo understood that far from de-
stroying her father, it exposed him. She was the only one who got it. We saw
each other in Paris. 'Finally, Mom,' she said, 'a woman of the family has decided to speak up.' "[68]

In long phone conversations with her father she shared her distress after
Elle printed an interview with him that was advertised as his reaction to the
book. In fact, he had granted no such interview and had systematically rejected all proposals. The interview had actually been published three years
earlier, by *Playboy*. Obviously, there was nothing in it about Denyse's book,
which had not yet been written. A French journalist, who happened to have
been one of the ghostwriters of *Un Oiseau pour le chat*, updated the old interview by peppering it with excerpts from the *Dictées* and adding a few items
about the book. It was presented as though Simenon were responding to
Denyse's attacks. A clever amalgam concocted by a press agency, it fooled
everyone, including the editor in chief of *Elle*, who said he had assumed, as

any reader would, that Simenon was speaking contemporaneously throughout.

Marie-Jo seemed as upset by the interview—dishonestly entitled "Simenon Replies to His Wife"—as by the book. More than ever, she had no idea whether her father or her mother was telling the truth. In an effort to reassure her, Simenon sent a correction to the magazine, which promised to print it. Marie-Jo phoned every day to ask when his statement would appear and went regularly to the newsstand. Her impatience was ill served by the delays typical of weeklies.[69]

A phone call from Paris. Simenon answers in Epalinges. It is Marie-Jo.

"Listen, Dad. Tell me you love me."

"I love my little girl."

"No. Just say, I love you."

"Yes, Marie-Jo, I love you."

"No. Just those three words."

"I love you."

They hang up simultaneously.[70]

The next day, in the late afternoon, Marie-Jo goes to have a coffee at her usual bistro. The counterman is struck by her expression:

"For the first time she was smiling. She finally seemed serene, free, as if she had just been released from some great suffering."[71]

Another phone call to Epalinges. This time it is Marc, calling to tell his father that Marie-Jo is dead, that she has shot herself in the chest with a .22 pistol.

Simenon was devastated, but when he recovered, there was no trace of aggression in his grief. He did not wail, "How could she do this to us?" For several weeks he was prey to a strange sensation, a mixture of annihilation and a kind of relief, both for her and for himself.

Her last wish was that she be cremated with the gold wedding band her father had given her and placed so often on her finger. At the funeral the family stood on one side, Denyse on the other. Bach and white lilacs. The next day, in accordance with his daughter's request, Simenon scattered her ashes in the garden of his small pink house. One day he would shock a Canadian television crew by claiming to have tasted the ashes and to have found them "salty."

Soon after the funeral he sent his collaborator Joyce Aitken to Paris to bring back the many documents Marie-Jo had left at her place for him: letters, manuscripts, cassettes. Meanwhile, Denyse sent her lawyer to recover a stack of love letters between her daughter and various Paris personalities: a publisher, an actor, a singer, and so on. These went into a safe-deposit box in a Swiss bank, where they were added to the love letters Simenon had sent to Denyse while she was in the Prangins clinic.[72]

Simenon stopped sitting on his bench in the garden. He still fed the pigeons, but from the terrace. Two months after the tragedy, when he sent a printed thank-you note to an old friend who had expressed condolences, he added a handwritten comment:

"Still a complete nightmare."[73]

Any child's suicide racks the parents with guilt, in one form or another, and Simenon was no exception. Officially, he said he had done all he could and did not feel at all responsible.[74] But although he had given her, for example, the money to buy and furnish an apartment, she might have been more touched had he helped her with the decoration. Just a gesture, but perhaps he should have done it. Could he have? Did he want to?

For weeks and months Simenon pondered the circumstances of this death too often foretold. The people around him testify that he did blame himself for some things: his passive attitude to relations between Marie-Jo and Denyse and the cowardice that prevented him from protecting the daughter from the mother; his rejection of both of them—"Women!"—when eight-year-old Marie-Jo seemed to take her mother's side; his lack of insight in failing to realize that at twenty his daughter needed both pressure and support; his impatient exasperation when he could no longer tolerate her coldness, lack of discipline and self-confidence, her dissipation, dilettantism, and self-destructiveness, the whining tone in which she spoke to him.

He even felt guilty about the perverse influence some of his novels may have had on her. It was by reading *Maigret et Monsieur Charles* (1972) that she learned of the existence of the Paris gunsmith Gastinne-Renette, where she got the pistol with which she killed herself. In *Les Autres* (1962) she found a sentence she pondered endlessly and finally took to heart: "I was too ambitious to exist." But it was most of all in *La Disparition d'Odile* (1971) that she inevitably saw herself.

He wrote this novel in the autumn of 1970. In it he recounted, several years in advance and with stunning foresight, the story of one Odile Pointet, a "lost" young woman of eighteen. Unable to tolerate the family atmosphere in Lausanne, she flees, taking with her a pistol and some barbiturates. She goes secretly to Paris, where she intends to kill herself. Her father, a historian regularly consulted by the media, thinks only of his books. Her mother acts as though Odile doesn't exist. Only her brother, four years her senior, loves her enough to rush to Paris to find her.

It is not difficult to see Georges Simenon in the character of Albert Pointet, an aging egotist obsessed by his work, a man whose daily activities—eating, working, sleeping—are timed like clockwork. It is not difficult to see Johnny Simenon in the character of Bobby, the devoted and protective big brother gifted with such strength of purpose.

And it is not difficult to see Marie-Jo in Odile. Simenon's heroine is a girl who never finds her footing in life. Proud, meddlesome, depressed, she lacks self-confidence. Obsessively self-destructive, haunted by the thought that she will wind up in a mental institution, she strikes out blindly, taking refuge in relationships with older men so as to escape realities with which she cannot deal. After one futile attempt to slash her wrists, she finds solace with a young medical student, her neighbor in the Latin Quarter hotel where she is living.

La Disparition d'Odile is a frightful portrait of father and daughter, especially in view of the context in which it was written and its fictionalized self-criticism. The end of the novel suggests that Odile has abandoned the thought of suicide, for she gives the student her weapon. But this seems merely a temporary decision. Was Simenon trying to exorcise the specter of a successful suicide by offering his daughter the happy ending she so desperately wanted?

After Marie-Jo's death he denied that there was any link between reality and fiction. The furthest he would go:

"Intuition perhaps? I don't know, and I don't intend to try to find out."[75]

Marie-Jo was more explicit. Several months after the novel came out, as she was about to leave Epalinges for Paris, she wrote to her father:

"By the time you read this letter, I'll be gone, my room will be empty, and—I don't know how you'll react. But most of all I don't want you to panic or be hurt. I'm not leaving to kill myself like 'Odile.' I'm leaving only because I feel so unbalanced inside that I would wind up in the hospital again, and I couldn't stand that."[76]

Marie-Jo's end would be far more tragic than Odile's, reality outstripping a fiction the author never wanted to finish. It is hard to see how the father of both heroines could have avoided feeling responsible.

He loved his daughter, most often clumsily. When she told him she had been deeply moved by *They Shoot Horses, Don't They?*, he did not bother to try to share her emotions and anxieties by going to see the film. Ten years earlier, however, he had gone out of his way to see Stanley Kubrick's *Dr. Strangelove* and Chaplin's *The Kid* again to make his son Johnny happy. He regretted not having been more generous with his time and affection and having dedicated *Feux rouges* (1953) to Marie-Jo when she was born, thus associating her with the most disturbing symbolism. He also regretted having been unable to attenuate the sense of self-deprecation that undermined her, and having failed to understand that it was unreasonable to demand that such a deeply depressed person exhibit strength of will. He was sorry he had not gone to Paris after her first suicide attempt, instead finding out how she was through Marc.

With the death of his daughter the author who so often and so masterfully depicted the tragedy of lack of communication between people came to understand that it was possible to love madly yet badly.

This absence, failure, and mystery would be his obsession for the rest of his life. He would never achieve the serenity he had dreamed of after finally freeing himself of the burden of his characters.

Simenon had never been sure whether his life was more comic or tragic. Now he was. He also knew that his Marie-Jo had been its sole victim. As the father he still was, he felt guilty. As the novelist he had been, he remembered that he was always on the victim's side.[77]

But the real irony of the story lies elsewhere, in a zone beyond his inner darkness, between an absence and a surfeit. This man who spent his life seeking the love his mother had denied him was ultimately overwhelmed by the love his daughter offered him.

Marie-Jo wrote letters to each of her brothers before she killed herself. But for her father she left not only many letters but also annotated books, song lyrics, poems, appointment books, and tapes.

He spent months studying the "Marie-Jo file," immersing himself in it in his effort to understand. Listening to the tapes was a journey through hell that he inflicted on himself as a daily punishment and purgatory. He conducted a kind of search for the fault line, never dreaming that it might have been in him.

"You ought to write your memoirs, Dad," his son Pierre said to him one day.

"Certainly not," he replied. "I have no desire at all to do that. Besides, I don't want the kind of legal trouble I had with *Pedigree*. It's not worth it."[78]

In his *Dictées* he mentioned the possibility only to reject it:

"To make myself the main character in some sort of long true-life novel is not my style."[79]

He also refused to write memoirs to be published after his death:

"A vulgar ruse."[80]

Yet in the end he decided to do it after all. In a letter to Fellini written early in 1980 he announced his plans to begin his next book, large in scope and broad in ambition. He expected it to take him a year or two.[81]

His intention was not only to refute Denyse's allegations but also to justify himself in his readers' eyes and to free himself from his own guilt. The circumstances of the tragedy had altered the image he had hoped to bequeath to posterity: that of an honest man in the old-fashioned sense of the word.[82] But *Mémoires intimes* (1981) was an expression less of authorial vanity than of determination to put his own character in order. It was as though he felt that drawing a balance sheet of his life would hasten his endless striving for peace and unattainable serenity.

He wanted to write *Mémoires intimes* for his daughter in the same spirit in which he had written *Pedigree* for his son. In both cases he needed a special reason to strike out into new territory, an excuse to indulge in an exercise that might appear extravagant. In 1940 it was his medical death sentence. Forty years later it was a real death.

Marie-Jo had wanted to be a writer. Her deepest desire was to be published, but her most intimate wish was to see her own byline alongside her father's. Simenon decided to fulfill that wish by adding a line to the cover, beneath the title: "including Marie-Jo's book." Despite the bulk of these memoirs, he flatly rejected any suggestion of publishing them in two volumes. He did not want to be separated from her. The memories of the one would stand alongside those of the other, father and daughter united for eternity.

It would also be an opportunity to preempt the "authorized biographies" being prepared in Britain and the United States. The one and only authorized biography would be his own.[83] To aid him in his reconstruction, Simenon asked Joyce Aitken to draw up a chronology of the major events of his life and a list of his novels, from the beginning. These would be the crutches of his memory.

He attached such importance to this undertaking that he added a codicil to his will. If he should die while writing the book, his companion, Teresa Sburelin, and his closest collaborator, Joyce Aitken, were to complete it. He believed that the former was the person best placed to write his biography, while the latter was the only one qualified to produce a monograph on the Simenon enterprise—complementary qualities that would enable the two women to compose his *Mémoires intimes* in his stead should the need arise. If for any reason they should fail to complete the project, Professor Maurice Piron of the University of Liège would inherit the delicate mission.

He had never spent so much time on any one book. He wrote from February to November 1980 and devoted February and March 1981 to the revision. For nearly a year he was, in his own words, "practically incommunicado,"[84] living like a "hermit,"[85] taking just one month off, July 1980, when he rested at the Valmont clinic in Glion-sur-Montreaux and took long walks in the forest.

At the age of seventy-seven, seven years after abandoning his typewriter for the tape recorder, he returned to an exhausting professional discipline. The *Mémoires intimes* were written by instinct, with a Parker fountain pen, on graph notebooks, from two in the afternoon until eight in the evening every day. Very few words crossed out, pages filled with his tiny, regular handwriting, so small it seemed as though he were hiding what he was writing. To type the text the secretaries had to microfilm it and project the enlarged image on a screen.

Several weeks into this regimen, he commented:

"I feel like a hundred-meter sprinter who suddenly goes out for a marathon.

In two months I have written the equivalent of four of my novels. I'm beginning to wonder whether my book might not turn out to be as big as a *Who's Who*. In the meantime, Teresa takes care of me as though I were an athlete in training."[86]

The ordeal was sometimes intolerable. He would burst into tears in the middle of writing. He was going further than he ever had, calling his wife responsible for their daughter's death in particular and for all the evils he suffered in general. Everything he says about her must be understood in the context of the divorce proceedings. Here was one "perpetrator" for whom he rarely found mitigating circumstances, other than mental illness.

The women in his life are more often nicknamed than named: D., Tigy, Boule. His mother exists only in relation to her son. Teresa has no last name. Marie-Jo alone is granted an autonomous existence, though she never had one in real life.

His memories unfold in a classical narrative framework (in chronological order) and not through the more Simenonian sensory associations of the *Dictées*. But he did not abandon all aspects of his novelistic technique: dialogues and descriptions, alternation of primary and secondary characters, first-person narration, epistolary passages (letters to his daughter). Some of his most cherished devices even appear, such as leitmotif ("Which was the real D.?") and the buried secret (the traumatic episode in Villars-sur-Ollon).

It would be charitable to say that Simenon spends little time talking about his work. He cites titles as though out of obligation, and there is a striking imbalance of treatment: an entire page devoted to baby food and a single line mentioning the writing of two new novels. There is no lack of anecdotes, but he was so irritated by his reading of Gertrude Stein's memoirs in 1973 (*The Autobiography of Alice B. Toklas*) that he was more reluctant than ever to name all the personalities of his scenario. That was also why he did not publish all the texts Marie-Jo left him. As he saw it, name-dropping would have been indecent. Yet he did not shrink from exhibiting dirty laundry, settling accounts, and boasting of his sexual exploits, recounting, for example, how he took the maid from behind as she did her chores, later making her his lifelong companion.

It is hard to see how details of this kind could be seen as homage to his dead little girl, and the gap between the book's avowed aim and its actual result outraged more than one reader. Some considered it sordid. The public was not accustomed to seeing a great writer expose his private life with such little reserve. Had the memoirs been aimed merely at getting even with a litigious spouse, they might have seemed more acceptable, a kind of picturesque provocation. But his daughter is the thread that runs through the book, and she ended a tragic life by killing herself.

What, then, is the explanation for Simenon's attitude? Possibly the famous "sense of propriety" inherited from his father, whereby religion, but not sex, was regarded as too intimate a subject to be treated in a novel. His self-justification required that he tell his children everything, out of respect for the tragedy they had experienced. He had to write without inhibition if the barriers were to come down and he were to sustain the illusion of being content with himself. In his mind, his account of his sexual epic reflected not immodesty but an absence of shame, for he had lived it quite naturally. He flatly rejected the idea that there was anything wrong with showing the reading public his private correspondence with his daughter. On the contrary, it was a dignified endeavor, and Marie-Jo wanted it that way—even at the risk of pandering to voyeurism rather than readers and of arousing a disquieting doubt: Had he gone as far as incest?

". . . and then legend took hold, and it was difficult even for him to make clear distinctions between truth, exaggeration, and lies," we read in *Le Petit Saint*.[87] It is hard not to think of *Mémoirs intimes,* a clever, pathos-ridden reconstruction of a story already spent by too many tellings.

On April 28, 1981, Joyce Aitken delivered the 2,400-page typescript to Presses de la Cité in Paris. It was the first time Simenon had ever given a text to a publisher without signing a contract first. Proof enough, were any needed, of this book's exceptional character. The contract, a sweet one indeed, came later: an advance of about 2 million francs, payable in several installments, graduated royalty rates beginning at 18 percent.

Despite the favorable terms, if ever there was a book not written for money, this was it. Simenon had given himself to it body and soul, out of moral commitment and fidelity to his four children and to honor Marie-Jo's memory.

Sven Nielsen, one of his few real friends, had died four years earlier, and Nielsen's son Claude had taken over management of the company. He was ready to back *Mémoires intimes,* even though he made no secret of his fears: the book would be big, bulky, and expensive to produce. The first print run would have to be high. It meant taking financial risks on a project that might well generate lawsuits.

Simenon proposed a bargain to ease his publisher's troubled mind: suspension of the payment of his advance until the book was in the shops and assured of distribution. He also put the house in Epalinges up as security for Presses de la Cité—just in case.

Claude Nielsen was touched, for he had asked for no such favor. He would have published the book anyway, and he could not imagine foreclosing on Simenon's home. But that was not the point: the author had made this highly symbolic gesture to prove, not least to himself, that he was ready for any sacrifice to see his daughter's name beside his own in the bookstores.

He was not inordinately concerned with Denyse's reaction. After all, she had not responded to several *Dictées* that were especially hostile to her, and she had already lost two trials against him. He hoped that this time her lawyers would think twice before following her into a lawsuit whose outcome was less than certain. But she did take the opportunity to publish a new book, *Le Phallus d'or* (The Golden Phallus), issued under the pseudonym Odile Dessane. It was accompanied by a promotional band announcing: "Intimate portrait of a celebrity."

Unlike Simenon, Claude Nielsen was more than a little uneasy. It was his business to consider how costly a successful lawsuit might be to his firm, and he looked at all the possibilities: a ban on sales, massive returns to the distributor, deleted pages, censored passages. A nightmare.

The author had already warned that he would accept only minor alterations, but Nielsen asked Robert Badinter, one of the most brilliant members of the Paris bar, to read the typescript. Unfortunately, the counselor had no sooner begun the enormous task than he had to abandon it, for François Mitterrand had just been elected president of the republic, and his prime minister, Pierre Mauroy, named Badinter minister of justice in the new cabinet. His associate Bernard Jouanneau therefore inherited the delicate task of making a provocative text unassailable without significantly pruning it.

It was clear that under French law the author of *Mémoires intimes* had violated the private lives of others. The only argument in his favor: To what extent was private life inviolable in the case of the secrets of a couple, which are necessarily shared?

The risk was obvious: seizure or pure and simple interdiction on grounds of invasion of privacy, defamation, divulging of highly personal letters, and so on. Major cuts were out of the question, for they would alter the very nature of the text. The lawyer suggested a few changes that the author accepted without too much resistance. He deleted a scene in a New York taxi that was considered too erotic and paraphrased some letters instead of reproducing them in full. But Simenon categorically refused when Jouanneau insistently begged him to delete an entire paragraph on page 1597 of the typescript. These were the lines in which Marie-Jo revealed the secret of her and Denyse's vacation at the chalet in Villars-sur-Ollon.

The lawyer persisted, and the writer stood his ground. He was informed that the passage could be grounds for prosecuting his wife for indecent assault on a minor. He didn't care. He would not let them truncate Marie-Jo's memory.

As soon as the book came out, Denyse Simenon's lawyers formally requested that the work be seized and that thirteen lines on pages 495 and 496 and seven lines on page 721 be deleted. The request was legally sound, for the serious violation of privacy was patent. Seizure, however, is an exceptional measure. In this case it would have been unjustified. To withdraw a 753-page book from the market because of twenty lines would be unreasonable.

On November 9, 1981, Marcel Caratini, presiding judge of the court in Paris hearing the case, issued a ruling under which Simenon was ordered to have opaque, self-adhesive stickers affixed to all existing copies of the book obliterating the following passage:

> The secret that has so tormented me I do not want to disclose in my own words. I prefer to reproduce several phrases of a cassette which, according to your appointment book, you recorded in March 1978, in an effort to ease your mind. These are your exact words. I only wish I could convey the heartrending tone of your voice.
>
> It concerns a scene that occurred when you were eleven years old and were alone with your mother in Villars. It is to her that you are speaking:
>
> "You always told me, when I was eleven, that I would never ever be able, I would never in my life be able, to be a real woman to a man, because I would always remember your image, the image of your open sex in front of me, before my eyes, the image of your fingers seeking pleasure and your cup of tea there beside you, there beside the bed, and me watching you, watching you the whole time."

That was Marie-Jo's secret. The rest, in which Simenon mentions "a kind of incest," was not censored.[88]

The author felt he had made out quite well financially. He congratulated Bernard Jouanneau and sent three cases of champagne to the staff of Presses de la Cité.

Marie-Jo had been careful to record her account on a cassette. Psychiatrists who heard it vouched for its authenticity. Other members of the Simenon household agreed, after hours of discussion. It was not an adolescent fantasy. The memorialist was therefore prepared to go to any lengths to unburden himself of the secret.[89]

Denyse denied the veracity of the incident:

"It's a vile falsehood, completely invented, made up out of whole cloth," she said.[90]

Simenon's only comment was "D. succeeded in censoring a dead woman."[91]

The publisher could consider himself lucky. *Mémoires intimes,* he said, sold 100,000 copies in two months. It was the literary event of the season. Reviews, while hailing the book's importance as a human document, were mixed. Some of Simenon's many ardent supporters among journalists and critics were a little nonplussed. They did not want to speak ill of the master, but the truth was that *Mémoires intimes* was virtually silent about its author's creative work, which was mentioned only incidentally. The hefty tombstone-shaped volume was wholly innocent of literature. As autobiography, it was of limited interest. Of the man there was pride and self-hatred, of his novelistic talent little or nothing. Whether out of admiration for his past achievements or respect for his pain as a bereaved father, Simenon was treated gently. But his memoirs were certainly not considered a masterpiece of the genre. It was Marie-Jo who rescued the book from banality, lending it a tragic dimension.

On the whole, then, the press was either enthusiastic or indulgent. Negative notices were rare. François Nourissier, writing in *Le Point,* was one of the few who dared vent his disappointment. He felt that the book left the Simenon mystery intact, and that the "display of trivial details, inanities, and violated secrets" rendered what remained insignificant. He concluded his review:

"One of the grand monsters of contemporary literature, a wild beast grown gray, a medium through whose voice a world was expressed, insists on sharing all the stages and details of his life. There is in this attitude a mixture of nobility, a craftsman's rage, a megalomaniac's temerity, and the arrogance of an old male at bay. It is beautiful and somehow ghastly. But it is not quite what is wanted of a book or of literary criticism."[92]

The writer Anthony Burgess was both admiring and harsh: "The pain is real, but real pain does not necessarily produce art. Dylan Thomas wrote a moving elegy for one Ann Jones, for whom he cared little. . . . The final irony is that a subject came into his life whose expression required a Sophoclean art. Maigret's creator had enormous talent, but he was no Sophocles."[93]

In the end, the normally accommodating Anglo-American critics were more exigent than the Europeans. His American publisher, Helen Wolff, actually suggested significant cuts in these overly loquacious memoirs. With the greatest trepidation she went to Lausanne to discuss them.

"It's fine," Simenon said, granting his approval. "You've done yeoman's service."

She deleted a total of about fifty pages, most of them having to do with America. Superfluous or inaccurate, they would only undermine the book's credibility. The same publisher had had the courage not to publish the *Dictées* in the United States, stalling when the author pressed.

"I didn't want to damage his reputation," Helen Wolff said.[94]

Mémoires intimes was Simenon's last book, this time for real. He was so sure of this that he granted many interviews, as though having decided that, when they were done, he would ring down the curtain forever. The richest and most powerful of these was a session with Bernard Pivot that became one of the vintage installments of the highly rated television series "Apostrophes." Filmed at Simenon's home, the program was entirely devoted to him.

Occasionally amusing, the interview was more often filled with pathos, for Simenon went so far as to listen to his daughter's voice on the tape while cameras recorded his every emotion. Though sufficiently at peace with himself to confront this ordeal without fear, he seemed increasingly vulnerable as the broadcast went on.

Bernard Pivot read from the first page of the book:

". . . Where did the single-shot twenty-two pistol come from? Who bought the bullets? . . . When the investigation was over and your body had been taken to the morgue, I was able to spare you an autopsy, but I did telephone the commissioner to ask that your doors be sealed."

The police atmosphere of these remarkable memoirs gave the interviewer the strange sensation that he was interrogating a suspect. Twice he asked who was the real author of this text: Marie-Jo's father or Inspector Maigret?

Simenon was shaken, unsettled, upset. Fighting back tears, he mumbled an inaudible reply.

"So, this is the voice of Inspector Maigret?"

"I like to reconstruct what happened earlier."

"It's both of them, then?"

"It's both," he answered with difficulty, after offering a technical explanation of why she would have been sure she would not miss with a single-shot pistol. "But more the father."

The journalist had put his finger on one of the author's great contradictions. But at what cost? When he watched the program again several years later, Pivot commented:

"When I repeat my question, I see that my insistence hurt him, that he found it cruel and inappropriate. Forgive me, Mr. Simenon."[95]

The writer had been caught in his own trap by allowing his exhibitionism to get the better of his long-standing voyeurism, two qualities he had always been able to balance. But not this time. The "Simenon sense of propriety" was found wanting, and the failure was especially regrettable in that this broadcast reached many more people than *Mémoires intimes* ever would. It was his last great interview aimed at the broad public, and it would linger in memory as his last word.

The "novelist in the glass cage" and the "man who made love to ten thousand women" would now forever be "Simenon whose daughter committed suicide."

He was now much like his characters: facing the void. Having withdrawn to his small pink house on the Avenue des Figuiers in Lausanne, he lived in an ever smaller space. This was the final demand of the anxiety and insecurity that had never left him: a house, a neighborhood, and furniture as cramped and ugly as those of his childhood.

He was finished traveling, too. Everything looked alike to a man who had seen it all, and he was appalled by *Homo touristicus,* who had ruined the places he had loved so much.

He feared death less than debilitation. Open and accessible despite appearances, he enjoyed exercising his memory by telling his three sons stories. He could still be impish now and then.

His withdrawal from the world was not a mere tactical retreat. He had nothing left to prove. No longer concerned about his image, he preferred to be hated for what he was rather than loved for what he was not.

Simenon believed that he had nothing more to learn and nothing more to understand. He disentangled himself from houses, objects, and people. Only his obsession with time remained. He couldn't stand the slightest unscheduled shift: the cancellation of a visit, a change in an appointment. Everything was still timed to the minute. Total and absolute order, which he saw as the royal road to a serenity so often promised but never attained.

At eighty he was beginning to feel his age. "The time has come to join the clan of old-timers," he said.[96] And: "Growing old is a succession of last times."[97]

Several years earlier, when some BBC producers proposed sending an interviewer to do a recording for the radio program "Desert Island Discs," he rejected the offer. He had stopped listening to records long ago. He wouldn't even have taken books to a desert island.

Yet reading remained one of his favorite activities. He had long since abandoned contemporary fiction, with a few exceptions here and there. One of the last had been just before beginning *Mémoires intimes,* when he read *La Guerre à neuf ans* and *Le Nain jaune,* by Pascal Jardin, who, with Michel Audiard, was among the best film adapters of his novels. He found both stories "extraordinary."[98] But for the most part he sought refuge in books of a completely different kind.

When he moved into his small pink house, he culled his library drastically. His choice of the books he wanted close at hand during his old age is revealing of his concerns and of the state of his curiosity.[99]

Medicine was the dominant subject. Within this discipline psychiatry was represented far more widely than his other passions. There were books by Henry Ey, Jean Delay, Konrad Lorenz, Freud, and Jung, but also several curiosities: a manual of gynecology, a treatise on obstetrics, a work on the illnesses of pregnant and postpartum women.

One shelf of his library was devoted to biographies (Beethoven, Oscar Wilde, Jean Renoir), another to collections of letters (Proust, Faulkner, Raimu, Jean Renoir), yet another to memoirs and private diaries (Roland Dorgèles, André Beucler, Anaïs Nin, Jean Renoir) and to unclassifiable works like the chronicles of Alexandre Vialatte. In a separate room Simenon had the complete works of Balzac, Gide, Maupassant, Mérimée, Brantôme, and Jules Romains, as well as a full set of the Pléiade collection.

It was here, among his books, that he spent most of his time. He also took walks and watched television. There were few visitors, except for close friends and family members. He jettisoned everything that seemed superfluous to him, transferring his valuable furniture and paintings to a storage facility across town and removing from his life anything that might remind him of his work.

Back in 1973 he had decided to donate the dozens of tapes of his *Dictées* to the University of Liège. Two years later he added more items to the collection: some of his original manuscripts, the voluminous files of clippings and articles sent to him by Argus over decades, letters (Pagnol, Miller, Fellini, Maugham, Gide, Cocteau), and French and foreign editions of his books. Thanks to the insistent efforts of Professor Maurice Piron, "Wallonian Walloon of Wallonia" and member of the Royal Academy of French Language and Literature, the Centre d'Etudes Georges Simenon of the University of Liège was officially founded in 1976.

Simenon yielded to Piron's pressure for two reasons: to facilitate research on his work and to make sure that his heirs would not scatter these documents at auctions after his death.[100] That was a spectacle he did not wish to contemplate.

He had four heirs: Denyse, who was still legally his wife, and his three sons— Marc, John, and Pierre. He had already stated that he would leave his companion, Teresa, "not even a trinket,"[101] but would instead deed her their house on the Avenue des Figuiers as a souvenir.

Apart from the comfortable support payments she received, Denyse owned an apartment in Nyon in the canton of Vaud, on the right bank of Lake Léman. She had new writing projects in the works and was now dabbling in psychoanalysis, wondering, for example, about the psychological consequences of the identity of her initials and her husband's father's and about the way their names seemed to reply to each other: "Si mais non? (Simenon.) Oui, mais . . . (Ouimet)."

As for the children: the oldest, a movie and television producer, divided his time between Paris and Porquerolles; the second, after graduating in the United States, worked in film distribution for Gaumont and then for Fox; the third lived in Boston, where he was studying law. His relations with them were free of the turbulence that racked his ties to Marie-Jo. "He was a good father," they report.[102]

Simenon planned to leave all his property to his sons, beginning with the estate in Epalinges, which was still unsold. Contrary to his expectations, zoning regulations prevented it from being turned into a clinic, since it was located in a residential area.

In 1987–1988 the tax department estimated his fortune at some 3.5 million Swiss francs, not counting the property. But his real fortune was elsewhere, in an apartment in Lausanne in which he had installed his secretariat and in which he never set foot. It was here that what he called the "Simenon factory" continued to work. He delegated full responsibility for it to Joyce Aitken.

Aitken had been hired as a secretary to Denyse in the early sixties, but since then she had become indispensable to him. He always called her by her last name, as in a Simenon novel, and she usually called him "Boss." She knew everything, saw everything, remembered everything. A rather exceptional instance of a working relationship based on trust and complicity. Aitken, whose husband was a lawyer, had Simenon's power of attorney and was executive director of his enterprise.

"Aitken takes care of my relations with television, and she does it perfectly. I therefore leave her a free hand, for she knows my principles better than anyone. I therefore approve what she decides," he told a friend.[103]

Simenon, Inc., did a booming business in the eighties. His novels continued to be translated worldwide. According to UNESCO's statistical directory for 1989, he is the eighteenth most translated author in the world. With eighty-seven translations in fifteen countries, he is the fourth most translated French-language author, behind Jules Verne, Charles Perrault, and René Goscinny, but ahead of Balzac, Dumas, and Stendhal. He is, of course, far and away the first among Belgians, well ahead of Hergé. People tend to forget that although he considered taking French, and later American, nationality, he ultimately insisted on remaining Belgian. When asked why, he replied with a witticism:

"Not everyone is lucky enough to be born in Liechtenstein or Monaco. Failing that, Belgian will do. Because it means nothing."[104]

In France itself he remained a strong-selling author even though readers knew there would never be any new titles. And despite his age, he had lost none of his commercial pugnacity. His correspondence with Claude Durand, chief executive officer of Fayard, shows that he consistently demanded the royalties due him for his old pseudonymous pulp novels, however small they were.

Some efforts were even made to woo him away from his publisher, just like in the old days. In 1987, when the Presses de la Cité group was about to change ownership, two Paris publishers who were friends of his paid a visit and tried to convince him to abandon ship surreptitiously, taking the rights to about thirty of his mass-market paperbacks with him. Simenon let them go on for a long time before reminding them that it was a principle of his to have just one publisher in each language. Then he stood up, restated his loyalty to the memory of his old friend Sven Nielsen, and proposed a toast: to the future of Presses de la Cité.

Despite all this, books had long ceased to be his main source of income. Publishing's share of the turnover of Simenon, Inc., had declined steadily, while remaining at an absolute level most authors would envy.

Since the sixties, television and the movies had taken first place. Not a week went by without some producer, somewhere in the world, requesting an option or buying film rights. The profits went far beyond those brought in by the sale of his books, despite the diversity of titles, new levies of readers, and the international audience.

There were a spate of Maigrets on the small screen. Millions of viewers identified the inspector with a particular actor: Jean Richard in France, Rupert Davies in Britain (Simenon's favorite by far), Gino Cervi in Italy, Heinz Ruhmann in West Germany, Jan Teuling in Holland. In 1966, when fourteen of his publishers and four television Maigrets gathered in Delfzijl, Holland, for the unveiling of a statue of the inspector, the photograph immortalizing the event showed the author surrounded not by publishers but by actors.

A new generation of filmmakers brought Simenon works to the screen, some remaining faithful to the original novels, others not: Claude Chabrol, Pierre Granier-Deferre, Bertrand Tavernier. Their predecessors were still on the scene as well. Renoir, increasingly obsessed by the preservation of his films and negatives as death drew near, was moved by his reading of *Il y a encore des noisetiers* (1969), identifying so closely with the hero that he wanted not only to make the film but also to play the leading role—at the age of seventy-five.[105] Marcel Carné, also in his seventies, sent Jean Gabin a script based on a Simenon novel. There was a perfect role in it for Gabin as a bistro owner, but by common agreement they abandoned the project, put off by the cinema's "frenzied consumption" of Simenon's work.[106]

The price of glory, as they say. Yet it is striking that many filmmakers, after paying dearly for the rights to Simenon novels, emptied the books of their substance when it came time to do a script. One paradox among many.

Simenon didn't care. As long as he was paid what was due him, it mattered little what was done to his books on the screen. Had he had any input, he would have expressed his deepest cinematic wish: to see Charles Aznavour, an unforgettable Kachoudas in *Les Fantômes du chapelier,* in the title role of *Le Petit Homme d'Arkhangelsk.* But since no one asked for his opinion, he kept it to himself, content to be the French-language novelist most often adapted for the screen, with fifty-five films in his portfolio and more to come.

1989: While repairs are being made to his home, Simenon spends several months in a suite in Lausanne's luxurious Hotel Beau Rivage, room 416. Whether you come by the stairs or the elevator, you need a special key to get in. He no longer walks, but rides in a wheelchair. Various operations over the past few years have eroded his intellect. His memory is spotty. He seems paralyzed on the left side. His cheek is swollen, his leg and arm immobile, his hand shriveled.

He listens attentively. Talks less and less. Now and then there are flashes.

Teresa acts as interpreter. She is his voice, and she remembers for both of them.

His pipes are neatly lined up. He still smokes constantly. The pipe is packed for him, the match struck. It takes time for him to bring the two together. His eyes are clear behind his glasses. His pipe in his mouth, a sly smile on his lips, he looks out at the boats on the lake, waiting for his walk.

He misses the atmosphere of the bistros. In the afternoon, he is taken by car or in his chair to the lakeshore. But there are too many stairways everywhere. Simenon pulls over in front of a café, hails a waiter who brings a beer to his car. He drinks it, pays, and is driven off. It would not have tasted the same in his hotel suite.

Tigy died not long ago in Porquerolles, at the age of eighty-five. They had remained very good friends. He had given her the house in Nieul, where she was a wonderful single grandmother to all the Simenon children and grandchildren.

Teresa's discretion, devotion, and simplicity help to soothe the anxieties of his retirement, as the children know better than anyone else.

"Without her I'd be dead," he tells them. "I have a piece under the bed, and I would have used it."[107]

Georges Simenon died at three-thirty in the morning on September 4, 1989. To spare his children what he went through when his own father died, he had asked that they not be told of his death until everything was all over. In accordance with his wish, he was cremated. Better flames than worms. He had organized it all, anticipating everything except the indiscretion of a municipal employee. The daily newspaper *La Suisse* announced the news prematurely, and the children heard on the radio a bulletin that would make front pages around the world the next day.

By night, shielded from prying eyes, Teresa hastily scattered his ashes in the garden, mixing them with his daughter's. He had died as he had dreamed of dying: old.

NOTES

Abbreviations

The formula "... to ..." indicates a letter. Most of the letters cited are unpublished.

Unless otherwise indicated, the city of publication is Paris.

ACGD Archives of Catherine Gide-Desvignes
ADV Departmental Archives of the Vendée
AEF Archives of Editions Fayard
AEG Archives of Editions Gallimard
AFB Archives of Fenton Bresler
AFD Archives of Frédéric Dard
AHW Archives of Helen Wolff
AMB Archives of Maurice Bessy
AMD Archives of Maurice Dumoncel
AMFAE Archives of the French Ministry of Foreign Affairs
AMG Archives of Maurice Garçon
AMI Archives of the French Ministry of the Interior
AN French National Archives
APSL Simenon's Private Archives in Lausanne
BN Bibliothèque Nationale
CDJC Centre de Documentation juive contemporaine
FSUL Fonds Simenon of the University of Liège
GS Georges Simenon
TS *Tout Simenon*
n.d. no date

Titles not preceded by an author's name refer to books by Georges Simenon. *Tout Simenon* (TS) is the twenty-five-volume edition of Simenon's works published by Presses de la Cité in its Omnibus collection. Most references to Simenon's novels are taken from this source.

Unless otherwise indicated, verbal testimony taken by the author was collected between 1989 and 1992. Certain quotations and information in Chapter 20 are unattributed, since the sources wished to remain anonymous.

Preface

1. Testimony of Federico Fellini, quoted by Claude Gauteur in *Simenon au cinéma* (Hatier, 1991).
2. GS to Doringe, September 28, 1954, APSL.

1: Altar Boy 1903–1919

1. *Je suis resté un enfant de chœur*, p. 52.
2. *Pedigree*, TS 2, p. 507.
3. See "Le Témoignage de l'enfant de chœur," written in 1946, TS 2; GS, "Le vélo de l'enfant de chœur," in *Gringoire*, Paris, March 21, 1940; Jean-Christophe Camus, "Une enquete judiciare sur Simenon enfant," in *La Libre Belgique*, March 19, 1990.
4. GS, interviewed by Jean Carlier, *Combat*, Paris, October 20, 1952.
5. GS, interview, *L'Illustré*, March 1967.
6. Ibid.
7. Ibid.
8. GS to his aunt, August 2, 1914, FSUL.
9. Memories of Pol d'Arzis, in *Le pays liégeois*, December 9, 1936.
10. *Je me souviens.*
11. GS, interview, Swiss radio and television, 1982.
12. Mathieu Rutten, *Simenon, ses origines, sa*

vie, son œuvre (Eugène Wahle, Nandrin, 1986).

13. GS, interview, *Patriote illustré*, Brussels, no. 46, November 12, 1967; GS interviewed by Andrivos, France-Culture.
14. *Des traces de pas*, p. 60.
15. *La Main*, TS 14, p. 288.
16. *Le Fils*, TS 9, pp. 9 and 13.
17. *L'Horloger d'Everton*, TS 7, p. 524. *Vent du nord*, pp. 8–9.
18. *L'Horloger d'Everton*, TS 7, p. 523.
19. *De la cave au grenier*, pp. 175–77.
20. Rutten, pp. 78–145.
21. *L'homme qui regardait passer les trains*, TS 21, p. 652; *Je me souviens, Pedigree, Lettre à ma mère* (p. 25), etc.
22. Rutten, p. 116.
23. *Mémoires intimes*, p. 339.
24. John Raymond, *Simenon in Court* (Hamish Hamilton, London, 1968), p. 178.
25. *La Main*, TS 14, p. 269.
26. *Lettre à ma mère*, pp. 10, 14, 122.
27. GS, interview, France-Culture.
28. GS, interview, *Médecine et hygiène*, Geneva, no. 828-bis, June 5, 1968.
29. GS, interviewed by his Russian translator, Eléonore Schraiber, Epalinges, July 1967, FSUL.
30. GS, interviewed by Andrivos, France-Culture.
31. Rutten, p. 158.
32. Fenton Bresler, *L'Enigme Georges Simenon* (Balland, 1985), pp. 29–30; *The Mystery of Georges Simenon* (Stein and Day, New York, 1985), pp. 24–25.
33. GS to Jean Mambrino, November 7, 1951, FSUL.
34. GS, interview, *Médecine et hygiène*.
35. Ibid.
36. Henri Guillemin, *Parcours* (Seuil, 1989), pp. 221–22.

2: Cub Reporter *1919–1922*

1. GS to André Gide, n.d. (probably April 1939), reproduced in Francis Lacassin and Gilbert Sigaux, *Simenon* (Plon, 1973), p. 409.
2. GS to André Gide, n.d. (probably January 1939), reproduced in Lacassin and Sigaux.
3. *Mémoires intimes*, p. 10.
4. Francis Lacassin, *Conversations avec Georges Simenon* (La Sirène/Alpen, Geneva, 1990).
5. GS interviewed by Francis Lacassin, reproduced in Georges Simenon, *A la découverte de la France*, UGE 10/18, 1976, pp. 12–14; Jean-Christophe Camus, *Simenon avant Simenon, les années de journalisme, 1919–1922*, vol. 1 (Didier-Hatier, Brussels, 1989), pp. 28–29; GS, interview, RTB, 1979.
6. Rutten, p. 78.
7. Camus, vol. 1, p. 46.
8. Claude Menguy, "Bibliographie des articles et reportages de Georges Simenon," in *Cahiers Simenon*, no. 4 (Les Amis de Georges Simenon, Brussels, 1990).
9. Georges Sim, "Impressions," in *Gazette de Liège*, July 15, 1919.
10. GS to Federico Fellini, November 24, 1976, FSUL.
11. "Un hotel mis en sac place de la République française," in *Gazette de Liège*, July 27, 1919.
12. "Les coulisses de la police," series published in *Paris-Soir*, January 26–February 11, 1934, and reprinted in *A la découverte de la France*, pp. 146–49.
13. *Destinées*, pp. 77, 78.
14. GS, interview, the program *Du coq à l'âne*, April 21, 1979.
15. GS interviewed by Victor Moremans, RTB, October 1969.
16. *Gazette de Liège*, March 9, 1920.
17. Ibid., March 10 and April 29, 1920. The comparison of Simenon's versions of the "Foch interview" was first done by Jean-Christophe Camus, pp. 123–27.
18. *Gazette de Liège*, October 14, 15, and 20, 1921.
19. Maurice Monnoyer, *Trois heures avec Simenon, chez l'auteur* (Montpellier, 1989), p. 35.
20. GS, article in *Le Courrier royal*, May 16, 1936.
21. Camus, vol. 1, pp. 115–16.
22. Christian Delcourt, *Un jeune reporter dans la guerre des journeaux liégeois, Georges Sim* (A. Vecqueray, Liège, 1977).
23. *Gazette de Liège*, August 4–5, 1921.
24. Ibid., August 10, 1921.
25. Ibid.
26. Ibid., September 8, 1921.

27. Ibid., September 22, 1921.
28. Ibid., October 6, 1921.
29. Ibid., September 1, 1921.
30. Ibid., October 6, 1921.
31. Ibid., April 15, 1919, cited by Corinne Forir, *La Question du mandat anglais en Palestine devant l'opinion liégeoise 1919–1923*, Mémoire d'histoire (University of Liège, 1981–1982), p. 53.
32. *Gazette de Liège*, August 20–21, 1922, cited by Forir, p. 63.
33. Ibid., cited by Camus, vol. 1, p. 141.
34. Forir, pp. 58 and 59.
35. Norman Cohn, *Histoire d'un mythe. La "Conspiration" juive et les Protocoles des Sages de Sion* (Gallimard 1967; reprint, Folio, 1992); *Les Protocoles des Sages de Sion. Introduction à l'étude des Protocoles, un faux et ses usages dans le siècle,* by Pierre-André Taguieff, vol. 1 (Berg International, 1992), pp. 39–44.
36. André Kaspi, "Henry Ford, roi de l'automobile," in *L'Histoire,* no. 136, Paris, September 1990; *Les Protocoles des Sages de Sion,* vol. 2, "Les Protocoles en Grande-Bretagne et aux USA," by Jean-François Moisan, pp. 165–216.
37. Forir, pp. 50, 51, 64–66.
38. *The Times,* August 16, 17, 18, 1921.
39. *Destinées,* p. 36.
40. Ibid., p. 37.
41. *Pedigree,* TS 2, p. 701.
42. GS to Jean-Christophe Camus, September 6, 1985, in Camus, vol.1, preface.
43. GS to Jean-Christophe Camus, August 27, 1985, in Camus, vol.1, p. 215.
44. *Revue sincère,* no. 7, April 15, 1923.
45. Georges Sim, *Un monsieur libidineux* (Prima, 1927), p. 57.
46. Christian Brulls (GS), *La Jeune Fille aux perles* (1932; reprint, Julliard, 1991), pp. 51 and 55.
47. Gaston Viallis (GS), *Lili-Sourire* (Ferenczi, 1930), pp. 6–9.
48. Georges Sim, *Deuxième Bureau* (Tallandier, 1933).
49. *Pietr-le-Letton,* TS 16, p. 394.
50. *Le Fou de Bergerac,* TS 17, pp. 498–500.
51. *Pietr-le-Letton,* TS 16, p. 394.
52. Charlotte Wardi, *Le Juif dans le roman français 1933–1948* (Nizet, 1973).
53. *Le Petit Homme d'Arkhangelsk,* TS 8, p. 651.
54. Charlotte Wardi, "Les 'petits juifs' de Georges Simenon," in *Travaux de linguistique et de littérature* (Centre de philologie et de littérature romanes, University of Strasbourg, 1974), XII, 2, p. 242.
55. "Le Petit Tailleur et le chapelier," TS 4. This short story, written in 1947, was the first version of *Les Fantômes du chapelier,* a novel written in 1948.
56. Chaïm Raphaël, "Simenon on the Jews," in *Midstream,* New York, January 1981, vol. 27, no. 1.
57. Wladimir Rabi, article in *La Terre retrouvée,* November 15, 1957.
58. "Europe 33," in *Voilà,* March 18–April 29, 1933, nos. 104 to 110; "Peuples qui ont faim," in *Le Jour,* April 4 to May 8, 1934; "Mare Nostrum," in *Marianne,* June 27, 1934. All these articles are collected in GS, *A la rencontre des autres,* UGE 10/18, 1989, pp. 152, 244, 336.
59. Maurice Einhorn, "De l'antisémitisme dans la littérature belge," in *Regards,* Brussels, no. 52, 1982.
60. GS to Chaïm Raphaël, January 13, 1981, APSL.
61. GS, speech in New York, 1945, reprinted in *The French Review,* February 1946, and in GS, *L'Age du roman* (Complexe, Brussels, 1988), pp. 35–70.
62. Olga Magnée, in *La Lanterne,* Brussels, September 7, 1989.
63. GS, in collaboration with Henri-J. Moers, *Le Bouton de col,* unpublished manuscript drafted in 1921 or 1922, FSUL. Quoted by Michel Lemoine, *L'Autre Univers de Simenon,* Editions du CLPCF (Liège, 1991), p. 51.
64. GS, reply to *Libération,* Paris, 1984, reprinted in Daniel Rondeau and Jean-François Fogel, *Pourquoi écrivez-vous?* (Le Livre de Poche, 1988), p. 48.

3: Budding Writer *1921–1922*

1. Camus, vol. 1, pp. 161–67.
2. Michel Lemoine, "Images de journalistes dans l'œuvre romanesque de Simenon," in *Cahiers Simenon,* no. 4 (Les Amis de Georges Simenon, Brussels, 1990), p. 37.
3. GS, "Mon premier rendez-vous avec l'art," in *La Meuse,* October 14, 1953.

4. Rutten, p. 59.
5. *Un homme comme un autre*, p. 19.
6. GS to Sven Nielsen, July 29, 1959, APSL.
7. Camus, vol. 1, p. 172.
8. Lemoine, *L'Autre Univers de Simenon*, p. 18.
9. Camus, vol. 1, p. 174.
10. *Au pont des Arches* was eventually republished by Editions Libro-Sciences (Liège-Brussels) in a facsimile edition, in a private run. Another edition, aimed at the broader public and also including *Jehan Pinaguet* and *Les Ridicules* was published by Presses de la Cité in spring 1991, in other words, after the author's death.
11. Article by GS, *Gazette de Liège*, May 9, 1952, quoted by Michel Lemoine in *L'Autre Univers de Simenon*.
12. *On dit que j'ai soixante-quinze ans*, p. 53.
13. *Jehan Pinaguet* (Julliard, 1991), pp. 73, 75.
14. *Les Ridicules* (Julliard, 1991).
15. Camus, vol. 1, pp. 187, 188.
16. Lemoine, *L'Autre Univers de Simenon*, pp. 24–26.
17. *Un homme comme un autre*, p. 258.
18. Roger Stéphane, *Portrait-souvenir de Georges Simenon* (Quai Voltaire, 1989), p. 66.
19. *Mémoires intimes*, p. 14.
20. *L'Âne rouge*, TS 18, p. 625.
21. GS, interview, Swiss television, 1975.
22. *De la cave au grenier*, p. 177.
23. *Le Fils*, TS 9, p. 21.
24. GS, interview, in *Nos Forces*, Brussels, March 15, 1962.
25. *Vent du nord*, pp. 49, 50.
26. Camus, pp. 195, 196.
27. *La Danseuse du Gai-Moulin*, TS 17, p. 59.
28. Jacques Dubois (collective), *Lire Simenon* (Nathan-Labor, Brussels, 1980), p. 23.
29. *Le Fils*, TS 19, p. 12.
30. GS, in *Voilà*, Brussels, May 2, 1941.
31. Michel Lemoine, *Liège dans l'œuvre de Simenon* (Faculté ouverte, Liège, 1989), p. 51.
32. Pol Vandromme, *Georges Simenon* (Pierre de Méyère, Brussels, 1962), p. 11.
33. Bernard Alavoine, *Les Sensations et l'atmosphère dans les romans de Georges Simenon* (doctoral thesis, University of Picardie, 1981), p. 73.

4: Crossing the Line
1922–1924

1. *Au-delà de ma porte-fenêtre*, p. 98.
2. Testimony of GS, in *La Meuse*, October 14, 1953.
3. GS to Jean Hélion, November 17, 1964, private archives of Jacqueline Hélion.
4. Jean Hélion, *Choses revues*, unpublished manuscript, 1984, archives of Jacqueline Hélion.
5. *L'Aîné des Ferchaux*, Folio, pp. 28, 29, 31.
6. *Destinées*, pp. 112, 113.
7. Luc Dorsan (GS), *Grande Clementine*, 1928, quoted by Michel Lemoine, *L'Autre Univers de Simenon*.
8. *Le Soir*, March 21, 1952.
9. GS, interview, *L'Expansion*, no. 38, February 1971; Stanley Eskin, *Simenon* (Presses de la Cité, 1990), February 1971.
10. Entry "Binet-Valmer," in Prevost and Roman d'Amat, *Dictionnaire de biographie française* (Letouzey, 1954); André de Fouquières, *Mon Paris et les Parisiens* (T.V., Pierre Horay, 1959), p. 62; Pierre Sipriot, *Montherlant sans masque*, vol. 1 (Robert Laffont, 1982), pp. 218, 220, 234.
11. GS to Jacques Péricard, January 2, 1939, APSL.
12. *Destinées*, p. 44.
13. Antoine Prost, *Les Anciens Combattants et la société française, 1914–1939* (Presses de la Fondation nationale des Sciences politiques, 1977).
14. Fouquières, p. 62.
15. Prost.
16. Georges Sim, in *La Revue sincère*, no. 6, March 15, 1923, reprinted in GS, *Portrait-souvenir de Balzac* (Christian Bourgois, 1991), pp. 81, 82.
17. GS, interview, *Le Patriote illustré*, Brussels, 1968.
18. *Les Noces de Poitiers*, (Gallimard, 1946), p. 60. See also pp. 39–48, 76.
19. *Les Noces de Poitiers*, pp. 34, 37.
20. *Mémoies intimes*, p. 17.
21. Ibid., pp. 17, 18.
22. Ibid., p. 12.
23. GS to his mother, n.d. (probably 1923), APSL.
24. Ibid.
25. *Mémoires intimes*, p. 16.
26. GS, unidentified radio interview.

27. *Deuxième Bureau.*
28. Testimony of the Marquis Claude de Tracy (son of Raymond de Tracy), to the author, and a visit to the site by the author.
29. This portrait of the Marquis de Tracy is based on testimony given to the author by his son.
30. GS interviewed by Charles-Henri Tauxe, *Georges Simenon, de l'humain au vide, essai de micropsychanalyse appliquée* (Buchet-Chastel, 1983).
31. GS interviewed by Robert and Rosine Georgin, RTBF, 1979, reprinted in *Simenon* (L'Age d'homme, Lausanne, 1980).
32. *Les Noces de Poitiers,* pp. 67, 68.
33. Ibid.
34. Ibid., January 17, 1924.
35. Ibid., March 16, 1924.
36. Ibid., March 12, 1924.
37. Ibid., March 24, 1924.
38. Ibid., March 2, 1924.
39. Testimony of Claude de Tracy to the author.
40. Ibid.
41. *Mémoires intimes,* p. 19.
42. GS, interviewed by Richard Cobb, *People and Places* (Oxford University Press, Oxford, 1985), pp. 93–101.
43. *Deuxième Bureau.*
44. *M. Gallet, décédé,* TS 16, p. 65.
45. Jean du Perry (GS), *L'Heureuse Fin,* 1925, pp. 14–15, quoted by Michel Lemoine, *L'Autre Univers de Simenon,* pp. 33, 34.
46. *Le Passage de la ligne,* TS 9, p. 688.
47. Ibid., pp. 620, 672, 720.
48. Ibid., p. 721.

5: Into the Whirlwind
1924–1927

1. *Destinées,* p. 114.
2. GS to his mother, n.d. (around 1924), APSL.
3. Ibid.
4. APSL.
5. *La Revue sincère,* April 15, 1923.
6. Ibid., May 15, 1923.
7. Ibid.
8. Ibid., June 15, 1923.
9. Ibid., July 15, 1923.
10. Ibid. All these portraits are reprinted in Lacassin-Sigaux, pp. 302–308.
11. Jean du Perry (GS), *Pour le sauver* (Ferenczi, 1925), quoted by Michel Lemoine, *L'Autre Univers de Simenon,* pp. 44–46.
12. Stanley Eskin, p. 80.
13. GS interviewed by Jean-Louis Ezine, *Les Nouvelles littéraires,* February 16, 1978.
14. Jean Hélion, notebook no. 40, June 3–4, 1958, unpublished. Archives of Jacqueline Hélion.
15. Maurice Martin du Gard, "Colette au *Matin,*" in *La Parisienne,* November 1954.
16. Roger Stéphane, p. 71.
17. Ibid.
18. *Destinées,* p. 114.
19. GS to Mauricio Restrepo, January 4, 1954, FSUL.
20. *Destinées,* p. 79.
21. Ibid., pp. 78–81. GS, interview, *Le Figaro,* April 7, 1938.
22. Distinction established by Michel Lemoine, "Quand Georges Sim préparait Simenon," in *La Revue nouvelle,* Brussels, 1991, pp. 46–47.
23. GS, "L'aventure est morte," speech in Pleyel hall, 1938.
24. Ibid.
25. Michel Lemoine, *L'Autre Univers de Simenon,* pp. 165, 304.
26. Francis Lacassin, *Conversations avec Simenon.*
27. Brendan Gill, *A New York Life: Of Friends and Others* (Poseidon Press, New York, 1990), pp. 231–52.
28. *Un monsieur libidineux,* pp. 62–63.
29. *Les Petits Hommes,* p. 76.
30. GS to Sven Nielsen, February 21, 1949, APSL.
31. Lemoine, "Quand Georges Sim préparait Simenon," p. 54.
32. GS to André Gide, n.d. (probably January 1939), FSUL.
33. *Mémoires intimes,* p. 25.
34. Interview with Mme Bonnot, secretary to GS, on his beginnings, in *Le Progrès de Lyon,* December 21, 1963.
35. *Mémoires intimes,* p. 259.
36. Ibid., p. 139.
37. Ibid., p. 107.
38. GS, speech in New York, reprinted in GS, *L'Âge du roman* (Complexe, Brussels, 1988), pp. 35–69.
39. Unpublished notebook, APSL.

40. AEF.
41. Interview with Fernand Brouty, in *Les Nouvelles littéraires,* July 30, 1953.
42. Max Favalelli, "J'ai vu naître Simenon," in *Gazette des Lettres,* October 15, 1950.
43. Lemoine, *L'Autre Univers de Simenon,* p. 266.
44. Testimony of Maurice Dumoncel, son of Rémy Dumoncel, to the author.
45. GS to Maurice Dumoncel, February 3, 1953, AMD.
46. *Paris-Soir,* June 5, 1925.
47. GS to Mauricio Restrepo, November 1, 1953, FSUL.
48. GS interviewed by Eléanore Schraiber, July 1967, FSUL.
49. Claude Arnaud, "Auteur du Bœuf sur le Toit," in Olivier Barrot and Pascal Ory, *Entre-deux-guerres* (François Bourin, 1990), pp. 289–314.
50. Florent Fels, *Voilà* (Fayard, 1957).
51. *Point-Virgule.*
52. GS, interviewed by Eléanore Schraiber.
53. Jean-Claude Klein, "La Revue nègre," in Barrot and Ory, pp. 365–77.
54. Article signed Georges Sim in *Le Merle rose,* 1928, reprinted in full in Lacassin, *Conversations avec Simenon,* pp. 136–39.
55. Phyllis Rose, *Josephine Baker* (Fayard, 1990), pp. 149, 150.
56. Testimony of Tigy to Fenton Bresler, in *l'Enigme Georges Simenon* (Balland, 1985), pp. 74–75.
57. *Mémoires intimes,* p. 24.
58. Lemoine, *L'Autre Univers de Simenon,* pp. 116, 141; Jean-Christophe Camus, *Simenon avant Simenon, les années parisiennes, 1923–1931,* vol. 2 (Dider-Hatier, 1990), pp. 122–32.
59. Quoted by Lemoine, *L'Autre Univers de Simenon,* p. 48.
60. Henri Jeanson, *Soixante-dix ans d'adolescence* (Stock, 1961), pp. 141–44; Pierre Lazareff, *Dernière Édition* (Brentano's, New York); *Le Crapouillot,* November 1938; *Destinées,* p. 83; Lacassin, *Conversations avec Simenon;* GS interviewed by Henri-Charles Tauxe; Jean-Christophe Camus, vol. 2, pp. 100–109.
61. *Deuxième Bureau, Les Forçats de Paris, Les Quatre Jours du pauvre homme,* quoted by Camus, vol. 2, pp. 104–105.
62. Raymond Barillon, *Le Cas Paris-Soir* (Armand Colin, 1959).
63. Jeanson, pp. 144–45.
64. Lacassin, *Conversations avec Simenon.*
65. Contract, FSUL, reprinted in ibid., p. 141.
66. FSUL.
67. *Les Nouvelles littéraires,* February 8, 1927; *La Wallonie,* February 8, 1927; *La Fronde,* February 4, 1927.
68. *Paris-Midi,* February 6, 1927.
69. *La Petite Gironde,* February 16, 1927.
70. *La Wallonie,* February 8, 1927.
71. *Le Canard enchaîné,* February 23, 1927, reprinted in full in Camus, vol. 2, p. 118. (The article is dated February 12, 1927.)
72. *Le Soir,* February 27, 1927.
73. *L'Intransigeant,* February 14, 1927, reprinted in full in Camus, vol. 2, p. 120.
74. GS interviewed by Marcel Sauvage, in *La Tribune de Lausanne,* August 17, 1958.
75. Youki Desnos, *Les Confidences de Youki* (Fayard, 1957), pp. 26–27.
76. André Warnod, *Drôle d'époque* (Fayard, 1960), pp. 40–42.
77. Fels, *Voilà,* p. 162.
78. *Vendredi,* November 17, 1938.
79. *Histoire de l'Edition française,* p. 514.

6: Waiting for Maigret
1928–1931

1. *Le Merle blanc,* February 5, 1927 (or 1928).
2. GS to Federico Fellini, January 3, 1977, FSUL.
3. GS to Henry Miller, August 3, 1954, FSUL.
4. GS, "Une France inconnue ou l'Aventure entre deux berges," in *Vu,* July 1, 1931, reprinted in *A la découverte de la France,* UGE 10/18, 1987, pp. 33–64.
5. GS to Jean Vigo, September 1933, in Jean Vigo, *Œuvre de cinéma* (La cinémathèque française/Lherminier, 1985).
6. *Sporting,* February 16, 1931.
7. GS to his mother, n.d., APSL.
8. GS, "Une France inconnue," p. 63.
9. *Mémoires intimes,* pp. 27–28.
10. GS, "Escales nordiques," in *Le Petit Journal,* March 1–12, 1931, reprinted in GS, *A la rencontre des autres,* UGE 10/18, pp. 15–18.

11. GS, "La naissance de Maigret," preface to *Œuvres complètes* (Rencontre, Lausanne, 1967–1973); *Je suis resté un enfant de chœur.*

12. GS, interview, *La Semaine,* July 12, 1942.

13. Christian Brulls (GS), *L'Amant sans nom* (Fayard, 1929), pp. 57 and 228, quoted by Claude Menguy and Pierre Deligny, "Les vrais débuts du commissaire Maigret," in *Races,* University of Liège, no. 1, 1989, pp. 28–30.

14. Michel Lemoine, "Maigret en gestation dans les romans populaires," in *Traces,* University of Liège, no. 1, 1989, pp. 61–65.

15. GS to Mauricio Restrepo, October 6, 1953, FSUL.

16. Robert Vellerut, "Supplément aux *Mémoires* de Maigret," unpublished, FSUL.

17. GS-Georges Kessel correspondence (several letters), 1929, APSL.

18. Georges Sadoul to GS, December 13, 1928, APSL.

19. Georges Sadoul to GS, February 19, 1929, APSL.

20. Georges Sadoul to GS, March 26, 1929, APSL.

21. Contracts dated April 15, 1929; July 15, 1928; and October 15, 1928, respectively, AEF.

22. Contracts of September 30, 1929; July 30 1929; September 18, 1929; June 14, 1930; and May 26, 1930, AEF.

23. GS recounted his conversations with Arthème Fayard on many occasions, in various forms, which I have synthesized, trying to eliminate the contradictions. For example: GS interviewed by Eléanore Schraiber; Carlo Rim, pp. 74, 75; GS to Sven Nielsen, February 28, 1950, APSL; Max Favalleli interviewed by France-Culture; GS interviewed by André Bourin, France-Culture; GS, speech in New York, pp. 57–58.

24. Testimony of Robert Toussaint to the author. (Mr. Toussaint went to work for Fayard in 1934 and later became the production manager and then the general secretary.)

25. Menguy and Deligny, "Les vrais débuts," pp. 37–40.

26. Pierre Boileau and Thomas Narcejac, *Tandem ou trente-cinq ans de suspense* (Denoël, 1986).

27. GS, speech in New York, pp. 56–57.

28. Article by Frédéric Lefèvre, *La République,* February 16, 1931; GS, interview, *Bulletin de Paris,* June 21, 1956; GS, interview, *Les Nouvelles littéraires,* December 30, 1966.

29. Testimony of Georges Charensol to the author.

30. GS interviewed by Georges Charensol, *Les Nouvelles littéraires,* August 22, 1931.

31. GS to André Gide, January 15, 1939, FSUL; Roger Stéphane, p. 78.

32. Gilles Henry, *Commissaire Maigret, qui êtes-vous?* (Plon, 1977), pp. 9–10.

33. GS, interview, *Le Havre,* March 18, 1952.

34. Stéphane, p. 107.

35. Testimony of GS to Fenton Bresler, p. 116.

36. GS, interview, *Comœdia,* October 10, 1933.

37. Pierre Boileau, "Quelque chose de changé dans le roman policier," in Lacassin and Sigaux, pp. 190–91.

38. Thomas Narcejac, *Le Cas Simenon* (Presses de la Cité, 1957), p. 22.

39. GS to Mauricio Restrepo, October 6, 1953, FSUL.

40. Carlo Rim, *Mémoires d'une vieille vague* (1961; reprint, Ramsay-Poche-Cinema, 1990), p. 75.

7: *Simenon Makes His Movie 1931–1932*

1. Carlo Rim, p. 77.

2. Paul Colin, *La Croûte, souvenirs* (La Table Rond, 1957).

3. *Paris-Midi,* February 21, 1931; *Paris-Soir,* February 22, 1931.

4. Ibid.

5. Rim, pp. 77–78.

6. *Paris-Soir; Candide,* February 26, 1931.

7. Pierre Descaves, *Européen,* February 25, 1931.

8. Georges Ravon, *Le Figaro,* February 23, 1931.

9. *Cyrano,* March 1, 1931.

10. *Le Canard enchaîné,* February 25, 1931.

11. GS, radio interview, 1952, rebroadcast by France-Culture. Stéphane.

12. *L'Œil de Paris,* March 28, 1931.

13. FSUL.
14. André Levinson, "Remarques nouvelles sur le roman policier," in *Radio-Magazine,* March 29, 1931; *D'Artagnan,* September 5, 1931; *Le Coup de patte,* September 19, 1931.
15. Lucien Farnoux-Reynaud, *Le Crapouillot,* April 1931.
16. GS, interview, *L'Eclaireur de Nice,* February 4, 1932.
17. *L'Antenne,* March 1, 1931.
18. *L'Eclaireur de Nice,* February 4, 1932.
19. Odette Pannetier, "Georges Simenon, candidat explorateur," in *Candide,* June 16, 1932.
20. *Les Nouvelles littéraires,* August 22, 1931.
21. J. K. Raymond-Millet, "Georges Simenon ou la naissance d'un romancier," in *Le Courrier cinématographique,* June 21, 1931.
22. Ibid.
23. GS–Jacques Haumont correspondence. Several letters between April 13, 1931, and September 14, 1931, APSL.
24. *L'Œil de Paris,* August 15, 1931.
25. GS–Haumont corresponence; Nino Frank, "Hypothèse à propos de Maigret," in Lacassin and Sigaux, p. 193.
26. *Vacances obligatoires,* p. 140.
27. GS to Man Ray, September 1931, APSL.
28. AEF.
29. GS to Fernand Brouty, December 2, 1931, AEF and APSL.
30. GS to Fernand Brouty, November 6, 1931, AEF; Fernand Brouty to GS, November 21, 1931.
31. Fernand Brouty to GS, December 31, 1931, AEF.
32. Curtis Brown to GS, April 21, 1931, APSL.
33. *The New Yorker,* October 24, 1931.
34. Articles cited by Camus, vol. 2, pp. 78–80.
35. GS to Fernand Brouty, December 28, 1931, AEF.
36. Contract of October 31, 1931, AEF.
37. GS to Jean Tarride, n.d., APSL.
38. Contract of October 31, 1931, AEF and FSUL.
39. Célia Bertin, *Jean Renoir* (Perrin, 1986), pp. 121–24.
40. Jean Renoir, *Ma vie et mes films* (Flammarion, 1974), pp. 106–107.
41. GS, article in *Paris-Soir,* April 16, 1932.
42. Bertin, pp. 121–24.
43. GS, article in *Paris-Soir,* April 16, 1932.
44. Pierre Braunberger, *Cinémamémoire* (CNC/Centre Pompidou, 1987), p. 89.
45. Renoir, pp. 106–107.
46. *Les Cahiers de la cinémathèque,* no. 26–27, 1979.
47. Testimony of GS to Fenton Bresler, p. 122.
48. GS interviewed by Maurice Piron and Robert Sacré, September 20, 1982, FSUL.
49. Ibid.
50. *La Revue française,* May 15, 1932.
51. Renoir, *Ma vie et mes films,* p. 107.
52. Ibid.
53. GS interviewed by Robert Sadoul, Radio-Lausanne, July-August 1957.
54. GS, interview, *Paris-Midi,* April 19, 1932.
55. Ewa Bérad, *La Vie tumultueuse de Ilia Ehrenbourg* (Ramsay, 1991), p. 168.
56. *Cinémonde,* May 19, 1932.
57. *Point-Virgule.*
58. Carlo Rim, p. 79.
59. *Mémoires intimes,* p. 299.
60. APSL.
61. GS to Charles Gouverneur Paulding, December 2, 1931. APSL.

8: Great Reporter, Failed Detective *1932–1935*

1. GS interviewed by Carlo Rim, in *Marianne,* January 3, 1934.
2. Testimony of Jacqueline Audaire, in *Sud-Ouest,* March 3, 1989.
3. *Marianne,* January 3, 1934.
4. Carlo Rim, p. 74.
5. Michel Georges-Michel, in *Aux écoutes,* November 25, 1933.
6. GS, "Le romancier," speech given in New York in 1945, pp. 54–55.
7. GS, "L'aventure est morte," speech at Pleyel hall, Paris.
8. GS, *A la rencontre des autres.*
9. Lemoine, "Quand Sim préparait Simenon," p. 74. Michel Lemoine, "Aventures exotiques dans les romans populaires de Georges Simenon," pp. 77–92.
10. Lacassin, *Conversations avec Georges Simenon.*
11. GS to Sven Nielsen, June 23, 1962, APSL.

12. Christian Simenon to his mother, n.d., APSL.
13. GS, interview, first television station, May 20, 1975.
14. GS, "L'heure du nègre," in *Voilà*, October 8 to November 12, 1932, reprinted in GS, *A la recherche de l'homme nu*, pp. 55, 106.
15. *A l'abri de notre arbre*, p. 132.
16. GS, "L'heure du nègre," in *A la recherche de l'homme nu*, pp. 55, 106.
17. Ibid., p. 70.
18. *Les Annales coloniales*, May 8, 1934.
19. *Marianne*, May 9, 1934.
20. *L'Intransigeant*, February 15, 1936.
21. GS, "Chez Trotski," in *Paris-Soir*, June 16, 1933.
22. GS, interview in *Fantasio*, December 16, 1933; GS, "Europe 33," in *Voilà*, April 22, 1933; GS, *A la rencontre des autres*, p. 149.
23. Ibid., p. 150.
24. *Mémoires intimes*, p. 529.
25. Pierre Broué, *Trotski* (Fayard, 1988).
26. Letter from Trotsky's secretary to GS June 4, 1933, and original text of the interview, FSUL.
27. GS, "Chez Trotski," in *Paris-Soir*, June 16 and 17, 1933, reprinted in *A la rencontre des autres*, p. 211.
28. GS, interviewed by Maurice Piron and Robert Sacré.
29. Ibid.
30. Henri Dubief, *Le Déclin de la IIIᵉ République* (Points-Seuil, 1976), p. 77.
31. Internal note, January 23, 1934; Affaire Stavisky-Prince. MI 25 377 and 25 378, AMI.
32. Claude Bellanger et al., *Histoire générale de la presse française* (PUF, 1972), pp. 521–27.
33. Lazareff, pp. 101–208.
34. According to Jacques Debû-Bridel, quoted by Eugène Weber, *L'Action française* (Fayard, 1985), p. 386.
35. GS to Jean Prouvost, April 23, 1934, APSL.
36. GS and H. Moers, *Le Bouton de col* (1921–1922), unpublished, quoted by Michel Lemoine, *L'Autre Univers de Simenon*, p. 25.
37. Albert Mambert, in *Le Radical de Marseille*, March 24, 1934.
38. Lazareff, pp. 191–208.
39. *Eastern Daily News*, March 26, 1934; *Daily Sketch*, March 26, 1934; *Daily Express*, March 20, 1934; *Irish Times*, March 21, 1934.
40. Jean Vertey, "Bistros du Paris d'aujourd'hui," in *Vendémiaire*, 1935.
41. Carlo Rim, "Maigret à l'œuvre," in *Marianne*, March 28, 1934.
42. Ibid.
43. *Destinées*, p. 84.
44. Interrogation of Lussats, March 28, 1934, by the examining magistrate, MI 25 362, cote 862, AMI.
45. *Le Huron*, September 6, 1934; *Le Populaire*, September 14, 1934.
46. Interrogation of Lussats.
47. Report of Inspector Bonny, March 27, 1934, MI 25 362 cote 789, AMI.
48. Philippe Lamour, *Le Cadran solaire* (Robert Laffont, 1980).
49. *Notre Temps*, May 25, 1934.
50. *Excelsior*, March 2, 1934.
51. *Mémoires de Georges Hainnaux, dit Jo-la-Terreur*, adapted by Maurice-Yvan Sicard (Nouvelles Editions latines, November 1934).
52. Lazareff.
53. Quoted by *Lu*, April 13, 1934.
54. *Destinées*, p. 85; GS, interview, in *Point de mire*, November 3, 1981; Tauxe, pp. 107–114.
55. Rim, *Mémoires*, pp. 80–87.
56. GS to Jean Prouvost, April 23, APSL.
57. Report of Inspector Guillaume, August 16, 1934, MI 25 365, AMI.
58. Testimony of Philippe Lamour to the author.
59. Director of the news service of *Paris-Soir* to the president of the union of journalists, November 23, 1934, APSL.
60. GS to Jean Prouvost, November 22, 1934, APSL.
61. Lazareff, pp. 191–208.
62. Articles collected in *A la recherche de l'homme nu*, pp. 107–278.
63. *Dictionnaire des mythes littéraires*, under the direction of Pierre Brunel (Editions du Rocher, 1988), pp. 1280–91.
64. André Parinaud, p. 410.
65. Contracts of June 3, June 8, and November 25, 1932, AEF.
66. APSL.
67. *La Nouvelle Revue des jeunes*, July 15, 1932.

9: A Novelist Among the Literati: *1935–1939*

1. Maurice de Vlaminck, *Portraits avant décès* (Flammarion, 1943), pp. 258–62.
2. GS to the Office des changes, March 22, 1948, APSL.
3. GS to Doringe, February 15 and 16, 1955, APSL.
4. Edmond Epardaud, in *Les Nouvelles littéraires,* April 17, 1937.
5. Angelo Brandis, *Histoire vécue d'un serviteur dévoué,* unpublished typed text, FSUL.
6. Angelo Brandis; Edmond Epardaud; Raoul Noilletas, in *Le République du Var,* August 9, 1955; *Paris-Soir,* September 23, 1937.
7. *Des traces de pas,* pp. 218–19.
8. Testimony of GS to Fenton Bresler, pp. 146–48.
9. Contract of October 18, 1933, AEG.
10. Louis-Daniel Hirsch to GS, October 15, 1937, APSL.
11. GS to Louis-Daniel Hirsch, October 19, 1937, APSL.
12. *La Nouvelle Revue française,* December 1937.
13. *Des traces de pas,* pp. 26, 27.
14. Jean-Jacques Gautier, in *L'Epoque,* January 19, 1938.
15. GS to the director of the Société des gens de lettres, November 20, 1938, AEG.
16. GS interviewed by Doringe, *Toute l'Edition,* February 8, 1938.
17. GS to Louis-Daniel Hirsch, November 5, 1935, APSL.
18. GS to Artine Artinian, October 28, 1938, Harry Ransom Humanities Research Center, University of Texas at Austin.
19. Lucien Descaves, in *L'Œuvre,* December 7, 1933.
20. Fonds Goncourt, Municipal Archives of Nancy.
21. Lucien Descaves, *Souvenirs d'un ours* (Editions de Paris, 1946).
22. Fonds Goncourt, Municipal Archives of Nancy.
23. GS to his mother, December 28, 1939, APSL.
24. Testimony of Viviane Carel-Fourrier to the author.
25. Fonds Goncourt, Municipal Archives of Nancy. Jacques Robichon, *Le Défi des Goncourt* (Denoël, 1975).
26. *Vendémaire,* October 7, 1936.
27. *Excelsior,* August 10, 1936; Michel Lemoine, "Evolution et parentés littéraires de Simenon selon la critique de 1931 à 1935," in *Traces,* University of Liège, no. 3, 1991, pp. 75, 84–89, 106, 107, 119; Michel Lemoine, "Simenon face à la critique de 1936 à 1940: jugements et rapprochements," in *Cahiers Simenon,* no. 5, Les Amis de Georges Simenon, Brussels, 1991.
28. Michel Lemoine.
29. GS to André Gide, January 15, 1939, reprinted in Lacassin and Sigaux, p. 397.
30. *Gringoire,* April 30, 1937; *L'Action française,* August 2, 1934.
31. GS to René Lalou, n.d. (May 13, 1937), BN, n.a.fr. 14692.
32. GS to Gaston Gallimard, December 3, 1938, APSL.
33. Lemoine, "Simenon face à la critique."
34. René Lalou, in *Nouveautés,* May 1937.
35. GS interviewed by André Rousseaux, May 23, 1935.
36. Lemoine, "Simenon face à la critique."
37. NRF publicity poster for GS, anonymous, 1942. Authorship has been attributed to Raymond Queneau.
38. Testimony of GS to Fenton Bresler, p. 149.
39. Anatole de Monzie to GS, March 25 and November 16, 1937, FSUL.
40. Emile Henriot to GS, March 26, 1937, FSUL.
41. François Mauriac to GS, April 23, 1937, FSUL.
42. *Au-delà de ma porte-fenêtre,* p. 121.
43. Paul Nizan, in *L'Humanité,* May 4, 1937, quoted by Lemoine, "Simenon face à la critique."
44. Jacques Copeau, *Journal,* vol. 2 (Seghers, 1992), pp. 481–82.
45. Emmanuel Berl and Jean d'Ormesson, *Tant que vous penserez à moi* (Grasset, 1992), p. 195.
46. Maria Van Rysselberghe, *Les cahiers de la petite dame,* vol. 5 (Gallimard, 1974), p. 383.
47. GS interviewed by André Parinaud.
48. GS, interview, in *Les Lettres françaises,* June 5, 1963; GS interviewed by Claude Mossé, in *Nice-Matin,* January 1978; Van Rysselberghe, p. 461.

49. André Gide to Roger Martin du Gard, May 18, 1935, in Gide–Martin du Gard, *Correspondance*, vol. 2 (Gallimard, 1968), p. 31.

50. Van Rysselberghe.

51. Ibid. (January 1938).

52. Testimony of Lucien Combelle to the author; Lucien Combelle, *Je dois à André Gide* (Frédéric Chambriand, 1951), pp. 34–35.

53. André Gide to GS, December 31, 1938, quoted in Lacassin and Sigaux, p. 393; Gaston Gallimard to GS, January 23, 1939, APSL; André Gide to GS, January 6, 1939, FSUL.

54. *A la recherche des autres*, p. 407.

55. GS to Louis-Daniel Hirsch, August 2, 1939, APSL.

56. GS to André Gide, n.d. (probably December 1938), reprinted in Lacassin and Sigaux, p. 391.

57. GS to André Gide, January 15, 1939, reprinted in Lacassin and Sigaux, p. 397.

58. *Cahiers du Nord*, no. 51–52, Charleroi, 1939.

59. GS, interview, *Le Petit Niçois*, May 9, 1937.

60. GS to Jean Prouvost, August 6, 1937, AMG/AN.

61. GS to Maurice Garçon, June 23, 1939, AMG/AN.

62. GS-*Paris-Soir* file, May-June 1938, AMG/AN.

63. GS to *Cinémonde*, January 23, 1939, AMB. GS to Maurice Bessy, n.d. (1939), AMB.

64. GS-François Hervé correspondence, 1935–1936, APSL; Georges Martin to GS, July 21, 1936, APSL; GS to Georges Martin, January 17, 1937, APSL.

65. GS to Maurice Garçon, May 15, 1937, AMG/AN.

66. *Quartier nègre* file, AMG/AN; *Paris-Soir*, March 25, 1939.

67. GS interviewed by Eléanore Schraiber.

68. GS to Gaston Gallimard, April 30, 1938, APSL-AEG; Gaston Gallimard to GS, May 9, 1938, APSL-AEG.

69. Hermann von Keyserling to GS, November 5, 1936, FSUL.

70. Von Keyserling.

71. Ibid.

72. GS interviewed by Pierre Lagarde, in *Les Nouvelles littéraires*, December 25, 1937.

73. GS to Fernand Brouty, December 10, 1939, AEF.

74. Article reprinted in *Cahiers du Nord*, no. 2–3, Charleroi, 1939.

75. T. Murray Ragg to GS, January 3, 1939, APSL.

76. Ibid., February 14, 1939.

77. GS to Gaston Gallimard, March 28, 1940, APSL-AEG.

78. Geoffrey Sainsbury to GS, June 4, 1939, APSL.

79. Interview, *La Nation belge*, November 30, 1936.

80. *La Gazette de Bruxelles*, November 30, 1936.

81. Gaston Baty to GS, January 10 and May 30, 1938, APSL.

82. *Le Jour*, November 1934, reprinted in *A la recherche de la France*, pp. 369 ff.

83. Henri Jeanson.

84. *Mémoires intimes*, p. 530.

85. *Le Testament Donadieu*, TS 20, p. 220.

86. GS interviewed by Doringe, *Pour vous*, March 12, 1936.

87. GS to Gaston Gallimard, January 22, 1938, APSL-AEG.

88. GS to Denise Barcheff-Tual, January 15, 1938, AMG/AN.

89. GS to Gaston Gallimard, n.d. (October 1938), APSL-AEG; Gaston Gallimard to GS, November 5, 1938, APSL-AEG; GS to Maurice Garçon, December 19, 1939, AMG/AN; GS to Gaston Gallimard, April 30 and September 19, 1938, APSL-AEG.

90. GS to Maurice Bessy, September 20, 1938, AMB.

91. GS to Maurice Garçon, December 19, 1939, AMG/AN.

92. GS to Routledge, August 2, 1939, APSL.

93. GS to Nicolas Vondas, December 5, 1939, and film contract for *Le Passager de la "Polarlys,"* AMG/AN.

94. GS to Gaston Gallimard, March 20, 1935, APSL-AEG; Gaston Gallimard to GS, April 30, 1935, APSL-AEG.

95. Gaston Gallimard to GS, February 24, 1936, APSL-AEG.

96. Gaston Gallimard to GS, April 14, 1937, APSL-AEG.

97. Internal note from Gaston Gallimard to Raymond Gallimard, November 3, 1937, AEG.

98. GS to Gaston Gallimard, November 19, 1938, APSL-AEG.

99. Gaston Gallimard to GS, January 10, 1938, APSL-AEG.
100. GS to Gaston Gallimard, January 3, 1938, APSL-AEG.
101. Gaston Gallimard to GS, November 5, 1938, APSL-AEG.
102. GS to Gaston Gallimard, n.d. (probably Nieul, November 16, 1938), APSL-AEG.
103. Gaston Gallimard to GS, November 18, 1938, APSL-AEG.
104. Ibid. GS to Gaston Gallimard, November 20, 1938, APSL-AEG; Gaston Gallimard to GS, February 27, 1939, APSL-AEG.
105. Gaston Gallimard to GS, August 1, 1939, APSL-AEG.
106. GS to Gaston Gallimard, August 10, 1939, APSL-AEG.

10: A Time of Commitment?
1939–1940

1. GS interviewed by Bernard Pivot, *Apostrophes,* 1981.
2. Testimony of Marc Simenon to the author.
3. *Le Fils,* TS 9, p. 17.
4. Testimony of Viviane Carel-Fourier to the author.
5. Testimony of Marc, John, and Pierre Simenon to the author.
6. Michel Lemoine, "Les villes charentaises et vendéennes dans l'œuvre romanesque de Georges Simenon," in *Cahiers Simenon,* no. 2 (Les Amis de Georges Simenon, Brussels, 1988).
7. GS to Lina Chavier, February 11, 1959, Archives of Lina Chavier.
8. André Gide to GS, Paris, January 6, 1939, ACGD.
9. *Mémoires intimes,* p. 64; *Des traces de pas,* p. 44.
10. *Le Fils,* TS 9, pp. 40–41.
11. GS to André Gide, December 1939, reprinted in Lacassin and Sigaux, pp. 411, 412.
12. GS to Geoffrey Sainsbury, March 8, 1947, APSL.
13. GS to Gaston Gallimard, September 28, 1939, APSL.
14. Gaston Gallimard to Marius Larique, December 27, 1939, AEG.
15. GS to André Gide, n.d. (December 1939), reprinted in Lacassin and Sigaux, p. 412.
16. Henri-Charles Tauxe. GS, interviewed by Claude Jadoul, *Le Matin,* March 10, 1978.
17. *Vacances obligatoires,* pp. 86–87.
18. GS, interview, *La Flandre libérale,* May 20, 1963; GS, interview, Swiss Television, 1975; GS interviewed by Jean-Claude Zylberstein, *Le Nouvel Observateur,* July 13, 1970.
19. GS interviewed by Eléanore Schraiber, August 16, 1979.
20. Quoted by Michel Lemoine, *L'Autre Univers de Simenon,* p. 156.
21. *Maigret revient* (Gallimard, 1964), p. 278.
22. *Le Président,* TS 9, p. 556.
23. *Quand j'étais vieux,* p. 43.
24. "L'aventure est morte," speech in Pleyel hall, November 1938, reprinted in GS, *Portrait-souvenir de Balzac,* pp. 107–153.
25. GS interviewed by Eléanore Schraiber, July 1967.
26. GS to Franz Winckler, December 18, 1938, APSL.
27. GS to Robert Aron, April 5, 1939, APSL.
28. Henri, comte de Paris, *Mémoires d'exil et de combat* (Atelier Marcel Jullian, 1979), pp. 105–33.
29. Eugène Weber, pp. 445–50.
30. *Courrier royal* to GS, August 13, 1935, APSL.
31. Ibid., November 30, 1935.
32. Ibid., January 25, 1936.
33. Editor in chief of *Courrier royal* to GS, November 14, 1935, APSL.
34. Ibid., December 9, 1935.
35. Ibid., February 19, 1936.
36. Count of Paris to GS, March 12, 1936, APSL.
37. GS to the Count of Paris, March 20, 1936, APSL; Count of Paris to GS, April 15, 1936, APSL.
38. Testimony of Mgr the Count of Paris to the author.
39. GS interviewed by Jean Jour in *Liège, Province d'Europe,* March-May 1977.
40. GS interviewed by Doringe, *Toute l'Edition,* February 8, 1938.
41. Lucien Descaves, in *Le Journal,* January 6, 1938.
42. *Je suis partout,* February 25, 1939.
43. *La Nouvelle Revue française,* May 1939.
44. *Les Mémoires de Maigret,* TS 4, p. 844.

45. Philippe Chastenet, "Les Charentes de Simenon," in *Sud-Ouest,* February 14, 1982.
46. *Mémoires intimes,* p. 74; GS to Maurice Garçon, October 18, 1949, AMG/AN.
47. "Résumé des déclarations faites au bureau des affaires belges par diverses personalités belges concernant l'ensemble des problèmes soulevés par l'émigration belge en France," report dated May 30, 1940, Dossier Hoppenot, AMFAE.
48. GS, "Comte rendu de mission au préfet de Charente-Maritime," La Rochelle, August 17, 1940. Typed text, FSUL.
49. Ibid.
50. "Le moral belge et les possibilités françaises d'après le contrôle postal," Vichy, July 17, 1940; Dossier Vichy-Europe, vol. 179, AMFAE.
51. See Michel Lemoine, *Index des person-nages de Georges Simenon* (Labor, Brussels, 1985).
52. Maxime Steinberg, *L'étoile et le fusil. Tome II, La question juive 1940–1942* (Editions Vie Ouvrière, Brussels, 1983), p. 89.
53. *Mémoires intimes,* pp. 77 and 524.
54. GS, "Comte rendu."
55. "Le moral belge."
56. Dedication of *Lettre à ma mère,* to Lina Chavier, Lina Chavier collection.
57. Belgian consul to Lina Caspescha, La Rochelle, August 22, 1940; archives of Lina Chavier.
58. Testimony of Lina Caspescha-Chavier to the author.
59. Notes of Pierre Bonardi on the Occupation in La Rochelle, in *L'Atlantique,* February 23, 1941.
60. M. F. Wansele, in *La Lanterne,* December 15, 1951, quoted by Michel Lemoine in *Cahiers Simenon,* no. 2, Les Amis de Georges Simenon, Brussels, 1988, pp. 50–60.
61. GS, interview, *Hausse 10* (Lausanne), 1960.
62. *Le Fils* TS 9, p. 15.
63. Dedication of *Le Clan des Ostendais* to Lina Chavier, 1961, Lina Chavier collection.
64. *Le Clan des Ostendais* (Gallimard, 1947), pp. 36, 38, 64, 76, 93, 97, 105, 111, 136, 138, 139, 159, 161.
65. GS to Gaston Gallimard, July 26, 1940, AEG and APSL.
66. GS to Brice Parain, September 23, 1940, APSL.
67. Ibid.

11: *Occupation 1940–1944*

1. GS to Brice Parain, September 8, 1940, APSL.
2. GS to Gaston Gallimard, January 4 and 12, 1941, APSL-AEG.
3. *Pour Elle,* nos. 21 and 22, January 1 and 8, 1941.
4. GS to Gaston Gallimard, April 4, 1941, AEG.
5. GS to Gaston Gallimard, January 12, 1941, AEG.
6. Testimony of Count Alain du Fontenioux to the author.
7. Ibid.
8. Michel Ragon, *Enfances vendéennes* (Editions Ouest-France, 1990), pp. 85–88.
9. Testimony of André Guiller and Raymond Belin to the author.
10. *Mémoires intimes,* pp. 79–83.
11. GS, interview, *L'Express,* February 6, 1958. Stéphane, p. 57.
12. Gill, *A New York Life,* pp. 231–52.
13. Testimony of Viviane Carel-Fourrier to the author.
14. Testimony of Odette Maury, née Bastian, to the author.
15. *Mémoires intimes,* pp. 82, 101–103; GS, interview, *La Presse,* March 22, 1952; Jean Cocteau, *Journal 1942–1945* (Gallimard, 1989), p. 486.
16. Bresler, pp. 177–78.
17. Testimony of Boule to the author.
18. Testimony of Alain du Fontenioux to the author.
19. Testimony of Dr. Cécile Artarit (Dr. Artarit's widow) to the author.
20. Testimony of Dr. René Laforge to the author.
21. APSL.
22. Report of Dr. Brunet, February 16, 1937, APSL.
23. Report of Dr. Papin to Nationale, n.d. (1937), APSL.
24. APSL.
25. GS to Mauricio Restrepo, November 9, 1953, FSUL.

26. *Pedigree* (Actes-Sud/Labor, Brussels, 1989), commentary of Danielle Racelle-Latin, p. 641.

27. *Mémoires intimes*, p. 81.

28. GS to André Gide, February 15, 1941, AEG.

29. GS to Gaston Gallimard, January 12, 1941, AEG-APSL.

30. GS to Lina Caspescha-Chavier, September 28, 1940, Chavier archives.

31. GS to Gaston Gallimard, January 12, 1941, AEG-APSL.

32. GS to André Gide, n.d. (February 15, 1941), ACGD.

33. GS to Gaston Gallimard, April 4, 1941, AEG.

34. Gaston Gallimard to GS, April 1, 1941, AEG.

35. Unpublished report by André Gide, to Gaston Gallimard, May 30, 1941, AEG.

36. André Gide to GS, June 5, 1941, ACGD.

37. GS to Gaston Gallimard, August 3, 1941, ACGD.

38. André Gide to GS, September 19, 1941, ACGD.

39. GS to Gaston Gallimard, November 18, 1941; December 18, 1941; January 27, 1942, APSL.

40. André Gide to GS, August 21, 1942, ACGD.

41. André Gide to GS, December 11, 1944, ACGD.

42. *La Semaine,* no. 79, February 5, 1942; testimony of Ernest Bourasseau (projectionist at the Ciné-Palace for fifty years) to the author.

43. GS to Alfred Greven, June 12, 1942, F21 (25), AN.

44. Jacques Siclier, *La France de Pétain et son cinéma* (Ramsay-Poche-Cinéma, 1990).

45. *Vedettes,* no. 92, September 5, 1942.

46. GS to Gaston Gallimard, April 4, 1941, AEG.

47. Decree of December 5, 1940, *Journal officiel.*

48. GS to M. Maurin, Inspecteur des Domaines, March 27, 1945, APSL; GS to Gaston Gallimard, February 3 and March 17, 1941, APSL; Gaston Gallimard to GS, January 31, 1941, APSL.

49. Director of the UGC to GS, June 7, 1948, AMG/AN.

50. Testimony of Maurice Bessy to the author. See also his *Histoire du cinéma français. Encyclopédie des films 1940–1950,* written with Raymond Chirat (Pygmalion/Gérard Watelet).

51. Testimony of Simone Signoret to the author (1985).

52. Jean-Pierre Bertin-Maghit, *Le Cinéma français sous l'Occupation* (Olivier Orban, 1989).

53. *Film,* June 7, 1941.

54. Continental to GS, September 17, 1941, F21 (25), AN.

55. GS to Alfred Greven, June 12, 1942, F21 (25), AN.

56. Contract of October 19, 1942; director of UGC to GS, June 7, 1948, AMG/AN.

57. Contract of July 2, 1941, AEF.

58. GS to Gaston Gallimard, April 4, 1941, APSL.

59. Ibid., December 24, 1940.

60. Michel Gallimard to GS, February (or December?) 22, 1942, AEG.

61. Gaston Gallimard to GS, June 12, 1941, APSL.

62. GS to A. Keller, August 23, 1941, F21 (25), AN.

63. GS to his mother, March 25, 1941, APSL.

64. Ibid., June 12, 1941.

65. *Le Jour,* November 1934.

66. F21 (25), AN.

67. GS to A. Keller, August 23, 1941, F21 (25), AN; GS to Gaston Gallimard, April 4, 1941, AEG.

68. *Gringoire,* June 20, 1941.

69. Pierre Costantini to Gaston Gallimard, November 18, 1941, AEG.

70. *Le Nouveau Journal,* January 20 to March 4, 1941; *La Legia,* February 4 to March 11, 1941 (found by Fabrice Schurmans, of Ans).

71. *La Nouvelle Revue française,* October 1, 1941; *Lectures 40,* May 25, 1941; *Aujourd'hui,* June 3, 1941; *Le Figaro,* October 24 and 31, 1942; *Tout et tout,* July 12, 1941.

72. Promotional document provided by the Centre de Documentation Raymond Queneau (Verviers); Florence Géhéniau, *Queneau analphabète. Répertoire de ses lectures de 1917 à 1976,* vol. 3 (IESE, Brussels, 1986).

73. GS to A. Keller, August 23, 1941, F21 (25), AN.

74. Ibid.

75. Claude Lévy, *Les Nouveaux Temps et l'idéologie de la collaboration* (Presses de la FNSP, 1974).

76. *L'Atlantique* (La Rochelle), June 8, 1941.

77. *La Gerbe,* July 30, 1942.
78. Ibid., August 6, 1942.
79. *Les Nouveaux Temps,* August 1, 1942.
80. GS to his mother, March 25, 1941, APSL; Secours national to GS, December 5, 1941, APSL; GS to Mauricio Restrepo, August 14, 1952, FSUL.
81. Tauxe, p. 136.
82. Testimony of René Serceau and Aimé Gerbaud to the author.
83. Report of the Renseignements Généraux de Vendée, August 12, 1949, no. 1020, 13M3996, ADV.
84. Ibid.
85. *Mémoires intimes,* p. 86.
86. Gérad Nocquet, *Le Vendée sous l'Occupation allemande 1940–1944,* Cahiers d'Histoire de la Seconde Guerre mondiale.
87. Police commissioner of Fonentay-le-Comte to the Subprefect, May 6, 1941, 13M3837, ADV; prefect of the Vendée to the director of the SCAP, January 31, 1942, AJ38965, AN.
88. Théo Dannecker to Captain Sézille, April 22, 1942; Captain Sézille to Théo Dannecker, May 5, 1942, XIa76, XIg108a, CDJC.
89. Director of the office of the General Commission for Jewish Questions to the director of the surveillance and investigations sections of the occupied zone, September 8, 1942, CXV, 87, CDJC.
90. *Mémoires intimes,* pp. 89–90.
91. Corinne Luchaire, *Ma drôle de vie* (Sun, 1949), pp. 146–47.
92. *La Petite Gironde,* February 16, 1927; *L'Œil de Paris,* March 28, 1931.
93. Maurice Garçon to GS, October 3, 1942, AMG/AN.
94. Testimony of Maurice Dumoncel to the author.
95. Chief of police for Jewish questions to his deputy delegate in Dijon, April 3, 1942, AJ38 1152, AN.
96. Principal commissioner to the General Intelligence Services of Poitiers, October 2, 1942, 13M3837, ADV. Ibid., CXV, 87, CDJC.
97. Chief of police for Jewish questions to the general commissioner for Jewish questions, October 8, 1942, CXV, 87, CDJC.
98. Chief of police for Jewish questions to Mr. Grimprey, October 29, 1942, CXV, 87, CDJC.
99. *Mémoires intimes,* pp. 90–91.
100. Principal commissioner of La Roche-Sur-Yon to the police deputy (General Intelligence Services of Poitiers), October 30, 1942, 13M3837, ADV.
101. General commissioner for Jewish questions to GS (Hotel Bristol), November 16, 1942, CXV, 87, CDJC.
102. Testimony of Dr. René Laforge to the author.
103. GS to Maurice Garçon, October 18, 1949, AMG/AN.
104. Testimony of René Pérochon, Paul Proust, Rémy Liboureau, Micheline Liboureau, Octave Soulard to the author. See also Louis-René Barbarit, "Un drôle de Parisien nommé Simenon," in *Presse-Océan,* September 6, 1985.
105. GS to Claude Gallimard, April 23, 1943, APSL; Claude Gallimard to GS, April 12, 1943, APSL.
106. GS to Jean Fayard, November 3, 1943, APSL.
107. Testimony of Frédéric Dard to the author; GS to Frédéric Dard, November 23, 1943, AFD.
108. Bertin-Maghit.
109. Director of the UGC to GS, June 7, 1948, AMG/AN.
110. GS to Alfred Greven, September 19, 1943, APSL.
111. Janine Spaak, *Charles Spaak, mon mari* (France-Empire, 1977), pp. 123–24.
112. Arys Nissotti to GS, July 1, 1943, APSL.
113. GS to Paul Morand, July 6, 1943, APSL.
114. GS to Louis-Emile Galey, July 6, 1943, APSL.
115. Louis-Emile Galey to GS, August 2, 1943, APSL.
116. Pierre-Marie Dioudonnat, *L'Argent nazi à la conquête de la presse française* (Jean Picollec, 1981), p. 250.
117. List dated April 15, 1943, APSL.
118. Testimony of René Pérochon to the author.
119. *Bir-Hakeim,* no. 7, November 1, 1943, and no. 9, January 1944.
120. Testimony of Rémy Liboureau to the author.
121. Général de La Barre de Nanteuil, *Historique des unités combattantes de la Résistance 1940–1944. Deux-Sèvres-Vendée* (Château de Vincennes, 1974), pp. 44, 91.
122. Testimony of René Pérochon to the author.

123. *Mémoires intimes,* pp. 109, 110, 112, 115; *Point-Virgule,* pp. 169–70.
124. GS to Maurice Garçon, October 18, 1949, AMG/AN.
125. Testimony of Constant Vaillant to the author.
126. Constant Vaillant, *Cerizay, villa historique et martyre* (Hérault, Maulévrier, 1980).
127. *Mémoires intimes,* p. 100; GS to Maurice Garçon, October 18, 1949, AMG/AN.
128. Testimony of Boule to the author.
129. Testimony of René Devaud to the author.
130. *Un homme comme un autre,* p. 215.

12: The Flight of Mr. Georges *1944–1945*

---

1. *Pedigree,* TS 2, pp. 883, 884.
2. Testimony of Jean Huguet to the author.
3. GS to Mr. Champenois (Belgian ambassador in Paris), January 31, 1945, AMG/AN.
4. Testimony of Jean Huguet to the author.
5. GS to Maurice Garçon, November 4, 1944, AMG/AN.
6. GS to Claude Gallimard, November 1, 1944, AEG.
7. GS to Maurice Garçon, November 14, 1944, AMG/AN.
8. GS to Champenois, January 31, 1945, AMG/AN.
9. GS, interview, *La Résistance,* August 1, 1955.
10. Prefect of the Vendée to Ropert, May 3, 1945, APSL.
11. *Ouest-France,* April 24, 1945.
12. Decree no. 45-1089, May 30, 1945, *Journal officiel.*
13. *Cahiers Céline,* no. 7, "Céline et l'actualité littéraire" (Gallimard, 1986).
14. Siclier.
15. Ibid.
16. *Les inconnus dans la maison,* Folio, p. 226.
17. GS to Sven Nielsen, November 21, 1945, APSL.
18. Francis Lacassin, *Simenon aux Presses de la Cité* (Plaquette h.c., 1988), pp. 5–8; Portrait of Sven Nielsen by Jean-Jacques Brichier, in *Magazine littéraire,* September 1968.
19. APSL.
20. Stanley Eskin has already made this point, p. 37.
21. *Malempin,* TS 22, p. 184.
22. *Le Fond de la bouteille,* TS 3, p. 336.
23. GS to his mother, April 23, 1943, and June 10, 1943, APSL.
24. Report on the internal organization of the Rexist movement during the war, drafted by a Belgian intelligence service, CERHSGM, Brussels, Fonds Rex, no. 87.
25. Alfred Lemaire, S.J., *Le Crime du 18 août* (Imprimerie Maison d'Editions, S.C., Couillet, Belgium, n.d.), pp. 47, 135, 136, 142, 276, 392, 397; interview with Francis Balace, professor of contemporary history at the University of Liège, by the author.
26. *Index des recherches pour crimes et délits contre la sûreté de l'Etat,* vol. 1, March 31, 1945, Auditorat général, Brussels.
27. GS to his mother, January 15, 1948, and February 4, 1948, APSL; GS to the president of the Tribunal de 1re instance de Usambura (Belgian Congo), February 26, 1950, APSL.
28. Testimony of Maurice Dumoncel to the author.
29. *Mémoires intimes,* p. 113.
30. Testimony of Tigy to Fenton Bresler, p. 210.
31. GS, "Problèmes du roman," 1943, in *L'Âge du roman,* p. 33.
32. Gill, *A New York Life,* pp. 231–52.
33. APSL.
34. GS to Maurice Garçon, September 28, 1947, AMG/AN.
35. AMG/AN.
36. *La Fuite de Monsieur Monde,* TS 1, pp. 126, 185, 194.
37. GS to André Gide, in Lacassin-Sigaux, p. 422.

13: A Bit of Happiness: *1945–1950*

---

1. Monnoyer, p. 42.
2. Gill, *A New York Life,* pp. 231–52.
3. GS to Sven Nielsen, July 2, 1951, APSL.
4. Ibid., November 13, 1946.
5. Justin O'Brien, *Portrait of André Gide* (Knopf, New York, 1953).

6. GS to Frédéric Dard, September 7, 1946, AFD. GS to Sven Nielsen, November 21, 1945, APSL.
7. Testimony of Boule to the author.
8. *Mémoires intimes,* pp. 107–108.
9. Ibid., pp. 133–34.
10. Ibid., pp. 135, 139–42.
11. *Quand vient le froid,* pp. 44–45; *Tant que je suis vivant,* pp. 159–63; *Un homme comme un autre,* p. 189.
12. Testimony of Denyse Simenon to the author.
13. *Mémoires intimes,* p. 155.
14. Testimony of Marc Simenon to the author.
15. *Mémoires intimes,* p. 168; GS, interview, in *Les Lettres françaises,* June 5, 1963.
16. *Trois chambres à Manhattan,* TS 1, p. 231.
17. GS, interviewed by André Parinaud.
18. GS to Frédéric Dard, May 20, 1949, AFD.
19. GS to Roland Saucier, February 7, 1950, APSL.
20. GS to Gaston Gallimard, December 12, 1945, APSL.
21. Gaston Gallimard to GS, January 7, 1946, APSL.
22. GS to Sven Nielsen, June 20, 1946, APSL.
23. Draft contract for *Pedigree,* August 26, 1946, APSL; GS to Gaston Gallimard, July 17, 1946, APSL; Gaston Gallimard to GS, April 2, 1947, APSL.
24. Sven Nielsen to GS, May 3, 1948, APSL.
25. GS to Sven Nielsen, May 10, 1948, APSL.
26. GS interviewed by Tauxe.
27. *Mémoires intimes,* pp. 360, 361.
28. *Pietr-le-Letton,* TS 16, p. 409.
29. *A la recherche de l'homme nu,* pp. 294, 343–49 (*France-Soir,* November 5–22 1946).
30. GS interviewed by André Parinaud, pp. 401–403.
31. GS to Sven Nielsen, November 13, 1946, APSL.
32. N. Tremblay, "Au Far West avec Georges Simenon," in *Les Nouvelles littéraires,* February 5, 1948.
33. GS to Sven Nielsen, October 14, 1947, and February 23, 1948, APSL; GS, interview, in *La Flandre libérale,* May 20, 1963.
34. GS to Sven Nielsen, December 26, 1946, APSL; GS to André Gide, October 4,

1948, quoted in Lacassin and Sigaux, pp. 440–44.
35. *Le Passage de la ligne,* TS 9, p. 620.
36. *Mémoires intimes,* pp. 205–206.
37. GS to A. C. Spectorsky (*Playboy* magazine, Chicago), December 17, 1968, Harry Ransom Humanities Research Center, University of Texas at Austin.
38. Lacassin, *Conversations avec Simenon.*
39. GS to *La Press,* May 25, 1946.
40. GS to George Adam, October 3, 1947, APSL.
41. Erskine Caldwell, *With All My Might. An Autobiography* (Peachtree Publishers, Atlanta, 1987), pp. 171, 209, 210, 228; GS, interview, *France-USA,* December 1954.
42. Testimony of Denyse Simenon to the author.
43. *Lettre à ma mère,* p. 107.
44. Testimony of Denyse Simenon to the author.
45. GS to his mother, January 15, 1948, APSL; GS to Maria Croissant, January 5, 1948, APSL; GS to General Salan, April 28, 1948, APSL; General Salan to GS, February 19, 1948, APSL; telegram to GS, January 14, 1948, APSL; *Lettre à ma mère,* p. 107.
46. *Mémoires intimes,* pp. 202 203; GS interviewed by André Parinaud.
47. GS to Frédéric Dard, January 7, 1949, AFD. See also GS to Sven Nielsen, February 25, 1950, APSL.
48. Geoffrey Sainsbury to GS, May 28, 1948, APSL; Jean Renoir to GS, December 30, 1950, and February 22, 1951, FSUL.
49. *Los Angeles Times,* January 7, 1950, quoted by Diane Johnson, *Dashiell Hammett, une vie* (Payot, 1989).
50. *Ici-Paris,* November 18, 1947.
51. Marcel Carné, *La Vie à belles dents* (Belfond, 1989), pp. 214–15.
52. *Mémoires intimes,* p. 216.
53. GS to Maurice Garçon, May 13, 1946, and May 24, 1948, AMG/AN; GS to Frédéric Dard, April 23, 1949, AFD.
54. Jean Renoir, *Lettres d'Amérique* (Presses de la naissance, 1984), (see letters of June 12 and October 1, 1948); Bertin, pp. 304, 309, 330, 331.
55. Jean Renoir to GS, March 2, 1948, in *Lettres d'Amérique.*
56. GS to Sven Nielsen, January 2, 1949, APSL.

57. GS to Sven Nielsen, August 6, 1949, APSL.
58. F 21-13, dossier 5, AN.
59. Maurice Garçon to GS, October 15, 1949, AMG/AN.
60. GS to Maurice Garçon, October 18, November 19, 20, and 26, 1949, AMG/AN.
61. Maurice Garçon to GS, November 21, 1949, AMG/AN.
62. GS to Maurice Garçon, January 7, 1950; Maurice Garçon to GS, February 2, 1950.
63. GS to Claude Gallimard, January 27, 1950; GS to Gaston Gallimard, February 15, 1950; Gaston Gallimard to GS, March 10, 1950; GS to Roland Saucier (Librairie Gallimard), February 7, 1950, AEG.
64. GS to Doringe, July 5, 1952, APSL.
65. Carlo Rim.
66. *Ici-Paris,* July 17, 1950.

14: *Lakeside* 1950–1952

---

1. GS to Sven Nielsen, August 8, 1950, APSL.
2. G. Campbell Becket, "History of Lakeville Chamber of Commerce Reviewed," in *The Lakeville Journal,* June 2, 1954.
3. Roy Hoopes, *Ralph Ingersoll. A Biography* (Atheneum, New York, 1985); Ralph McAllister Ingersoll, *Point of Departure. An Adventure in Autobiography* (Harcourt Brace Jovanovich, New York, 1961).
4. GS interviewed by Piron and Sacré.
5. GS to Maurice Garçon, October 25, 1951, AMG/AN; GS to Maurice Garçon, November 2, 1951, AMG/AN.
6. *Des traces de pas,* p. 130; *Mémoires intimes,* p. 183; *Le Prix d'un homme,* pp. 49–51.
7. *Quand vient le froid,* pp. 125, 126.
8. *Mémoires intimes,* pp. 311–13.
9. GS to Helen Wolff, August 15, 1984, Archives of Helen Wolff.
10. *Mémoires intimes,* p. 364.
11. *The Lakeville Journal,* July 12, 1951.
12. *Trois Chambres à Manhattan,* TS 1, pp. 214, 244, 248.
13. "Les Petits Cochons sans queue," TS 4, p. 411.
14. *Le Fond de la bouteille,* TS 3, p. 327.
15. *Maigret chez le ministre,* TS 7, p. 562.
16. GS to Doringe, September 25, 1951, APSL.
17. GS to Geoffrey Sainsbury, March 26, 1951, APSL; James King, *The Last Modern. A Life of Herbert Read* (Weidenfield, London, 1990), pp. 195, 202, 274; GS to Doringe, August 13, 1951, APSL; Art Buchwald, *New York Herald Tribune,* December 9, 1956; GS to Mauricio Restrepo, February 8, 1954, FSUL.
18. GS to Sven Nielsen, July 2, 1951, APSL.
19. GS to Sven Nielsen, May 27, 1950, APSL.
20. GS to Mauricio Restrepo, November 9, 1953, FSUL.
21. Narcejac, pp. 10. 11, 29, 115, 116.
22. GS to Sven Nielsen, February 23, 1951, APSL.
23. Article by Gaetan Picon, in *Le Figaro littéraire,* January 12, 1970.
24. Claude Martin, "André Gide critique de Georges Simenon," in *Bulletin des amis d'André Gide,* April 1977, no. 34, pp. 39–44; Gérard Cleisz, in Lacassin and Sigaux, pp. 387–452. See also Claude Dirick, "Georges Simenon et André Gide," in *Traces,* no. 3, 1991, University of Liège, pp. 25–40.
25. GS to André Gide, January 18, 1948, ACGD.
26. GS to André Gide, January 15, 1948, ACGD.
27. Ibid.
28. GS to André Gide, July 16, 1949, ACGD.
29. GS to André Gide, February 26, 1948, ACGD.
30. GS to André Gide, March 29, 1948, ACGD.
31. Testimony of Catherine Gide-Desvignes to the author.
32. "GS" file, ACGD.
33. *Au-delà de ma porte-fenêtre,* p. 121.
34. *Quand j'étais vieux,* pp. 170–71.
35. Carvel Collins.
36. GS to Blanche Montel, August 29, 1949, APSL; GS to Frédéric Dard, n.d. (1951), AFD; GS to Frédéric Dard, August 20, 1947, AFD; GS to Frédéric Dard, December 16, 1948, AFD.
37. GS to Frédéric Dard, November 5, 1946, AFD; GS to Frédéric Dard, December 16, 1948, AFD. See also Jean-Baptiste Baornian, "Rencontre du troisième type," in *Cahiers Simenon,* no. 5, Les Amis de Georges Simenon, Brussels, 1991, pp. 165–69.

38. GS to Frédéric Dard, March (or May?) 12, 1946, AFD; *La Crève* was reprinted in 1989 by Fleuve Noir.
39. GS to Frédéric Dard, February 21, 1951, AFD.
40. GS to Frédéric Dard, February 23, 1951, AFD; Frédéric Dard to GS, February 13, 1951, AFD.
41. Testimony of Pierre Simenon to the author.
42. Agenda 1952, APSL.
43. *La Meuse,* March 19, 1952.
44. Testimony of Denyse Simenon to the author.
45. *Mémoires intimes,* p. 321.
46. *Samedi-Soir,* March 22, 1952.
47. Carlo Rim, Memoires.
48. GS interviewed by Micheline Sandrel, radio.
49. Testimony of Frédéric Dard to the author.
50. GS to Mauricio Restrepo, November 1, 1953, FSUL.
51. GS to Doringe, June 27, 1956, APSL.
52. Testimony of Frédéric Dard to the author.
53. Jean Paulhan to Etiemble, November 7, 1967, in Jeanine Kohn-Etiemble, *226 lettres inédites de Jean Paulhan* (Klincksieck, 1975), pp. 418–19.
54. Rim, *Mémoires,* pp. 87–92.
55. Jean Cocteau, *Le Passé défini. Journal I, 1951–1952* (Gallimard, 1983), pp. 180–82.
56. Testimony of Jacques Laurent to the author.
57. *Mémoires intimes,* p. 323.
58. Testimony of Denyse Simenon to the author.
59. Rim, *Mémoires.*
60. *1934,* April 11, 1934.
61. *Les Nouvelles littéraires,* August 22, 1931.
62. Ibid.
63. Ibid.
64. GS to Maurice Garçon, April 3, 1950, AMG/AN.
65. *Gazette de Liège,* June 23, 1949.
66. GS to Maurice Garçon, July 18, 1949, AMG/AN.
67. GS to Maurice Garçon, December 12, 1949, AMG/AN.
68. *Pedigree* case, AMG/AN.
69. Maurice Garçon to GS, May 25, 1950, AMG/AN.
70. Ibid.
71. GS to Maurice Garçon, May 16, 1950, AMG/AN.
72. GS to Maurice Garçon, May 24, 1951, and January 18, 1952, AMG/AN.
73. GS to Maurice Garçon, October 10, 1950, AMG/AN.
74. *Mémoires intimes,* p. 326.
75. *Lettre à ma mère,* p. 40; Gill, pp. 231–52.
76. GS to his mother, June 16 and August 10, 1949, APSL.
77. *Le Monde* (Paris) and *Le Jour* (Verviers), May 5, 1952.
78. Stanley Eskin, p. 263.
79. Ruling of the Tribunal de 1re instance of Verviers, 1er Chambre, June 16, 1952.
80. GS to Sven Nielsen, August 17, 1955, APSL.
81. *Gazette de Liège,* May 6, 1952.
82. *Lettre à ma mère,* p. 38; testimony of the Baron Pierre Clerdent to the author.
83. *Lettre à ma mère,* pp. 32, 33; *Mémoires intimes,* pp. 330–32.
84. GS to his mother, July 2, 1952, APSL.
85. *Quand j'étais vieux,* p. 191.
86. GS to Maurice Garçon, October 25, 1951, AMG/AN.
87. Carlo Bronne, "Simenon académicien," in *La Grive,* no. 74, July 1952.
88. GS to Doringe, March 1, 1952, APSL; GS to Mauricio Restrepo, November 27, 1953, FSUL.
89. Jean Gorini, in *Radar,* May 18, 1952.
90. Claude Gauteur, *Michel Simon* (Edilig, 1987).
91. GS to Jean Carlier, in *Combat,* October 20, 1952.

15: The Color of Business
1952–1955

---

1. *Tant que je suis vivant,* pp. 123–24.
2. GS to Sven Nielsen, September 16, 1949, APSL.
3. GS to his mother, July 11, 1950, APSL.
4. Testimony of Denyse Simenon to the author.
5. Ibid.
6. GS to Henry Miller, August 3, 1954, FSUL.
7. GS to Doringe, September 25, 1951, APSL.
8. Extract from Maurice Dumoncel, *Le Journal inédit,* February 1954, AMD.
9. GS to Fernand Brouty (Fayard), July 12, 1952, AEF.

10. GS to Sven Nielsen, February 22, 1955, APSL.

11. GS to Gaston Gallimard, February 23, 1953, APSL.

12. GS to Mauricio Restrepo, January 4, 1954, FSUL.

13. Gaston Gallimard to GS, June 27, 1952, and May 16, 1953, APSL; GS to Gaston Gallimard, May 23, 1953, APSL.

14. GS to Doringe, June 9, 1954, APSL.

15. GS to Mauricio Restrepo, January 4, 1954, FSUL.

16. GS to Sven Nielsen, September 21, 1955, APSL.

17. Brendan Gill, "Profiles Out of the Dark," in *The New Yorker,* January 24, 1953, pp. 35–49. See also GS to Mauricio Restrepo, January 4, 1954, FSUL.

18. Gill, "Profiles Out of the Dark," p. 242.

19. GS, interview, France-USA, December 1954.

20. Dorothy B. Hughes, *Erle Stanley Gardner: The Case of the Real Perry Mason* (William Morrow, New York, 1978), p. 161.

21. GS to Thornton Wilder, August 5, 1954, FSUL.

22. Testimony of Georges Belmont, in Mary Dearborn, *Henry Miller, biographie* (Belfond, 1991), pp. 339–77.

23. Henry Miller to GS, March 23, 1954, FSUL.

24. Henry Miller to GS, April 23, 1954, FSUL.

25. Henry Miller to GS, May 27, 1954, FSUL.

26. Henry Miller to GS, June 23, 1954, FSUL.

27. Henry Miller to GS, August 6, 1954, FSUL.

28. Homage to Henry Miller by GS, in *Synthèses,* no. 249–50, Paris-Brussels, March 1967.

29. GS to Henry Miller, September 16, 1954, FSUL.

30. Henry Miller to GS, April 23, 1954, and May 27, 1954, FSUL.

31. Letters from John Cowper Powys, translated and published by Xavier Jaujard, in *Le Monde,* September 8, 1989.

32. GS interviewed by Fenton Bresler, recording unpublished, AFB.

33. Letter from Herbert Read to C.A. Franklin, October 1, 1953, Routledge archives, quoted by James King.

34. GS interviewed by Fenton Bresler, recording unpublished, AFB.

35. GS to Sven Nielsen, March 12, 1954, APSL.

36. *Mémoires intimes,* p. 353.

37. Roger Machell (director at Hamish Hamilton) to GS, January 1954; Hamish Hamilton to GS, February 3, 1954. APSL.

38. GS to Sven Nielsen, March 12, 1954, and April 12, 1954, APSL; GS, homage to Hamish Hamilton for the fiftieth anniversary of his firm.

39. Robert Calder, *Willie. The Life of W. S. Maugham* (Heinemann, London, 1989).

40. T. S. Eliot to GS, March 5, 1955, FSUL.

41. Julian Symons, *Bloody Murder: From the Detective Story to the Crime Novel* (Penguin Books, Harmondsworth, 1985), pp. 133–37.

42. *Le Figaro,* November 17, 1954.

43. Testimony of Nane Poirson to the author. (Mme Poirson was Gilbert Sigaux's assistant for this recording.)

44. GS to Sven Nielsen, February 7, 1955, APSL.

45. *Mémoires intimes,* p. 369; *On dit que j'ai soixante-quinze ans,* pp. 149–50.

46. GS to Sven Nielsen, March 2, 1955, APSL.

47. GS to Sven Nielsen, March 4, 1951, APSL.

48. GS interviewed by Jean Jour.

49. Letter of the Federal Bureau of Investigation to the author, July 25, 1991; article by Christian Millau in *Le Nouveau Candide,* March 5, 1964.

50. GS to Mauricio Restrepo, January 4, 1954, FSUL.

51. Testimony of Helen Wolff, Brendan Gill, and Maurice Dumoncel to the author.

52. Testimony of Vicki Silvert-Oppenheimer to the author.

53. Article by Vicki Silvert in *The Lakeville Journal,* February 25, 1954.

54. Testimony of Denyse Simenon to the author.

55. *Vacances obligatoires,* p. 93.

56. *Mémoires intimes,* p. 370.

16: To Live and Write in Noland 1955–1963

1. Jean Renoir to GS, April 15, 1957, FSUL.
2. GS to Doringe, February 15, 1955 (letter not sent), APSL.
3. APSL document.
4. Contract of February 7, 1956, between Fayard and Simenon, AEF; testimony of Robert Toussaint (Fayard) to the author; GS interviewed by Fenton Bresler, pp. 149–51.
5. GS to Brice Parain, June 12, 1941, APSL.
6. Letter of April 1954 published in *The Third Degree,* reprinted in Dorothy Gardner and Katherine Sorley Walker, ed., *Raymond Chandler Speaking* (Penguin, Harmondsworth, 1988), p. 93.
7. GS, "Sur la propriété littéraire," in *Arts,* no. 587, October 1956, reprinted in full in Lacassin and Sigaux, pp. 373–79, and GS, *Portrait-souvenir de Balzac,* pp. 218–25.
8. *L'Ours en peluche,* TS 10, pp. 609–11.
9. GS to Sven Nielsen, April 10, 1960, APSL.
10. Ibid.
11. GS interviewed by Jean-Louis Ezine; *Les Petits hommes,* p. 94; *Mémoires intimes,* pp. 445–46.
12. *Mémoires intimes,* p. 441.
13. Statements of GS in *Bulletin quotidien du festival,* May 9, 1956, and May 6, 1957; Maurice Bessy, *Les Passagers du souvenir* (Albin Michel, 1977), p. 214.
14. Interview by Pierre Granier-Deferre, in *Simenon Travelling,* pp. 35–46.
15. GS, radio interview (origin undetermined).
16. Jean Renoir to GS, October 3, 1954, FSUL.
17. *Paris-Presse,* March 20, 1952.
18. Jean Renoir to GS, March 29, 1957, FSUL; interview with Jean Renoir, in *Les Cahiers du cinéma,* no. 78, Christmas 1957.
19. Testimony of Maurice Le Roux and Maurice Bessy to the author. *Mémoires intimes,* pp. 441–43; *Tant que je suis vivant,* p. 118.
20. Mary Dearborn.
21. *L'Express,* no. 465, May 12, 1950.
22. *Le Monde,* May 20, 1960.
23. *Le Monde,* May 12, 1960.
24. GS, text on Fellini, March 22, 1976, FSUL.
25. *Tant que je suis vivant,* p. 119.
26. Henry Miller to GS, April 20, 1961, FSUL.
27. Henry Miller, article in *Candide,* May 11, 1961; Henry Miller to GS, March 9, 1960, FSUL.
28. Roger Nimier to GS, February 16, 1962, APSL.
29. Paul Morand to GS, October 10, 1959, FSUL.
30. GS, *Portrait-souvenir de Balzac,* pp. 21–50.
31. Somerset Maugham to GS, December 8, n.d., FSUL; Robert Calder.
32. *Les Nouvelles Littéraires,* June 21, 1962.
33. *Des traces de pas,* p. 81; *Tant que je suis vivant,* p. 33.
34. GS to Federico Fellini, January 3, 1977, FSUL.
35. *Gazette de Liège,* November 24, 1920.
36. *Les Scrupules de Maigret,* TS 9, pp. 408, 410, 422, 435–37, 443–44.
37. GS, interview, *La Press de Tunisie,* May 15, 1963.
38. GS, interview, *Les Lettres françaises,* June 5, 1963.
39. Raymond Olivier to GS, September 12, 1962; Dr. Lemoine to GS, September 17, 1962; Dr. Cruchard to GS, September 1, 1962 (in *Anneaux de Bicêtre* file, FSUL).
40. GS to Sven Nielsen, December 8, 1962, APSL.
41. GS to Sven Nielsen, December 16, 1948, APSL.
42. Sven Nielsen to GS, March 26, 1963, APSL.
43. *France-Soir,* May 9, 1963.
44. Jean Paulhan, in Lacassin and Sigaux, pp. 280–82.
45. *Le Monde,* June 5, 1963.
46. *L'Express,* May 30, 1963.
47. *Le Figaro Littéraire,* May 11–18, 1963.
48. *Minute,* May 3, 1963.
49. *Les Anneaux de Bicêtre,* TS 11, pp. 738, 739.
50. Ibid., p. 670.
51. Testimony of Helen Wolff to the author.
52. Michael Ermarth, ed., *Kurt Wolf. A Portrait in Essays and Letters* (University of Chicago Press, 1991).
53. *Tant que je suis vivant,* p. 95; *Des traces de pas,* p. 38.

54. Testimony of Helen Wolff to the author.
55. *Tant que je suis vivant,* p. 134.
56. Testimony of Marc Simenon to the author.
57. *Le Fils,* TS 9, p. 87.
58. Denyse Simenon to Fernand Brouty, July 4, 1955, FSUL.
59. GS to Mauricio Restrepo, July 3, 1955, FSUL.
60. *Mémoires intimes,* p. 381.
61. Ibid.
62. Ibid.
63. *Pedigree,* TS 2, p. 554.
64. *Lettre à mon juge,* TS 1, pp. 705, 739.
65. Testimony of Denyse Simenon to the author.
66. *Le Passager clandestin,* TS 2, p. 220.
67. Testimony of GS to the author.
68. Roger Stéphane, "Deux ou trois choses qu'il me faut rappeler," in *Portrait-souvenir de Georges Simenon,* pp. 7–9.
69. GS to Doringe, November 8, 1962, APSL.

17: *Deliverance* 1964–1972

1. Testimony of Helen Wolff to the author.
2. Testimony of Pierre Simenon to the author.
3. Testimony of Joyce Aitken to the author.
4. Testimony of Denyse Simenon to the author.
5. Testimony of Helen Wolff to the author.
6. *La Main,* TS 14, p. 316.
7. Testimony of Yves Salgues to the author.
8. Yves Salgues, *Le Testament d'un esclave* (Stock, 1991), pp. 332–33.
9. *Mémoires intimes,* pp. 404–405.
10. Testimony of Yves Salgues to the author.
11. *Mémoires intimes,* pp. 533–34.
12. Testimony of Marc Simenon to the author.
13. *Mémoires intimes,* p. 504.
14. GS to Sven Nielsen, January 10, 1966, APSL; GS interviewed by Fenton Bresler, unpublished recording, AFB.
15. GS to Sven Nielsen, October 15, 1964, APSL.
16. GS interviewed by Fenton Bresler, unpublished recording, AFB; GS interviewed by Eléanore Schraiber, FSUL; GS to Sven Nielsen, May 14, 1965, APSL.
17. Note from Helen Wolff to William Jovanovich, January 27, 1965, AHW.
18. Thomas Narcejac, in Lacassin and Sigaux, p. 21.
19. Pierre MacOrlan to GS, June 16, 1965, FSUL.
20. *Au-delà de mon porte-fenêtre,* pp. 140–41.
21. Testimony of Pierre Simenon to the author. *Quand j'étais vieux,* p. 149.
22. Charles Chaplin to GS, June 9, 1965, FSUL.
23. *Des traces de pas,* pp. 168–69; Tauxe.
24. Charles Chaplin, *Ma vie* (Presses Pocket, 1989), p. 472.
25. GS to Maurice Bessy, August 26, 1978, AMB.
26. GS to Sven Nielsen, March 9, 1962, APSL.
27. GS interviewed by Fenton Bresler, unpublished recording, AFB.
28. *Le Figaro littéraire,* April 9, 1964.
29. GS, interview, *Germinal,* October 1966.
30. GS interviewed by Eléanore Schraiber, August 1971, FSUL.
31. The interview in *Médecine et hygiène* is reprinted in Alain Bertrand, *Georges Simenon* (La Manufacture, Lyons, 1988), pp. 180–214.
32. Testimony of Dr. Pierre Rentchnik to the author.
33. *Quand vient le froid,* p. 36.
34. GS, interview, *La Lanterne,* November 13, 1951.
35. Brendan Gill, pp. 231–52.
36. *Lettre à ma mère,* pp. 90–91.
37. André Parinaud.
38. GS, interview, Swiss Radio and Television, 1982.
39. FSUL.
40. *Mémoires intimes,* p. 589.
41. GS, interview, *L'Express,* February 6, 1958.
42. Stéphane, p. 149.

18: *Style Is Rhythm* 1972

1. GS to André Gide, January 15, 1939.
2. Denyse Simenon, interview, Radio Canada, 1978.
3. GS, interview, Swiss Radio and Television, 1982.

4. See especially *Paris-Centre,* March 31, 1923.

5. GS, interview, in *Monitor. An Anthology,* edited by Hugh Weldon (MacDonald, London, 1962), p. 109.

6. Ian Fleming, interview, in *Le Figaro Littéraire,* April 9, 1964.

7. GS, interview, in Hugh Weldon.

8. Testimony of Marc Simenon to the author.

9. *Mémoires intimes,* p. 278; GS interviewed by Claude Mossé, in *Le Soir,* February 13, 1978.

10. Carlo Rim.

11. *Mémoires intimes,* p. 46.

12. André Gide to GS, January 6, 1939, in Lacassin and Sigaux, p. 394; GS to André Gide, January 15, 1939, in Lacassin and Sigaux; GS interviewed by André Parinaud, 1955.

13. GS, preface to *Traqué,* by Arthur Omre.

14. Félicien Marceau, in *Arts,* September 12, 1954.

15. GS interviewed by Carvell Collins, pp. 91, 92.

16. Jacques Dubois, "Simenon et la déviance," in *Littérature,* no. 1, February 1971, pp. 62–72.

17. GS to Geoffrey Sainsbury, November 24, 1949, APSL.

18. GS to Sven Nielsen, June 21, 1961, APSL.

19. *Un homme comme un autre,* p. 28.

20. Roger Nimier, *Journées de lecture* (Gallimard, 1965), p. 265.

21. GS to Mauricio Restrepo, December 11, 1953.

22. GS to Robert Vouin, October 10, 1950, APSL.

23. *Le Testament Donadieu,* TS 20, p. 245.

24. *Le Voyageur de la Toussaint,* TS 22, p. 860, pp. 166, 167.

25. Testimony of Pierre Simenon to the author.

26. *Le Président,* TS 9, p. 538.

27. GS to his mother, n.d. (1934), APSL.

28. GS to his mother, December 28, 1939, APSL.

29. GS to Sven Nielsen, April 29, 1961, APSL.

30. GS to Annette de Bretagne, April 12, 1960, APSL.

31. GS to Sven Nielsen, September 23, 1964, APSL.

32. Claudine Gothot-Mersch, "Genèse des romans de Simenon: le problème des titres," in *Traces,* no. 1, University of Liège, 1989, pp. 139–48.

33. GS interviewed by Robert Sadoul.

34. André Parinaud, p. 405.

35. GS to Louis-Daniel Hirsch, August 21, 1939, APSL; GS to Sven Nielsen, January 23, 1948, APSL; Philippe Zoummeroff collection. FSUL.

36. GS to Doringe, October 4, 1951, APSL.

37. GS to André Gillon (Larousse), July 3, 1952, APSL.

38. GS interviewed by André Parinaud, radio.

39. GS interviewed by Thérèse de Saint-Phalle, *Le Monde,* June 5, 1965.

40. *Le Destin des Malous,* TS 1, p. 852; *Mémoires intimes,* p. 441; *Le Petit Saint,* TS 12, p. 651; *Le Chat,* TS 13, p. 455.

41. *Le Petit Saint,* TS 12, pp. 663, 691; *Le Testament Donadieu,* TS 20, p. 77.

42. *Le Destin des Malou,* TS 1, p. 872; *Malempin,* TS 22, p. 215.

43. *Le Passager clandestin,* TS 2, p. 195.

44. *L'Ours en peluche,* TS 10, pp. 551, 553, 618, 619.

45. GS to Gaston Gallimard, December 5, 1939, APSL.

46. Marie-Hélène André-Nihant, pp. 125–29.

47. *La Mort de Belle,* TS 6, p. 105.

48. GS to André Gide, January 15, 1939, in Lacassin and Sigaux; GS, interview, *L'Indépendance Belge,* December 5, 1936.

49. GS, interview, *La Libre Belgique,* June 8, 1956.

50. GS interviewed by Pierre de Boisdeffre, in *Les Nouvelles littéraires,* December 17, 1953.

51. GS to Sven Nielsen, June 25, 1962, APSL.

52. Ibid.

53. GS, interview, *Les Lettres françaises,* June 5, 1963.

54. André Thérive, *Le Temps,* May 9, 1935.

55. Jacques Festy to GS, November 4, 1941, APSL.

56. GS to Sven Nielsen, August 7, 1964, APSL.

57. GS to Sven Nielsen, June 27, 1962, APSL.

58. Ibid., and March 28, 1963, APSL.

59. GS to Doringe, March 27, 1960, APSL.

60. GS to Paul Alexandre (production manager), January 15, 1957, APSL.

61. GS to Sven Nielsen, February 28, 1950, APSL.

62. GS to Sven Nielsen, March 7, 1950, APSL.

63. GS to Sven Nielsen, March 25 and 14, 1950, APSL.

64. Federico Fellini to GS, December 27, 1976, FSUL.

65. Jean Fabre, "Nécessité de Maigret," in *Traces,* no. 1, University of Liège, 1989, pp. 81–90.

66. *L'Express,* March 8, 1962, p. 31.

67. *Tout et tout,* July 12, 1941.

68. Gilbert Sigaux, in Lacassin and Sigaux, pp. 14–17.

69. GS, interview, *Lettres françaises,* June 5, 1963.

70. GS to André Gide, January 15, 1939, in Lacassin and Sigaux, pp. 396–404.

19: Unattainable Serenity
1973–1989

1. GS interviewed by Pierre Lagarde, in *Les Nouvelles Littéraires,* December 25, 1937.

2. GS to Sven Nielsen, November 17, 1951, APSL.

3. Gaston Gallimard to GS, April 9, 1943, APSL.

4. GS interviewed by Bernard Pivot, *Apostrophes,* November 27, 1981.

5. *Les Nouvelles Littéraires,* November 1951.

6. GS to Sven Nielsen, November 17, 1951, APSL.

7. Ibid.

8. Testimony of Denyse Simenon to the author.

9. *Quand j'étais vieux,* p. 337.

10. Hermann von Keyserling.

11. Sven Nielsen to GS, December 2, 1949, APSL.

12. Daniel-Rops to GS, October 2, 1959, FSUL.

13. Testimony of Maurice Druon to the author.

14. *Tant que je suis vivant,* pp. 45–46.

15. *Quand j'étais vieux,* p. 215.

16. GS interviewed by André Parinaud, in *Opéra,* March 26, 1956.

17. *Vacances obligatoires,* p. 56.

18. Alphonse Boudard, *Cinoche* (La Table Ronde, 1974; reprint, Le Livre de Poche), pp. 136–37.

19. *Je suis resté un enfant de chœur,* p. 183.

20. Quoted by Michel Lemoine, in *Cahiers de l'Association des romanistes,* University of Liège, p. 8.

21. Stanley Eskin, p. 285.

22. François Truffaut to GS, November 23, 1977, in François Truffaut, *Correspondance* (Hatier, 1988), pp. 532, 533.

23. *De la cave au grenier.*

24. *Vacances obligatoires,* pp. 105, 107, 130.

25. *A l'abri de notre arbre,* p. 35.

26. *Des traces de pas,* p. 85.

27. *La Main dans la main,* p. 120.

28. *Des traces de pas,* p. 9.

29. *Tant que je suis vivant,* p. 38.

30. Ibid.

31. *La Femme endormie,* p. 121.

32. *Les Petits Hommes,* pp. 93, 94.

33. Testimony of Denyse Simenon to the author.

34. GS to his mother, March 13, 1964, APSL.

35. *Lettre à ma mère,* p. 81.

36. Ibid., pp. 10, 18, 63, 79, 122.

37. *Vent du nord, vent du sud,* p. 28.

38. *Au-delà de ma porte-fenêtre,* pp. 88, 89.

39. Testimony of Emmanuel Berl to his biographer Bernard Morlino.

40. *La Femme endormie,* p. 137.

41. *La Main,* TS 14, p. 281; *Le Chat,* TS 13, p. 473; *Le Destin des Malou,* TS 1, p. 783; *La Chambre bleue,* TS 12, p. 260; *En cas de malheur,* TS 8, pp. 472, 473.

42. GS interviewed by Fenton Bresler, unpublished.

43. Testimony of Boule to the author.

44. GS to Federico Fellini, August 18, 1976, FSUL.

45. Federico Fellini to GS, August 1976, FSUL.

46. *L'Express,* no. 1337, February 21–27, 1977, p. 130.

47. GS interviewed by Jacques Chancel, Radioscopie, France-Inter, 1982.

48. *La Femme endormie,* p. 52.

49. Tigy interviewed by Patrick and Philippe Chastenet.

50. GS to Frédéric Dard, May 20, 1949, AFD.

51. Testimony of Denyse Simenon to the author.

52. *Mémoires intimes,* pp. 216, 220, 264, 314, 341, 603, 604, 572, 573, 575, 603.

53. *Les Petits Hommes,* p. 93.

54. Testimony of Lina Chavier to the author.

55. Testimony of Michel Friedman to the author. The three other ghostwriters were Louis Valentin, Jean-Pierre Spilmont, and Dimitri Davidenko.

56. *On dit que j'ai soixante-quinze ans,* p. 68.
57. GS interviewed by André Bourin, France-Culture, November 1981.
58. *Mémoires intimes,* pp. 354–56, 578; *On dit que j'ai soixante-quinze ans,* pp. 80–82.
59. Testimony of Denyse Simenon to the author.
60. Article by Christian Guy in *Votre enfant,* no. 28, February 1955.
61. *Mémoires intimes,* pp. 435, 436, 612; *On dit que j'ai soixante-quinze ans,* pp. 94, 95.
62. Testimony of Denyse Simenon to the author.
63. Testimony of Pierre Simenon to the author.
64. *La Femme endormie,* p. 43; *Vacances obligatoires,* p. 78; GS interviewed by Fenton Bresler, unpublished.
65. Testimony of Roger Mirmont to the author.
66. *Mémoires intimes,* pp. 585, 642, 651, 599, 608, 716, 752.
67. *Quand vient le froid,* p. 44.
68. Testimony of Denyse Simenon to the author.
69. GS to Jean-Pierre Farkas (*Elle*), June 2, 1978, APSL.
70. GS interviewed by Pierre Lhoste, radio; *Mémoires intimes,* p. 607.
71. Testimony of Marc Simenon to the author.
72. Testimony of Denyse Simenon to the author.
73. GS to Maurice Bessy, June 24, 1978, AMB.
74. GS interviewed by Pierre Lhoste, radio.
75. *Mémoires intimes,* p. 572.
76. Ibid., pp. 584, 585.
77. GS interviewed by Claude Chabrol, 1982, published in *Studio,* no. 31, October 1989, p. 96.
78. Testimony of Pierre Simenon to the author.
79. *Un homme comme un autre,* p. 51.
80. *Je suis resté un enfant de chœur,* p. 49.
81. GS to Federico Fellini, January 11, 1980, FSUL.
82. *Vacances obligatoires,* p. 19.
83. GS to Hamish Hamilton, April 13, 1981, APSL; GS to Fenton Bresler, April 13, 1981, APSL.
84. GS to Federico Fellini, August 13, 1980, FSUL.
85. GS to Fenton Bresler, June 6, 1980, AFB.
86. GS to Fenton Bresler, April 9, 1980, AFB.
87. TS 12, pp. 696, 697.
88. *Mémoires intimes,* pp. 495, 496.
89. Ibid.
90. Testimony of Denyse Simenon to the author.
91. GS, interview, Swiss radio and television, 1982.
92. *Le Point,* November 16, 1981.
93. Anthony Burgess, *Homage à Qwert Yiop* (Grasset, 1988), pp. 195–98.
94. Testimony of Helen Wolff to the author. On the reception of *Intimate Memoirs* in America, see GS, interviewed by Leslie Garis, *The New York Times Magazine,* April 22, 1984.
95. Notes of Bernard Pivot, in *Lire,* October 1989, p. 11.
96. GS to Pierre Clerdent, June 15, 1984, letter communicated to the author by the Baron Clerdent.
97. Testimony of Frédéric Dard to the author.
98. GS interviewed by Eléanore Schraiber, August 16, 1979, FSUL.
99. List established and communicated to the author by Teresa Sburelin.
100. GS to Maurice Piron, November 4, 1975, in *Traces,* no. 1, University of Liège, 1989.
101. *Les Petits Hommes,* p. 53.
102. Testimony of Marc, John, and Pierre Simenon to the author.
103. GS to Maurice Bessy, June 22, 1982, AMB.
104. Testimony of Gabrielle Rolin to the author.
105. Jean Renoir to GS, May 12, 1969, FSUL.
106. Marcel Carné, p. 333.
107. Testimony of Pierre Simenon to the author.

SOURCES

Bibliography

The following lists of Simenon's works have been established thanks to the research of Claude Menguy, Pierre Deligny, Michel Lemoine, Maurice Dubourg, Maurice Piron, Mathieu Rutten, Gilbert Sigaux, Bernard de Fallois, and Francis Lacassin.

Unless otherwise indicated, works appear in chronological order of their release. The dates are the years of publication; the city of publication is Paris unless otherwise indicated. The names of the publishers are given after each title.

The letter *S* in parentheses after a work indicates that the title concerned is a collection of short stories. The letter *M* indicates that the book is a Maigret, the letter *D* that it is one of the autobiographical *Dictées* (Dictations).

I. Works Published Under Pseudonyms

1921
Georges Sim, *Au pont des Arches*, Bénard, Liège (reissued by Presses de la Cité, 1991).

1924
Jean du Perry, *Le Roman d'une dactylo*, Ferenczi.
Jean du Perry, *Amour d'exilée*, Ferenczi.
Georges Sim, *Les Larmes avant le bonheur*, Ferenczi.

1925
Georges Martin-Georges, *L'orgueil qui meurt*, Tallandier.
Gom Gut, *Un viol aux "Quat'z'Arts,"* Prima.
Jean du Perry, *L'Heureuse Fin*, Ferenczi.

Georges d'Isly, *Etoile de cinéma*, Rouff.
Jean du Perry, *L'Oiseau blessé*, Ferenczi.
Christian Brulls, *La Prêtresse des Vaudoux*, Tallandier.
Jean du Perry, *La Fiancée fugitive*, Ferenczi.
Jean du Perry, *Entre deux haines*, Ferenczi.
Gom Gut, *Aux vingt-huit négresses*, Prima.
Jean du Perry, *Pour le sauver*, Ferenczi.
Jean du Perry, *Ceux qu'on avait oubliés*, Ferenczi.
Jean du Perry, *Pour qu'il soit heureux*, Ferenczi.
Gom Gut, *La Noce à Montmartre*, Prima.
Jean du Perry, *Amour d'Afrique*, Ferenczi.
Jean du Perry, *A l'assaut d'un cœur*, Ferenczi.

1926
Luc Dorsan, *Nuit de Noces,* followed by *Double noces* and *Les Noces ardentes*, Prima (S).
Luc Dorsan, *Histoire d'un pantalon*, Prima.
Christian Brulls, *Sa Ma Tsien, le sacrificateur*, Tallandier.
Jean du Perry, *L'Orgueil d'aimer*, Ferenczi.
Luc Dorsan, *Nini violée*, Prima.
Jean du Perry, *Celle qui est aimée*, Ferenczi.
Jean du Perry, *Les yeux qui ordonnent*, Ferenczi.
Gom Gut, *Une Petite très sensuelle*, Prima.
Jean du Perry, *Que ma mère l'ignore!*, Ferenczi.
Jean du Perry, *De la rue au bonheur*, Ferenczi.
Jean du Perry, *Un péché de jeunesse*, Ferenczi.
Gom Gut, *Orgies bourgeoises*, Prima.
Christian Brulls, *Nox l'insaisissable*, Ferenczi.

1927
Georges Sim, *Un monsieur libidineux*, Prima.
Luc Dorsan, *La Pucelle de Bénouville*, Prima.
Georges Sim, *Le Cercle de la soif*, Ferenczi.
Gom Gut, *L'Homme aux douze étreintes*, Prima.
Georges Sim, *Le Feu s'éteint*, Fayard.
Jean du Perry, *Lili-Tristesse*, Ferenczi.
Jean du Perry, *Un tout petit cœur*, Tallandier.
Gom Gut, *Etreintes passionées*, Prima.
Georges Sim, *Défense d'aimer*, Ferenczi.

Georges Sim, *Les Voleurs de navires*, Tallandier.

1928

Christian Brulls, *Dolorosa*, Fayard.
Christian Brulls, *Le Désert du froid qui tue*, Ferenczi.
Georges Sim, *Le Monstre blanc de la Terre de feu*, Ferenczi.
Georges Sim, *Le Roi des glaces*, Tallandier.
Georges Sim, *Miss Baby*, Fayard.
Christian Brulls, *Mademoiselle X . . .*, Fayard.
Georges Sim, *Chair de beauté*, Fayard.
Jean du Perry, *Le Fou d'amour*, Ferenczi.
Gom Gut, *L'Amour à Montparnasse*, Ferenczi.
Gom Gut, *Madame veut un amant*, Ferenczi.
Georges Sim, *Les Cœurs perdus*, Tallandier.
Georges Sim, *Le Secret des lamas*, Tallandier.
Luc Dorsan, *Une petite dessalée*, Ferenczi.
Gom Gut, *Les Distractions d'Hélène*, Ferenczi.
Jacques Dersonne, *Un seul baiser*, Ferenczi.
Georges-Martin Georges, *Un soir de vertige*, Ferenczi.
Georges Sim, *Les Maudits du Pacifique*, Tallandier.
Jean du Perry, *Cœur exalté*, Ferenczi.
Gaston Vialis, *Un petit corps blessé*, Ferenczi.
Georges Sim, *La Maison sans soleil*, Fayard.
Georges-Martin Georges, *Brin d'amour*, Ferenczi.
Christian Brulls, *Les Adolescents passionés*, Fayard.
Georges Sim, *Le Semeur de larmes*, Ferenczi.
Gaston Vialis, *Haïr à force d'aimer*, Ferenczi.
Jean du Perry, *Trois Cœurs dans la tempête*, Ferenczi.
Georges Sim, *Le Sous-Marin dans la forêt*, Tallandier.
Jean du Perry, *Les Amants de la mansarde*, Ferenczi.
Christian Brulls, *Annie, danseuse*, Ferenczi.
Georges Sim, *Aimer d'amour*, Ferenczi.
Georges Sim, *Songes d'été*, Ferenczi.
Georges-Martin Georges, *Les Cœurs vides*, Ferenczi.
Georges-Martin Georges, *Cabotine*, Ferenczi.
Georges Sim, *Les Nains des cataractes*, Tallandier.
Gom Gut, *L'Amant fantôme*, Prima.
Jean du Perry, *Un jour de soleil*, Ferenczi.
Georges Sim, *La Lac d'angoisse*, Ferenczi.
Georges Sim, *Le Sang des gitanes*, Ferenczi.
G. Vialo, *L'Etreinte tragique*, Ferenczi.

1929

Georges Sim, *La femme qui tue*, Fayard.
Georges Sim, *Le Gorille roi*, Tallandier.
Christian Brulls, *L'Amant sans nom*, Fayard.
Georges Sim, *La Fiancée aux mains de glace*, Fayard.
Georges Sim, *Les Mémoires d'un prostitué par lui-même*, Prima.
Georges Sim, *En Robe de mariée*, Tallandier.
Jean Dorsage, *L'Amour méconnu*, Ferenczi.
G. Violis, *Rien que pour toi*, Ferenczi.
Luc Dorsan, *Un drôle de coco*, Prima.
Jean du Perry, *La Fille de l'autre*, Ferenczi.
Georges-Martin Georges, *Aimer, mourir*, Ferenczi.
Georges Sim, *Destinées*, Fayard.
G. Violis, *Trop beau pour elle!*, Ferenczi.
Georges Sim, *L.53*, Fayard.
J. K. Charles, *La Police scientifique*, Fayard.
Georges-Martin Georges, *Voleuse d'amour*, Ferenczi.
Jean du Perry, *L'Amour et l'argent*, Ferenczi.
Jean Dorsage, *Celle qui revient*, Ferenczi.
Georges Sim, *Les Bandits de Chicago*, Fayard.
Georges Sim, *L'Ile des hommes roux*, Tallandier.
Jean du Perry, *Cœur de poupée*, Ferenczi.
Jean du Perry, *Une femme qui a tué*, Ferenczi.
Germain d'Antibes, *Hélas! je t'aime*, Ferenczi.
Christian Brulls, *Un drame au pôle sud*, Fayard.
Georges Sim, *Le Roi du Pacifique*, Ferenczi.
Georges-Martin Georges, *Une ombre dans la nuit*, Ferenczi.
Christian Brulls, *Captain S.O.S.*, Fayard.
Jean du Perry, *Deux Cœurs de femmes*, Ferenczi.
Jean du Perry, *L'Epave d'amour*, Ferenczi.
Georges Sim, *Les Contrebandiers de l'alcool*, Fayard.
Jean du Perry, *Le Mirage de Paris*, Ferenczi.
Christian Brulls, *Les Pirates du Texas*, Ferenczi.
Georges-Martin Georges, *Nuit de Paris*, Ferenczi.
Georges-Martin Georges, *La Victime*, Ferenczi.
Georges Sim, *L'Ile des maudits*, Ferenczi.
Jean Dossage, *Les Deux Maîtresses*, Ferenczi.
Jacques Dersonne, *La Merveilleuse Aventure*, Ferenczi.
Georges Sim, *La Femme en deuil*, Tallandier.

1930

Christian Brulls, *Jacques d'Antifer, roi des Iles du Vent*, Ferenczi.

Georges Sim, *Nez d'argent*, Ferenczi.
Georges Sim, *La Femme 47*, Fayard.
Georges Sim, *Mademoiselle Million*, Fayard.
Christian Brulls, *Train de nuit*, Fayard
    (reissued Julliard, 1991).
Jean Dorsage, *Cœur de jeune fille*, Ferenczi.
Jean du Perry, *Celle qui passe*, Ferenczi.
Georges-Martin Georges, *Un nid d'amour*,
    Ferenczi.
Georges Sim, *Le Pêcheur des bouées*, Tallandier.
Jean du Perry, *Petite Exilée*, Ferenczi.
Jean du Perry, *Les Amants du malheur*,
    Ferenczi.
Georges-Martin Georges, *Bobette, mannequin*,
    Ferenczi.
Gaston Viallis, *Lili-Sourire*, Ferenczi.
Jean du Perry, *La Femme ardente*, Ferenczi.
Jean du Perry, *La Porte close*, Ferenczi.
Jacques Dersonne, *Les Etapes du mensonge*,
    Ferenczi.
Georges-Martin Georges, *La Puissance du*
    souvenir, Ferenczi.
Jean du Perry, *La Poupée brisée*, Ferenczi.
Gaston Viallis, *Folie d'un soir*, Ferenczi.
Georges-Martin Georges, *Le Bonheur de Lili*,
    Ferenczi.

1931
Jean du Perry, *Marie-Mystère*, Fayard.
Georges Sim, *L'Homme à la cigarette*,
    Tallandier (reissued Julliard, 1991).
Georges Sim, *Katia, acrobate*, Fayard.
Georges Sim, *L'Homme de proie*, Fayard.
Christian Brulls, *La Maison de la haine*, Fayard.
Georges Sim, *Les Errants*, Fayard.
Jacques Dersonne, *Baisers mortels*, Ferenczi.
Georges-Martin Georges, *La Double Vie*,
    Ferenczi.
Jean Dorsage, *Les Chercheurs de bonheur*,
    Ferenczi.
Jean du Perry, *Pauvre amante!*, Ferenczi.
Gaston Viallis, *Ame de jeune fille*, Ferenczi.
Christian Brulls, *Pour venger son père*, Ferenczi.
Jacques Dersonne, *Victime de son fils*, Ferenczi.
Jean du Perry, *Le rêve qui meurt*, Rouff.

1932
Christian Brulls, *La Figurante*, Fayard (reissued
    Julliard, 1991, under the title *La Jeune*
    Fille aux perles).
Georges Sim, *Matricule 12*, Tallandier.
Georges Sim, *La Maison de l'inquiétude*,
    Tallandier (reissued Julliard, 1991).
Georges Sim, *L'Epave*, Fayard.
Christian Brulls, *Fièvre*, Fayard.

Christian Brulls, *Les Forçats de Paris*, Fayard.
Georges Sim, *La Fiancée du diable*, Fayard.

1933
Georges Sim, *Deuxième Bureau*, Tallandier.
Georges Sim, *La Femme rousse*, Tallandier
    (reissued Julliard, 1991).
Georges Sim, *Le Château des sables rouges*,
    Tallandier (reissued Julliard, 1991).

1934
Christian Brulls, *L'Evasion*, Fayard.

1937
Christian Brulls, *Seul parmi les gorilles*,
    Ferenczi.
Christian Brulls, *L'Ile empoisonnée*, Ferenczi.
(These two novels probably written in 1928.)

1991
Georges Sim, *Jehan Pinaguet. Histoire d'un*
    homme simple, Presses de la Cité (novel
    written in 1921, unpublished until
    1991).

II. WORKS PUBLISHED UNDER HIS OWN NAME

Titles that have been published in English are
given in italics. When the book bore different
titles in Britain and the United States, both are
given. Titles that have not been published in
English are translated literally, in roman type.

1931
Monsieur Gallet, décédé, Fayard (M). *The Death*
    of Monsieur Gallet.
Le Pendu de Saint-Pholien, Fayard (M). *Maigret*
    and the Hundred Gibbets (Britain). *The*
    Crime of Inspector Maigret (US).
Le Charretier de "La Providence," Fayard (M).
    The Crime at Lock 14.
Le Chien jaune, Fayard (M). *A Face for a Clue*.
Pietr-le-Letton, Fayard (M). *The Case of Peter*
    the Lett (Britain). *The Strange Case of*
    Peter the Lett (US).
La Nuit du carrefour, Fayard (M). *The*
    Crossroad Murders.
Un crime en Hollande, Fayard (M). *A Crime in*
    Holland.
La Folle d'Itteville, Jacques Haumont. The
    Madwoman of Itteville.
Au Rendez-vous des Terres-Neuvas, Fayard
    (M). *The Sailors' Rendez-vous*.

La Tête d'un homme, Fayard (M). *A Battle of Nerves*.

Le Relais d'Alsace, Fayard. *The Man from Everywhere*.

La Danseuse du Gai-Moulin, Fayard (M). *At the Gai-Moulin*.

1932

La Guinguette à deux sous, Fayard (M). *The Guinguette by the Seine*.

L'Ombre chinoise, Fayard (M). *The Shadow in the Courtyard*.

L'Affair Saint-Fiacre, Fayard (M). *The Saint-Fiacre Affair*.

Chez les Flamands, Fayard (M). *The Flemish Shop*.

Le Fou de Bergerac, Fayard (M). *The Madman of Bergerac*.

Le Port des brumes, Fayard (M). *Death of a Harbour Master*.

Le Passager du "Polarlys," Fayard. *The Mystery of the "Polarlys"* (Britain). *Danger at Sea* (US).

"Liberty Bar," Fayard (M). *Liberty Bar*.

Les Treize Coupables, Fayard. Thirteen Guilty Men.

Les Treize Énigmes, Fayard. Thirteen Enigmas.

Les Treize Mystères, Fayard. Thirteen Mysteries.

1933

Les Fiançailles de M. Hire, Fayard. *Mr. Hire's Engagement*.

Le Coup de lune, Fayard. *Tropic Moon*.

La Maison du canal, Fayard. *The House by the Canal*.

L'Ecluse no. 1, Fayard (M). *The Lock at Charenton*.

L'Âne rouge, Fayard. *The Nightclub*.

Les Gens d'en face, Fayard. *The Window Over the Way* (Britain). *Danger Ashore* (US).

Le Haut Mal, Fayard. *The Woman of the Grey House*.

1934

L'Homme de Londres, Fayard. *Newhaven–Dieppe*.

Maigret, Fayard (M). *Maigret Returns*.

Le Locataire, Gallimard. *The Lodger*.

Les Suicidés, Gallimard. *One Way Out*.

1935

Les Pitard, Gallimard. *A Wife at Sea*.

Les Clients d'Avernos, Gallimard. The Clients of Avernos.

Quartier nègre, Gallimard. Negro Quarter.

1936

L'Evadé, Gallimard. *The Disintegration of J.P.G.*

Long Cours, Gallimard. *The Long Exile*.

Les Demoiselles de Concarneau, Gallimard. *The Breton Sisters*.

45° à l'ombre, Gallimard. *Aboard the Aquitaine*.

1937

Le Testament Donadieu, Gallimard. *The Shadow Falls*.

L'Assassin, Gallimard. *The Murderer*.

Le Blanc à lunettes, Gallimard. *Talatala*.

Faubourg, Gallimard. *Home Town*.

1938

Ceux de la soif, Gallimard. *They Who Thirst*.

Chemin sans issue, Gallimard. *Blind Path* (Britain). *Blind Alley* (US).

Les Sept Minutes (S: "Le Grand Langoustier," "La Nuit des sept minutes," and "l'Enigme de la Marie-Galante"), Gallimard.

Les Rescapés du Télémaque, Gallimard. *The Survivors*.

Les Trois Crimes de mes amis, Gallimard. My Friends' Three Crimes.

La Mauvaise Etoile, Gallimard. Unlucky Star.

Le Suspect, Gallimard. *The Green Thermos*.

Les Sœurs Lacroix, Gallimard. *Poisoned Relations*.

Touriste de bananes, Gallimard. *Banana Tourist*.

Monsieur la Souris, Gallimard. *Monsieur La Souris*.

La Marie du port, Gallimard. *A Chit of a Girl*.

L'homme qui regardait passer les trains, Gallimard. *The Man Who Watched the Trains Go By*.

Le Cheval-Blanc, Gallimard. *The White Horse Inn*.

1939

Le Coup de vague, Gallimard. The Breaking Wave.

Chez Krull, Gallimard. *Chez Krull*.

Le Bourgmestre de Furnes, Gallimard. *The Burgomaster of Furnes*.

1940

Malempin, Gallimard. *The Family Lie*.

Les Inconnus dans la maison, Gallimard. *The Strangers in the House*.

1941

Cour d'assises, Gallimard. *Justice*.

Bergelon, Gallimard. *The Country Doctor* (Britain). *The Delivery* (US).

L'Outlaw, Gallimard. *The Outlaw.*

Il pleut, bergère . . . , Gallimard. *Black Rain.*

Le Voyageur de la Toussaint, Gallimard. *Strange Inheritance.*

La Maison des sept jeunes filles, Gallimard. The House of Seven Girls.

1942

Oncle Charles s'est enfermé, Gallimard. Uncle Charles Has Locked Himself Away.

La Veuve Couderc, Gallimard. *Ticket of Leave* (Britain). *The Widow* (US).

Maigret revient . . . , (Containing: *Cécile est morte, Les Caves du Majestic,* and *La Maison du juge*), Gallimard (M). *Maigret and the Spinster, Maigret and the Hotel Majestic,* and *Maigret in Exile.*

Le Fils Cardinaud, Gallimard. *Young Cardinaud.*

La Verité sur Bébé Donge, Gallimard. *The Trial of Bébé Donge* (Britain). *I Take This Woman* (US).

1943

Le Petit Docteur (S: "Le Flair du Petit Docteur," "La Demoiselle en bleu pâle," "Une Femme a crié," "La Bonne Fortune du Hollandais," "Le Passager et son nègre," "La Piste de l'homme roux," "L'Amiral a disparu," "La Sonnette d'alarme," "Le Château de l'arsenic," and "L'Amoureux aux pantoufles"), Gallimard.

Les Dossiers de l'Agence O (S: "La Cage d'Emile," "La Cabane en bois," "L'Homme tout nu," "L'Arrestation du musicien," "L'Etrangleur de Moret," "Le Vieillard au porte-mine," "Les trois bateaux de la calanque," "La Fleuriste de Deauville," "Le Ticket de métro," "Emile à Bruxelles," "Le Prisonnier de Lagny," "Le Club des vieilles dames," "Le Docteur Tant-Pis," and "Le Chantage de l'Agence O"), Gallimard.

1944

Signé Picpus (S: "Signé Picpus" (M), "L'Inspecteur Cadavre" (M), "Félicie est là" (M), "L'Escale de Buenaventura," "Un crime au Gabon," "Le Policier d'Istanbul," "L'Enquête de Mlle Doche," and "La Ligne du désert"), Gallimard. "Signé Picpus": "To Any Lengths." "L'Inspecteur Cadavre": "Maigret's

Rival." "Félicie est là": "Maigret and the Toy Village."

Le Rapport du Gendarme, Gallimard. *The Gendarme's Report.*

Les Nouvelles Enquêtes de Maigret (S: "La Péniche aux deux pendus," "L'Affaire du boulevard Beaumarchais," "La Fenêtre ouverte," "Monsieur Lundi," "Jeumont," "51 minutes d'arrêt," "Peine de mort," "Les Larmes de bougie," "Rue Pigalle," "Une Erreur de Maigret," "L'Amoureux de Mme Maigret," "La Vieille Dame de Bayeux," "L'Auberge aux noyés," "Stan-le-Terreur," "L'Etoile du Nord," "Tempête sur la Manche," "Mademoiselle Berthe et son amant," and "Le Notaire de Châteauneuf"), Gallimard (M).

1945

La Fenêtre des Rouet, La Jeune Parque. *Across the Street.*

La Fuite de Monsieur Monde, La Jeune Parque. *Monsieur Monde Vanishes.*

L'Aventure (speech delivered in 1937), Editions de Savoie, Lyons. Adventure.

L'Aîné des Ferchaux, Gallimard. *The First-Born.*

Je me souviens . . . , Presses de la Cité. I Remember . . .

1946

Les Noces de Poitiers, Gallimard. *The Couple from Poitiers.*

Trois Chambres à Manhattan, Presses de la Cité. *Three Beds in Manhattan.*

Le Cercle de Mahé, Gallimard. Mahé's Circle.

1947

Au bout du rouleau, Presses de la Cité. Running on Empty.

On ne tue pas les pauvres types, Fayard (S). Poor Guys Don't Get Killed.

Maigret se fâche, followed by *La Pipe de Maigret* (S), Presses de la Cité (M). *Maigret in Retirement.*

Maigret à New York, Presses de la Cité (M). *Inspector Maigret in New York's Underworld.*

Lettre à mon juge, Presses de la Cité. *Act of Passion.*

Le Clan des Ostendais, Gallimard. *The Ostenders.*

Le Destin des Malou, Presses de la Cité. *The Fate of the Malous.*

Maigret et l'inspecteur malchanceux, reprinted as *Maigret et l'inspecteur malgracieux* (S: "Maigret et l'inspecteur malchanceux,"

"Le Témoignage de l'enfant de chœur,"
"Le Client le plus obstiné du monde,"
and "On ne tue pas les pauvres types"),
Presses de la Cité (M). Maigret and the
Unlucky/Ungainly Inspector. An Altar
Boy's Testimony. The World's Most
Obstinate Client. Poor Guys Don't Get
Killed.

La Passager clandestin, La Jeune Parque. *The
Stowaway.*

1948

Le Bilan Malétras, Gallimard. *The Reckoning.*

La Jument perdue, Presses de la Cité. The Lost
Mare.

Maigret et son mort, Presses de la Cité (M).
Maigret's Special Murder (Britain).
Maigret's Dead Man (US).

Les Vacances de Maigret, Presses de la Cité (M).
Maigret on Holiday (Britain). *No Vacation
for Maigret* (US).

La Neige était sale, Presses de la Cité. *The Stain
on the Snow* (Britain). *The Snow Was
Black* (US).

Pedigree, Presses de la Cité. *Pedigree.*

1949

Le Fond de la bouteille, Presses de la Cité. *The
Bottom of the Bottle.*

La Première Enquête de Maigret (1913), Presses
de la Cité (M). *Maigret's First Case.*

Les Fantômes du chapelier, Presses de la Cité.
The Hatter's Ghosts.

Mon ami Maigret, Presses de la Cité. *My Friend
Maigret* (Britain). *The Methods of Maigret*
(US).

Les Quatre Jours du pauvre homme, Presses de
la Cité. *Four Days in a Lifetime.*

Maigret chez le coroner, Presses de la Cité (M).
Maigret and the Coroner.

1950

Un nouveau dans la ville, Presses de la Cité. *A
New Man in Town.*

Maigret et la vieille dame, Presses de la Cité
(M). *Maigret and the Old Lady.*

L'Amie de Madame Maigret, Presses de la Cité
(M). *Mme Maigret's Friend* (Britain).
Madame Maigret's Own Case (US).

L'Enterrement de M. Bouvet, Presses de la Cité.
Inquest on Bouvet (Britain). *The Burial of
Monsieur Bouvet* (US).

Maigret et les petits cochons sans queue (S: "Les
Petits Cochons sans queue," "Sous peine
de mort," "Le Petit Tailleur et le

chapelier," "Un certain Monsieur
Berquin," "L'Escale de Buenaventura,"
"L'Homme dans la rue," "Vente à la
bougie," "Le Deuil de Fonsine," and
"Madame Quatre et ses enfants"), Presses
de la Cité (M). Maigret and the Little
Tailless Pigs.

Les Volets verts, Presses de la Cité. *The Heart
of a Man.*

1951

Tante Jeanne, Presses de la Cité. *Aunt Jeanne.*

Les Mémoires de Maigret, Presses de la Cité
(M). *Maigret's Memoirs.*

La Neige était sale (play, adapted with Frédéric
Dard), Fayard.

Le Temps d'Anaïs, Presses de la Cité. *The Girl
in His Past.*

Un Noël de Maigret (S: "Un Noël de Maigret,"
"Sept Petites Croix dans un carnet," and
"Le Petit Restaurant des Ternes"), Presses
de la Cité (M). *Maigret's Christmas.*

Maigret au Picratt's, Presses de la Cité (M).
Maigret in Montmartre (Britain). *Inspector
Maigret and the Strangled Stripper* (US).

Maigret enmeublé, Presses de la Cité (M).
Maigret Takes a Room (Britain). *Maigret
Rents a Room* (US).

Une vie comme neuve, Presses de la Cité. *A New
Lease of Life.*

Maigret et la grande perche, Presses de la Cité
(M). *Maigret and the Burglar's Wife*
(Britain). *Inspector Maigret and the
Burglar's Wife* (US).

1952

Marie qui louche, Presses de la Cité. *The Girl
with a Squint.*

Maigret, Lognon et les gangsters, Presses de
la Cité (M). *Maigret and the Gangsters*
(Britain). *Inspector Maigret and the
Killers* (US).

Long Cours sur les rivières et canaux, Dynamo,
Liège. Along the Rivers and Canals.

La Mort de Belle, Presses de la Cité. *Belle.*

Le Revolver de Maigret, Presses de la Cité (M).
Maigret's Revolver.

Les Frères Rico, Presses de la Cité. *The Brothers
Rico.*

1953

Maigret et l'homme du banc, Presses de la Cité
(M). *Maigret and the Man on the Bench.*

Antoine et Julie, Presses de la Cité. *The
Magician* (Britain). *Antoine and Julie* (US).

Maigret a peur, Presses de la Cité (M). *Maigret Afraid.*

L'Escalier de fer, Presses de la Cité. *The Iron Staircase.*

Feux rouges, Presses de la Cité. *Red Lights* (Britain). *The Hitchhiker* (US).

Maigret se trompe, Presses de la Cité (M). *Maigret's Mistake.*

1954

Crime impuni, Presses de la Cité. *Account Unsettled* (Britain). *The Fugitive* (US).

Maigret à l'école, Presses de la Cité (M). *Maigret Goes to School.*

Le Bateau d'Emile (S: "La Femme du pilote," "Le Doigt de Barraquier," "Valérie s'en va," "L'Epingle en fer à cheval," "Le Baron de l'ecluse ou la croisière du 'Potam,' " "Le nègre s'est endormi," "Le Deuil de Fonsine," "L'Homme à barbe," and "Le Bateau d'Emile"), Gallimard. Emile's Boat.

Maigret et la jeune morte, Presses de la Cité (M). *Maigret and the Young Girl* (Britain). *Maigret and the Dead Girl* (US).

L'Horloger d'Everton, Presses de la Cité. *The Watchmaker of Everton.*

Maigret chez le ministre, Presses de la Cité (M). *Maigret and the Minister* (Britain). *Maigret and the Calame Report* (US).

Le Grand Bob, Presses de la Cité. *Big Bob.*

1955

Les Témoins, Presses de la Cité. *The Witnesses.*

Maigret et le corps sans tête, Presses de la Cité (M). *Maigret and the Headless Corpse.*

La Boule noir, Presses de la Cité. *The Black Ball.*

Maigret tend un piège, Presses de la Cité (M). *Maigret Sets a Trap.*

1956

Les Complices, Presses de la Cité. *The Accomplices.*

En cas de malheur, Presses de la Cité. *In Case of Emergency.*

Un échec de Maigret, Presses de la Cité (M). *Maigret's Failure.*

Le Petit Homme d'Arkhangelsk, Presses de la Cité. *The Little Man from Archangel.*

1957

Maigret s'amuse, Presses de la Cité (M). *Maigret's Little Joke* (Britain). *None of Maigret's Business* (US).

Le Fils, Presses de la Cité. *The Son.*

Le Nègre, Presses de la Cité. *The Negro.*

1958

Maigret voyage, Presses de la Cité (M). *Maigret and the Millionaires.*

Strip-Tease, Presses de la Cité. *Striptease.*

Les Scrupules de Maigret, Presses de la Cité (M). *Maigret Has Scruples.*

Le Président, Presses de la Cité. *The Premier.*

Le Passage de la ligne, Presses de la Cité. *Crossing the Line.*

1959

Dimanche, Presses de la Cité. *Sunday.*

La Femme en France (photographic album), Presses de la Cité. *Women of France.*

Maigret et les témoins récalcitrants, Presses de la Cité (M). *Maigret and the Reluctant Witness.*

Le Roman de l'homme, Presses de la Cité. *The Novel of a Man.*

Une confidence de Maigret, Presses de la Cité (M). *Maigret Has Doubts.*

La Vieille, Presses de la Cité. *The Grandmother.*

Le Veuf, Presses de la Cité. *The Widower.*

1960

Maigret aux assises, Presses de la Cité (M). *Maigret in Court.*

L'Ours en peluche, Presses de la Cité. *Teddy Bear.*

Maigret et les vieillards, Presses de la Cité (M). *Maigret in Society.*

1961

Betty, Presses de la Cité. *Betty.*

Le Train, Presses de la Cité. *The Train.*

Maigret et le voleur paresseux, Presses de la Cité (M). *Maigret and the Lazy Burglar.*

1962

La Porte, Presses de la Cité. *The Door.*

Les Autres, Presses de la Cité. *The Others.*

Maigret et les braves gens, Presses de la Cité (M). *Maigret and the Black Sheep.*

Maigret et le client du samedi, Presses de la Cité (M). *Maigret and the Saturday Caller.*

1963

Maigret et le clochard, Presses de la Cité (M). *Maigret and the Dosser* (Britain). *Maigret and the Bum* (US).

Les Anneaux de Bicêtre, Presses de la Cité. *The Patient* (Britain). *The Bells of Bicêtre* (US).

La Rue aux trois poussins (S: "La Rue aux trois poussins," "Le Comique du 'Saint-Antoine,' " "Le mari de Mélie," "Le Capitaine du 'Vasco,' " "Le Deuil de Fonsine," "Le Crime du Malgracieux," "Le Docteur de Kirkenes," "La Piste du Hollandais," "Les Demoiselles de Queue de vache," "Le Matin des trois absoutes," "Le Naufrage de l'Armoire à glace," "Les Mains pleines," "Nicolas," and "Annette et la dame blonde"), Presses de la Cité. *The Street with Three Chicks.*

La Colère de Maigret, Presses de la Cité (M). *Maigret Loses His Temper.*

1964

La Chambre bleu, Presses de la Cité. *The Blue Room.*

L'Homme au petit chien, Presses de la Cité. *The Man with the Little Dog.*

Maigret et le fantôme, Presses de la Cité (M). *Maigret and the Ghost* (Britain). *Maigret and the Apparition* (US).

Maigret se défend, Presses de la Cité (M). *Maigret on the Defensive.*

1965

Le Petit Saint, Presses de la Cité. *The Little Saint.*

Le Train de Venise, Presses de la Cité. *The Venice Train.*

La Patience de Maigret, Presses de la Cité (M). *The Patience of Maigret.*

1966

Le Confessional, Presses de la Cité. *The Confessional.*

La Mort d'Auguste, Presses de la Cité. *The Old Man Dies.*

1967

Maigret et l'affaire Nahour, Presses de la Cité (M). *Maigret and the Nahour Case.*

Le Chat, Presses de la Cité. *The Cat.*

Le Voleur de Maigret, Presses de la Cité (M). *Maigret's Pickpocket.*

Le Déménagement, Presses de la Cité. *The Neighbors* (Britain). *The Move* (US).

1968

Maigret à Vichy, Presses de la Cité (M). *Maigret Takes the Waters* (Britain). *Maigret in Vichy* (US).

La Prison, Presses de la Cité. *The Prison.*

Maigret hésite, Presses de la Cité (M). *Maigret Hesitates.*

La Main, Presses de la Cité. *The Man on the Bench in the Barn.*

L'Ami d'enfance de Maigret, Presses de la Cité (M). *Maigret's Boyhood Friend.*

1969

Il y a encore des noisetiers, Presses de la Cité. *There Are Still Some Hazel Trees.*

Novembre, Presses de la Cité. *November.*

Maigret et le tueur, Presses de la Cité (M). *Maigret and the Killer.*

1970

Maigret et le marchand de vin, Presses de la Cité (M). *Maigret and the Wine Merchant.*

Quand j'étais vieux, Presses de la Cité. *When I Was Old.*

Le Riche Homme, Presses de la Cité. *The Rich Man.*

La Folle de Maigret, Presses de la Cité (M). *Maigret and the Madwoman.*

1971

La Disparition d'Odile, Presses de la Cité. *The Disappearance of Odile.*

Maigret et l'homme tout seul, Presses de la Cité (M). *Maigret and the Loner.*

La Cage de verre, Presses de la Cité. *The Glass Cage.*

Maigret et l'indicateur, Presses de la Cité (M). *Maigret and the Flea* (Britain). *Maigret and the Informer* (US).

1972

Les Innocents, Presses de la Cité. *The Innocents.*

Maigret et Monsieur Charles, Presses de la Cité (M). *Maigret and Monsieur Charles.*

1974

Lettre à ma mère, Presses de la Cité. *Letter to My Mother.*

1975 (beginning of the Dictées)

Un homme comme un autre, Presses de la Cité (D). *A Man Like Any Other.*

Des traces de pas, Presses de la Cité (D). *Footprints.*

1976

Les Petits Hommes, Presses de la Cité (D). *Ordinary Men.*

Vent du Nord, Vent du sud, Presses de la Cité
(D). North Wind, South Wind.

1977
Un banc au soleil, Presses de la Cité (D). A
Bench in the Sun.
De la cave au grenier, Presses de la Cité (D).
From Cellar to Attic.
A l'abri de notre arbre, Presses de la Cité (D). In
the Shelter of Our Tree.

1978
Tant que je suis vivant, Presses de la Cité (D).
So Long as I Live.
Vacances obligatoires, Presses de la Cité (D).
Compulsory Holiday.
La Main dans la main, Presses de la Cité (D).
Hand in Hand.
Au-delà de ma porte-fenêtre, Presses de la Cité
(D). Beyond My Window.

1979
Je suis resté un enfant de chœur, Presses de la
Cité (D). Still an Altar Boy.
A quoi bon jurer?, Presses de la Cité (D). Why
Bother to Swear?
Point-Virgule, Presses de la Cité (D). Semicolon.

1980
Le Prix d'un homme, Presses de la Cité (D). A
Man's Price.
On dit que j'ai soixante-quinze ans, Presses de
la Cité (D). They Say I'm Seventy-five.
Quand vient le froid, Presses de la Cité (D).
When It Turns Cold.
Les Libertés qu'il nous reste, Presses de la Cité
(D). The Freedoms Left Us.

1981
La Femme endormie, Presses de la Cité (D).
Woman Asleep.
Jour et nuit, Presses de la Cité (D). Day and
Night.
Destinées, Presses de la Cité (D). Destinies.
Mémoires intimes, Presses de la Cité. *Intimate
Memoirs.*

Some of the articles Simenon wrote in the press
between the two World Wars and just after
World War II were collected by Francis Lacassin and Gilbert Sigaux and published in
three volumes, 1987–89, by 10/18 of Paris,
under the titles *A la rencontre des autres, A la
découverte de la France,* and *A la recherche de
l'homme nu.*

Various writings by Simenon between 1919
and 1966, dealing with writers, literature, Maigret, and other matters were collected by Francis Lacassin and published by Christian
Bourgeois, Paris, 1991, under the title *Portrait-
Souvenir de Balzac.* Others have appeared under
the title *L'Age du roman* (Complexe, Brussels,
1988). Pierre Deligny published Simenon's reportage entitled *Le Drame mystérieux des îles
Galápagos* under the auspices of Les Amis de
Georges Simenon, Brussels, 1991.

III. On Simenon

1. Books

Bertrand, Alain. *Georges Simenon.* Lyons: La
Manufacture, 1988.
Boutry, Marie-Paul. *Les 300 vies de Simenon.*
Claire Martin du Gard, 1990.
Bresler, Fenton. *The Mystery of Georges
Simenon.* New York: Stein and Day, 1985.
Camus, Jean-Christophe. *Simenon avant
Simenon. Les années de journalisme
(1919–1922).* Brussels: Didier Hatier,
1989.
————. *Les Années parisiennes. Simenon avant
Simenon (1923–1931).* Brussels: Didier
Hatier, 1990.
Chastenet, Patrick and Philippe. *Simenon,
album de famille. Les années Tigy.* Presses
de la Cité, 1981.
Courtine, Robert-J. *Le Cahier de recettes de
Madame Maigret.* Robert Laffont, 1974.
Debray-Ritzen, Pierre. *Georges Simenon,
romancier de l'instinct.* Lausanne: Editions
Pierre-Marcel Favre, 1989 (includes
Simenon, avocat des hommes, signed
Quentin Ritzen and published by Le
Livre contemporain, 1961).
Delcourt, Christian. *Un jeune reporter dans la
guerre des journaux liégeois, Georges Sim.*
Liège: A. Vecqueray, 1977.
Dessane, Odile. *Le Phallus d'or.* Encre, 1981.
Dubourg, Maurice, and Claude Menguy.
*Georges Sim ou les années d'apprentissage
de Georges Simenon,* 1980, unpublished,
FSUL.
Dumortier, Jean-Louis. *Georges Simenon.*
Brussels: Labor-Bruxelles, 1985.
Eskin, Stanley. *Simenon. Une biographie.*
Presses de la Cité, 1990.
Fabre, Jean. *Enquête sur un enquêteur, Maigret.
Un essai de sociocritique.* Montpellier:
Editions du CERES, 1981.

Fallois, Bernard de. *Simenon*. Gallimard, 1961; updated second edition, Lausanne: Editions Rencontre, 1971.

Gautier, Claude. *Simenon au cinéma*. Hatier, 1991.

Gilles, Henry. *La véritable histoire du commissaire Maigret*. Condé-sur-Noireau: Editions Charles Corlet, 1989 (includes *Maigret, qui êtes-vous?*, Plon, 1977).

Gothot-Mersch, Claudine, Jacques Dubois, Jean-Marie Klinkenberg, Danièle Racelle-Latin, and Christian Delcourt. *Lire Simenon. Réalité/Fiction/Ecriture*. Brussels: Fernand Nathan-Editions Labor, 1980.

Jour, Jean. *Simenon et Pedigree*. Liège: Editions de l'essai, 1963.

———. *Simenon, enfant de Liège*. Brussels, 1980.

Lacassin, Francis. *Conversations avec Simenon*. La Sirène/Alpen, 1990.

Lacassin, Francis, and Gilbert Sigaux. *Simenon* (collection with many contributions). Plon, 1973.

Lemoine, Michel. *Index des personnages de Simenon*. Brussels: Labor, 1985.

———. *Liège dans l'œuvre de Simenon*. Liège: Faculté ouverte, 1989.

———. *L'Autre Univers de Simenon. Guide complet des romans populaires publiés sous pseudonymes*. Liège: Editions du CLPCF, 1991.

Marnham, Patrick. *The Man Who Wasn't Maigret. A Portrait of Georges Simenon*. London: Bloomsbury, 1992.

Monnoyer, Maurice. *Trois Heures avec Simenon*. Montpellier: Chez l'auteur, 1989.

Narcejac, Thomas. *Le Cas Simenon*. Presses de la Cité, 1957.

Ouimet, Denyse. *Un oiseau pour le chat*. Jean-Claude Simoën, 1978.

Parinaud, André. *Connaissance de Georges Simenon*. Presses de la Cité, 1957

Piron, Maurice, with the collaboration of Michel Lemoine. *L'Univers de Simenon*. Presses de la Cité, 1983.

Raymond, John. *Simenon in Court*. London: Hamish Hamilton, 1968.

Richter, Anne. *Georges Simenon et l'homme désintégré*. Brussels: La Renaissance du Livre, 1964.

Rutten, Mathieu. *Simenon. Ses origines, sa vie, son œuvre*. Nandrin: Eugène Wahle, 1986.

Simenon Travelling (collection), Catalog of the Eleventh International Festival of the Roman Noir and the Film Noir, Grenoble, October 1989.

Stéphane, Roger. *Le Dossier Simenon* (interviews). Tallandier, 1963; reissued by Quai Voltaire, 1989.

Tauxe, Henri-Charles. *Georges Simenon. De l'humain au vide. Essai de micropsychanalyse appliqué*. Buchet-Chastel, 1983.

Thoorens, Léon. *Qui êtes-vous . . . Georges Simenon?* Verviers: Marabout Flash, 1959.

Tillinac, Denis. *Le Mystère Simenon*. Calmann-Lévy, 1980.

Vandromme, Pol. *Georges Simenon*. Brussels; Pierre de Méyère, 1962.

Vanoncini, André. *Simenon et l'affair Maigret*. Librairie Honoré Champion, 1990.

Veldmann, Hendrik. *La Tentation de l'inaccessible. Structure narrative chez Simenon*. Amsterdam: Rodopi, 1981.

Vellerut, Robert. *Supplément aux Mémoires de Maigret*, unpublished, FSUL.

2. Major Magazine Articles

Adam, International Review, special issue on Simenon, no. 328-330, University of Rochester, New York, 1969.

Alavoine, Bernard. "Simenon, la littérature et ses institutions," in *Cahiers Simenon no. 5*, Les Amis de Georges Simenon, Brussels, 1991.

Andrianne, René. "Pour une biographie de Simenon," in *Cahiers Simenon no. 3*, Les Amis de Georges Simenon, Brussels, 1989.

———. "Simenon dans les histoires de la littérature française," in *Cahiers Simenon no. 5*, Les Amis de Georges Simenon, Brussels, 1991.

Baronian, Jean-Baptiste. "Bruxelles, une ville de passage," in *Cahiers Simenon no. 2*, Les Amis de Georges Simenon, Brussels, 1988.

———. "Simenon conteur et nouvelliste," in *Traces no. 1*, University of Liège, 1989.

Bedner, Jules. "Maigret et le mythe de l'enquêteur infallible," in *Cahiers Simenon no. 2*, Les Amis de Georges Simenon, Brussels, 1988.

Bertrand, Alain. "Georges Simenon et ses doubles: Jules Maigret et Honoré de Balzac," in *Cahiers Simenon no. 3*, Les Amis de Georges Simenon, Brussels, 1989.

————. "Georges Simenon et le genre policier," in *Traces no. 3,* University of Liège, 1991.

Cahiers du Nord (contributions from André Gide, Jean Cassou, Max Jacob, Maurice de Vlaminck et al.), no. 51–52, Charleroi, 1939.

Decaudin, Michel. "Topographie et imaginaire chez Simenon," in *La Licorne no. 12,* Troyes, 1986.

Delbouille, Paul. "Notes pour une étude du récit de paroles," in *Traces no. 1,* University of Liège, 1989.

————. "La place de Simenon dans les dictionnaires et encyclopédies," in *Traces no. 3,* University of Liège, 1991.

Dirick, Claude. "Georges Simenon et André Gide," in *Traces no. 3,* University of Liège, 1991.

Dubois, Jacques. "Simenon et la déviance," in *Littérature no. 1,* February 1971.

————. "Politique de Maigret," in *Traces no. 2,* University of Liège, 1990.

————. "Situation de Simenon," in *Traces no. 3,* University of Liège, 1991.

Dumortier, Jean-Louis. "Les scrupules de Maigret," in *Traces no. 2,* University of Liège, 1990.

Fabre, Jean. "Sur Simenon, un regard socio-psychanalytique," in *Simenon Travelling,* see above.

————. "Nécessité de Maigret," in *Traces no. 1,* University of Liège, 1989.

Fallois, Bernard de. "J'ai perdu un ami," in *Cahiers Simenon no. 3,* Les Amis de Georges Simenon, Brussels, 1989.

Gautier, Claude. "Le personnage de Maigret" (in the cinema), in *Cahiers Simenon no. 1,* Les Amis de Georges Simenon, Brussels, 1988.

Gill, Brendan. "Profile," in *The New Yorker,* January 24, 1953.

Gossiaux, Pol P. "L'Afrique nue de Simenon," in *Traces no. 1,* University of Liège, 1989.

Gothot-Mersch, Claudine. "Genèse des romans de Simenon: le problème des titres," in *Traces no. 1,* University of Liège, 1989.

————. "Simenon et la gestion de l'écriture romanesque," in *Traces no. 2,* University of Liège, 1990.

Lemoine, Michel. "Les villes charentaises et vendéennes dans l'œuvre de George Simenon," in *Cahiers Simenon no. 2,* Les Amis de Georges Simenon, Brussels, 1988.

————. "Errance parmi les romans populaires de Georges Simenon," in *Simenon Travelling,* see above.

————. "Traces autobiographiques d'origine liégeoise dans l'œuvre romanesque de Georges Simenon," in *Cahiers Simenon no. 3,* Les Amis de Georges Simenon, Brussels, 1989.

————. "Images de journalistes dans l'œuvre romanesque de Simenon," in *Cahiers Simenon no. 4,* Les Amis de Georges Simenon, Brussels, 1990.

————. "Simenon face à la critique de 1936 à 1940: jugements et approchements," in *Cahiers Simenon no. 5,* Les Amis de Georges Simenon, Brussels, 1991.

————. "Maigret en gestation dans les romans populaires," in *Traces no. 1,* University of Liège, 1989.

————. "Des romans de Maigret aux romans de la destinée: unité de l'œuvre de Simenon?" in *Traces no.2,* University of Liège, 1989.

————. "Evolution et parentés littéraires de Simenon selon la critique de 1931 à 1935," in *Traces no. 3,* University of Liège, 1991.

————. "Quand Georges Sim préparait Georges Simenon," in *La Revue nouvelle,* Brussels, October 1991.

Menguy, Claude. "Bibliographie des éditions originales de Georges Simenon y compris les œuvres publiées sous des pseudonymes," in *Le Livre et l'estampe,* nos. 49–50, 1967.

————. "Additions et corrections à la Bibliographie des éditions originales de Georges Simenon," in *Le Livre et l'estampe,* nos. 67–68, 1971.

————. "Les vrais débuts du commissaire Maigret," in *Traces no. 1,* University of Liège, 1989.

Magazine Littéraire. "Dossier Simenon," no. 107, December 1975.

Martin, Claude. "André Gide critique de Georges Simenon," in *Bulletin des Amis d'André Gide,* April 1977, no. 34.

Mercier, Paul. "Je ne suis donc pas le seul, je ne suis donc pas un monstre," in *Simenon Travelling,* see above.

————. "Maigret à travers le miroir," in *Traces no. 2,* University of Liège, 1990.

————. "Simenon sociologue? Simenon, sociologue raté ou les deux bouts de la vie," in *Traces no. 3,* University of Liège, 1991.

Monde médical magazine, Le. "Simenon et les médecins," no. 82, Brussels, November 23, 1989.

Nord. "Dossier Simenon," no. 7, Lille, June 1986.

Raphaël, Chaïm. "Simenon on the Jews," in *Midstream,* New York, January 1981, vol. 27, no. 1.

Richter, Anne. "Simenon ou le bonheur n'existe pas," in *Cahiers Simenon no. 1,* Les Amis de Georges Simenon, Brussels, 1988.

Veldman, Hendrick. "Des 'Maigret' aux romans noncycliques: continuité de structure, discontinuité de forme," in *Traces no. 1,* University of Liège, 1989.

Wardi, Charlotte. "Les 'petits juifs' de Georges Simenon," in *Travaux linguistique et de la littérature,* Centre de philologie et de littérature romanes, University of Strasbourg, vol. 12, no. 2, 1974.

The major newspaper obituaries of Georges Simenon are collected in a pamphlet entitled *Au revoir Georges Simenon!,* published by Les Amis de Georges Simenon, Brussels, 1989.

3. Major Memoirs and University Theses

Alavoine, Bernard. *Les Sensations et l'atmosphère dans les romans de Georges Simenon.* Doctoral thesis, University of Picardie, January 1981.

Astori, Gabriella. *Simenon sans Maigret.* Bocconi University of Milan, 1967–68.

Bertrand, Alain. *Les Ambiguïtés de l'indicible dans "Lettre à mon juge."* Catholic University of Louvain, 1981.

Bertrand-Abbas, Marie. *La Question du familiale dans l'œuvre de Georges Simenon.* University of Lille III, 1987.

Boulanger, André. *Georges Simenon: apologie des femmes par un misogyne. Etude des caractères dans les romans psychologiques.* Free University of Brussels, 1985–86.

Decolle, Brigitte. *Le Juge d'instruction chez Simenon.* University of Liège, 1984–85.

Decombas-Boutry, Marie-Paule. *L'Univers de Georges Simenon: espaces familliers, espaces familiaux.* University of Lyons II, 1984.

Drysdale, Dennis H. *Georges Simenon, a Study of Humanity.* Doctoral thesis, University of Nottingham, 1973.

Gillet, Pascale. *La Paternité dans les romans psychologiques de Simenon: une impossibilité.* University of Liège, 1980–81.

Jadoul, Francis. *Simenon et le "mythe" de Maigret.* University of Liège, 1968–69.

Lacroix, Jean-François. *L'Érotisme et le sentiment du mal dans l'œuvre de Georges Simenon.* University of Liège, 1972–73.

Mans, Christian. *Les Romans liégeois de Georges Simenon.* University of Liège, 1974–75.

Nihant-André, Marie-Hélène. *Impressionisme de Simenon? Le thème de la lumière et ses implications à travers l'œuvre romanesque.* Master's thesis, University of Liège, 1980–81.

Nisolle, Pierre. *Le Thème de la solitude humaine dans l'œuvre de Georges Simenon.* University of Liège, 1959–60.

Oudin, Gilbert. *Médecins et malades dans l'œuvre de Georges Simenon.* University of Amiens, 1975.

Robert, Cécile. *La Légende Simenon, Essai d'étude critique de la représentation de Simenon dans la presse.* University of Liège, 1972–73.

Robesco, Marie-Catherine. *Romans populaires sous pseudonymes ou les débuts littéraires d'un écrivain mondialement célèbre: Simenon.* University of Liège, 1989–90.

Spengler, Dominique. *Le Héros dans l'œuvre de Georges Simenon.* Faculté de Médecine-Necker-enfants-malades, Paris, 1984.

4. Major Works Mentioning Georges Simenon

Bertin, Célia. *Jean Renoir.* Perrin, 1986.

Boudard, Alphonse. *Cinoche.* La Table Rond, 1974.

Carné, Marcel. *La Vie à belles dents.* Belfond, 1989.

Cobb, Richard. *People and Places.* Oxford: Oxford University Press, 1985.

Colin, Paul. *La Croûte, souvenirs.* La Table Rond, 1957.

Collins, Carvel. "Interview with Simenon," in *Writers at Work, The Paris Review Interviews,* ed. Malcolm Cowley. New York: Penguin, 1977; reprinted in GS, *L'Age du roman,* Brussels: Complexe, 1988.

Desnos, Youki. *Les Confidences de Youki.* Fayard, 1957.

Ezine, Jean-Louis. *Les Écrivains sur la sellette.* Seuil, 1981.

Fels, Florent. *Voilà.* Fayard, 1957.

Gill, Brendan. *A New York Life: Of Friends and Others.* New York: Poseidon Press, 1990.

Guillemin, Henri. *Parcours.* Seuil, 1989.

———. *Vérités complémentaires.* Seuil, 1990.

Hainnaux, Georges. *Mémoires de Georges Hainnaux dit Jo-la-Terreur.* adapted by Maurice-Ivan Sicard. Nouvelles Éditions latines, 1934.

Jeanson, Henri. *70 ans d'adolescence.* Stock, 1971.

Keyserling, Hermann von. *Voyage dans le temps.* Stock 1961.

Lacassin, Francis. *Mythologie du roman policier,* vol. 2. 10/18, UGE, 1987.

———. et al. *Entretiens sur la paralittérature.* Plon, 1970.

Lazareff, Pierre. *Dernière Édition.* New York: Brentano's, 1942.

Mauriac, Claude. *L'Allitérature contemporaine.* Albin Michel, 1958.

Montarron, Marcel. *La Foudre de Dieu.* Gallimard, 1969.

Nimier, Roger. *Journées de lecture.* Gallimard, 1965.

Ragon, Michel. *Enfances vendéennes.* Editions Ouest-France, 1990.

Régent, Roger. *Cinéma de France.* Bellefaye, 1948.

Renoir, Jean. *Ma vie et mes films.* Flammarion, 1974.

Rim, Carlo. *Mémoires d'une vieille vague.* Gallimard, 1961, Réédition Ramsay-Poche-Cinéma, 1990.

Rivière, François. *Les Couleurs du noir. Biographie d'un genre.* Chêne, 1989.

Poulet, Robert. *La Lanterne magique.* Debresse, 1956.

Sauvage, Marcel. *Les Mémoires de Joséphine Baker.* Corréa, 1949.

Spaak, Janine. *Charles Spaak, mon mari.* France-Empire, 1977.

Symons, Julian. *Bloody Murder. From the Detective Story to the Crime Novel: a History.* Harmondsworth: Penguin, 1985.

Vlaminck, Maurice de. *Portraits avant décès.* Flammarion, 1943.

5. *Archives*

LAUSANNE
Private archives of Georges Simenon at his secretariat

LIÈGE
Fonds Simenon of the University (château de Colonster)

PARIS
National Archives
Bibliothèque nationale

Ministry of the Interior
Ministry of Foreign Affairs
Centre de documentation juive contemporaine
Institut d'Histoire du Temps présent (CNRS)
Editions Gallimard
Editions Fayard
Personal collection of Mme Catherine Gide-Desvignes
Personal collection of Maurice Bessy
Personal collection of Maurice Dumoncel
Personal collection of Mme Jacqueline Hélion
Association de la Noblesse française

LA ROCHE-SUR-YON
Departmental archives of the Vendée

LA ROCHELLE
Personal collection of Mme Lina Caspescha-Chavier
Personal collection of Mme Odette Bastian-Maury

NANCY
Fonds Goncourt in the Municipal Archives

CANTON OF VAUD (SWITZERLAND)
Personal collection of Frédéric Dard

LONDON
Personal collection of Fenton Bresler

WASHINGTON, D.C.
Department of Justice (FBI)

HANOVER, NEW HAMPSHIRE
Personal collection of Helen Wolff

LAKEVILLE, CONNECTICUT
Archives of the *Lakeville Journal*

AUSTIN, TEXAS
Harry Ransom Humanities Research Center, University of Texas at Austin

FOR MORE INFORMATION

Fonds Simenon
Université au Sart-Tilman
Château de Colonster
B-4000 Liège
Belgium
Tel.: (41) 56-30-22
Fax: (41) 88-15-55

Les Amis de Georges Simenon

Secretariat: Michel Schepens
291, Beigemsesteenweg
1852-Beigem
Belgium
Tel.: (02) 269-47-87

Filmography

The following list owes much to the research of Maurice Dubourg and Claude Gauteur.

The dates refer to the years the films were released. The name immediately after the film title identifies the director.

Unless otherwise indicated, the films were adapted from the novel or short story of the same name.

1932
La Nuit du carrefour, Jean Renoir, starring Pierre Renoir.
Le Chien jaune, Jean Tarride, starring Abel Tarride.

1933
La Tête d'un homme, Julien Duvivier, starring Harry Baur.

1938
Sept Amoureuses, Franck Borzage (American release), adapted from *La Maison des sept jeunes filles.*

1939
Dernier Refuge, Jacques Constant, starring Mireille Balin, adapted from *Le Locataire.*

1942
Annette et la dame blonde, Jean Dréville, starring Louise Carletti.
La Maison des sept jeunes filles, Albert Valentin, starring Jean Tissier.
Les Inconnus dans la maison, Henri Decoin, starring Raimu.
Monsieur la Souris, Georges Lacombe, starring Raimu.

1943
Picpus, Richard Pottier, starring Albert Préjean and Jean Tissier.
Le Voyageur de la Toussaint, Louis Daquin, starring Jean Desailly and Jules Berry.

L'Homme de Londres, Henri Decoin, starring Fernand Ledoux, Jules Berry, and Suzy Prim.

1944
Cécile est morte, Maurice Tourneur, starring Albert Préjean.

1945
Les Caves du Majestic, Richard Pottier, starring Albert Préjean and Gabriello.

1947
Panique, Julien Duvivier, starring Michel Simon and Viviane Romance, adapted from *Les Fiançailles de M. Hire.*
Dernier Refuge, Marc Maurette, starring Raymond Rouleau, adapted from *Le Locataire.*

1948
Temptation Harbour, Lance Confort, starring Robert Newton, Simone Simon, and Dalio, adapted from *L'Homme de Londres.*

1950
The Man on the Eiffel Tower, Burgess Meredith, starring Charles Laughton, adapted from *La Tête d'un homme.*
La Marie du port, Marcel Carné, starring Jean Gabin and Nicole Courcel.
Midnight Episode, Gordon Parry, starring Stanley Holloway, adapted from *Monsieur La Souris.*

1952
Brelan d'as, Henri Verneuil, starring Michel Simon, adapted from "Le Témoignage de l'enfant de chœur."
La Vérité sur Bébé Donge, Henri Decoin, starring Jean Gabin and Danielle Darrieux.
La Fruit défendu, Henri Verneuil, starring Fernandel and Françoise Arnoul, adapted from *Lettre à mon juge.*

1953
The Man Who Watched Trains Go By, Harold French, starring Claude Rains, adapted from *L'homme qui regardait passer les trains.*

1954
La Neige était sale, Luis Saslavsky, starring Daniel Gélin and Valentine Tessier.

Sources

1955

A Life in the Balance, Harry Horner, starring Ricardo Montalban, Lee Marvin, and Anne Bancroft, adapted from "Sept Petites Croix dans un carnet."

1956

Maigret dirige l'enquête, Stany Cordier, starring Maurice Manson, adapted from three Maigret stories.

The Bottom of the Bottle, Henry Hathaway, starring Van Johnson and Joseph Cotten, adapted from *Le Fond de la bouteille.*

Le Sang à la tête, Gilles Grangier, starring Jean Gabin, Monique Mélinand, and Paul Frankeur, adapted from *Le Fils Cardinaud.*

1958

Maigret tend un piège, Jean Delannoy, starring Jean Gabin and Annie Girardot.

Le Passager clandestin, Ralph Habib, starring Martine Carol, Karl-Heinz Boehm, Arletty, and Serge Reggiani.

The Brothers Rico, Phil Karlson, starring Richard Conte, adapted from *Les Frères Rico.*

En cas de malheur, Claude Autant-Lara, starring Jean Gabin, Brigitte Bardot, and Edwige Feuillère.

1959

Maigret et l'affair Saint-Fiacre, Jean Delannoy, starring Jean Gabin, Valentine Tessier, and Michel Auclair, adapted from *L'Affaire Saint-Fiacre.*

1960

Le Baron de l'écluse, Jean Delannoy, starring Jean Gabin and Micheline Presle.

1961

Le Président, Henri Verneuil, starring Jean Gabin and Bernard Blier.

La Mort de Belle, Edoardo Molinaro, starring Jean Desailly and Alexandra Stewart.

1962

Le Bateau d'Emile, Denys de la Patellière, starring Annie Girardot, Lino Ventura, Pierre Brasseur, and Michel Simon.

1963

Maigret voit rouge, Gilles Grangier, starring Jean Gabin and Françoise Fabian, adapted from *Maigret, Lognon et les gangsters.*

L'Aîné des Ferchaux, Jean-Pierre Melville, starring Jean-Paul Belmondo and Charles Vanel.

1965

Trois Chambres à Manhattan, Marcel Carné, starring Annie Girardot, Maurice Ronet, and Roland Lesaffre.

1966

Maigret fait mouche, Alfred Weidenmann, starring Heinz Rühmann, adapted from *La Danseuse du Gai Moulin.*

1967

Le Commissaire Maigret à Pigalle, Mario Landi, starring Gino Cervi, adapted from *Maigret au Picratt's.*

A Stranger in the House, Pierre Rouve, starring James Mason and Geraldine Chaplin, adapted from *Les Inconnus dans la maison.*

1971

Le Chat, Pierre Granier-Deferre, starring Jean Gabin and Simone Signoret.

La Veuve Couderc, Pierre Granier-Deferre, starring Simone Signoret and Alain Delon.

1973

Le Train, Pierre Granier-Deferre, starring Jean-Louis Trintignant and Romy Schneider.

1974

L'Horloger de Saint-Paul, Bernard Tavernier, starring Philippe Noiret, Jean Rochefort, and Jacques Denis, adapted from *L'Horloger d'Everton.*

1979

Der Mörder, Ottokar Runze, starring Gerhard Olschewski, adapted from *L'Assassin.*

1982

L'Etoile du nord, Pierre Granier-Deferre, starring Simone Signoret and Philippe Noiret, adapted from *Le Locataire.*

Les Fantômes du chapelier, Claude Chabrol, starring Michel Serrault, Charles Aznavour, Aurore Clément, and Monique Chaumette.

433

1983

Equateur, Serge Gainsbourg, starring Barbara
  Sukowa and Francis Huster, adapted
  from *Le Coup de lune.*

1989

Monsieur Hire, Patrice Leconte, starring
  Michel Blanc and Sandrine Bonnaire,
  adapted from *Les Fiançailles de M. Hire.*

1992

Betty, Claude Chabrol, starring Marie
  Trintignant and Stéphane Audran.

Announced for 1992–93

Les Inconnus dans la maison, Georges Lautner,
  starring Jean-Paul Belmondo.
L'Ours en peluche, Pierre Granier-Deferre,
  starring Alain Delon.

ACKNOWLEDGMENTS

This book could not have been written without the invaluable aid of Georges Simenon; his sons, Marc, John, and Pierre; and his companion, Teresa Sburelin. Let me thank them yet again.

May I also express my gratitude to two people who helped me throughout my inquiry, from beginning to end: Joyce Aitken in Lausanne and Christine Swings in Liège. They know how much I owe them.

François Samuelson, my agent, played a pivotal role from the book's conception, in a spirit of unfailing cooperation. I will not forget it.

Elisabeth Gille, Stéphane Khémis, Jean-Maurice de Montremy, and Jean-Pierre Bertin-Maghit did me the favor of reading the manuscript, red pencil in hand. I am unlikely to forget that either.

Angela, my wife, and Meryl and Kate, our daughters, gave me admirable support during the ordeal. They are unlikely to forget it.

Mme Catherine Gide-Desvignes and Messrs Frédéric Dard, Antoine Gallimard, Claude Durand, Pierre Maurice Garçon, Maurice Bessy, and Maurice Dumoncel offered me inestimable aid by opening their archives to me.

I would like to offer special thanks to Michel Lemoine, one of the most reliable connoisseurs of Simenon's work, and to pay homage to all those who aided me in various ways:

Mesdames or Mesdemoiselles: Laure Adler, Dr. Cécile Artarit, Danielle Bajomée, Elise Becket, Annabelle Buffet, Florence Callu, Viviane Carel-Fourrier, Lina Caspescha, Myriam Cendrars, Françoise Constantin-Weyer, Marianne Czernin, Mylène Demongeot, Pascale Frey, Florence Géhéniau, Jacqueline Hélion, Henriette "Boule" Liberge, Micheline Liboureau, Nancy Longley, Anne McCormick, Odette Maury, Marie-Hélène Nihant-André, Vicki Oppenheimer, Nane Poirson, Denyse Simenon, Chantal de Tourtier-Bonazzi, Danielle Vincken, Charlotte Wardi, Helen Wolff.

Misters: Frédéric d'Agay, Bernard Alavoine, Jean-Marc Ancian, Francis Balace, Louis-Marie Barbarit, Jean-Baptiste Baronian, Joseph Barry, Raymond Belin, Alain Bertrand, Alphonse Boudard, Ernest Bourasseau, Christian Bourgeois, Jean-Manuel Bourgois, André Bourin, Fenton Bresler, Bernard Buffet, Jean-Christophe Camus, Georges Charensol, Pierre

Clerdent, Yves Courrière, Jim Dandurand, Jean-Pierre Dauphin, Paul Delbouille, Christian Delcourt, Pierre Deligny, René Devaud, William Doolittle, Jacques Drouin, Michel Drouin, Jacques Dubois, Jean-Arnaud Dyens, Kjell Espmark, Roger Faligot, Jean Favier, Thomas Ferenczi, Alain du Fontenioux, Henri du Fontenioux, Michel Freidman, Aimé Gerbaud, Brendan Gill, André Guiller, Thierry Heckman, Jean Huguet, Vidar Jacobsen, Manfred Graf von Keyserling, Francis Lacassin, Dr. René Laforge, Jean Lambert, Philippe Lamour, Maurice Le Roux, Rémy Liboureau, Claude Menguy, Pascal Mercier, Dominique Michonneau, Roger Mirmont, Bernard Morlino, Gérard Nocquet. Dr. Gilbert Oudin, Mgr the Count de Paris, Pierre Pasquereau, René Pérochon, Mark Polizzotti, Dr. Lucien Porte, Paul Proust, Dr. Pierre Rentchnick, Yves Salgues, John Sargent, Fabrice Schurmans, René Serceau, Octave Soulard, Henri Thyssens, Robert Toussaint, Claude de Tracy, Constant Vaillant, Louis Valentin, André Versaille, Eric Vigne, Philippe Zoummeroff.

INDEX

A NOTE ON THE TYPE

The text of this book was composed in Apollo, the first
typeface ever originated specifically for film composition.
Designed by Adrian Frutiger and issued by the Monotype
Corporation of London in 1964, Apollo is not only a
versatile typeface suitable for many uses but also pleasant
to read in all of its sizes.

Composed by Crane Typesetting Service,
Charlotte Harbor, Florida

Printed and bound by Quebecor Printing,
Martinsburg, West Virginia

Designed by Misha Beletsky

92 S4894AS
Assouline, Pierre.
Simenon
32953006159265